Advanced Praise
Relationsh...

"This is a brilliant book about Inte... their practice form. I know of no book ... more thorough form. It definitely has my highest recommendation!"

    Ken Wilber, *The Religion of Tomorrow*

"Not since Eric Fromm's classic, *The Art of Loving*, have we seen such a rich exposition on intimate relationships, and how to create and maintain them."

    Allan Combs, PhD, Author of *Consciousness Explained Better*, *The Radiance of Being*, and other titles

"In this encyclopedic work, Martin Ucik delivers a comprehensive look at how he has been applying Integral Theory to the subject of intimate relating. It covers so many topics, expanding outside the bounds of Integral Theory, covering such topics as truth-telling, shame, polarities, and purpose. If you were going to teach a year-long course in intimacy, this could be your curriculum. I highly recommend this book."

    Susan Campbell, PhD, Author of *Getting Real*, *From Triggered to Tranquil*, and other titles

"Human worlds are constituted relationally and are destroyed when relationality ruptures. The transgenerational transmission that scaffolds relational development is a casualty of our cultural crisis. The ways in which social media trivializes and twists the heart of relationality is only one of the vectors of cultural crisis. This book, robust also with current theory, is truly intended as a manual for practitioners. While primary bonding is its focus, relating is an essential practice for all of us, making Martin's book useful to anyone interested in growing relational capability through relational practice.

    Aftab Omer, PhD, President, Meridian University
    meridianuniversity.edu

"Written with humor, wisdom, and depth, this is a comprehensive manual for exploring the complex territory of our personal relationships. As a guide to facilitating group process, the experiential exercises provide ways to embody the wide variety of themes in the theoretical material. Anyone wishing to discover more about their partner, and their own relationship behavior and prepare themselves for deeper intimacy and fulfillment will find this an extensive resource. And as Ucik argues—having rich, healthy, integral relationships is truly the key to hope for the future."

Barbara J Hunt, Author of Forgiveness Made Easy

"In his third book on Integral Relationships, Martin Ucik presents a truly all-encompassing coverage of the topic through applied practice and step-by-step description and instructions. The book is organized into 26 modules, each covering a different aspect of relationships from an Integral perspective and from other related disciplines. This comprehensive reference combines decades of wisdom, clearly laid out in a practical and applicable manner. I cannot recommend this book enough."

Khaled ElSherbini, PhD, Transpersonal Psychologist and Consciousness Mentor, Founder of The Consciousness Academy and Enneagram Egypt

"Martin's book is a valuable resource for anyone who values nourishing, meaningful, healthy relationships. He has skillfully woven together multiple approaches to create a multifaceted model of how relationships work and can evolve. The practical exercises take you along a step-by-step path that leads to an in-depth understanding of your own way of relating, areas for development, and strategies for creating a fulfilling relationship. Highly recommended."

Jan Day, Author and Teacher of Living Tantra

"Being, becoming, and relating are intertwined and need to be informed and enacted in the light of art, science, and spirituality, of East and West. And Martin's *Integral Relationship Practice* accomplishes that magnificently. It also complements the previous two books by skillfully connecting the tried and tested Integral theory with corresponding practices, hence cultivating true and authentic embodiment. A la Ken Wilber, if reality tetra-arises, so do our relationships. And Martin's manual provides holonic performatives for the co-creation of waking up, growing up, cleaning up, showing up, linking up, lifting up, and opening up, in mutuality, passionately, and purposefully. It's a tall order but as Spinoza said, 'All noble things are as difficult as they are rare.'"

Nomi Naeem, Senior Librarian, Central Brooklyn Public Library, New York, Editor at Light on Light Press

"In this, the third installment of his Integral Relationship opus, Martin Ucik offers us a mind-bogglingly comprehensive manual for how to co-create integrally informed romantic relationships. His promise is that through the fire of personal and spiritual work necessary to forge enlightened love relationships, we can co-create the foundation for an authentic second-tier future culture. Martin feels that the fulfilment of the promise of integral theory lies in the coming of age of the progeny of spiritually awakened adults. If he is right, we will all have a lot to thank him for."

Andrew Cohen, Author of Evolutionary Enlightenment, Founder of Manifest Nirvana, www.manifest-nirvana.com

"Martin puts together an integral vision of relationships that is brilliant. He has a rare mind that can see how the parts and the whole interrelate. He intuitively knows what's truly relevant in relationships. Comprehensiveness is important for a full understanding, and this book provides it beautifully. His book ensures that we don't overlook our blind spots. I don't know where else you can get this kind of intelligent comprehensiveness! More and more people are realizing that we need to awaken and heal together in relationship and in community. Martin integrates the relationship wisdom of others yet authentically comes from his own unique, transcendent but grounded, fully human wisdom. I gained a lot, going through all 26 modules with Martin, and I came to know him on a beautiful soul level. I invite you to receive his gifts and give them to others. As a practicing psychologist specializing in relationships, I can't recommend his book enough."

Wayne Carr, PhD, Executive Director of Center for Growth and Healing, Psychologist, Seattle

"Martin is an absolute genius, and we are so very grateful for him and his work and his beautiful way of bringing it all together in a practical, fun, and easily digestible way. His ten core tenets say it all, and our favorite is number ten: 'Healthy love relationships don't just happen, the skills must be learned.' What a wonderful teacher of those skills he is, and here he compiles everything together in one complete and comprehensive manual.

We were lucky enough to study under Martin's guidance and are huge fans of his work. His new manual is a must for singles, couples, coaches, and facilitators. He is an inspiration, and we're so excited for what his work is doing for this world!"

Natalie Kalkbrenner and Beau Jess, Relationship and Mindset Consultants

"As a couple who met as students in Martin's 26-week Integral Relationship Facilitator Training, we got to know each other by engaging with this book's practices together each week. What a gift! We frequently return to insights from the practices as a shared foundation for understanding our relationship dynamics. The practices in this book have brought us greater awareness of ourselves and one another. They have helped us develop new skills and a wider view as we explore, negotiate, and grow our being together. We can think of no one who is working harder, more creatively, and with a more inspired vision in support of the success of our, and every, partnership relationship than Martin. Thank you Martin!"

Nick Boyar and Jean Garofoli

"I have been inspired by Martin's work since 2011 when I first read *Integral Relationships: A Manual for Men*. Martin's new book contains a great balance of theory and practice that will be useful for everyone, for personal use or to facilitate groups, whether familiar with the Integral perspective or not. With each of the 26 practice Modules, I discovered, learned, or deepened my knowledge of relationships, with state-of-the-art contributions selected, ordered, and revisited by Martin's acute Integral eye. Each chapter is worth reading, practicing, reading again, practicing again…, as the richness and density of Martin's work progressively unfolds, and the pieces of the puzzle fit together better and better. I am very grateful to Martin for generously bringing this masterpiece to the world in times when love is needed more than ever."

Guillaume Thouvenel, NonViolent Communication Certified Trainer, Relationship Coach, France

"This book is a massive undertaking. Incredibly comprehensive. And considering the wealth of information and insight it holds within, remarkably compact. To have all this material in one place, laid out like this, will undoubtedly be invaluable to seminar leaders, workshop participants, and dedicated students of love and loving relationships. Like the course it accompanies, this book examines in theoretical breadth and experiential depth 14 essential dimensions of relationships in astounding detail, with plenty of footnotes for further exploration.

We all know the old parable of the six blind men and the elephant, where each mistakes his personal experience for absolute truth. In contrast, here in these 26 practice modules, Martin gets us to experience a multifaceted array of perspectives that provide a continuing spring of 'aha moments' to anyone serious about understanding their partner—and themselves."

Lee Liebner, PhD, Author of How to Get Through to Your Guy

"This book reflects the complexity of our current world and modern-day relationship dynamics. The practices provide us with the mindset to build, maintain, evolve, and reform our love relationships. Martin collected a wide range of views, systems, methods, and techniques about relationships from a practical, scientific, psychological, and spiritual perspective and connected them together. He zooms in from broad areas such as politics, society, and human evolution to specific aspects of intimate relationships. From a facilitator perspective, I am unspeakably thankful for the birth of this book, as it gives me confidence to start leading Integral Relationship groups."

Renata Kiss, Integral Psychology Counselor, Socio- and Art Therapist

"Martin's books have helped me more than any others that I've read on relationships, communication, or intimacy. Despite all the work I'd done in relating, there were a few very painful experiences that kept repeating and seemed to cast a shadow on my enjoyment of my partners. Martin's books gave me context to frame the content of my personal experience so that I could see the path forward. I'm endlessly grateful and excited for all those who choose to deepen their capacity to love through this work."

Dr. Matt Kreinheder, Founder of META Mastermind

"*Integral Relationship Practice* is the cumulation of many years of study, observation, and practice by Martin Ucik. The book is Integral in that it includes many systems of understanding the complexity of human relationship. It is Integral in that there are didactic and experiential components, with the added fun of suggested movies to transmit content. Martin is precise, organized, and complete. There is something to learn for everyone, whether you are a beginner in the intrepid world of relationship or an experienced explorer or you wish to facilitate Integral Relationship groups."

Eva Giedt, Psychotherapist in Marin, California, Assistant and Teacher for Thomas Huebl

"I have been enriched by participating in Martin Ucik's extensive Integral Relationship Training and have recommended it to clients and friends, as I will his new book, *Integral Relationship Practice*. In it, Martin's commitment to higher, deeper, and more meaningful relationships, and to the next-level flourishing of the Human Experiment, shines brightly from the compelling pages. It is filled with perspective and practices, techniques and tools to deepen and widen your capacity to consciously contain your subjective experience, thereby freeing the space between us for next-level connection and co-creation."

> Daniel Piatek, Founder of The Way of the Practical Mystic and The Hero Academy

"In his usual enthusiastic and integral way, Martin presents us with a host of possibilities for engaging with life and our (future) life partner ever more deeply and fully. One can read the book as a preparation for integral dating, like I did, or use its modules, one at the time, as 'relational acupuncture points'. I found doing the practices to bring more clarity and initiate fresh momentum, which is especially useful when 'something' in a dating or relationship flow feels off and you can't precisely put your finger on it yet. From start to finish the book covers a wide range of important topics and new perspectives as well as points of disagreement, all thoroughly infused with a growth potential eagerly waiting to be unpacked."

> drs. Marielle de Natris, Retired Psychotherapist, Author of Conscious Interconnection Volume 1: Bodymind Basics for Healthy Living and Working

"How lucky was I to get a preview of Martin's new book. Martin is a modern-day alchemist, leading the way in consciousness, elevation, and relating. A fascinating read from beginning to end in easy-to-understand, bite-size chunks, creating a symphonic concoction of awareness. The new MUST read for 'conscious' people."

> Anthony Abis, Founder of www.bu-evolution.com

"The Path to Healthy Love Relationships is Clear! Once again, Martin Ucik has taken a much-needed step in laying a clear path for those looking to have the greatest of love relationships. We owe Martin a great debt for his dedication to fostering Integral love relationships with greater purpose and meaning, an antidote to the disconnection and division being created in our world. I, for one, continue to benefit from the magnitude and depth of his work, both in my professional career supporting individuals, couples, and families in creating healthier lives, and in my personal life, which has become not only stronger but also deeper through his amazing ability to find the great nuance in loving relationships and his guidance to navigate its stormy waters. This book can be returned to again and again and will continue to add value to any relationship for those willing to be vulnerable enough to face themselves and each other with open hearts."

Ben Calder, Founder and Director of Centre for Integral Health UK

"Martin's new book offers a comprehensive and well-organized Integral approach to relationships! He brilliantly introduces most of the cutting-edge theories and practices that are necessary for co-creating thriving relationships in the 21st century. The book also provides an abundance of suggestions for further reading in endnotes if you wish to further research any of the 26 practice modules. Last but not least, you find information about the root causes of problems that plague most relationships—such as the fear-shame downward spiral."

Valdo Lallemand, Founder of Happy Couples Play Together

"Amazing! Integral approach in action! *Integral Relationship Practice* is the most comprehensive step-by-step repository of invaluable information for couple's work. Martin has brilliantly created a collection of practical exercises and detailed instructions for practitioners that are easy to follow and implement. Talk about being a solution! I hear his invaluable message of building a better world through co-creating healthy love relationships loud and clear and cannot wait to get out there and start building a community that will benefit from his work and watch the results ripple out in expanding circles."

Lana Koyadinovich, Transformational Coach, Integral Relationship and Authentic Relating Facilitator, www.theinterrelated.com

This manual is a wonderful tool in the way that it is written, structured, and explained. Many times, people say that a book changed their life; this manual is certainly one of them for me. I already ordered six copies for my best friends. The understanding drawn from the explanations and exercises will clarify many doubts, not only about the importance of relationships in the 21st century and how to successfully create them, but also about the validity and practical application of Ken Wilber's Integral philosophy.

J.C. Subias, Airline Captain, Theatre Producer, Certified Integral Relationship Professional

"This manual goes far beyond applying Integral theory to romantic relationships. If you're a perpetually evolving person, then Martin's comprehensive books can take you into a completely new dimension of being, inter-becoming, and a full holistic, integral way of living, relating, and loving. This is not another self-help book that you will read and then reflect on a bit; rather, it's a life companion. Integrating and embodying all practices will benefit you in every step of your journey."

Matija Rukavina, Certified Integral Relationship Professional

"Martin's continuing masterpiece on relationships is a gift to humanity. Our relation to self, others and community are foundational to living well together. The journey is inherently a mystery, and Martin offers a beautiful map with which to navigate. His humble diligence demonstrates that we can know more about this mystery than we think, feel or sense. The brilliant tapestry he's woven from insights and practices empowers people to be present in their relationships and avail themselves to new horizons of possibility, dancing in the mystery with embodied abundance."

Steve Caram, Integral Master Coach™

"In his book, *Integral Relationship Practice*, Martin Ucik applies Integral theory and covers a vast amount of theoretical and practical territory. His groundbreaking work helps couples to connect with their transformational and transcendental purpose to improve their lives, deepen their relationships, and ultimately make the world a better place."

Gael McCool, Author of Be Wise Now: A Guide to Conscious Living

"A tour de force: Martin lays out his vision of a society based on healthy integral relationships and gives couples and those seeking healthy coupledom the necessary tools. The kind of deeply fulfilling and mutually supportive conscious relationships that most people desire are not created and maintained without work, and this book is a must-have for those who seek them."

Richard Theobald, Integral Relationship Coach, California

"This manual provides a plethora of relationship insights, as well as step-by-step coaching instructions, that can (and should) be used with clients. Become familiar with this material. Learn the exercises. Pass on these learnings to your clients. Make your copies of his books well-worn with highlights and side notes. Join Integral Relationship workshops live or online to hone your skills. Integrate the concepts into your practice. You will help clients understand people in general, as well as how to set themselves up for success in their intimate relationships. Where else can you get such a vast array of coaching tools all for the price of a paperback?"

Mary Gordon, Clinical Hypnotherapist, Integral Relationship Professional and Group Facilitator

"This masterpiece from Martin Ucik is a must-read for every relationship coach, trainer, and couple as well. The content is brilliant, unique, and extensive. It offers a deep understanding of the multiple angles of relationship issues and supports the evolution of consciousness through Integral relationships."

Yves Mayer, Heart Intelligence Coach and Trainer

"Martin Ucik's *Integral Relationship Practice* is obviously a labor of love, as it offers transparent access to his lifetime of learning. This manual provides a comprehensive collection of highly relevant perspectives for you and your partner to explore. In the process, I assure you that awareness of the dynamics in your relationship will come alive. Some of those perspectives may be familiar to you, while one or more may shock you when they awaken you to THE BLINDSPOT(S) that have bedeviled you for decades. When that awareness emerges, you will discover the consequential gift this book offers: embodied wisdom rooted in lived experience."

Rodney Dueck, MD

Martin has, in this book, given us an incredibly comprehensive compendium of resources that inform relationship development. *Integral Relationship Practice* is a valuable roadmap that guides us through a very thick territory in service to couples, those preparing to be part of a couple, and, indeed, anyone interested in relationships.

Daniel Kirkpatrick, Consultant and Author, Educational Design Associates

"The world needs this book more than ever. We should start teaching integral relationship in our schools. It's time to find our way back to each other's heart for a more peaceful world.

The dedication and passion Martin put into this book has touched my heart, and I hope it touches the hearts of others too."

Ali Mobarez

Praise for Sex Purpose Love

"Martin Ucik has continued his ground-breaking work in applying Integral Theory to the whole complex issue of relationships. Like his first book in this area, it is fully grounded in Integral Theory, and continues adding new, interesting, and relevant material to it, to bring a truly up-to-date overview of today's relationships and how to make them work from the very highest potentials possible. Some of it is controversial, but that's what you expect from any truly great pioneering approaches, and this is certainly that. Given the fractured and fragmented state of relationships as they exist now, nothing is more important for today than a truly comprehensive and inclusive and leading-edge guide. Highly recommended for men and women alike who are looking for a relationship today that will actually last. One thing is for sure—not taking into account all the information, insights, and wisdom that is contained in this book is to almost guarantee any relationship will not last. So check this out, you'll be very glad you did!"
   Ken Wilber, Author of *The Religion of Tomorrow*

"Martin Ucik has given us another beautiful book on love relationships, including along the way many insights about integral living as well."
   Allan Combs, PhD, CIIS Professor of Consciousness Studies, President of The Society for Consciousness Studies, Editor of Consciousness: Ideas and Research for the 21st Century

"*Sex Purpose Love* sheds new light on intimate relations. In his new book, Martin Ucik builds a bridge between a Californian way of feeling and the continental philosophy of life. A really instructive and salutary read!"
   Dr. Ferdinand Fellmann, Prof. Emeritus for Philosophy at Chemnitz University and Author of The Couple: Intimate Relations in a New Key

"I have always believed that for romantic and sexual relationships to flourish and be truly enduring, it was essential that both parties share the same hopes, values, and existential aspirations. In *Sex Purpose Love* Martin Ucik lays out a bold utopian vision in which integrally inspired romantic couples who share both biological and transcendental purpose, endeavor to bond at all levels. What is driving their tantric passions is not merely a quest for personal fulfillment but the highest aspiration: that their radical and inclusive union/communion can form the enlightened nuclei or building blocks of a better, more evolved world to come.

This evolutionary manifesto is both a detailed guidebook and a compelling argument that brings to light our unexamined beliefs, assumptions, hidden hopes and fears about sex and love. Boldly, Ucik has paved new and exciting territory into the captivating world of the possible for us all."

Andrew Cohen, Founder of Evolutionary Enlightenment

"The Integral approach is all about multiple perspectives. The more ways we can experience each moment, the more complete our view and the more choices we have. Many studies have found that satisfying relationships are the main contributors to happiness, and that modern intimacy is challenging. *Sex, Purpose, Love: Couples in Integral Relationships Creating a Better World* provides countless perspectives and insights, organized around the Integral model to help individuals and couples grow in their abilities to love and serve throughout a lifetime. Highly recommended!"

Keith Witt, PhD, Author of Integral Mindfulness: From Clueless to Dialed-In, and Shadow Light: Illuminations at the Edge of Darkness

"Martin Ucik has produced a sweeping opus and seminal meta-analysis regarding the past, present, and future of co-creative love relationships. *Sex Purpose Love* is a well-researched and comprehensive guide into the intricacies of human development, relationships, sexual dynamics, and Integral theory. It leads us to a marvelous critical discourse on the direction and fate of human flourishing. The call toward living our individual ultimate purpose and finding shared evolutionary purpose with another is both loving and imploring."

Wesly Feuquay, M.Ed., Prof. of Consciousness Studies - Maricopa Colleges, AZ, Founder and Director of The PSYLOGIA Institute for the Development of Consciousness, Purpose, and Transformation

"Martin Ucik's new book is a great gift for all of us who are struggling to make sense of self and relationships in an increasingly chaotic and tribal world.

His passion, compassion and sincerity are weaved into every sentence. It's so palpable to me. As a librarian I love to spread the good word and I can't wait to spread it far and wide. Martin has brought Integral theory down-to-earth where it is needed the most. *Sex Purpose Love* is a bodhisattvic, scholarly and passionate blend of wisdom from the East and West, from the sacred and scientific, and from the intrinsic and extrinsic that can help tremendously in making our tribal as well as our transcendental unconscious conscious, and thereby developing our highest but often unrealized human potentials for loving sincerely and living meaningfully--and inspiring others to do the same."

Nomi Naeem, Senior Librarian, Central Brooklyn Public Library, Integral New York

"A much-needed contribution, written to reach many who are interested in the intricacies of coupling. This book provides the reader with an easily understood application of integral theory while elucidating the obstacles and joys in couple development."

Tom Habib, PhD, Clinical Psychologist, Carlsbad, California

Praise for Integral Relationships

"It's a terrific book, Buddy. The more and more I read, the more and more I was just really astounded how much territory you cover. I will read sections of the book and hopefully people will get a sense of just how complete this thing is. Honestly, I haven't seen anything quite like it [chuckles] — it's very impressive."
Ken Wilber, The Integral Vision

"Get this book and pay attention to what it has to say."
Prof. Allan Combs, CIIS

"I read the pages you suggested and am impressed by your scholarship! You must be one of the first people in history to put the postmodern predicament as it relates to sex and romance on the integral map, and you've done an impressive job. I don't have any particular feedback to give you. It was clear that your ideas regarding what truly evolved transpersonal relationships would actually look like were somewhat speculative, but what else could they be? We're not there yet.... "
Andrew Cohen, Founder of Evolutionary Enlightenment

"I read *Integral Relationships: A Manual for Men* this morning and found it to be an insightful and powerful application of the Integral model to what has to be the most compelling developmental topic in the world. I especially appreciated your straightforward and candid style; it was refreshing in a landscape littered with cloying fluff."
Robb Smith, Chief Executive Officer, Integral Institute

"I have only glanced over your book but find it intriguing enough to add to our library of carefully selected relationship books as we enter into the process of writing our own, which is a giant compliment in itself — you know how much is out there."
Dr. David Feinstein, Co-Author of **The Promise of Energy Psychology**

"*Integral Relationships* is one of the most important books I have ever read in my life, and I am a guy with 4000 books in his personal library. Bravo! I really regret not having this when in my 20s, so much pain and heartbreak over the years could have been avoided. Your book has made my life so much easier, for now I know what sort of person is optimal for me and how I need to go about it, instead of having my heart torn out at predictable intervals. Much appreciated, and more power to you."

Rohit Arya, Navi Mumbai, India

"Martin Ucik's book, written as a manual for men, will be recognized as one of the most important books of the early 21st century."

Dr. Marj Britt, Senior Minister Emeritus, Unity of Tustin, CA

"A very intelligent, original, enlightening, and well-written analysis of male-female relationships as they are experienced in our contemporary culture. After reading this book, one is left with an acute sense of the difficulties of human love, but also with a vision of the ideal worth striving for: a personal love relationship that Ucik simply but profoundly calls–following Wilber–Integral."

Michael Morrissey, PhD, Department of Philosophy and Religion, Dominican University San Rafael, CA

"I love your book and have suggested it to the New York Integral community. It is one of the best ways to get introduced to–or revisit–Integral theory. I am a librarian and experiment with different representations of information. I have found that people who find Wilber intimidating, but want to learn about relationships, can do both from your book and become a little bit more Integral in the process. Bows. Maybe now I can better appreciate that "choices" in relationships are based on the capacity to simultaneously hold multiple perspectives, and also on the mutual interactions of levels of development (preconventional, conventional, postconventional) in important lines/intelligences/potentials that Wilber identifies."

Nomi Naeem, Senior Librarian, Brooklyn Library, Integral New York

"Prior to your work, I considered David Deida's "The Way of the Superior Man..." to be the best book out there on understanding relationships. He, like you, didn't pull any punches. But now your book gets top honors with me. And let me compliment your command of English. Being from Germany, I realize it's a second language for you. You write better than many Americans."

Richard Oliver, Integral Author and Teacher

"I said it once, and I'm to saying it again... this book, *Integral Relationships: A Manual for Men*, is a must, must, must read for men AND women! I hope it becomes a favorite, well-worn accompaniment to coffee tables across the globe. ~moi, whose MA in Marriage and Family Therapy underwhelms by comparison."

Susan Hodges, MA, MFT, Certified Integral Coach

"I think I read the first 50 pages in the first sitting. Then a couple weeks ago I heard the interview with Ken Wilber and couldn't stop laughing as he took the words right out of my mouth at the beginning...."I've never seen anything quite like it." So much of the book helped to make sense of my past relationships, especially the matrix on page 154. "Oh my God, well no wonder!" 2002 me at Green dating Red on the surface it LOOKED like Green Thank You. Congrats on your exceptional work and on all you are doing."

Mark Lorenzon, Awaken Beyond

INTEGRAL RELATIONSHIP PRACTICE

A Manual for Singles, Couples, Helping Professionals, and Group Facilitators

Martin Ucik
Edited by Dr. Cynthia Deitering

First Edition 2022

Integral Relationship Practice: A Manual for Singles, Couples, Helping Professionals, and Group Facilitators

Copyright © 2022 by Martin Ucik

Published and distributed worldwide by Light on Light Press

All Rights Reserved. No part of this book may be reproduced or distributed in any form or by any means, or stored in a database or retrieval system, without the prior written permission by the author.

ISBN-13: 9798839443723
Library of Congress Control Number: 2022912072

Cover design by Rizwana Kausar
Inside illustrations by Özer Koç, Sahra Özdoğan, Muzzammil Baig, and Annette Berlin
Book layout by Feroz Ahmed
Edited by Dr. Cynthia Deitering

Dedication

To my dear friend, Liza Braude-Glidden

Short Table of Contents

Advanced Praise for Integral Relationship Practice	I
Praise for Sex Purpose Love	XIII
Praise for Integral Relationships	XVII
INTEGRAL RELATIONSHIP PRACTICE	i
Dedication	iii
Short Table of Contents	v
Detailed Table of Contents	ix
List of Figures	xix
List of Tables	xxiii
Acknowledgments	xxv
My Ten Core Tenets	xxvii
Preface	xxix
Introduction	1
Preliminary Practice Module	9
Ego-Transcendence and Unconditional Love	9
Practice Module 1	29
Four Dimensions of Being and Relating	29
Practice Module 2	49
Archaic, Magic, and Egocentric Stages	49
Practice Module 3	71
Mythic and Rational Stages	71

Practice Module 4	81
Pluralistic Stage	81
Practice Module 5	91
Integral and Transpersonal Stages	91
Practice Module 6	109
Nonviolent Compassionate Communication	109
Practice Module 7	125
Need-Based Communication	125
Practice Module 8	145
Integral and Transpersonal Communication	145
Practice Module 9	159
Biological Differences and Learned Gender Roles	159
Practice Module 10	171
Avoiding the Fear–Shame Downward Spiral	171
Practice Module 11	183
Feminine-Masculine Polarities	183
Practice Module 12	207
Spiritual Development	207
Practice Module 13	235
Sexual Development	235
Practice Module 14	255
Anima/Animus Complex Development	255
Practice Module 15	275
The Five Love Languages	275

Practice Module 16	289
Enneagram Types	289
Practice Module 17	319
Attachment Styles	319
Practice Module 18	337
The Unconscious and Emotional Availability	337
Practice Module 19	349
Healing your Shadow/Unconscious	349
Practice Module 20	367
Forms, Levels, and States of Love	367
Practice Module 21	391
Personality Disorders	391
Practice Module 22	417
Biological and Transformational Purpose	417
Practice Module 23	435
Transcendental Purpose and Love	435
Practice Module 24	475
Soulmates	475
Practice Module 25	497
Co-Creation at the Level of the Seven Chakras	497
Practice Module 26	523
Why Relationships Matter	523
Live Event Script	551
Hosting and facilitating Integral Relationship events	551

Afterword	**561**
Appendix I	**565**
Links, updates, and resources	**565**
Endnotes	**567**
Index	**689**

Detailed Table of Contents

Advanced Praise for Integral Relationship Practice	I
Praise for Sex Purpose Love	XIII
Praise for Integral Relationships	XVII
INTEGRAL RELATIONSHIP PRACTICE	i
Dedication	iii
Short Table of Contents	v
Detailed Table of Contents	ix
List of Figures	xix
List of Tables	xxiii
Acknowledgments	xxv
My Ten Core Tenets	xxvii
Preface	xxix
Introduction	1
Preliminary Practice Module	**9**
Ego-Transcendence and Unconditional Love	**9**
Module Description	9
Introduction	10
Purpose and application	12
Exercises: Meditation and love circle	12
Unconditional love circle affirmations	21
Follow-up questions	27
Additional information and resources	27
Practice Module 1	**29**
Four Dimensions of Being and Relating	**29**

Module description	29
Introduction	30
Purpose and application of Module 1	33
Exercises: Experiencing the four dimensions	34
Worksheet: Four-quadrant questions	36
Follow-up questions	37
Additional information and resources	38
Suggested movie: *Her* (2013)	47

Practice Module 2 — 49

Archaic, Magic, and Egocentric Stages — 49

Module description	49
Introduction	50
Purpose and application	60
Exercise: First three stages of consciousness development	61
Worksheet: Stages one to three of consciousness development	62
Follow-up questions	66
Additional information and resources	67
Suggested movie: *Into the Wild* (2007)	69

Practice Module 3 — 71

Mythic and Rational Stages — 71

Module description	71
Introduction	72
Purpose and application of the module	74
Exercise: Stages four and five of consciousness development	74
Worksheet: Stages four and five of consciousness development	74
Follow-up questions	76
Additional information and resources	77
Suggested movie: *Groundhog Day* (1993)	79

Practice Module 4 — 81

Pluralistic Stage — 81

Module description	81
Introduction	82
Purpose and application of the module	84
Exercise: Stage six of development	85

xi | Detailed Table of Contents

Worksheet: Stage six of consciousness development	85
Follow-up questions	86
Additional information and resources	87
Suggested movie: *Same Time, Next Year* (1978)	89

Practice Module 5 — 91

Integral and Transpersonal Stages — 91

Module description	91
Introduction	92
Purpose and application of the module	95
Exercise: Stages seven and eight of consciousness development	95
Worksheet: Stages seven and eight of consciousness development	96
Follow-up questions	98
Additional information and resources	98
Suggested movie: *American Beauty* (1999)	107

Practice Module 6 — 109

Nonviolent Compassionate Communication — 109

Module description	109
Introduction	110
Purpose and application of the module	114
Exercises: Nonviolent Compassionate Communication	114
Worksheet: Nonviolent Compassionate Communication	117
Additional lists of human being needs	121
Follow-up questions	123
Additional information and resources	123
Suggested movie: *Gandhi* (1982)	123

Practice Module 7 — 125

Need-Based Communication — 125

Module description	125
Introduction	126
Purpose and application of the module	127
Exercises: Need-based communication	128
Worksheet: Need-based communication	139
Follow-up questions	142
Additional information and resources	142

Suggested movie: *The Invention of Lying* (2009) — 142

Practice Module 8 — 145

Integral and Transpersonal Communication — 145

Module description — 145
Introduction — 146
Purpose and application of the module — 150
Exercises: Integral and transpersonal communication — 151
Worksheet: Integral and transpersonal communication — 154
Follow-up questions — 157
Additional information and resources — 157
Suggested movie: *The Imitation Game* (2014) — 158

Practice Module 9 — 159

Biological Differences and Learned Gender Roles — 159

Module description — 159
Introduction — 160
Purpose and application of the module — 161
Exercises: Sex and gender differences — 162
Worksheet: Sex and gender exercise — 164
Follow-up questions — 165
Additional information and resources — 166
Suggested movie: *The Red Pill* (2016) — 169

Practice Module 10 — 171

Avoiding the Fear–Shame Downward Spiral — 171

Module description — 171
Introduction — 172
Purpose and application of the module — 176
Exercises: Fear-shame downward spiral — 176
Worksheets: Fear-shame downward spiral — 178
Follow-up questions — 181
Additional information and resources — 181
Suggested movie: *Little Miss Sunshine* (2006) — 182

Practice Module 11 — 183

Feminine-Masculine Polarities	**183**
Module description	183
Introduction	184
Purpose and application of the module	188
Exercises: Feminine-masculine polarities	188
Worksheet: Feminine-masculine polarities	198
Follow-up questions	200
Additional information and resources	200
Suggested movie: *The Tree of Life* (2011)	205
Practice Module 12	**207**
Spiritual Development	**207**
Module description	207
Introduction	208
Purpose and application of the module	225
Exercises: Spiritual development	226
Follow-up questions	229
Worksheets: Spiritual development	229
Additional information and resources	229
Suggested movie: *I Heart Huckabees* (2004)	232
Practice Module 13	**235**
Sexual Development	**235**
Module description	235
Introduction	236
Purpose and application of the module	244
Exercises: Sexual development	244
Worksheet: Sexual development	248
Follow-up questions	249
Additional information and resources	249
Suggested movie: *Bliss* (1997)	252
Practice Module 14	**255**
Anima/Animus Complex Development	**255**
Module description	255
Introduction	255

Purpose and application of the module ... 257
Exercise: Anima/animus complex ... 258
Worksheet: Anima/animus complex ... 260
Follow-up questions ... 262
Additional information and resources ... 262
Suggested movie: *Marriage Story* (2019) ... 273

Practice Module 15 — 275

The Five Love Languages — 275

Module description ... 275
Introduction ... 276
Purpose and application of the module ... 280
Exercises: Personality types and five love languages ... 281
Worksheet for practitioners ... 282
Follow-up questions ... 285
Additional information and resources ... 286
Suggested Movie: *Love Actually* (2003) ... 287

Practice Module 16 — 289

Enneagram Types — 289

Module description ... 289
Introduction ... 289
Purpose and application of the module ... 291
Exercises: Enneagram ... 292
Worksheet: Enneagram test ... 293
Instinctual variants ... 311
Follow-up questions ... 314
Additional information and resources ... 315
Suggested movie: *Winnie the Pooh* (2011) ... 317

Practice Module 17 — 319

Attachment Styles — 319

Module description ... 319
Introduction ... 319
Purpose and application of the module ... 321
Exercises: Attachment styles ... 322
Worksheet: Attachment styles ... 322

Follow-up questions	330
Additional information and resources	330
Suggested movie: *As Good As It Gets* (1997)	335

Practice Module 18 — 337

The Unconscious and Emotional Availability — 337

Module description	337
Introduction	338
Purpose and application of the module	342
Exercises: Emotional availability	344
Worksheet: Emotional availability	345
Follow-up questions	346
Additional information and resources	346
Suggested movie: *Prince of Tides* (1991)	348

Practice Module 19 — 349

Healing your Shadow/Unconscious — 349

Module description	349
Introduction	350
Purpose and application of the module	355
Exercise: Healing your shadow	356
Worksheets: Healing your shadow	358
Follow-up questions	364
Additional information and resources	364
Suggested movie: *Good Will Hunting* (1997)	365

Practice Module 20 — 367

Forms, Levels, and States of Love — 367

Module description	367
Introduction	368
Purpose and application of the module	378
Exercises: Forms, levels, and states of love	378
Additional information and resources	387
Suggested movies:	388
The Mirror Has Two Faces (1996)	388
When Harry Met Sally (1989)	388

Practice Module 21 — 391
Personality Disorders — 391

Module description — 391
Introduction — 392
Purpose and application of the module — 405
Exercises: Personality disorders — 405
Worksheets: Personality disorders — 406
Additional information and resources — 412
Suggested Movie: *Eternal Sunshine of the Spotless Mind* (2004) — 416

Practice Module 22 — 417
Biological and Transformational Purpose — 417

Module description — 417
Introduction — 418
Purpose and application of the module — 421
Exercises: Biological and transformational purpose and love — 422
Biological purpose — 423
Asymmetrical, transactional, need-based love relationships — 424
Transformational purpose and transformational love — 431
Follow-up questions — 432
Additional information and resources — 433
Suggested movie: *Quest for Fire* (1981) — 433

Practice Module 23 — 435
Transcendental Purpose and Love — 435

Module description — 435
Introduction — 436
Purpose and application of the module — 444
Exercises: Transcendental purpose and love — 445
Worksheet: Immunity To Change — 446
Voice dialogue — 446
Worksheet: Voice dialogue — 447
Five purpose discovery methods — 450
Depth of expression — 457
Levels of callings — 458
Stages of Maturity — 460

Global challenges	462
Focus and circle of influence	463
Sharing your transcendental purpose	465
Moving from transactional to transcendent(al) love	466
Follow-up questions	470
Additional information and resources	470
Suggested movie: *Cloud Atlas* (2012)	470

Practice Module 24 — 475

Soulmates — 475

Module description	475
Introduction	475
Three unfolding levels of soulmates	479
Purpose and application of the module	481
Exercises: Soulmates	481
Removing psychological blocks and barriers to love	482
Worksheet: Immunity To Change	484
Defining your soulmate	484
Worksheet: Defining your soulmate	486
Soulmate selection process	490
Finding, attracting, or inviting your soulmate	491
Exercise six: Dating strategy for singles	492
Identifying, qualifying, and choosing your soulmate	492
Acceptance	493
Follow-up questions	493
Additional information and resources	494
Suggested movie: *Grace and Grit* (2021)	494

Practice Module 25 — 497

Co-Creation at the Level of the Seven Chakras — 497

Module description	497
Introduction	498
The seven chakras	498
Purpose and application of the module	501
Exercises: Co-creation at the level of the seven chakras	502
Worksheet: Chakra meditation	506
Pointers to chakras and quadrants	507

Worksheet: Chakra co-creation in the four dimensions	516
Chakra	516
Co-Creation	516
Integral Relationship	518
Follow-up questions	519
Additional information and resources	519
Suggested movies:	520
Frida (2002)	520
Inside Bill's Brain: Decoding Bill Gates (2019)	520

Practice Module 26 — 523

Why Relationships Matter — 523

Module description	523
Introduction	524
Purpose and application of the module	527
Time–money–sex	527
Exercises: Why relationships matter	528
Eight additonal reasons why relationships matter	529
Follow-up questions	548
Additional information and resources	548
Suggested movies:	549
Idiocracy (2006)	549
Tomorrow Ever After (2016)	549

Live Event Script — 551

Hosting and facilitating Integral Relationship events — 551

Goals of events	551
Marketing	551
Event logistics and structure	553

Afterword — 561

Appendix I — 565

Links, updates, and resources — 565

Endnotes — 567

Index — 689

List of Figures

Figure 1: The 14 essential dimensions of an Integral Relationship 4
Figure 2: Integral Relationship co-created along the seven chakras 6
Figure 3: Unconditional love circle 16
Figure 4: The four dimensions of being 32
Figure 5: The four dimensions of relating 33
Figure 6: Manifestations in the four dimensions/quadrants 39
Figure 7: The eight zones and their major fields of study 44
Figure 8: Perspectives of the eight zones 45
Figure 9: Eight developmental stages in the four dimensions of being ... 46
Figure 10: Age and developmental potentials of mental complexity 51
Figure 11: Development through integration and transformation 54
Figure 12: Levels/stages of consciousness development 55
Figure 13: Consciousness ladders 56
Figure 14: Transcend and include/exclude nested dolls 58
Figure 15: Interior and exterior control 73
Figure 16: Young-old woman 83
Figure 17: Different person when looking from a distance 84
Figure 18: Compatibility Matrix 100
Figure 19: Male-female dynamic in consciousness growth 101
Figure 20: Divergent psychological complexity of men and women 102
Figure 21: The STAGES Matrix 105
Figure 22: Organon model of language with levels of consciousness 129
Figure 23: Explicit versus implicit (tacit) use of language 131
Figure 24: Dreaded Drama Triangle 132
Figure 25: Drama and empowerment triangles 134
Figure 26: Four basic steps for conflict resolution 136
Figure 27: The primary sexual fantasy dynamic 166
Figure 28: The 10 phases of the fear–shame downward spiral 174
Figure 29: River with masculine banks and feminine flow 185
Figure 30: Personality matrix 187
Figure 31: Leading and following hula hoop exercise 192
Figure 32: Subtle co-creation hula hoop exercise 194
Figure 33: Exercise ascending, descending, agency, communion 197
Figure 34: Ascending, descending, agency, communion 198
Figure 35: Feminine-masculine in the four dimensions 204
Figure 36: The Wilber-Combs matrix with spiritual state-stages 214

Integral Relationship Practice | xx

Figure 37: Four levels of selfhood and reality in religions 230
Figure 38: Four dimensions of integral sexuality 237
Figure 39: Wilber-Combs matrix adopted for sexual state-stages 243
Figure 40: Forms of non-monogamy 251
Figure 41: Examples of lunch/dinner table drawings 260
Figure 42: The Five Love Languages 280
Figure 43: The nine Enneagram types 295
Figure 44: Four attachment styles 328
Figure 45: Primary emotions and vulnerable feelings 339
Figure 46: Layers of emotion, feeling, false belief, and fear 352
Figure 47: The triangle of love 370
Figure 48: Compatible and incompatible triangles of love 371
Figure 49: Eight forms of love 371
Figure 50: US statistics for origin of humans 420
Figure 51: Acceptance of evolutionary theory 421
Figure 52: Biological purpose 423
Figure 53: Cause and response in male-female relationships 424
Figure 54: Seven chakras 425
Figure 55: Transactional desire and love 427
Figure 56: Transactional love chakra-consciousness matrix 428
Figure 57: Four dimensions, chakras, and consciousness 429
Figure 58: The good, true, beautiful, and functional quadrants 437
Figure 59: Sapiosexual woman 441
Figure 60: Meiosis 441
Figure 61: Genetically predisposed talents 442
Figure 62: Skill development based on talents 442
Figure 63: Development and expression of talents 443
Figure 64: Ikigai 455
Figure 65: Ikigai and connection to the four dimensions 456
Figure 66: Bill Plotkin's Eight Stages of Maturity 461
Figure 67: Millennium Project 15 global challenges 462
Figure 68: United Nations global issues overview 463
Figure 69: Circle of influence and concern 464
Figure 70: Example of enactment of purpose 464
Figure 71: Combining talents 466
Figure 72: Transcendental desire and love 467
Figure 73: Co-created transcendental love between the seven chakras. 468
Figure 74: Transcendental love chakra matrix 469
Figure 75: Cloud Atlas timeline and characters 472

Figure 76: Metaphor of co-creative impulse...477
Figure 77: Metaphorical transformational soulmates development.......478
Figure 78: The seven chakras 499
Figure 79: Seven chakra co-creation in the four dimensions of relating 515
Figure 80: Integral couple making the world a better place 518
Figure 81: Natural world, lifeworld, and system 531
Figure 82: Ecological footprint of single versus family living 534
Figure 83: World fertility rate map...535
Figure 84: Japan, China, and US populations age 536
Figure 85: German population age distribution 1910, 2005, and 2025....536
Figure 86: Fertility rates and overall decline in consciousness................538
Figure 87: Israel's projected demographic shift..539
Figure 88: Female in domestic, and male in public sphere 540
Figure 89: Female and male in the domestic and public spheres...........540
Figure 90: Individual and social holons...542
Figure 91: Size, depth, and span of individual and social holons...........543
Figure 92: Holonic structure with highest depth given to couples.........544
Figure 93: Collapsing social holons...545
Figure 94: Closing circle with touching hands and thumbs up...............559
Figure 95: Enneagram holy ideas...602
Figure 96: Enneagram specific reactions..603
Figure 97: Enneagram specific delusions...604
Figure 98: The NARM healing cycle...628
Figure 99: Marriages per 1000 People...676
Figure 100: US statistic men and women looking for partner..............678
Figure 101: US statistic men and women looking for partner..............679
Figure 102: Societal secularism as fertility determinant.....................685
Figure 103: Secularism in various countries....................................686

List of Tables

Table 1: Structure of the 26 Modules 5
Table 2: Connection survival style 63
Table 3: Attunement survival style 64
Table 4: Trust survival style 65
Table 5: Autonomy survival style 66
Table 6: Love-Sexuality adaptive survival style 76
Table 7: Developmental lines 106
Table 8: NVC Card 113
Table 9: List of needs 117
Table 10: Interpretations versus feelings 119
Table 11: Manfred Max-Neef's fundamental human needs 123
Table 12: Biology and gender exercise 165
Table 13: Feminine-masculine exercise 190
Table 14: Love languages test 285
Table 15: Attachment style test 325
Table 16: What do you like/not like about being in relationship/single . 327
Table 17: Borderline personality disorder 407
Table 18: Histrionic personality disorder 409
Table 19: Narcissistic personality disorder 410
Table 20: Cloud Atlas cast and characters (main in bold) 473
Table 21: Ego and Soul 482
Table 22: Soulmate worksheet 489
Table 23: Chakra charge worksheet 506
Table 24: Four dimensions chakra co-creation worksheet 517
Table 25: My path to an Integral soulmate relationship 547
Table 26: Difference between ethics and morals 583
Table 27: Different forms of therapy 633
Table 28: Transcendental Purpose immunity to change examples 656
Table 29: Ego versus Soul 667
Table 30: Soulmate immunity to change examples 668
Table 31: List of Passions and Interests 670
Table 32: List of capacities, value and ideals 672
Table 33: Examples Co-Creation at 1st and 2nd Chakra 674

Acknowledgments

As I reflect on a long and fulfilled life, I am full of gratitude for the countless kind and wise people who helped me arrive at this place where I feel called to pass on the accumulated understanding and practices of how to co-create a healthy love relationship and teach the necessary skills to others. While there are too many to thank directly for their love, support, friendship, mentorship, and generosity, I want to thank certain people who were instrumental in creating this practice manual.

My first and foremost thanks go to all the practitioners from around the world who took part in our live workshops and online trainings over the past eleven years and provided invaluable feedback and suggestions for improvements in the teaching material and experiential exercises: most notably, Dr. Wayne Carr for introducing me to the NARM process that is used in Module 2, 3, and 19; Kirsten Kristensen for her suggestions in improving the NVC Module 6; Jan Day for her feedback on the Sexuality Module 13; Dr. Khaled El Sherbini for his contributions to the Enneagram Module 16; and Barbara J. Hunt for her Forgiveness Made Easy work in Module 20. And a special thank you to those graduates who now incorporate the 26 Modules into their work.

Secondly, I am full of gratitude for my fellow soulmate-searcher Liza Braude-Glidden, whom I met 19 years ago. She introduced me to the world of polyamory and undefended love; took me to Harbin Hot Springs, where I had deep transformative state experiences over the years; accompanied me to my first Human Awareness Institute[1] workshop about love, intimacy, and sexuality; and led me to the work of Ken Wilber by way of gifting me the 12-hour Kosmic Consciousness CD set. She is a true pioneer in the areas of love, spirituality, sexuality, femininity, consciousness development, and political activism, and I am deeply honored to call her my friend.

My deep love goes out to my late maternal grandparents, Eugen and Mina Geiger, and to my parents, Heinrich and Renate Ucik, who are still my primary examples of couples who work together as equals and opposites to make the world a better place.

I am eternally grateful for my amazing daughters, Laura, Lisa, and Anna Lea, who are now adult women and leave their positive mark in the world and who keep me on my toes with their feedback about my views as an "old white man." I love you more than anything else.

I am also deeply indebted to Ken Wilber for his incredible body of work that changed my life and enabled me to write my two previous books and now this manual, and for his kind friendship and generous support of the *Integral Relationship Vision*. I'm indebted, too, to Prof. Allan Combs for his mentorship, his inspiration to watch movies through an Integral lens, and for the brilliant Wilber-Combs Matrix that explains so much about the complexity of consciousness development, and to Andrew Cohen for opening my eyes to evolutionary spirituality and for our inspiring conversations about the importance of co-creation and procreation in Integral Love Relationships for human evolution and a better world.

My deep appreciation goes to Allyson and Alex Grey, one of the best examples of an Integral couple, for their invitation to contribute an essay to their *CoSM Journal* (vol. 10, focusing on Love) and to facilitate a workshop at the Chapel of Sacred Mirrors in Wappinger, NY.

I also want to thank my team that tirelessly works on spreading the Integral Relationship Vision and supporting our clients, trainees, and workshop participants.

Last, but certainly not least, my gratitude goes to Dr. Cynthia Deitering for her guidance and excellent editing of this manual, Rizwana Kausar for the cover design, Özer Koç, Sahra Özdoğan, Annette Berlin, and Muzzammil Baig for contributing inside graphics, and Firuj Ahmed for creating the index and formatting the text. I could not have done it without you!

My Ten Core Tenets

Love is unconditional, relationships are not.

Humans are not social atoms but social beings.

We can only practice our simultaneous wholeness and partialness at all levels of our being in intimate love relationships.

The more we learn to love ourselves, the more we need to learn to love others. Anything else leads to uneven development.

If we want to contribute to creating a peaceful and sustainable future for all humanity, we need to begin by co-creating a peaceful and sustainable love relationship with one person.

If we want to raise consciousness on the planet, we also need to raise conscious children.

It takes two partners to co-create an embodied love relationship, but only one to end it.

We can only heal our relationship wounds in relationships.

Humans are happiest when they are in healthy relationships and live on purpose.

Healthy love relationships don't just happen, the skills must be learned.

Preface

It is not a measure of health to be well adjusted to a profoundly sick society.
~ Jiddu Krishnamurti ~

As I write this, there is an unexpected backslide in many crucial domains of human well-being, happiness, flourishing, and progress. Putin's invasion of the Ukraine—causing the biggest war in Europe since 1945 and a possible global food crisis—has been raging on for five months now, with no end in sight, while fears of other international armed conflicts are growing. Around the world, we see a rise of illiberal democracies, in which elections still take place but autocratic and corrupt leaders control the media and repress, jail, or even kill their opponents. We saw the UK leave the European Union, and the defeating Taliban retaking of power in Afghanistan. We hear now from the US House committee investigating the January 6 attack how former President Donald Trump and his allies almost succeeded in reversing the 2020 election results by staging a coup to overthrow the legitimately elected US government. We are astonished to hear from liberal world leaders that defending democracies is now the biggest challenge facing humanity, as they see an independent media and fair and free elections as the foundation for human progress. We are assailed daily with news of environmental disasters such as floods, droughts, wildfires, and megastorms, all caused by preventable global warming and climate change that threatens millions, and soon billions, of humans, animals, and plants. We are compelled to witness horrible images of migrants who are stranded in refugee camps or perish on their journey to find better lives in developed countries. Almost everyone knows someone who suffered or died during the Coronavirus pandemic, a global health crisis which could have been much better managed or even prevented if humans would have acted more responsibly. We have an illegal drug and opioid epidemic, with increasing numbers of deaths of despair, including suicides, especially among men. As described by Warren Farrell,[2] we face a "boy crisis" in 63 developed nations, where girls will graduate from college at up to twice the rate of boys who, in turn, feel increasingly vulnerable to female sexual and relationship rejection, as women prefer winners and see losers who approach them as either harassers (if they come on too strong) or wimps (if they are too cautious). Consequently, these "boys," who often grow up without fathers, may, as men, stay involuntarily single and celibate and become vulnerable to be radicalized by both the left and right.[3] Along with all of this, we see an ongoing upward distribution of wealth and power, as well as rising inflation around the world, with threats of economic decline and maybe even collapse in some nations.

Why do I share all of this at the beginning of a relationship book? When I entered the spiritual New-Age scene in Northern California in 2000, I initially bought into the teachings and practices that were adopted and propagated by the communities and groups that I joined—that we would find happiness by living in the now, surrendering to what is, finding inner peace, loving ourselves, creating our own reality, awakening the giant within, activating our genius code, or getting over our fears of success, and that we would contribute to making the world a better place by raising consciousness on the planet through our heightened individual awareness and spiritual realizations.

When, after several years, I rarely saw any positive effects for individuals or any noticeable progress towards a more peaceful and sustainable world by following these ideas, I began to wonder why. The only common denominator I noticed was that most practitioners and teachers in these circles were either die-hard singles or struggled in their love relationships and rarely had children. When I questioned how people could be loving and contribute to creating a peaceful and sustainable world if they could not even co-create a loving, happy, peaceful, and sustainable relationship with one person, and how they imagined raising consciousness on the planet without raising conscious children, I was kicked out of most of these groups (who paradoxically maintained that everyone was welcome—except for me.)

I gained a better understanding of why most people in these communities continued to struggle in their lives and relationships, and why they seemingly failed to effectively contribute to making the world a better place when I was introduced to the Integral Philosophy of Ken Wilber in January 2006.

Through reading him and other Integral authors, and joining the Integral Salon in Santa Rosa, CA, I learned that there are multiple stages of consciousness and spiritual development, or ego building and ego transcendence, both of which are essential. I realized that functional social holons such as couples, families, communities, and nations are co-created by humans who are able to be simultaneously whole and part through balancing their healthy feminine and masculine polarities. And I was introduced to the idea of an underlying evolutionary impulse, Eros, or higher/causal intelligence, that supposedly drives human evolution towards ever increasing levels of consciousness that create more goodness, truth, beauty, and functioning in the world. Wilber and his followers maintained then that soon over 10 percent of the world's population would advance into a new stage called Integral. This advance would create tectonic shifts and progress for humanity comparable to those caused by the invention of agriculture some 8,000 years ago and the scientific discoveries that emerged during the Enlightenment era that began 500 years ago and led to the many achievements of modernity and postmodernity. At this new post-postmodern Integral level, humans would integrate all the positive capacities, achievements, virtues, values, and worldviews of the preceding levels and transcend their liabilities and limited views, thus ending human conflict and suffering by creating a peaceful, sustainable, eudaemonic world in which everyone would flourish. I was very excited and fully on board to be part of this transformation.

Alas, 16 years later, there is mounting evidence that we are not even near that 10 percent number and, instead, that overall human progress through cultural and social evolution has actually come to a grinding halt and is even in decline in crucial areas.

The only conceivable reason why this new transformation has not taken place is the same as why spiritual New-Age communities failed to create lasting happiness and a peaceful sustainable future for humanity: progressives at higher levels of consciousness development often fail to co-create healthy sustainable love relationships and rarely have children. The cause for this unprecedented worldwide increase in singles and childless couples, and the subsequent falling birth rates—far below sustainable replacement levels—was a shift away from traditional religiously motivated family and community values[4] and conventional gender roles as defended by right-leaning conservatives, towards hyperindividualistic social atomism and the empowerment and education of women, as promoted by left-leaning progressive modern liberals. Along with this shift came the transformation of local citizens into global consumers and the rise of liberal political parties. Their main aim became to protect the rights and freedoms of individuals, many of which became increasingly dependent on governmental support and protection, which, paradoxically, eventually deprived them of their freedoms and led to their discontent. As a consequence, right-leaning illiberal conservative political parties have of late regained momentum around the globe, as their supporters see themselves as the victims of meritocratic liberalization, modernization, globalization, multiculturalization, immigration, degenderization, and eroded traditional gender roles and family values. This resurgence of a radical conservatism and the resulting extreme polarization in politics and social life is aptly analyzed in the book, *Why Liberalism Failed*, by Patrick J. Deneen who writes in its preface:

> My basic assumption was that the underpinnings of our inherited civilized order—norms learned in families, in communities, through religion and a supporting culture— would inevitably erode under the influence of the liberal social

and political state. From that vantage, I hinted that such a political condition was ultimately untenable, and that the likely popular reaction to an increasingly oppressive liberal order might be forms of authoritarian illiberalism that would promise citizens power over those forces that no longer seemed under their control: government, economy, and the dissolution of social norms and unsettled ways of life. For liberals, this would prove the need for tighter enforcement of a liberal regime, but they would be blind to how this crisis of legitimacy had been created by liberalism itself. Today's widespread yearning for a strong leader, one with the will to take back popular control over liberalism's forms of bureaucratized government and globalized economy, comes after decades of liberal dismantling of cultural norms and political habits essential to self-governance. The breakdown of family, community, and religious norms and institutions, especially among those benefiting least from liberalism's advance, has not led liberalism's discontents to seek a restoration of those norms. That would take effort and sacrifice in a culture that now diminishes the value of both. Rather, many now look to deploy the statist powers of liberalism against its own ruling class. Meanwhile, huge energies are spent in mass protest rather than in self-legislation and deliberation, reflecting less a renewal of democratic governance than political fury and despair. Liberalism created the conditions, and the tools, for the ascent of its own worst nightmare, yet it lacks the self-knowledge to understand its own culpability. While I end this volume by calling on political philosophers for help in finding a way out of the vise in which we now find ourselves—the mental grip of those revolutionary ideologies inaugurated in modernity first by liberalism itself— the better course lies not in any political revolution but in the patient encouragement of new forms of community that can serve as havens in our depersonalized political and economic order. As the Czech dissident Václav Havel wrote in "The

Power of the Powerless": "A better system will not automatically ensure a better life. In fact, the opposite is true: only by creating a better life can a better system be developed." Only a politics grounded in the experience of a polis—lives shared with a sense of common purpose, with obligations and gratitude arising from sorrows, hopes, and joys lived in generational time, and with the cultivation of capacities of trust and faith—can begin to take the place of our era's distrust, estrangement, hostility, and hatreds.

If we accept Deneen's analysis that progressive liberalism is failing to create a better world because of its support of hyperindividualism through ever-increasing government interventions and social spending to protect the freedom of individuals to do whatever they please; and if we also reject the idea that the solutions to the challenges faced by humanity are found in a return to conservatism with the enforcement of traditional religious and patriarchal family values by illiberal, corrupt, autocratic, fascist, or dictatorial leaders and their supporters of the radical right; and if we admit that we will most likely not see a political evolution or revolution towards a depolarized society and government at an integral level (as envisioned by integral politics philosopher Steve McIntosh in his well-argued book, *Developmental Politics: How America Can Grow Into a Better Version of Itself*)[5] anytime soon—or, as McIntosh admits, maybe never; and if we realize that people are happiest and healthiest when they are in flourishing love relationships and live on purpose in supportive communities—then we need a different solution.

I offer that solution in this book and invite you to become a part of it: that we move towards *holonism* that transcends liberalism and conservatism by learning and practicing how to co-create healthy love relationships between opposite and equal partners in our own lives and teach the necessary relationship skills that can be applied by people from all walks of life, levels of consciousness and spiritual development, religious beliefs, race, ethnic and cultural backgrounds, sexual orientations, and political affiliations in our schools, communities, institutions, and workplaces. In this way, we can contribute to making the world a better place by allowing our own healthy love relationships and those of others to become the foundation for functional nuclear families, thriving communities, flourishing societies, and a peaceful and sustainable future for humanity. See more in Module 26.

Please contact me at martin@integralrelationship.com if I can be of any support to you to become an Integral Relationship practitioner and teacher to make this vision a reality.

Introduction

Experience without theory is blind, but theory without experience is mere intellectual play.
~ Immanuel Kant ~

This manual is for singles and couples who are not only interested in the theory of Integral Relationships as outlined in my previous two books, *Integral Relationships: A Manual for Men* and *Sex Purpose Love: Couples in Integral Relationships Creating a Better World*,[6] but also in the deep understanding that can only be gained through embodied practices and experiences. It is for those who realize that for us to become fully human means to develop the capacity to be simultaneously whole in ourselves AND part of healthy, sustainable love relationships and nuclear families, who then form the foundation for thriving communities and flourishing societies. And it is for those who understand that cultural and biological evolution are intertwined—that we need to raise conscious children if we want to raise consciousness on the planet to create a better world and a peaceful, sustainable future for humanity.

This manual is also intended for helping professionals who want to support their clients in co-creating healthy love relationships, and for group facilitators who feel called to lead events, workshops, and trainings in which the participants sharpen their relationships skills together with others in their local communities through experiential exercises. If the latter is your intention, see detailed instructions of how to market and set up your events under "Live Event Script," on page 551. My wish for all readers is that they co-create Integral Relationships and inspire and teach others so that the Integral Relationship vision can ripple out into the world and make it a better place.

In the context of relationships, the term *integral* means to differentiate the essential dimensions of our human being and relating, and to integrate them into a functional whole in co-created healthy, sustainable love relationships.

As a useful metaphor to understand this integration, consider the essential dimensions of a flourishing garden, such as soil, water, air, seeds, trees, light, shade, insects, fertilizers, structures, paths, etc., that need to be brought into a functional whole for the plants to thrive and realize their full growth potentials. Neglecting any of these essential or necessary dimensions would lead to dysfunction and, ultimately, the withering of the whole.

The same is true for healthy love relationships and, consequently, for our families, communities, societies, and humanity. We need to have knowledge and experience of all our essential human dimensions and how they interact with each other so that we can realize our full potentials in the context of our love relationships.

The 14 essential dimensions of an Integral Relationship, as outlined and illustrated in *Figure 1* (below), allow singles and couples to achieve the following:

1. Become aware, connect, and co-create in all four dimensions of their being and relating.
2. Identify eight levels of consciousness development to learn, heal, and grow together with an equal and opposite partner.
3. Communicate with each other at their shared level of consciousness so that both are heard and understood, thus able to reach agreement on how to best meet both of their needs.
4. Understand biological and gender differences of males/men and females/women in order to a) end the gender wars through understanding and compassion, and b) return to love and romance for those who went down the infamous Fear-Shame spiral that ultimately leads to relationship crashes.
5. Balance and harmonize their healthy feminine and masculine polarities to maintain their simultaneous wholeness and partialness in their relationships and to create synergy and sexual passion.

6. Awaken together through the five state-stages of spiritual development.
7. Co-create a healthy, exciting, and rewarding sex life by healing and growing towards sacred and tantric sexuality.
8. Understand their anima/animus complex to co-create a healthy love relationship at stages three or five.
9. Become aware of various personality types in order to understand and accept different fundamental human needs, preferences, passions, virtues, and drives that guide each partner's thoughts and behaviors.
10. Move towards earned secure attachment through creating a coherent narrative and healing their childhood trauma and attachment wounds.
11. Own the emotional reactions to their partner's reality instead of blaming him or her and making demands, consequently healing their underlying false identities in order to move towards undefended love.
12. Create compassion and healthy boundaries when they are attracted to or in a love relationship with a highly seductive, complex, and challenging partner who may display symptoms of personality disorders.
13. Awaken to their biological, transformational, and transcendental purpose and define, find/attract/invite, identify, and choose a soulmate who shares their passion, purpose, vision, and mission.
14. Co-create a deeply rewarding love relationship with their soulmate through intimacy, passion, and commitment in all four dimensions of their being, at the level of the seven chakras, by balancing and harmonizing healthy feminine and masculine polarities in the four dimensions of their being to make the world a better place.

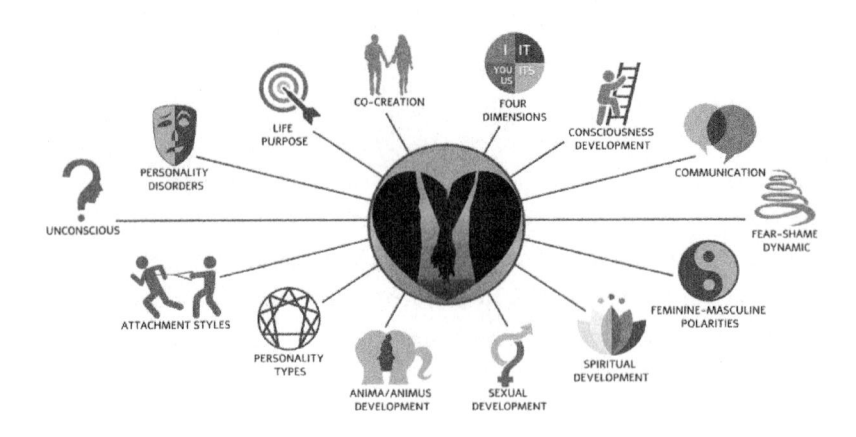

Figure 1: The 14 essential dimensions of an Integral Relationship

These 14 dimensions are further divided into the 26 practice modules that are described in detail in this manual. They were developed, tested, refined, and validated between 2011 and 2022 in over 600 experiential Integral Relationship live workshops and online training sessions with monogamous and non-monogamous heterosexual, same-sex, and gender fluid singles, couples, helping professionals, teachers, and workshop leaders of all adult ages from over 40 countries in the East and West. The universality of their experiences around love relationships, despite their cultural, gender, sexual, and age differences, was striking.

Each of the 26 practice modules has the same structure:

1.	A general description of the module.[7]
2.	A short introduction to the theory that underlies the exercises.
3.	The purpose and practical application of each module.
4.	Detailed descriptions of the exercises.
5.	Worksheets for the exercises.[8]
6.	Follow-up questions for the practitioners.
7.	Additional information, resources, book references, and tinyurl links[i] to websites for a deeper understanding of the module. Also see Appendix I.
8.	Descriptions of suggested movies that depict the modules.

Table 1: Structure of the 26 Modules

The knowledge and practices that are offered in this manual allow you and your date or partner, your clients, and/or the participants in your groups, workshops, and trainings to understand and embody the 14 essential dimensions of an Integral Relationship to co-create healthy, lasting love relationships in which equal and opposite partners realize their fullest human potentials through sharing their biological purpose (including raising children, if possible); their transformational purpose of ongoing learning, healing, growing, and awakening; and their transcendental purpose of creating more goodness, truth, beauty, and functioning in the world by maintaining their simultaneous wholeness and partialness through balancing and harmonizing their healthy feminine and masculine polarities in the four dimensions of their being and relating along their seven chakras in the safe container of intimacy, passion and commitment as shown below.

---

[i] The links to websites throughout the manual are provided as short tinyurls for easy typing and in full original length in the endnotes.

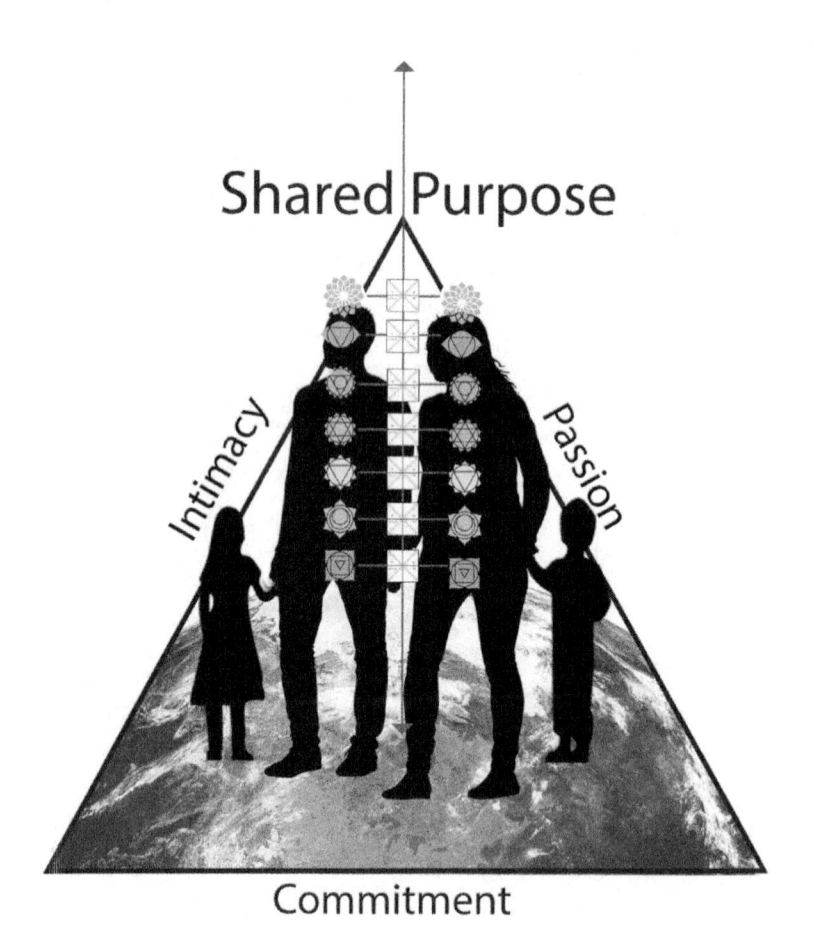

Figure 2: Integral Relationship co-created along the seven chakras

Module 26 provides eight philosophical arguments for why Integral Relationships matter not only for your own well-being but also for addressing the wicked problems that humanity is facing, so you may want to start there if this subject is of primary interest to you and your audience.

To keep the text succinct and flowing, I have added an abundance of endnotes in which you will find additional information, details, references, and resources for further reading.

As mentioned above, keep in mind that the map is not the territory, no more than a recipe is the meal. Maps and words are only simplified reflections of reality. The gap between the map (your or your client's vision of a healthy, happy love relationship and a better world) and the territory (your or your client's reality of being single, in an unfulfilling partnership, or living in a less than perfect world) is called the reality gap. This is where you come in, to bridge this gap. Only if you apply the 26 Modules of the Integral Relationship model and the related practices to your real-life dating strategy, your love relationships, and your work as a helping professional or facilitator can you make the model work for you and contribute to creating a better world.

Also be aware that there are limitations to the empirical findings upon which this manual is based, especially those findings that result from social and gender studies. The studies may tell a lot about randomly selected groups of men and women—such as "on average, men are taller than women" or "women are more emotional than men"—but little to nothing about individuals. There are also no stereotypical types *of* people but only contextual and fluid types *in* people.

While based on the latest scientific research from the West and enduring wisdom traditions from the East, the content of this manual can only serve as a *generalizing orientation* that needs your careful verification on an individual level (such as, "Am I really taller or less emotionally available than my partner?").

The same holds true for the nature of the exercises. Some of them are based and phrased in the experience of heterosexual singles and couples, even though the exercises may also apply to people with other gender identities and sexual orientations. In no way should you use what you learn and practice in the following pages to label, discriminate against, or take advantage of others.

Throughout the manual, we will refer to people with whom you romantically relate as *partners* and to love relationships as *partnerships*, in order to distinguish them from the relationships you have with other people, even though most of the exercises will help to improve those relationships as well.

Thank you very much for supporting the Integral Relationship vision that makes the world a better place through your own practice and by being a role model, and thank you for sharing the theory and experiential exercises with others

Preliminary Practice Module
Ego-Transcendence and Unconditional Love

The ego cannot love, it always wants something.
~ Eckhart Tolle ~

Module Description

Join us for a guided ego-transcending mindfulness meditation that is followed by an unconditional love circle to deepen the connection with yourself, your partner, and others. Develop meta-cognition during the subject-object mindfulness meditation by strengthening your witnessing self (or subject) that is aware of objects. Transcend your separate false sense of self (or ego) that cannot love. Let go of fear, which is the opposite of love. Free yourself from desire, attachment, delusion, and hatred/aversion, all of which create pain and suffering.

Become fully present in the here and now, and surrender, without judgment, to what arises in your awareness from moment to moment. Enter a state of pure being, or witnessing consciousness, through disidentifying from material objects, from your body, from your mind/thoughts, from your feelings and emotions, and even from the experience of enlightenment, or full awakening, itself. Integrate all dimensions of your being by entering into a state of nondual awareness in an Integral Relationship.

Open your heart and remove all the barriers that prevent love by staying fully present in the now with yourself and your partner to deeply connect in the we-space that is created in the unconditional love circle. Understand why love is unconditional and relationships are not.

Introduction

The deepest yearnings of our human soul, essence, or nature are to feel fully alive, to love and be loved, and to live on purpose in a healthy love relationship with a soulmate at all levels of our being, including the material, physical, mental, emotional, and spiritual.

These yearnings are driven by an underlying co-creative life force (sometimes called Eros or evolutionary impulse) that exists a priori[9] as unconditional love before any manifestation or human experience of conditional love and relationships can arise.

The manifestation of this co-creative life force is often inhibited by the ego. The ego, in the sense that spiritual teachers like Eckhart Tolle and poets like Rumi use the term, is our conditioned, wounded, fearful, separate—and thus false—sense of self that cannot love because it lives in the past and future, is disconnected from the co-creative life force, has no purpose, and always wants something from outside itself to be happy. This impaired capacity of the ego results in diminished aliveness and in an inability to love and to live on purpose. It is caused by hidden dimensions of the self that underlie most psychological and many physiological challenges. Unfortunately, we are often unaware of these impairments that have developed in reaction to emotional pain and developmental shock trauma during childhood; consequently, the related nervous system dysregulations, disruptions in secure attachment, and distortions of identity may have caused us to live in fear and shame, which are the opposites of love.[10]

Because of ego impairments, an increasing number of people struggle in their love relationships. Some even avoid them altogether in the name of not having to deal with the pain from the past, selfish hedonism, misguided pursuits of becoming whole without simultaneously being part of a healthy love relationship, pathological ascending transcendence without healthy descending immanence (see page 198), and spiritual bypassing (see page 217).

Others project their endless ego-driven deficiency needs and desires outward onto their partners, loving them only as long as they make the ego-driven partner happy.

In contrast, healthy ego development takes place in a relational context through mindful presence—healing our psychological wounds and continually expanding our capacities and perspectives while transcending limited views in order to fulfill our souls yearning to co-create more goodness, truth, beauty, and functionality in a loving relationship with our soulmate at the gross, subtle, and causal level of our being:

1. At the gross, material, and physical level, our soul yearns to co-create with a compatible mate to meet our survival needs for food, shelter, safety, money, goods, mobility, and procreation.
2. At the subtle mental and emotional level, our soul yearns to co-create with a compatible mate to meet our being-needs for connection, attunement, trust, autonomy, and sexuality through ongoing learning, healing, growing, and awakening. (See an extended list of being-needs on page 117.)
3. At the causal level of our mystical spiritual nature, essence, or being, our soul yearns to co-create with a compatible mate to meet our inter-becoming needs by combining our different natural talents to co-create more goodness, truth, beauty, and functioning in service of the well-being of others and in order to contribute to making the world a better place.

In other words, both ego transcendence through **disidentification** (not dissociating, repressing, splitting off, denying, ignoring, bypassing, etc.) from our separate, false, wounded—and thus fearful—sense of self and limiting views, **and** healthy ego development through **integration** of ever-wider perspectives and capacities to love are necessary to fulfill our souls' yearning to feel fully alive and to share our purpose in a flourishing love relationship with a soulmate.

We practice this ego transcending disidentification in this preliminary module by creating a safe container of *unconditional love* and acceptance for everything that arises from moment to moment without judgement, desire, attachment, delusion, and hatred/aversion. This experience provides us with the foundation to safely explore the multiple dimensions of healing and integration through healthy ego development in *conditional relationships* in the following 26 practice modules for co-creating an Integral Love Relationship with our soulmate.

Purpose and application

1. Realize why love is unconditional but relationships are not.
2. Understand that the ego cannot love because it always wants something.
3. Be introduced to an ego-transcending, subject-object, mindfulness meditation.
4. Experience pure witness consciousness or metacognition.
5. Let go of fear and shame, the opposite of love.
6. Create a safe container of unconditional love and acceptance in which your love relationships can flourish as you participate in the practice module exercises that follow.
7. Use affirmations to create intimacy, love, and connection.
8. Have a peak experience of full aliveness and unconditional love.
9. Stay fully present with the thoughts and feelings of your partner and the other practitioners, without judgment or reactions arising from old wounds.
10. Develop empathy and compassion for the reality of others.
11. Move your body and have fun in the sock name game that follows the love circle.

Exercises: Meditation and love circle

The following are individual, paired, and group exercises.
1. If this exercise is followed by Module 1, mention that we will do personal introductions later.

2. Make the four agreements for confidentiality, responsibility, healthy boundaries, I-statements, and sharing, as outlined on page 556.
3. If you practice alone with your partner, sit across from each other during the meditation, as outlined below, and at the end of the meditation gaze into his or her left eye for about 10–15 minutes, without drifting off into thought. You may then share some of the affirmations from page 21 (below). Alternately, you may lie down or sit on your partner's lap and hold each other, and one by one consciously breath together into your seven chakras (see Module 25 on page 506) to deepen your connection and experience of unconditional love.
4. If you facilitate a live group event, begin with all practitioners sitting in a circle for the guided meditation, as outlined on page 12 below, and directly follow the meditation with the unconditional love circle in which all participants connect with each other, one by one, through eye gazing, handholding, affirmations (see list below), and hugging. This releases the bonding, feel-good, love-and-cuddle hormones, Dopamine and Oxytocin,[11] in the practitioners; lowers their stress hormone, cortisol[12]; and opens them up to safely explore the exercises, with vulnerability, in the practice module(s) that follow(s).
5. You may explain that the meditation and unconditional love circle are based on Eckhart Tolle's insight that "the Ego cannot love; it always wants something." With that insight, Tolle points to our separate and false illusionary sense of self that confuses love with getting what it wants to feel happy (such as, ice cream, money, or a person).
6. You may also point out that the subject-object mindfulness meditation is rooted in the Buddhist insights about suffering—that it is caused by desire, attachment, delusion, ignorance, and hatred/aversion in the material, physical, mental, emotional, and even spiritual realms of

our being. During the meditation, we will disidentify or "un-fuse" from these realms by observing them as objects in a consciousness that no longer defines who we truly are; in this way, we will transcend our false and separate sense of self or ego. This is like peeling off the layers of an onion or removing layers of veils that cover a precious jewel. What is left will be pure witness consciousness or being or, metaphorically speaking, the seed from which the onion originated. This process will be followed by re-integrating all levels of the participants' being in nondual awareness during the unconditional love circle.

Explain and demonstrate the unconditional love circle

It is important to demonstrate the unconditional love circle with your assistant or a participant with whom you have practiced, in private, before the event. Say and show the following:

1. At the end of the meditation, I will ring the bell.
2. You will then stand up without talking (stay seated while we demonstrate) and form a double circle by each of you standing across from another person, with one of you facing the center of the room and the other facing the wall (demonstrate with your partner).
3. Look your partner in the eyes.
4. Either put your hands on your heart or hold hands with your partner.
5. Experiment with this step, and if your partner does not want to hold hands, avoid taking it personally by staying present with your feelings.
6. I will be the only one speaking, saying, for example, "I see you; I hear you; and I feel you."
7. After the affirmation, either bow a Namaste or share a hug.
8. Demonstrate the Namaste bow.
9. If you share a hug, we will first show you four ways NOT to hug: (1) "The A-Frame," where only your shoulders are

15 | Ego-Transcendence and Unconditional Love

touching; (2) "The Burper," where you pat your partner on the back; (3) "The Grind," where you grind your groins together; and (4) "The Butt Grab," where you place your hands below the waistline and grab your partner's butt (you can smilingly say that this is for another workshop …). Make sure that the person with whom you demonstrate these hugs is amenable to demonstrating, especially 3 and 4.

10. Demonstrate the way you do want the practitioners to hug by asking the taller person to bend their knees (the built-in lift) so that they are at the same height as their partner. Then, demonstrate how they should gently embrace each other so that their bellies touch, breathing in and out together to feel their bellies rise and fall.
11. Show that the hug is over when one person lifts his or her arms, and demonstrate that the other person does not hang on.
12. Then, say and demonstrate "step to the left," so that each participant will face a new person when they participate in the actual circle after the meditation.
13. Say and demonstrate that if the practitioners are with the facilitator or the designated person (and ONLY with this person, nobody else!!!), they will be switched from the inside to the outside or vice versa when the facilitator says, "step to the left." They will then move in the other direction around the circle to meet the participants they have not yet met. (Instruct your assistant or the designated person how to do this and watch that he or she is doing it every time; otherwise, the circle becomes disorganized!)
14. Mention that it does not matter who they begin the circle with, as they will eventually meet everyone.
15. Ask practitioners not to leave the room during the meditation and love circle. Ask them to go to the bathroom now if they must. Wait for them to return.
16. Ask participants to leave (the room) if they don't want to do the meditation and love circle, as this is an

experiential/participatory activity and not a spectator event/workshop.
17. Take a count of the group to determine whether you will be in the love circle (if it is an even number of practitioners, including yourself).
18. Make sure you have the affirmations sheet and bell ready.
19. After demonstrating the love circle, facilitate the meditation as described below.
20. See image below and love circle demo video at tinyurl.com/irpm101[13]

Figure 3: Unconditional love circle

Exercise one: Guided meditation

See video of guided meditation at tinyurl.com/irpm98[14]
1. Invite practitioners to assume the (meditation) position and to look spiritual (joke).
2. Ask practitioners to put their hand on their belly/abdomen and to take a few deep, natural breaths, feeling their belly rise and fall (some practitioners need to learn how to deeply and

17 | Ego-Transcendence and Unconditional Love

   naturally breath into their abdomen by relaxing it while breathing in deeply.)
3. Optional: Facilitate the raisin exercise about desire, attachment, and hatred found on page 226.
4. Ask practitioners to follow the sound of the bell arising out of silence and fading back into silence. Ring the bell, bowl, or chime.
5. Guide practitioners to bring their attention into their physical body: to wiggle their toes a little; to feel the surface (pillow, chair, floor) that supports their body, feel the gravity of the earth that keeps them firmly grounded; and to relax every muscle in their body, starting from their feet, legs, abdomen (deep breath), taking back their shoulders a little to fully open and remove barriers around their heart, to relax their chest, to relax their shoulders, arms, and hands.
6. Ask practitioners to gently turn their heads to the left, right, front, and back to find that perfect balancing point for their head on top of their spine.
7. Finally, ask them to relax every muscle in their face and release any tension that they may hold in their jaw.
8. They may also relax their tongue, slightly touching it on the inside of their lower front teeth.
9. When you are fully present in the moment with your body, say the following to the participants: realize that you have a body but that you are not your body. You, as the self, witness, consciousness, or subject, are not defined by your body's looks, size, age, sex, gender, race, health, etc. This allows you to be the steward or master of your body by taking care of it through healthy eating, exercise, sleep, body work, yoga, meditation, and medication as needed.
10. Next, invite the practitioners to focus their attention on their breath, to become fully present in the now, without drifting off into thought about the past or future, and to take ten conscious, natural, relaxed, in-and-out breaths, feeling their bellies rise and fall. Remind them, after 6 breaths, to focus on

breath. Suggest that they practice daily at home to count about 160 conscious breaths without drifting off into thought until they can stay present indefinitely with their breath, without counting.

11. When you are fully present with your breathing, guide the practitioners to watch their mind, waiting for the next thought to arise (using the metaphor of a cat watching a mouse hole, waiting for the mouse to stick out its head) and to release that thought once it arises by bringing their attention back into the present moment, using their conscious breathing and the body as an "anchor" in the here and now. Ask practitioners to repeat this process until their mind is still or they maintain a witnessing state of observing thought (like lucid dreaming.) Say the following: realize that you may have thoughts or no thought, but you are not your thoughts or your mind. You are the self, witness, consciousness, awareness, or subject, that is aware of thought or no thought but not defined by your thoughts or mind. This allows you to quiet your mind and become fully present or use it for creative thoughts, contemplation, problem-solving, intuition, visioning, etc., in the now, instead of being used by it.

12. When you are fully present in the now, guide the practitioners to also become present in the space between one thought ending and another beginning in order to allow the "vertical drop" into the causal realm, with experiences of presence, surrender, stillness, joy, peace, connectedness, oneness, empathy, compassion, love, insight, etc., and even full awakening or enlightenment. They may also experience feelings of pain, (suffering is optional), sadness, or fear. Ask them to stay present with those feelings, without repressing or dissociating. When you are in this state, say the following: realize that you may have feelings and realizations in the causal realm below thoughts, but you are not your feelings and realizations, including the experience of full awakening or enlightenment. You, as the witnessing self, consciousness,

awareness, or subject, are not defined by your feelings and spiritual realizations.
13. When you are pure witnessing consciousness, point to the eternal, infinite, timeless, and spaceless ground, source, oneness, or "God," from which time, space and all manifestation arise. To that which pervades everything and is not separate from any manifestation or experience. To that which is the witness that cannot be witnessed. To the subject that cannot be made into an object. That which can cannot be spoken of, thought about, or experienced, as that would make it into an object in consciousness. That which has never been born, never entered the stream of time, will never die, and therefore knows no pain of the past or fear of the future. "It" just "is."
14. Sit for a while in this blissful state of pure witness consciousness (not making "it" into something, e.g., an "experience").
15. Ring the bell or say the following: "Thus, it has been said that those who speak do not know, and those who know do not speak" and/or that "the Dao that can be spoken is not the eternal (true/real) Dao. The name that can be named is not the eternal name. The Dao that can be understood cannot be the primal, or cosmic, Dao, just as an idea that can be expressed in words cannot be the infinite idea. There are ways, but the Way is uncharted."
16. You may also joke that "there should be a conference for enlightened people and everyone who goes is automatically disqualified."
17. Point to the realization that the ability to retain the pure witness state while also being fully engaged in the manifest world is called Nondual Awareness or Enlightenment.
18. Ring the bell.

Exercise two: Love circle

1. If you have a very small group or if you practice with your partner, you may meditate in pairs, then eye gaze for 10–15 minutes. Follow this by either sharing some of the affirmations below, holding each other, and consciously breathing into your seven chakras, or by doing a chant together (for example, Deva Premal & Miten: "Om Namo Bhagvate Vasudevaya." tinyurl.com/irpm104)[15]
2. If you have a group of six or more, start playing soft instrumental music (for example, Jim Wilson "Northern Seascape")[16]
3. Ask practitioners to stand up without talking and to form the love circle as you demonstrated earlier. You may have to assist a little with forming the circle.
4. IMORTANT! Make sure to remember a couple in the circle or the participant with whom you started the love circle, so that you know when the circle is completed!
5. If you participate in the circle, start by looking inside out (towards the wall) and be the first to turn/be turned so that you will then always look from the outside in (towards the center). This way, you can better monitor the group to see if there are any problems; check on whether the designated person is doing the turning correctly with every partner; make sure that everyone steps to the left; notice if someone is leaving the circle (in which case you or your assistant can step in or out); offer support if someone is in distress; or intervene if practitioners don't follow the instructions and agreements.
6. Facilitate the circle as described above.
7. When the practitioners return to the partner with whom they started the circle, say the following: "Wow, it looks like we met a long time ago. Thank you for beginning this journey with me. I notice that you are more present, open, and loving, and I notice the same in myself." Add any affirmation that seems appropriate. Invite the practitioners to share a final hug (or bow a Namaste).

21 | Ego-Transcendence and Unconditional Love

8. Afterwards, ask the participants to form a big circle. Say, "If we could love each other unconditionally, the way you just experienced, then we would not need to learn any relationships skills. But as most of us have "painfully" experienced, Love is (or may be) unconditional, but relationships are not. That is why we will now learn about and practice healthy relationship skills.

Unconditional love circle affirmations

Short affirmations

1. Thank you for being here; your presence is a gift to all of us.
2. Thank you for taking the risk to share yourself in an authentic way.
3. You are my teacher; I look forward to everything I can know, understand, and learn from you.
4. You are loved and lovable, valid, and valuable, in every way, now and every day.
5. I know that your inner world is a whole universe, equal and different from mine.
6. I see you; I hear you; and I feel you.
7. Thank you for taking the risk to reveal yourself and to reach out to others/me.
8. As I see the good in myself, I also see the good in you.
9. I appreciate your strengths, and I accept if they are different from mine.
10. As I see the God/dess in myself, I see the God/dess in you.
11. I understand that change is inevitable. I welcome change and adapt myself to change.
12. I deserve and receive goodness from the world, and, in turn, I give goodness back to the world.
13. Thank you for all the gifts that you bring to the world.
14. Thank you for your commitment to your relationship life.
15. I love, respect, and accept you as you are.
16. I am a spiritual being having a human experience.

17. I am open to love.
18. Thank you for giving your gift of love to me/this group.
19. I feel good about myself and about everybody around me.
20. The past is gone. I live only in the present.
21. I am a loving, forgiving, gentle, and kind person.
22. I am surrounded by love, and everything is fine.
23. My heart is always open, and I radiate love.
24. All my relationships are long-lasting and loving.
25. My current or future partner is the love of my life and the center of my universe.
26. In life, I always get what I give out, and I always give out love.
27. I encounter love in all my relationships, and I love these encounters.
28. I see everything with loving eyes, and I love everything I see.
29. I deserve love, and I get it in abundance.
30. I love myself and everybody else—and, in return, everybody loves me.
31. Everywhere I go, I find love. Life is joyous.
32. I let go of all past pain and hurt and concentrate only on the present.
33. My life is full of joy and happiness, and I radiate joy and happiness.
34. I easily attract love into my life.
35. The warmth of love surrounds me.
36. I am ready for a relationship filled with love to enter my life.
37. I am willing to give to someone else.
38. I appreciate those who love me.
39. I give my love unconditionally.
40. I am ready to be in love.
41. I love you just the way you are.
42. There is one partner meant for me, and I already love him or her.

Long affirmations

1. Look into your partner's face. Notice the nose, mouth, forehead, cheeks, chin, ears, hair or no hair. Find one thing that you would have created differently—one thing that is not perfect, not acceptable to you. If you don't find anything, then you know that you are both beautiful, perfect, and lovable as you are.

2. Notice the color of your partners iris. Is it brown, blues, green, black, grey or something else? You may even see the unique pattern of your partners iris. Also notice the pupil and realize what a miracle it is that we can see. The eyes are the window to the soul. I see you; I feel you; I accept you; I love you, just the way you are.

3. Imagine that all humans would make an agreement to pause every day at noon, find a stranger or an enemy, stand across from him or her, look each other in the eyes, hold hands, and after a few minutes share a hug. Could people still hate or fear each other because of their different gender, skin color, sexual orientation, age, looks, political affiliation, religious beliefs, nationality, cultural background? Why do we create so many binaries and divisions between us when we are all humans who want to love and be loved? Imagine such a world.

4. Take a deep breath and make an "ahh" sound on the outbreath. Ask them to do it again and louder. Thank you for brushing your teeth this morning/before coming here. I love to see your smiling face. I see the little boy, the little girl, in you having fun.

5. Feel back 13.7 billion years. We were all very close together, and it was very hot. Then the universe came into existence, and about 3.7 billion years ago the first life forms emerged on earth. About 140 million years ago, mammals populated the

earth. Humans entered the scene some 2 million years ago. They made love with each other, and many generations later your ancestors were born. Then your grandparents, and eventually your parents, arrived in the world. You may know how your parents met and conceived you. When they made love, out of about 40 million sperms the one that co-created you won the race to the egg, and eventually you were born. You already won the race. What a miracle you are. A precious gift to all of us and the world. I am so glad and honored that you are here with me right now. I love you. You are amazing.

6. Out beyond ideas of wrongdoing and rightdoing,
   there is a field. I'll meet you there.
   When the soul lies down in that grass,
   he world is too full to talk about.
   Ideas, language, even the phrase "each other"
   doesn't make any sense.
Jalal Rumi

What had Rumi realized when he wrote this poem some 800 years ago? When we are fully present with each other as you are right now, without any thought or judgment, then we become one on the level of our human souls, and the phrase "each other" no longer makes sense. Thank you for giving me the gift of love through your presence without judgment.

Optional affirmations

1. It doesn't interest me what you do for a living. I want to know what you ache for and if you dare to dream of meeting your heart's longing.
2. It doesn't interest me how old you are. I want to know if you will risk looking like a fool for love, for your dream, for the adventure of being alive.
3. It doesn't interest me what planets are squaring your moon. I want to know if you have touched the center of your own

sorrow, if you have been opened by life's betrayals or have become shriveled and closed from fear of further pain.
4. I want to know if you can sit with pain, mine or your own, without moving to hide it, or fade it, or fix it.
5. I want to know if you can be with joy, mine or your own; if you can dance with wildness and let the ecstasy fill you to the tips of your fingers and toes without cautioning us to be careful, be realistic, remember the limitations of being human.
6. It doesn't interest me if the story you are telling me is true. I want to know if you can disappoint another to be true to yourself. If you can bear the accusation of betrayal and not betray your own soul. If you can be faithless and therefore trustworthy.
7. I want to know if you can see Beauty even when it is not pretty every day. And if you can source your own life from its presence.
8. I want to know if you can live with failure, yours and mine, and still stand at the edge of the lake and shout to the silver of the full moon, "Yes."
9. It does not interest me to know where you live or how much money you have. I want to know if you can get up after the night of grief and despair, weary and bruised to the bone and do what needs to be done to feed the children.
10. It does not interest me who you know or how you came to be here. I want to know if you will stand in the center of the fire with me and not shrink back.
11. It does not interest me where or what or with whom you have studied. I want to know what sustains you from the inside when all else falls away.
12. I want to know if you can be alone with yourself and if you truly like the company you keep in the empty moments.

"The Invitation" Oriah Mountain Dreamer

1. I love myself the way I am, there's nothing I need to change, I'll always be the perfect me there's nothing to rearrange, I'm

beautiful and capable of being the best me I can, and I love myself just the way I am.
2. I love you just the way you are there's nothing you need to do, when I feel the love inside myself it's easy to love you, behind your fears, your rage and tears, I see your shining star, and I love you just the way you are.
3. I love myself the way I am and still I want to grow. But change outside can only come when deep inside I know, I'm beautiful and capable of being the best me I can, and I love myself just the way I am, I love myself just the way I am.
4. I love the world the way it is, cause I can clearly see, that all the things I judge are done by people just like me, so till the birth of peace on earth, that only love can bring, I'll help it grow by loving everything.

Jai Josefs

Exercise three: The sock game

This is a fun game that gets practitioners moving, laughing, and learning their names.
1. Prepare a shopping bag containing 10 pairs of folded socks or soft balls from a pet or toy store.
2. Take out one pair of folded socks or a ball and demonstrate how to gently throw it to a person in the circle, saying his or her name.
3. Remember who you threw it to!
4. Ask that person to gently throw the socks/ball to a person in the circle who has not yet received it, to say his/her name, and to remember that person!!!
5. Ask the practitioners to continue until everyone in the circle has had the socks/ball once.
6. Ask the last person to throw the socks/ball back to you.
7. Do another round to make sure each person throws the socks/ball to the same person they threw it to before and says their name (some practitioners may not remember, so help them with names).

8. If needed, do another test round.
9. When the circle is working, throw additional socks/balls, every few seconds, to the person you started with, so that socks/balls keep flying. After a while, collect all socks and place them back in your bag.
10. Optional: Ask practitioners to reverse the circle by throwing the socks/ball to the person they received it from and saying their name— first with one pair of socks/ball and again with all of them.
11. Invite the participants to give a round of applause.
12. Have a bathroom break and offer snacks and beverages.

Follow-up questions

1. How do you feel after this exercise?
2. What was your experience during the meditation?
3. Which levels (gross material/physical, subtle mind, causal mystical) could you disidentify from and stay present with?
4. What was your experience during the love circle?
5. Were you able to stay fully present with each partner?
6. What did you experience while eye-gazing, holding hands, hugging?
7. Was there a difference in your experience based on gender or partners?
8. How did you feel at the beginning, during, and at the end of the love circle? What changed?
9. Did you become more open, connected, and loving, or more closed, disconnected, and fearful—and what do you think was the cause?
10. What did you experience during the sock game?

Additional information and resources

Link for affirmation sheet
tinyurl.com/irpm576[17]
The Power of Now: A Guide to Spiritual Enlightenment by Eckhart Tolle
tinyurl.com/irpm105[18]

Practice Module 1
Four Dimensions of Being and Relating

A hundred times every day I remind myself that my inner and outer life are based on the labors of other men, living and dead.
~ Albert Einstein ~

Module description

Learn and practice how to build a solid foundation for a healthy sustainable Integral Love Relationship. Realize that four essential dimensions of your human being and relating come into intimate contact with each other when you fall in love and enter a committed romantic relationship, regardless of whether or not you and your partner are consciously aware of them. See how these four dimensions are arranged in four quadrants:

1. Your individual, subjective, interior mind and feelings, represented by the Upper Left quadrant.
2. Your collective, inter-subjective, interior cultural background, values, and communication, represented by the Lower Left quadrant.
3. Your individual, objective, exterior physical body and behavior, represented by the Upper Right quadrant.
4. Your collective, inter-objective, exterior social environment, represented by the Lower Right quadrant.

Understand why it is foundational for any healthy love relationship to integrate, balance, and harmonize these four dimensions. Notice whether you and your partner are attracted to each other and focused on co-creating in only one or two of these four dimensions/quadrants, while neglecting or ignoring the others, or focused on co-creating in all of them. Avoid potential relationship conflicts and breakdowns, especially when you focus on relating and co-creating in different dimensions: for example, one of you on the Upper Right physical/sexual and Lower Left cultural, and the other on the Upper Left mental and Lower Right social dimensions. Experience all four dimensions in an embodied exercise.

Introduction

Our existence or being has four essential dimensions or "relationships" that you can experience right now:

1. A relationship with your individual interior awareness that is best experienced when you close your eyes and focus your attention inward on your thoughts, feelings, intuitions, intentions, dreams, values, needs, vision, purpose, meaning of life, etc.—in other words, what is alive inside of you right now.
2. A relationship with your collective interior or culture when you focus your attention outward and ask yourself: How does my cultural background and conditioning live in me? How have my relationships with parents, family, friends, teachers, etc. formed who I am today? How do I relate my inner world to others through shared language, values, meaning, and understanding? How do I understand the inner world of others? What are our shared languages, identities, ethics, and morals, and how do we create mutual understanding and agreement? In other words, what is alive between you and others?

Individuals cannot exist without the cultural collective environment and, at the same time, without co-creating it with others. You may ask, "To what extent do I live in my culture, and to what extent does my culture live in me?"

3. A relationship with your individual, objective, exterior, physical body, including your muscles, bones, organs, hormones, sex organs, brain activities, etc. This also includes your physical behavior.
4. A relationship with your collective, exterior, physical environment with which you directly or indirectly interact in order to sustain your body—such as, the space you are in right now, the air you breathe, the food you eat, as well as your money, housing, transportation, job, plants, animals, etc. It also includes social norms and behaviors that you adopted, e.g., how you dress, travel, or make money, and how you coordinate your actions with others.

Individuals cannot exist without the collective social environment that they co-create with others. You may ask, "To what extent do I live in my social environment, and to what extent does my social environment live in me?"

If you facilitate an online group or work with clients, you may verbally guide them through the four dimensions, as described above.

In Integral Theory, these four dimensions are called The Four Quadrants. They are labeled the Upper Left (UL) "I," Lower Left (LL) "We," Upper Right (UR) "It," and Lower Right (LR) "Its" quadrants, as shown below. Going forward, we will refer to them using these terms.

Figure 4: The four dimensions of being

Unlike in any other human relationships, in romantic sexual love relationships, all four dimensions come into a unique and often challenging intimate contact with each other, as each partner brings his or her unique background, experiences, needs, desires, and unconscious to the relationship, as shown below.

Figure 5: The four dimensions of relating

In Integral Relationships, compatible partners balance and harmonize the four dimensions in healthy ways.

Purpose and application of Module 1

1. Become aware and learn about the four essential dimensions (quadrants) of our human being.
2. Experience and embody the four dimensions so that you can relate with others through all of them, especially in your intimate love relationships.
3. Avoid quadrant absolutism, which means to see and interpret the world and your relationships from one quadrant only.
4. Share about yourself and show curiosity about others in all four dimensions of your being and relating.
5. Practice active listening (reflecting on what you heard/understood/felt) in each of the four dimensions during the exercise and, subsequently, in all of your relationships.

Integral Relationship Practice | 34

6. Realize that we often falsely assume that we or our partner and others hear, understand, and retain everything correctly, as it was communicated (also see Modules 6-8 on pages 109-158 about communication).
7. Identify to what extent you, your date or partner, your clients, or your event participants are healthy and balanced in all four dimensions.
8. Become healthier and more balanced in all four dimensions through an Integral Life Practice:[19] (UL) mentally/spiritually/emotionally; (UR) physically/sexually; (LL) ethically/morally; and (LR) socially/professionally.

This experience becomes the foundation for our Integral Relationship Practice.

Exercises: Experiencing the four dimensions

The following is a paired exercise.
1. Prepare a kitchen timer, bells, two 30-foot/10-meter ropes, the four quadrant identifier sheets, a two-minute sand timer (hourglass), and worksheets for the practitioners.
2. Make the four agreements for confidentiality, responsibility, healthy boundaries, I-statements, and sharing, as outlined on page 556.

Exercise one: Get to know your partner

1. Bring out the ropes. You may jokingly say that you start with a bonding exercise.
2. Divide the room into four quadrants by placing the two ropes on the floor so that they intersect in the center of the room.
3. Place the "I," "We," "It," and "Its" sheets in the respective quadrant where the two ropes intersect.[20]
4. Hand out the worksheets.
5. Demonstrate the exercise with a participant or your assistant by moving into each quadrant and offering examples of what to share there (see worksheet).

6. Encourage the practitioners to be vulnerable and stretch themselves in giving their answers.
7. Ask practitioners in a live event to pair up with someone they do not know yet (this means that couples and friends should not do this exercise together in groups unless they insist.) If you facilitate an online event, pair up practitioners in breakout rooms.
8. Allow three minutes or more per quadrant for each pair to get to know each other, depending on the available time and on the attention span and size of the group.
9. Instruct practitioners that they can start in any quadrant they like and stand or sit.
10. Practice "pass the shush" (or "sushi") by asking all practitioners to make a "shhh" sound together when you say "pass the shush/sushi" to quiet the room.
11. Use the kitchen timer and bell for signaling to the practitioners when to switch to their partner and when to move on to the next quadrant (one that they have not yet covered).
12. Ask the practitioners to begin in the quadrant of their choice.
13. Ring the bell and say "pass the shush" to announce when the first three or more minutes are over, and again when six or more minutes are over. Then ask practitioners to move to a new dimension/quadrant they have not yet covered.
14. Do not tell the practitioners about exercise two (below) yet, and do not allow them to take notes.

Exercise two: Introducing the partner

1. After all four quadrants have been covered, ask the couples to sit down next to each other in a big circle.
2. Invite the couples, one by one, to introduce their partner to the group by moving through the four quadrants and sharing what they learned about him or her.
3. Allow about 30 seconds per person for the introduction in each quadrant, depending on the size of the group.

4. The practitioner who is making the introduction may use the two-minute sand timer as a "talking stick" and timekeeper.
5. If you have a very large group and limited time, you may put the couples into subgroups (e.g., 6 and 6) to introduce their partners.
6. Ask for an applause at the end of each introduction.

Worksheet: Four-quadrant questions

If I would deeply know you, what would I know about?

Upper Left "I" Subjectivity:
- What is alive inside of you right now (thoughts, feelings, awareness?)
- What are you most passionate about?
- What is of ultimate concern to you?
- What is beautiful to you?
- What is your spiritual practice and shadow work?
- What individual interior potentials would you like to develop and share with a/your partner?

Lower Left "We" Intersubjectivity:
- What are significant relationships in your past and now? (Think family, romantic partners, teachers, mentors, etc.)
- How have these relationships formed who you are today and how you see the world, such as culture, values, virtues, ethics?
- What does "being good" mean to you?
- What collective interior (cultural) relationship potentials would you like to realize (partner, friends, family, community)?

Upper Right "It" Objectivity:
- How do you feel about your body, health, and (if you like to share) sexuality?
- How do you take care of your body? Think exercise, nutrition, rest, meditation, bodywork etc.
- How do you know or define what is objectively true?

- What physical, health, sexual, and objective truth (understanding) potentials would you like to develop and share with a/your partner?

Lower Right "Its" Inter-objectivity:
- Where and how do you live?
- What is the social environment that sustains your life (work, lifestyle, economic and ecological)?
- How do you contribute to society?
- What social potentials and lifestyle would you like to realize and share with a/your partner?

Follow-up questions

1. Was it easier to speak or to listen?
2. When did time pass more quickly, while you were listening or speaking?
3. Was there enough time, too much time, not enough time, to answer the questions?
4. Did you prefer the communication in some quadrants over others?
5. Which quadrants were the easiest and hardest to share in?
6. Which quadrants do you typically talk about with others/with your partner?
7. In which quadrants did you withhold information, feel an edge, feel uncomfortable?
8. In which quadrants did you deepen intimacy by becoming vulnerable?
9. What did you realize about the interconnectedness of the quadrants and how they impact each other?
10. How did you feel when you introduced your partner?
11. How do you feel about what you remembered and forgot?
12. How did you feel when you were introduced?
13. Did you feel heard and understood and well-represented by your partner?

14. How does this experience reflect your real-life experiences—for example, how you relate and communicate with your partner/others?
15. Which quadrants elicit your primary attraction and focus when you relate romantically with others?
16. Thinking back on your life, how did you become who you are today in each of the quadrants?
17. When did or do you experience relationships that were/are not balanced in all quadrants? In what way?
18. What qualities do you want to develop in each quadrant (learn, heal, grow, awaken) so that you can have an Integral Relationship that is healthy and balanced in all four dimensions of your being and relating?
19. What would you like to co-create in each quadrant with your partner?
20. How will you practice covering all four dimensions of your being and relating (quadrants) in your conversations and intimate relationships?

Additional information and resources

Below is an image that illustrates various fields of experiences and disciplines for each of the four dimensions/quadrants, followed by suggested questions to create a deeper connection with your partner.

39 | Four Dimensions of Being and Relating

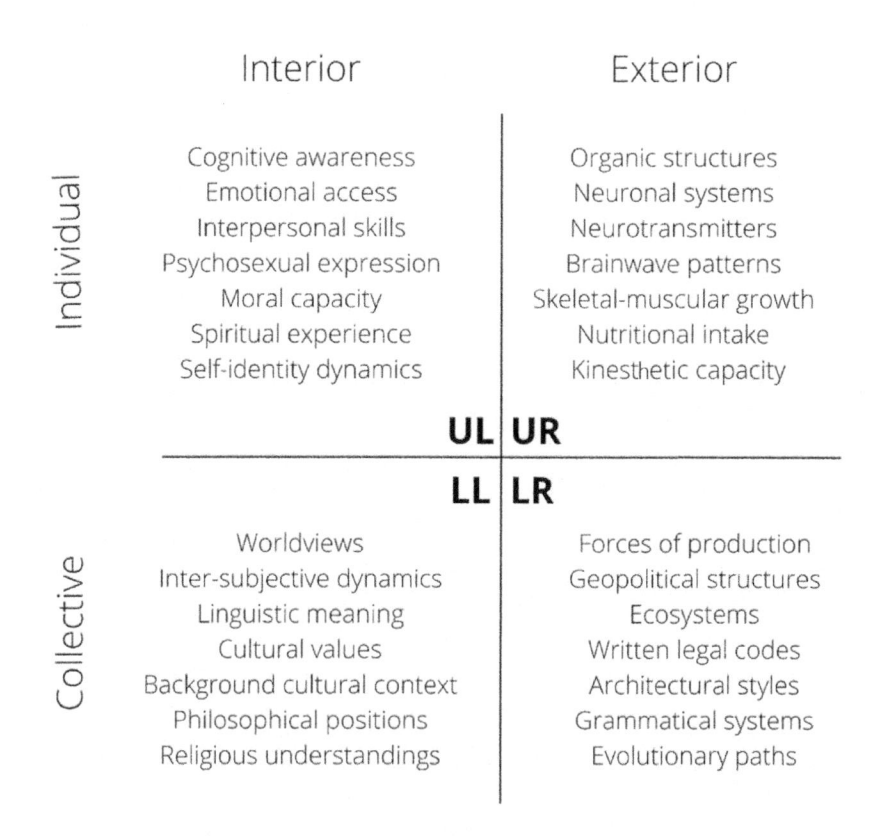

	Interior	Exterior
Individual	Cognitive awareness Emotional access Interpersonal skills Psychosexual expression Moral capacity Spiritual experience Self-identity dynamics	Organic structures Neuronal systems Neurotransmitters Brainwave patterns Skeletal-muscular growth Nutritional intake Kinesthetic capacity
	UL	**UR**
	LL	**LR**
Collective	Worldviews Inter-subjective dynamics Linguistic meaning Cultural values Background cultural context Philosophical positions Religious understandings	Forces of production Geopolitical structures Ecosystems Written legal codes Architectural styles Grammatical systems Evolutionary paths

Figure 6: Manifestations in the four dimensions/quadrants

Additional Upper Left quadrant "I" questions

1. Who are you?
2. What is of ultimate concern to you?
3. What are your emotional needs?
4. What are your values? (See list in endnote 464.)
5. What dreams, visions, and goals do you have for your future?
6. What is beauty or beautiful to you?
7. What is the purpose of life in general, and what is your life's purpose and mission in particular?
8. What is the highest aspiration you hold for yourself?
9. In what areas of your life would you like to grow, and what steps are you willing to take towards your goals?
10. What have you been passionate about throughout your life?

11. How do you make choices?
12. What does love mean to you?
13. What does unconditional love mean to you?
14. In which way do you create your own reality?
15. What does spirituality mean to you, and do you have a spiritual practice or path? (See more questions about spirituality in Module 12.)
16. What do you think about paranormal experiences, and have you had any?
17. What do you think about miracles?

Additional Upper Right quadrant "It" questions

1. How do you feel about your age?
2. How do you feel about your looks?
3. How do you feel about your height?
4. How do you feel about your weight?
5. What physical exercise(s) do you do and would like to do?
6. How often do you exercise—and where and when?
7. What is your diet and favorite food?
8. When, where, and how often do you eat?
9. Do you drink alcohol and/or take other drugs? What, when, why, and how often?
10. Do you take medicines?
11. What is the difference between objectivity and subjectivity for you?
12. How do you feel about the education you received?
13. What is your view on science and empiricism?
14. How do you feel about fake news or alternative facts?
15. How do you feel about the statement "everyone is entitled to their own opinion but not their own facts"?
16. What do you think about free speech? What would be limitations and how should they be enforced?
17. See questions about sexuality on page 248.

Additional Lower Left quadrant "We" questions

1. What is your relationship with your family, children, friends, co-workers, and neighbors?
2. How is your relationship with your father and mother?
3. Who are your best friends, what do you like about them, and what are they interested in?
4. What is your love relationship history?
5. What attracted you to your former partners, why/how did the relationships end, and who ended them?
6. How do you feel about the ending?
7. What is your relationship with your former partners now?
8. What have you learned from the ending of your love relationships, and what do want to do differently now and in the future?
9. What do you see as the downsides and upsides of being in a relationship?
10. What makes you feel loved?
11. What makes you upset in love relationships?
12. What are the emotional rewards and challenges of being in a relationship for you?
13. What would it take for you to make a long-term commitment to a partner?
14. Would you get together again with your current partner or a former partner?
15. What thoughts do you have about your current or former partner that you have not shared with him?
16. Why did or didn't you have children?
17. In what ways do you feel inferior or superior to others?
18. What has your current or former partner done that created distance or intimacy for you?
19. Under what circumstances would a white lie and lying by omission be acceptable?
20. What ethical and moral values or virtues are most important for you to share in a love relationship?

21. For which ethical reasons (e.g., violation of values and agreements) would you leave a committed partnership?
22. When have you felt betrayed by others in your relationships?
23. What does the word integrity mean to you?
24. What is your responsibility towards other people and how far does it extend?
25. What are your political views and how were they formed?
26. How do you feel about the sentence, "If you are human you have to be a humanist"?[21]
27. What is your position on abortion rights?
28. What do you think is worth fighting for?
29. What are your thoughts and values around gender equality and feminism?
30. If there is room for 10 people in a lifeboat (otherwise, it would sink) and 13 people want to get in, who do you think should be rejected and drown, and by whom and how should this be decided?
31. When do you think civil disobedience is appropriate?
32. How do you feel about a child dying every second from hunger or a preventable disease, and what do you think humanity should do about it (if anything)?
33. Do you believe in a God, Spirit, or Higher Power, and what is your relationship with him/her/it?

Additional Lower Right quadrant "Its" questions

1. Where and how do you live?
2. Where and how did you grow up, and how did that impact you?
3. What do/did your parents do for a living, and what is/was their economic status? How did that influence you?
4. What schools did you go to, did you choose them, and what degrees did you earn?
5. What do you do professionally, and why did you choose this career?

6. What social accomplishments are you most proud of in your life?
7. How do you feel about financial responsibilities and dependence between partners?
8. What are your hobbies and interests in the social realm?
9. Where and how do you spend your vacations?
10. What and where do you like to eat and drink?
11. What is your view of the media (TV, newspapers, social media, etc.)?
12. What do you think about environmental issues such as global warming and sustainability?
13. What substance addictions and/or compulsive behaviors do you have?
14. What kind of music, books, TV shows, and movies do you like, and how do they speak to you/touch you?
15. What do you want to accomplish in the future?
16. What do you see as the role of (or how do you see) men and women in our society?
17. How would your lifestyle be improved if you were with a wonderful partner, or how would you like to improve your lifestyle with your current partner?
18. What do you see as potential social downsides of a partnership?
19. What changes would you be willing to make in your lifestyle and what would you give up in your life to be in (or stay in) a healthy love relationship?
20. Under which socioeconomic circumstances would you leave a committed partnership?

Eight zones of being and relating

The two images below show that each quadrant can be looked at and studied through two major methodological approaches: from either the inside (i.e., your own or a person's first-person perspective) or from the outside (i.e., your partner's or another person's third-person perspective.) These inside and outside views result in eight distinct zones of human inquiry and research. This is particularly interesting for romantic love relationships, as each partner has his or her own first-person experience in each of the four quadrants, while the other is observing and interpreting it from a third-person perspective.

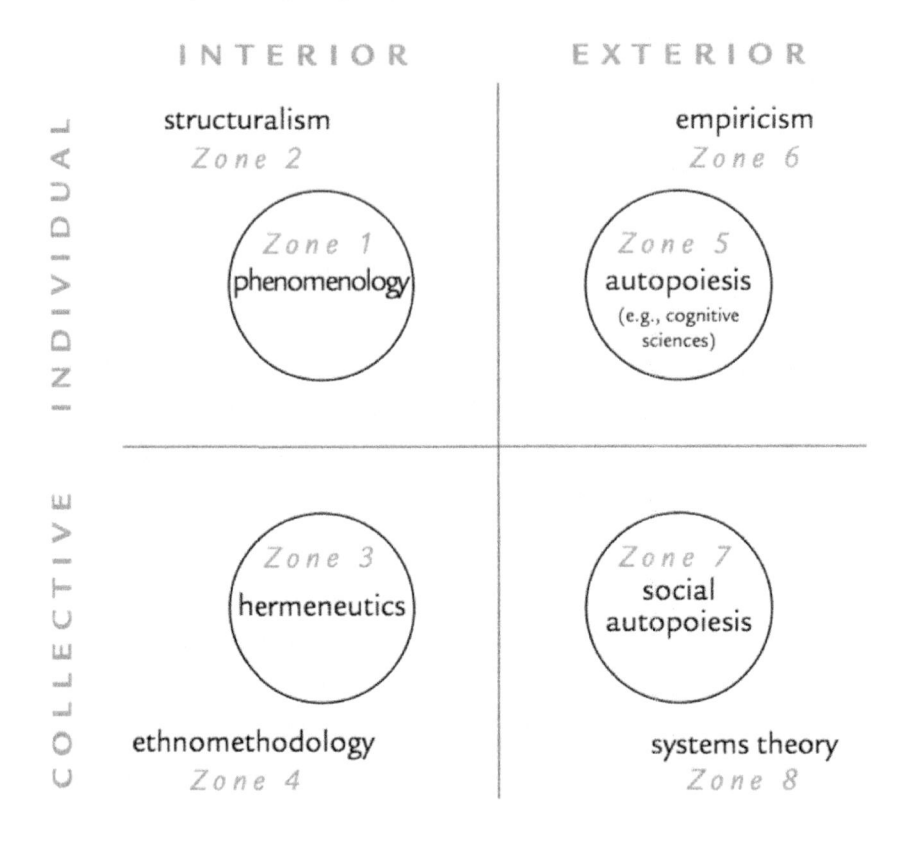

	INTERIOR	EXTERIOR
INDIVIDUAL	structuralism *Zone 2* *Zone 1* phenomenology	empiricism *Zone 6* *Zone 5* autopoiesis (e.g., cognitive sciences)
COLLECTIVE	*Zone 3* hermeneutics ethnomethodology *Zone 4*	*Zone 7* social autopoiesis systems theory *Zone 8*

Figure 7: The eight zones and their major fields of study

Notice that nondual awareness, which we will cover in Module 12 (about spirituality, on pages 207–232), is located in the center of the Eight Zones in the second image, indicating that there is no more separation or duality between the eight zones.

Four Dimensions of Being and Relating

Particular (Local)
4 AGENCY ZONES

Interior | Exterior

Singular

- Moral / Natural — *Subjective* — Zone 2 — Structuralism
- Spiritual / Creational — *Intra-Subjective* — Zone 1 — Phenomenology
- Emotional / Vital — *Intra-Objective* — Zone 5 — Autopoiesis
- Material / Behavioral — *Objective* — Zone 6 — Empiricism

Individual

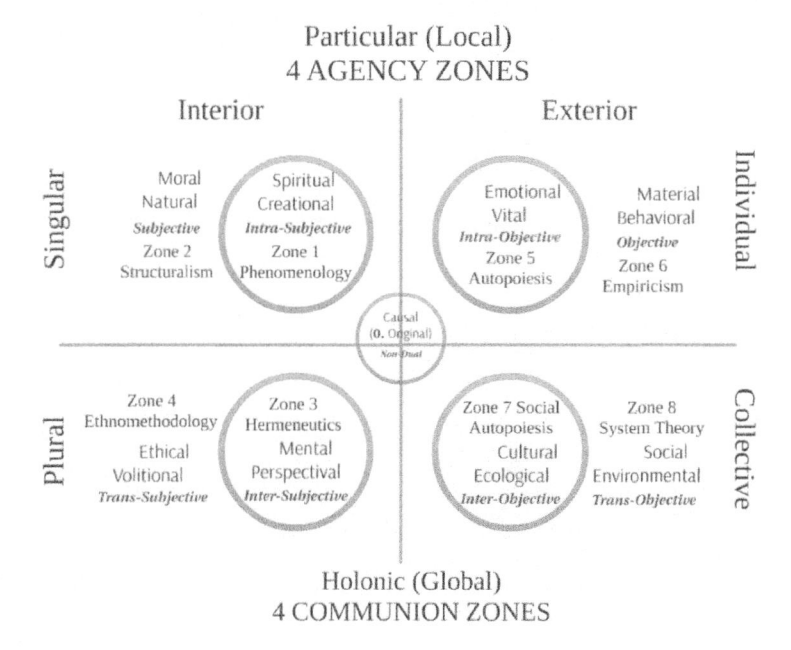

Causal (0. Original)
Non-Dual

Plural

- Zone 4 — Ethnomethodology — Ethical / Volitional — *Trans-Subjective*
- Zone 3 — Hermeneutics — Mental / Perspectival — *Inter-Subjective*
- Zone 7 Social Autopoiesis — Cultural / Ecological — *Inter-Objective*
- Zone 8 System Theory — Social / Environmental — *Trans-Objective*

Collective

Holonic (Global)
4 COMMUNION ZONES

Figure 8: Perspectives of the eight zones

Other philosophies using three/four dimensions

Not surprisingly, we see three or all four dimensions in many other philosophies, meta models, and human achievement awards.

- Plato's (UL) beauty, (UR) truth, and (LL) good.
- Immanuel Kant's three critiques of (UL) judgement, (UR) pure reason, and (LL) practical (moral) reason.
- Jürgen Habermas's validity claims to (UL) truthfulness, (UR) truth, and (LL) moral rightness.[22]
- Edgar Morin's model of uniduality between (UL) psychic, (UR) cerebral, (LL) cultural, and (LR) natural dimensions.
- Roy Bhaskar's four planar theory in critical dialectical realism of (UL) intra-subjectivity, (UR) material transactions with nature, (LL) inter-personal action, and (LR) social relations.
- Nobel prizes: (UL) literature, (UR) chemistry, physics, medicine, (LL) peace, and (LR) economics.

Development in the four dimensions

One of Ken Wilber's greatest philosophical contributions in general and to the Integral Relationship model in particular is his deep insight into stages or levels of development in each of the four dimensions; how these stages co-arise (tetra arise) in individuals, cultures, and societies; and how they impact our relationships.

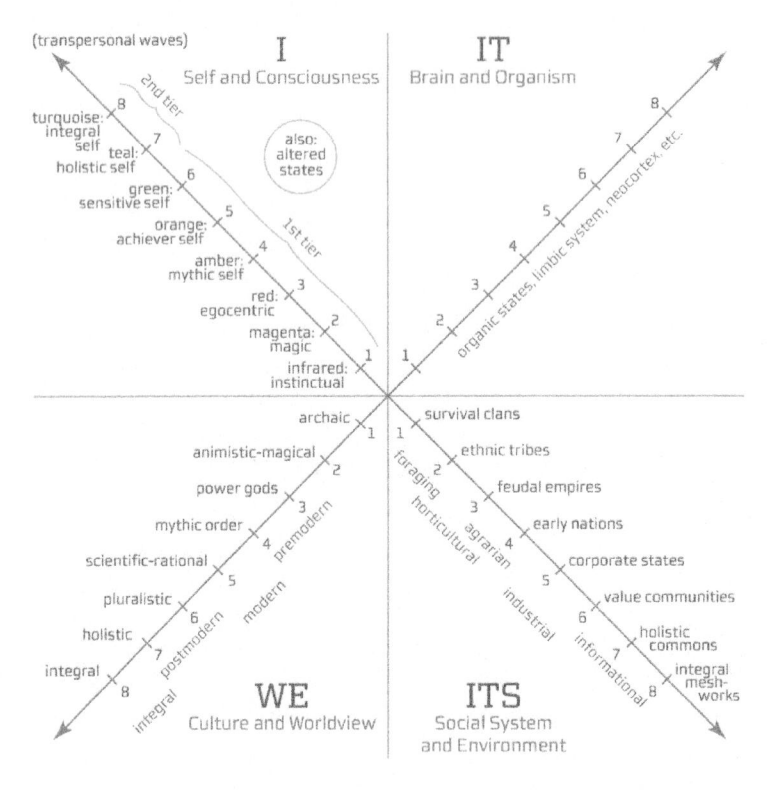

Figure 9: Eight developmental stages in the four dimensions of being

In the following seven modules, we will explore the eight developmental stages in each of the four dimensions, as shown above: how they impact our love relationships and how we validate what is (LL) morally good/right, (UR) objectively true/rational, (UL) subjectively truthful/beautiful, and (LR) practical/functional in our communication.

Sex Purpose Love book reference
Pages 17–23

Suggested movie: *Her* (2013)

Watch this Oscar-winning movie for best screenplay to see that healthy love relationships can only flourish if they are co-created and balanced and harmonized in all four dimensions of being and relating between opposite and equal partners.

The main protagonist, Theodore (Joaquin Phoenix), is a heartbroken, sensitive, and soulful man who lives in a not-so-distant future, where he earns a living by writing personal letters for other people. His recently ended marriage seems to have mostly focused on the right-hand exterior quadrants.

Ten minutes into the movie, he sees an advertisement that poses a few "simple questions": "Who are you? What can you be? Where are you going? What's out there? What are the possibilities?" The ad is for "OS1," a new intuitive and conscious artificially intelligent operating system that promises to listen to him, understand him, and to know him. Theodore is intrigued.

After installing OS1 and answering a few personal questions, he is introduced to "Samantha" (Scarlett Johansson), a computer-generated voice that reveals a sensitive and playful personality. Though "friends" initially, they soon develop a deeper connection. As their relationship in the left-hand interior dimensions deepens, Theodore falls in love with Samantha, who becomes increasingly emotionally intelligent and "conscious" through their connection, but also more challenging, as it is often the case in real-life relationships. Despite their best efforts to extend their relationship into the right-hand exterior dimensions, and Theodor's efforts to keep up with her evolving consciousness and emotional complexity, they increasingly struggle, and she (spoiler alert!!!!) eventually exceeds his level of development and breaks up with him.

Practice Module 2
Archaic, Magic, and Egocentric Stages

You have to know the past to understand the present.
~ Carl Sagan ~

Module description

Learn and explore how the archaic, magic, and egocentric stages of consciousness developed in your earlier life and how they impact your love relationships today. Receive an introduction to cultural and individual developmental stages of consciousness and learn how they evolved through solving the significant problems and limitations of earlier stages.

Learn about the archaic stage that entails biological survival needs, such as food, shelter, physical health, work, sex, and fight-flight-freeze reactions, which are the foundation of all love relationships.

Investigate the second stage, called magic, which entails the magical and mysterious aspects of love relationships and your needs for safety and belonging. Look at potential narcissistic tendencies between you and your partner that are characterized by childish selfishness, a sense of unrealistic entitlement, a lack of empathy between partners, and pervasive needs for admiration. Understand how people who are exclusively at this stage of development often feel insecure and victimized, are superstitious, and engage in magical thinking and irrational conspiracy theories.

Examine the third stage of consciousness development, called egocentric, which entails desires for instant gratification, respect, freedom, narrow boundaries, autonomy, and dominance over others. Understand its impacts on your relationship.

Look at the healthy needs and expressions of each of these three stages, as well as the unhealthy aspects and limited views. Understand how lack of healthy integration and attachments to limited views at these stages are often the cause of relationship conflicts and breakups, especially when one partner is at a later or earlier stage of development than the other.

Introduction

There are things (events, physical objects, thoughts, feelings, sensations, etc.) and there is consciousness that is aware of things. In humans, consciousness not only means to be awake and aware of things, but also how we think about and interpret what we are aware of, where our focus and interest lies, what we care for and are most concerned and passionate about, what is of importance and value to us—or, in short, how conscious we are. This consciousness varies significantly in people and cultures.

Most people accept the fact that children develop into adulthood through predictable stages of consciousness or mental complexity as they learn to include increasing numbers of perspectives (from me, to you, to we, to us, to all of us, to all of it; or, first-, second-, third-, and fourth-person perspectives). Likewise, most people accept that cultures have evolved throughout human history through stages of development, from archaic to postmodern.

A relatively new insight from developmental studies is that adults have the potential to continue their growth and development in mental complexity and consciousness throughout their lifetime, as shown in the image below, taken from the book, *Immunity to Change,* by Robert Kegan, renowned developmental psychologist and Meehan Professor in Adult Learning and Professional Development at Harvard University.

51 | Archaic, Magic, and Egocentric Stages

Age and mental complexity: The revised view today

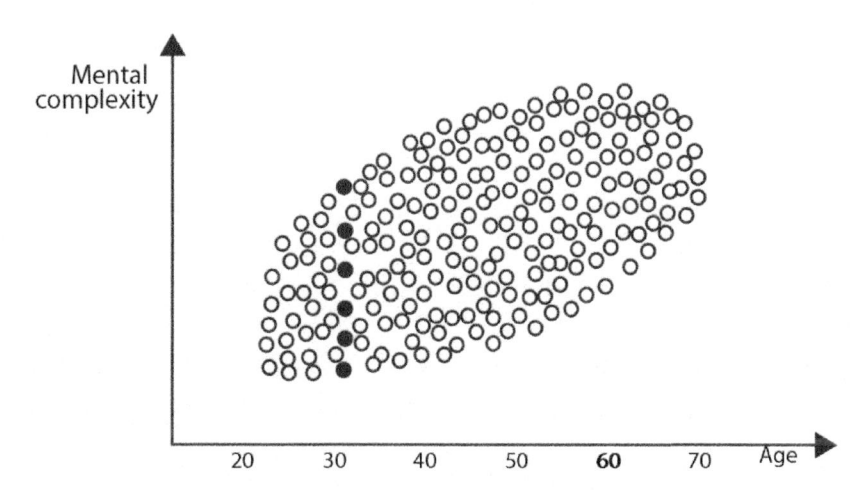

Figure 10: Age and developmental potentials of mental complexity

The integral philosopher Ken Wilber describes these ongoing potentials of consciousness developmental in individuals, cultures, and societies in over 20 of his books, drawing from many evolutionary thinkers who preceded him.

Georg Wilhelm Friedrich Hegel recognized that history progresses in a dialectical process of thesis, anthesis, and synthesis to resolve conflicts that result from dissatisfaction with a current situation (as we also see in evolving love relationships.)

Henri Bergson developed a spiritual context for Darwin's evolutionary science, emphasizing the interior nature of things as well as their exterior outward manifestations, as we explored in the four quadrants in Module 1.

Alfred North Whitehead went on to examine the conflicts between religion and science and proposed a reconciliation.

Sri Aurobindo developed a spiritual practice called Integral Yoga to transform ordinary human life into a divine life in a divine body.

Pierre Teilhard de Chardin took this direction further and conceived the idea of successive enveloping spheres of evolutionary activity from matter into the geosphere, biosphere, and noosphere of human consciousness, and onward to a supreme consciousness or Omega Point.

Jean Gebser had a clear intuition that human history would soon produce an emergent new structure of consciousness and culture, which he termed Integral consciousness.

Clare W. Graves observed that the emergence of new bio-psycho-social systems within humans, in response to the interplay of external conditions, follows a hierarchy which was later popularized by Don Edward Beck and Christopher Cowan as Spiral Dynamics.

Eminent critical social philosopher Jürgen Habermas[22] had the insight that ethical and moral actions need to be based in rational ethical discourse in which the participants make validity claims to truth, truthfulness, goodness, and beauty (see below in integral and transpersonal communication), and that each higher stage of development solves the problems of the previous stage but eventually creates its own challenges that increase in complexity.[23]

Metamodern evolutionary metatheories have been conceived by a new generation of deep thinkers such Roy Bhaskar,[24] Emil Ejner Friis, Daniel Görtz (writing as Hanzi Freinacht),[25] and Integral politics philosopher Steve McIntosh.[26] They refer to a broad range of current developments in individuals, culture, and society that appear as an oscillation between aspects of modernism and postmodernism, and integrate them with premodern indigenous and traditional ethical and cultural codes.

While all these evolutionary thinkers realized the importance of raising consciousness to solve the significant problems facing individuals and societies, none of them seem to make the connection to the underlying necessity to also raise conscious children in functional families that are co-created by evolved parents.

As mentioned above, most practitioners will be able to relate to consciousness development either through cognitive development in children (from sensorimotor to preoperational, to concrete operational and formal-operational), as researched by Jean Piaget, or through stages of cultural evolution (from archaic survival to tribal magic, heroic egocentric, traditional mythic, progressive modern, pluralistic postmodern, to the potential of integral post-postmodern), as researched by Jean Gebser. Some practitioners may also liken consciousness development to the seven chakras or to Abraham Maslow's hierarchy of needs. These comparisons, however, are misleading, as they describe potentials that are available at all stages of cultural evolution and individual development, and thus represent levels of integration rather than stages of transformation, as we will see in this and following modules.

In the Integral Relationship model, we use eight levels, stages, or altitudes (we use these terms interchangeably) of consciousness development. They are derived from the research of Clare W. Graves (1914–1986),[27] who was a contemporary and colleague of Abraham Maslow.

As shown below, transformational growth to the next higher level takes place when the available tools or interior mental and emotional complexity are no longer sufficient to address the exterior complexity and challenges that we face—including, and especially during, conflicts in our intimate relationships—and, consequently, we "hit a wall."

Each higher stage then solves the problems of the previous stage and eventually creates new problems that increase in complexity. Einstein and his colleagues famously noted this dynamic by saying that "the significant problems we face cannot be solved at the same level of thinking (consciousness) we were at when we created them,"[28] and Jürgen Habermas later further elaborated on this need to evolve consciousness.

In other words, when horizontal "integration" through developing better tools and skills (for example, communication) at any particular level no longer solves the fundamental problems and challenges that we are facing at any given level, then the only way out is the way up, through transformation to the next higher level, which usually takes several years and, unfortunately, never happens for some people.

Integral Growth Relationships through Transformation to Higher Complexity

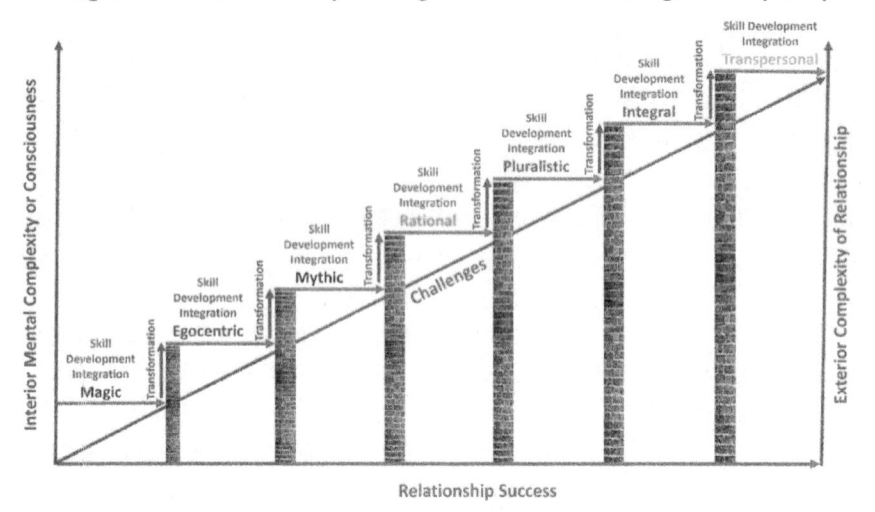

Figure 11: Development through integration and transformation

After Graves's death, his students, Dr. Don Edward Beck and Christopher C. Cowan, adopted and popularized his research in their book, *Spiral Dynamics*, [29] which initially found widespread application in organizational development and politics, and later in personal growth and spirituality. Beck and Cowan introduced a color-coding system, from Beige to Turquoise (see below), for each of the eight stages, which Wilber adopted and later slightly changed to the color spectrum from Infrared to Turquoise.[30] Going forward, we will use both color schemes.

55 | Archaic, Magic, and Egocentric Stages

Consciousness Development

8. Turquoise—Transpersonal—interpenetrative or interpretive

7. Yellow/Teal—Integral—integrated or partial

Second Tier
———————
First Tier

6. Green—Pluralistic—sensitive or indifferent

5. Orange—Rational—win or lose

4. Blue/Amber—Mythic—right or wrong

3. Red—Egocentric—good or bad

2. Purple/Magenta—Magic—safe or unsafe

1. Beige/Infrared—Archaic—dead or alive

Figure 12: Levels/stages of consciousness development

Ladder-climber-view

In his 2006 book, *Integral Spirituality*, Wilber likened the transformation to higher stages of consciousness to developing the rungs and then climbing a ladder, thereby increasing our altitude and view. To illustrate this concept to the practitioners, you may imagine or draw the side rails of two ladders (one for each partner in a relationship) next to each other in Zoom or on a whiteboard and then insert the rungs one by one, as described below, with holes in the rungs to indicate lack of integration.

Consciousness Ladders

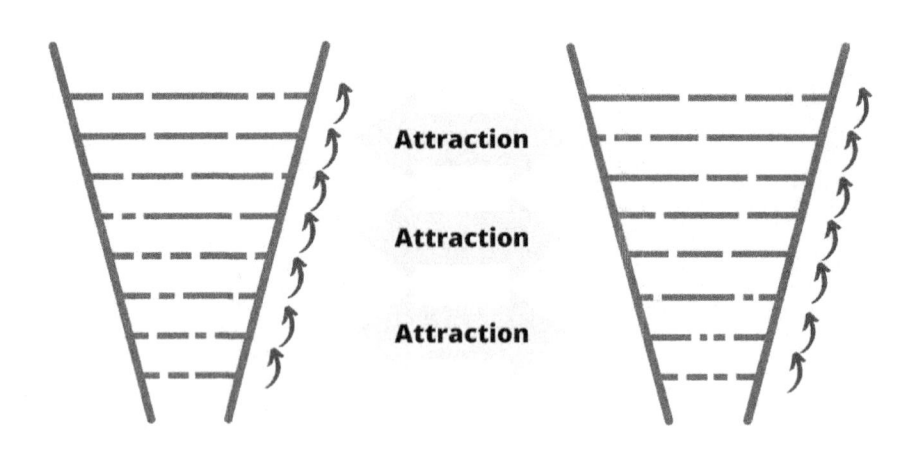

Figure 13: Consciousness ladders

Explain (and draw) that everyone starts out with developing the first rung during gestation and the first few years after birth, as they acquire the basic capacities for survival. This stage can be loosely associated with the reptilian brain, which regulates basic bodily functions and sexuality. When there is no more room for horizontal growth and integration to address the environmental challenges that are faced, then, by necessity, transformational growth takes place when the self slowly develops and climbs to the next rung or level, and, in the process, transcends or leaves behind the limited views of the previous level while retaining the basic capacities.

Next, children and cultures develop the second metaphoric rung, which we call magic. It mainly concerns bonding and safety. This stage can be loosely associated with the functions of the limbic brain system—with the amygdala, hippocampus, and hypothalamus, which regulate emotions, memory, and fight-flight-freeze (and fawn) responses. In cultural evolution, it is the tribal stage. To illustrate, draw the second rungs in each of the two ladders, with holes in them, as well.

This is followed by developing the egocentric rung or stage (very loosely associated with the neocortex, our conscious, verbal, creative, and thinking brain) and so on (see the descriptions in the worksheet below).

Nobody moves through this integration and transformation perfectly. We all have "holes" in our development/rungs through lack of integration, and we retain limited views from earlier levels through lack of transcendence. These holes are then projected onto others, especially onto romantic partners, initially as attraction (I love you, you complete me) and eventually as challenging conflicts (I fear you, you no longer make me happy). Both attraction and conflicts are opportunities for ongoing learning, healing, growing, and awakening in Integral Relationships, based on the insight that we can only heal our relationship wounds in relationships.

Consequently, the more we evolve in consciousness and increase our mental complexity, the more opportunities we have to "mess up" our development, and thus our love relationships increase in complexity.

While all levels of consciousness that we have developed are alive in us, we normally operate from the highest altitude that we have reached. However, when we fall in love (which has been called the only socially accepted form of insanity), during relationship stress, or when we are heartbroken, we often regress to earlier stages. This is metaphorically shown in the nested dolls image below.

Figure 14: Transcend and include/exclude nested dolls

During relationship conflicts, it is important that one partner stays in his or her "adult self" to support the other in his or her healing (see Modules 19–21).[31]

Five phases of change

Spiral Dynamics offers us the following five phases of transformational change, from one stage to the next:

1. The ALPHA fit: Everything is (more or less) in order and things are going well at a particular level.
2. The BETA condition: Times of uncertainty and questioning. Current systems and relationships are proven to be dysfunctional.
3. The GAMMA trap: State of anger and hopelessness. No vision or hope of improvement.
4. The DELTA surge: Constraints are released, positive change and advancement is ever-present.

5. The new ALPHA: New values and worldviews have been consolidated. Procedures, systems, and relationships are functional again.

The GAMMA trap does not necessarily have to occur and can be avoided by good guidance and leadership. In this case, one can directly advance from the BETA condition to the DELTA surge to form the new functional ALPHA fit at the next level. Lack of guidance may keep people too long in the GAMMA trap and result in collapse or breakdown of a person, relationship, or system.

See an animated PowerPoint slide in Google Drive, courtesy of Robert Kaiser. tinyurl.com/irpm10[32]

Three conditions of change

1. Open: Being able to take in new things and understanding one's insights as not being absolutes.
2. Arrested: Not being able to advance because of a disbelief that conditions can change externally.
3. Closed: Being blindsided that there is no internal reality beyond the one at the current level.

Types of people versus types in people

An important aspect related to evaluating stages of consciousness development is not to judge what people do (e.g., becoming a vegetarian, getting married, being polyamorous, believing in conspiracy theories, or buying an electric vehicle), but to be curious about why they do it. What are their motives, values, needs, feelings and reasoning in the given context and what level of development do they reflect?

It is thus not about types *of* people—such as rich and poor, uneducated and educated, religious and atheists, men and women, native-born and foreigners, environmentalists and materialists, white and non-white, etc.—but rather fluid types *in* people. Why do people respond to the world in the way they do? How do they make meaning of their experiences? How do they see themselves?

Who do they want to be and become? What are they most concerned and passionate about? How many perspectives can they take? How much of the past do they consider (how did I/we get here), and how much about their own future and that of others are they concerned about (where do I/we want to go, what future impact do my/our actions have today)? What do they consider to be healthy and functional human beings? How do they validate what is good, true, beautiful, and functional?

Purpose and application

1. Gain basic insights into stages of consciousness development or mental complexity.
2. Understand the first three of eight stages/levels of consciousness development: archaic, magic, and egocentric.
3. Explore to what extent you and others have evolved through these stages in all four dimensions/quadrants of your being and relating by sharing your biography.
4. Feel into which limited or false views you and your partner have transcended, and which basic/healthy/essential capacities you have included at the various stages as you evolved.
5. Identify the stages of consciousness to which you and your partner may regress during the love-struck phase and during relationship conflict.
6. Understand how the different stages impact your (love) relationships in multiple ways.
7. Understand how the lack of integration and transcendence at each stage leads to defensiveness, projections, regression, and conflicts, especially in intimate love relationships.
8. Gain insights about the transformational process to the next higher stage through evolution or revolution when better integration at the previous stage is no longer sufficient to solve the significant problems and challenges that you face.
9. Understand how often irresolvable conflicts arise between individuals, couples, groups, communities, and even societies, who are at different stages of consciousness development.

61 | Archaic, Magic, and Egocentric Stages

10. Develop compassion for those at earlier stages (while maintaining healthy boundaries); connect with people at your level (your peers); and learn from those at later stages (your teachers, mentors, elders, or role models.)

Exercise: First three stages of consciousness development

The following is a paired exercise.
1. Have tissues ready.
2. Have a timer and bell ready to indicate when practitioners should cover the next stage.
3. Print out one worksheet for each practitioner.
4. Make the four agreements for confidentiality, responsibility, healthy boundaries, I-statements, and sharing, as outlined on page 556.
5. Hand out the participant worksheet.
6. Clarify the questions at the top of the worksheet.
7. Give a few examples from your personal life of how you experienced and lived through the stages that are covered in this module.
8. Ask practitioners who already have experience with developmental models to pair up with someone who is less experienced.
9. Ask couples to do the exercise together and support them as needed.
10. Focus on the questions at the top of the worksheet below, based on the available time and experience of the practitioners.
11. Ask practitioners to have a conversation about each stage by reflecting on some or all the questions at the top of the worksheet.
12. Invite questions about how to do the exercise.
13. Give practitioners about 10–30 minutes or more per each stage that you cover, depending on the practitioners' familiarity and understanding of stage development.

It is advised that the facilitator does not take part in the exercise so that s/he can support the practitioners who have questions during the exercise.

Worksheet: Stages one to three of consciousness development

Share with your partner in an autobiographical way how you grew through the stages below. How did your views and your life change in each of the four dimensions of your being and relating (quadrants) as you evolved? Which limited views did you transcend; which basic capacities did you include? How does each stage impact your love relationships today? What attracts you to a/your partner? What needs do you project onto a/your partner based on these levels? When do you regress (in love relationships,) and at what levels do you become defensive (fight, flight, freeze, fawn)? What do you want to co-create at each level in your love relationship?

1. Beige/ Infrared — archaic — dead or alive (Interior controls or dominates exterior–freedom)[ii]

Core capacities: Concerns basic survival needs: Food, shelter, warmth, and sex. Behavior is guided by instincts and impulses for

---

[ii] In the odd-numbered levels 1, 3, 5, and 7, the individual interior and exterior upper "I" and "it" is focused on gaining control over the collective interior and exterior lower "we" and "its" dimensions, with a focus on ego-affirming "becoming" self-expression and the ability to control, dominate, and manipulate the collective external world.

This alternates with the even-numbered levels 2, 4, 6, and 8, where the individual interior and exterior upper "I" and "it" is focused on "being" and surrendering to the collective interior and exterior lower "we" and "its" dimensions, with a focus on seeking peace with the external world through surrender in a self-sacrificing, ego-transcending way, and on aligning with external forces, groups, or authorities.

See details on page 73.

physical well-being. Fight, flight, and freeze reactions. Primal jealousy. World is primarily perceived through the senses.

NARM[33] **Connection:**[306] We feel that we belong in the world. We are in touch with our body and our emotions and capable of consistent connection with others.

Limited views: No conscious awareness of interior, past or future. Fusion with the environment, which is called a-duality, is sometimes confused with higher stages of nonduality.

NARM Adaptive Survival Style	Disconnected from physical and emotional self. Difficulty relating to others.	
Connection	Shame-Based Identifications	Pride-Based Counter-Identifications
	Shame at existing. Feeling like a burden. Feeling of not belonging.	Pride in being a loner. Pride in not needing others. Pride in not being emotional.

Table 2: Connection survival style

As a couple: We need each other to survive and to procreate.

2. Purple/Magenta — magic — safe or unsafe (Interior surrenders to exterior – peace)

Core capacities: Obey desires of spirit beings. Show allegiance to elders, custom, clan. Preserve sacred places, objects, rituals. Bond together with family, group, or tribe to endure and find safety. Live in an enchanted, magical community, village, tribe, world. Seek harmony with nature's rhythms. To be full of wonder about the world.

NARM Attunement:[307] The ability to attune to our needs and emotions. To know what we need. To recognize, reach out for, and take in physical and emotional nourishment. To take in the abundance that life offers.

NARM Trust:[308] An inherent trust in ourselves and others. We feel safe enough to allow a healthy interdependence with others.

Limited views: Very limited or no individuality, sense of past and future, and connection with other "tribes/cultures." False beliefs in magic. Childish. Believes in pre-rational (versus transrational) magical fairy tales, law of attraction, karma, synchronicities, astrology, energy-healing, etc. New-Age narcissism. Is superstitious, irrational, and often confuses cause and effect.

NARM Adaptive Survival Style	Difficulty knowing what we need. Feeling our needs do not deserve to be met.	
Attunement[34]	Shame-Based Identifications	Pride-Based Counter-Identifications
	Needy. Unfulfilled. Empty. Undeserving.	Caretaker. Pride in being the shoulder that everyone cries on. Make themselves indispensable and needed. Pride in not having needs.

Table 3: Attunement survival style

NARM Adaptive Survival Style	Feeling we cannot depend on anyone but ourselves. Feeling we must always be in control.	
Trust	Shame-Based Identifications	Pride-Based Counter-Identifications
	Small. Powerless. Used. Betrayed.	Strong and in control. Successful. Larger than life. User, betrayer.

Table 4: Trust survival style

As a couple: We need each other to create a magical relationship and feel safe in a hostile and dangerous world.

3. Red—egocentric—good or bad (Interior controls or dominates exterior–freedom)

Core capacities: Power, independence, spontaneity, uninhibited, carefree, alive, authentic, expressive, refreshingly open. Escape domination by others and nature. Avoid shame, feel no guilt, demand respect, set narrow boundaries.

NARM Autonomy:[309] Capacity for healthy dependence and interdependence. To be able to say no and set limits with others. To speak one's mind without guilt or fear.

Limited views: Selfish. Express self, to hell with others. Aggressive or passive-aggressive. Wants it all and wants it now, without concern for future consequences. Fight to gain control at any cost. Gratify impulses and senses immediately. Ignoring the past and future brings bliss.

NARM Adaptive Survival Style	Feeling burdened and pressured. Difficulty setting limits and saying no directly.	
Autonomy	Shame-Based Identifications	Pride-Based Counter-Identifications
	Angry. Resentful of Authority. Rebellious. Enjoys disappointing others.	Nice. Sweet. Compliant. Good boy/girl. Fear of disappointing others.

Table 5: Autonomy survival style

As a couple: We need each other to make us feel good about ourselves and get respect, no matter what.

Follow-up questions

1. How do you feel after this exercise?
2. What insights did you gain as you shared with your partner about these first three levels of development?
3. Are you and/or your partner currently in an alpha, beta, gamma, delta, or new alpha phase in your relationship?
4. Are you and/or your partner currently in an open, arrested, or closed condition in your relationship?
5. How do unconscious aspects and possible trauma from these stages affect your love relationships?
6. What kind of healing would you like to do to deepen connection, attunement, trust, and autonomy in your love relationships?

Additional information and resources

Why and how did humans evolve in consciousness?

We will probably never know why, when, and how humans became self-conscious and to what extent other species are self-conscious.[35] However, there is ample evidence that important factors in the evolution of human consciousness are the male sex drive and competition for attractive females with the best reproductive capabilities (young, good-looking, caring, receptive), and the female sexual selection process for tall, strong, and aggressive males (good sperm donors) who also offer them and their offspring the best chances of survival and highest quality of life through their productive capabilities, which are enhanced by being smarter, more creative, kinder (to their partner and offspring), and more practical than their competitors. As there is no apparent upper limit to the desire of females for the safety and material abundance that is provided by males or to the creativity of males to meet these desires, the genes and memes[36] of the most conscious/successful couples were handed down to future generations. (See more in Practice Module 22: Biological and Transformational Purpose, on page 417, and in Practice Module 23: Transcendental Purpose and Love, on page 435.

A salient question of concern is whether cultural evolution will continue or eventually center around the mythic level that we cover below, as females at later stages of development, with higher levels of education and incomes, enter into relationships and procreate much less than females at earlier levels, or not at all.

See more in Practice Module 26: Why Relationships Matter, on page 523.

Why do some people grow further than others?

As mentioned above, growth and development occur when the available skills and inner complexity of feeling and thinking no longer match the complexity and challenges of the outside world, thus causing the individual to suffer.

One aspect of potentials for individuals' consciousness development is the stage of cultural evolution, or center of gravity, of the family, community, and society in which they grow up and live. It is quite difficult or even impossible to grow beyond because both theoretical knowledge and challenging experiences are necessary in order to advance to and fully embody a higher stage.

Genetic predispositions[37] and the resulting personality traits, as we explore in Modules 15 and 16, may be other factors that impact growth in consciousness development. And, finally, personal circumstances, opportunities, challenges, and sheer luck or fate may play important roles, as well.

States of consciousness

You may mention that temporary-state experiences, when the synapses of our brains fire during hormonally or drug-induced altered states (for example, when we fall in love, during spiritual and other peak experiences, or during orgasm), are also essential for consciousness development, as they provide glimpses of higher potentials that we can then realize and make permanently accessible through practice, learning, healing, and awakening. Practitioners who engage in the exercises outlined in this manual frequently have this temporarily elevated state or peak experiences.

We will cover temporary states of consciousness of spiritual awakening in Module 12 (page 207), states of sexual experience in Module 13, on page 235, and states of falling in love in Module 20, on page 367.

Suggested relationship books for the magic stage

The Everything Love Signs Book: Use astrology to find your perfect partner! (2012)
by Jenni Kosarin
tinyurl.com/irpm107[38]

Suggested relationship books for the egocentric stage

The Rules: Time-tested Secrets for Capturing the Heart of Mr. Right (1995) by Ellen Fein and Sherrie Schneider
tinyurl.com/irpm109[39]

The Game: Penetrating the Secret Society of Pickup Artists (2005) by Neil Strauss
tinyurl.com/irpm111[40]

See Appendix I in *Integral Relationships: A Manual for Men*, pages 206–207, for reviews of the books listed above.

The Pickup Artist: The New and Improved Art of Seduction (2010) by Mystery (aka Erik von Markovik)
tinyurl.com/irpm110[41]

Sex Purpose Love book reference

Page 45–48

Suggested movie: *Into the Wild* (2007)

Watch this movie that is based on the true story of Christopher McCandless, aka "Alexander Supertramp" (Emile Hirsch), written by Jon Krakauer and directed by Sean Penn, to see an idealistic, rebellious, complex young man who grew up in a dysfunctional family regress to a Red egocentric, Purple/Infrared magic, and finally Beige/Infrared archaic stage of pure survival.

After graduating from Emory University, where he was a top student and athlete, McCandless abandons his possessions, gives his entire $24,000 in savings to charity, and eventually hitchhikes to Alaska to "live off the land" in the wilderness, where he eventually perishes.

Along the way, McCandless encounters a series of characters at different levels of first-tier consciousness development who shape his perspectives on life.

His final entry into his journal is a motto for Integral Relationships: "Happiness is only real when shared."

Practice Module 3
Mythic and Rational Stages

The significant problems that we face cannot be solved at the same level of thinking we were at when we created them.
~ Albert Einstein ~

Module description

Learn and practice how/if the mythic and modern stages of consciousness developed in your life, and how they impact your love relationships today.

Gain insights into the fourth stage, which is called mythic or traditional, in which you seek to satisfy your needs for stability, order, purpose, hope, recognition, right and wrong morals, and future rewards for right behavior through establishing law and order, including clearly divided gender roles and rules to which women and men are compelled to conform. See how these rules and roles are often based in religious and other myths about humans and the world (such as, "Men are from Mars and Women are from Venus") rather than in rationality.

Investigate the fifth stage, which is called rational or modern, in which you gravitate towards objective reasoning, scientific methods, individual freedoms and responsibilities, and democratic capitalism to satisfy your desires for individual choice. In the fifth stage, you are also focused on pursuing success through taking controlled risks; gaining personal liberty, individuality, equality, rights, self-expression; and seeking the good life through attaining material abundance, higher educations, objective information, a successful career, money, and win-win thinking. Notice how the focus in love relationships at this level is to augment the couple's quality of life, social status, and worldly success, and to support each other to reach their individual goals.

Look at the healthy needs and expressions of each of these two stages, as well as the unhealthy aspects and limited views. Understand how lack of healthy integration and attachments to limited views at these stages are often the cause for relationship conflicts and breakups, especially when one partner is at a later or earlier stage of development than the other.

Introduction

We continue our exploration of consciousness development with stage four and five.

The mythic stage emerged about 12,000 years ago when agriculture took root in parts of the world and replaced traditional hunter-gatherer lifestyles. This caused the emergence of cities and civilizations because crops and animals could now be farmed and often produced surplus food supplies to meet the demands of the growing populations. Along with this stage emerged the ownership of property by males and patriarchies, and, later, by mythic monotheistic religions.[42]

The rational "modern" stage emerged when Gutenberg invented the printing press around 1439; Columbus discovered America in 1492 and proved that the world is round; Luther posted his 95 Theses on the church door of Wittenberg in 1517; and Copernicus, Galileo, Kepler, Bacon, Hobbes, Descartes, Newton, Kant, Hegel, Marx, Freud, and countless other scientists, explorers, philosophers, artists, and social reformers developed new approaches to physics, astronomy, ethics, art, and governance between the sixteenth and twentieth centuries. They questioned the feudalistic systems and supreme powers of monarchies and challenged traditional dogmata of religions. This changed the way people came to think about many things and led to the rise of late modernity, with the industrial age, democracies, the information age, and globalization as we know it today.

Control and surrender

At this point, you may want to further explain that individuals advance through the stages via swinging back and forth between an exterior locus of control in the stages with the uneven numbers (1, 3, 5, and 7), or "warm" colors (Beige/Infrared, Red, Orange, and Yellow/Teal), and the stages with the even numbers (2, 4, 6, and 8), or "cool" colors (Purple/Magenta, Blue/Amber, Green, and Turquoise). Hence the term Spiral Dynamics. In the warm color stages, the self tends to control or dominate its environment and takes more responsibility for its own choices and destiny. In the cold color stages, the self tends to surrender to its environment and seeks peace by fitting in with others and following the rules and values of the group, while taking less responsibility for its faith and destiny.

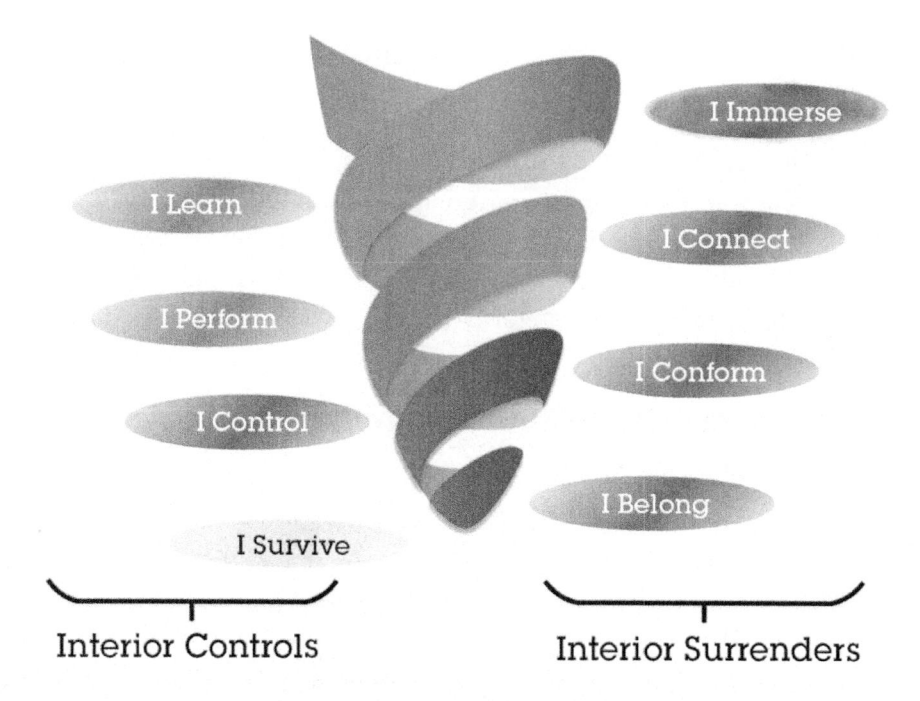

Figure 15: Interior and exterior control

If people and groups don't integrate stages in healthy ways (females sometimes 3, 5, and 7, and males sometimes 2, 4, and 6), they regress under stress to the stage below the one they skipped (e.g., 7 to 5 to 3, or 6 to 4 to 2.)

Purpose and application of the module

1. Become aware of the fourth and fifth (mythic and rational) of the eight stages/levels of consciousness development and how you and others advanced through them.
2. Realize how you and others advanced through the stages by swinging back and forth between an exterior and interior locus of control and how this impacted your love relationships.
3. For more, see "Purpose and application" in Module 2 on page 60.

Exercise: Stages four and five of consciousness development

The following is a paired exercise.
1. See page 60 for the preparation and explanation of the exercise.
2. Make the four agreements for confidentiality, responsibility, healthy boundaries, I-statements, and sharing, as outlined on page 556.

Worksheet: Stages four and five of consciousness development

Share with your partner in an autobiographical way how you grew through the stages below. How did your views and life change in each of the four dimensions of your being and relating (quadrants) as you evolved? Which limited views did you transcend, which basic capacities did you include? How does each stage impact your love relationships today? What attracts you to a/your partner? What needs do you project onto a/your partner based on these levels? When do you regress (in love relationships) and at what levels do you become defensive (fight, flight, freeze, fawn)? What do you want to co-create at each level in your love relationship?

4. Blue/Amber — mythic — right or wrong (Interior surrenders to exterior –peace)

Core capacities: Find meaning, hope, and purpose in life through affiliation with a higher authority. Sacrifice self for the one true way. Bring order and stability, and be loyal to receive future recognition and reward. Honor the recent past and consider future generation. Control impulsivity through guilt. Enforce strict mythic morals, rules, and principles of rightful living. Master plan puts people in their proper places in the hierarchy. Clearly defined gender roles ("Men are from Mars, Women from Venus"). Patriarchal and sometimes matrifocal (women are head of household).

NARM Love-Sexuality:[310] Capacity to live with an open heart. Capacity to integrate a loving, committed relationship with a vital sexuality.

Limited views: Dogmatic. Mythic beliefs and interpretations (e.g., scripture). Often rejects modern science. Only one right way. Us-versus-them thinking. Marginalizes or eliminates non-conformists. Inflexible, rigid, controlling. Men seen as superior to women. Accepts slavery.

NARM Adaptive Survival Style	Difficulty integrating heart and sexuality. Self-esteem based on looks and performance.	
Love-Sexuality	Shame-Based Identifications	Pride-Based Counter-Identifications
	Hurt. Rejected. Physically flawed. Unloved and unlovable.	Rejects first. Perfect. Does not allow for mistakes. "Seamless," having everything together.

Table 6: Love-Sexuality adaptive survival style

As a couple: We need each other to fulfill our gender roles as husband and wife, to have children, and to continue the family traditions.

5. Orange—rational—win or lose (Interior controls or dominates exterior–freedom)

Core capacities: Objective, democratic, humanistic. Pursuit of life, liberty, and happiness. Ends slavery and repression. Strive for autonomy and adapt to constant change. Equal rights and responsibilities for all, including women as seen in liberal feminism. Knowledge is power. Seek out the good life and abundance. Make progress through the best solutions. Enhance living for many through technology and wealth. Play to win and enjoy competition. Learn through tried-and-true experiences.

Limited views: Materialistic. Overly rational, calculating, cold, and driven by status and success. Little consideration for nature, animals, and "losers."

As a couple: We need each other to increase our status, further our careers, support each other's success, and to enjoy life to the fullest.

Follow-up questions

1. How do you feel after this exercise?
2. What insights did you gain as you shared with your partner about the fourth and fifth stage of consciousness development?
3. How have the transitions from an interior to an exterior locus of control impacted your relationships?
4. How do unconscious aspects and possible trauma from these stages affect your love relationships?
5. What kind of healing would you like to do to deepen connection, attunement, trust, and autonomy in your love relationships?

Additional information and resources
Suggested relationship books for the mythic stage
See Appendix I in *Integral Relationships: A Manual for Men*, pages 208–212, for reviews of the books listed below.

The Art of Loving (1956) by Erich Fromm
tinyurl.com/irpm112[43]

The Seven Principles for Making Marriage Work (1999) by John Gottman and Nan Silver
tinyurl.com/irpm115[44]

For Men Only: A Straightforward Guide to the Inner Lives of Women (2006) by Shaunti and Jeff Feldhahn
tinyurl.com/irpm118[45]

For Women Only: What You Need to Know about the Inner Lives of Men (2004) by Shaunti Feldhahn
tinyurl.com/irpm121[46]

Why Mars and Venus Collide: Improving Relationships by Understanding How Men and Women Cope Differently with Stress (2007) by John Gray
tinyurl.com/irpm123[47]

How to Improve Your Marriage Without Talking About It, (2007) by Patricia Love and Steven Stosny
tinyurl.com/irpm125[48]

For single women at the Amber stage
Making Sense of Men: A Woman's Guide to a Lifetime of Love, Care and Attention from All Men, (2008) by Alison Armstrong
tinyurl.com/irpm127[49]

Suggested relationship books for the rational stage

See Appendix I in *Integral Relationships: A Manual for Men*, pages 213–220, for reviews of the books listed below.

Why We Love: The Nature and Chemistry of Romantic Love (2004) by Helen Fisher
tinyurl.com/irpm128[50]

Real Love: The Truth About Finding Unconditional Love & Fulfilling Relationships (2003) by Greg Baer
tinyurl.com/irpm131[51]

Getting the Love You Want: A Guide for Couples, (2005) by Harville Hendrix
tinyurl.com/irpm132[52]

The New Rules of Marriage: What You Need to Know to Make Love Work (2007) by Terrence Real
tinyurl.com/irpm134[53]

Passionate Marriage: Keeping Love and Intimacy Alive in Committed Relationships (1997) by David Schnarch
tinyurl.com/irpm267[54]

Hold Me Tight: Seven Conversations for a Lifetime of Love (2008) by Sue Johnson
tinyurl.com/irpm268[55]

For single women at the rational stage

Is He Mr. Right?: Everything You Need to Know Before You Commit (2006) by Mira Kirshenbaum
tinyurl.com/irpm269[56]

The Intelligent Woman's Guide to Online Dating (2008) by Dale Koppel
tinyurl.com/irpm271[57]

For single men at the rational stage

Stumbling Naked in the Dark: Overcoming Mistakes that Men Make with Women (2003) by Bradley Fenton
tinyurl.com/irpm273[58]

For single women and men at the rational stage

Relationship Roulette: Improve Your Odds at Lasting Love (2010) by Carol Diamond
tinyurl.com/irpm274[59]

Sex Purpose Love book reference

Pages 49–52

Suggested movie: *Groundhog Day* (1993)

Watch this now classic movie to see Phil Connors (Bill Murray) evolve from the egocentric to the mythic level of consciousness development to win the heart of Rita (Andie MacDowell).

Connors is a cynical egocentric television weatherman who is sent to Punxsutawney, PA, for the fourth time in as many years to cover the story of a weather-forecasting groundhog. There, he becomes trapped in a time loop, forcing him to relive February 2 again and again.

He first uses his "power" to take advantage of others and to do whatever brings him pleasure, as any egocentric person would do, and even believes himself to be godlike.

When he realizes that he is stuck in this time loop forever and no longer finds fulfillment, he tries to kill himself, an act that we can see as a metaphor of the necessary "ego death" before a new stage can emerge. As so often happens in real life, he realizes that if he wants to win Rita's heart and entice her to spend the night with him, he needs to meet her expectations by becoming a better man.

He does this through transforming to the next higher Blue/Amber mythic level of consciousness development, which seemingly takes a few years, by cultivating his natural talents for creating more goodness and beauty in service of his community.

Practice Module 4
Pluralistic Stage

Each higher stage of development solves the problems of the previous stage but eventually creates its own challenges that increase in complexity.
~ Jürgen Habermas ~

Module description

Learn and practice how/if the pluralistic stage of consciousness developed in your life, and how it impacts your love relationships today. Feel how this stage allows for greater compassion, idealism, and involvement by providing a sense that all human beings—regardless of race, gender, sexual orientation, cultural background, or class—are born equal and should be equally treated, heard, and respected.

Realize how people in this stage reject hierarchy/patriarchy and establish lateral social structures with an emphasis on values such as communion, empathy, peace, compassion, nonviolence, and consensus among all.

Develop a sense that all souls are connected in a web of life. Develop a deep caring for Mother Earth and all its inhabitants and, along with it, the desire to find peace and happiness within, which triggers an exploration of the feelings and inner experiences of the self and others, with an increasing attention to the unconscious and subjective.

Recognize the potential downside of this worldview, as rationality is dismissed and the feminine is established as being superior to the masculine. This perspective can lead to New-Age narcissism and relativism, along with unending discussions in which all parties add divergent observations and feelings without ever achieving consensus and reaching decisions. Such continual, unresolved discussions, despite the best intentions, often make love relationships challenging and unstable.

Look at the healthy needs and expressions of this fascinating stage, as well as the unhealthy aspects and limited views. Understand how a lack of healthy integration at this stage, as well as attachments to limited views, are often the cause for relationship conflicts and breakups, especially when one partner is at a later or earlier stage of development than the other.

Introduction

Postmodernity challenged the worldviews that are associated with the rational Enlightenment era that began in the seventeenth century and with many values of the industrial and late modern era that followed. Postmodernity is associated with pluralism, relativism, existentialism, and the radical progressive left.

Postmodernists are skeptical of explanations which claim to be fundamental and valid for all individuals, groups, cultures, traditions, or races, and instead focus on the relative truths of each person. They consider "reality" to be a mentally and culturally conditioned construct, or created by our perceptions or consciousness, and reject the possibility of an unmediated reality or objective rational knowledge, asserting that all interpretations are contingent on the perspective and conditioning from which they are made. Simple examples are the questions: "If a tree falls in a forest, and no one is there to listen, is there still a sound? (hint, there isn't)"[60] and "What do you see in the two images below (hints, an old or a young woman, Einstein or … if you look at the image from a distance)?"

83 | Pluralistic Stage

Figure 16: Young-old woman

Figure 17: Different person when looking from a distance

Purpose and application of the module

1. Become aware of the sixth of the eight stages/levels of consciousness development (pluralistic) and how you and others advanced to this stage.
2. Understand the performative contradictions and different forms of pluralism that make love relationships at this level very complex.
3. Learn about the pre-trans or pre/post fallacy (pre-rational versus transrational; pre-personal versus transpersonal; and preconventional versus postconventional stages) and how they impact your relationships.
4. For more, see "Purpose and application" in Module 2, on page 60.

Exercise: Stage six of development

The following is a paired exercise.
1. See page 60 for the preparation and explanation of the exercise.
2. Make the four agreements for confidentiality, responsibility, healthy boundaries, I-statements, and sharing, as outlined on page 556.

Worksheet: Stage six of consciousness development

Share with your partner in an autobiographical way how you grew through the stages below. How did your views and life change in each of the four dimensions of your being and relating (quadrants) as you evolved? Which limited views did you transcend, which basic capacities did you include? How does each stage impact your love relationships today? What attracts you to a/your partner? What needs do you project onto a/your partner based on these levels? When do you regress (in love relationships) and at what levels do you become defensive (fight, flight, freeze, fawn)? What do you want to co-create at each level in your love relationship?

6. Green—pluralistic—sensitive or indifferent (Interior surrenders to exterior–peace)

Core capacities: Humanistic. Nonjudgmental, holistic, caring, environmentally conscious. Celebrates the feminine, animal rights, sexual freedoms, and authentic polyamory. Liberates humans from greed and dogma. Shows compassion. Explores the inner beings of self/others. Promotes community and unity. Shares society's resources among all. Cares about the planet and all living things. Reaches decisions through consensus. Refreshes spirituality and brings harmony. Elevates the feminine and envisions cultures based on matriarchy and on radical, social, and ecofeminism.

Limited views: Relativism, no absolute truths. Rejects science. Self-diagnoses illnesses (e.g., food allergies) and applies unproven natural remedies. Endless processing and inability to reach decisions. Shows (idiot) compassion.[iii] Falls for the pre/trans pre/post fallacy (confuses pre-rational, pre-personal, or preconventional with transrational, transpersonal or postconventional stages); confuses natural hierarchies with dominator hierarchies. Engages in performative contradictions (no absolute truths is an absolute truth; judging judgments; no hierarchies are better than hierarchies (and thus creating a hierarchy); shouldng people not to should; all relative truths are equal; include/love/accept all except those who don't include/love/accept all etc.). Marginalizes men and all forms of the masculine as toxic; elevates the feminine/Goddess image. New-Age narcissism.

As a couple: We need each other to learn to love unconditionally.

Follow-up questions

1. How do you feel after this exercise?
2. What insights did you gain as you shared about the sixth stage of consciousness development with your partner?

[iii] "Idiot compassion" is a term attributed to the late Chogyam Trungpa Rinpoche, although he may have borrowed it from the Russian spiritual teacher George Gurdjieff. Idiot compassion can take several forms.

Rinpoche related it to "doing good" as an act of self-gratification: "Idiot compassion is the highly conceptualized idea that you want to do good to somebody. At this point, good is purely related with pleasure. Idiot compassion also stems from not having enough courage to say no."

Trungpa's student, Pema Chödron, elaborated:"It refers to something we all do a lot of and call it compassion. In some ways, it's what's called enabling. It's the general tendency to give people what they want because you can't bear to see them suffer. Basically, you're not giving them what they need (and keeping them in their dependence). You're trying to get away from your feeling of 'I can't bear to see them suffer.' In other words, you're doing it for yourself. You're not really doing it for them."

3. Did you experience defensiveness about the Green stage six—especially about developmental stages in general, the elevation of the feminine over the masculine, performative contradictions, and the pre/trans and pre/post fallacy—as it is often the case for people at this level?
4. Was there a recognition of the limited views and maybe some painful experiences at the Green stage six?
5. What kind of healing and forgiveness do you need to do in order to integrate healthy aspects and transcend limited views from this stage?

Additional information and resources

As we have seen, the Green pluralistic stage six is very complex and full of contradictions and paradoxes. (Also see Module 26 about the end of Green radical progressive liberalism.) One of the reasons is that, on the surface, people at this stage attempt to welcome and include all others and their views, only to become confused and frustrated, often regressing to absolutistic behaviors of the Blue/Amber stage when others don't conform to the ideals of Green (known as the mean green meme), or even falling back further into the tribal victim stage of Purple/Magenta.

It is, therefore, helpful to understand different forms of pluralism that may look like Green but are not.

Five forms of pluralism

On page 137–138 in the book, *Pragmatism: An Introduction*, by Michael Bacon, Richard J. Bernstein distinguishes between four forms of pluralism (below) that he thinks are best to be set aside in favor of the desirable fifth form:
1. **Fragmented pluralism,** in which different groups are pushed apart and no communication takes place between them. (Purple/ Magenta tribalism or New-Age narcissism)
2. **Flabby pluralism** is the superficial acceptance of other ideas without any serious attempt to understand them. (Orange rational, we agree to disagree.)

3. **Polemic pluralism** respects diversity until one is in a position to set it aside in order to install one's own view as the single truth. (Blue/Amber absolutistic)
4. **Defensive pluralism** demands the freedom to act as one desires without being held responsible or accountable to others. (Red egocentric)

None of these are really open to alternatives. They all confine one's interest to a specific group out of the belief that there is nothing of value to be learned from others.

5. **Engaged fallibilistic pluralism** seeks to understand other views and, in the process of so doing, criticizes its own views as well as those it encounters (dialectic). This requires openness and fairness, a willingness to change, and imagination/creativity for the new possible, which eventual leads to the seventh integral stage.

Suggested relationship books for the pluralistic stage

See Appendix I in *Integral Relationships: A Manual for Men*, pages 220–227, for reviews of the books listed below.

The Way of the Superior Man: A Spiritual Guide to Mastering the Challenges of Women, Work, and Sexual Desire (1997) by David Deida
tinyurl.com/irpm275[61]

The Path to Love: Spiritual Strategies for Healing (1996) by Deepak Chopra
tinyurl.com/irpm278[62]

Undefended Love (2000) by Jett Psaris and Marlena Lyons
tinyurl.com/irpm279[63]

How to Be an Adult in Relationships: The Five Keys to Mindful Loving (2002) by David Richo
tinyurl.com/irpm280[64]

Love and Awakening: Discovering the Sacred Path of Intimate Relationship (1996) by John Welwood
tinyurl.com/irpm281[65]

The Heart's Wisdom: A Practical Guide to Growing through Love (1999) by Joyce and Barry Vissell
tinyurl.com/irpm282[66]

Books for pluralistic singles

If the Buddha Dated: A Handbook for Finding Love on a Spiritual Path (1999) by Charlotte Kasl
tinyurl.com/irpm284[67]

Calling in "the One": 7 Weeks to Attract the Love of Your Life (2004) by Katherine Woodward Thomas
tinyurl.com/irpm288[68]

Sex Purpose Love book reference

Page 52–54

Suggested movie: *Same Time, Next Year* (1978)

Watch this movie to see the two main characters, Doris (Ellen Burstyn) and George (Alan Alda), evolve from the Red egocentric to the Blue/Amber mythic, Orange rational, and eventually Green Pluralistic stages of consciousness development over the time span of 26 years, from 1951 to 1977.

George and Doris meet by chance over dinner at a romantic Northern California inn. Although both are married to others, they find themselves in the same bed the next morning, questioning how this could have happened. Regardless, they agree to return on the same weekend each year to continue their affair.

Originally a stage play by Bernard Slade, the movie follows the two characters as they are seen changing in different scenes, five years apart, always in the same room. As time goes on, each is helped through a transformative personal crisis by the other, often without either of them understanding what is going on.

As their values and concerns noticeably change with every encounter that we witness, we also see feminine-masculine polarity reversal between them in the Green pluralistic stage, which we will explore in Module 11, on page 183.

Practice Module 5
Integral and Transpersonal Stages

*Is it possible to evolve beyond the need to be in a romantic relationship?
No, that would be like playing checkers with ourselves.*
~ Ken Wilber ~

Module description

Learn and practice how/if the integral and transpersonal stages of consciousness development emerged in your life, and how they impact your love relationships today.

Realize why people at the previous "first-tier" levels of consciousness development insist that their particular views, beliefs, and values are the best and only "right" way to see the world and to make their love relationships work. Understand why people react negatively and lash out in defense whenever their views are challenged or threatened, using the tools that are available to them.

Understand why people in "second-tier" integral and transpersonal levels of consciousness intuitively recognize the importance of all preceding levels—including the process of development itself. Integrate the essential qualities and basic capacities of each preceding level while transcending the limited views through ongoing learning, healing, growing, and awakening.

Balance and harmonize healthy masculine agency/ascending and feminine communion/descending polarities in all four dimensions of your being and relating in order to co-create attraction, synergy, and flow in your love relationships. Meet others at earlier levels of consciousness development with understanding and compassion, supporting them in their development without getting entangled in their drama, and co-create a love relationship with an equal and opposite partner.

Look at the healthy needs and expressions of each of these two stages, as well as the unhealthy aspects and limited views. Understand how a lack of healthy integration at these stages, as well as attachments to limited views, are often the cause for relationship conflicts and breakups, especially when one partner is at a later or earlier stage of development than the other.

Introduction

The integral post-postmodern, metamodern, or supermodern stage emerged in the early twentieth century in India and Europe[69] and was widely recognized by pioneering U.S. psychologists and social researchers in the 1970s as a step beyond the ontological emptiness and relativism of postmodernity.[70]

The integral Yellow/Teal stage is not just another level but marks the shift into what is called second-tier consciousness. People at previous levels insist that their particular views are the only right way to see the world. Whenever threatened, people at the magic Purple/Magenta stage lash out and defend themselves with voodoo-like spells; people at the egocentric Red stage with anger and crude violence; people at the mythic Blue/Amber stage with religious wars and shaming; people at the modern Orange stage with cold logic and collateral damage; and people at the postmodern Green stage through its cancel culture, wokeness, emasculations, and endless processing.

Unlike people at the Green level, who discard developmental hierarchies and maintain that all humans are equal, integral people see the liabilities, contributions, benefits, values, and limitations of each previous stage. They communicate with others at their level of consciousness, facilitate others' healthy growth through the stages, and acknowledge that higher levels of development are always possible, recognizing that the prevailing world order is a result of the existence of developmental stages as well as the movement of individuals and groups through those stages.

Integral people can feel quickly discouraged, bored, and frustrated, as they think they have seen and had it all—and in a way they often have. And while they can easily connect with others in earlier stages of development when making the effort, they often feel isolated and alone, as they get tired of the limited worldviews, self-created drama, narrow-minded labeling, and naive stereotyping of people in first-tier consciousness.

In turn, seen from the perspective of first-tier consciousness, people at the integral stage may seem to be cold, calculating, opportunistic, manipulative, analytical, distant, cynical, or arrogant—and sometimes they are, when they show a certain aloofness, edginess, or bitterness, and would rather win the argument than maintain the relationship.

People at an Integral level can be prone to fall in love with others who have personality disorders. They are attracted to the other's inner complexity, seductiveness, and psychological and spiritual pursuits of finding solutions to their problems. Unfortunately, these relationships frequently turn into one-way streets and eventually break down when the integral empath and helper burns out and either gives up or is left by his or her partner. We will explore this further in Module 21 (on page 391) about personality disorders.

The Turquoise stage is called transpersonal (or post/super-integral)[71] and in our exploration represents all the stages above integral. While people in the integral stage tend to observe, analyze, and often evaluate the inner and outer world of others in an analytical, left-brained, righteous, emotionally distant, and ascending way, without authentically engaging, individuals at Turquoise and higher stages naturally meet others where they are and would rather lose the argument and maintain the relationship. They display an actual embodiment, full embrace, and interweaving of the healthy qualities of the previous stages, with a new focus on love and compassion that transcends Green's localized/selective love and its indiscriminate and suffering-perpetuating "idiot compassion."

People in post-Integral stages recognize the importance of co-creative couples who raise children to create sustainable goodness, truth, beauty, and functioning in the world—and not just the importance of raising individual and group consciousness without offspring.

They weave together bottom-up and top-down approaches in "classic tantric" ways and deeply resonate with the limited views of the previous developmental stages as parts of the whole, while continuously working to embody the healthy capacities of those earlier stages.

Conflicts in Turquoise are resolved by finding a higher (transcendental) truth through dialectical processes (or absenting of absences) of thesis (or abstract), antithesis (or negation) and synthesis (or overcoming through the negation of the negation.)

As you explore this final module about consciousness development, you may also touch on the fact that there is often a lack of integration in males of the stages with the even numbers (2, 4, 6 and 8) or "cool" colors Purple/Magenta, Blue/Amber, Green, and Turquoise; similarly, there is often a lack of integration in females of the stages with the uneven numbers (1, 3, 5 and 7) or "warm" colors Beige/Infrared, Red, Orange, and Yellow/Teal. This can lead to initial attraction and, later, relationship conflicts, but it also offers an invitation to heal and better integrate the stages that were skimmed.

You may also notice how people often locate themselves two stages higher on a cognitive level of understanding than they really are on a level of experience, embodiment, and enactment. Purple/Magenta thinks it is Blue/Amber; Red thinks it is Orange; Blue/Amber thinks it is Green; Orange thinks it is Yellow/Teal; and Green feels that it is Turquoise. Green may also sense that it was born at, or moved into, the Turquoise stage early in life, falling for the pre/trans fallacy.

This confusion about the stages also has to do with the interior locus of control and, consequently, the resonance between the stage with the unevenly numbered warm colors and the exterior locus of control of the evenly numbered cool colors.

Finally, we will see how females tend to grow through the stages by "transcending and including" basic capacities and limited views, and males tend to grow by "transcending and excluding" basic capacities and limited views.

We will then set the stages into a relational context in the compatibility matrix.

Purpose and application of the module

1. Become aware of the seventh and eighth of the eight stages of second-tier consciousness development and how they are fundamentally different from first-tier consciousness.
2. Understand the tendency in males to skim or skip the stages with the evenly numbered "cool" colors, and the tendency in females to skim or skip the unevenly numbered, "warm"-color stages.
3. See how people often locate themselves two stages higher on a cognitive level than they really are on a level of embodiment.
4. See how females tend to grow through the stages by "transcending and including" and males by "transcending and excluding."
5. Understand and apply the Compatibility Matrix in *Figure 18: Compatibility Matrix* (on page 100).
6. For more, see "Purpose and application" in Module 2, on page 60.

Exercise: Stages seven and eight of consciousness development

The following is a paired exercise.
1. See page 60 for the preparation and explanation of the exercise.
2. Make the four agreements for confidentiality, responsibility, healthy boundaries, I-statements, and sharing, as outlined on page 556.

Worksheet: Stages seven and eight of consciousness development

Share with your partner in an autobiographical way how you grew through the stages below. How did your views and life change in each of the four dimensions of your being and relating (quadrants) as you evolved? Which limited views did you transcend, which basic capacities did you include? How does each stage impact your love relationships today? What attracts you to a/your partner? What needs do you project onto a/your partner based on these levels? When do you regress (in love relationships) and at what levels do you become defensive (fight, flight, freeze, fawn)? What do you want to co-create at each level in your love relationship?

7. Teal/Yellow—Integral—integrated or partial/fragmented (Interior controls or dominates exterior–freedom)

Core capacities: Recognizes the importance of all preceding levels, including the process of development itself (consciously competent about stages). Is curious and open. Does not force its own values onto others. Self-interested without doing harm to others. Knowledge, competency, and functionality supersede rank, power, gender, or status. Flexibility, spontaneity, and adaptability become the highest priority. Establishes truths and norms through intersubjectivity and inter-objectivity. Accepts the inevitability of nature's flows and hierarchies. Integrates feminine and masculine polarities. Considers what is good, true, beautiful, and functional (four dimensions of our being and relating—quadrants/perspectives). Finds natural mix of conflicting (half) "truths." Utilitarian (greatest good/happiness for largest number of people, or greatest depth for the largest span). Supports people in their development (translation/integration and transformation).

Limited views: Would rather win the argument and lose the relationship. More interested in the map/model than in the territory (menu vs. meal). Easily frustrated, especially with Green. Can be (seen as) cynical, cold, calculating, distant, pompous, arrogant, opportunistic, manipulative, and overly analytical. Can feel quickly discouraged and bored, as it can think it has seen and had it all. Isolates itself (and writes books). Often only ascending spirituality. Attracted to (or attracts) complex people/partners with personality disorders. Potentially problematic sexual relationships with partners in first-tier consciousness.

As a couple: We need each other to learn, heal, grow, and awaken together in the four dimensions of our being.

8. Turquoise—transpersonal—interpenetrative or interpretive (Interior surrenders to exterior–peace)

Core capacities: Full and healthy embrace/embodiment (and not only "knowledge") of previous stages (unconsciously competent about stages). Deep drive to contribute to creating a eudemonic world and future in which everyone can flourish through living meaningful lives. Would rather lose arguments to maintain relationships. More interested in the territory than in the map (meal vs. recipe), which is embodied. Humble. Compassion for the suffering of all beings—present and future. Deep ecology. Blending, harmonizing, inviting. Strong collective. Focus on the good of all living entities. Authentic "traditional tantric" and possibly transpersonal/nondual spirituality. Self is part of the collective (un)conscious whole. Global networking seen as routine. Acts for minimalist living, so less is more. Does not enter into sexual relationships with partners in first-tier consciousness. Linguistically construct-aware (see Module 8) and philosophically pragmatic/critically realistic.

Limited views: Fear of being dragged down into the drama of earlier stages and wasting too much time and energy there. Getting lost in metatheories of metatheories. May have difficulties in forming deep friendships and love relationships because of a lack of peers and a general surrender to what is. Conflicted about charging for services and thus making money. As a result, an inability to create sustainable organizational structures and communities.[72] Fear of co-creators leaving relationship or community, especially if there is no shared biological, transformational, or transcendental purpose.

As a couple: We need each other for ego transcendence and full embodiment of all previous stages to co-create (and if possible) procreate at the level of all seven chakras to make the world a better place.

Follow-up questions

1. How do you feel after this exercise?
2. What insights did you gain as you shared with your partner about the seventh and eighth stages of consciousness development?
3. Did you notice a lack of integration in yourself at some of the levels?
4. Did you sense that you and/or your partner have a cognitive understanding of higher stages but lack integration through experience and embodiment (aka "integrity" or "walking your talk")?
5. Do you often unconsciously flow to earlier stages by identifying with their limited views or lack of healthy integration?
6. What kind of healing and forgiveness do you need to do to integrate healthy aspects and transcend limited views from this stage?

Additional information and resources

Compatibility matrix

As we have seen above, our level of consciousness development or altitude defines how we view the world, ourselves, and others. This obviously has a major impact on our love relationships, especially when conflicts arise. Who we fall in love with is primarily determined by unconscious processes in our limbic and reptilian brains. The hormones that are released when our primary fantasies are met and we fall in love (see Module 20, page 367) often cause us to temporarily ignore red flags that signal incompatibilities which are based on differing levels of consciousness. Once the honeymoon phase is over and the intoxicating love hormones wear off, potential differences become apparent. No matter how much we may be sexually attracted to our partner, or complement each other in our psychological makeup and unconscious, or share interests, lifestyle choices, dreams, values, and passions, the quality and outcome of our love relationship will ultimately be determined by our own and our partner's level of consciousness.

If we place the eight levels of consciousness development, as outlined above, on a vertical axis for one partner, and on a horizontal axis for the other, we get 64 possible combinations of (in)compatibilities.

To use the matrix, simply locate the highest level of consciousness that you and your partner have reached individually, and find a short description of the relationship that is most likely to exist or develop between the two of you in the intersecting field.

Generally speaking, we can say that individuals who are fully actualized at their highest level of consciousness are most compatible with partners who are at the same altitude, as indicated by the shaded fields in the matrix shown below. Women who are in transition from one stage to the next higher stage will be attracted to men at the level they are moving into. Most men will find women at the stage that they are transitioning into as too threatening, challenging, and sometimes emasculating. Women who typically want to "marry up" find men who are transitioning into the woman's level to be immature and needy. The biggest challenges for conflict resolution arise between first-tier couples who are fully actualized at their respective altitude and one level apart (Green fights Orange, which most vehemently rejects Amber, which is utterly frustrated by Red). People who are more than one level apart in first-tier consciousness don't resonate, either, in their values and worldviews, except for the pre/post fallacy between preconventional Purple/Magenta/Red and postconventional Green (which are both "unconventional") or between Red and Orange (in "sugar daddy," "trophy wife," "boy toy," and "cougar" relationships.)

Fundamental major conflicts that arise between partners who have grown apart or who realize, after the "love-struck phase" is over, that they are at different stages of development can't be simply resolved through better communication or other means of reconciliation. Their relationships are basically doomed ... sorry.[73]

Male \ Female	Archaic	Magic	Egocentric	Mythic	Rational	Pluralistic	Integral	Transpersonal
Transpersonal	Caretaker/ Dependent	Mystic-Connection	Compassion	Friendship	Mentor / Guide / Friendship	Mentor/Friendship Unconditional Love	Mentor / Teacher / Guru / Guide	Transpersonal Inter-becoming Embodied
Integral	Caretaker/ Dependent	Caretaker/ Dependent	Conflict/ Fights	Friendship	Support / Friendship / Lovers	Female Challenging Emasculating	Interbeing Equals & Opposites Learning, Healing, Growing, Awakening	Mentor / Teacher / Guru / Guide
Pluralistic	Caretaker/ Dependent	Prerational/ Transrational Fallacy	Preconventional /Postconventional Fallacy	No Partnership	Green Male Frustration Divorce	Interdependence Feminine/Masculine Role Reversal Pre-Post Fallacy	Inspiring Male to Become Integral	Mentor/Friendship Unconditional Love
Rational	Caretaker/ Dependent	No Partnership	Trophy Wife	Independence Male - Female Gender Roles or Divorce	Independence Equals Not Opposites	Orange Male Offering Financial Support / Lovers	Support / Friendship / Lovers	Mentor / Guide / Friendship
Mythic	Caretaker/ Dependent	No Partnership	Frustration/ Divorce	Dependence Mythic Opposites Not Equals	Independence Male - Female Gender Roles or Divorce	No Partnership	Friendship	Friendship
Egocentric	No Relationship	Red Abuse of Magenta	Codependence Fight -> Flight Makeup Sex	Frustration / Divorce	Boy Toy	Preconventional /Postconventional Fallacy	Conflict/ Fights	Compassion
Magic	Survival-Bond	Tribal, Fused Survival-Bond	Red Abuse of Magenta	No Partnership	No Partnership	Prerational/ Transrational Fallacy	Caretaker / Dependent	Mystic-Connection
Archaic	Living side by side, Survival and Procreation	Survival-Bond	No Relationship	Caretaker / Dependent	Caretaker/ Dependent	Caretaker/ Dependent	Caretaker/ Dependent	Caretaker / Dependent

Figure 18: Compatibility Matrix

See an interactive version of the Compatibility Matrix by David Fonsbo at tinyurl.com/irpm419[74]

Transcend and include/exclude

Males and females often grow through the stages of first-tier consciousness differently. Males tend to be single-focused (agentic) and growth-oriented (ascending), advancing through the stages by *transcending and excluding* the limited views but also the basic capacities of the previous levels through negation, dissociation, and repression.

Because females are conditioned by evolution to rear children (who naturally all start out at the Infrared level) and to accommodate a male protector/provider, they are often more relational (communal) and fulfillment-oriented (descending), and thus tend to *transcend and include* the limited views and basic capacities of the previous stages through attachment, fusion, and preservation, and through unconsciously floating between the first-tier stages that they have transcended.

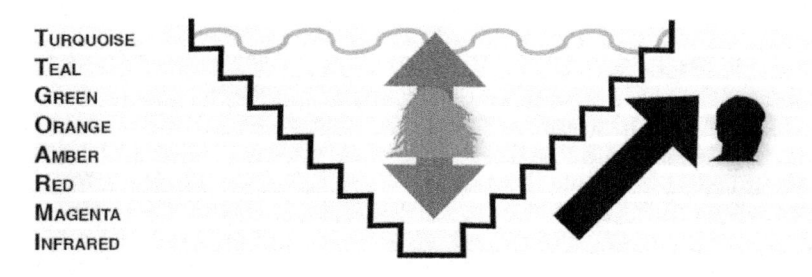

Figure 19: Male-female dynamic in consciousness growth[75]

As a consequence, males in first-tier consciousness act more consistently from the highest level or altitude they have reached and have a hard time tolerating the behavior, values, and worldviews of people in stages below or above them (i.e., let's force our views onto others by getting them up to our standards or rein them in to our level).[76]

In contrast, females in first-tier consciousness unconsciously flow between the stages and tend to be more tolerant towards people with differing values. The fluidity of females in moving between the stages also explains why most women in first-tier consciousness don't think hierarchically and either reject altogether the idea of vertical stage development or conceive only men not women, as moving through individual stages of development after adolescence.[77] If women experience growth and development, it is often likened to a waning and waxing horizontal movement, or to the moon, or to the expanding waves of a pebble thrown into a pond, rather than a clumsy vertical climb up a hierarchical ladder, as it is perceived for males.

Male/female difference in emotional complexity

The gender difference in development through the first-tier stages makes the personality of females seemingly more complex than that of males. This complexity is portrayed in many male-female jokes, in literature and movies, and is illustrated in the image below.

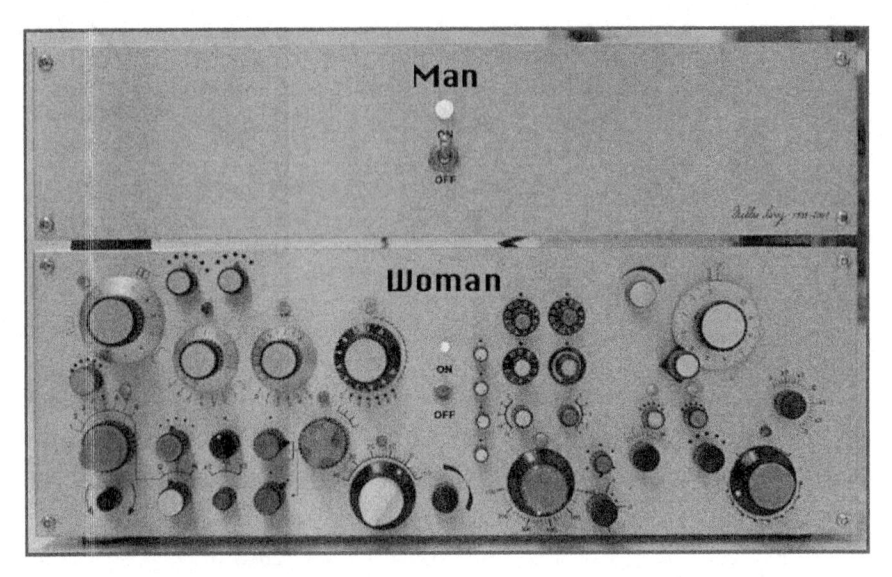

Figure 20: Divergent psychological complexity of men and women

More developmental models of consciousness

There are many other models of human developmental. Some of them are listed below—or see a comprehensive, mind-dazzling overview of these models and their sources in *Integral Psychology* by Ken Wilber (pages 197–217).tinyurl.com/irpm12[78]

Georg Wilhelm Friedrich Hegel: (1770-1831): Dialectic—"Sturm und Drang," Eros -> Perfection.
Charles Darwin: (1809-1882): Evolutionary theory.
Jean Piaget (1896-1980): Age 0–2, sensorimotor; age 2–7, pre-operational (magical, not mental, only one perspective); age 7–11,

concrete operation (conserve, imagine, second-person perspective); age 11–17, formal operational (abstract, imaginary thinking).
Jean Gebser: (1905–1973): Structures of human development archaic to integral.
Abraham Maslow: (19081970): Being values and needs: survival, safety, love/belonging, self-esteem, self-actualization, integration (hierarchy is questionable).
Clare Graves (1914-1986) and his late students and creators of *Spiral Dynamics*, Don Beck and Christopher Cowan: Levels of human nature, existence, values, worldviews, consciousness, meaning-making. What is a healthy personality? What is of concern?
Lawrence Kohlberg (1927-1987): Stages of moral development: preconventional (1–punishment, 2–self-interest); conventional (3–good behavior, being nice, 4–law and order); and postconventional (5–social contract, 6–universal ethics).
Jane Loevinger (1918-2008): Ego/personal development. Impulsive, self-protective, conformist, self-aware, conscientious (careful, diligent, serious), individualistic, autonomous, integrated (empathy, ongoing learning).
Susanne Cook-Greuter (1945-): Mature ego development.
1. The Symbiotic Stage.
2. The Impulsive.
3. The Opportunist (or self- protective).
4. The Diplomat (or conformist).
5. The Expert (efficient, problem-solving, dogmatic, seeking recognition for uniqueness and expertise).
6. The Achiever (cultural version of mature adulthood: success oriented, achievement based, initiating, win-lose mentality, operating within cultural structures).
7. The Individualist (focuses on self and experience in the moment, looks inward, takes a system approach, questions norms, inclusive of others' perspectives).
8. The Strategist (or autonomous). (Focused on becoming the most one can be; guided by big-picture principles; thriving on human complexity and variety, as viewed from a coherent,

complex, and separate core sense of self; alive and aware that what one sees depends on level of development; creative; inclusive and pragmatic leadership).
9. The Magician (construct aware). (Self as separate from the rest of reality comes into question, as Magicians see that language and storytelling has shaped but limited our understanding of who we are. Self now becomes understood as a part of one reality with no true separateness. One becomes more identified as having a global or planetary self-sense).
10. The Unitive (ego-aware). (Creative practitioners in the ongoing evolutionary and creative journey of humanity; a deep and continual cherishing and honoring of all humans, non-judging; an experienced state of being that is beyond language; self-identity based on inner knowing, the higher self).

Robert Kegan (1946-): Pre-social, impulsive, opportunistic, conformist, conscientious, and autonomous meaning making.

STAGES model and assessments

Human development is a highly complex subject with many facets. The outline above was created to support practitioners in gaining a basic understanding of developmental models and stages, and how they impact love relationships. For those interested in a deeper exploration and assessments of levels of consciousness development, the STAGES model, shown below,[79] created by Terri O'Fallon and Kim Barta and based on Susanne Cook Greuter's work on ego development, offers an advanced view of human development and assessments based on the sentence completion test.[80]

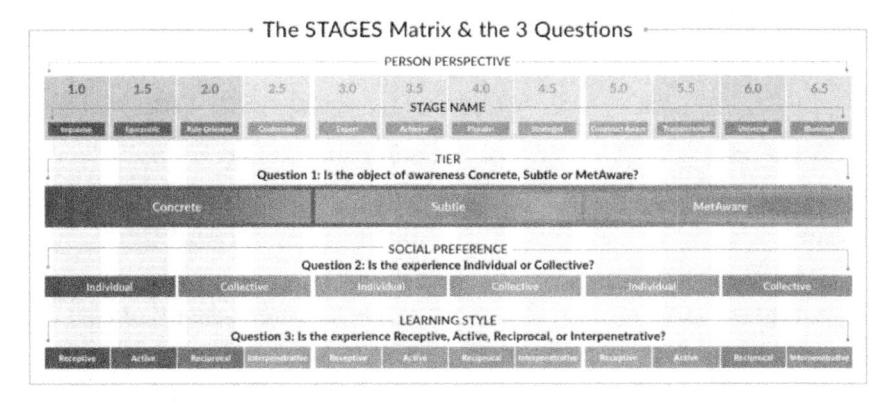

Figure 21: The STAGES Matrix

www.stagesinternational.com/about/#the-model
A PDF about the model is at tinyurl.com/irpm18[81]

For an important critique of the STAGES model and a rebuttal, see tinyurl.com/irpm22[82]

Other developmental lines

Ken Wilber lists the following developmental lines in various parts of his work. In our training, we cover the bolded lines below.

aesthetics (what is beautiful) affect/emotion (feelings about things) altruism anima animus complex care cognition (awareness of what is) communicative competence what is of concern to you creativity death seizure (dying to an old self) culinary defense mechanisms empathy gender identity idea of the good (moral/ethics)	interpersonal capacity kinesthetic mathematical meditative stages morals/ethics (what to do) modes of space and time musical needs (immediate needs for well-being) psychosexual (expression of Eros) role-taking self-esteem self-identity (who are you?) socioemotional capacity spiritual (what are you identified with?)

Table 7: Developmental lines

Suggested relationship books

Truth in Dating: Finding Love by Getting Real (2003) by Susan Campbell
tinyurl.com/irpm578[83]

Integral Relationship: A Manual for Men (2010) by Martin Ucik
tinyurl.com/irpm581[84]

Transpersonal stage

Sex Purpose Love: Couples in Integral Relationships Creating a Better World (2017) by Martin Ucik
tinyurl.com/irpm582[85]

Sex Purpose Love book reference
Page 55–62

Suggested movie: *American Beauty* (1999)

Watch this truly Integral movie to see how people at different levels of consciousness development collide with each other in their daily lives. On the surface, the movie is about the breakdown and disintegration of a middle-class American family. On a deeper level, we painfully see how people at five different levels of consciousness development (archaic, magic, egocentric, mythic, rational, and pluralistic), with their divergent values, concerns, needs and worldviews, get into irresolvable conflicts with each other, and how an integral person critically reflects and engages with them all. At the end of the movie, we even offered a glimpse into the transpersonal stage.

Lester Burnham (Kevin Spacey) is the husband of real estate agent Carolyn Burnham (Annette Bening) and father to high school student Janie Burnham (Thora Birch). Although Lester and Carolyn were once in love, they now merely tolerate each other. Typical "Red/egocentric" wallflower Janie hates both of her parents. "Orange/rational" Carolyn wants to create the persona of success to further her career in real estate. Initially "Orange/rational" Lester walks mindlessly through life, including at his job in advertising, until he falls in love at first sight with Janie's "Purple/Magenta/magic" classmate, Angela Hays (Mena Suvari). His infatuation "transforms" Lester into the "Green/Pluralistic" stage—with plenty of the pre/trans fallacy—where he no longer cares what anyone thinks about him (except for Angela). When homophobic disciplinarian, "Blue/Amber mythic" Marine Colonel Frank Fitts (Chris Cooper), his demented "Beige/Infrared/archaic" wife, Barbara Fitts (Allison Janney), and their seemingly "Teal/Yellow/integral" eighteen-year-old son, Ricky Fitts (Wes Bentley) move in next door, the drama unfolds, and eventually all of the players are forced to confront their demons.

Practice Module 6
Nonviolent Compassionate Communication

We may never be strong enough to be entirely nonviolent in thought, word and deed. But we must keep nonviolence as our goal and make strong progress towards it.
~ Mahatma Gandhi ~

In an ever-changing, incomprehensible world, the masses had reached the point where they would, at the same time, believe everything and nothing, think that everything was possible and that nothing was true.
~ Hanna Arendt ~

Module description

Learn and practice how to communicate your observations and related feelings in a nonviolent and compassionate way in order to get your needs met by your partner.

Identify your specific needs when relating with others, especially in your love relationships. Separate your observations of your partner's behavior from the feelings that are stimulated in you when your needs are not met. Express these feelings in an authentic, nonthreatening way by distinguishing them from interpretations and strategies. Without being attached to an outcome other than compassionate connection and mutual understanding, make doable requests that clearly communicate what and why, when, where, and how you want your partner to meet your needs. Understand the difference between needs and neediness. Offer your partner empathy when he or she is in distress by guessing his or her observation, the feeling created, and the unmet need—and then make an offer to reestablish love and connection.

Introduction

Because communication at the Green level six of consciousness development is quite complex, we will start there with our exploration of how people at the eight levels of consciousness development communicate in different ways to create mutual understanding, coordinate their actions, and have their needs met.

As we established above, people and groups at the pluralistic Green level reject the idea of objective, absolute truths. They stress the importance that every observation or experience must be put into a relative culturally constructed context and that individual subjective observations, experiences, and truths must be considered, respected, and validated. Rather than trusting the mind, reason, and sense perceptions, the focus in their communications shifts to expressing subjective observations, feelings, unmet needs, and to making requests (rather than demands).

This way of creating mutual understanding has become known as Nonviolent Communication (NVC) or sometimes called Compassionate Communication. It was initially conceived by Carl Rogers, who was one of the founders of humanistic psychology and who developed a client-centered therapy.[86] His student, Marshall Rosenberg,[87] who was also inspired by Mahatma Gandhi, Martin Luther King, and Nelson Mandela, later refined and popularized the method.

The main goal of NVC is to achieve interpersonal harmony through empathy and understanding of universal needs; there is a lesser intent—or none at all—to expect or demand concrete results or actions beyond creating compassion and mutual understanding.

Nonviolent communication is based in the idea that unmet needs and vulnerable feelings of others will resonate with us through empathy and compassion (suffering with others) if we also recognize our own human needs and feelings, even if they are different, which then inspires and motivates us to be more open to meet each other's needs.

NVC is also a spiritual way of communication, as it requires insight, presence, surrender, non-attachment, compassion, and openness (being nonjudgmental).

The NVC processes to resolve relationship conflicts and to restore intimate connection entails the following four steps:

Observation—Feeling—Need—Request

1. Express an objective observation (e.g., words or actions) without making an evaluation of the person.
2. Express an authentic feeling or emotional reaction (not an interpretation) that was stimulated by the observation.
3. Express an unfulfilled underlying need that stimulated the emotional reaction.
4. Express a doable request for connection or behavior that is concrete in kind, time, and place.

This four-step process is abbreviated as OFNR (Observation-Feeling-Need-Request).

Similarly, if your partner or someone else is in emotional distress and cannot provide you with empathy, you may make an empathy guess that has the following four steps:

Empathy Guess

1. Express an objective observation (e.g., words or actions) without making an evaluation of your partner.
2. Guess a feeling or emotional reaction (not interpretation) that was stimulated in your partner.
3. Guess an unfulfilled underlying need that stimulated the emotional reaction in your partner.
4. Suggest a doable action that is concrete in kind, time, and place to restore connection with your partner.

NVC Guidelines

Explain the following NVC guidelines:
1. Don't be attached to any specific outcomes, other than authentic empathic human connection.
2. Avoid criticism and "shoulding"; denial of responsibility (response-ability); demands with threats of blame and punishment; and declarations of who deserves reward or punishment.
3. Do not provoke fear, shame, or guilt in others.
4. Do not mix objective observations with subjective evaluations (s/he is/isn't; you are ...; you never ...; you always ...; etc.)
5. Always make "I" statements.
6. Understand that behind every request or demand is a person with an unmet need.
7. Focus on all feelings.
8. Wait until all is expressed (ask, "Is there anything else?"). Especially for men, wait 10 seconds before responding.[88]
9. Understand when no empathy can be given by another person, he/she needs empathy from you.
10. Listen actively and paraphrase.
11. Do not advise, compare, educate, reassure, story-tell, tell not to feel, sympathize, gather data, or apologize. Instead, share authentically what you feel.

113 | Nonviolent Compassionate Communication

Nonviolent Compassionate Communication Card
1. Avoid:
- Criticism and shielding.
- Denial of responsibility.
- Demands with threats of blame and punishment.
- Declarations of who deserves reward or punishment.
2. Do not mix observations with evaluations.
3. Make "I" statements:
When I observed or heard X, I felt Y, because I have a need for Z.
4. Make a doable request that is precise in kind, time, and place.
Observation -> Feeling -> Need -> Request
5. Behind every message is a person with an unmet need:
Focus on all feelings. Wait until all is expressed (is there anything else?) When no empathy is given, empathy is needed.
6. Listen and paraphrase. Do not:
Advise, compare, educate, reassure, story-tell, tell not to feel, sympathize, gather data, apologize. Instead, share how you feel.
7. Make an empathy guess:
State what was observed by your partner (when I did/said ...)
Guess the feeling that was stimulated in your partner.
Guess the unfulfilled need of your partner.
Make an offer what you will do differently going forward.

Table 8: NVC Card

Copy, fold, and laminate the card with packing tape for your wallet and hand it out to your clients.[89]

Purpose and application of the module

1. Identify your needs in relationships.
2. Differentiate feelings from interpretations and needs from neediness.
3. Take responsibility for your needs and emotional reactions when they are not met.
4. Learn and practice how to communicate your feelings and needs in a nonviolent, compassionate way.
5. Make clear and doable requests that are nonthreatening to your partner.
6. Learn not to be attached to any specific outcomes other than compassionate loving human connection.
7. Return to love instead of judgment and conflict.
8. Show empathy when empathy cannot be given to you.
9. Apply the insights and practices of this module in Modules 7, 10, 18, and 19.

Exercises: Nonviolent Compassionate Communication

The following are individual and paired exercises.
1. In a group setting, it is advised that couples do the exercise together.
2. For the rest of the group, it can be helpful if practitioners who are already familiar with expressing feelings and needs pair up with less experienced partners.
3. Print out the worksheet below, double-sided.
4. Make the four agreements for confidentiality, responsibility, healthy boundaries, I-statements, and sharing, as outlined on page 556.

Exercise one: Needs

What are your needs or interests?
1. In the worksheet below, ask practitioners to circle the most important of the needs they would like to have met by their

partner in their love relationship, based on the expectation of having bad, difficult, or challenging "negative"[90] emotional reactions and feelings when these needs are not met on an ongoing basis.
2. Ask practitioners to pair up with someone and share what they circled; why they circled it; what doable acts that are specific in kind, time, and place would meet these needs; and how it would make them feel if these needs were not met on an ongoing basis.
3. Invite group shares and questions about the exercise.
4. Explain the difference between "being needs" at different levels of consciousness development and neediness, which is the projection of our needs onto others and punishing them if they do not meet them.
5. Explain transforming needs into desires, desires into wants, wants into preferences, and preferences into no preference (as suggested in the book *Undefended Love*—see more on page 353 in Module 18), which opens us up to being less needy and to finding mutually beneficial ways to meet our own needs and the needs of our partner.
6. Explain need versus strategy. Needs are universal driving energies of life. Strategies are ways to fulfill needs. Needs are often intangible and difficult to measure, while strategies refer to visible or doable actions or words (e.g., getting money, finding shelter, or receiving affirmations are "strategies" or necessities, in certain contexts, to meet needs.)[91]

Exercise two: OFNR
1. Explain feelings versus interpretations (see worksheet below).
2. Explain that feelings are always expressed after "I feel ..." and never after "I feel like ..." or "I feel that ...," etc.
3. Explain and demonstrate the OFNR exercise (see worksheet below).
4. Invite practitioners to pair up again with the same partner with whom they worked in the first exercise.

5. Ask practitioners to think about a contentious situation when their needs were not met and they had a difficult emotional reaction or feeling.
6. Ask practitioners to practice OFNR (allow about 20–30 minutes).
7. Invite shares and answer questions.

Exercise three: Empathy guess

1. Explain and demonstrate the empathy guess exercise (see worksheet below.)
2. Invite practitioners to pair up again with the same partner as before.
3. Ask practitioners to think about a contentious situation when their partner's need was not met.
4. Ask practitioners to practice the empathy guess exercise.
5. Invite shares and answer questions.

Worksheet: Nonviolent Compassionate Communication

List of needs:	connection	inspiration	security
acceptance	consciousness	integrity	self-expression
adventure	contribution	intimacy	self-responsibility
affection	cooperation	joy	
aliveness	creativity	kindness	
appreciation	direction	learning	sex
attention	discovery	leisure	significance*
attraction	ease	masculinity	space
attunement	effectiveness	moderation	spirituality
authenticity	efficacy	mutuality	spontaneity
autonomy	empathy	nurturing	stability
awareness	equality	oneness	support
beauty	fallibility	opinions	to matter
belonging	femininity	order	touch
celebration	flexibility	participation	trust
certainty*	freedom	peace	uncertainty* (not knowing)
challenge	fun	play	
choice	generosity	presence	understanding
clarity	growth	protection	warmth
closeness	harmony	purpose	wildness (uninhibited)
co-creation	honesty	quality time	will (to live)
communion	humor	respect	Others:
community	inclusion	rest/reset	
companionship	independence	safety	

Table 9: List of needs

*Needs, as seen by Tony Robbins, that are not part of NVC needs inventory. He also sees intimacy, growth, and contribution as needs.

List of seven/ten universal primary emotions

The following emotions are universally experienced and recognized through facial expressions:[92] anger, sadness, disgust, fear, surprise, shame, joy (sometimes added are guilt, contempt, excitement).

Feelings when needs are satisfied

AFFECTIONATE: *Compassionate, friendly, loving, open-hearted, sympathetic, tender, warm*
CONFIDENT: *Empowered, open, proud, safe, secure*
ENGAGED: *Absorbed, alert, curious, engrossed, enchanted, entranced, fascinated, interested, intrigued, involved, spellbound, stimulated*
INSPIRED: *Amazed, awed, wonder*
EXCITED: *Animated, ardent, aroused, astonished, dazzled, eager, energetic, enthusiastic, giddy, invigorated, lively, passionate, surprised, vibrant*
EXHILARATED: *Blissful, ecstatic, elated, enthralled, exuberant, radiant, rapturous, thrilled*
GRATEFUL: *Appreciative, moved, thankful, touched*
HOPEFUL: *Expectant, encouraged, optimistic*
JOYFUL: *Amused, delighted, glad, happy, jubilant, pleased, tickled*
PEACEFUL: *Calm, clear-headed, comfortable, centered, content, equanimous, fulfilled, mellow, quiet, relaxed, relieved, satisfied, serene, still, tranquil, trusting*
REFRESHED: *Enlivened, rejuvenated, renewed, rested, restored, revived*

Feelings when needs are not satisfied

AFRAID: *Apprehensive, dread, foreboding, frightened, mistrustful, panicked, petrified, scared, suspicious, terrified, wary, worried*
ANNOYED: *Aggravated, dismayed, disgruntled, displeased, exasperated, frustrated, impatient, irritated, jerked*
ANGRY: *Enraged, furious, incensed, indignant, irate, livid, outraged, resentful*
AVERSION: *Animosity, appalled, contempt, disgusted, dislike, hate, horrified, hostile, repulsed*

CONFUSED: *Ambivalent, baffled, bewildered, dazed, hesitant, lost, mystified, perplexed, puzzled, torn*

DISCONNECTED: *Alienated, aloof, apathetic, bored, cold, detached, distant, distracted, indifferent, numb, removed, uninterested, withdrawn*

DISQUIET: *Agitated, alarmed, discombobulated, disconcerted, disturbed, perturbed, rattled, tasteless, shocked, startled, surprised, troubled, turbulent, turmoil, uncomfortable, uneasy, unnerved, unsettled, upset*

EMBARRASSED: *Ashamed, chagrined, flustered, guilty, mortified, self-conscious*

FATIGUE: *Beat, burnt out, depleted, exhausted, lethargic, listless, sleepy, tired, weary, worn out*

PAIN: *Agony, anguished, bereaved, devastated, grief, heartbroken, hurt, lonely, miserable, regretful, remorseful*

SAD: *Depressed, dejected, despair, despondent, disappointed, discouraged, disheartened, forlorn, gloomy, heavy-hearted, hopeless, melancholy, unhappy, wretched*

TENSE: *Anxious, cranky, distressed, distraught, edgy, fidgety, frazzled, irritable, jittery, nervous, overwhelmed, restless, stressed out*

VULNERABLE: *Fragile, guarded, helpless, insecure, leery, reserved, sensitive, shaky.*

YEARNING: *Envious, jealous, longing, nostalgic, pining, wistful*

Interpretations versus feelings

Words such as "ignored" express how we interpret the behavior or reality of others, rather than how we feel. Below is a sample of words that do not express authentic feelings but interpretations:

abandoned	co-opted	taken for granted	provoked
abused	cornered	let down	threatened
attacked	diminished	manipulated	unappreciated
betrayed	distrusted	misunderstood	unheard
boxed in	interrupted	neglected	unseen
bullied	intimidated	overworked	used
cheated	put down	patronized	unsupported
coerced	rejected	pressured	unwanted

Table 10: Interpretations versus feelings

To express feelings and needs in a nonthreatening, non-blaming, or inoffensive way (so they don't create fear in females and shame in males, thus triggering the fear-shame downward spiral as described in Module 10, page 171) is to put them into a sentence that expresses (1) an objective observation, (2) the feeling that was stimulated, (3) an underlying need that was not met, and (4) a doable request which is specific in kind, time, and place (in short, an OFNR—Observation, Feeling, Need, Request).

It goes like this:
1. State an observation that is factual (when you ... e.g., showed up later than I understood we had agreed upon; did not buy milk on your way home as I understood you had promised; etc.).
2. Describe the feeling that was stimulated for you—which is called owning your feelings by making an "I statement" (such as, I felt ...e.g., irritated, frustrated, etc.).
3. State the need that was not met (because I have a need for ... e.g., consideration, respect, reliability, certainty); and...
4. Make a doable request that is specific in time, place, and kind (would you be willing to ... e.g., call me on my cell phone 15 minutes ahead when you are later than we agreed? Inform me ahead of time when you are unable to run an errand? Set a reminder in your calendar, etc.?).

If the answer is no, you can either make another request (e.g., would you be willing to accept that I won't wait for you and meet you later at ...? Cook sauerkraut instead of making pancakes?) or state in the same structure how you feel about not getting a yes to your request. Alternatively, you can accept what he or she is saying yes to by saying no to you, and see how you can meet your need in other ways, or make an empathy guess as shown below.

Empathy guess:

To connect with the feelings and needs of others, especially if they are not responding empathetically to an OFNR, is to guess them without interpretation or judgment in the following way:
1. Guess his/her feeling (are you feeling ... e.g., frustrated?)
2. State or guess a fact why s/he may feel that way (because I watched TV while you talked to me?)
3. Guess a need (and you have a need for/to ... e.g., be heard and understood?); and...
4. Make a doable/realistic offer that is specific in kind, time, and place (would you like me to ... e.g., listen to you tonight at home in the living room from seven to eight?)

Additional lists of human being needs

11 Dimensions of well-being

(1) High positive emotions, (2) low negative emotions, (3) life satisfaction, (4) autonomy, (5) environmental mastery, (6) personal growth, (7) positive relations, (8) self-acceptance, (9) purpose and meaning in life (eudaimonia), (10) engagement in life, (11) accomplishment.

The World Happiness Report

Ranks countries on six key variables that support well-being and happiness:
(1) GDP per capita, (2) social support, (3) healthy life expectancy, (4) sense of freedom to make life choices, (5) generosity, and (6) perception of corruption.[93]

Maslow's hierarchy of needs

Physiological (survival), safety, love/belonging, (self)esteem, self-actualization. At the end of his life, Maslow himself questioned whether this is really a valid hierarchy, and most people think today it is not. We see these needs as a horizontal integration of well-being at any level of consciousness development rather than a vertical transformation. The same is true for the need inventory below:

Manfred Max-Neef's fundamental human needs[94]

Fundamental Human Needs	Being (Qualities)	Having (Things)	Doing (Actions)	Interacting (Settings)
Subsistence	Physical and mental health	Food, shelter, work	Feed, clothe, rest, work	Living environment social setting
Protection	Care, adaptability, autonomy	Social security, health systems, work	Cooperate, plan, take care of, help	Social environment dwelling
Affection	Respect, sense of humor, generosity, sensuality	Friendships, family, relationships with nature	Share, take care of, make love, express emotions	Privacy, intimate spaces of togetherness
Understanding	Critical capacity, curiosity, intuition	Literature, teachers, policies educational	Analyze, study, meditate investigate	Schools, families, universities, communities
Participation	Receptiveness, dedication, sense of humor	Responsibilities, duties, work, rights	Cooperate, dissent, express opinions	Associations, parties, churches, neighborhoods
Leisure	Imagination, tranquility spontaneity	Games, parties, peace of mind	Daydream, remember, relax, have fun	Landscapes, intimate spaces, places to be alone
Creation	Imagination, boldness, inventiveness, curiosity	Abilities, skills, work, techniques	Invent, build, design, work, compose, interpret	Spaces for expression, workshops, audiences

Identity	Sense of belonging, self-esteem, consistency	Language, religions, work, customs, values, norms	Get to know oneself, grow, commit oneself	Places one belongs to, everyday settings
Freedom	Autonomy, passion, self-esteem, open-mindedness	Equal rights	Dissent, choose, run risks, develop awareness	Anywhere

Table 11: Manfred Max-Neef's fundamental human needs

Follow-up questions

1. How do you feel after the exercises?
2. How will you apply nonviolent compassionate communication in your relationships?
3. What difficulties do you see with practicing nonviolent compassionate communication in your relationships?
4. What would support you in practicing nonviolent compassionate communication in your relationships?
5. In what situations may nonviolent compassionate communication not be effective for you or feel manipulative?

Additional information and resources

Nonviolent Communication: A Language of Life (2015) by Marshall B. Rosenberg
tinyurl.com/irpm293[95]

Integral Relationship book reference

Page 35–39

Suggested movie: *Gandhi* (1982)

Watch this profound multiple Oscar-winning movie to see how Mahatma Gandhi (Ben Kingsley) became the famed father of the modern nonviolence movement and Green icon through his leadership of the Indian revolts against the British rule and his philosophy of nonviolent protest.

In 1893, Gandhi, who has just become a UK-trained lawyer, is thrown off a South African train for being an Indian and traveling in first class. He realizes that the laws are biased against Indians and decides to start a nonviolent protest campaign. After numerous arrests, the government finally relents by recognizing rights for Indians. After this victory, Gandhi is invited back to India and urged to take up the fight for India's independence from the British Empire. Gandhi agrees and mounts a nonviolent non-cooperation campaign of unprecedented scale, coordinating millions of Indians nationwide. The campaign generates great attention, and Britain finally grants India's independence. Religious tensions between Hindus and Muslims erupt into nationwide violence. Gandhi declares a hunger strike and the fighting eventually stops, but the country becomes divided into today's predominantly Hindu India, and Muslim-majority Pakistan and Bangladesh. Gandhi opposes the idea, but the partition of India is carried out, nevertheless. Gandhi spends his last days trying to bring about peace between both nations and thereby angers dissidents on both sides, one of whom finally gets close enough to assassinate him.

Practice Module 7
Need-Based Communication

The single biggest problem with communication is the illusion that it has taken place.
~ George Bernard Shaw ~

Module description

Learn and practice how people at the first six levels of consciousness development communicate differently to validate their views and behaviors to get their needs met.

Realize that it is generally true that the most important skill to make relationships work is effective communication, but that people who are at different levels of consciousness development often cannot create mutual understanding, have their needs met, and solve their significant relationship conflicts through better communication.

Understand how people at the archaic, magic, egocentric, mythic, rational, and pluralistic stages make different feminine and masculine validity claims as to what is objectively true, subjectively truthful, morally/ethically right, aesthetically beautiful, and functional/practical from their view.

Consider a useful metaphor that likens communicating from different stages to speaking different languages, such as Greek and Chinese, resulting in a lack of communication that leads to irresolvable conflicts.

Practice communicating with others at their level of consciousness development by showing curiosity and empathy so that they feel heard and understood. Think win-win by focusing on your shared interests and needs; resolving conflicts by agreeing to disagree; or ending contentious conversations or relationships with love and compassion (instead of causing ongoing suffering for yourself and others) when conflicts become irresolvable because of developmental differences.

Introduction

Good communication is often hailed as the holy grail—the most important skill to make relationships work. While this is generally true, from an integrally informed perspective we understand that people at different levels of consciousness development make unique feminine and masculine validity claims as to what is beautiful, good, true, and/or practical/functional in order to justify their beliefs, needs, and behaviors.

These four essential validity claims correlate with the four dimensions of being and relating (quadrants), as shown in Module 1 on page 32. The "self" in the center communicates experiences, knowledge, observations, beliefs, requests, etc., from one or more quadrants.

1. Good LL "We" Intersubjective: We share, we agree/disagree (values), we believe, we connect, we understand, we resonate, etc. Validity claims to what is morally and ethically good and right (for us) and why.[96]
2. True UR "It" Objective: My body, my perceptions and observations of the exterior physical world. Validity claims to what is true (to me) and why.
3. Beautiful UL "I" Subjective: I feel, I think, I envision, what is alive in me, etc. Validity claims to what is truthful and beautiful to me and why.
4. Functional/Practical LL "Its" Inter-objective: Our shared outer physical reality and coordinated actions—for example, our social environment, our home, our money, our children, our natural environment. Validity claims to what is practical and functional (to us) and why.

People in a pure survival stage or state, which can be real or imagined, demand/require immediate and full attention and action to save or rescue them.

People at the magic level are often superstitious and fearful and perceive all kinds of imagined threats and dangers.

People at the egocentric level demand respect and validation for their subjective needs and truths and believe that nobody can be trusted.

People on a mythic/conformist level argue that what is good, true, beautiful, and practical is determined by higher authorities and powers instead of individuals.

People at the rational level argue that only practical experience, objective reason, and scientific empiricism can deliver what is good, true, beautiful, and practical.

People at the pluralistic level shift their communication to subjective cultural relativism and reject the ideas of norms and absolutes about what is good, true, beautiful, and practical.

Purpose and application of the module

1. Understand and practice how people at each level of first-tier consciousness development validate and communicate their worldviews, concerns, interests, and needs in different ways.
2. Go beyond a cognitive understanding of the different stages by deeply connecting, feeling, and identifying with them in yourself through role-playing each level with your partner.
3. Notice from which level you and others communicate. What kind of validity claims do you and they make (altitude, perspective, and feminine-masculine?)
4. Get a better understanding that everyone, including you, is right from his or her own view (altitude) and perspective (quadrants).
5. Gain insights into your own unresolved attachments and limited views at each level.
6. Become sensitive to what worldviews, values, and needs you and others are defensive about?

7. Realize why conflicts between people and partners in first-tier consciousness cannot be resolved through better communication techniques or strategies. If these kinds of conflict could be resolved, we would all live in a peaceful world and in peaceful love relationships with each other; however, we would no longer grow and develop/evolve.

Exercises: Need-based communication

The following are group and paired exercises.
1. Print out the worksheet below double sided.
2. Make the four agreements for confidentiality, responsibility, healthy boundaries, I-statements, and sharing, as outlined on page 556.

Exercise one: Why do we communicate verbally?

Exercise one is a group activity:
1. Ask practitioners why—and what—humans communicate through words? What purpose does verbal communication serve?
2. Use a whiteboard or flipchart to write down the practitioners' answers.
3. You may assign the answers to the four dimensions of being/quadrants for later exploration (see *Figure 4: The four dimensions* of being on page 32 and the description of the four dimensions on page 126 above.)
4. Practitioners may use the following list as they mention reasons for communicating.

To advise, affirm, apologize, appreciate, argue, ask for help, attack, attract a mate, belong, brag, comfort, complain, congratulate, connect, co-create, coordinate actions, counter, create world,[iv] defend, entertain, explain, flirt, get feedback, get help, heal,

---

[iv] Ludwig Wittgenstein stated in his Tractatus Logico-Philosophicus: "The limits of my language mean the limits of my world." For example, indigenous tribes who only know airplanes as shiny objects that leave a white trail in the sky may name it a God that sends

greet, invite, influence, inform, inquire, introspect, instruct, justify, learn, manifest, manipulate, make validity claims (give reasons for what is true, truthful, good, beautiful, functional/practical), mirror, motivate, order, plan, pray, promise, question, refuse, repel, request, seduce, self-express/share (feelings, emotions, thoughts, needs), set boundaries, show empathy (love, compassion), stay sane, support, teach, tell stories/poetry/memories, think out loud, understand/be understood, verify that one is not insane, warn.

Organon model of language

Karl Bühler's Organon, as shown below (expanded by levels of consciousness development and feminine/masculine validity claims), illustrates the three necessary functions for communication to take place.

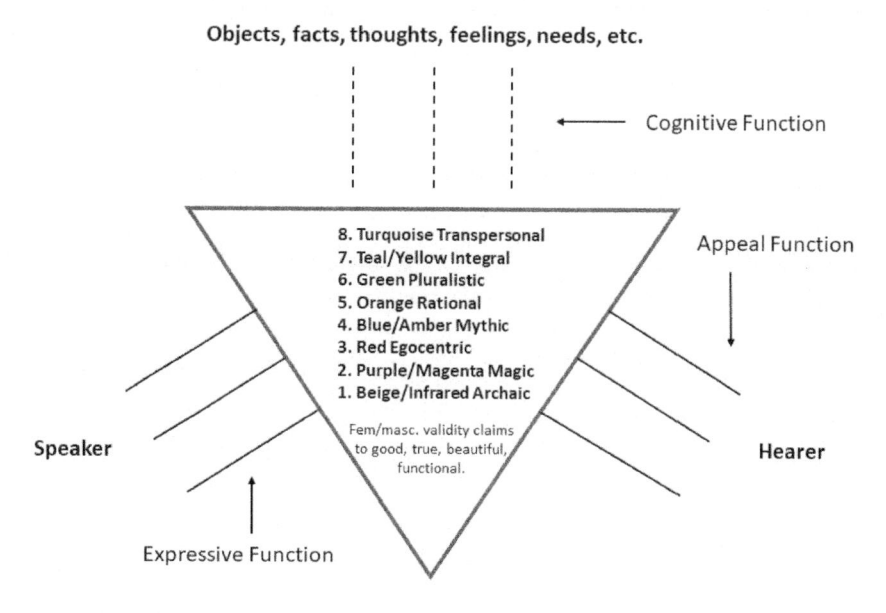

Figure 22: Organon model of language with levels of consciousness

---

them a message—such as, "move in this direction"—as they have no conception of airplanes. On the other hand, as Wittgenstein later realized, we may have experiences that we can't name, language can be very imprecise, or it does not describe or lead to action—such as saying "hello."

First, there must be an object, fact, thought, feeling, need, desire, etc., that we can cognitively grasp, experience, or be aware of. This cognition is shaped through our level of consciousness or inner mental complexity. The speaker then expresses his or her cognition through verbal language. The hearer filters and interprets the words based on his or her level of consciousness/cognitive complexity, which determines the appeal or what the hearer cognitively or experientially understands (understanding is knowledge plus experience). This is either followed by some explicit or implicit "tacit" resonance or mutual understanding and agreement which often leads to coordinated actions, or to an indifference/disconnect reaction of "whatever," or to a dissonance that leads to conflict.

Explicit versus implicit or tacit use of language

The definition of implicit/tacit is "implied or understood though not plainly or directly expressed."[97] For example, "walk in someone else's shoes"; "I am dying of hunger;" "my heart stopped"; "I love you to the moon and back"; etc., are obviously not meant to be taken literally, but we know what the speaker means.

We also implicitly (without being spoken) assume certain things: for example, if I buy something in a store, I must pay for it; if two people passionately kiss each other, they must be in a love relationship; if people drive a car, they have a driver's license; if someone reaches out their hand, they want me to shake it; etc.

131 | Need-Based Communication

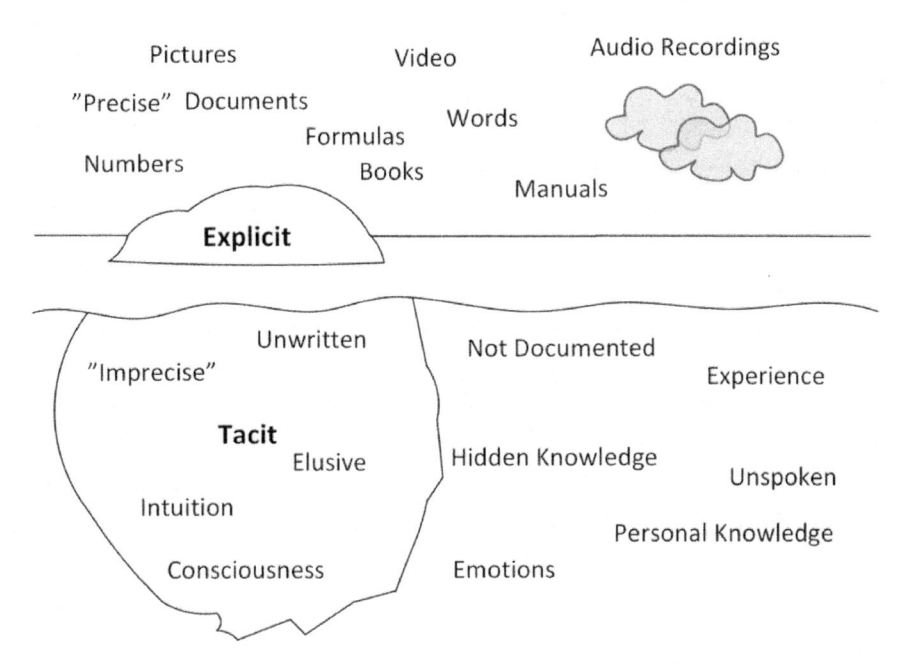

```
        Pictures          Video       Audio Recordings
   "Precise" Documents         Words
                    Formulas
       Numbers              Books
                                    Manuals
   ─────────────── Explicit ───────────────────────

                Unwritten      Not Documented
    "Imprecise"                                Experience
              Tacit
                     Elusive   Hidden Knowledge
                                              Unspoken
        Intuition
                                      Personal Knowledge
           Consciousness       Emotions
```

Figure 23: Explicit versus implicit (tacit) use of language

The Finnish comedian Ismo, who lives in the US, performs funny sketches about the many implicit meanings of words like "shit" and "ass":

"You don't know shit. I know shit. This is shit. This is the shit. I give you shit. I give a shit. Are you shitting me? You are full of shit. You are the shit. I take shit. I take a shit. This is my shit. Take care of your shit. Clean up your shit. I have shit to do (except actually shitting). This is deep shit. I like to travel—and shit. Holy shit. This is a piece of shit. I do not understand this shit."

tinyurl.com/irpm297[98]

"Bad ass (is good). Dumb ass (is bad). Smart ass. Move your ass. My ass (either means no, or my butt). You are an ass. That was a half-assed effort. You are a piece of ass. You are a pain in the ass. I had to pull it out of my ass."

tinyurl.com/irpm299[99]

Bernard Weber said, "Between what I think, what I want to say, what I believe I say, what I say, what you want to hear, what you believe you hear, what you hear, what you want to understand, what you think you understand, what you understand ... there are ten possibilities that we might have some problem communicating. But let's try anyway ..."

In *The Imitation Game* movie, the character of Alan Turing says, "When people talk to each other, they never say what they mean. They say something else, and you're expected to just know what they mean." In another scene, his colleagues tell Turing several times, "Alan, we are going to have lunch." He replies only after they say, "We are hungry," to which Turing responds, "I am hungry too."

The Dreaded Drama Triangle

Stephen B. Karpman's "Dreaded Drama Triangle,"[100] as shown below, can play out inside one person or between two or three people, with shifting roles, especially in codependent relationships.

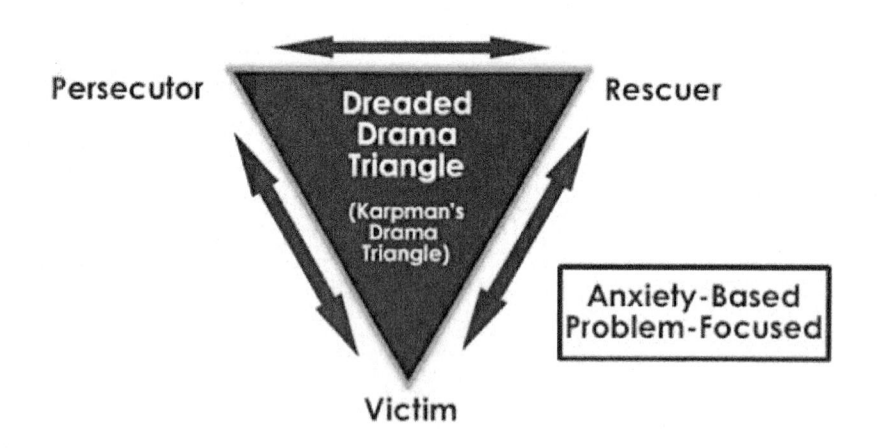

Figure 24: Dreaded Drama Triangle

Victims, shown at the bottom of the triangle, feel that they have no power to choose their response in any given situation by either changing, accepting, or leaving the circumstances in which they find themselves. Victims often have an insidious interest in confirming their problems as unsolvable. This is not to deny that bad things happen to people, but rather to say that their ability to respond (response-ability) determines whether they stay in victimhood—often to get attention or sympathy, or to blame and even exploit others for their own gain—or they heal, learn, grow, and awaken through the situations they find themselves in, and, if warranted, see their own role in creating them. This focus on the significance of the victim's role and response reflects Victor Frankl's insight:

> Everything can be taken from a man but one thing: the last of the human freedoms—to choose one's attitude in any given set of circumstances, to choose one's own way. When we are no longer able to change a situation, we are challenged to change ourselves. Between stimulus and response there is a space. In that space is our power to choose our response. In our response lies our growth and our freedom.[101]

Persecutors, shown at the top left of the triangle, are people or circumstances (illnesses, natural disasters, accidents, poverty, etc.) that the victims blame for their situation, especially in codependent relationships. Since the victims feel powerless, they look for supposed rescuers to solve their problems.

Rescuers, shown at the top right of the triangle, are sought out by victims to solve their problems, without the victims taking responsibility for themselves. In turn, rescuers seem to want to help the victims, but, in reality, act in ways that are geared towards their own desires to be noticed, needed, paid, or to assume positions of control or power, thus keeping the victims in their dependent situations.

It is important to understand that when we talk about rescuers, we do not mean people like firefighters or other first responders who are saving victims in real emergencies. The definition of rescuers in the drama triangle is people who appear to be striving to solve the problems of the victims, but actually do so in ways that result in the victims having less power, and the rescuers benefiting more than the victims.

David Emerald's "The Power of TED"[102]

In "The Empowerment Dynamic" (TED), a new triangle is conceived, as shown below in the top triangle:

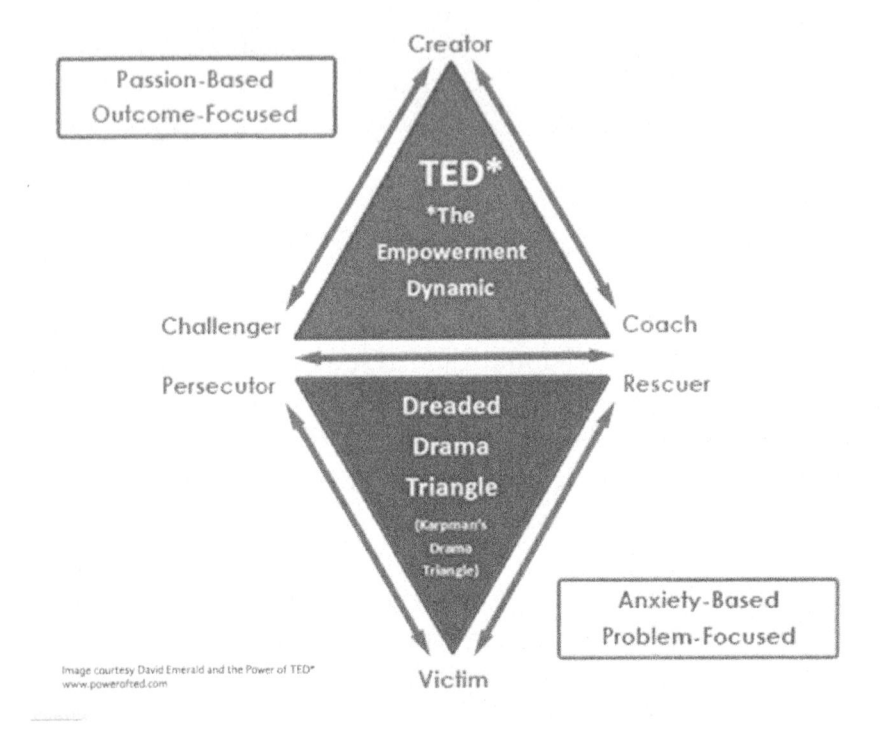

Figure 25: Drama and empowerment triangles

Victims becomes creators, as shown at the top of the TED Triangle, by realizing their own role in reacting to the situation they are in and realizing their freedom and power to choose their own response.

The persecutor becomes seen as the challenge(r), shown at the bottom left of the triangle, providing an opportunity for learning, healing, growing, and awakening to either accept, change, or leave a situation by being proactive, instead of remaining stuck in it.

The rescuer assumes the new role of coach (or friend, partner, consultant, teacher, therapist, lawyer, etc.), shown at the bottom right of the triangle, who supports and empowers the creator to face and solve their challenges and to become more empowered, liberated, and emancipated through them.

Getting to Yes: Negotiating agreement without giving in

The communication strategies that are outlined in the book, *Getting to Yes*, are based on the work of the Harvard Negotiation Project, whose mission is to improve the theory and practice of conflict resolution and negotiation by working on real world conflict interventions, theory building, education, training, and writing and disseminating new ideas for resolving domestic, business, and political conflicts.[103]

The six steps of Getting to Yes:
1. Keep feelings and emotions out of the conversation.
2. Separate the people and their emotions from the problem.
3. Focus on interests, not positions.
4. Invent options for mutual gain.
5. Insist on using objective criteria.
6. Know your BATNA; your Best Alternative To a Negotiated Agreement.

This way of communication resonates mostly with people at the Orange level who make masculine validity claims as to what is good, true, beautiful, and practical; it is often rejected by people at the Green level, as being insensitive, and people at earlier levels, as being disrespectful.

CIRCLE CHART

THE FOUR BASIC STEPS IN INVENTING OPTIONS

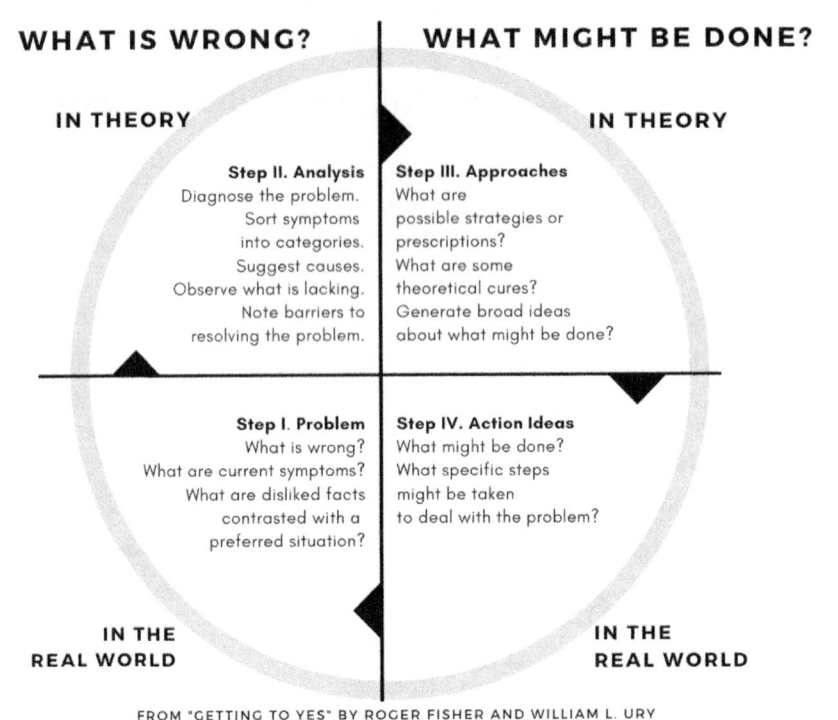

WHAT IS WRONG?	WHAT MIGHT BE DONE?
IN THEORY	**IN THEORY**
Step II. Analysis Diagnose the problem. Sort symptoms into categories. Suggest causes. Observe what is lacking. Note barriers to resolving the problem.	**Step III. Approaches** What are possible strategies or prescriptions? What are some theoretical cures? Generate broad ideas about what might be done?
Step I. Problem What is wrong? What are current symptoms? What are disliked facts contrasted with a preferred situation?	**Step IV. Action Ideas** What might be done? What specific steps might be taken to deal with the problem?
IN THE REAL WORLD	**IN THE REAL WORLD**

FROM "GETTING TO YES" BY ROGER FISHER AND WILLIAM L. URY

Figure 26: Four basic steps for conflict resolution

Understanding, agreement, and conflict

In most day-to-day communications, there is either mutual understanding, agreement and acceptance, or people simply give up and move on, thus avoiding major conflicts. Conflicts emerge when interlocutors (the people who communicate) are more emotionally bonded or otherwise dependent on each other (for example, financially or existentially).

Conflicts and miscommunication arise between individuals and groups who are at different levels of consciousness and spiritual development (see Wilber-Combs Matrix/Lattice on page 214) when they make and accept validity claims from only one perspective (dimension/quadrant), which is called quadrant absolutism; or only make and accept feminine validity claims of care, compassion, relationship, and feelings, or masculine claims of autonomy, rights, justice, and rationality (see Module 11 on page 183), instead of considering all of them. These interlocutors will have difficulties in reaching mutual understanding and agreement as encapsulated in the German word "Verständigung," which means both, to understand each other and to agree about what actions to take.

Thus, every level has developed its own communication styles and validity claims: Beige/Infrared—"I need to be rescued right now"; Purple/Magenta—"we are victims and threatened by evil magical forces"; Red—"me against the rest of the world, I do whatever brings instant gratification and demand respect"; Blue/Amber—"us versus them, we are morally right, based on our higher authority/laws, those who do not agree are wrong"; Orange—"everyone can win, alas, some people may lose, and reason tells us what is true/false"; Green— "we accept everyone's feelings and needs as equally valid, are non-judgmental, compassionate, and peaceful."

Notice if the practitioners have grown apart in consciousness and spiritual development (what you and others desire, are attached to or hate, see page 207) and thus have difficulties in creating mutual understanding and agreement.

In general, couples at different levels of consciousness development can usually not resolve major relationship conflicts through better communication. However, they may still be able to stay together if they have enough in common (values, interests, passions/purpose, children, work); are tolerant enough to focus on what works in their relationship and simply accept/ignore their differences; have their unmet needs fulfilled outside the relationship (ideally with the consent from their partner); or have clearly defined gender roles with their respective rights and responsibilities.

Exercise two: Conflicts in first-tier communication

Exercise two is a paired exercise.
1. Ideally, have baseball caps available in different colors that match the eight levels of consciousness development (Beige, Purple/Magenta, Red, Blue/Amber, Orange, and Green for Module 7, and Yellow/Teal and Turquoise for the exercises in Module 8).[104]
2. You may also make hats out of colored paper or have other colored items available to indicate from which level the practitioners are communicating.
3. In a group setting, it is advised that couples do the exercise together.
4. For the rest of the group, it is helpful to have practitioners who are well versed in levels of consciousness development pair up with partners who are less familiar or less experienced.
5. Try not to participate in the exercise if you are the facilitator, so that you can help practitioners who have difficulties.
6. Allow about 40 minutes or longer for this exercise.

Think of a conflict you had with an intimate partner. For example:
1. Definition of commitment.
2. Commitment/communion versus autonomy.
3. Issues around work, making and spending money.
4. Differences around lifestyle choices, interests, hobbies.
5. Different Love Languages (words, quality time, gifts, acts of service, touch).
6. How to spend time together/apart?
7. Issues around family, friends, and jealousy.
8. Sexual needs.
9. Monogamy versus non-monogamy.
10. Having a child or not.
11. How to raise children/parenting/roles.
12. Healing wounds, processing childhood trauma, doing therapy, personality disorders.
13. Moving or staying in a particular location (city, country).

14. Issues around boundaries.
15. Issues around shared purpose.

Follow the exercise structure below:
1. Practitioner one explains to a practice partner the conflict situation that he or she has/had with a real-life person or group.
2. Practitioners argue back and forth with each other from different levels of first-tier consciousness—if possible from each of the four dimensions of being/quadrants—and indicate which level they speak from by wearing the hats with the corresponding colors for level-one survival; level-two safety; level-three respect/freedom; level-four right/wrong rules and roles; level- five interests and true/false rationality; and level-six emotional connection, as described in more detail in the worksheet below.
3. Ask practitioners to first argue from their own position and then from the opposing person's or group's position by switching roles (putting themselves into the other person's or group's shoes.)
4. Then argue about a conflict situation of practitioner two in the same way.

Worksheet: Need-based communication

Find a topic of contention that you had with a partner or someone else. Briefly explain the situation to your practice partner. Make arguments (or validity claims) from different levels of consciousness development, as described below, for both sides, ideally from each of the four quadrants, while wearing the hat with the corresponding color.

1. Archaic—Beige Hat: Dead or alive. Control or dominate environment.

People at this level experience real or perceived issues and dangers that threaten their lives. Immediate action is needed for survival or to save life. Uncontrollable primal fight, flight, and freeze reactions. Issues around primal sexual lust and jealousy.

2. Magic—Purple/Magenta Hat: Safe or unsafe, superstitions, tribal belonging. Surrender to environment.

People on the magic level are superstitious and perceive all kinds of imagined threats and dangers to their safety. Their communication is irrational, with beliefs in miracles, magical powers, unseen outside forces, and their own narcissistic "poor-me" victim perceptions (drama triangle). Good, true, beautiful, and functional is what unites the tribal identity, brings luck, and fends off real or imagined evil threats through rituals, ceremonies, dress, artifacts, etc. People at this level expect others to make them feel safe through compassion and affirmations and join like-minded tribes and communities who share their needs and concerns. They may get lost in the fear-based drama triangle of victim-persecutor-rescuer.

3. Egocentric—Red Hat: Good or bad for me. Boundaries. Control or dominate environment.

Egocentric people demand respect and validation for their subjective needs and truths, think that nobody can be trusted, believe that everyone should fend for themselves, and that their desires must be immediately met, without consideration of the needs of others or of negative consequences for their future. They insist that whatever brings instant gratification and strengthens their self-identity is good, true, beautiful, and functional. They argue that if everyone takes care of themselves, then everyone is taken care of, and if everybody takes responsibility for their own happiness, then everybody is happy.

4. Mythic—Blue/Amber Hat: Right or wrong thinking. Higher authority. Surrender to environment.

Mythic people argue for the need to conform to rules, laws, and hereditary or bestowed hierarchies that guaranty order and stability. For them, what is good, true, beautiful, and functional is decided by a mythic higher authority (typically male) to which they adhere, and which is not to be questioned. They are conservative, they fear change and taking risks, and they control impulsivity through guilt. They believe that making sacrifices, rightful living, and submitting to law and order will bring future rewards, and that violations will be punished.

5. Rational—Orange Hat: True or false. Win or lose. Control or dominate environment.

Rational people argue that only objective experience, reason, and empiricism can deliver what is good, true, beautiful, and functional, and assign these four fundamental domains of human experience and investigation to separate disciplines of research and authority. Rational people tend to (1) keep feelings and emotions out of the conversation; (2) separate people from the problem; (3) focus on interests instead of fixed positions; (4) search for multiple options for mutual gains (think win-win, but accept if the other loses); (5) insist on using objective criteria; and (6) know their best alternative to a negotiated agreement in case that they can't win (see book *Getting to Yes*). They strive for autonomy and change, seek out the good life and abundance, and pursue progress through the best solutions. They shift the drama triangle from persecutor, victim, and rescuer to outcome-focused creator, challenger, and coach.

6. Pluralistic—Green Hat: Sensitive or indifferent. Surrender to environment.

Pluralistic people shift their communication from goal-oriented objective rationality to expressing subjective observations, feelings, unmet needs, and making requests (rather than demands), known as nonviolent or compassionate communication. They explore the inner beings of self/others and prioritize a more feminine authentic human connection and care over finding practical/rational solutions. They insist that individual subjectivity determines what is good, true, beautiful, and functional, as there are no moral, scientific, aesthetic, or pragmatic absolutes, and everyone is equally right from their own view and perspective (different from Red, who is intolerant).

Follow-up questions

1. How do you feel after this exercise?
2. What insights did you gain through the exercise?
3. Could you feel yourself into the different levels while arguing from each of them?
4. Which levels resonated most with you, and which were the hardest to argue from?
5. How was it for you to put yourself into your partner's shoes (implicit/tacit language) and argue from his/her side?

Additional information and resources

Rational Stage:

Getting to Yes: Negotiating Agreement Without Giving In (2011) (Revised Edition) by Roger Fisher, William L. Ury, Bruce Patton
tinyurl.com/irpm303[105]

Pluralistic stage:

Nonviolent Communication: A Language of Life (2015) by Marshall B. Rosenberg
tinyurl.com/irpm307[106]

Sex Purpose Love book reference

N/A

Suggested movie: *The Invention of Lying* (2009)

Watch this at times silly but nonetheless provocative movie to discern and discuss concepts such as belief, knowing, truth, honesty, truthfulness, rightness, validity, communicating, understanding, agreeing, and intimacy (in-to-me-you-see), and the opposing concepts of untruths, lies, deceptions, etc., at different levels of consciousness development, and how all of these concepts impact our love relationships. This star-studded semi-romantic comedy also touches on subjects such as the primary sexual fantasies, which we will cover in Module 9, and religion, which we will touch on in Module 12.

Mark Bellison (Ricky Gervais) is a physically unappealing unsuccessful screenwriter who lives in a world that has no concept of untruth. As his life moves further and further into despair, he stumbles across the concept of lying. Everyone believes whatever he says, and he becomes successful, rich, and famous. But he can't get the one thing he really wants—the love of Anna McDoogles (Jennifer Garner), a beautiful woman who is generally out of his league—because he does not match her primary sexual fantasy of a physically attractive person. In a crucial moment when Mark could have lied to Anna to win her over, he tells the truth, and Anna finally realizes that she loves him.

After watching the movie, you may explore the following:
- What would happen if we always truthfully shared what we think and feel, and never lied? What happens if we truly believe things that are not true?
- What is truth and how can we know it?
- Why do people believe different things to be true?
- Why do we lie?
- Are white lies okay?
- Does lying ever serve a purpose, such as being kind or not hurting others?
- Do we really want others to be totally honest?
- Is radical honesty the best way to go through life and create a better world?
- Should we only say what is true, truthful, kind, and necessary?

Practice Module 8
Integral and Transpersonal Communication

The limits of my language mean the limits of my world.
~ Ludwig Wittgenstein ~

Module description

Learn and practice how people at the seventh integral and eighth transpersonal level of consciousness communicate to validate their views and behaviors in order to get their needs met.

Realize why everyone is right (but not equally right) from the viewpoint of what is called their "Kosmic Address," which is defined by the combination of their level of consciousness development or altitude, the perspectives they take from one or more of the four dimensions of being (quadrants), and the feminine/masculine validity claims they make. See that all views hold partial truths, as nobody is stupid enough to be wrong all of the time or smart enough to be right all of the time.

See how people and groups at the seventh integral level of consciousness development shift from need-based to being-based communication by moving away from the narrow judgments and beliefs of people in the previous six levels towards curiosity and openness about what they consider to be good, true, beautiful, and functional. See, too, how people and groups at this level validate their own views by referring to what the most competent and peer-reviewed experts in any given field agree on as serving the greatest good or happiness for the largest number of people.

Advance into the eighth transpersonal stage in which a new sense of humility, beginner's mind, and compassion emerge, and communication becomes more authentic, personal, vulnerable, and dialectical to advance into novelty. Recognize the shift away from looking and talking down at people in first-tier consciousness from the integral level (which can be perceived as being arrogant and superior) towards a deep caring, love, kindness, and bonding that becomes the hallmark of creating mutual understanding with others and serves the greatest good for all living things.

Introduction

As people evolve into the integral and transpersonal stages, their ways of communication and problem-solving become more differentiated and flexible and, in the transpersonal stage, reach the limits of language to describe reality and experiences. This is often puzzling to people (including romantic partners) in first-tier consciousness, and they either try to pull people in second-tier consciousness down to their level, or, if they don't succeed, feel threatened and reject and ostracize those more evolved people for seeming to be arrogant, pompous, elitist, and uncaring asses. This kind of reaction often leaves people in second-tier consciousness speechless and feeling alone when they attempt to make differentiated validity claims as to what is good, true, beautiful, and functional and explain how although different views are valid from the observer's perspective, some views are more correct, inclusive, and loving than others.

While people in second-tier consciousness can adjust their communication to the level of people in first-tier consciousness, they often get frustrated when they themselves are not heard, understood, or met, and they consequently get into double binds. They then sometimes would rather win the argument and lose the relationship or withdraw and end up feeling alone and isolated.

Double binds

Integral people often find themselves in situations in which they cannot say anything, cannot leave, and cannot win. These situations are called double/triple binds.

Double bind theory was first described by Gregory Bateson and his colleagues in the 1950s.[107]

A double bind is a dilemma in communication in which an individual (or group) receives two or more conflicting messages, with one negating the other. In some circumstances (particularly in families and love relationships), this becomes emotionally distressing. It creates a situation in which a successful response to one message results in a failed response to the other (and vice versa), so that the person will automatically be wrong and potentially be punished, regardless of their response. The double bind occurs when the person cannot confront the inherent dilemma and, therefore, can neither resolve it nor opt out of the situation.

The double bind often happens for integral and spiritually evolved people when less evolved people demand that their limited views and behaviors are accepted, even though they cannot see how they create suffering for themselves and others.

Sometimes, people at a transpersonal level can get out of the double binds by advancing into novelty through dialectical processes.

Dialectic

Hegelian dialectic comprises three phases of an argument: first, the thesis, a statement of an idea that eventually becomes seen as flawed, limited, or problematic; second, the antithesis, a reaction that contradicts or negates the thesis; and, third, the synthesis or negation of the negation, a statement or resolution through which the differences between the two points are resolved in a process of sublation (translation of the German word "Aufhebung," which has a triple meaning of keeping, saving or preserving, lifting or picking up, and canceling) that retains the useful portions of the thesis or idea while eliminating its limitations or flaws, so that new novel ideas or solutions can emerge through inter-becoming.

Another way to resolve conflict by advancing into novelty or creativity is called Bohm(ian) dialog, which is similar to brainstorming or mind-mapping, but goes beyond it, as the participants deeply get to know themselves and others in the process.

Bohmian (group) dialog

Below are the basic steps for this form of dialog:[108]

1. The couple or group agrees that no group-level decisions will be made in the conversation. In the dialogue group, the participants are not going to decide what to do about anything. This is crucial. Otherwise, they are not free. They must have an empty space where they are not obliged to anything, to come to any conclusions, or to say anything or not say anything. It's open and free (Bohm, "On Dialogue," page 18–19). Each individual agrees to suspend judgment in the conversation (specifically, if the individual hears an idea he or she doesn't like, thus not attacking that idea):
   > ...people in any group will bring to it assumptions, and as the group continues meeting, those assumptions will come up. What is called for is to suspend those assumptions, so that they neither carry them out nor suppress them. They don't believe them, nor do they disbelieve them; they don't judge them as good or bad.... (Bohm, "On Dialogue," page 22)
2. As these individuals suspend judgment, they are also simultaneously as honest and transparent as possible. (Specifically, if individuals have a "good idea" that they might otherwise hold back from the group because the idea is too controversial, they will share that idea in the conversation.)
3. Individuals in the conversation try to build on other individuals' ideas in the conversation. (The group often comes up with ideas that are far beyond what any of the individuals thought possible before the conversation began.)

A foundational practice within Bohm's dialogue is the attention-based practice of suspension. Suspension helps practitioners cultivate a firsthand experience of the nature of thought, the limits of rationality, and the creative possibilities of a consciousness-informed process of inquiry. Over time, suspension practice helps individuals become less identified with their habits of mind and points of view.

Communicative action and discourse ethics

According to Habermas's critical social philosophy, couples and groups should only move forward with cooperative action after mutual deliberation and argumentation based in discourse ethics, with following presuppositions:

1. All participants in communicative exchange are using the same linguistic expressions in the same way (meaning they agree on the meaning of words).
2. No relevant arguments for what is good, true, truthful, beautiful and functional are suppressed or excluded by the participants.
3. No force except that of the better argument is exerted.
4. All participants are motivated only by a concern for the better argument.
5. Everyone agrees with the universal validity of the claims thematized.
6. Everyone capable of speech and action is entitled to participate, and everyone is equally entitled to introduce new topics or express attitudes needs or desires.[109]

Critical realism

A critical realist approach to communication distinguishes three domains:

1. The "real" refers to causal powers that cannot be directly known or perceived—for example, what exists outside time and space; what is the color of a surface; or why are we attracted to a certain person (also see Module 12: Spiritual Development).
2. The "actual" refers to what happens when these powers are activated and produce phenomenon and change—for

example, social uprisings, color perception, changes in nature, or falling in love.
3. The "empirical" is the study of the actual—for example, social studies, climate research, light waves and the retina, or hormonal changes in lovers.

While empirical studies can influence natural processes and the views and behavior of people and, hence, what happens, much of the physical and social world exists regardless of scientific research and regardless of actors experiencing, understanding, and describing them through language.[110]

The science of reasoning with unreasonable people

Psychologists found that when people listened carefully and called attention to the nuances in the thinking of other people with whom they may disagree, they became less extreme and more open in their views.

Asking people how their preferred view or position might work in practice and solve problems, rather than asking why they favored those approaches, was more effective in opening people's minds. These people could then be asked if they see any downsides and what their concerns and fears are.[111]

For example:
How would you stop the pandemic?
How would you run the country?
How would you address global warming?

Purpose and application of the module

1. Communicate with people in first-tier consciousness at their level of development.
2. Stay open, curious, and compassionate (instead of defensive or judgmental) when people make validity claims that you don't understand or agree with.

3. Notice whether being right is more important to you than maintaining the relationship.
4. Experience how interlocutors at the integral level create mutual understanding and resolve conflicts by making validity claims as to what is objectively true, morally right, aesthetically beautiful, and practically functional.
5. Explore how people at the transpersonal level recognize and transcend the limitations of language; make feminine and masculine validity claims; and advance into novelty through nondual, critically realistic, ethical, dialectical discourse.
6. See how people in second-tier consciousness either accept, change, or leave a situation or relationship before deeper and irresolvable conflicts emerge, or before their values get compromised and their boundaries get violated.

Exercises: Integral and transpersonal communication

The following are all paired exercises.
1. In a group setting, it is advised that couples do the exercises below together. If they struggle, a more experienced participant or the facilitator may support them.
2. For the rest of the group, it is helpful if practitioners who are well versed in all the levels of consciousness development that we cover pair up with those who are less familiar or experienced.
3. As in Module 7, ideally, you will have available baseball caps with the additional colors for the two levels of second-tier consciousness—Yellow/Teal and Turquoise. You can also make hats with colored paper or have other colored items to indicate what level the practitioners are arguing from.
4. Allow about 40 minutes or longer for this exercise.
5. Make the four agreements for confidentiality, responsibility, healthy boundaries, I-statements, and sharing, as outlined on page 556.

Exercise one: Second-tier with first-tier communication

In this paired exercise, practitioners experience how people in second-tier consciousness communicate with people in first-tier consciousness at their various levels of development (from archaic to pluralistic) by showing curiosity (integral level) and compassion (transpersonal level). The second-tier partners ask questions, empathize, and acknowledge the needs and worldviews of the partners who role-play a person in first-tier consciousness, while preventing them from violently imposing their limited views onto others or doing harm to themselves.

If you can, use a conflict from your own life that involved all first-tier levels, or make up a topic.

1. Partner one explains the conflict situation with a real-life partner to partner two.
2. Argue back and forth, with partner one using all levels of first-tier consciousness, as indicated by wearing different hats/color, and partner two meeting him or her from second-tier consciousness.
3. Argue from your own and your real-life partner's view–if you can, from each quadrant—by switching roles.
4. Then switch and argue in the same way about a contentious situation of partner two.

Examples:
1. See examples in Module 7, on page 138, above.
2. You co-parent or teach children who are at different levels of development.
3. Your family comes together for the holidays and members are at different levels.
4. You run a team/company/organization.
5. You facilitate an Integral Relationship group, and first-tier people challenge you.
6. You are the president of a nation.

7. You may also use the metaphor of a house with seven floors, where people on the first six floors in first-tier consciousness have conflicts with each other, or with you on the seventh floor in second-tier consciousness (e.g., if they cannot grasp what you are practicing in your Integral Relationship groups and feel threatened by it).

Exercise two: Integral communication

In this paired exercise, practitioners will practice "interbeing" communication between interlocutors at the integral level of second-tier consciousness by looking at a situation through all four dimensions of being and relating (quadrants) and making utilitarian, pragmatic validity claims for what is good, true, beautiful, and functional. They can use the same conflict as in exercise one above or chose a different conflict or situation.

Practitioners may also explore unconscious dimensions or lack of integration and transcendence of first-tier levels by seeing every unresolved situation as an AFGO (Another Fine/Fucking Growth Opportunity) to learn, heal, grow, and awaken.

Follow the structure of exercise one above.

Exercise three: Transpersonal communication

In this paired exercise, practitioners experience "inter-becoming based" communication at the transpersonal level of second-tier consciousness by entering a dialectical process of advancing into novelty by recognizing that the views of both partners are limited if they cannot see the other persons view and find mutual agreement at a higher level. They will also notice the limitations of words and language to grasp what is real and tap into their individual and collective unconscious. In the process, practitioners will not only look at and show curiosity about the views of people in first-tier consciousness, but also show compassion for their own and the suffering of others.

The practitioners may use a relationship conflict from their own life or use one of the examples from the above exercise, and either role-play how to resolve the conflict at a transpersonal level or imagine how others whom they perceive as being at that level would resolve the conflict.

Examples for dialectical problem-solving:
1. Materialism versus idealism = co-emergence (panpsychism).
2. Feudalism versus capitalism = communism.

In a relational context you may mention:
3. Sexual faithfulness versus cheating = polyamory.
4. Feminine versus masculine = healthy feminine and masculine.
5. Loving yourself versus loving others = loving what is co-created.
6. Wholeness versus partialness = holonic (see more about holons on page 540).

Or simpler:
1. Cooking at home versus dining out = having food delivered.
2. My place or your place = a third place.
3. Spend money on education or vacation = study abroad/learning vacation.
4. Wearing a hat (sweat), or no hat (sunburn) = use sunscreen.

Worksheet: Integral and transpersonal communication

Find a topic of contention that you had or have with a partner or someone else. Briefly explain the situation to your practice partner. Switch roles as you assume the role of an interlocutor at the second-tier integral or transpersonal level who argues (or makes validity claims) first with a partner, person, or group in first-tier consciousness, and then with interlocutors at the integral level, and finally with interlocutors at the transpersonal level. Wear the hats with the corresponding colors as you shift roles.

7. Integral—Yellow/Teal Hat: Integrated or partial. Control or dominate environment. Interbeing.

People at an integral level use a more individualistic masculine discourse again (autonomy, rights, justice, rationality). They shift from judgment and expressing feelings and needs to curiosity. For them, creating context by looking through the AQAL lens or at the map (quadrants, lines, levels, states, types) is everything. They become consciously competent about perspectives and development and are often more interested in the map than the territory! They demand flexibility and open systems and make pragmatic (what practical difference does it make, and what words do rather than what they say), utilitarian validity claims as to what provides the greatest good, truth, beauty, and functioning for the largest number of people. They consider what the most competent persons/experts agree on, as well as the enduring "perennial" wisdoms and practices from the East and West.

Integral people communicate with others at the other's level of consciousness, make invitations, and acknowledge the healthy and valid aspects of their interlocutors' respective stages, while trying to prevent them from (violently) imposing their limited views and "half-truths" onto others. Thus, integral people act in their self-interest without harming others. However, when challenged, they would rather win the argument and lose the relationship, or they find themselves in double binds (see above). They are interested in learning, healing, growing, and awakening, especially with other integrally informed people. Some use the third-, second-, and first-person (3-2-1) shadow process (see below) to identify and integrate parts of the self that are repressed or denied and see every challenge as an AFGO (Another Fine/Fucking Growth Opportunity).

8. Transpersonal—Turquoise Hat: Emergent/embodied or fixated/disembodied. Surrender to environment. Inter-becoming.

People at the transpersonal stage go beyond mere curiosity and become deeply compassionate and humble. They question their own limited views (event horizons), including the limits of experience, thought, knowledge, and language itself (that which is beyond the map or no longer accurate). They become more relational again and interested in the lived experience in the territory rather than the map. Rather than just looking at others from above through an integral lens or map, people at the transpersonal stage see themselves and others as part of an open, global, holonic, dialectical, emergent, evolving (or devolving) conscious and unconscious whole, with creative frictions and inevitable necessary conflicts.

They may take a critical realist approach to communication by distinguishing between the "real" (causal powers that cannot be directly known or perceived); the "actual" (visible experienced and knowable phenomenon); and the "empirical" (study and description of the phenomenon through language).

Transpersonal people expand on Habermas's communicative rationality and discourse ethics which inherently considers every rational, reasonable person who makes intersubjective and interobjective validity claims as to what is good, true, truthful, beautiful, and functional by integrating healthy feminine descending and communal care, compassion, feelings, and relationships, as well as healthy masculine ascending and agentic autonomy, rights, justice, and rationality at the level of all seven chakras.

Thus, transpersonal people expand and revise the map as they are in the territory and find solutions through dialectical processes of thesis, antithesis, and synthesis to advance into new possibilities (novelty) and potentials by "absenting absences" (bringing forth something that is missing).

People in this stage see the necessity for all people to live out their conflicts as part of their learning, healing, growing, and awakening process; show compassion for others' suffering; and give support when warranted without getting lost in the drama of others or showing idiot compassion.

Follow-up questions

1. How do you feel after the exercises?
2. What insights have you gained through the exercises?
3. Could you feel yourself into the different levels while arguing from each of them?
4. Which levels resonated most with you, and which were the hardest to argue from?
5. How was it for you to put yourself into your partner's shoes and argue from his/her side?
6. What learning, healing, growing, and awakening potentials do you see for yourself to improve your ability to communicate more effectively?

Additional information and resources

Getting Real: Ten Truth Skills You Need to Live an Authentic Life (2001) by Susan Campbell
https://www.amazon.com/Getting-Real-Truth-Skills-Authentic/dp/0915811928/

Habermas: A Very Short Introduction (2005) by Gordon Finlayson
tinyurl.com/irpm309[112]

Pragmatism: An Introduction (2012) by Michael Bacon
tinyurl.com/irpm311[113]

Metatheory for the Twenty-First Century: Critical Realism and Integral Theory in Dialogue (2015) Edited by Roy Bhaskar, Sean Esbjörn-Hargens, Nicholas Hedlund-de Witt, Mervyn Hartwig.
tinyurl.com/irpm312[114]
A Complex Integral Realist Perspective: Towards A New Axial Vision (2016) by Paul Marshall tinyurl.com/irpm314[115]

Non-Dual Dialectical Critical Realism
tinyurl.com/irpm316[116]

Sex Purpose Love book reference
Page N/A

Suggested movie: *The Imitation Game* (2014)

Watch this movie to see the complexity of communication, including implicit and explicit language, advancements into novelty, artificial intelligence, and codes.

Loosely based on true events, the movie focuses on Alan Turing (Benedict Cumberbatch), who is hired in 1939 to crack Nazi codes — including Enigma, which was thought unbreakable. With help from fellow mathematicians and linguists, including Joan Clarke (Keira Knightley), he builds what later became called "a computer." He was inspired by a friend who told him earlier in his life that sometimes it is the people no one imagines anything of who do the things that no one can imagine.

Historians estimate that breaking Enigma shortened WWII by more than two years, saving over fourteen million lives. Turing's work inspired generations of research into what scientists called "Turing machines," now known as computers.

Turing also proposed an experiment that became known as the Turing test, an attempt to define a standard by which a machine can be defined as "intelligent." He postulated that a computer could be said to "think" if a human interrogator could not distinguish it from a human being through conversation.

The quiet genius encountered disgrace in 1952, when UK authorities revealed that he was gay, and it is speculated that Turing killed himself in 1954, after a year of debilitating government-mandated hormonal therapy as an alternative to being sent to prison.

Practice Module 9
Biological Differences and Learned Gender Roles

In this country, you gotta make the money first. Then when you get the money, you get the power. Then when you get the power, then you get the women.
~ Al Pacino in *Scarface* ~

Women marry men, hoping that they will change. Men marry women, hoping they will not. So each is inevitably disappointed.
~ Albert Einstein ~

Module description

Learn and practice how to understand the opposite sex as never before, by hearing about their deepest secrets, truths, fears, shame, frustrations, desires, hopes, attractions, joys, appreciations, and needs.

Distinguish between biological/natural sex differences, and divergent culturally nurtured and socially conditioned and adopted gender roles of men and women.

Gain a better understanding of your own and the opposite sex by sharing your own experiences and listening to what others share about sex and gender—what is nature, and what is nurture?

See how the perspectives from the four dimensions of being and relating (quadrants) and levels of consciousness development impact individuals' views on sex and gender, the feminist perspective, and views from gender studies discourse.

Explore questions like the following: How can we better understand the opposite sex if we have never walked in their shoes (or lived in their bodies)? Why do these differences exist, and how did they develop? Are we still in our essence (male) hunters and (female) gatherers? Do different gender roles make sense—and when? Why do we have gender conflicts, and how can we resolve them? Find answers through open listening, vulnerable sharing, deep understanding, nonjudgmental acceptance, authentic empathy, and caring compassion. Join us in a safe environment for an engaging and eye-opening experiential exploration of these exciting and important topics. Make peace with yourself and the opposite sex. Live happily ever after in a healthy love relationship!

Introduction

In Module 9, we will move from creating the theoretical framework of the Integral Relationship model, theory, or map of quadrants and levels of consciousness development into the lived territory or reality of love relationships.

In the Integral Relationship model, we don't simply differentiate between men (are from Mars) and women (are from Venus) and other gender stereotypes and superficial traits, but we go deeper by making distinctions between (1) given natural male and female biological sex differences and behavioral patterns in the Upper Right quadrant of our being—such as, different sex organs, body features, hormones (testosterone, estrogen, cortisol, adrenaline), mate preferences based on looks, etc.; (2) different socially constructed gender roles and norms (e.g., job preferences, sports, clothing, makeup, etc.) in the Lower Right quadrant; (3) different culturally conditioned values and norms around sex and gender in the Lower Left quadrant (such as, who initiates romantic contact, proposes, buys the diamond ring, makes decisions about contraception/abortions, earns and spends money, etc.); and (4) different gender identities in the Upper Left dimension (such as, straight, heterosexual, lesbian, gay, bisexual, transgender, transsexual, two-spirit, queer, questioning, intersex, asexual, ally, pansexual, agender, gender queer, bigender, gender variant, pangender, etc.)[117] and individual shadows, feelings, fears, shame, spirituality, communication styles, etc., related to sex and gender.

See *Figure 4: The four dimensions of being and relating*, on page 32

Some male and female behavioral patterns and needs are seemingly driven by our instincts and are hard or impossible to override: for example, men more often risk their lives to protect women, while women more often call for help when men are in danger (this difference makes evolutionary sense, for men to act as the disposable sex); and most women are choosier and take more time in the sexual selection process than men. Understanding these differences can help couples to develop empathy and compassion for their related struggles with the opposite sex.

In Module 10, on page 171, we will dive into the Fear-Shame dynamic between males and females.

In Module 11, on page 183, we will differentiate sex and gender further by exploring feminine and masculine polarities, which can be embodied equally by both sexes.

In Module 14, on page 255, we will make an additional distinction between the sexes by exploring the five stages of the unconscious female animus and the male anima complex which is projected onto the opposite sex.

Purpose and application of the module

1. Gain a better understanding between biological "evolutionary" givens of what is hardwired for each sex by nature, and thus hard or impossible to change or overwrite, and what is socially, culturally, and individually conditioned and can, therefore, more easily be changed, healed, or transcended.
2. Understand the differences between learned gender roles for men and women—and where and how the two interact and overlap.
3. Notice how Green tries to argue away any biological and gender differences by giving extreme examples and insisting that all differences are culturally constructed.
4. Deeply listen to the "opposite sex" and develop empathy and compassion about their pain, challenges, desires, and appreciation.

5. Prepare practitioners to further differentiate between feminine and masculine polarities in Module 11, and the Anima/Animus complex in Module 14.

Exercises: Sex and gender differences

These are group exercises.
1. Print out the small worksheets and cut them.
2. In the first exercise, female and male practitioners are separated into two groups, ideally in different rooms.
3. You may also conduct this exercise in a "fishbowl" format in which males and females sit separately in an inner and outer circle, with both groups facing towards the center. In the inner circle or inside the fishbowl, the practitioners answer the questions while the practitioners in the outer circle first listen and then may ask questions. Then the groups switch. This format is not recommended because it takes longer and can lead to practitioners withholding, especially if things get out of control when the listening group starts to make comments, laugh, or become bored or distracted.
4. Make the four agreements for confidentiality, responsibility, healthy boundaries, I-statements, and sharing, as outlined on page 556.

Exercise one: Female and male sex and gender experiences

1. Check with the group to see if everyone identifies with being either male or female and feels comfortable about being assigned (or assigning themselves) to the respective group, especially when you offer this exercise online.
2. Note that even though this exercise uses male-female language, similar dynamics may play out in same-sex and gender-fluid couples.
3. Optional if necessary: Form a third group for practitioners who don't identify with either sex/gender or who want to be in a mixed group.

4. Hand out the worksheet with the questions below to each participant, explain the exercise, give examples, and answer questions.
5. Explain that one person in each group will take notes of all the answers and then share them after the two groups come back together again for exercise two.
6. Tell the notetaker to write down what was agreed on by all, what most agreed on, and what were some of the diverse views.
7. Ask practitioners to make generalizing orientations—such as, "on average, males are taller than females" or "males tend to have more testosterone than females" or "almost all females are born with ovaries and a vagina."
8. For gender roles generalizations, they may say: "most women wear makeup, men don't"; "most women cover their chests when swimming in public, men don't"; "women may wear skirts, most men don't"; "men typically pay for dinner dates, women don't"; "most men don't cry (in public?), women do"; "women feel, men think"; etc. See a link to lists from previous groups in this endnote.[118]
9. In a group with mostly integral practitioners, you may ask them to locate the differences in the respective quadrants.
10. Emphasize again (especially in a group with many practitioners at the sixth Green stage, who often feel uncomfortable with this exercise) that there are, of course, variations and exceptions to everything. Remind them that it is not the purpose of this exercise to focus on the exceptions! It is about the personal experiences and views of the practitioners in the group and what applies to most males and females, and not about other people.
11. Give about 45 minutes or more for this part of the exercise, and frequently check in with each group to see if there are questions and if they need more time.

12. Begin the exercise in a live group by inviting "the weaker sex" to decide where they want to do the exercise (this is, of course, a trick-question to start the conversation.)
13. Separate the groups.

Exercise two: Sex and gender sharing

1. Bring the group back together.
2. Ask the practitioners if they feel a difference between being with their own gender versus being back in a mixed group?
3. Check in to see how the exercise was for each group.
4. Give "the weaker sex" the choice to share either first or second.
5. Ask practitioners to be sensitive, tolerant, respectful, and quiet while listening to the answers from each group.
6. Have the notetaker for group one share their answers to question one, followed by the notetaker for group two.
7. Invite participants to share how they feel as they listened and to comment and ask questions.
8. Invite the notetaker for group one to share the answers to question two.
9. Keep going back and forth through answers to all the questions.
10. Invite discussion, sharing insights, and reflections.

Worksheet: Sex and gender exercise

Create two columns for the answers to question one below.
1. What qualities are hardwired by evolution/nature for each sex, and what qualities are learned/nurtured gender roles?

Biological/Hardwired/Nature in Females	Biological/Hardwired/Nature in Males
Females have … Females have … Females have …	Males have … Males have … Males have …
Learned/Conditioned/Nurtured Gender Roles — Women	Learned/Conditioned/Nurtured Gender Roles — Men
Women … Women … Women …	Men … Men … Men …

Table 12: Biology and gender exercise

2. What is the most important thing the opposite sex should know about what it means to be your gender?
3. What pain does/has the opposite sex create(d) for you?
4. What is most difficult for you when relating to the opposite sex?
5. What makes the opposite sex attractive to you?
6. What do you appreciate about the opposite sex/your partner?
7. How would you and your gender feel and act if the opposite sex would disappear from the world?

Follow-up questions

1. How do you feel after this exercise?
2. What insights about the opposite sex have you gained through the exercise?
3. What touched you the most?

4. When did you feel most challenged?
5. What learning, healing, and growing potentials around sex and gender do you want to realize?
6. How may you contribute to end the battle between the sexes?

Additional information and resources

You may also explain the Primary Sexual Fantasy Dynamic, as shown below.

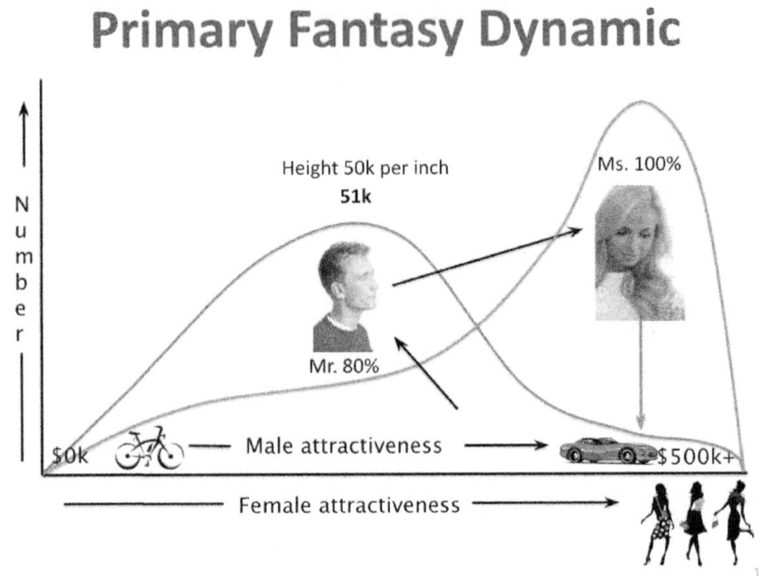

Primary Fantasy Dynamic

[Chart showing Number (y-axis) vs. Male attractiveness ($0k bicycle to $500k+ sports car) and Female attractiveness. Mr. 80%, Height 50k per inch, 51k. Ms. 100%.]

Figure 27: The primary sexual fantasy dynamic

The divergent primary sexual fantasies of males and females were first described by Donald Symons in his book, *The Evolution of Human Sexuality*, and later adopted by Warren Farrell in *The Myth of Male Power*. Also see research in the books, *Warrior Lovers* by Donald Symons and Catherine Salmon,[119] *The Evolution of Desire: Strategies of Human Mating* by David M. Buss, and *Dataclysm: Love, Sex, Race, and Identity: What Our Online Lives Tell Us about Our Offline Selves"* by Christian Rudder,[120] all confirming the universal primary fantasy dynamic that most people are aware of through their own experiences and observations of others.[121]

The primary attractiveness of males to women is measured by increasing income/wealth/power, $0 to $500k+ annual income, and height that goes from very short to very tall. The median income of working males in the US in 2021 was about 51k (of all males, 39k).[122] The average height of US males is 175.4 cm (approx. 5 ft., 9 in.). Depending on the location, most women in the US want men in the $150k (10% of males) to 500k+ (1% of males) income bracket[123] who are strong/aggressive and above average in height, all of which indicate ability to provide and protect. Men can compensate for being below average in height by making roughly $50k more per year per inch than their taller competitors. Most men would be thrilled to settle for 80 percent of what they want in a mate. Women are usually NOT willing to settle for anything less than 100 percent of what they want in a mate.[124]

While the primary male attractiveness can be measured objectively, female attractiveness is mostly in the eye of the beholder and influenced by features such as age, height/weight proportionality, waist to hip ratio (WHR) of 0.7, shiny hair, smooth skin, large eyes, perky breasts etc., (features which are often labeled as sexist, but are, in fact, indicative of women's ability to give birth to healthy children).

The Evolution of Human Sexuality (1979) by Donald Symons
tinyurl.com/irpm317[125]

The Myth of Male Power: Why Men are the Disposable Sex (1993) by Warren Farrell
tinyurl.com/irpm320[126]

Warrior Lovers: Erotic Fiction, Evolution and Female Sexuality (2003) by Donald Symons and Catherine Salmon
tinyurl.com/irpm321[127]

The Evolution of Desire: Strategies of Human Mating (2003) by David M. Buss
tinyurl.com/irpm323[128]

The Mating Mind: How Sexual Choice Shaped the Evolution of Human Nature (2001) by Geoffrey Miller
tinyurl.com/irpm325[129]

Redefining Seduction: Women Initiating Courtship, Partnership and Peace (2009) by Donna Sheehan with Paul Reffell
tinyurl.com/irpm326[130]

Dataclysm: Love, Sex, Race, and Identity — What Our Online Lives Tell Us about Our Offline Selves (2015) by Christian Rudder
tinyurl.com/irpm327[131]

From Women to Men
tinyurl.com/irpm328[132]

The Battle is Over: From Men to Women
tinyurl.com/irpm329[133]

Critical Realist views on gender:

Read about interesting Critical Realist perspectives on gender by Lena Gunnarsson, even though she does not have (or apply) the developmental insights of the Integral Relationship model and solutions of co-creation between equal and opposite partners along the seven chakras (see Module 25 on page 497), but rather portrays females as victims of patriarchy and further polarizes the sexes by demonizing males instead of offering solutions that hold both sexes accountable. tinyurl.com/irpm365[134]

Sex Purpose Love book reference

Page 173–204

Suggested movie: *The Red Pill* (2016)

Watch this movie to see the journey of feminist filmmaker Cassie Jaye from San Anselmo, CA, as she explores today's gender wars and asks the question: "What is the future of gender equality?" She interviews radical feminists and leaders of the mysterious and polarizing Men's Rights Movement (MRM), among them the intellectual godfather of the movement, Warren Farrell, author of the *The Myth of Male Power: Why Men are the Disposable Sex*.

As an illustration of male powerlessness, MRM members point out that men are the only sex drafted to fight wars; to traditionally take on high-risk jobs in mining, agriculture, forestry, and fishing; are 11 times more likely than women to die on the job; have much higher suicide rates; and are three times more likely than women to be murder victims. Moreover, women live five years longer on average than men. MRM members also argue that fathers' rights are legally secondary to mothers' rights in family court and child custody cases, and although death rates for breast cancer and prostate cancer are about the same, six times more money is spent on breast cancer research in the U.S.

The male and female feminists in the movie counterargue that these arguments all come from whiny men who still hold all the power and that "nobody believes that what they say is true," so they should just shut up.[135]

Practice Module 10
Avoiding the Fear–Shame Downward Spiral

In the arithmetic of love, one plus one equals everything, and two minus one equals nothing.
~ Mignon McLaughlin ~

Module description

Learn and practice how to avoid going down the fear-shame spiral that eventually leads to relationship crash, and how to make amends and return to love if the spiral has already happened for you and your partner.

Realize why nearly 50 percent of relationships end because couples unconsciously descend through the ten phases of the fear-shame spiral. Avoid the unnecessary emotionally frustrating, financially devastating, socially disruptive, physically harmful, and children-traumatizing ending of relationships by understanding why most women experience fear under relationship stress and why most men experience shame. Recognize and understand the ten phases of the downward spiral and why they unfold in the order that they do.

Practice how to reverse the path down the spiral by emotionally connecting with your own and your partner's feelings in order to no longer stimulate fear or shame in each other. Make amends and return to the romance, love, and intimacy that you experienced at the beginning of your relationship. Become able to not only make your own love relationship crash-proof but also to support family members, friends, and clients who are going down the spiral in finding their way back to love.

Introduction

This module is based on the book, *How to Improve Your Marriage Without Talking About It*, by Patricia Love and Steven Stosny. Rooted in our evolutionary given biological programming that we explored in Module 9, most females consciously or unconsciously have a fear of being abandoned, unsupported, or otherwise harmed when they feel a disconnect and lack of love from their male protector and provider.[136] Males, on the other hand, often feel shame of not being good and successful enough professionally, in (sports) competitions, in bed, and in making their partner happy when they are rejected, belittled, humiliated, challenged, criticized, and unappreciated. When males feel fear, it usually covers up the shame of being weak and not good enough. When females feel shame, it usually covers up their fear of not being desirable and lovable. Both have to do with our underlying need for belonging.

Brené Brown defines shame as "the intensely painful feeling or experience of believing that we are flawed and therefore unworthy of love and belonging." She maintains that there are three things we really need to know about shame: (1) we all have it; (2) we're all afraid to talk about it; and (3) the less we talk about it, the more control it has over our lives.

Yet, women and men experience shame differently, she says. For women, shame is a web of unattainable expectations that say, "Do it all, do it perfectly, and never let them see you struggle." For men, the primary shame mandate is "Do not be perceived as weak."

When Brown asked women what tended to trigger shame, the primary response was how they looked—despite years of consciousness raising and critical awareness, women still tend to feel shame about not being thin, young, and beautiful enough.

Men's most common response was that shame was triggered by a sense of failure—whether it was at work, on the football field, in bed, in marriage, or with children.

Unfortunately, most men are not aware of the inherent fear responses in women under relationship stress, and women are not aware of the inherent shame responses in men; consequently, both act in counterproductive ways that adds insult to injury and makes things worse.

The downward spiral

We often notice that after men "win" a woman's heart and have frequent sex with her, they stop being romantic, because their evolutionary purpose to pass on their genes has been fulfilled. Instead, they naturally withdraw and switch to protecting (sometimes in unhealthy possessive and controlling ways) and providing for their partner and children by focusing on work and recreation. This is partly caused by a drop of the romance hormone dopamine to normal levels.

Women, on the other hand, often stop being charming, seductive, receptive, and appreciative after the romance phase, as it is also no longer necessary for them from a purely evolutionary perspective, and start what is perceived by men as complaining and nagging when they experience waning levels of attention, connection, love, support, and romance. Men usually experience this desire for connection as shaming them for not being good enough. This then leads men to withdraw into their man-cave instead of understanding the fear-based needs of their partner and leaning into the relationship, and, to make things worse, to become angry and aggressive or passive-aggressive, after they resurface, when they feel emasculated. This can lead to sexual or emotional infidelity, which prepares the ground for the crash of the relationship as shown below.

Integral Relationship Practice | 174

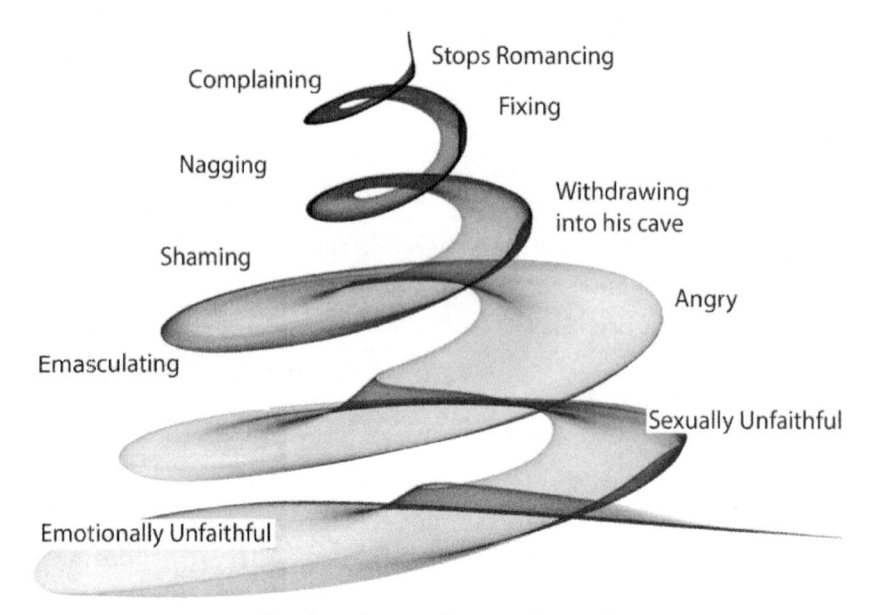

```
                    Stops Romancing
     Complaining
                        Fixing
        Nagging
                        Withdrawing
                        into his cave
        Shaming
                                Angry
    Emasculating
                            Sexually Unfaithful
  Emotionally Unfaithful
```

Relationship Crash

Figure 28: The 10 phases of the fear–shame downward spiral

While men generally like to be challenged to improve for their own sake and for the world,[137] they don't want to be nagged, compared, or emasculated by women and given the feeling that they are not good enough for them. On the other hand, men need to understand that when women complain, they don't feel safe, supported, understood, or no longer trust them and miss a deeper emotional and physical connection.

The practice in this module is to notice when the fear-shame dynamic sets in and, for men, to stop withdrawing, and, instead, to actively listen to their partners (without trying to fix their problems unless specifically asked) and to reaffirm their commitment, love, and support. For women, the practice is to stop nagging, criticizing, and shaming their partners, and, instead, appreciating, affirming, and celebrating them (see the *Celebrating Men, Satisfying Women* work of Alison Armstrong on page 424) instead of talking about the problems they experience in the relationship (hence the title of the book.)

If this approach does not stop the fear-shame downward spiral, couples at the Green and higher stages of development are advised to openly talk about what triggers their fear and shame by using the NVC OFNR (as described in Module 6, page 109): "When you do this, I experience/feel this, because I have a need for .... Would you be willing to ...?"

Couples at the Orange level may come to some win-win agreements by focusing on their interests and outcomes rather than on problems and feelings, and couples at the Blue/Amber level may be able to establish certain traditional gender roles and rules (Men are from Mars, Women are from Venus) to return to love.

If you facilitate this module, notice where the practitioners are in the downward spiral, and at what level of consciousness development the fear and shame is created, as each level has its own needs, sensibilities, and triggers. It often takes time to rebuild trust, so baby steps are needed. If couples struggle during the exercise, then consider in which of the four dimensions of being (quadrants) the fear and shame is stimulated, what stage of anima/animus complex development they are in (Module 14); what their Love Languages (Module 15), Enneagram types and instincts (Module 16), and attachment styles are (Module 17); and if there are psychological wounds and false identities that need to be healed (Modules 18 and 19).

See if the couples can work themselves back up the spiral and return to the level of "First Love"—how they felt when they first fell in love—which may require that they are at the same level of consciousness and spiritual and sexual development.

When made conscious, the fear-shame dynamic becomes an incredible opportunity for healing and growth for both partners.

Purpose and application of the module
1. Bring awareness to the fear-shame downward spiral and the behavior that causes it.
2. Prevent the downward spiral by avoiding stimulating fear in females and shame in males, or by openly sharing when these emotions are triggered.
3. Make amends and offers of future behaviors to avoid the fear-shame downward spiral and learn how to ask for support from their partner if necessary.
4. Take responsibility for feelings of fear and shame instead of projecting them outward.
5. Practice returning to love and romance if a couple is already descending the spiral.
6. Understand that reversing the fear-shame downward spiral is often the prerequisite to addressing other issues in the relationship.
7. Prevent others from going down the fear-shame spiral by bringing attention to it.

Exercises: Fear-shame downward spiral
The following are a group and a paired exercise.
1. Print out the two worksheets.
2. For the first exercise, ask practitioners to separate into male and female groups, ideally in two separate rooms.
3. Refer to the exercise description in Module 9 on page 162 about sensitivities around gender identifications. Even though this exercise uses male-female language, the same fear-shame dynamics may play out in same-sex, gender- fluid, etc. couples.
4. This is followed by group sharing and a paired exercise.
5. Make the four agreements for confidentiality, responsibility, healthy boundaries, I-statements, and sharing, as outlined on page 556.

Exercise one: Female fear, male shame

1. Hand out the sheets with the four questions below.
2. Explain that one person in each group will take notes of all the answers and then share them after the two groups come back together again for exercise two.
3. Ask notetakers to write down what was agreed on by all, what most agreed on, and some of the individual experiences. See a link to lists from previous groups in this endnote.[138]
4. Allow about 20–40 minutes time for this exercise.

One person takes notes and then reports to the joined group.

Exercise two: Restoring love

This exercise is based in the Nonviolent Compassionate Communication (NVC) model.

1. Print one worksheet below (front and back) for each practitioner.
2. Ask the practitioners to pair up with someone who is already experienced with NVC or similar psychological processes.
3. Encourage couples to do the exercise together, unless they feel too vulnerable, in which case they may choose another participant for the exercise.
4. Hand out the worksheet.
5. Refer to or hand out the Nonviolent Compassionate Communication worksheet from Module 6, page 118, about needs, feelings, and interpretations.
6. Go through the entire fear-shame worksheet, give examples and answer questions.
7. Have tissues ready for the exercise, as it can bring up deep emotions and tears.

Worksheets: Fear-shame downward spiral

Worksheet 1

Answer the following questions:

Female practitioners:
1. In which situations have you felt fear/anxiety in your relationship?
2. What triggered it?
3. How did you react?
4. How did your partner react?

Male practitioners:
1. In which situations did you feel shame in your relationship?
2. What triggered it?
3. How did you react?
4. How did your partner react?

Worksheet two

Complete the sentence stems for each of the five fear-shame dynamic pairs below.

1–2: Stops Romancing–Complaining

Man: I now realize that I stopped being romantic when I no longer ... instead of showing my love and caring for you by ... (think of romantic things you did before).

I am very sorry and feel ... that this confused, disappointed, and scared you. Going forward, I will ... (think about her love languages—see Module 15—and creative ideas about how to show your love and be romantic again.)

Woman: I now realize that when I perceived that you stopped being romantic, I stopped being seductive/receptive/appreciative and started to "improve/fix" you and complain about ... instead of celebrating and encouraging you. I am very sorry and feel ... for complaining this way. Going forward, I will ... (think about being more seductive again, telling him how you want to be loved, sharing your needs, and appreciating/celebrating him for what he does for you). Also see Alison Armstrong on *Celebrating Men, Satisfying Women,* page 424.

3–4: Fixing–Nagging

Man: I now realize that I was trying to fix things (or you) when I perceived you as complaining, instead of empathically listening to you. I am very sorry and feel... that this upset and frustrated you. Going forward, I will ... (think about making time for asking her questions; listening to her empathetically when she needs attention, closeness, and reassurance; having intimate conversations; sharing withholds; etc., instead of fixing her. See video, *It's Not About the Nail*, at tinyurl.com/irpm476[139]

Woman: I now realize that I started nagging you about ... when I was frustrated when I felt a lag of attention, empathy, and care from you instead of being curious. I am very sorry and feel ... for shaming you this way. Going forward I will ... (think about giving him a list of things that you want him to do for you and making doable requests that are clear in kind, time, and place.)

5–6: Withdrawing into Cave–Shaming

Man: I now realize that I was withdrawing into my cave by ... when I perceived you as nagging, instead of trying to understand and meet your needs and desires that would have made you feel loved and cared for. I am very sorry and feel ... that this hurt and scared you. Going forward, I will ... (think about telling her that you sometimes need a time-out and when you come back, listen to her, share your feelings and needs, and do something romantic with her.)

Woman: I now realize that I was shaming you when you came out of your cave by... instead of giving you space and welcoming you back with love, care, and encouragement. I am very sorry and feel ... for shaming you this way. Going forward I will ... (think welcoming him back with love and showing curiosity and care).

7–8: Anger–Emasculating

Man: I now realize that I was (passive) aggressive by ... when I perceived you as shaming me for withdrawing, instead of holding you and reaffirming our love and my commitment to us. I am very sorry and feel ... that this hurt and scared you. Going forward, I will ... (think owning and "presencing" your anger instead of projecting it outward, and look at your underlying wounds—see false identity process in Module 19 on page 349).

Woman: I now realize that I was emasculating you when you were (passive) aggressive by ... instead of understanding what triggered you, showing empathy, and supporting you in your learning, healing, growing and awakening process. I am very sorry and feel ... for shaming you this way. Going forward, I will (think making amends by "handing back his balls" and looking at your own unmet needs and underlying wounds that caused you to provoke and degrade him this way).

9–10: Sexually Unfaithful–Emotionally Unfaithful

Man: I now realize that I was deeply hurting you when I was (sexually) unfaithful (flirting, watching porn, etc.) by ... instead of sharing my shame, loneliness, and frustration with you and finding a way out together with you. I am deeply sorry and feel ... for betraying, hurting, and scaring you this way, and making you lose your trust and hope in me. Going forward, I will ... (think about taking the risk of being vulnerable by using self-validating intimacy (see David Schnarch's book, *Passionate Marriage*, page 106-111, and Susan Campbell's book, *Truth in Dating*), even if that will mean losing her, because you realize that being authentic and truthful is the only way to create intimacy and a healthy love relationship with her.

Woman: I now realize that I was going behind your back when I complained about you and our relationship by telling an intimate/romantic friend about ... instead of having the courage to share my feelings and fears with you directly. I am very sorry and feel ... for not trusting you to be strong enough to hear my deepest truth and fears, and for shaming you this way by telling others and trusting them more. Going forward, I will ... (think about taking the risk of being vulnerable by using self-validating intimacy—see above—even if that will mean losing him, because you realize that being authentic and truthful is the only way to create intimacy and a healthy love relationship with him.)

Follow-up questions

1. How do you feel after this exercise?
2. What insights have you gained about the fear/shame that you stimulated in your partner?
3. What touched you the most?
4. How will you respond differently in the future when you or your partner experience fear or shame in your relationship?
5. In what ways can you be more seductive and receptive, and appreciate and celebrate your (male) partner?
6. In what ways can you be more present and make your (female) partner feel seen, safe, connected, loved, protected, and provided for?

Additional information and resources

How to Improve Your Marriage Without Talking About It (2008) by Patricia Love and Steven Stosny
tinyurl.com/irpm330[140]

Passionate Marriage: Keeping Love and Intimacy Alive in Committed Relationships (1997) by David Schnarch
tinyurl.com/irpm332[141]

Making Sense of Men: A Woman's Guide to a Lifetime of Love, Care and Attention from All Men (2008) by Alison Armstrong
tinyurl.com/irpm333[142]

Brené Brown Ted Talk: *Listening to Shame*
tinyurl.com/irpm334[143]

Sex Purpose Love book reference
Page 26–27

Suggested movie: *Little Miss Sunshine* (2006)

Watch this hilarious and touching movie to see elements of the fear-shame downward spiral. On one hand, this is a very funny comedy. On the other hand, it painfully shows the shame of males about failing professionally, and the fears of the two female characters around their safety and not being beautiful enough.

The plot revolves around a somewhat dysfunctional multigeneration family that is determined to get their youngest member Olive Hoover (Abigail Breslin) to the finals of the "Little Miss Sunshine" beauty pageant. Father Richard (Greg Kinnear), his wife, Sheryl (Toni Collette), her gay brother, Frank (Steve Carell), her Nietzsche-admiring son, Dwayne (Paul Dano), and Richard's grandfather, Edwin (Alan Arkin) embark on the 800-mile (1300 km) trip in their ailing yellow VW bus, traveling from Albuquerque, New Mexico, to Redondo Beach, California. On the way, they must overcome several obstacles and challenges that bring them closer together.

Practice Module 11
Feminine-Masculine Polarities

If any human being is to reach full maturity, both the masculine and the feminine sides of the personality must be brought up into consciousness.
~ Mary Esther Harding ~

If we keep on talking about masculine and feminine and following those stereotypes, then we will make women suppress and despise their so-called masculine qualities and men suppress and despise their so-called feminine ones, and that's where all the trouble starts.
~ Gloria Steinem ~

Module description

Learn and practice how to develop, balance, and harmonize healthy feminine and masculine polarities for the co-creation of sexual attraction and synergy in a healthy, sustainable love relationship.

Define what feminine and masculine means to you. See how the healthy expressions of both polarities can be equally embodied by males and females and are necessary for maintaining their wholeness and partialness in love relationships through descending, communion, ascending, and agency. Engage in several embodied exercises, with music and movement, to feel into movement and stillness, leading and following, transcendence and immanence, and autonomy and connection.

Realize your healing and growth potentials around your feminine and masculine polarities for the co-creation of a healthy love relationship. Do away with the postmodern notion that everything feminine is positive, good, or divine, and everything masculine is negative, bad, or toxic, by realizing that both polarities have healthy and unhealthy expressions.

Introduction

In Module 11, we differentiate further between the sexes by exploring feminine and masculine polarities (also called energy, charge, traits, temperaments, attitudes, schematizations, identities, roles, or potentials) which can be equally embodied by males and females! The meanings of masculine and feminine polarities are necessarily contrastive and contextual, shift in different situations (for example work/home, alone/together), and are largely culturally conditioned.[144] They originated from shared cultural conceptions of what it means to be male or female and are transmitted through parents, peers, and institutions such as religion or the educational systems. Females became conditioned to be expressive, warm, and submissive, and males to be instrumental, rational, and dominant.

As we see in the Personality Matrix on page 187, this conditioning tends to shift when females enter the modern Orange rational stage and develop their masculine side, and when males enter the postmodern Green pluralistic stage and develop their feminine side. These shifts allow both sexes to embody both polarities in the integral and higher stages.

David Deida uses the metaphor of a river. He likens the masculine to the directional, goal-oriented, focused, empty presence and stillness that is often compared to the banks of a river or canal. The feminine is characterized by pure boundless energy that moves freely without any direction. The containing masculine banks and the fluid feminine flow co-create the river. The stronger and higher the banks, the more flow of sexual energy and synergy can appear. If the banks are too rigid (like a concrete canal), the feminine will feel stifled, restrained, limited, controlled, and dominated. Alternatively, the feminine may not provide enough flow to fill the riverbed, which leads the masculine to feel unmoved, uninspired, unchallenged, unattracted, and useless. If the banks are too low or weak, the feminine will flow over and further erode the banks of the masculine, and thus feel uncontained and aimless. If both partners are too masculine, there is too much rigidity; if both are too feminine, there is no containment and direction.

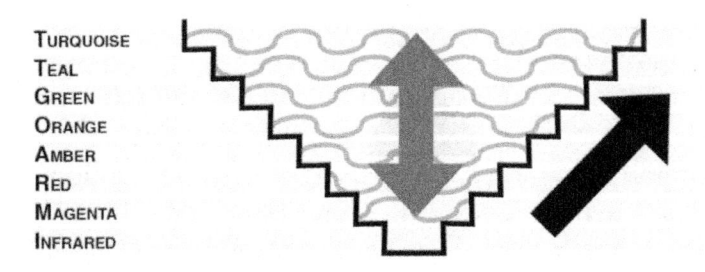

TURQUOISE
TEAL
GREEN
ORANGE
AMBER
RED
MAGENTA
INFRARED

Figure 29: River with masculine banks and feminine flow

In eastern traditions, this dynamic is often referred to as the yin (feminine) and yang (masculine).

The greater the polarities and their expression in healthy ways, the greater the synergy and sexual attraction that is created. Therefore, this module is very experiential through various exercises that show that both sexes can embody both polarities or traits, even though individuals may feel a certain natural essence or tendencies for one or the other.

Pre/post fallacy in love relationships

Couples frequently struggle in their relationships when feminine-masculine polarities are expressed in unhealthy ways; become neutralized when women and men embody too much of their masculine energy in the Orange stage (like the banks of the river above), which leads to power struggles when both want to lead; or when polarities become reversed when men develop their feminine and sensitive side and women manifest their "feminine power" in the Green stage. In the latter situation, women then often feel annoyed and put off by needy, weak, overly sensitive and emoting "hairy females" or SNAG's (Sensitive New-Age Guys) who are no longer aggressive towards others and no longer focused on competing, worldly success, power, protecting, and providing, and thus lose their sexual attractiveness. Conversely, the SNAGS find women in this stage to be overly challenging, condescending, demanding, insensitive, cold, and emasculating towards them.

This dynamic often leads to the devastating pre/post fallacy in love relationships, when postconventional Green males become attracted to and fall in love with preconventional seductive, sexy, immature, childish, needy, and clingy females in the magical Purple/Magenta stage, and Green females become attracted to the powerful, uninhibited, raw, and strong sexual masculinity of egocentric males in the Red stage. Because Green rejects hierarchies and tends to romanticize the preconventional magical superstitions and tribal earthliness of Purple/Magenta, as well as the "living in the now," uninhibited, shameless "I-take-what-I-want" spontaneity of Red, Green can initially not see the difference between the pre- and postconventional stages as they are both unconventional. Thus, the energies of the pre- and postconventional stages often resonate with each other in very confused and destructive ways.

These relationships usually end badly for the Green partners and leaves them confused, heartbroken, and devastated because they blame themselves for being judgmental, for not loving unconditionally, for not having done everything they could to make the relationship work, and for ending the relationship when they could no longer live with the neglect and abuse from their preconventional partners, who, in turn, play the victim and blame their postconventional partners for being judgmental, unloving, unevolved, ignorant, unenlightened, arrogant, uncaring, insensitive, and disloyal (when it was actually the other way around).

This dynamic is shown in the Personality Matrix below. Women up to the Blue/Amber mythical stage of development are traditionally conditioned through their upbringing and role models to be more feminine, and men to be more masculine. They are opposites, but often not equals in their power.

In the rational Orange stage, women often develop their masculine side and become equals but are no longer opposites.

In the pluralistic Green stage, men often develop their feminine side, while women continue to strengthen their masculine polarity. They are now opposites, potentially equals but with reversed polarities. This often leads to the preconventional/postconventional fallacy in relationships, as described above. In the second-tier integral and transpersonal stages, women and men can move towards embodying and expressing both polarities in healthy ways as opposites and equals.

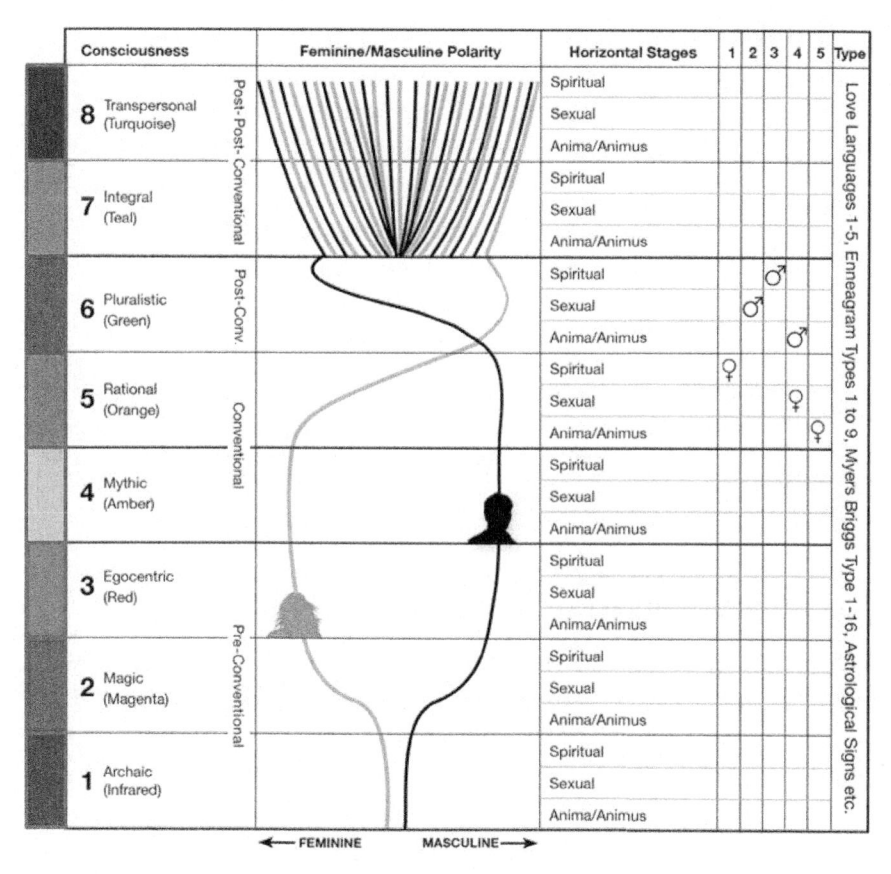

Figure 30: Personality matrix

Purpose and application of the module
1. Differentiate feminine-masculine polarities from biological differences between males and females and learned gender roles of men and women.
2. Feel and embody the feminine-masculine polarities—and not just conceptualize them intellectually—through the exercises.
3. Notice which polarities you and others embody at any given moment, and whether the expressions are healthy or unhealthy.
4. Realize your growth potentials towards embodying the feminine-masculine polarities in healthy ways.
5. Notice any fear or shame that are related to your feminine-masculine polarities, and heal related wounds and trauma.
6. Practice how to create flow and synergy between the polarities, like the energy flow between the positive and negative poles of a battery, to create sexual attraction and polarity, synergy, movement, flow, and growth.
7. Avoid the pre/post fallacy by having healthy boundaries in relationships around preconventional Purple/Magenta/Red partners if you are at the postconventional pluralistic Green stage.
8. Play and have fun with the feminine-masculine polarities!

Exercises: Feminine-masculine polarities
The following are group and paired exercises. They are designed to give the practitioners not only an intellectual understanding of the feminine and masculine polarities but also an embodied experience.

1. Explain how biological sex and learned gender roles are different from feminine-masculine polarities, as the latter always has opposites, like light and dark, inside and outside, up and down, hot and cold, singular and plural, positive and negative, etc., and can be equally embodied by males and females.

2. Make the four agreements for confidentiality, responsibility, healthy boundaries, I-statements, and sharing, as outlined on page 556.

Exercise one: Imagine a forest

Ask practitioners to close their eyes and to imagine or visualize a forest. After about 30 seconds, ask them to open their eyes and to give a show of hands as to who saw the forest from the outside (masculine) and who saw it from the inside (feminine). Most groups are equally divided, and the results are not related to gender.

Exercise two: Folding arms

Ask practitioners to fold their arms. Most people have one hand on top of their upper arm and the other hand tugged under. Ask for a show of hands as to who had their left hand on top and who had their right hand on top. Then ask the practitioners to reverse how they fold their arms. This exercise illustrates that we have certain genetically conditioned and learned preferences, essences, or opposites, such as feminine or masculine polarities, but that we can change them through practice.

Exercise three: Healthy and unhealthy feminine-masculine expressions

1. Separate males and females into two groups or conduct the activity as a shared group exercise or in a fishbowl format, as described in Module 9 on page 162.
2. Refer to the exercise description in Module 9, on page 162, about sensitivity around gender identifications. Even though this exercise uses male-female language, the same feminine-masculine polarity dynamics play out in same-sex, gender-fluid, etc., couples.
3. Ask each group to first make a list of what they think are masculine and feminine polarities (traits, energies, drives, tendencies, potentials) and then write down examples of

healthy and unhealthy or toxic expressions in a table, as shown below. See lists with answers from previous workshop and training participants at tinyurl.com/irpm569.[145]

Feminine/ Yin	Healthy	Unhealthy/ toxic	Masculine /Yang	Healthy	Unhealthy/ toxic
Inside	Connected	Withdrawn	Outside	Alert	Aloof

Table 13: Feminine-masculine exercise

4. Allow about 30 minutes or more, depending on the size and engagement of the group.
5. Ask one person to take notes and report afterwards to the joint group.
6. Bring the group back together.
7. Encourage practitioners to share how it feels to be in a mixed gender group again.
8. Invite the notetakers in each group to read their lists, starting with feminine-masculine traits first, then switching, and then reading the healthy and unhealthy expressions second.
9. Invite feedback and sharing about the exercise.

Exercise four: Grounded and flowing

1. Ask practitioners to stand up and to choose a practice partner (ideally male/female pairs).
2. Demonstrate and guide the practitioners with the shorter hair in each pair to stay unmoving and firmly grounded — feeling

like a rock or a tree with roots in the floor—by having their feet separated to shoulder width, bending their knees a little, feeling the floor under their feet, and breathing in and out calmly and deeply.
3. Demonstrate and guide the practitioner with the longer hair in each pair to move in front of their partner in a flowing, smiling, seductive way, but without physically touching (he/she can get close), trying to get their partner to move, including fascial expressions.
4. Ask the practitioners to switch roles after about two minutes.
5. Invite sharing and feedback how each role felt.

Exercise five: Leading and following[146]

1. For this exercise you need simple hula hoops (one for every two practitioners) that are about 90 cm (36 in.) or larger in diameter.[147]
2. Ask practitioners to pair up, ideally male/female, and encourage couples to do the exercise together.
3. Play soft, rhythmic music, with about 50 beats per second (for example, tinyurl.com/irpm23.[148]
4. Explain that the exercise has four phases as outlined below.
5. Demonstrate each of the four phases with a partner before each phase.
6. See a short demo video with all four phases at tinyurl.com/irpm27.[149]

Figure 31: Leading and following hula hoop exercise

Phase one

One practitioner is inside the hoop and holds on to it with both hands and with eyes closed. The other practitioner is holding the hoop from the outside with both hands and with eyes open. The practitioners outside lead the practitioners inside the hoop around the room, while the inside partners surrender and follow. After about two minutes, the practitioners switch who is inside and outside for another two-minute round, with the outside practitioners leading and the inside practitioners following, with eyes closed.

Invite feedback/sharing

1. Was it easier/more familiar or natural to lead or to follow?
2. How did it feel to lead, how did it feel to follow?
3. Is leading or following more familiar/natural for you in your day-to-day life and relationships?

4. Did you trust your partner when you were lead?
5. Did your partner inside the hoop surrender, trust, and follow you?
6. Were you confident and grounded in leading?

Phase two

One practitioner is inside the hoop and holds on to it, with eyes open, giving non-verbal directions through eye contact and body language to the practitioner who is holding the hoop from the outside and leading, as shown in *Figure 31* on page 192. This second phase is like partner dancing or, metaphorically speaking, one partner expressing a desire (I want a massage, I want to go out to dinner, I want to go to the ocean, etc.) and the other fulfilling it by leading. After about two minutes, the practitioners switch roles for another two-minute round of leading and following in the same way.

Invite feedback/sharing

1. How was this experience different from the previous exercise?
2. How did it feel to lead, how did it feel to follow this time?
3. Was it easier/more familiar to lead or to follow?
4. Were you in tune with each other?
5. Did your partner inside the hoop give clear signals and then surrender and follow?
6. Were you confident and grounded to lead?

Phase three

Both practitioners hold the hoop from the outside with both hands and alternate between leading and following, making eye contact, and feeling each other energetically through the hoop. This can be very playful and creative: for example, one practitioner briefly going inside the hoop, both inside the hoop, hoop vertical, hoop horizontal, practitioners very close or far apart, etc.

Invite feedback/sharing

1. How was this experience different from the previous exercise?

2. Were you in tune with each other?
3. Did you switch between leading and following and feel the different energy?
4. Was leading or following more enjoyable?
5. Were there moments when you both tried to lead or wanted to follow and, if yes, how did that feel?
6. Did following or leading feel more natural?

Phase four

Both practitioners gently balance the hoop from the outside on their fingertips, make eye contact, and feel each other energetically through the hoop as shown in *Figure 32* below. Ask them to deeply breath in and out together, become fully present, and notice and follow any subtle movement of the hoop. Instead of moving the hoop, the hoop is moving them.

At the end, you may invite the practitioners to share a hug.

Figure 32: Subtle co-creation hula hoop exercise

Invite feedback/sharing

1. How was this experience different from the previous exercise?
2. Were you present and in tune with each other?
3. Was there movement or stillness?
4. Did you feel the subtle energy flow between you through the hoop?
5. Did you feel drawn to each other or distanced?
6. How were all four phases of this exercise for you?
7. What insights did you gain?
8. How can you translate the experience in all four phases into your relational and sex life?

See a great video about leading and following and the politics around gender roles at tinyurl.com/irpm7.[150]

Exercise six: Ascending, descending, agency, communion

1. Place a stable table, on which several people can safely stand, at one end of the room for experiencing ascending and a pillow/blanket pile (maybe on yoga mats or a carpet) at the other end of the room for experiencing descending. As you can see in the picture below, you may use a door that is mounted onto two stable tables.
2. Begin this exercise by explaining that practitioners will have an embodied experience of the polarities between masculine ascending or self-transcendence (reaching up) which is opposed by feminine descending or self-immanence (reaching down), and masculine agency (acting by one's own choice or maintaining wholeness) that is opposed by feminine communion (acting in harmony with others or partialness). Remind the practitioners that males and females have equal potentials to embody each of the four polarities in healthy or unhealthy ways.

3. The two opposing polarities can be visualized as a graph (shown below) that you may draw on a whiteboard, with ascending and descending on a vertical axis, and communion and agency on a horizontal axis.
4. Explain that we can either experience an agentic or communal, or ascending or descending polarity, charge, or energy, but not both simultaneously—just as it is impossible to simultaneously breathe in (descending) and out (ascending), or to be physically together (communion) and apart (agentic). This means that ascending or descending appear in either an agentic or communal way—or, as a metaphor, you can go either up or down in an elevator by yourself or in a group, but not both simultaneously. The resulting intersection between the two lines provides you with your feminine or masculine polarity or charge at any given time.
5. Demonstrate how practitioners can experience the four polarities by moving into each of them, as described below.

Ascending

Standing on the table, maybe holding up hands, allowing themselves to be seen by others while looking down at them. Practitioners below may look up at them admiringly and/or submissively, bow, or prostrate themselves to the people on the table.

Descending

Submerging themselves into the pillow pile, closing their eyes, covering themselves with a blanket, going into a fetal position, feeling into their bodies, connecting with the floor and earth.

Agency:

Facing the table, going to the right side of the room and moving around independently on their own, avoiding any eye contact or interaction with other practitioners.

Communion

Facing the table, going to the left side of the room and moving/dancing in a group with other practitioners (or waiting to be joined), holding hands, making eye contact, making sounds/laughter, feeling if they lead or follow in the group, and noticing how it feels to join the group (fear of rejection?), having to fit in, and leaving (guilt or happiness?).

Figure 33: Exercise ascending, descending, agency, communion

6. Play the same soft, rhythmic music, with about 50 beats per second, that you used for the hula hoops exercise above.
7. Invite practitioners to start exploring by trying each polarity three or more times, for about one minute or longer each (so the exercise is about 12–20 minutes).
8. Stop the music at the end and ask the practitioners to move into the space that felt most resonant or familiar to them.

9. Invite each participant to share what resonated with them about the polarity they chose, how the other three polarities felt, and how this reflects their relationship experiences and life.

Worksheet: Feminine-masculine polarities

While there are many feminine and masculine traits, the Integral model equates them with ascending, descending, agency, and communion, each with healthy and unhealthy expressions, and related fears. These polarities are mainly felt energetically as drives or tendencies to maintain our simultaneous wholeness and partialness and to co-create synergy and sexual attraction in relationships.

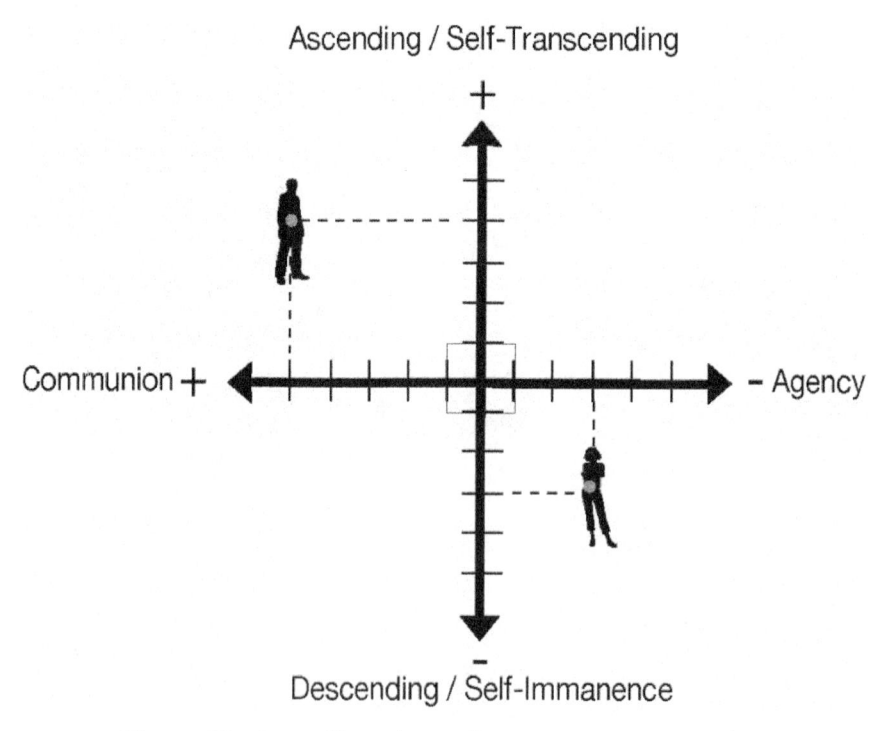

Figure 34: Ascending, descending, agency, communion

Masculine ascending

Healthy ascending is characterized by a desire to improve, to go beyond, to grow, to transcend, to create, and to think big. This is accomplished by gaining wider perspectives of the self and the nature of things. It requires a willingness to change by letting go of old paradigms and not sweating the small stuff.

Unhealthy ascending ignores, represses, controls, and dominates the lower, instead of embracing and caring for it. It denies feelings, the body, sexuality, and nature.

The fear of ascenders is to get dragged down, engulfed, absorbed, and lost.

Feminine descending

Healthy descending means to be connected with, and sensitive to, the richness and fullness of the world, to be down-to-earth and in touch with one's body, feelings, emotions, and sexuality.

Unhealthy descending means to be overwhelmed, fused with, and run by the many details of life and its manifestations, feelings, earthly desires, and needs.

The fear of descenders is to lose touch, to get lost, or to be dissociated from the fullness of life and its forces.

Masculine agency

Healthy agency supports the autonomous functioning of the individual, group, family, community, organization, or society.

Unhealthy agency leads to alienation and dissociation from others.

The fear of agentic people is to lose the freedom to make independent choices and to become dependent on others for their well-being.

Feminine communion

Healthy communion is expressed through the peaceful, responsible (response-able), considerate, and caring connection between people.

Unhealthy communion leads to fusion, dependency, neediness, and clinging—with the loss of one's own will, individuality, and autonomy—which eventually leads to resentment.

The fear of communion-oriented (communal) people is to be abandoned, unsupported, and alone.

Follow-up questions

1. How do you feel after the exercises?
2. What insights about the feminine-masculine polarities and healthy and unhealthy expressions have you gained?
3. What touched you the most when listening to others?
4. Are there areas in your life where the polarities are more or less balanced?
5. What healing and growth potentials around your feminine-masculine polarities do you see?
6. How will you respond differently in the future when you or your partner express unhealthy or toxic forms of the feminine-masculine polarities?
7. How can expressing healthy feminine-masculine polarities improve your sex life?

Additional information and resources

Below are more detailed descriptions of the feminine-masculine polarities.

Ascending

Ascending (or self-transcendence) is characterized as "the love that reaches up" (Eros) and brings forth new creations by arranging whole parts into larger wholes with their own unique characteristics or properties, such as atoms which form molecules (think of a single oxygen and two hydrogen atoms, with their unique properties that bond together to form a unique water molecule); individual musical notes that become parts of whole symphonies; food ingredients that become parts of whole meals;

words that form sentences; individuals who form couples; or communities that form societies.

Ascenders see reality from above and see fractions as part of the larger whole or a greater totality. They perceive the world from an extended view and try to rise ever higher in consciousness to encompass everything. Ascending energy expresses itself through wisdom, creativity, novelty, visionary concepts, emptiness, and stillness.

Descending

Descending (or self-immanence) is characterized as "the love that reaches down" (Agape) towards the many and the parts, embracing everything—including earth and all its inhabitants—with selfless compassion and devotion. Descenders celebrate life and its many manifestations, the body, and their sexuality. They go with the flow, are in touch with the richness of the manifest world, and experience things from the fullness of existence by diving in deep.

Descending energy expresses itself through feelings, compassion, emotions, warmth, movement, surrender, fullness, and flow. A descender perceives the world and the body from the inside.

Agency

Agency (or self-preservation) is the drive towards maintaining wholeness, acting through one's own will, making independent choices, and exerting one's own power. People with a tendency towards agency have a desire to maintain their own identity, personality, individuality, independence, and autonomy. They focus on rights, rules, laws, and justice that protect and serve the interests of the individual or wholeness of the group (for example, couple or family).

Agentic people or groups define themselves by their own decisions, success, and free will, rather than their environment and the opinion of others. Their motto is that failing at living one's own life is better than succeeding at living someone else's.

Communion

Communion (or self-adaptation) is the drive to connect (commune) with others, to be part of and act in the interest of everyone in the unit or group, and to cooperate. Communion is expressed through qualities of care, responsibility (ability to respond to others' needs), relationship, lateral bonding, connection, communication, empathy, intimacy, joining, altruism, and participation.

Communal people feel that their well-being depends on their ability to contribute, trust, depend on others, fit into their environment, and maintain a mutual support system of give-and-take.

Balance and harmonize

To maintain our simultaneous wholeness and partialness in healthy love relationships (and life in general), we need to balance and harmonize healthy agency, communion, ascending, and descending.

You as an individual whole and collective part, called a holon (see more on page 540), can feel into these four polarities right now in a relational context:

Ascending (self-transcendence)

In its healthy form, it is your drive towards co-creating a healthy love relationship; to surrender your separate sense of self or Ego and to show humility; to recognize that, as one person put it, "One plus one equals everything, and two minus one equals nothing"; to co-create synergy, to advance into novelty with your partner; to serve a purpose that is larger than either individual and is put into service for the well-being of others by creating more goodness, truth, beauty, and functioning.

In its unhealthy forms, the ascending drive will neglect the needs of the individual holons (you and your partner) that make up the larger whole (the love relationship).

Descending (self-immanence)

In its healthy form, it is your drive to care for yourself and your partner as parts of the relationship, to maintain the wellness of your physical body through a wholesome diet, exercise, and rest, and to connect on the level of feelings and sexuality.

In its unhealthy form, the descending drive will lead to the dissolution, decomposition, or deconstruction of the larger whole (the love relationship) by focusing too much on yourself (often in an egocentric or narcissistic way, including New Age narcissism), loving yourself or a pet more than a partner, and losing sight of the greater good.

Agency (self-preservation)

In its healthy form, it is your drive to maintain your own wholeness, and the integrity, independence, and autonomy of the larger holon, such as your love relationship, family, team, organization, community, country, etc.; to be stable, faithful, and devoted.

In its unhealthy form, agency leads to separation, conflict, isolation, alienation, and loneliness.

Communion (self-adaptation)

In its healthy form, it is your drive towards acting in partnership with others, to connect, join, communicate, participate, fit in, consider, take responsibility, compromise, cooperate, and to show empathy.

In its unhealthy form, communion leads to dependence, fusion, and loss of independent functioning and free will.

Quadrants and feminine-masculine polarities

We can either experience the drive towards certain polarities in a harmonized way in all four dimensions of our being and relating (quadrants), as shown below, or feel a dissonance between the interior, exterior, individual, and collective quadrants, which gives us 16 different combinations (for example, feeling drawn inward while we are in a group or having an outward focus while we are hiking by ourselves).[151]

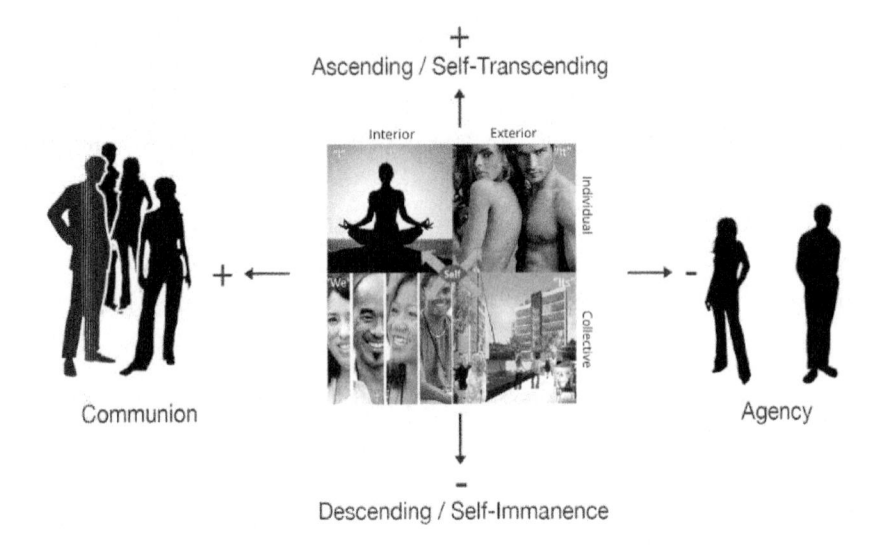

Figure 35: Feminine-masculine in the four dimensions

Books

Intimate Communion: Awakening Your Sexual Essence (1995) by David Deida
tinyurl.com/irpm336[152]

Sex and the Seasoned Woman (2007) by Gail Sheehy
tinyurl.com/irpm338[153]

New Passages (1996) by Gail Sheehy
tinyurl.com/irpm340[154]

Sex Purpose Love book reference

Page 32–37

Suggested movie: *The Tree of Life* (2011)

Watch this profound and complex movie to see the masculine ascending and agency, and feminine descending and communion interacting at all levels of the evolutionary process, including our human life and death.

The Tree of Life is both an experimental film and an epic drama, written and directed by American filmmaker Terrence Malick. In it we see the main character, Jack (Sean Penn), looking back at his childhood in a 1950s Texas family where he is conflicted between the way of grace, as embodied by his demurring feminine mother (Jessica Chastain), and that of nature, as embodied by his patriarchal masculine father (Brad Pitt). Also see the formation of his anima complex (Module 14) and the tensions between the archaic, magic, egocentric, mythic, and rational stages of the characters.

The movie is interspersed with imagery and sounds of the origins of the known universe and the inception of life on Earth and features amazing music.

Practice Module 12
Spiritual Development

The proof of the depth and embodiment of your spiritual realization will be seen in your love relationship. That's where the proof is in the pudding.
If it all collapses in your relationship, you have some work to do. And people do have a lot of difficulties in their relationships.
~ Adyashanti ~

Module description

Learn and practice how to identify five states of spiritual experiences or "waking up" through a guided meditation. Realize how these state experiences are interpreted differently from eight levels of consciousness development or "growing up," and how they impact your love relationships. Become inspired to make these temporary state experiences into permanently accessibly state-stages through a daily mindfulness meditation practice.

Explore five states or realms of spiritual awakening or realization, as identified by Eastern wisdom traditions and described by Ken Wilber in his many books. Strengthen your witnessing self or "subject" during a guided meditation by becoming fully present with "gross" physical objects and your body, your breath, your "subtle" thoughts/mind, and your "causal" mystical pure being, spiritual essence, or soul, before you become one with the "pure witness" or subject that cannot be made into an object, witnessed, or thought and talked about, but only pointed to.

Fully awaken to end your own suffering and the suffering you create for others by freeing yourself from any desire, attachment, delusion, and hatred—even about "enlightenment"—through disidentifying from objects in your consciousness.

Integrate the four state-stages into nondual awareness by avoiding the spiritual bypassing (page 217) of dissociating, repressing, denying, rejecting, or splitting off, and, instead, embracing everything and avoiding nothing in present moment-to-moment awareness, without judgment.

Have one of the most important insights of the Integral (Relationship) model—how the five state-stages of "waking up" are interpreted differently from each of the eight stages of consciousness development or "growing up"—in order to understand why we may deeply resonate and fall in love with a partner on a spiritual level, but struggle to co-create a healthy love relationship because of differing needs, values, concerns, and worldviews, and because of spiritual bypassing.

See how you can further grow and awaken in the four dimensions of your being in an Integral Love Relationship with an equal and opposite partner.

Introduction

State-stages of spiritual development

Unlike structure stages or levels of vertical consciousness development (growing up), which have to be "earned" through personal growth work, temporary states of spiritual and other peak experiences have been described by Wilber as "free" because they can arise in individuals at every level of vertical development. What requires work (usually years of meditation, mindfulness, therapy, or other contemplative practices) is to make them permanently accessible as a stage. Hence the name state-stages.

The word *spiritual* means "that which is not bound to time, the physical world, or mental concepts," which are all the domain of the mind and our senses. To be spiritual means different things to different people: (1) random spiritual and paranormal phenomena; (2) a particular attitude or quality; (3) superhuman achievements in one or several of the developmental lines; (4) being in touch with feelings and inner experiences; and (5) a permanent level or stage of spiritual realization or freedom that is attained through practices such as meditation, yoga, tantra, or contemplative prayer.

So how can we even talk about spirituality without making it into something it is not, thus engaging in spiritual materialism?[155] We can't! We can only guide practitioners to witness and disidentify from the "gross" material and physical, "subtle" mental and emotional, and "causal" mystical realms of their conditioned, timebound separate sense of self. Through this practice, they can awaken to the infinite and eternal "unknowable" source or ground of all being, out of which experiences such as time, space, being, existence, and even being fully awake or enlightened arise, and they can include these experiences in nondual awareness.

1. Gross/waking

The initial level of spiritual realization is called the gross/waking state-stage. It marks the major transition of awakening by disidentifying from the material and physical realm. This state-stage emerges with the realization that nothing material or physical that you desire, possess, are attached to, or reject defines who you truly are. This awakening allows you to respond in mindful and responsible ways by creating a "space" between bodily impulses and previously unhealthy habitual reactions, and, instead, consciously choose a response in any given moment that serves your own material and physical well-being, as well as that of others, thus becoming the master of your physical realm instead of its slave. The first two phases of the meditation practice support this awakening. This is followed by a breathing practice that serves as a bridge to the subtle realm.

The feminine in this state-stage tends to move consciously into the body (descend) and the manifest world. This downward movement gave rise to earth-bound and Goddess-worshipping religions such as paganism. The masculine tends to move away from the body (ascend) and deny its pleasures, as seen in male God-worshipping religions such as Christianity, Buddhism, Hinduism, and Islam, in their fundamentalist forms.

2. Subtle/dreaming

Awakening to the subtle or psychic state-stage is marked by the realization that we are not our thoughts, mind, and beliefs. Like awakening from a dream after sleeping, we realize that random and unobserved thoughts (assumptions, projections, prejudices, etc.), which are frequently fed by pain from the past and fears/hopes about the future, are just as unreal as our dreams at night.

When we enter the subtle state-stage, we awaken from this nightmare and develop metacognition or become construct aware. Strengthening our witnessing self by observing thoughts as "objects in consciousness" allows us to disidentify from desires, attachments, delusions, and defenses of our mind and, instead, use it for creative thinking, problem-solving, learning, planning, contemplation, visioning, etc., through present moment-to-moment awareness, instead of being used by it. Observing and "quieting" our mind may lead to experiences of lucid dreaming, subtle illuminations, and other paranormal phenomena, such as, remote viewing or psychic experiences. Note that attempts to stop our mind or thinking are misconceptions of this stage and don't lead to liberation or enlightenment. Instead, it is about witnessing our thoughts.

The feminine tends to strengthen the self and connect more deeply with feelings and the heart, while the masculine tends towards repressing and dissociating from emotions and the ego.

3. Causal/deep sleep

Entering the causal state may feel like a "vertical drop" out of our head into a state of present stillness or pure being that can be likened to deep dreamless sleep, except that there is still a witness that is aware of this mystical experience of deep peace, joy, love, connectedness, surrender, oneness, joy, acceptance, allowing, empathy, compassion, intuition, creativity, full awakening or enlightenment that many mystics and spiritual teachers have been and are still pointing to, and that spiritual seekers are seeking. It is called "causal" because it is seen and experienced as the cause, ground, or seed of the subtle and gross realms. In philosophy, it is the branch of metaphysics that studies the fundamental nature of reality, the first principles of being, identity and change, space and time, causality, necessity, and possibility.[156] Strengthening the witnessing self by observing causal feelings and mystical experiences allows us to disidentify from desires, attachments, aversions, defenses, and delusions about how we want or don't want to feel (present, joyful, compassion, suffering), or what we want to experience (sunset, great sex, freedom), or about being fully awake or enlightened, which is called spiritual materialism or spiritual bypassing (see page 217).

Experiencing this state can be deeply disorienting and scary when it brings up repressed pain and trauma,[157] or leads to "depersonalization"[158] when we become a detached observer (for example, during an out-of-body experience).

The masculine tends to experience this state as radical stillness and emptiness; the feminine experiences it as radical fullness and flow.

4. Pure witness

The pure witness state-stage cannot be experienced and talked about as such and is therefore often not seen as a separate level of spiritual realization. However, it can be conceptualized as the witness that cannot witness itself, or the subject that cannot be made into an object. It goes one step further than the causal state-stage when the experience(d) and the experiencer of the causal stage, or the inside and the outside, are no longer separate. If you experienced the causal state-stage, you may ask yourself: what was experiencing it; what is the subject that was aware of the causal as an object in consciousness; what caused the experience. It was no longer a separate you, so what was it? You cannot answer this question, not even with the word "emptiness," so it is the end of story. Hence silent retreats and the sayings, "Those who speak do not know, those who know do not speak" and "There should be a conference for enlightened beings and everyone who goes is automatically disqualified."

Another way of conceptualizing this state-stage is the insight that the perception of our inner and outer reality is ultimately created or caused in our mind as qualia (think colors, sounds, taste etc.) and then interpreted through a combination of prior experiences and labeled through language. If we relinquish any prior conception, memory, or experience, and become fully present, the perceived and the perceiver become one. We may call this direct or immediate experience or, as Wilber calls it, "One Taste." It happens when our separate sense of self is completely transcended with a loss of the sense of time and space. What remains is "isness," "suchness," or "dasein" (German word for "being there," "presence," or "existence") that is completely devoid of desire, attachment, delusion, and hatred/aversion.

In this state-stage, the feminine-masculine duality is fully transcended.

5. Nondual

In the preceding witness state-stage, one can become completely absorbed or lost in immediate or direct experience of "The Now." Nonduality can be conceptualized as the transcendence and inclusion of all the preceding state-stages and dualities of being and becoming, singular and plural, creator and created, exterior and interior, feminine and masculine, and emptiness (the unmanifest) and form (the manifest) through the dialectical processes of intersubjectivity and inter-objectivity in tantric weaving or union. Like the pure witness, nonduality cannot be experienced or talked about by a separate self, as that would create a subject-object duality.

Wilber describes nonduality as reaching the top of a pole and then climbing one step further. What follows is a complete emptying of the subject into the object, so that there is no more subject-object duality at all. Nonduality is devoid of any looking out on the world from any vantage point that is apart from it. The self is then the world's perspective or one with Godhead.

Nonduality is often confused with the preverbal a-dual, non-self-aware or fused stage that babies and (most?) animals are in. Because no separate sense of self has developed in them, they can also not transcend it. Or as Jack Engler wrote in the '70s, "You have to be somebody before you can be nobody." A good example is the mirror test.[159] Babies and most animals don't realize that a mirror reflects the environment. They see the reflection as part of their surroundings, and their self-image as another being, whereas there is an awareness of the reflective quality in nonduality.

See meditation video at tinyurl.com/irpm9.[160]

Wilber-Combs Lattice/Matrix

In the Wilber-Combs Lattice (or Matrix) below, which Wilber conceived together with Dr. Allan Combs, we see that all spiritual state-stages are interpreted from the individual's level of consciousness, maturity, or structure stages. This updates Wilber's earlier writings in which he stacked spiritual state-stages on top of structure stages, which would have meant that tribal shamans or the Buddha or Jesus, who lived in pre-rational/premodern times, could not have had spiritual realizations. This is important to realize, as many people falsely assume that if someone is spiritually awake, he or she is also consciously developed and psychologically healthy (which is often not the case.)

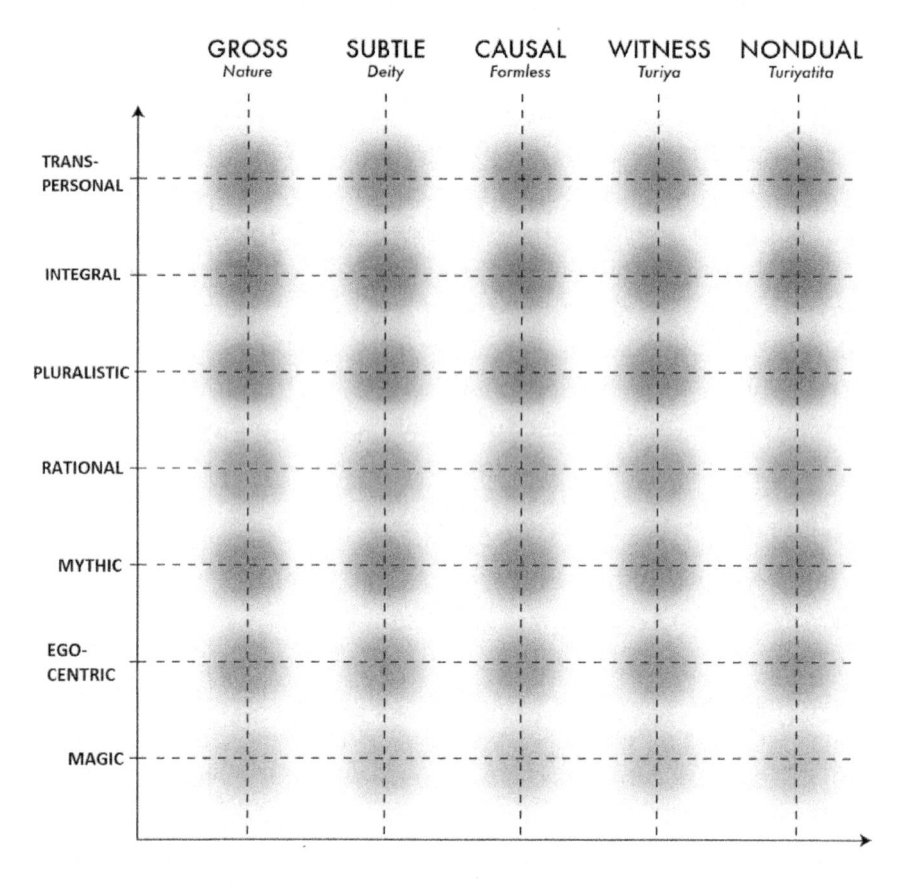

Figure 36: The Wilber-Combs matrix with spiritual state-stages

Interpretation of spiritual state-stage experiences

- People (or animals) at the archaic level cannot have spiritual state experiences, as they have no separate sense of self. As mentioned earlier, you must be somebody before you can be nobody.
- People at the magical superstitious level may interpret their spiritual experiences as having outside visions of spirits, ghosts, energies, forces, angels, or animals that speak or interact with them and whose voices they obey.
- People at the egocentric level may interpret their spiritual experiences as having attained some unique realizations that

make them special and that they can do whatever they please, as they are totally liberated and free and that (from an enlightened perspective) "nothing matters." They just live in "The Now." To mediate this egocentric impulse, Eckhart Tolle writes in *The Power of Now*, "Nothing matters, but everything is honored."

- People at the mythic conformist level may interpret their spiritual experiences as grace from their God, or special encounters, experiences, guidance, or visions, and create (or follow) all kinds of mythic rituals and rules (Religion) that please their creator and establish right and wrong actions that lead to salvation or condemnation.
- People at the rational level may interpret spiritual peak experiences as created by random or deliberately induced altered brain states, using religious or creative activities, meditation, music, dancing, breathing exercises, physical exercise, sexual intercourse, or consumption of psychotropic drugs (see, for example, the book *Zen and the Brain*).
- People at the pluralistic level may interpret their spiritual experiences as a unity with all creation through unconditional love for everything that arises by transcending their separateness (we are one with everything, no separation, no boundaries, etc.)
- People at the integral level may interpret their spiritual experiences through the four dimensions of their being (interior-exterior and singular-plural; body, mind, cultural, and social environment) and see these experiences as being a result of a mindfulness practice that aligns them with Eros or an evolutionary impulse (intelligent design).
- People at the transpersonal level no longer create an identity out of their spiritual experiences and deepen their compassion for the suffering of all beings—present and future. They further their deep desire to contribute to creating a eudaimonic world by co-creating more goodness, truth, beauty, and functioning

through balancing and harmonizing healthy feminine and masculine polarities.

We now see that there is a big difference between growing up, cleaning-up (doing shadow and trauma work and dealing with other unresolved developmental issues, including personality disorders) and waking up. Ignoring the former is now summarized under the term "spiritual bypassing."

Love relationships are essential, as they are the best and sometimes only way to become aware of our desires, attachments, delusions, and hatreds/aversions at the levels of the gross material and physical body, the subtle mental, causal "phenomenal," and even the pure witness, and to avoid spiritual bypassing, as love relationships are the only realm in which these dimensions come into intimate contact and our unconscious attachment wounds get triggered.

Also see Ken Wilber's, *Integral Spirituality* (pages 88–93), *The Integral Vision* (page 143), *Integral Meditation* (pages 92-94), and Allan Combs' *Consciousness Explained Better* (pages 90–102).

Personality matrix and five spiritual state-stages

Accordingly, we place the five spiritual state-stages on a horizontal axis in the Integral Relationship Personality Matrix, as shown in *Figure 30: Personality matrix* on page 187.

This is important to realize, as many people falsely assume that if someone is spiritually developed, they are also at a later stage of consciousness and psychologically healthy. We now see that there is a big difference between growing up, cleaning-up (doing shadow and trauma work and dealing with other unresolved developmental issues, including personality disorders) and waking up. Ignoring the former is now summarized under the term, "spiritual bypassing."

Spiritual bypassing

The term *spiritual bypassing* was introduced in the early 1980s by John Welwood, a Buddhist teacher and psychotherapist. A spiritual bypass or spiritual bypassing is a "tendency to use spiritual ideas and practices to sidestep or avoid facing unresolved emotional issues, psychological wounds, and unfinished developmental tasks."

Spiritual bypassing can be addressed with various forms of psychotherapy. We should keep in mind that there are important differences between (1) identification or fusion, (2) disidentification or un-fusing, and (3) dissociating, splitting off, or repressing. The first two words describe the self which is identified or fused with external material objects—for example, money, the physical body, and interior "objects in consciousness" such as thoughts, beliefs, feelings, emotions, or mystical experiences. The second two words describe objects that are "owned" but don't define us anymore—such as "I (as subject) have possessions, a body, thoughts, feelings, emotions, experiences, and I value and care about them in a non-attached way." The third (dissociation, repression, splitting off) are attempts to disown objects (including objects in consciousness) and deny them as illusions or energies that are not ours or us. Herein lies a danger. This attempt to disown can lead to outward projection, spiritual bypassing, and disconnecting from personal responsibility: Money is just "energy" that flows in and out of life; I am not angry—you make me angry; all thinking is bad, thoughts are just Ego; I am not ill—illness is a mental concept; feelings are not real—they are just caused by thoughts.[161]

Mindfulness

Mindfulness is the combination of traditional Eastern meditation practices and modern Western insights from philosophy, psychology, and neuroscience. The term was coined by the Buddhist scholar T. W. Rhys Davids at the dawn of the twentieth century.

Researchers who reviewed more than 200 studies found that mindfulness-based therapy was especially effective for reducing stress, anxiety, depression, pain, and addictions such as smoking.[162] Other benefits may include reducing the risk for heart disease by bringing down blood pressure; decreasing cognitive decline due to aging and Alzheimer's disease; improving the immune system by increasing levels of disease-fighting T-cells and their activity (found in patients with HIV or breast cancer); sharpening attention and creativity; increasing compassion; and improving relationships.[163]

The best way to practice mindfulness is to create a specific meditation space in your home and to follow the Zen suggestion to sit in meditation for about 20 minutes every morning—unless you're too busy; then you should sit for an hour.

Below are some short definitions and aspects of mindfulness that you may consider for your own practice, when working with clients, and when facilitating groups.

Being mindful

Jon Kabat-Zinn defines mindfulness as "awareness that arises through paying attention, on purpose, in the present moment, nonjudgmentally, in the service of self-understanding and wisdom."

Daniel Siegel defines mindfulness as "not being swept away by the mind, but to be able to discern through metacognition" and uses the acronyms "coal" for being curious, open, accepting, and loving, and "faces" for being flexible, adaptive, coherent (holding experiences and memories together dynamically over time), energized, and stable.

Mark Leary provides the following definitions for being mindful and mentally healthy:
1. Displaying a lack of genuine psychopathology and mental illness (see Module 21: Personality Disorders, on page 391).
2. The ability to get along with other people and maintain supportive close relationships.

3. The ability to define, pursue, and achieve goals based on purpose.
4. The motive to achieve and be successful in living one's purpose.
5. The ability to cope with problems and challenges that arise in life in a mature way.
6. A sense of subjective well-being.
7. The motive to interact with other people.
8. The motive to positively influence other people.
9. Psychological consistency, self-esteem, and authenticity.
10. Ability to experience and own emotions such as anger, joy, guilt, and sadness without projecting them on others.
11. Having positive values, moral foundations, virtues, and character strengths.
12. Ability to make sound decisions quickly, critically evaluate beliefs, and enjoy thinking.
13. Being clear about your identity (who you think you are); self-efficacy (what you're capable of doing); self-esteem (evaluation of yourself); and self-compassion (how you think about yourself when bad things happen.)

Brain and mind

The brain and the mind are not the same. The brain regulates the process and flow of energy and information through the firing of neurons, which is indicated through increased blood flow and oxygen consumption in the activated regions, as seen in PET scans. The mind involves our thoughts and cultural values, as seen in individual and group reactions to phenomena. The mind is using the brain to create itself. We use awareness to start shaping activity in our neural system.

The mind and brain interact with each other in ways that are still not understood to create consciousness, which we may define as levels of self-awareness of internal and external existence and, importantly, what we are interested in and passionate and concerned about, and the number of perspectives we can take.

Subcortical system

Very simply put, below the level of conscious awareness in the neocortex operate multiple unconscious regions in the limbic and basal ganglia (reptilian) areas of our brains that are not well understood.

Regions in the limbic area are believed to control affect, motivation, memory, intuition, appraisal of meaning (important-or-not-important filter), and attachment in intimate relationships.

- Amygdala: Fear/shame responses ... also emotion, affect, and feeling states.
- Hippocampus: Stores and makes implicit memory explicit.
- Hypothalamus: Plays a crucial role in many important functions, including releasing hormones such as oxytocin, adrenaline, and cortisol.
- Thalamus: Relays information of the sensory system (except for smell) between different subcortical areas and the cerebral cortex.
- Insula: Brings information upward from the body and the limbic area into the neocortex, and from the cortex down into the limbic area and on into the body.
- Regions in the basal ganglia (reptilian brain) control the body's vital functions, such as, heart rate, breathing, body temperature, hunger, thirst, balance, sexuality, and the motor system (for example, walking.)

A mindfulness practice furthers the healthy differentiation and integration of these and other parts of the brain for better functioning.

Implicit and explicit memory

Memories are remembered experiences from the past that shape us in the present and influence how we may act, think, and feel in the future. Memory is much more than what comes to mind when we try to recall something.

Implicit memories are emotions, perceptions, bodily actions, and bodily memories that are mainly stored in the amygdala, without markers for the time they occurred.

Explicit memories are things that we can recall or remember and are stored in the hippocampus, with markers for time and place.

Adrenaline and cortisol can inhibit or shut down the hippocampus under stress to protect us from creating traumatic memories, while the amygdala is still online and "recording" to stimulate "unconscious" fight, flight, and freeze "reactions" to protect us from dangerous situations.

Balancing the BIS/BAS system

Mindfulness can help us to balance the genetically and developmentally conditioned patterns of over- and underactivity in the dopamine, norepinephrine, and serotonin systems of our brains that are believed to impact the tendencies in our "behavioral approach system" (BAS) that drives us to move toward something desired, and the opposing "behavioral inhibition (avoidance) system" (BIS) that is said to regulate aversive motives in which the goal is to move away from something unpleasant.[164]

Left and right brain

The left brain is sometimes called the digital brain and believed to be associated with language, words, reading, writing, computations, sequencing, reason, certainty, predictability, right/wrong, true/false, and being linear, orderly, logical, rational, analytical, methodical, factual, mathematical, and controlling.

The right brain is sometimes referred to as the analog brain and is believed to be associated with being nonverbal, spontaneous, intuitive, spatial, visual, musical, creative, imaginative, holistic, and less organized. The right brain is also associated with facial expressions, body language, the arts, rhythm, feeling, flowing, and daydreaming.

List of prefrontal cortex functions

Dr. Daniel Siegel offers the following nine descriptions of essential brain functions for healthy relationships that are improved through relational mindfulness practices:[165]

1. Body regulation: Improves the autonomous nervous system that works as the accelerator and brakes of bodily functions (see above under BIS/BAS system.)
2. Attuned communication: Improves how we perceive another person's signals and respond back.
3. Emotional balance: Improves the capacity to enable or calm the lower limbic and brainstem regions that create healthy effects of states (emotional availability) through hormones that are transported through inhibitory fibers. If there is not enough calming, emotions get out of control and life becomes chaotic. If there is too much, we shut down emotionally and become rigid, and life loses vitality and meaning.
4. Response flexibility: Improves ability to pause before we act and allows us to choose between various options and the most effective and appropriate response.
5. Insight: Improves the way we connect the past with the present and anticipate the future to understand what is happening right now. Through a coherent sense of continuity across time and space, we become active authors of our own story.
6. Empathy and compassion: Improve our understanding of other persons' points of view by having an image of other persons minds in our own mind and to feel their suffering.
7. Fear modulation: Improves our ability to deal with unwarranted fears (false evidence appearing real). Trauma is embedded in the firing patterns of subcortical structures. To calm and transcend unhealthy fear responses, we need to increase the number of fibers that transport inhibitory peptides (GABA—gamma-aminobutyric acid) toward the amygdala to diminish its firing. Under stress, the subcortically embedded GABA fibers are less or not active to squelch the fear response.
8. Accessing intuition: Improves the ability of bringing the wisdom of the body (especially the neural networks around the bowel and heart) into awareness.

9. Morality: Improves how we act for the larger social good, even when we are alone.

Nine domains of integration

Below is Dr. Siegel's list of mindful integration domains for the co-creation of healthy relationships.[166]

1. Integration of consciousness: Awareness of the body, mental/emotional, relational, and outside world. Openness to things as they are.
2. Bilateral integration: Left and right hemispheres working in synchrony.
3. Vertical integration: Gut, heart, and lungs all have neural networks that seek to communicate with the brain. Many people are disconnected from body awareness (also see chakra charge and co-creation meditation on page 502).
4. Memory integration: Implicit and explicit memory integration. When traumas become implicit memory, we are stuck in the past. To integrate memory, we make implicit memories explicit (see Module 18 on page 337, and Module 19 on page 349.)
5. Narrative integration: Biographical memory needs to be included through creating a coherent narrative (see endnote 268). Facing and healing trauma and not running away from it, using the NARM process.
6. State integration: Honoring our interior states and accepting that they can be in conflict or in harmony. This includes the spiritual state-stages of the gross, subtle, causal, witness, and their nondual integration, as outlined above.
7. Interpersonal integration: Honoring and supporting the differences between self and others promotes neural integration in the brain. Mind is energy and information flow. Communicating thoughts and feelings between people creates and strengthens integrative fibers in the brain.
8. Temporal integration: Learning and accepting that our lives are limited and that death is an inevitable part of our lives.

Temporal integration directly confronts this organizational role of time and confronts our transient lives, in helping us to consider the deep questions of our purpose in life (see Module 22 on page 417, and Module 23 on page 435).
9. Transpirational integration: The identity of a bodily self that expands beyond the boundary of the skin, sensing our interconnection with time, place, and culture; the "integration of integration" or we-space consciousness.

Removing top-down constraints

Perceptions that enter our conscious mind through our senses are experienced as arriving from the "bottom-up." Young children are not limited or inhibited by so-called top-down constraints that are created through past experiences and judgments. For them, information from the senses flows freely from the bottom-up. Learning shapes the way we encounter bottom-up data and create top-down constraints. This means that when we perceive things that are familiar, our brains tend to push down and suffocate the experience. On one hand, this protects us from sensory overload. On the other hand, it separates us from experiencing the fullness of life in the "Now" and gives us a sense of disconnection and being out of touch with the co-creative life force. This "top-down" way makes us miss out on the fullness of life.

As we get older, this suffocation increases and may make our lives seem dull. We lose the sense of wonder and excitement of being alive and the connectedness with everything that arises in the world around us, including deeply resonating with other human beings. This suffocation also disconnects us from body sensations (which we may additionally distort or numb with alcohol, caffeine, or other drugs, including psychopharmaca), intuition, empathy, compassion, creativity, etc., and thus from love and from our purpose. Through mindful awareness, we practice diminishing the top-down constraints and so may connect more consciously to our inner and outer world, transcend our separate and false sense of self, and feel more fully alive and connected to others and the world.

Purpose and application of the module

1. Understand what people mean when they use the term spiritual.
2. Understand and experience the difference between temporary states of consciousness and permanently accessible stages of spiritual and other developmental lines.
3. Differentiate between the subject (or self/witness) and objects in consciousness.
4. Understand the difference between healthy differentiation, disidentification, and integration versus fusion, dissociation, splitting off, repressing, denying, ignoring, and projecting.
5. Stop creating your own suffering and that of others by relinquishing desire, attachment, delusion, and hatred.
6. Experience and integrate the five levels of spiritual realization (gross, subtle, causal, and pure witness) in nondual awareness through a guided meditation.
7. Explore how these five state-stages of spiritual realization (waking up) are interpreted by people from their level of consciousness development or maturity (growing up).
8. Stop conflating spiritual development with consciousness development.
9. Locate yourself and your partner in the Wilber-Combs Lattice/Matrix, on page 213, by noticing what you are defensive about and what you identify with.
10. Avoid spiritual bypassing and spiritual materialism.
11. Learn about the benefits of mindfulness practices and therapy.
12. Integrate the embodied feminine polarities of descending and communion with the transcendent masculine polarities of ascending and agency.

Exercises: Spiritual development

The following are an individual and a paired exercise.
1. Prepare a bowl with raisins, a bell or singing bowl, and a clock/timer to facilitate this exercise.
2. Print out the worksheets.
3. Make the four agreements for confidentiality, responsibility, I-statements, and sharing, as outlined on page 556.

Exercise one: Desire, attachment, delusion, hatred

This optional exercise illustrates how quickly we desire what others have; how quickly we get attached to what we have; how we can be delusional/judgmental; and how we can develop hatred or aversion if we feel treated unfairly. Desire, attachment, and hatred (along with delusion and ignorance) are often referred to in Buddhism as the three poisons of the mind that cause suffering or duhkha.[167]

1. Ask the practitioners what they are aware of (sometimes called what they are conscious of) in this moment. They may mention items in the room, body sensations, thoughts, feelings, world events, knowledge, understanding, etc.
2. Point out that there are things or "objects in consciousness" and a self or subject that is aware or conscious of things/objects.
3. To give the practitioners an experience of desire, attachment, delusion, hatred/aversion, pass around a bowl with raisins.
4. Ask everyone to carefully pick one raisin that they feel called to and that reflects their personality, and to hold it in their hand.
5. As the bowl is passed around, tell one person that they do not get a raisin and to pass the bowl to the next person.
6. Once everyone has taken a raisin, ask the person whom you singled out how he or she felt.
7. Ask everyone in the group how they felt about you singling out one of the practitioners.

8. Ask the person next to you to show you their raisin and then take it away from him or her.
9. Ask how he or she feels.
10. Offer the person who was singled out earlier to take as many raisins as he or she wants and point out that now others may feel treated unfairly because they got only one.
11. Explain that suffering is created through desire for, attachment to, delusion about, and hatred of things — in this case, the raisin. Most practitioners will get the point.
12. Invite the practitioners to consciously observe the raisin in their hand and become fully present with it. They may also focus on physical objects around the room or on a candle or other item, maybe on an altar, for a minute or two.
13. Ask the practitioners to notice how their mind verbally labels objects (the raisin).
14. Ask what they see when they suspend the concept of raisin? Does their mind see or label it as something else (a stone, a small brain, etc.)?
15. What happens if they suspend any labeling?
16. Point out that they, as a consciousness, self, awareness, or witness are not (defined by) the objects they are aware of, desire, possess, are attached to, or hate (reject).
17. Ask practitioners to close their eyes or to lower their gaze and to put the raisin into their mouth and roll it around for a while.
18. Invite them to gently bite on it and sense the sweet taste of glucose molecules interacting with their taste buds, to feel the saliva rushing into their mouth, to notice the sweet juice going down their throat/esophagus, and the glucose entering their bloodstream.
19. Ask the practitioners to feel the object dissolve in their mouth.

Integral Relationship Practice | 228

Exercise two: Guided meditation

Invite the practitioners to the guided subject-object mindfulness meditation as described in the Preliminary Module on page 16, in which they experience four of the five state-stages of spiritual realization by strengthening the witness (self, subject, or consciousness) that is or becomes aware of objects in consciousness through differentiation and disidentification (not dissociation, repression, splitting off).

Exercise three: Spiritual bypassing

Robert Augustus Masters describes the following aspects of spiritual bypassing in his excellent and highly recommended book, *Spiritual Bypassing: When Spirituality Disconnects Us from What Really Matters.*

1. Exaggerated detachment
2. Emotional numbing and repression
3. Overemphasis on the positive
4. Anger phobia
5. Blind or overly tolerant compassion
6. Weak or too-porous boundaries
7. Lopsided development (cognitive intelligence often being far ahead of emotional and moral intelligence)
8. Debilitating judgment about one's negativity or shadow elements
9. Devaluation of the personal relative to the spiritual
10. Delusions of having arrived at a higher level of being or enlightenment

Give a brief description for each aspect and then either pair up practitioners to share about their experience with each of them or invite group sharing and discussion.

Follow-up questions

1. How do you feel after the meditation?
2. What states (gross, subtle, causal, pure witness) did you experience during the meditation?
3. What are you attached to; what do you desire/need; what do you hate or reject; what are you delusional about?
4. What do you have control over as the subject? Your body? Your mind? Your feelings (including spiritual experiences)?
5. What forms of spiritual bypassing have you engaged in?
6. How have the state-stages of spiritual experience and realizations, your level of consciousness development, and spiritual bypassing in you and your partner(s) impacted your love relationship(s)?

Worksheets: Spiritual development

You may print the Wilber-Combs Lattice/Matrix, on page 213, and the 10 forms of spiritual bypassing above.

Additional information and resources

Religions

Each religion has a gross (materialistic/atheistic), subtle (polytheistic/psychic), causal (monotheistic/divine), and pure witness (mystical/spiritual) branch, as shown below. So we can't simply assume that religious people are all at a mythic level of consciousness development or have magical beliefs in Gods or spirits.

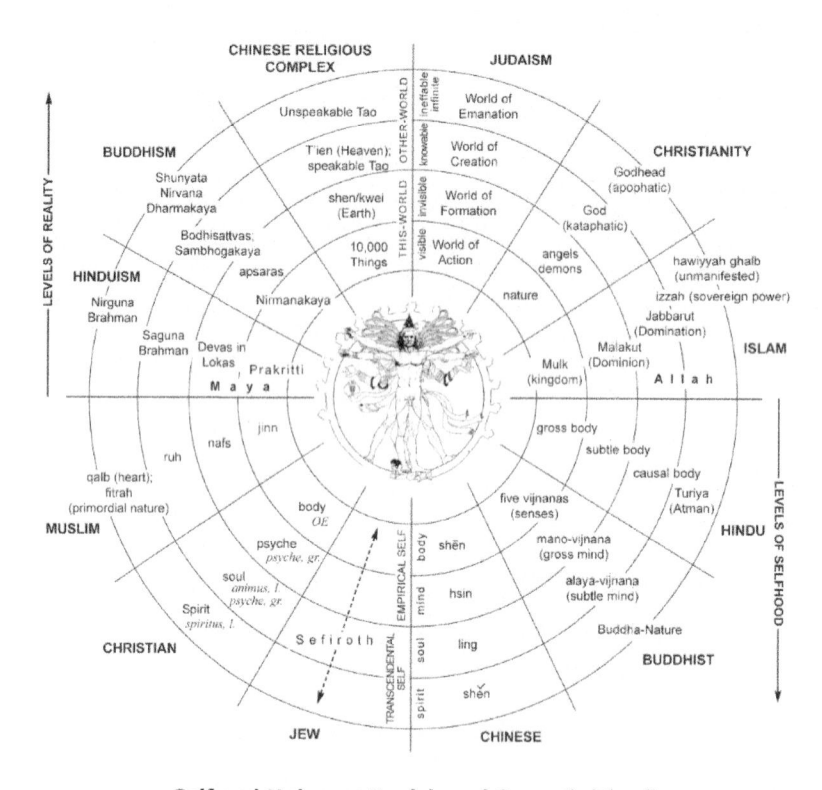

Self and Universe Envisioned Cross-Culturally
(from Huston Smith)

Figure 37: Four levels of selfhood and reality in religions

Books

The Power of Now: A Guide to Spiritual Enlightenment (2004) by Eckhart Tolle
tinyurl.com/irpm341[168]

Integral Spirituality: A Startling New Role for Religion in the Modern and Postmodern World (2007) by Ken Wilber
tinyurl.com/irpm343[169]

Integral Meditation: Mindfulness as a Way to Grow Up, Wake Up, and Show Up in Your Life (2016) by Ken Wilber

tinyurl.com/irpm344[170]

Cutting Through Spiritual Materialism (2002) by Chögyam Trungpa
tinyurl.com/irpm345[171]

SQ21: The Twenty-One Skills of Spiritual Intelligence (2012) by Cindy Wigglesworth
tinyurl.com/irpm347[172]

Spiritual Bypassing: When Spirituality Disconnects Us from What Really Matters (2010) by Robert Augustus Masters
tinyurl.com/irpm349[173]

Love and Awakening: Discovering the Sacred Path of Intimate Relationship (1997) by John Welwood
tinyurl.com/irpm351[174]

Journey of the Heart: The Path of Conscious Love (1996) by John Welwood
tinyurl.com/irpm352[175]

Toward a Psychology of Awakening: Buddhism, Psychotherapy, and the Path of Personal and Spiritual Transformation (2002) by John Welwood
tinyurl.com/irpm354[176]

Perfect Love, Imperfect Relationships: Healing the Wound of the Heart (2007) by John Welwood
tinyurl.com/irpm355[177]

Evolutionary Enlightenment: A New Path to Spiritual Awakening (2011) by Andrew Cohen. The book fails to establish ethical and moral norms and the importance of procreation for human evolution, but takes enlightenment teachings to an important new level.
tinyurl.com/irpm356[178]

The Neurobiology of "We": How Relationships, the Mind, and the Brain Interact to Shape Who We Are (Sounds True Audio Learning Course) Unabridged Edition (2008) by Daniel Siegel, MD
tinyurl.com/irpm359[179]

Links to articles about the health benefits of meditation and mindfulness:
www.newsweek.com/topic/mindfulness
tinyurl.com/irpm361[180]

Sex Purpose Love book reference
Page 62–69

Suggested movie: *I Heart Huckabees* (2004)

Watch this chaotic, funny, and thought-provoking spiritual/philosophical comedy to see elements of desire, attachment, delusions, and hatred at the gross, subtle, causal, and pure witness level of spiritual development come into paradoxical conflicts with each other.

The plot follows "existential" detectives Bernard Jaffe (Dustin Hoffman) and his wife, Vivian (Lily Tomlin), who are hired to investigate certain events and the possible underlying meanings in the lives of their clients Albert Markovski (Jason Schwartzman), Tommy Corn (Mark Wahlberg), Brad Stand (Jude Law), and Dawn Campbell (Naomi Watts). Vivian and Bernard are of the general Buddhist view that everything is connected and has meaning, and that our ego and unconscious separates us from this realization, thus creating suffering.

As the different investigations cross paths and chaos ensues, their former student and now rival and nemesis, Caterine Vauban (Isabelle Huppert), enters the scene. She drags Albert and Tommy into her nihilistic and cynical view that life is nothing but cruelty, manipulation, meaninglessness, and suffering that cannot be escaped and so is best endured by being present in the now and surrendering to what is—which leads to pure being (reminiscent of Eckhart Tolle).

At the end of the movie, the potential of a synthesis between the two opposing views emerges.

Practice Module 13
Sexual Development

I am not saying renounce sex, I am saying transform it. It need not remain just biological: bring some spirituality to it. While making love, meditate too. While making love, be prayerful. Love should not be just a physical act; pour your soul into it.
~ Osho ~

Module description

Learn and practice how to identify five state-stages of sexual development, ranging from repressed to sacred, tantric, and transcendent. Understand why it is vital for thriving love relationships that couples move towards the fourth "making love" stage—in which sexuality becomes an expression of their vitality, deep care, and heart connection—and on to stage five of sacred sexuality.

Agree with your partner to reserve regular and ample time for your lovemaking in order to create a warm and intimate environment and to practice how to get each other "in the mood." Engage in ongoing learning about your own and your partner's sexual preferences and desires; expand your sexual boundaries in healthy ways; heal emotional wounds and trauma; transcend fears and shame around your sexuality; and keep advancing your love life to keep it vital and exciting.

Advance to stage five, in which sexuality becomes a part of your spiritual practice and deep soul connection with your partner. Practice how to become fully embodied and present with each other through ecstatic dancing to different rhythms (soul motion or 5Rhythms); shared meditation; prolonged eye gazing; breathing together into your seven chakras; chanting and praying together; giving and receiving tantric massages; making love with eyes open in the lotus position; and moving kundalini energy up your spine.

Join us for an intimate partner meditation, sensual unconditional touch, and a verbal exploration of the five state-stages of sexual development through questions and answers. Identify the state-stage of your own and your partner's sexual development and realize your sexual learning, healing, growing, and awakening potentials.

Introduction

In the Integral Relationship model, we identify five state-stages of sexual development, from repressed to fucking, having sex, making love, and sacred/tantric/transcendent. Like the temporary states of spiritual experiences, the higher states of sexual experience are "free," as they can arise spontaneously in lovers at any level of vertical structure stages of consciousness development that have to be "earned" through personal growth work. These states can then be made into permanently accessible state-stages through practice.

Four dimensions of integral sexuality

As shown below, integral sexuality includes awareness and practices in all four dimensions of our being and relating (quadrants):

1. In the Upper Left "I" singular interior quadrant, we locate our spiritual practice, balancing and harmonizing healthy feminine and masculine polarities, shadow and trauma work, gender identity, etc.
2. In the Upper Right "It" singular exterior quadrant, we locate setting aside ample time for lovemaking, physical exercise, nutrition, rest, hygiene, PC muscle strengthening, sexual preferences, dancing, eye gazing, showering or bathing together, exchanging sensual massages, and any other behavioral physical aspects of sexual expression.
3. In the Lower Left "We" plural interior quadrant, we locate sharing of vulnerable feelings and sexual fantasies; breaking of cultural restrictions around sexual norms; sex therapy;

respecting healthy boundaries; and honoring agreements—for example, around (non)monogamy, etc.
4. In the Lower Right collective exterior quadrant, we locate creating sacred space for sexuality; wearing sarongs/pareos; using various angled sex pillows or wedges, tantra chairs, sensual foods, sex toys, massage oils, blindfolds, ties for bondage, lingerie, and other props for sensual pleasure and sexual play; reading books and watching videos about sexuality together, etc.

Figure 38: Four dimensions of integral sexuality

Five state-stages of sexual development

There are five broad state-stages of sexual development and expression that are the result of the lover's genetic makeup (e.g., libido), previous sexual experiences and practice, as well as their physical, psychological, and spiritual health.

1. Repressed sexuality

In this lowest stage, the body and sex are often viewed with suspicion and as something negative and dirty. Usually driven by repression, shame, guilt, and fear that originate from childhood trauma and abuse, or by a very low libido (lowered levels of testosterone in males and estrogen in females), adults at this level avoid sexual activities altogether or perform them out of duty in a dissociated way with eyes closed, under the sheets, in the dark. Oral sex or similarly playful sensual activities are usually out of the question for couples at this stage, where modesty is confused with shame.

2. Fucking

In the fucking stage, sexuality is animalistic, self-serving, and limited to the purely physical pleasures of the body, often only for one partner. Partners and fuck buddies at this stage tend to objectify each other without seeking a deeper personal and emotional connection. They want to have fun, even at the other's expense, "get off," and usually don't care much about their partner's physical needs, boundaries, feelings, or sexual desires. There is no shame or guilt, and "everything goes," an aspect that can be confused with the higher, unrestrained forms of transcendent sexuality and consensual passionate ravishing. In this stage, males may dominate and manipulate females into having intercourse and engaging in hurtful practices such as unwanted anal sex, or deep throating/gagging.

Thus, in the fucking stage, everything is seen as acceptable, as long as the partner seemingly cooperates—or, at least, does not call the police. Rarely is there a prior conversation about consent, sexual preferences, sexual history, sexually transmitted diseases (STD's), no-no's, safe words, expectations about the relationship afterwards, or possible consequences such as emotional/sexual dependence or pregnancy. Women at this stage may have an unspoken expectation that their partner will make an exclusive commitment after intercourse and feel used and abused if he simply moves on or is not monogamous. Women may also become nonconsensually pregnant to "hook" a partner and/or to collect child support and social security payments.

Once the excitement of the newness of a sexual partner wanes or vanishes, couples in this stage often lose interest in sex with each other and either stop having sex or seek a new fuck buddy.

3. Having sex

In this stage, partners go beyond the purely physical aspects of sexuality (fucking). They see each other as human subjects, and consent comes into play. Sex becomes a conscious choice between couples that have a mutual understanding and agreement about the implications and consequences of becoming sexual. Having sex is seen as a beautiful and important activity which brings two people closer together and provides many physical and emotional health benefits.[181] There is usually an agreement for monogamy or a hidden, unspoken acceptance of the various forms of non-monogamy (see below). Partners try to find the time and energy to be sexual with each other when both are in the mood. They focus on pleasing the other within the context of their respective boundaries.

All the same, this strong focus on pleasing the other can prevent the open expression of one's own sexual needs, desires, and fantasies. Not having one's sexual needs met by a partner can lead to sexuality at the lowest common denominator and leave both partners unfulfilled and wanting over time.

At this stage, relationship difficulties such as power struggles, conflicts, or emotional withdrawal tend to be carried into the bedroom but don't get resolved there. Instead of addressing deeper underlying relationship issues, couples may try to improve their sexual play through new positions or locations, engage in role playing, apply sex toys, watch porn movies, or join swinger clubs to keep their sex life interesting. Unless they evolve to the next higher stage of sexual development, merely having sex will eventually turn stale, cease completely, or become so difficult that their partnership ends when one of them falls in love/lust with a new sex partner.

4. Making love

In the lovemaking stage, a couple's sexuality becomes the expression of their genuine love, mutual acceptance, deep emotional intimacy, and the joy and gratitude of being together. Body, mind, and heart become integrated in their lovemaking, which is no longer just "a thing that couples do" but an expression of who they are as loving, caring, sexual human beings. No special effort to find the time or energy to get into the mood and being sexual needs to be made by them. Their lovemaking becomes a life-enhancing and rejuvenating affirmation of their bond and the depth of their connection. They are open to talking about their desires and exploring all forms of healthy sexual play that brings pleasure to each other and deepens their union. They naturally stay in verbal and nonverbal communication (eye contact, focusing on the breath, etc.) with each other during their lovemaking.

Sex at this level is not used to cover up conflicts, keep score, or manipulate each other. Instead, sexual and emotional blocks that may arise are worked out between them, and therapeutic help is sought if they can't resolve the challenges they may face in and outside the bedroom.

5. Sacred tantric transcendent sexuality

This stage represents all advanced sacred, transcendent, and tantric sexual practices that lead to spiritual state-stage experiences through sexual union, such as Kundalini[182] awakenings, which transcend the lovers' sense of separation from each other and the universe. This kind of sexuality emerges as a state-stage between partners who share a deep soul connection; enjoy a high level of physical, emotional, and relational health; and have reached an advanced stage of spiritual development (see Module 12: Spiritual development), with the ability for intense presence and full surrender. Spiritual practices such as shared meditation, partner yoga, and ecstatic dance are often interwoven into this form of lovemaking.

Partners who consciously engage in transcendent sexuality allocate ample quality time for their lovemaking (instead of waiting until they are in the mood), create a sacred space in their home or away (think of a tastefully decorated warm room, soft sheets, dimmed lights, scented candles, burning incense, veils around the bed, oils and lotions, soft sacred music, etc.), and co-create a wide range of experiences through rituals such as sharing sensual food (think strawberries, chocolate, ice-cream, etc.); eye gazing; erotic dance; synchronized conscious breathing into the seven chakra; reciting of mantras; reading of poems; alternate giving and receiving of sensual touch and massage; playfulness with objects (think feathers, boas, silk, flower petals, ice cubes); gentle intercourse; or unrestrained consensual ravaging, which may be falsely interpreted as a form of rape.

A common position for deep tantric connection is for the man to sit cross-legged (or on a chair) and the woman on top of him, allowing them to meet each other face-to-face as opposites and equals. The goal of transcendent sexuality is not solely to derive pleasure and to reach orgasms, but to move (Kundalini) energy up the spine or through the seven chakras and to deepen the soul connection between the lovers that leads them to consciously experience the divine, instead of unconsciously exclaiming, "oh my God," during a short orgasmic release. This requires the ability for men to delay or avoid orgasm, and/or to have orgasms without ejaculating by squeezing their PC muscle.[183] Often, deeply rooted emotional blocks that are embedded in the body and inhibit a further spiritual awakening are revealed and can be released through transcendent sex. In fact, a University of California–Davis study showed that deeply connected lovers unconsciously sync their heart rates and breathe in and out at the same intervals.[184]

Sexual Wilber-Combs Lattice or Matrix

Similar to the spiritual Wilber-Combs Lattice/Matrix, on page 213, that outlines how individuals at any level of vertical consciousness development can experience advanced spiritual states and then interpret those states from their level of consciousness, advanced sexual states can be temporarily experienced in the same way. This is important to realize, as many people falsely assume that if someone is highly developed sexually, he or she is also consciously developed and psychologically healthy (which is often not the case).

To make these temporary sexual states permanently accessible as state-stages requires work and practice, such as meditation, yoga, opening of the seven chakras, possibly therapy to heal sexual wounds and trauma, physical exercise, healthy nutrition, detoxification, and sexual practice.

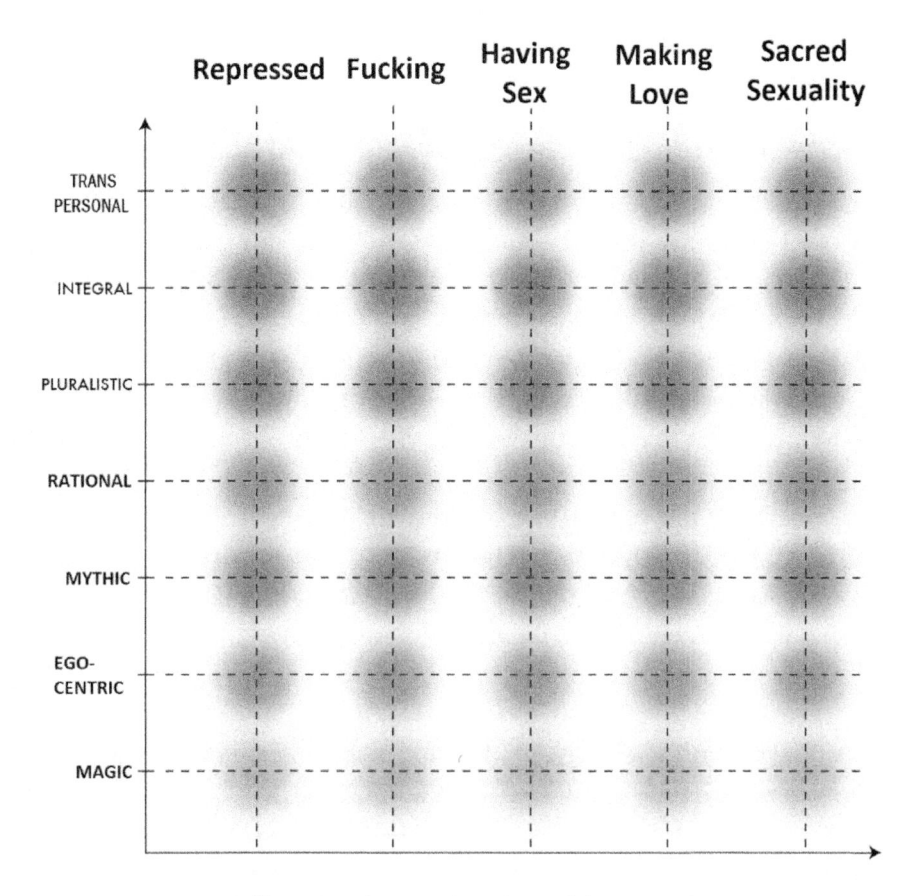

Figure 39: Wilber-Combs matrix adopted for sexual state-stages

Personality matrix

Accordingly, we place the five sexual state-stages on a horizontal axis in the Integral Relationship Personality Matrix, as shown in *Figure 30: Personality matrix,* on page 187.

We now see that there is a big difference between growing up, cleaning-up (doing shadow and trauma work, and dealing with other unresolved developmental issues, including personality disorders), waking up, and the sexual state-stages (except for sacred sexuality, which also requires at least a subtle level of spiritual realization). Realizing this is especially important between lovers at the preconventional and postconventional stages of consciousness development as described under Pre/post fallacy in love relationships on page 185.

Purpose and application of the module

1. Realize that bringing awareness into all four dimensions of our being and relating (quadrants) at the making love or higher stage of sexuality is essential for an Integral Relationship.
2. Learn about the importance and benefits of a healthy sex life for your physical, mental, emotional, and spiritual health.
3. Learn about the five state-stages of sexuality, from repressed to transcendent/sacred/tantric.
4. Transform temporary sexual state experiences into permanently accessible state-stages.
5. Balance and harmonize healthy feminine and masculine polarities to create sexual attraction and flow.
6. Create and deepen intimacy and trust between you and your partner.
7. Have an intimate conversation about your and your partner's sexuality, including desires and fantasies.
8. Notice your and your partner's state-stage of sexual development and realize that sexuality usually takes place at the lowest common denominator.
9. Create environments and engage in practices that allow for elevated sexual state experiences that can be transformed into permanently accessible state-stages.
10. Heal sexual trauma and wounds (see for example the book, *Passionate Marriage*, by David Schnarch.)
11. Expand your sexual horizons through play.

Exercises: Sexual development

The following is a paired exercise.
It takes the practitioners through four phases to create a safe container and heart connection in order to explore the five state-stages of sexual development.

1. Prepare a bell and clock/timer to facilitate the exercise.
2. Print out the worksheet.
3. Have tissues (Kleenex) available, as participants may tear up during the exercise.
4. Ask couples to do the exercise together.
5. Ask the other practitioners to choose a partner with whom they feel safe and comfortable—ideally of the opposite sex, for heterosexual participants.
6. Invite the practitioners to sit on the floor or chairs, with enough space to first sit across from each other and then, in the third phase of the exercise, next to each other's right side.
7. Make the agreements for confidentiality, responsibility, healthy boundaries, I-statements, and group sharing, as outlined on page 556.

Phase one

Invite the practitioners to sit across from each other on cushions (half or full lotus position, if possible) or on chairs so that their knees (almost) touch and they can comfortably look into each other's eyes.

Like the exercise about spiritual development, begin with a guided subject-object meditation in which the practitioners strengthen the witness (the self, or subject, or consciousness) by becoming fully present with the material, physical, mental, emotional/feeling, and "spiritual" mystical dimensions of their being. This allows them to disidentify from these dimensions (not dissociate or repress) and then integrate them in their sexuality.

See page 12 for the guided meditation, which you may modify by pointing out that disidentifying from their body, mind, and challenging emotions allows the practitioners to release any fear or shame around their sexuality.

Phase two

After the meditation with closed eyes or lowered gaze (about 20–30 minutes), invite the practitioners to remain fully present in the here and now, and to gently look into their partner's left eye in a quiet, calm, and relaxed way for 10–15 minutes without drifting off into thought about the past, future, or daydreams until you ring the bell.

Phase three

Begin by playing soft music (e.g., Jim Wilson "Northern Seascape" album). tinyurl.com/irpm32[185]
or tinyurl.com/irpm41[186]

Invite the partners to move next to each other on their right side so that their thighs gently touch each other.

Ask them to continue to look into each other's eyes.

Invite the partners with the shorter hair to ask the partners with the longer hair for a nonverbal permission (by nodding their head, etc.) to hold their right hand between his or her hands (which is usually granted).

Invite the partners with the shorter hair to gently turn their partner's hand so that they can see the palm of the hand and ask for a nonverbal permission to stroke the hand tenderly.

When permission is given, ask the recipients of the touch to close their eyes, to continue to consciously breathe in and out, and to receive this nonsexual, unconditional touch as a gift for which nothing needs to be given back or done.

Tell the partners who provide the nonsexual, unconditional touch to stroke the hand gently and tenderly, to notice the lines in the hand, and to become aware of what this hand may have done in its life and never received any recognition for. Mention the following as examples:

1. Prepared a meal.
2. Gave another person a healing touch.
3. Planted a tree.
4. Wrote a love letter.
5. Held a newborn child.
6. Gave a relaxing massage
7. Held a lost child by the hand.

8. Gave a dying person soothing a touch.
9. Nursed a sick person back to health.
10. Played a musical instrument.
11. Painted a picture.
12. Wrote a love letter or poem.
13. Repaired something.

Then invite the partners who provide the touch to gently turn the hand over, and to stroke the back of the hand slowly, respectfully, and tenderly.

After a few minutes, ask the giving partner to stop the touching and to hold the hand of the receiving partner between his or her hands.

Invite the couple to look lovingly into each other's eyes again, sending a nonverbal "thank you for allowing me to give you this gift of nonsexual, unconditional touch" to the receiving partner and a nonverbal "thank you for giving me this gift of nonsexual, unconditional touch" to the sending partner.

Invite the couples to hug each other and to whisper a "thank you" and other appreciations into each other's ears. They may also say things like "thank you for your care (or presence, kindness, warmth, love, tenderness, vulnerability, sensitivity, openness, receptivity, understanding, courage, or our connection)."

After the hug ends, invite the partners with the longer hair to ask the partners with the shorter hair to give a non-verbal permission (by nodding their head, etc.) to hold their right hand between his or her hands (which is usually granted.)

Repeat the exercise above after permission is given, ending with the shared hug and whispering appreciations into each other's ears.

Phase four

Invite the partners to continue holding their hands and to share about their experiences during the meditation, eye gazing, hand stroking, and hugging.

Phase five

When the couples are finished with sharing about their experiences, hand them the worksheet below, with questions about their sexuality, and ask them to share the answers with each other while staying physically connected. Allow about 30–60 minutes for the exchange and encourage the practitioners to share their appreciation afterwards.

After a short break, bring all practitioners back into a big circle again and invite them to share about their experiences and insights during all five phases (meditation, eye gazing, hand stroking, hugging, and conversation about their sexuality) with the group.

Worksheet: Sexual development

1. Please let me know if I say or ask something that is too vulnerable or intimate for you to answer.
2. How do you feel talking about your sexuality in general and with me specifically right now?
3. What is your sexual orientation?
4. What role does sexuality play for you in a partnership?
5. How do you equate sex with love and spirituality?
6. What is your definition of great sex?
7. Do you have any experiences with sacred/tantric/transcendental sexuality and, if yes, what were they?
8. Has your sexuality evolved over the years and, if yes, how?
9. Do you orgasm, how often, what makes you come, and what is the most enjoyable way for you?
10. What would you like to improve, learn, or experience around your sexuality?
11. What are sexual blocks that you are aware of and what sexual practices are not acceptable to you?
12. Under what circumstances did you withhold sex or get turned off in the past?
13. Were your sexual boundaries ever violated as a child or in your youth?

14. If yes, how has that affected your sexuality?
15. Which sexual fantasies would you like to realize?
16. What else would you like to share with me about your sexuality?

Follow-up questions

1. How do you feel after the five phases of the exercise?
2. What is the sexual state-stage (repressed, fucking, having sex, making love, sacred sexuality) that you typically co-create or experience?
3. What forms of sexual development would you like to realize?
4. How have the state-stages of sexual development in you and your partners impacted your love relationships?

Additional information and resources

Non-monogamy

It has become popular in recent years to call any form of non-monogamy polyamory.

However, as half-jokingly shown in the image below, there are many forms of consensual and nonconsensual non-monogamy, and each developmental stage has its own socially accepted forms.[187] The term and concept of polyamory (many loves) emerged in the Green pluralistic stage of development and was first outlined in a 1990 article by Morning Glory Zell-Ravenheart to describe the practice of, or desire for, intimate relationships with more than one partner, with the informed consent of all partners involved. In its original form, it was intended to be practiced in a primary, fully committed love relationship or marriage, with consensual (consensual) secondary love relationships by one or both partners as an alternative to cheating, breaking up, or repressing loving feelings and sexual attraction towards others, and included the processing and honoring of feelings and needs between all partners involved.

In an ideal situation, polyamorous relationships lead to compersion or mudita (the opposite of jealousy), terms that are used in the polyamorous scene to describe the vicarious joy associated with seeing one's partner having an exciting, loving, romantic, sexual relationship with someone else. In the worst case, it leads to polyagony,[188] a term used to describe the emotional and practical challenges experienced by partners who cannot handle the feelings of fear, shame, insecurity, abandonment, jealousy, or social discrimination of a polyamorous relationship.

From an integral perspective, authentic polyamory is a valid developmental aspect of the communal Green stage—of going broad with multiple partners (who are sometimes at the magical or egocentric stage, which creates the challenges described above) and dealing with the associated insecurities and chaos, including fear of commitment, and sometimes feeding love and sex addictions, before going deeper with one partner at the integral and later stages.

There are also practical limitations to non-monogamy, including polyamory, as it is often difficult for people at integral and higher stages to find even one compatible partner, let alone multiple lovers. Singles in second-tier consciousness usually would rather focus back on ongoing learning, healing, growing, and awakening, and living their purpose while staying fully open to be with their soulmate in order to make the world a better place, instead of self-indulging, time-consuming sexual relationships with multiple lovers.

In addition, moving towards healthy integral monogamous relationships and creating nuclear families (versus polygamy, polyamory, and other forms of non-monogamy in which men often have multiple female partners who are monogamous) creates stable communities and societies, as it allows most men to find a partner.[189]

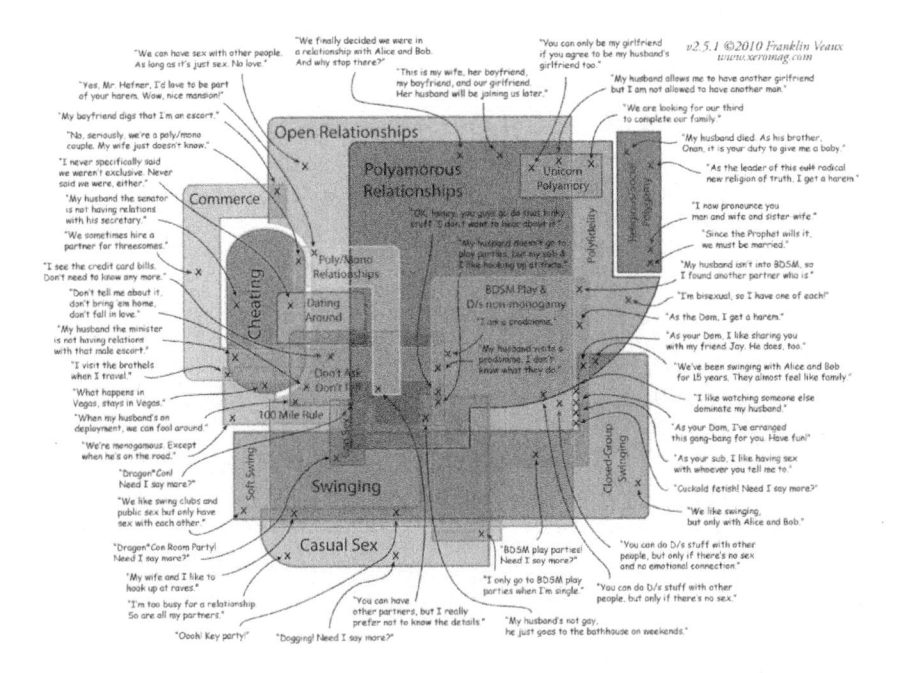

Figure 40: Forms of non-monogamy

Books

Stage 3:

Mars and Venus in the Bedroom: A Guide to Lasting Romance and Passion (2009) by John Gray
tinyurl.com/irpm363[190]

Stage 4:

Passionate Marriage: Keeping Love and Intimacy Alive in Committed Relationships (2009) by David Schnarch
tinyurl.com/irpm369[191]

Stage 5:

Transcendent Sex: When Lovemaking Opens the Veil (2004), by Jenny Wade.
tinyurl.com/irpm370[192]

Intimate Communion: Awakening Your Sexual Essence (1995) by David Deida
tinyurl.com/irpm371[193]

Finding God Through Sex: Awakening the One of Spirit Through the Two of Flesh (2005) by David Deida
tinyurl.com/irpm372[194]

Dear Lover: A Woman's Guide to Men, Sex, and Love's Deepest Bliss (2004) by David Deida
tinyurl.com/irpm374[195]

Sex Purpose Love book reference

Page 69–73

Suggested movie: *Bliss* (1997)

Watch this movie to see many elements that we explored in the previous modules and that we will address as we move forward, including the four dimensions of being and relating, levels of consciousness development, sex and gender, fear-shame downward spiral, feminine-masculine polarities, spiritual and sexual development, tantra, developmental trauma, anima/animus complex, personality types, personality disorders, psychological healing, and the seven chakras. At times, it may feel that the script was just written for us.

Bliss is a deeply emotional movie that tells the story of a couple who are in love but have many challenges, especially with their sex life. Within six months, they're telling their problems to the therapist, Alfred (Spalding Gray), who uses a traditional psychoanalytic approach. In addition, the wife, Maria (Sheryl Lee), is sneaking to secret sessions with a sex therapist named Baltazar (Terence Stamp), who "operates on the edge of the law" to heal sexual trauma. (Disclaimer: If you have experienced sexual trauma and feel vulnerable, this movie may be disturbing to watch.) Soon after, her husband, Joseph (Craig Sheffer), finds out. After an initial hostility towards Baltazar that discloses that Joseph is better than his wife at hiding his anger and other vulnerable feelings (go figure), Joseph also becomes Baltazar's client to learn about sex as bliss, which is nine on Baltazar's erotic scale and far above simple orgasm, which is around level four on the scale. Eventually, the two therapists meet and gain important information that validates each of their approaches, as Maria and Joseph heal and deepen their relationship.

Practice Module 14
Anima/Animus Complex Development

The shadow can be realized only through a relation to a partner, and anima and animus only through a relation to a partner of the opposite sex, because only in such a relation do their projections become operative.
~ Carl Gustav Jung ~

Module description

Learn and practice how to identify five possible stages of the animus complex development in females and five possible stages of anima complex development in males, and how they profoundly impact their love relationships.

Take a deep dive into your early childhood memories through a visual exercise. Realize how your gender and relationship with your mother and father caused you to repress certain traits of the opposite sex into your unconscious. See how you now unconsciously project the shadow that was created onto the opposite sex in various ways. Heal and grow to overcome this complex to co-create a healthy sustainable Integral Love Relationship with an equal and opposite partner at stage three of five stages.

Introduction

In Module 9 we differentiated between biological sex differences and learned gender roles, and in Module 11 between feminine and masculine traits. In Module 14, we make one more distinction around gender by exploring how early childhood experiences with our parents and other caregivers created various intensities of the unconscious anima/animus complex that we later project as adults onto the opposite sex in five possible stages (not state-stages) that profoundly impact our romantic love relationships.

It is important to point out that unlike other developmental lines, not everyone starts out in stage one of their anima/animus complex but may land in stage two or three as a young adult and may then advance from there.

This module is based on the book, *Female Authority*, by Polly Young-Eisendrath and Florence L. Wiedemann.

In Jungian psychology, the anima and animus are seen as the bridge to the soul. The soul is the unique core of our existence that knows nothing about the duality of the opposite sex, gender, or the feminine-masculine polarities.[196]

As our self-identification as boys or girls develops during childhood, we invariably cover up, split off, disown, repress, or dismiss qualities of the opposite sex to various degrees. Since we are all born to a mother, this intricate process is different for males and females.

Little boys soon learn that they are not like mother, painfully dissociate from her, and identify with their father and other male figures, while little girls learn that they are like her, but not like father, who becomes somewhat of a mystery to them. Carl Jung[197] discovered this split off and called the disowned feminine in males the anima, and the disowned masculine in females the animus.[198] The parts of these disowned (and therefore unconscious) realities that are not recognized and reclaimed in later life appear as inward shadows that cover parts of the soul and, consequently, become outward projections onto the opposite sex, which is called a complex.[199]

Men experience the projection of their anima when they feel a strong emotional (versus sexual or otherwise) attraction to, or threat from, a woman's feminine presence and energy. Women experience the projection of their animus when they feel a strong sexual (versus emotional or otherwise) attraction to, or threat from, a man's masculine presence and energy.[200]

If the attraction is mutual and they decide to become a couple, it will feel as if they have found and come home to their long lost other, their soulmate, or "twin flame."[201] The blissful feelings of completeness when they are harmoniously together, the longings that they feel when they are apart, and the fears of loss and abandonment that they experience when one or both withdraw are expressed in the lyrics of many love songs, such as "when I found you, there was no more emptiness inside" or "if you leave me now, you take away the biggest part of me" or "this is it, I finally found the one who makes me feel complete," and are represented in movie dialogues such as "I love you, you complete me" and "you had me at hello."[202]

Lovers with these experiences have fallen in love with a partner who has a compatible anima/animus complex. These relationships can be healthy and sustainable, especially between couples in stages three and five, if the couple is at the same level of development in other crucial lines that we explored above; knows how to resolve conflicts and return to love; avoids the fear-shame downward spiral; and shares the same purpose, as described in Modules 22 and 23. Relationships often end when one partner advances to the next stage of his or her anima/animus complex development, or evolves in other developmental lines and leaves the other behind.

At this point, you may give only a brief overview—without too much detail of the five stages of anima complex development in females and anima stages in males—to allow practitioners to first have experiences during the exercise without overanalyzing or starting inquisitive discussions and stirring up premature questions.

Purpose and application of the module

1. Learn about the five stages of the anima complex in males, and animus complex in females.
2. Remember your relationship with your parents and other caregivers during your childhood.
3. See how their relationship with each other and with you shaped how you relate with the opposite sex as an adult.

Integral Relationship Practice | 258

4. Learn about the childhood experiences of your partner and clients.
5. Identify your own, your partner's, and your client's level of anima/animus complex development.
6. Understand that the complex creates not only attraction but also conflict, especially between partners at different levels of their anima/animus complex development.
7. Realize why it is almost impossible to have a committed healthy love relationship with a partner in stage four.
8. Heal your own anima/animus complex to move towards stage five and support others in their development.

Exercise: Anima/animus complex

The following is an individual and a paired exercise.
1. The practitioners will first make a drawing and then share about their childhood experience with their partner.
2. Print out the worksheet below.
3. Make the four agreements for confidentiality, responsibility, healthy boundaries, I-statements, and sharing, as outlined on page 556.
4. Place multiple crayons of different colors (about 6–10 crayons for each participant) and blank paper in the middle of the room.
5. Have paper tissues/Kleenex ready (practitioners may cry during the exercise).
6. Ask practitioners to choose a partner. Couples should do this exercise together.
7. Ask practitioners to remember as far back as possible into their childhood, thinking about how they felt in relationship to their primary caregivers and other family members at the dinner or lunch table.
8. Demonstrate how you want them to draw the dinner table and all people around it, including themselves, in different colors, sizes, shapes, positions, and distance from the table, to represent the perceived energy of each person. They may also

draw lines between the people that represent their connections and energies.
9. Ask the practitioners to withdraw into a quiet space (maybe even outside the workshop room) to make the drawing.
10. Play soft instrumental music.
11. Tell the practitioners to rejoin their partners when they are both finished with the drawing and to explain their drawings to each other. Who are the people on the table? Why are they drawn that way? What is the relationship between them as perceived and remembered?
12. Hand out the participant worksheet below and ask the practitioners to answer the questions.
13. When they are finished, they may do the following additional exercise: The partner of a woman asks, "What is a man?" The woman gives a spontaneous **one-word!** answer without thinking or conceptualizing. Then partner one asks again, in a different tone of voice, "What is a man?" and the woman gives another one-word answer in the same way. This continues until words become repetitive, until she needs to think, or until no more words are coming. Then they switch, and partner two asks the question. If his or her partner is a man, the question is "What is a woman?"
14. Also see the "filler" exercises/additional questions at the end of the worksheet below.
15. Invite shares and answer questions.
16. Explain how the anima/animus complex development unfolds in stages (not related to spiritual or sexual state-stages) independently from consciousness development, as shown in the Personality Matrix and as described below under additional resources.

Figure 41: Examples of lunch/dinner table drawings

Worksheet: Anima/animus complex

1. How did your mother (or female caregiver) feel about being your mother?
2. How did your father (or male caregiver) feel about being your father?
3. What were significant disappointments or trauma you endured during childhood?
4. How do your parent's feelings about you and your childhood experiences affect your relationships with the opposite sex today?
5. What is attractive and challenging about the opposite sex for you?
6. What are your fantasies, desires, demands, expectations, and requirements that you project onto a (potential) partner? He/she must/should be ….
7. When are you able to trust the opposite sex?

8. What is a man/woman? (Wait for instructions.)[v]

For the back of the worksheet:

- Stage 1: Males as alien outsider: she fears, hates, and is strangely attracted to them.
- Stage 2: Males as father, God, or king: she wants their approval.
- Stage 3: Male as hero: she wants to look up to him (marry up to him).
- Stage 4: Males as independent beings: she wants to find out who she is outside of male relationships.
- Stage 5: Male as equal partner: she sees him as an equal and opposite partner.

- Stage 1: Female as mother: he wants a mommy to take care of him.
- Stage 2: Females as sex objects: he wants them to admire him and be sexually submissive.
- Stage 3: Female as supportive partner: he wants her to be his caring, loving wife who he protects and provides for.
- Stage 4: Females as creative/spiritual guides: they challenge him to find meaning/love from a source other than women.
- Stage 5: Female as equal partner: he sees her as an equal and opposite partner.

Additional or filler questions

Below are additional questions you can use at the end of most of the following exercises to explore more deeply or to fill the time for couples in groups who finish early with the main questions.

1. What do you like about being in a love relationship?
2. What do you not like about being in a love relationship?
3. What do you like about being single?

---

[v] See instruction above, under step 13 of the exercise description.

4. What do you not like about being single?
5. What attracted you to your former partner(s)?
6. Why did the relationship(s) end?
7. Who ended the relationship(s)?
8. What did you learn from the ending of the relationship(s)?
9. What do you want to do differently in your next relationship(s)?

Follow-up questions

1. How do you feel after this exercise? What insights have you gained?
2. In what stage of anima/animus complex are you and your current or former partner?
3. How have your own and your partner's anima/animus complex impacted your relationships?
4. What healing and growth potentials around your anima/animus complex would you like to realize?
5. What kind of support would you need to move towards stage three or five?

Additional information and resources

The five stages of the anima/animus complex development that are outlined below provide you with a generalizing orientation of a woman's animus and a man's anima development and how they may evolve in the future. As you read through the descriptions, one or more stages may resonate with your own level of development and that of your current or former partners. Note how stage five is almost identical for both sexes. Also remember that not everyone starts out in stage one but may land in stage two or even three as a young adult.

Stages of animus complex development in women

1. Men as alien outsiders

She fears, hates, and is strangely curious about him.

Because of abuse or abandonment from men with whom she identified during childhood, such as her father, a fatherly figure, older brother, male relative, or family friend, a woman in this stage completely denies and suppresses her animus as alien inside and outside of herself. She trusts her mother and other females, while she distrusts, hates, or fears men. This is often countered by a strange curiosity about men, which confuses her and the men she tries to date.

This ambivalence can make her extremely seductive, needy, and clingy, and can cause severe symptoms of the "seduce-and-withhold" syndrome. As soon as a man gets close to her, she withdraws, only to come back to ask for more after he becomes distant. She can break the heart of a weak man, who tries to prove that he is different, attempts to rescue her from her fears, and so becomes codependent as she lures him into her pathological cat-and-mouse game.

Within the limits of her domain in household, family, and female-oriented work environment (e.g., schoolteacher, nurse, artist, gardener, therapist, healer, animal-care worker, etc.), such a woman may seem grounded and self-confident. Outside those limits, she leaves the work and responsibility for creating thriving communities and functional societies to men and to psychologically healthier women.

2. Men as father, God, or king

She wants his approval.

The self-esteem of a woman in this stage is directly connected to the response and approval that she receives from men. She is often driven by a need to be seen as the most attractive female, and constantly monitors her value by her internalized masculine judgment and through externalized male reflection. This may lead to a split in her personality when at times she imitates male behavior in order to be liked by men, and at other times presents herself as a sexually seductive femme fatale (such as in the movie, *Basic Instinct*) to be desired.

She either hides behind a feminine mask of beautiful appearance, a graceful, charming manner, and entertaining wit, or she develops a tomboyish attitude through teasing, competing, and challenging, or some other facade that suggests success. Women in this stage gravitate towards men whom they perceive to be more attractive, intelligent, and exciting than they themselves could ever be. They often try to live up to desirable men's expectations of the perfect mate through dietary restrictions, vigorous physical exercise, cosmetic surgery, adaptation to men's intellectual interests, development of new talents, and sexual availability.

If a woman remains in this stage, she is at great risk of entering a profound depression when her beauty and sexual attractiveness wane, and the number of heads that she turns and men who admire her diminishes.

She may then isolate herself from all intimate relationships because her perfectionism overrides her ability to be compassionate and to forgive her own and others' mistakes. This may lead her to withdraw into a cold and bitter self-denial in which her anxieties create all kinds of psychosomatic illnesses, such as panic attacks, vomiting, heart problems, fatigue, and body aches.

A strong, conscious, and patient man (or a good psychotherapist) can support a woman in this stage to find her own worth, passions, and identity—independent of male approval—which then allows her to enter stage three of her animus complex development.

3. Men as hero

She wants him to take care of her.

A woman in stage three wants a man as a protector and provider, with strength, courage, and ability, who can meet her needs, cherish her, and marry her. He represents her ideal (if often unrealistic) image of the knight in shining armor who fulfills her expectations for good looks, intelligence, solid reputation, stable finances, generosity, loyalty, humor, kindness, care, integrity, and faithfulness.

To be in a good bargaining position, this woman will focus on her appearance, health, and fitness, and will adapt to the world of men by seeking a higher education, pursuing a career, fighting for social justice, or saving a failing business. She will appear as self-affirming and expects something in return. She functions well in the competitive world of men, sees herself as equal, is willing to share responsibilities, and will contribute and perform as long as her partner is able to provide more in return—as she wants to marry up in social status.

As long as he meets her expectations for financial security, social status, and devotion, she will support him to achieve his full potential, while often denying such achievements to herself. This can lead later to feelings of resentment and anger when she sees that she has been "denied" the right to experience her own competence, and when her partner/husband fails to live up to her ever-growing expectations for more (the bigger house, car, vacation, career, income, etc.)

Some women in this stage will enter an inward journey once they acknowledge the transitory nature of their physical attractiveness, question their ability to succeed with men, bump up against the limitations of finding acceptance in the male world, or hit the proverbial glass ceiling. This may lead women to the restoration of their female authority as they take responsibility for their own identity and move into stage four of their animus complex development.

4. Men as independent beings

She wants her independence.

A woman in stage four makes an active choice in favor of her self-interest and self-fulfillment, independent of men, a partner, or husband. This transition takes place with the realization that she has constructed her own experiences throughout her lifetime in relationship to men, and now wants to find her own identity. She will stop trying to be perfect in all things to please her partner (who was a heroic father figure in the previous stage), as she becomes emotionally free from his approval and support. Having discovered her own source of worthiness and foundation, she is working to restore her female authority. Financial independence through her own labor or through other sources of money that are often only available to women, such as "divorcing well," alimony and child-support payments, generous lovers, support from parents, or Social Security benefits, are the prerequisite for this transition.

Men can notice when their partners enter stage four of their animus development when they start to challenge them more often, care less about their partner's needs, seek their financial independence, and refuse to take responsibility for holding the relationship together. If a man is in partnership with a woman in this stage, it is important to know that it is not his fault that her pain of staying will eventually be greater than her fear of leaving, and that there is nothing he can do but to take care of himself emotionally and sexually, protect the financial assets that are legitimately his (if necessary, with the help of a CPA or lawyer), and, if he can, support his former partner with love and compassion in her transition. Once separated and/or divorced, she will feel free from the evaluation and needs of men for the first time in her life.

These newly single women are then much occupied with challenging work, their animals (often one or more dogs who they prefer over men), their children, social activities, educational advancements, maintaining their households, hobbies, world travel, and their (mostly female) friendships. At the same time, they look down at women who show more feminine or balanced qualities and who desire to be (or are) in a committed partnership with men. To women in stage four, partnered women still seem to be in the pitiful stages two or three of dependence on male partners (which they have just escaped). However, married women may have actually advanced into stage five, which women in stage four cannot yet fathom. They discredit partnered women as unevolved and often compete socially and professionally with them in merciless ways. Women in stage four frequently break with the conventional role of a caring mother, show tough love, and feel fulfilled outside of partnerships with men.

Still, there remains an underlying fear of isolation, especially in older women, when concerns about the disappearance of their skills and autonomy during a crisis arise. This often leads to feelings of ambivalence. On one side, there is a secret longing for the stability and support that a partnership with a man could provide during times of stress, fatigue, loneliness, or desire for sex. On the other side, there is the fear of becoming emotionally dependent and enmeshed, taken advantage of, dominated, or repressed again.

Frequent complaints about the lack of good younger men who are physically fit and attractive, highly intelligent, successful, accomplished, mature, kind, loving, generous, evolved, supportive, spiritual, and available when they need/want them, but who remain flexible, undemanding, and unattached otherwise, are a hallmark of women in stage four. Becoming men-hating, die-hard singles, settling for "friends with benefits" whom they string along, or engaging in serial monogamy (calling in the "next" 'One' after "consciously uncoupling" from the previous partner) are often the only solutions that seem to resolve their dilemma.

Also see Carol Gilligan's book, *In A Different Voice*, in which she outlines in the introduction, page 20 (xx), that "men think by knowing themselves they will understand women, while women think by knowing others they will come to know themselves," and on page 16 where she quotes Virginia Woolf as saying, "It is obvious that the values of women differ very often from the values which have been made by the other sex. Naturally, this is so. Yet, it is the masculine values that prevail." Woolf adds, "As a result, women come to question the normality of their feelings and alter their judgments in deference to the opinion of others."

5. Men as equal partners

She wants him as an equal and opposite partner.

A woman in stage five of her animus development has accepted that conflict and ambivalence are intrinsic to human relationships and has realized the significance of a partnership to balance her further psychological growth and spiritual awakening. Having fully claimed her own authority after transcending her animus complex, she no longer sees men as alien, superior, inferior, or independent. She finally comes to realize that the idea of living and going at it alone was a distorted conception of human existence because no one lives alone.

She sees that in being human, we have a variety of economic, physical, sexual, psychological, and spiritual needs that cannot be met by living alone. At last, she has the insight that a balanced personality at all levels of her being always develops in a self-other conception, and never through the discovery of an independent self, which is an illusion. This woman then desires the material, intellectual, emotional, sexual, and spiritual synergy that is co-created with a man who meets her as an opposite and equal (which means opposite feminine and masculine polarities with equal levels of consciousness, rights and responsibilities). Since she may have never experienced a stage-five partnership, she needs guidance from a man in stage five of his anima development who is able to meet her in an integrally informed way. These couples can then form inter-becoming partnerships in which they heal, learn, grow, and awaken together, and enjoy family and social activities together, while contributing to the well-being of others.

Stages of anima complex development in men

1. Women as mother

He needs a mommy to take care of him.

In this first stage, a man's anima is completely tied up with the mother. She is not necessarily his personal mother but the image of a woman who is a faithful provider of nourishment, security, and love. She represents all that is natural, instinctual, and biological in a mother. A man with an anima complex of this type cannot function well without a vital connection to a woman, and easily falls prey to being controlled and exploited by her. He frequently suffers from impotence or has no sexual desire at all and is therefore called a mama's boy. This type of anima possession also manifests through fear of accidents or disease, or a dullness of personality. The Greek Sirens and the German Lorelei personify these dangerous aspects of the anima, which may even lead a man to his death through suicide over a lost love relationship.

2. Women as sex object

He wants her to make him feel good.

In the second stage, the anima is a collective sexual image. She is a Marilyn Monroe, Madonna, or Playboy model. Men in stage two are often Don Juans who see all women as sex objects, and engage in repeated sexual adventures, which sometimes develop into sexual addictions. These relationships are invariably short-lived, because he is not faithful, is always looking for his next conquest, and no woman can ever live up to his unrealistic image of the ideal female partner.

3. Women as wife

He wants her loyalty and support.

In the third stage of his anima complex development, a man becomes ready to care for a wife and be devoted to his family. He is the loving protector and provider that women in the equivalent stage three of their animus development seek. Men with this anima accept their partner as she is, as long as she fulfills her role as supportive, undemanding, caring, and faithful wife, available sex partner, and loving mother to his children. His sexuality is usually integrated into their relationship and not an autonomous function that drives him into promiscuity. He can differentiate between love and lust, which allows him to create a lasting partnership (if she stays), because he can tell the difference between making someone the object of his sexual desire and deriving the benefits of being a faithful husband to his partner.

4. Women as guide to creativity and awakening

He struggles with her need for independence.

In the fourth stage, a man's anima functions as a guide to his inner life. As women in stage four of their animus complex development become emotionally and financially independent from men, they often turn away and abandon their husbands/partners against their will. This turn of events often challenges the men who are left behind to seek other sources of appreciation, value, significance, fulfillment, happiness, aliveness, passion, joy, purpose, peace, and love outside a relationship. Through their quest, a desire often emerges to answer life's deeper questions of "who am I," "where do I come from," "why am I here," "what is the meaning of my life," "what should I do," "what is my purpose," and "where do I go."

Contemplating these questions, reading books like the one that you are holding right now, meditating, or seeking a bond with others on a similar path in men's groups, New Age churches, and personal-growth workshops allow men in this stage to bring deeper levels of their unconscious anima into awareness. As they do so, they experience a liberating process of awakening to their authentic nature, true purpose, genuine passions, and capacity to love "unconditionally"—all independently of a partnership with a woman.

On the flip side, these men may act like they are having a midlife crisis, become commitment-phobic, avoid deeper intimacy with women altogether, or engage in serial monogamy or polyamory so as to avoid sacrificing their newfound freedom or being limited by one partnership. As such, this entire experience represents only a partial awakening, as the idea of living alone is not integral or fully realized and is not the ultimate realization of human development. This partial awakening is transcended when a man enters stage five of his anima development.

5. Women as equal partner

He meets her as an opposite and equal partner.

Similar to a woman in this stage (see above), a man in stage five of his anima complex development has accepted the fact that conflicts and ambivalence are intrinsic to human relationships and sees how their resolution contributes to his ongoing healing, personal growth, and spiritual realization. He feels confident, secure, and comfortable to express his authentic sexual essence (which tends to be masculine in heterosexual men), while he embraces his feminine (anima). This self-acceptance allows him to invite differing views, experiences, and feelings of his female partner without feeling threatened, offended, or puzzled by them.

Her authentic stage-five feminine qualities naturally complement his masculinity and vice versa. Since he has found his own purposeful identity that does not depend on her inspiration, support, or approval, he appreciates his partner's independent authority and doesn't feel responsibility, shame, or insecurity if she is unhappy—even though he shows empathy, care, and devotion, and is supportive when requested—and enjoys her even more when she is happy.

He neither clings nor pushes her away, but fully opens to embrace her at all levels of their being when they are together and stays content and fulfilled when they are apart. This all-embracing equanimity allows him to enter into a mature, monogamous relationship as an opposite and equal partner, which itself opens the door to radically new life experiences, emotional healing processes, and deeper spiritual realizations, which in turn often become the foundation for altruistic acts of kindness and service towards others.

Personality Matrix

Accordingly, we place the five stages of the anima/animus complex development on a horizontal axis in the Integral Relationship Personality Matrix, as shown in *Figure 30: Personality matrix*, on page 187.

This is important to realize, as many people falsely assume that if someone has reached a higher stage of their anima/animus complex development, that they are also at a higher level of consciousness or in other developmental lines, which is not necessarily the case.

Books

Female Authority: Empowering Women Through Psychotherapy: A Jungian Approach (1990) by Polly Young-Eisendrath and Florence L. Wiedemann
tinyurl.com/irpm375[203]

In a Different Voice: Psychological Theory and Women's Development (1982/2016) by Carol Gilligan
tinyurl.com/irpm378[204]

The Way of the Superior Man: A Spiritual Guide to Mastering the Challenges of Women, Work, and Sexual Desire (1997) by David Deida
tinyurl.com/irpm383[205]

The Masculine in Relationship: A Blueprint for Inspiring the Trust, Lust, and Devotion of a Strong Woman (2019) by G. S. Youngblood
tinyurl.com/irpm386[206]

King, Warrior, Magician, Lover: Rediscovering the Archetypes of the Mature Masculine (1990) by Robert L. Moore and Douglas Gillette
tinyurl.com/irpm387[207]

Fire in the Belly: On Being a Man (1992) by Sam Keen
tinyurl.com/irpm388[208]

Iron John: A Book about Men (1990/2015) by Robert Bly
tinyurl.com/irpm389[209]

Sex Purpose Love **book reference**
Page 73–81

Suggested movie: *Marriage Story* (2019)

Watch this Oscar-nominated Netflix movie to see the story of a painful divorce between the New York-based theater director, Charlie Barber (Adam Driver), who is stuck in stage three of his anima complex development, and his wife, Nicole Barber (Scarlett Johansson), an actress originally from Los Angeles, who moved into stage four of her animus complex.

Charlie is especially clueless about the needs of his wife and the dynamic that is slowly and painfully unfolding between them, since for him everything seems to be fine in their life and marriage, as is typical for men in this stage. He simply can't understand why she needs to claim her female authority by finding her own independent identity. The movie's conclusion offers a glimpse that Charlie has moved into his anima complex stage four and has come to peace with their separation.

This movie couldn't be more perfect to illustrate the anima/animus stage three and four dynamic between a couple; it's a must-see for everyone who is in such a situation or wants to understand it better.

Practice Module 15
The Five Love Languages

Understanding the idea of types of humans was so important to our ancestors that they projected it onto the stars.
~ Mark Hezinger ~

Module description

Learn and practice how to improve your dates and love relationships by becoming aware of personality types in general and The Five Love Languages in particular.

Identify in which of five ways you and your partner naturally tend to show and receive love and appreciation. Participate in a simple test that will reveal the answer. Learn about each love language and people's different favorite expressions in a group exercise. Create a list of how you like to give and receive love and exchange it with your partner. Contemplate if you'd rather be with a partner who shares your primary and secondary love languages, or if you prefer to be with someone who complements your love languages so that you can create synergy, expand your horizon, and spice up your relationship, or if it does not matter to you one way or the other.

Send the test to your dates before you meet and gain valuable insights. Engage in great conversations about the love languages that go deeper than just talking about the weather or how your day was.

Create a list with 30 or more acts that make you feel loved if you become or are a couple and share it with each other. Develop a habit of doing one or more things from each other's list every day. Become creative once you have a better understanding of what makes your partner feel loved, and surprise him or her with your own ideas.

Realize that The Five Love Languages are relevant not only for couples, but also for children, family members, friends, and coworkers, and deepen your connection with them by learning about their preferences and what makes them feel loved and cared for as well.

Introduction

In Module 15, we explore the topic of personality types in general before we turn to The Five Love Languages, based on Garry Chapman's 1992 bestselling book of the same title.

As humans, we possess certain genetically predisposed[210] and environmentally conditioned personality characteristics, traits, or types that impact how we make meaning of our experiences and respond to our environment. These traits stay consistent throughout our lifetime and consciousness development and change only in degree or healthy/unhealthy expression, not in kind; for example, you will always be either an introvert or an extrovert (aka extravert). The Integral model refers to these fixed character traits as personality types or, simply, types.

Popular typologies include Type A (impatient, hostile) and Type B (calm, laid-back); the forementioned introvert and extravert; the nine types of the Enneagram (which we will cover in Module 16); NLP types;[211] the Myers-Briggs type indicator;[212] Human Design;[213] DISC;[214] and the infamous astrological signs of the zodiac. There are probably hundreds of typologies.

Knowledge about viable personality types and their integration with the other elements/dimensions of the Integral Relationship model provide us with crucial information that can make or break love relationships. Unfortunately, people often reduce questions of compatibility to types (s/he is just not my type; I don't get along with Capricorns; I don't like introverts; etc.), so knowing about the traits and validity of different typologies is useful. Exploring and analyzing types is relatively easy, can be fun, usually resonates with people (including astrology), and can provide many insights. On the other hand, some people become defensive and feel put into a box, judged, or reduced when they feel (stereo)typed by others. Professionals in the field of typologies recommend that this kind of (stereo)typing of others should be avoided, as we can never know the motives that underlie the behavior of others.

The Big Five

The only scientifically studied and validated personality traits are The Big Five.[215] This taxonomy describes the following five traits (plus a sixth) on a spectrum, using a scale from 1–5 (lowest to highest) for each of them.

1. Openness to experience (inventive/curious <-> consistent/cautious).
2. Conscientiousness (efficient/organized <-> extravagant/careless).
3. Extraversion (outgoing/energetic <-> solitary/reserved).
4. Agreeableness (friendly/compassionate <-> critical/rational).
5. Neuroticism/Emotionality (sensitive/nervous <-> resilient/confident).
6. A sixth trait for Honesty-Humility (sincere/honest/faithful/loyal/modest/unassuming <-> sly/deceitful/greedy/pretentious/hypocritical/boastful/pompous), based on the HEXACO model of personality structures, has been widely accepted.[216]

The labels for the five traits can be remembered by using the acronym OCEAN. They were derived by relating thousands of words that describe traits in humans and using factor analysis[217] to find overlaps. For example, people who are described as "conscientious" are also seen as being "always prepared" rather than "messy." Even though these overlaps result in far fewer than the theoretical 3,125 possible types (five traits and five tendencies for each, from lowest to highest, so 5x5x5x5x5), the Big Five give us an idea about the complexity of types in people and prevent us from oversimplified stereotyping.

Moreover, the expressions of all personality types are about 50 percent situational, further adding to the fallacy of typing other people based on their behavior, which is discouraged by professionals.

Thus, some people are averse to or critical about typologies and feel judged, stereotyped, or put into a box when typed. Paradoxically, this aversion to typologies indicates certain types in people, such as being defensive, skeptical, private, etc., versus those who are open, curious, tolerant, etc., and find typologies interesting, useful, or even essential for human understanding and relating. Either way, as with all modules in this book, it is preferable to be in a love relationship with someone who shares your views, values, and interests—in this case, about personality types.

The Five Love Languages

There are five ways, as listed below, in which people in general and romantic partners, in particular, naturally, and often unconsciously, express and experience love. A deeper connection between couples can be accomplished by showing love and care in the love language that the recipient appreciates.

A: **Words of affirmation** (NLP auditory) such as "I love you," "you are wonderful," "I miss you," and sending appreciative emails, text messages, cards, handwritten notes, or love letters.

B: **Quality time** spent together doing enjoyable things such as going to the movies, playing board/card games, dancing, sharing time with friends and family, shopping , playing sports, cooking, or travelling.

C: **Gifts** (NLP visual) such as chocolate, flowers, candles, books, CDs, clothes, jewelry, a car, boat, house, island, or country.

D: **Acts of service** for one's partner such as cooking dinner, cleaning the house, bringing breakfast to bed, driving the car, fixing things, or running errands.

E: **Physical touch** (NLP kinesthetic) such as holding hands, cuddling, kissing, giving and receiving massages, showering or taking baths together, cuddling, or lovemaking.

People tend to show their love in the same way they prefer to receive it. Most people have a primary and secondary love language and resonate to a lesser degree with the other three. We can discover another person's love language by observing the way they express love; by analyzing what they complain about most often when they feel unloved or unappreciated (you never…); and by paying attention to what they most often request from their significant other. Another way to learn another person's love language is to take the love languages test (see exercise two below).

Unfortunately, partners are often not aware of their different love languages and therefore miscommunicate their affection and appreciation for each other, for example, when he washes her car and buys her gifts to show his love, while she would rather receive a love letter and cuddle with him.

Even though understanding your own love languages and the those of others addresses only one of many aspects of human relating, and is a bit overblown in Chapman's various books, it is one of the essential facets for co-creating a healthy sustainable Integral love relationship.

Figure 42: The Five Love Languages

Purpose and application of the module

1. Learn about personality types in general, and The Five Love Languages in particular, which can be essential for thriving love relationships.
2. Understand which typologies (if any) are relevant and important for you and your partner.
3. Learn about your own love languages and those of your partner.
4. Share about how you want to be loved and create lists, with concrete acts, that you exchange with your partner.
5. Support others in identifying and sharing their love languages and seeing it as an invitation for fun and growth.

Exercises: Personality types and five love languages

1. The following are group, individual and paired exercises.
2. Print out the love languages test (double-sided) and have pens or pencils ready.
3. Present a general introduction to personality types.
4. Make the four agreements for confidentiality, responsibility, healthy boundaries, I-statements, and sharing, as outlined on page 556.

Exercise one: What personality types are you familiar with?

1. The English language includes over 3,000 words for characteristics or traits in people.
2. Ask practitioners to mention words that they may use to describe traits in themselves and others, such as outgoing, quiet, aggressive, calm, driven, smart, creative, lazy, busy, joyful, depressed, curious, humble, greedy, thoughtful, intense, modest, etc.
3. Ask practitioners what typologies they are familiar with and use in their relationships, such as the Enneagram or astrology.

Exercise two: Love languages test

1. It is preferable to begin this exercise with the test, before describing the five love languages, so that the practitioners are not influenced.
2. Hand out the test and explain it. There are 30 pairs of statements. The practitioners should circle the letter behind the statement that would make them feel most loved.
3. Point out that it is important not to choose based on their current situation and needs, but on their whole love life. Some needs can fluctuate in the short term due to hormones or life situations.

4. When they are finished, ask practitioners to add up the number of A's, B's, C's, D's, and E's.
5. When all practitioners have added up the number of letters they have chosen, give them the answers (see below) and offer the short descriptions of the love languages above.
6. Invite sharing, and answer questions.

Worksheet for practitioners

1. I like it when you give me notes of affirmation. _____A
I like it when you hug me. _____E

2. I like to spend one-on-one time with you. _____B
I feel loved when you give me practical help. _____D

3. I like it when you give me gifts. _____C
I like leisurely visits with friends and loved ones. _____B

4. I feel loved when you do things to help me. _____D
I feel loved when you touch me. _____E

5. I feel loved when you hold me in your arms. _____E
I feel loved when I receive a gift. _____C

6. I like to go places with you. _____B
I like to hold hands with you. _____E

7. Visible symbols of love (gifts) are very important to me. _C
I feel loved when you affirm me. _____A

8. I like to sit close to you. _____E
I like for you to tell me that I am attractive/handsome. _____A

9. I like to spend time with you. _____B
I like to receive little gifts from you. _____C

10. Your words of acceptance are important to me. _____ A
I know you love me when you help me. _____ D

11. I like to be together when we do things. _____ B
I like it when you say kind words to me. _____ A

12. What you do affects me more than what you say. _____ D
I feel whole when we hug. _____ E

13. I value your praise and try to avoid your criticism. _____ A
Several inexpensive gifts from you mean more to me
than one large gift. _____ C

14. I feel close when we are talking or doing something
together. _____ B
I feel closer to you when you touch me often. _____ E

15. I like it when you compliment my achievements. _____ A
I know you love me when you do things for me that you
don't enjoy doing. _____ D

16. I like for you to touch me when I walk by. _____ E
I like it when you listen to me sympathetically. _____ B

17. I feel loved when you help me with my jobs around
the house. _____ D
I really enjoy receiving gifts from you. _____ C

18. I like for you to compliment my appearance. _____ A
I feel loved when you take time to understand my feelings. _ B

19. I feel secure when you are touching me. _____ E
Your acts of service make me feel loved. _____ D

20. I appreciate the many things you do for me. _____D
I like receiving gifts that you make. _____C

21. I really enjoy the feeling I get when you give me your
undivided attention. _____B
I really enjoy the feeling I get when you do some acts
of service for me. _____D

22. I feel loved when you celebrate my birthday with a gift. _C
I feel loved when you celebrate my birthday with
meaningful words. _____A

23. I know you are thinking of me when you give me a gift. _C
I feel loved when you help me out with my chores. _____D

24. I appreciate it when you listen to me patiently and don't
interrupt me. _____B
I appreciate it when you remember special days with a gift.__C

25. I like to know you are concerned enough to help me
with my daily tasks. _____D
I enjoy extended trips with you. _____B

26. Kissing me unexpectedly excites me. _____E
Giving me a gift for no special occasion excites me. _____C

27. I like to be told that you appreciate me. _____A
I like for you to look at me when we are talking. _____B

28. Your gifts are always special to me. _____C
I feel good when you are touching me. _____E

29. I feel loved when you enthusiastically do some
tasks I have requested. _____D
I feel loved when you tell me how much you appreciate me. _A

30. I like to be touched several times every day. _____ E
I need your words of affirmation daily. _____ A

A:____ B: ____ C: ____ D: ____ E: ____

Table 14: Love languages test

For group facilitators only: A: Words of affirmation, B: Quality time, C: Gifts, D: Acts of Service, E: Physical touch.

Exercise three: What makes you feel loved?

1. Divide the group according to the practitioners' primary love languages, and ask each group to create a list of at least 20 actions through which they express love and feel loved. Give about 20–30 minutes to complete.
2. Bring the group back together and ask one person from each group to share their list.
3. Invite sharing and discussion about the experience and insights that the practitioners gained.

Exercise four: Expressing your love languages

1. You may invite the practitioners to explore the follow-up questions below in pairs, small groups, or in a large-group format.

Follow-up questions

1. How do you feel after this exercise?
2. How have the love languages impacted your relationships?
3. What have you projected (or project) onto your partner(s) around the love languages?
4. Is your "giving" love language different from your "receiving" love language?
5. Have you received and expressed love differently as you evolved through the levels of consciousness development?

6. Have the love languages changed throughout your life in certain relationships or situations?
7. Have early (traumatic or otherwise) childhood experiences affected your love languages?
8. Are there inappropriate or pathological forms of expressing love languages (manipulative compliments, acting in dangerous ways, hoarding, conditional acts of service, inappropriate touching, etc.)?
9. Would you rather be with someone who has the same or different love languages as you, or does it not matter?
10. How important is it to you that someone shares your love languages?
11. How do you give yourself love in your primary and secondary love languages?

Additional information and resources

Why You Are Who You Are: Investigations into Human Personality, The Great Courses (2018) by Mark Leary,
tinyurl.com/irpm390[218]

The H Factor of Personality: Why Some People are Manipulative, Self-Entitled, Materialistic, and Exploitive—And Why It Matters for Everyone (2012) by Kibeom Lee and Michael C. Ashton
tinyurl.com/irpm392[219]

The 5 Love Languages: The Secret to Love that Lasts (1992/2015) by Gary Chapman
tinyurl.com/irpm396[220]

For a Love Languages Quiz
tinyurl.com/irpm398[221]

Sex Purpose Love book reference

Page 88–89

Suggested Movie: *Love Actually* (2003)

Watch this classic British romantic comedy to see the different Love Languages and, as a preview for the following Module 16, Nine Enneagram types play out, as you follow eight very different couples in dealing with their love lives in various loosely interrelated tales, all set during a frantic month before Christmas in modern London.

While this star-studded movie (Alan Rickman as Harry; Emma Thompson as Karen; Hugh Grant as David, the Prime Minister; Keira Knightley as Juliet; Colin Firth as Jamie; Liam Neeson as Daniel; Bill Nighy as Billy Mack; Martine McCutcheon as Natalie; Laura Linney as Sarah; Martin Freeman as John; Olivia Olson as Joanna; Billy Bob Thornton as the US President; Claudia Schiffer as Carol) can be fun to watch, it also painfully shows the misguided shallow notion that all it takes to enter a happy love relationship is to muster up the courage to say; "I love you."

As in *He's Just Not That Into You* and similar movies, the protagonists have nothing visibly in common, such as shared values, interests, or passions, beyond having a (hormonal) crush on each other and being at a more or less rational stage of development.

Other things that we may critically notice from today's perspective are the objectification of women; sexist references to the characters' weight; suggestions and attempts to repress feelings, especially in males, so as not to be seen as weak; the strange "relationship" between Peter and his best friend's new wife; and a not-so-subtle anti-Americanism.

Practice Module 16
Enneagram Types

If we observe ourselves truthfully and non-judgmentally, seeing the mechanisms of our personality in action, we can wake up, and our lives can be a miraculous unfolding of beauty and joy.
~ Don Riso ~

Module description

Learn and practice how to identify which of the nine Enneagram types you and your partner resonate with most. Feel into your "wings"—the type(s) next to the primary type that you identify with—and the types you move towards under stress and when you relax. Understand how your type combinations positively and negatively impact your love relationship by comparing them online. Put your type in the context of the unhealthy, average, and healthy levels of expression.

Explore how to communicate your own values and needs and how to meet those of your partner. Identify whether you and your partner resonate most with the self-preservation, social, or attraction/intensity/sexual instinctual variant, and why compatibility, or at least acceptance, are crucial for you to meet each other's needs. Co-create a rewarding and thriving love relationship by creating synergy between your Enneagram types.

Introduction

History of the Enneagram

The Enneagram is a synthesis of several ancient mystical wisdom traditions and archetypes, including Greek philosophy, Jewish Kabbalah, Christian deadly sins and temptations, and Islamic Sufi esoterism.[222]

The term "Enneagram" is derived from two Greek words, *ennea* (nine) and *gramma* (something written or drawn). It was coined by the Russian philosopher, mystic, and spiritual teacher George Ivanovich Gurdjieff (1872–1949), who developed his own mystical interpretation of the symbol in the early twentieth century. Oscar Ichazo (1931–2020), a Bolivian-born philosopher, is generally recognized as the principal source of the contemporary Enneagram of ego-fixations, holy ideas, passions, and virtues. In the early '70s, Chilean-born psychiatrist Claudio Naranjo (1932–2019) popularized his own understanding of the Enneagram in the United States. A.H. Almaas integrated the Enneagram into his Diamond Approach work. This and other sources became the inspiration for Don Richard Riso (1946-2012) and Russ Hudson, who created the Riso–Hudson Enneagram Type Indicator (RHETI), founded the Enneagram Institute in 1995, and published the 1999 book, *The Wisdom of the Enneagram*, on which this module is largely based.

The Symbol

The Enneagram symbol is composed of three interlaced "triangles" that form a geometric figure with nine points around a circle, each of them representing a specific personality type. The nine types are grouped into head/thinking, heart/feeling, and gut/instinct types. It is common to find a little of yourself in all the types, although one of them will stand out prominently as being closest to yourself and will motivate the healthy integration of the other types.

The two adjacent numbers to your main type represent one or two secondary motivators or "wings," while the two inner lines that lead away from your main type point to the corresponding types toward which individuals tend to move when under stress/disintegration and during healthy integration/growth (relaxation).ABwings, stress, and relax types can lead to mistyping of people under certain conditions.

Criticism

The Enneagram received the same criticism as many other typologies (except "The Big Five") as being pseudoscience, subject to wide interpretations, difficult to test or validate scientifically, and prone to shoehorn people into one of the nine types. One of the reasons is that the behavior of people in response to their environment is highly situational and that we cannot assess the underlying motives of *what* people do and say through observing or even their self-reporting, but would need to deeply understand the underlying *why*, which is often guided by cultural conditioning and social pressures rather than their authentic, essential self. This is also the reason why people sometimes mistype themselves.

However, when used for authentic self-examination, psychological healing, and spiritual liberation, (especially in a relational context), the Enneagram (along with the Myers Briggs Type indicator) is one of the most popular typologies today that helps people to understand consistent patterns that drive and motivate their relational behavior and how they manage their emotions and fears. The Enneagram is widely applied in business (team building and change management), psychotherapy, personal growth, spirituality,[223] and, of course, love relationships, which will be our focus in this module.

Purpose and application of the module

1. Learn about the nine types of the Enneagram, including wings, stress, and relax lines, and the three instinctual variants.
2. Identify your own type and that of your partner through the simple test below or through more elaborate tests online.
3. Locate which of the nine levels of development of your own and your partner's type resonate most with you and realize your healing and growth potentials.
4. Show curiosity and compassion for your own and your partner's type—including wings, stress, and relax lines.
5. Review the positive aspects that each of you bring to the relationship, and learn about potential trouble spots and negative issues between you and your partner based on your type combination. See tinyurl.com/irpm586[224]

6. See how you can strengthen and benefit from what each of you brings to the relationship, and avoid conflicts based on trouble spots and issues.
7. Learn about your instinctual variants through the descriptions below or through a test at tinyurl.com/irpm45[225]

Exercises: Enneagram

The following are individual and paired exercises.
1. Print the Enneagram test below on one side, and the symbol and short descriptions on the other.
2. Make the four agreements for confidentiality, responsibility, healthy boundaries, I-statements, and sharing, as outlined on page 556.
3. Present a short introduction to the history and applications of the Enneagram.

Exercise one: What is your Enneagram Type?

1. Hand out the Enneagram test and invite the practitioners to take it by feeling into their whole adult life.
2. Mention that this test is about 70% accurate. More accurate results can be obtained by taking free or affordable assessment tests on the internet or by working with an Enneagram coach.[226]
3. Ask the practitioners what their primary type is and read the short descriptions together.
4. Invite the practitioners to share whether they find themselves in the descriptions (sometimes people don't like their own type or aspects of it).
5. Explain wings and stress/relax arrows.
6. Invite the practitioners to share whether they find themselves in the descriptions of wings and stress/relax types.
7. Point to or review the nine levels of development for each type.

Worksheet: Enneagram test

From the book, *The Wisdom of the Enneagram,* by Don Richard Riso and Russ Hudson.[227]

Select one paragraph in each of the following two groups. Select the one that resonates most with you over your lifespan, that your gut feeling says is right. Do not overanalyze it, it does not have to be perfect. Write down the two letters, e.g., A/Y

Group 1:

A: I have tended to be fairly independent and assertive: I've felt that life works best when you meet it head-on. I set my own goals, get involved, and want to make things happen. I don't like sitting around—I want to achieve something big and have an impact. I don't necessarily seek confrontations, but I don't let people push me around, either. Most of the time I know what I want, and I go for it. I tend to work hard and to play hard.

B: I have tended to be quiet and am used to being on my own. I usually don't draw much attention to myself socially, and it's generally unusual for me to assert myself all that forcefully. I don't feel comfortable taking the lead or being as competitive as others. Many would probably say that I'm something of a dreamer—a lot of my excitement goes on in my imagination. I can be quite content without feeling I have to be active all the time.

C: I have tended to be extremely responsible and dedicated. I feel terrible if I don't keep my commitments and do what's expected of me. I want people to know that I'm there for them and that I'll do what I believe is best for them. I've often made great personal sacrifices for the sake of others, whether they know it or not. I often don't take adequate care of myself—I do the work that needs to be done and then relax (and do what I really want) if there's time left.

Group 2:

X: I am a person who usually maintains a positive outlook and feels that things will work out for the best. I can usually find something to be enthusiastic about and different ways to occupy myself. I like being around people and helping others to be happy—I enjoy sharing my own well-being with them. (I don't always feel great, but I try not to show it to anyone!) However, staying positive has sometimes meant that I've put off dealing with my own problems for too long.

Y: I am a person who has strong feelings about things—most people can tell when I'm unhappy about something. I can be guarded with people, but I'm more sensitive than I let on. I want to know where I stand with others and who and what I can count on—it's pretty clear to most people where they stand with me. When I'm upset about something, I want others to respond and to get as worked up as I am. I know the rules, but I don't want people telling me what to do. I want to decide for myself.

Z: I tend to be self-controlled and logical—I am uncomfortable dealing with feelings. I am efficient—even perfectionistic—and prefer working on my own. When there are problems or personal conflicts, I try not to bring my feelings into the situation. Some say I'm too cool and detached, but I don't want my emotional reactions to distract me from what's really important to me. I usually don't show my reactions when others "get to me."

Key for facilitator: (AX=7, AY=8, AZ=3, BX=9, BY=4, BZ=5, CX=2, CY=6, CZ=1)

The Enneagram symbol and types

THE ENNEAGRAM

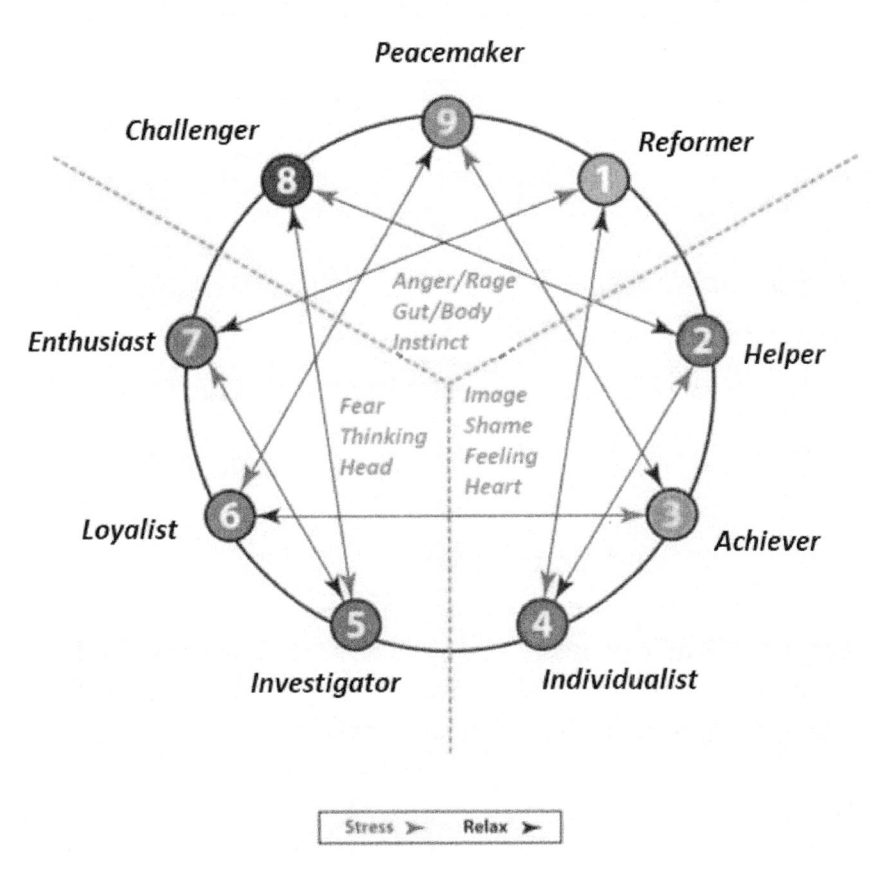

Figure 43: The nine Enneagram types

1. The reformer, judge, perfectionist

Is focused on personal integrity and seeks truth. Can be a teacher, crusader, or advocate for change. Is often ignorant of his/her own flaws and overly critical of others. Fears being corrupt, evil, or defective—wants to be good, balanced, perfect, and have integrity. See examples of famous people for each type in the endnotes.[228]

2. The helper, giver, caretaker

Is compassionate, attentive, generous, and caring. Can be clingy, needy, flattering, people-pleasing, and manipulative. Often well-meaning and driven to be close to others but can slip into doing things for others in order to be needed. Fears being unwanted and unlovable—wants to be loved and needed.[229]

3. The achiever, performer, status seeker

Is adaptable and changeable. Walks the world with confidence and acts in ways that will bring approval and accomplishments, sometimes at the expense of his/her true self. Fears failure and being worthless—wants to feel valuable and worthwhile.[230]

4. The individualist, romantic, aesthete

Is driven by the desire to understand and to find his/her place in the world. Embraces individualism, is creative, intuitive, and humane. Fears having no identity or personal significance—wants to be significant.[231]

5. The investigator, expert, thinker

Is driven to understand the world and derives self-worth through contribution, can be withdrawn, observant, and quiet, until he/she can impress with a witty remark. Fears incompetency or uselessness—wants to be capable and knowledgeable above all else.[232]

6. The loyalist, hero, rebel, defender

Longs for secure stability and exhibits unwavering loyalty and responsibility. Is slow to trust again if betrayed and prone to fearful thinking. Displays emotional anxiety, as well as reactionary and paranoid behavior. Fears being without support and guidance—wants to have security and support.[233]

7. The enthusiast, adventurer, sensationalist

Is adventurous and constantly busy, embraces life with all its various joys and wonders, and moves frantically from one new experience to another. Fears being unable to provide for him/herself and is afraid of missing out on life with all of its richness—wants to be satisfied, content, and to have his/her needs fulfilled.[234]

8. The challenger, boss, maverick

Is strong, with a desire to be a powerful and controlling leader. Can be friendly and charitable, or dictatorial, manipulative, ruthless, and willing to destroy anything that stands in the way. Fears being harmed or controlled by others—seeks self-protection and wants to be in control of life and destiny.[235]

9. The peacemaker, mediator, preservationist

Is empathetic, receptive, gentle, calm, and at peace with the world. Avoids conflict, withdraws, shuts down, and goes along with other people's wishes. Is prone to dissociation and passive-aggressive behavior. Fears loss and separation—wants to have inner stability and peace of mind.[236]

Levels of development

Each of the nine types has unhealthy, average, and healthy levels of expressions (or strengths and weaknesses).

Type One—Levels of development

Healthy Levels

Level 1: (At Their Best): Become extraordinarily wise and discerning. By accepting what is, they become transcendentally realistic, knowing the best action to take in each moment. Humane, inspiring, and hopeful: the truth will be heard.

Level 2: Conscientious, with strong personal convictions: they have an intense sense of right and wrong, personal religious and moral values. Wish to be rational, reasonable, self-disciplined, mature, moderate in all things.

Level 3: Extremely principled, always want to be fair, objective, and ethical: truth and justice primary values. Sense of responsibility, personal integrity, and of having a higher purpose often make them teachers and witnesses to the truth.

Average Levels

Level 4: Dissatisfied with reality, they become high-minded idealists, feeling that it is up to them to improve everything: crusaders, advocates, critics. Into "causes" and explaining to others how things "ought" to be.

Level 5: Afraid of making a mistake: everything must be consistent with their ideals. Become orderly and well-organized, but impersonal, puritanical, emotionally constricted, rigidly keeping their feelings and impulses in check. Often workaholics — "anal-compulsive," punctual, pedantic, and fastidious.

Level 6: Highly critical both of self and others: picky, judgmental, perfectionistic. Very opinionated about everything: correcting people and badgering them to "do the right thing" — as they see it. Impatient, never satisfied with anything unless it is done according to their prescriptions. Moralizing, scolding, abrasive, and indignantly angry.

Unhealthy Levels

Level 7: Can be highly dogmatic, self-righteous, intolerant, and inflexible. Begin dealing in absolutes: they alone know "The Truth." Everyone else is wrong: very severe in judgments, while rationalizing own actions.

Level 8: Become obsessive about imperfection and the wrongdoing of others, although they may fall into contradictory actions, hypocritically doing the opposite of what they preach.

Level 9: Become condemnatory toward others, punitive and cruel to rid themselves of wrongdoers. Severe depressions, nervous breakdowns, and suicide attempts are likely. Generally corresponds to the Obsessive-Compulsive and Depressive personality disorders.

Type Two—Levels of development

Healthy Levels

Level 1: (At Their Best): Become deeply unselfish, humble, and altruistic: giving unconditional love to self and others. Feel it is a privilege to be in the lives of others.

Level 2: Empathetic, compassionate, feeling for others. Caring and concerned about their needs. Thoughtful, warm-hearted, forgiving, and sincere.

Level 3: Encouraging and appreciative, able to see the good in others. Service is important, but takes care of self, too: nurturing, generous, and giving—a truly loving person.

Average Levels

Level 4: Want to be closer to others, so start "people pleasing," becoming overly friendly, emotionally demonstrative, and full of "good intentions" about everything. Give seductive attention: approval, "strokes," flattery. Love is their supreme value, and they talk about it constantly.

Level 5: Become overly intimate and intrusive: they need to be needed, so they hover, meddle, and control in the name of love. Want others to depend on them: give, but expect a return: send double messages. Enveloping and possessive: the codependent, self-sacrificial person who cannot do enough for others—wearing themselves out for everyone, creating needs for themselves to fulfill.

Level 6: Increasingly self-important and self-satisfied, feel they are indispensable, although they overrate their efforts on others' behalf. Hypochondria, becoming a "martyr" for others. Overbearing, patronizing, presumptuous.

Unhealthy Levels

Level 7: Can be manipulative and self-serving, instilling guilt by telling others how much they owe them and making them suffer. Abuse food and medication to "stuff feelings" and get sympathy. Undermine people, making belittling, disparaging remarks.

Extremely self-deceptive about their motives and how aggressive and/or selfish their behavior is.

Level 8: Domineering and coercive: feel entitled to get anything they want from others: the repayment of old debts, money, sexual favors.

Level 9: Able to excuse and rationalize what they do since they feel abused and victimized by others and are bitterly resentful and angry. Somatization of their aggressions results in chronic health problems, as they vindicate themselves by "falling apart" and burdening others. Generally, corresponds to the Histrionic personality disorder and Factitious disorder.

Type Three—Levels of development

Healthy Levels

Level 1: (At Their Best): Self-accepting, inner-directed, and authentic, everything they seem to be. Modest and charitable, self-deprecatory humor and a fullness of heart emerge. Gentle and benevolent.

Level 2: Self-assured, energetic, and competent with high self-esteem: they believe in themselves and their own value. Adaptable, desirable, charming, and gracious.

Level 3: Ambitious to improve themselves, to be "the best they can be"—often become outstanding, a human ideal, embodying widely admired cultural qualities. Highly effective: others are motivated to be like them in some positive way.

Average Levels

Level 4: Highly concerned with their performance, doing their job well, constantly driving self to achieve goals as if self-worth depends on it. Terrified of failure. Compare self with others in search of status and success. Become careerists, social climbers, invested in exclusivity and being the "best."

Level 5: Become image-conscious, highly concerned with how they are perceived. Begin to package themselves according to the expectations of others and what they need to do to be successful.

Pragmatic and efficient, but also premeditated, losing touch with their own feelings beneath a smooth facade. Problems with intimacy, credibility, and "phoniness" emerge.

Level 6: Want to impress others with their superiority: constantly promoting themselves, making themselves sound better than they really are. Narcissistic, with grandiose, inflated notions about themselves and their talents. Exhibitionistic and seductive, as if saying "Look at me!" Arrogance and contempt for others is a defense against feeling jealous of others and their success.

Unhealthy Levels

Level 7: Fearing failure and humiliation, they can be exploitative and opportunistic, covetous of the success of others, and willing to do "whatever it takes" to preserve the illusion of their superiority.

Level 8: Devious and deceptive so that their mistakes and wrongdoings will not be exposed. Untrustworthy, maliciously betraying or sabotaging people to triumph over them. Delusionally jealous of others

Level 9: Become vindictive, attempting to ruin others' happiness. Relentless, obsessive about destroying whatever reminds them of their own shortcomings and failures. Psychopathic behavior. Generally corresponds to the Narcissistic Personality Disorder.

Type Four—Levels of development

Healthy Levels

Level 1: (At Their Best): Profoundly creative, expressing the personal and the universal, possibly in a work of art. Inspired, self-renewing and regenerating: able to transform all their experiences into something valuable: self-creative.

Level 2: Self-aware, introspective, on the "search for self," aware of feelings and inner impulses. Sensitive and intuitive both to self and others: gentle, tactful, compassionate.

Level 3: Highly personal, individualistic, "true to self." Self-revealing, emotionally honest, humane. Ironic view of self and life: can be serious and funny, vulnerable and emotionally strong.

Average Levels

Level 4: Take an artistic, romantic orientation to life, creating a beautiful, aesthetic environment to cultivate and prolong personal feelings. Heighten reality through fantasy, passionate feelings, and the imagination.

Level 5: To stay in touch with feelings, they interiorize everything, taking everything personally, but become self-absorbed and introverted, moody and hypersensitive, shy and self-conscious, unable to be spontaneous or to "get out of themselves." Stay withdrawn to protect their self-image and to buy time to sort out feelings.

Level 6: Gradually think that they are different from others and feel that they are exempt from living as everyone else does. They become melancholy dreamers, disdainful, decadent, and sensual, living in a fantasy world. Self-pity and envy of others leads to self-indulgence and to becoming increasingly impractical, unproductive, effete, and precious.

Unhealthy Levels

Level 7: When dreams fail, becomes self-inhibiting and angry at self, depressed and alienated from self and others, blocked and emotionally paralyzed. Ashamed of self, fatigued, and unable to function.

Level 8: Tormented by delusional self-contempt, self-reproaches, self-hatred, and morbid thoughts: everything is a source of torment. Blaming others, they drive away anyone who tries to help them.

Level 9: Despairing, feel hopeless and become self-destructive, possibly abusing alcohol or drugs to escape. In the extreme: emotional breakdown or suicide is likely. Generally corresponds to the Avoidant, Depressive, and Narcissistic personality disorders.

Type Five—Levels of development

Healthy Levels

Level 1: (At Their Best): Become visionaries, broadly comprehending the world while penetrating it profoundly. Open-minded, take things in whole, in their true context. Make pioneering discoveries and find entirely new ways of doing and perceiving things.

Level 2: Observe everything with extraordinary perceptiveness and insight. Most mentally alert, curious, searching intelligence: nothing escapes their notice. Foresight and prediction. Able to concentrate: become engrossed in what has caught their attention.

Level 3: Attain skillful mastery of whatever interests them. Excited by knowledge: often become expert in some field. Innovative and inventive, producing extremely valuable, original works. Highly independent, idiosyncratic, and whimsical.

Average Levels

Level 4: Begin conceptualizing and fine-tuning everything before acting—working things out in their minds: model building, preparing, practicing, and gathering more resources. Studious, acquiring technique. Become specialized and often "intellectual," challenging accepted ways of doing things.

Level 5: Increasingly detached as they become involved with complicated ideas or imaginary worlds. Become preoccupied with their visions and interpretations rather than with reality. Are fascinated by off-beat, esoteric subjects, even those involving dark and disturbing elements. Detached from the practical world, a "disembodied mind," although high-strung and intense.

Level 6: Begin to take an antagonistic stance toward anything which would interfere with their inner world and personal vision. Become provocative and abrasive, with intentionally extreme and radical views. Cynical and argumentative.

Unhealthy Levels

Level 7: Become reclusive and isolated from reality, eccentric and nihilistic. Highly unstable and fearful of aggressions: they reject and repel others and all social attachments.

Level 8: Get obsessed yet frightened by their threatening ideas, becoming horrified, delirious, and prey to gross distortions and phobias.

Level 9: Seeking oblivion, they may commit suicide or have a psychotic break with reality. Deranged, explosively self-destructive, with schizophrenic overtones. Generally, corresponds to the Schizoid Avoidant and Schizotypal personality disorders.

Type Six—Levels of development

Healthy Levels

Level 1: (At Their Best): Become self-affirming, trusting of self and others, independent yet symbiotically interdependent and cooperative as an equal. Belief in self leads to true courage, positive thinking, leadership, and rich self-expression.

Level 2: Able to elicit strong emotional responses from others: very appealing, endearing, lovable, affectionate. Trust is important: bonding with others, forming permanent relationships and alliances.

Level 3: Dedicated to individuals and movements in which they deeply believe. Community builders: responsible, reliable, trustworthy. Hard-working and persevering, sacrificing for others, they create stability and security in their world, bringing a cooperative spirit.

Average Levels

Level 4: Start investing their time and energy in whatever they believe will be safe and stable. Organizing and structuring, they look to alliances and authorities for security and continuity. Constantly vigilant, anticipating problems.

Level 5: To resist having more demands made on them, they react against others passive-aggressively. Become evasive, indecisive, cautious, procrastinating, and ambivalent. Are highly reactive, anxious, and negative, giving contradictory "mixed signals." Internal confusion makes them react unpredictably.

Level 6: To compensate for insecurities, they become sarcastic and belligerent, blaming others for their problems, taking a tough stance toward "outsiders." Highly reactive and defensive, dividing people into friends and enemies, while looking for threats to their own security. Authoritarian, while fearful of authority; highly suspicious, yet conspiratorial; fear-instilling to silence their own fears.

Unhealthy Levels

Level 7: Fearing that they have ruined their security, they become panicky, volatile, and self-disparaging, with acute inferiority feelings. Seeing themselves as defenseless, they seek out a stronger authority or belief to resolve all problems. Highly divisive; disparaging, and berating others

Level 8: Feeling persecuted, that others are "out to get them," they lash out and act irrationally, bringing about what they fear. Fanaticism, violence.

Level 9: Hysterical and seeking to escape punishment, they become self-destructive and suicidal. Alcoholism, drug overdoses, "skid row," self-abasing behavior. Generally corresponds to the Passive-Aggressive and Paranoid personality disorders.

Type Seven—Levels of development

Healthy Levels

Level 1: (At Their Best): Assimilate experiences in depth, making them deeply grateful and appreciative for what they have. Become awed by the simple wonders of life: joyous and ecstatic. Intimations of spiritual reality, of the boundless goodness of life.

Level 2: Highly responsive, excitable, enthusiastic about sensation and experience. Most extroverted type: stimuli bring immediate responses—they find everything invigorating. Lively, vivacious, eager, spontaneous, resilient, cheerful.

Level 3: Easily become accomplished achievers, generalists who do many different things well: multi-talented. Practical, productive, usually prolific, cross-fertilizing areas of interest.

Average Levels

Level 4: As restlessness increases, want to have more options and choices available to them. Become adventurous and "worldly wise," but less focused, constantly seeking new things and experiences: the sophisticate, connoisseur, and consumer. Money, variety, keeping up with the latest trends important.

Level 5: Unable to discriminate what they really need, become hyperactive, unable to say "no" to themselves, throwing self into constant activity. Uninhibited, doing and saying whatever comes to mind: storytelling, flamboyant exaggerations, witty wisecracking, performing. Fear being bored: in perpetual motion but do too many things—many ideas but little follow through.

Level 6: Indulge in conspicuous consumption and all forms of excess. Self-centered, materialistic, and greedy, never feeling that they have enough. Demanding and pushy, yet unsatisfied and jaded. Addictive, hardened, and insensitive.

Unhealthy Levels

Level 7: Desperate to quell their anxieties; can be impulsive and infantile; do not know when to stop. Addictions and excess take their toll: debauched, depraved, dissipated escapists, offensive and abusive.

Level 8: In flight from self, acting out impulses rather than dealing with anxiety or frustrations: loss of control, erratic mood swings, and compulsive actions (manias).

Level 9: Finally, their energy and health are completely spent: become claustrophobic and panic-stricken. Often give up on themselves and life: deep depression and despair, self-destructive overdoses, impulsive suicide. Generally, corresponds to Bipolar disorder and Histrionic personality disorder.

Type Eight—Levels of development

Healthy Levels

Level 1: (At Their Best): Become self-restrained and magnanimous, merciful and forbearing, mastering self through their self-surrender to a higher authority. Courageous, willing to put self in serious jeopardy to achieve their vision and have a lasting influence. May achieve true heroism and historical greatness.

Level 2: Self-assertive, self-confident, and strong: have learned to stand up for what they need and want. A resourceful "can do" attitude and passionate inner drive.

Level 3: Decisive, authoritative, and commanding: the natural leader others look up to. Take initiative, make things happen: champion people; provider, protective, and honorable, carrying others with their strength.

Average Levels

Level 4: Self-sufficiency, financial independence, and having enough resources are important concerns: become enterprising, pragmatic, "rugged individualists," wheeler-dealers. Risk-taking, hardworking, denying own emotional needs.

Level 5: Begin to dominate their environment, including others: want to feel that others are behind them, supporting their efforts. Swaggering, boastful, forceful, and expansive: the "boss" whose word is law. Proud, egocentric, want to impose their will and vision on everything, not seeing others as equals or treating them with respect.

Level 6: Become highly combative and intimidating to get their way: confrontational, belligerent, creating adversarial relationships. Everything a test of wills, and they will not back down. Use threats and reprisals to get obedience from other and to keep others off balance and insecure. However, unjust treatment makes others fear and resent them, possibly banding together against them.

Unhealthy Levels

Level 7: Defying any attempt to control them, become completely ruthless, dictatorial, "might makes right." The criminal and outlaw, renegade, and con artist. Hard-hearted, immoral, and potentially violent.

Level 8: Develop delusional ideas about their power, invincibility, and ability to prevail: megalomania, feeling omnipotent, invulnerable. Recklessly over-extending self.

Level 9: If they are in danger, they may brutally destroy everything that has not conformed to their will rather than surrender to anyone else. Vengeful, barbaric, murderous. Sociopathic tendencies. Generally corresponds to Antisocial Personality Disorder.

Type Nine—Levels of development

Healthy Levels

Level 1: (At Their Best): Become self-possessed, feeling autonomous and fulfilled: have great equanimity and contentment because they are present to themselves. Paradoxically, at one with self and thus able to form more profound relationships. Intensely alive, fully connected to self and others.

Level 2: Deeply receptive, accepting, unselfconscious, emotionally stable and serene. Trusting of self and others, at ease with self and life, innocent and simple. Patient, unpretentious, good-natured, genuinely nice people.

Level 3: Optimistic, reassuring, supportive: have a healing and calming influence—harmonizing groups, bringing people together. A good mediator, synthesizer, and communicator.

Average Levels

Level 4: Fear conflicts, so become self-effacing and accommodating, idealizing others and "going along" with their wishes, saying "yes" to things they do not really want to do. Fall into conventional roles and expectations. Use philosophies and stock sayings to deflect others.

Level 5: Active, but disengaged, unreflective, and inattentive. Do not want to be affected, so become unresponsive and complacent, walking away from problems and "sweeping them under the rug." Thinking becomes hazy and ruminative, mostly comforting fantasies, as they begin to "tune out" reality, becoming oblivious. Emotionally indolent, unwilling to exert self or to focus on problems: indifference.

Level 6: Begin to minimize problems, to appease others, and to have "peace at any price." Stubborn, fatalistic, and resigned, as if nothing could be done to change anything. Into wishful thinking and magical solutions. Others frustrated and angry by their procrastination and unresponsiveness.

Unhealthy Levels

Level 7: Can be highly repressed, undeveloped, and ineffectual. Feel incapable of facing problems: become obstinate, dissociating self from all conflicts. Neglectful and dangerous to others.

Level 8: Wanting to block out of awareness anything that could affect them, they dissociate so much that they eventually cannot function: numb, depersonalized.

Level 9: They finally become severely disoriented and catatonic, abandoning themselves, turning into shattered shells. Multiple personalities possible. Generally, corresponds to the Schizoid and Dependent personality disorders.

Enneagram type combinations

After people learn about their Enneagram type, the next question is invariably "What types go well together?" or "Who should I be with?"

The answer is that no pairing of types is particularly blessed or doomed. One can have a relationship with any type if the two people are healthy. Since this is not always the case, knowing the type, the level of health, and the instinctual variant (see below) of each person can provide more insight. Two highly self-aware people have the best chances of success. Two highly unaware people may be able to continue in a relationship, but it is usually characterized by problems. If one person is highly self-aware and the other is not, at some point the relationship usually just stops making sense. The two people will not understand each other enough to continue.

At tinyurl.com/irpm583[237], you can find an overview to help you understand the positive aspects that each of you brings to the relationship and learn about potential trouble spots and negative issues that are likely to arise between any two types.[238]

Lynn Roulo did a study with 457 couples to find out the most common combinations. The results don't mean these are the most successful combinations; they just happened with the most frequency.[239]

Compatibility or high awareness of Instincts (see below) also play a big role in the compatibility between partners.

Exercise two: The Enneagram in your relationships

Invite the practitioners to a paired exercise in which they answer the following questions about their Enneagram type and how it has manifested in their relationships.

1. How have your type, wings, relax/growth and stress/regression types impacted your life?
2. Do or did you know the type of your partner(s)?
3. How did this knowledge impact your relationships?
4. What is the level of health (1 being highest to 9 being lowest) in your Enneagram type expression?
5. What is it about your type that you do not like and sometimes struggle with?

Instinctual variants

There are three Enneagram instincts or instinctual variants (often erroneously called "subtypes") that are part of our personality and are extremely important for understanding ourselves and others in relationships.

Self-preservation variant

People of this instinctual variant are preoccupied with basic survival needs as they translate in our contemporary society. Thus, self-preservation types are concerned with money, food, housing, health, physical safety, and comfort.

Being safe and physically comfortable are priorities. These people are quick to notice any problems in a room, such as poor lighting or uncomfortable chairs, or prone to be dissatisfied with the room temperature. They often have issues connected with food and drink, either overdoing it or having strict dietary requirements. In the healthy to average levels of the three instinctual types, self-preservation types are the most practical in the sense of taking care of basic life necessities—paying bills, maintaining the home and workplace, acquiring useful skills, and so forth.

When these types deteriorate, they tend to distort the instinct to the degree that they are poor at taking care of themselves. Unhealthy self-preservation types eat and sleep poorly or become obsessed with health issues. They often have difficulty handling money and may act out in deliberately self-destructive ways. In a nutshell, self-preservation types are focused on enhancing their personal security and physical comfort.

Social variant

People with this variant are focused on their interactions with other people and with the sense of value or esteem that they derive from their participation in collective activities. These include work, family, hobbies, clubs—basically any arena in which social types can interact with others for some shared purpose.

Within that social instinct, however, are many other implicit imperatives, and primary among them is the understanding of "place" within a hierarchical social structure. This is as true for dogs and gorillas as it is for human beings. Thus, the desire for attention, recognition, honor, success, fame, leadership, appreciation, and the safety of belonging can all be seen as manifestations of the social instinct.

Social types like to know what is going on around them and want to make some contribution to the human enterprise. There is often an interest in the events and activities of one's own culture, or, sometimes, of another culture.

In general, social types enjoy interacting with people, but they avoid intimacy. In their imbalanced, unhealthy forms, these types can become profoundly antisocial, detesting people and resenting their society, or having poorly developed social skills. In a nutshell, social types are focused on interacting with people in ways that will build their personal value, their sense of accomplishment, and their security of "place" with others.

Sexual/attraction variant

Many people originally identify themselves as this variant, perhaps confusing the idea of a sexual instinctual type with being a "sexy" person.

Sexual types are the "intimacy junkies" of the instinctual types, often neglecting pressing obligations or even basic "maintenance" if they are swept up in someone or something that has captivated them. This gives a wide-ranging, exploratory approach to life, but also a lack of focus on one's own priorities.

In their neurotic forms, this type can manifest with a wandering lack of focus, sexual promiscuity, and acting out—or just the opposite, with a fearful, dysfunctional attitude toward sex and intimacy. Sexual types, however, will be intense, even about their avoidances.

Much has been said about this type preferring "one-on-one" relationships versus the social type's preference for "larger groups," but a quick poll of one's acquaintances will reveal that almost all people prefer communicating one-on-one to communicating in a group. The question is more about the intensity of contact and the strength of the desire for intimacy. This intensity could be found in a great conversation or an exciting movie.

In a nutshell, sexual types are focused on having intense, intimate interactions and experiences with others and with the environment to give them a powerful sense of "aliveness." In healthy to average sexual types, there is a desire for intensity of experience—not just sexual experience but having a similar "charge."

Exercise three:

This is an individual and paired exercise.
1. Invite the practitioners to explore the different degrees of their self-preservation, social, and sexual/attraction variants by examining their thoughts, feelings, needs, attention, focus, and behavior when they receive an invitation to a party or event and when they arrive there.

2. Ask the practitioners which of the three descriptions below resonates most with them. What are the parallels in their life in general and their needs in their love relationships, in particular.
3. After they have heard the three descriptions of being invited to a party (below), invite the practitioners to a paired exercise in which they share how their instinctual variant impact(ed) their love relationship(s)?

The party

1. Is your main concern with the safety of the neighborhood, location, and how to get there: if the place will be clean and comfortable, with sanitary bathrooms, fresh air, enough light, appropriate seating, not too much noise, clean dishes and food, fire exits, etc.?
2. Or do you wonder who will be there and what kind of group activities will take place, how you will be welcomed and introduced to the group, how you will be valued, what the vibes will be, if you will feel a sense of belonging, make new friends, etc.?
3. Or is your main interest in meeting fascinating people who share your deepest passions and concerns to form a deeply intimate, arousing, inspiring, and interesting connection with through intense conversation in which you can totally lose yourself (like having passionate sex)?[240]

If you can't detect your own and your partner's instinctual variants from the descriptions above, then it is strongly suggested that you take a test online.[241]

Follow-up questions

1. How do you feel after this exercise?
2. How have the nine Enneagram types and instinctual variants impacted your relationship(s)?

3. What have you projected (or project) onto your partner(s) around the nine Enneagram types?
4. Has the expression of the nine Enneagram types changed as you evolved through the levels of consciousness?
5. Have the nine Enneagram types changed throughout your life or in certain relationships?
6. Would you rather be with someone who has a particular Enneagram type, or does it not matter to you?

Additional information and resources

Authors/teachers/coaches/trainings

Dr. Khaled ElSherbini tinyurl.com/irpm400[242]
Dr. David Daniels: tinyurl.com/irpm406[243]
Helen Palmer: tinyurl.com/irpm408[244]
Ginger Lapid Bogda tinyurl.com/irpm410[245]
Lynn Roulo www.lynnroulo.com/

Tests and Information

tinyurl.com/irpm411[246]
www.9types.com
Free test Max Marmer: tinyurl.com/irpm413[247] (also see https://www.blog.trueself.io/)

Type combinations (very helpful):

Enneagram Institute: tinyurl.com/irpm402[248]
David Daniels: tinyurl.com/irpm403[249]
Lynn Roulo: tinyurl.com/irpm415[250]

Instincts tests

Enneagram Institute: tinyurl.com/irpm416[251]
Similar Minds: tinyurl.com/irpm418[252]
(Use Google search to find more tests)

Videos:

Dr. Khaled ElSherbini tinyurl.com/irpm424[253]
Joshua French (look for his Enneagram Videos)

tinyurl.com/irpm495[254]
Josh Keefe: The Enneagram Explained with Movie Characters
tinyurl.com/irpm425[255]

Enneagram apps:

tinyurl.com/irpm426[256]

Books

All Enneagram books on Amazon:
tinyurl.com/irpm428[257]

The Wisdom of the Enneagram: The Complete Guide to Psychological and Spiritual Growth for the Nine Personality Types (1999) by Don Richard Riso and Russ Hudson
tinyurl.com/irpm430[258]

Facets of Unity: The Enneagram of Holy Ideas (2000) by A. H. Almaas
tinyurl.com/irpm431[259]

The Nine Keys: A Guide Book To Unlock Your Relationships Using Kundalini Yoga and the Enneagram (2018) by Lynn Roulo
tinyurl.com/irpm433[260]

The Enneagram, Relationships, and Intimacy: Understanding One Another Leads to Loving Better and Living More Fully (2018) by David Daniels and Suzanne Dion.
tinyurl.com/irpm434[261]

The Enneagram in Love and Work: Understanding Your Intimate and Business Relationships (1995) by Helen Palmer
tinyurl.com/irpm435[262] (See Palmer's other books as well).

Sex Purpose Love **book reference**

Page 89–94

Suggested movie: *Winnie the Pooh* (2011)

Watch this and other movies from Disney's *Winnie the Pooh* series (Disney-Buena Vista Home Videos) or read the books to see that most of the Pooh characters clearly fit one of the nine different Enneagram styles, which is one of the reasons these stories are both charming and memorable. Here is the list of characters and their corresponding Enneagram types:[263]

1. The Reformer: Rabbit
2. The Helper: Kanga (mother of Roo)
3. The Achiever: Gopher
4. The Individualist: Eeyore
5. The Investigator: Owl
6. The Loyalist: Piglet
7. The Enthusiast: Tigger
8. The Challenger: Gorilla
9. The Mediator: Pooh

While searching for honey, Pooh and his friends embark on an adventure to find Eeyore's missing tail and rescue Christopher Robin from an unknown monster called The Backson.

Practice Module 17
Attachment Styles

Your task is not to seek for love, but merely to seek and find all the barriers within yourself that you have built against it.
~ Jalal Rumi ~

Module description

Learn and practice how to identify your and your partner's attachment style through a test and conversation about how you feel about intimate relationships and react under relationship stress. Gain a deeper understanding of the four attachment styles that are formed in early childhood and remain with you into your adult life: secure, anxious, avoidant, and anxious-avoidant (also called disorganized, disoriented, or ambivalent). Explore how your genetic predisposition and your relationship with your parents and other caregivers formed your attachment style. Realize that you can heal your relationship wounds only in intimate love relationships, ideally with a partner who is more secure than you are.

Move towards earned secure autonomous attachment by creating a coherent narrative that supports you in removing psychological blocks and healing childhood wounds that limit you emotionally in your capacity to form a healthy sustainable love relationship. Support others in learning about their attachment style and becoming more secure.

Introduction

Closely related to personality types are four attachment styles that are formed through genetic predispositions and early childhood experiences with our primary caregiver(s)/parents: (1) secure, (2) anxious, (3) avoidant, and (4) anxious-avoidant (aka ambivalent, disoriented, or disorganized).[264] Once established, the style remains into adulthood and emerges in how we relate in intimate relationships and in how we parent our children. The difference between personality types and attachment styles is that the former tend to be fixed and have healthy and unhealthy expressions, while attachment styles can be steered or transformed from the three unhealthy styles towards healthy earned secure autonomous attachment.

The general patterns of different attachment styles were discovered in the 1940's and 1950's by the British psychologist, John Bowlby (1907–1990), who observed higher rates of maladaptation and delinquency in children who were separated from their families during the war. His findings were refined in the 1960's and 1970's by Bowlby's collaborator, the Canadian developmental psychologist Mary Ainsworth (1913–1999). She developed the Strange Situation Test, in which she observed how small children behaved when a caregiver left the room and returned after some time.[265] The American psychologist Mary Main (1943-), who was Ainsworth's student, later discovered the fourth anxious-avoidant style and created the Adult Attachment Interview and coding system (see below) for assessing different states of mind regarding attachment.

Their combined findings showed that young children need to develop a dependable relationship with at least one primary caregiver (usually the mother) for their social and emotional development to occur normally. Without this security, they will suffer serious psychological and social difficulties. How the parents or caregivers respond to their infants in the first two years, particularly during times of distress, establishes the attachment style of their children. This childhood style will proceed to guide their feelings, thoughts, and expectations in their adult relationships in profound and enduring ways and will also be transmitted to their own children.

For example, if the main caregiver, who is supposed to make the child feel safe and secure, is threatening, absent, confusing, or ambivalent, it will result in one of the "insecure" attachment styles. Hardly anyone feels 100 percent secure in their love relationships all of the time; however, when and how the insecure attachment styles are triggered, as well as the form and degree of expression and the way of dealing with them, varies greatly between people.

Understanding attachment styles is essential because of the insights they offer into how partners may have felt and developed in childhood, and into how they may be emotionally limited in their capacity to relate. This understanding of their own fundamental orientation towards other people can greatly help them to realize what they may need to change to improve their relationships, including the relationships with their own children.[266]

Purpose and application of the module

1. Learn about the four attachment styles.
2. Identify your and your partner's attachment style through a test and through sharing about your childhood and adult relationship experiences.
3. Notice when you move from a secure into an insecure style.
4. Learn to self-regulate through mindful awareness and staying present with the fear/pain/terror that you may experience under relationship stress instead of acting out of the old wounds and behavioral patterns.
5. Create and share a coherent narrative about your childhood experiences.
6. Communicate your feelings and needs to your partner without being clingy or avoidant, and assure him or her that you will return to secure connection and love when you have calmed your nervous system.
7. Seek help from a trained therapist if self-help measures in this module and the given resources are ineffective to address your attachment wounds.
8. Accept that in rare cases people cannot heal their attachment wounds and co-create healthy love relationships, especially if they are combined with severe personality disorders (see Module 21 on page 391) and deep trauma.
9. Support others in identifying their attachment styles and becoming more secure.

Exercises: Attachment styles

The following are individual and paired exercises.
1. Print out the attachment style quiz below (double-sided).
2. Present a short introduction to the history of attachment style research.
3. Make the four agreements for confidentiality, responsibility, healthy boundaries, I-statements, and sharing, as outlined on page 556.

Exercise one: Attachment style quiz

1. Explain the attachment style quiz below, which can be a bit confusing to fill out.
2. Make sure everyone understands how to take the test.
3. Ask practitioners to take the test by feeling into the times when they experienced relationship stress.
4. Invite the practitioners to share the results with the group. You may mention that there is no shame in any style, as nobody chose their genetic predisposition and parents.

Worksheet: Attachment styles

Feel into a time when you were (madly) in love, (terribly) heartbroken, or had relationship stress.

Mark the small circle next to each statement that is TRUE for you. If the statement does not apply or is NOT true for you, do not mark the circle and go to the next statement. At the end, count all A, B, and C circles that you marked.

	True		
	A	B	C
1. I often worry that my partner will stop loving me.	O		
2. I find it easy to be affectionate with my partner.		O	
3. I fear that once someone gets to know the real me, s/he won't like who I am.	O		

4. I find that I bounce back quickly after a breakup. It's weird how I can just put someone out of my mind.				O
5. When I'm not involved in a relationship, I feel somewhat anxious and incomplete.	O			
6. I find it difficult to emotionally support my partner when s/he is feeling down.				O
7. When my partner is away, I'm afraid that s/he might become interested in someone else.	O			
8. I feel comfortable depending on romantic partners.			O	
9. My independence is more important to me than my relationships.				O
10. I prefer not to share my innermost feelings with my partner.				O
11. When I show my partner how I feel, I'm afraid s/he will not feel the same about me.	O			
12. I am generally satisfied with my romantic relationships.			O	
13. I don't feel the need to act out much in my romantic relationships.			O	
14. I think about my relationships a lot.	O			
15. I find it difficult to depend on romantic partners.				O
16. I tend to get very quickly attached to a romantic partner.	O			
17. I have little difficulty expressing my needs and wants to my partner.			O	
18. I sometimes feel angry or annoyed with my partner without knowing why.				O
19. I am very sensitive to my partner's moods.	O			
20. I believe most people are essentially honest and dependable.			O	

21. I prefer casual sex with uncommitted partners to intimate sex with one person.			O
22. I'm comfortable sharing my personal thoughts and feelings with my partner.		O	
23. I worry that if my partner leaves me, I might never find someone else.	O		
24. It makes me nervous when my partner gets too close.			O
25. During a conflict, I tend to impulsively do or say things I later regret, rather than being able to reason about things.	O		
26. An argument with my partner doesn't usually cause me to question our entire relationship.		O	
27. My partners often want me to be more intimate than I feel comfortable being.			O
28. I worry that I'm not attractive enough.	O		
29. Sometimes people see me as boring because I create little drama in relationships.		O	
30. I miss my partner when we're apart, but then when we're together I feel the need to escape.			O
31. When I disagree with someone, I feel comfortable expressing my opinions.		O	
32. I hate feeling that other people depend on me.			O
33. If I notice that someone I'm interested in is checking out other people, I don't let it faze me. I might feel a pang of jealousy, but it's fleeting.		O	
34. If I notice that someone I'm interested in is checking out other people, I feel relieved—it means s/he's not looking to make things exclusive.			O
35. If I notice that someone I'm interested in is checking out other people, it makes me feel depressed.	O		

36. If someone I've been dating begins to act cold and distant, I may wonder what's happened, but I'll know it's probably not about me.		O	
37. If someone I've been dating begins to act cold and distant, I'll probably be indifferent; I might even be relieved.			O
38. If someone I've been dating begins to act cold and distant, I'll worry that I've done something wrong.	O		
39. If my partner was to break up with me, I'd try my best to show her/him what s/he is missing (a little jealousy can't hurt).	O		
40. If someone I've been dating for several months tells me s/he wants to stop seeing me, I'd feel hurt at first, but I'd get over it.		O	
41. Sometimes when I get what I want in a relationship, I'm not sure what I want anymore.			O
42. I won't have much of a problem staying in touch with my ex (strictly platonic)—after all, we have a lot in common.		O	

Table 15: Attachment style test

From the book *Attached*: adapted from Fraley, Waller, and Brennan's (2000) ECR-R Questionnaire.

Add up all your checked circles in column A: _____ Anxious

Add up all your checked circles in column B: _____ Secure

Add up all your checked circles in column C: _____ Avoidant

Short description of attachment styles

Anxiously attached: These adults seek high levels of intimacy, approval, and responsiveness from their partners.

Securely attached: Adults with this style tend to have positive views of themselves, their partners, and their relationships.

Avoidant: These adults desire a high level of independence and often avoid attachment altogether.

Anxious-Avoidant: Describes adults who show high anxiety and high avoidance and constantly live in an ambivalent state in which they are afraid of being both too close and too distant from others.

Exercise two: Liking/not liking about relationship/being single?

This can be an additional individual or paired exercise to support the practitioners in determining their attachment style.
1. Invite the practitioners to feel into the four questions below and to note as many answers as come up for them.
2. Ask practitioners to chart the positive and challenging "negative" (fearful) feelings in their answers along the vertical and horizontal line of low or high avoidance/anxiety of relationships, as shown in the graph below, to get pointers on their attachment style.

What do you like about being in a relationship? (Low anxiety)	What do you like about being alone (single)? (High avoidance)
What do you not like about being in a relationship? (High anxiety)	What do you not like about being alone (single)? (Low avoidance)

Table 16: What do you like/not like about being in relationship/single

```
                    LOW
                 AVOIDANCE
                     ▲            ANXIOUSLY
      SECURE         │             ATTACHED
           ↖         │         ↗
              ↖      │      ↗
                 ↖   │   ↗
   LOW              │              HIGH
 ANXIETY ◄──────────┼──────────► ANXIETY
                 ↙   │   ↘
              ↙      │      ↘
           ↙         │         ↘
                     │             ANXIOUS
     AVOIDANT        │            AVOIDANT
                     ▼
                    HIGH
                 AVOIDANCE
```

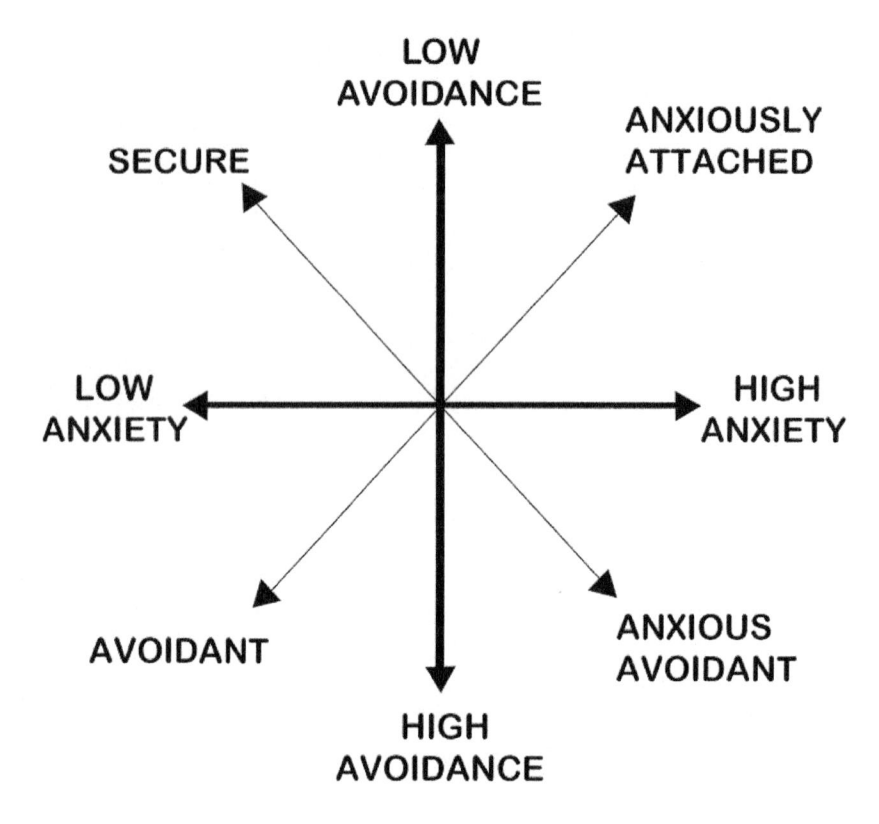

Figure 44: Four attachment styles

Optional Exercise

1. Watch/share the three-minute video about the "still-face experiment," with Dr. Edward Tronick, (tinyurl.com/irpm49)[267] in which we see a baby reacting to being ignored by her mother.
2. Invite the practitioners to share their feelings after seeing the video

Exercise three: Share about your attachment style

The following is a paired exercise in which practitioners answer the following questions to each other.

1. Provide an example of how to create a coherent narrative as described in the endnote[268] and why this is helpful for becoming more secure.
2. Encourage couples to do this exercise together.
3. Ask individuals with little experience to pair up with someone more experienced.
4. Invite group sharing after the exercise.

Attachment style exercise questions

1. In what specific situations has an insecure attachment style been triggered in your past relationships and in your current relationship?
2. How did you react, how did your partner react?
3. How would a person with a secure attachment style have reacted?
4. In which concrete situations was an insecure attachment style triggered in your partner(s) in past relationships and in your current relationship?
5. How did he or she react, how did you react?
6. How would a person with a safe attachment style have reacted?
7. Has your attachment style changed over the years?
8. What do you want to change to become more secure in your relationships?
9. What would be the "coherent narrative" (a retelling that makes sense) about your childhood?

Optional questions from the *Adult Attachment Interview Protocol*[269] (for emotionally stable practitioners only!)

1. How do you think your early childhood relationship with your primary caregivers/parents shaped your attachment style?
2. Name at least five adjectives from your early childhood memories that describe your main caregiver.
3. To which caregiver/parent did you feel the closest connection? Why not to the other?

4. If you were upset/angry as a child, what did you do?
5. Have you ever been threatened or abused by your primary caregivers— consciously or unconsciously?
6. How did your relationship with your primary caregivers shape you as an adult?
7. Why do you think your primary caregivers behaved the way they did?
8. Did you lose a primary caregiver in your childhood?
9. Did you have other traumatic experiences with primary caregivers in your childhood?
10. What is (or was) your current relationship with your primary caregivers and has it changed?

Follow-up questions

1. How do you feel after this exercise?
2. Do you need any support in processing the feelings that came up for you?
3. What insights have you gained through the quiz and paired exercise?
4. How will your experience and insights inform your current and future relationships?
5. Will you share the test with your dates and partners?

Additional information and resources

Below are short descriptions of the four attachment styles and processes to move towards secure attachment. Please refer to the book and website resources below for deepening your understanding and for healing of your attachment wounds.

Securely attached

Adults with this style tend to have positive views of themselves, their partners, and their relationships. They feel comfortable with intimacy and independence by balancing the two; are reliable and consistent; make decisions with their partner; communicate relationship issues well; can reach compromise during arguments;

are not afraid of commitment and healthy dependency; don't view relationships as hard work; create closeness that creates further closeness; introduce friends and family early on; naturally express feelings for their partner; and don't play games.

Anxiously attached

These adults seek high levels of intimacy, approval, and responsiveness from their partner, can become overly dependent, and may exhibit high levels of emotional expressiveness, worry, and impulsiveness in their relationships. They want a lot of closeness in the relationship; express insecurities such as angst about being rejected; are unhappy when not in a relationship; play games to keep the attention and interest of their partner; have difficulties explaining what's bothering them; expect their partner to guess their feelings and needs correctly; are preoccupied with the relationship; fear that small missteps will ruin the relationship; believe that they must work hard to keep their partner interested; and are suspicious that their partner may be unfaithful.

Avoidant

These adults desire a high level of independence and often avoid attachment altogether. They view themselves as self-sufficient; are invulnerable to attachment feelings; don't need close relationships for their well-being; suppress vulnerable feelings; deal with rejection by distancing themselves from partners (of whom they often have a poor opinion); are less trusting; send mixed signals; value their independence greatly; devalue their current or previous partners; use emotional and physical distancing strategies; emphasize boundaries in the relationship; have an unrealistically romantic view of how a relationship should be; fear being taken advantage of by a partner; have a rigid view of relationships and uncompromising rules; get away during disagreements or explode; don't make their intentions clear; and may have difficulty talking about what's going on between themselves and their partner.

Anxious-Avoidant

Sometimes called disorganized, disoriented or ambivalent, this fourth additional style describes adults who show high anxiety and high avoidance or patterns of attachment and constantly live in an ambivalent state in which they are afraid of being both too close and too distant from others. They can't avoid their anxiety or run away from their feelings. Instead, they are overwhelmed by their reactions and often experience emotional storms. They tend to be mixed up or unpredictable in their moods. They see their relationships from the working model that you need to go toward others to have your needs met but that if you get too close to others, they will hurt you. In other words, the person they want to go to for safety is the same person they are frightened to be close to.

Anxious-avoidant people attempt to keep their feelings at bay but are unable to do so. Since they detached from their feelings during times of trauma as children, they continue to be somewhat detached from themselves. They desire relationships and are comfortable in them until they become emotionally close. At this point, the feelings that were repressed in childhood begin to resurface and, with no awareness that the feelings come from the past, these people experience them as being in the present. In fact, the person is not present in the here and now at all but is suddenly reliving an old trauma. These people's lives are not balanced: they do not have a coherent sense of themselves, nor do they have a clear connection with others. As a result, they have no organized strategy for getting their needs met by others and find themselves in rocky or dramatic relationships with many highs and lows. They often have fears of being abandoned but also struggle with being intimate. They may cling to their partner when they feel rejected, then feel trapped when they are close. Often, the timing seems to be off between themselves and their partner. A person with anxious-avoidant attachment may even wind up in an abusive relationship.

Becoming Secure

In his book *The Developing Mind: How Relationships and the Brain Interact to Shape Who We Are*, Dr. Dan Siegel coined the term "Earned Secure/Autonomous Attachment." Although attachment styles begin to be formed in infancy, he maintains that it is possible to make sense of them and overcome the unhealthy patterns from which they arose by writing a "coherent narrative" with the help of a trained therapist. The process supports clients in understanding how childhood experiences are still affecting them in their adult relational lives. Through creating a "coherent narrative," their brains rewire themselves to build healthier, more secure attachments through building emotional resilience and security in relationships.

Because the ability for secure attachment was broken in early relationships, it is only possible to fix the lingering damage from them while in a love relationship or by methodically analyzing and reliving a partnership that ended dramatically. Siegel's colleague, Dr. Lisa Firestone, says, "One of the proven ways to change our attachment style is by forming an attachment with someone who had a more secure attachment style than what we've experienced. We can also talk to a therapist, as the therapeutic relationship can help create a more secure attachment. We can continue to get to know ourselves through understanding our past experiences, allowing ourselves to make sense and feel the full pain of our stories, then moving forward as separate, differentiated adults. In doing this, we move through the world with an internal sense of security that helps us better withstand the natural hurts that life can bring."[270]

As with all personality types, we carry traits of each attachment style in us. A person who is generally securely attached may slip into avoidant, anxious, or anxious-avoidant patterns when he or she falls in love and comes under relational stress.

Bringing awareness to your and your partner's attachment style will support you in healing early childhood wounds and catching each other when you fall back into old patterns.

Other attachment style tests

Attachment Metaproject tinyurl.com/irpm437[271] (great website with good resources)
Greatist 5 Attachment Style Quizzes tinyurl.com/irpm442[272]
Diane Poole Heller's Attachment Styles Test tinyurl.com/irpm444[273]
Attachment Styles and Close Relationships tinyurl.com/irpm446[274]
Video about attachment styles: tinyurl.com/irpm50[275]

Books:

Attached: The New Science of Adult Attachment and How It Can Help You Find—and Keep—Love (2012) by Amir Levine and Rachel Heller
tinyurl.com/irpm450[276]

Polysecure: Attachment, Trauma and Consensual Nonmonogamy (2020) by Jessica Fern
tinyurl.com/irpm451[277]

The Developing Mind, Second Edition: How Relationships and the Brain Interact to Shape Who We Are (2015) by Daniel J. Siegel
tinyurl.com/irpm453[278]

Attachment Disturbances in Adults: Treatment for Comprehensive Repair (2016) by Daniel P. Brown, PhD, and David S. Elliott, PhD
tinyurl.com/irpm455[279]

Attachment in Psychotherapie (2015) by David J. Wallin
tinyurl.com/irpm458[280]

Healing Developmental Trauma: How Early Trauma Affects Self-Regulation, Self-Image, and the Capacity for Relationship (2012) by Laurence Heller, PhD, and Aline LaPierre PsyD
tinyurl.com/irpm459[281]

Websites

CDC–Kaiser Permanente Adverse Childhood Experiences (ACE) Study tinyurl.com/irpm460[282]

tinyurl.com/irpm461[283]

Write a Coherent Narrative
Huffington Post tinyurl.com/irpm462[284]
Ecourse Psychalive tinyurl.com/irpm463[285]

Books on Amazon about interviewing your parents:
Mom tinyurl.com/irpm464[286]
Dad tinyurl.com/irpm467[287]
Story Worth Questions tinyurl.com/irpm468[288]

Sex Purpose Love **book reference**
Page 96–100

Suggested movie: *As Good As It Gets* (1997)

Watch this movie to see the misanthropic, obsessive-compulsive, egocentric, cynical, and manipulative best-selling romance novelist, Melvin Udall (Jack Nicholson), as he struggles with his anxious-avoiding attachment style after he falls in love with the waitress Carol Connelly (Helen Hunt), who displays an avoidant attachment style (or healthy boundaries, depending on your view).

After his neighbor, the sensitive gay artist Simon Bishop (Greg Kinnear), is assaulted and nearly killed during a robbery in his New York apartment, Melvin is forced to take care of Simon's dog, Verdell, to whom he becomes emotionally attached. This softens his relationship with Carol. Melvin's life is turned upside down when Carol leaves her job to care for her acutely asthmatic son, Spencer (Jesse James). To reconnect with her, Melvin hires a doctor to take care of her son and invites Carol to go on a road-trip with him and Simon, who is by now broke and needs to ask his parents for money. At dinner with Carol during the trip, Melvin lets down his guard and confesses to her, "You make me want to be a better man"—only to ruin the romantic moment a minute later when he suggests that Carol should have sex with Simon to help him "get over" his gayness. After returning to New York, Carol tells Melvin that she does not want him in her life anymore but later regrets her statement and calls to apologize. After Melvin is persuaded by Simon to meet Carol in the middle of the night and declare his love for her, Carol hesitantly agrees to establish a relationship with him.

Practice Module 18
The Unconscious and Emotional Availability

Everything that irritates us about others can lead us to an understanding of ourselves.
~ Carl Gustav Jung ~

Module description

Learn and practice how to become emotionally available and deepen your love relationship by taking full responsibility for your primary emotional fight, flight, or freeze reactions to your partner's reality, instead of projecting them outward onto him or her through blaming. Separate your observations and perceptions from your emotional reactions. Realize that your partner is not "creating" painful emotions and feelings in you, but rather "stimulates" or "triggers" already present unconscious psychological wounds and trauma in you. Create a space between these triggers and your response, instead of reacting from your wounded self. Get in touch with underlying vulnerable and painful feelings that are protected by your primary emotional reactions.

Integrate your feelings by differentiating and (re-)owning them (I have feelings, but I am not my feelings) instead of dissociating, repressing, denying, ignoring, or splitting them off. Re-enter the communication with your partner in a sensible and vulnerable way that is not defended by your unconscious wounds, trauma, and unrealized potentials once you feel calmer and more in tune with yourself, instead of fighting and separating.

Enjoy the benefits of this "undefended love" approach that leads to increasing peace, joy, aliveness, vulnerability, compassion, intimacy, and connection in all your relationships. Become ready for the deep healing process, in practice Module 19, through facing your false beliefs and deepest fears and recognizing your true identity.

Introduction

In Module 18, we explore the first two steps of the "healing your shadow/unconscious" process that we will practice in the following Module 19.

The two modules are about restoring and deepening the connection with ourselves and others that fulfills our longing to feel loved and fully alive in a healthy love relationship. An impaired capacity for connection to self and others, and the ensuing diminished aliveness, are caused by hidden unconscious dimensions that underlie most psychological and many physiological challenges. Unfortunately, we are often unaware of these inner roadblocks that keep us from experiencing the connection, love, aliveness, meaning, and purpose for which we all yearn. These roadblocks developed in reaction to developmental and shock trauma and the related nervous systems dysregulations, attachment disruptions, and distortions of our identity.[289]

The exercise begins with the first two steps of the Nonviolent Compassionate Communication process of expressing objective observations and subjective feelings that we practiced in Module 6. But instead of continuing with stating unmet needs and making requests for changed behaviors in our partner (which has its place in certain situations, especially when being-needs, agreements, or values are violated), we will use a psycho-spiritual process of transforming needs into desires, desires into wants, wants into preferences, and preferences into no preferences (surrendering and accepting what is in the present moment) that allows us to sense deeper into the vulnerable and often unconscious feelings that are protected and defended by our primary emotional reactions such as anger, sadness, disgust, fear, surprise, and shame, as shown in the wheel below and listed in the worksheet of feelings and interpretations in Module 6, on page 117.

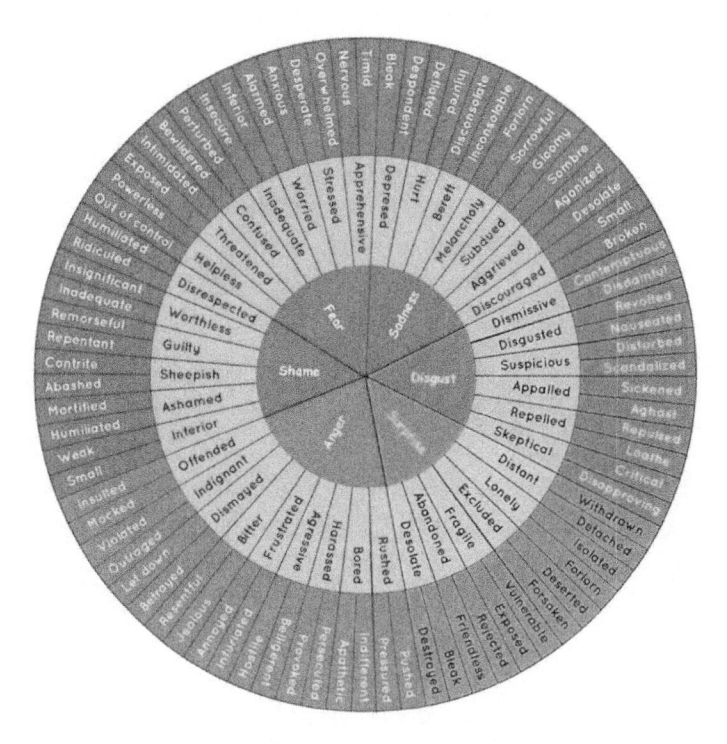

Figure 45: Primary emotions and vulnerable feelings

This process will lead us to become more emotionally available by creating a space between primary emotional triggers and our response, by taking full responsibility for the vulnerable feelings, and by making them into an "object" that we own through disidentifying (I experience anger, fear, shame, etc., but am not my anger, etc.), instead of repressing or being overwhelmed by them, and withdrawing or becoming defensive and projecting them onto our partner.[290]

Mutually compatible pathologies

Humans appear to have an intuitive capacity to scan another person's unconscious blueprint. In the book *Blink: The Power of Thinking Without Thinking*, by Malcom Gladwell, this capacity is described as "our ability to use limited information from a very narrow period of experience to come to a conclusion." Partners to whom we feel most drawn emotionally (rather than sexually or rationally) and who make us happy complement our unconscious in multiple ways.[291]

Alas, someone who has the power to attract us and make us happy also has the power to annoy us and make us unhappy when he or she triggers old childhood wounds or challenges us in ways that are outside of our comfort zone, beyond our event horizon, or "over our head."

As described above, instead of becoming defensive when "emotional buttons get pushed that our partner did not install," we learn to see these triggers as an invitation to look and feel intently into ourselves, take the information we gathered through the "looking" step, strengthen our "true identity or essential self" through mindful meta-awareness or witness consciousness, and own the emotions and feelings that enter our awareness instead of projecting them onto our partner.

With time and effort, you'll notice a difference in your reactions and self-awareness. Then celebrate the progress you've made in becoming more in tune with your true self or essence and with your partner.

In other words, Integral couples see emotional triggers as an opportunity to learn from each other, heal their unconscious, grow in all developmental lines, and awaken together.

The five forms of the unconscious

We all carry psychological blueprints that hold the details and lingering imprints of our genes, heritage, trauma, culture, and potentials.

The repressed, unacknowledged, or undeveloped parts of this unconscious blueprint contain the information that drives our irrational fears, anxieties, coping mechanisms, and defenses, as well as our growth potentials, creativity, yearnings, and passions. In this context, people often speak of "shadow," which are aspects of painful past experiences that are repressed into our unconscious. However, there are other forms of the unconscious, which Ken

Wilber describes in his book *The Atman Project*,[292] that are of relevance for the mysterious magnetism and resulting healing and growth potentials that lovers experience at various times in their relationships at the levels of their bodies, minds, hearts, souls, and spirits.

The ground unconscious

Represents our shared unrealized embedded potentials. All humans carry the potential, after conception, to grow in their physicality and in their consciousness (from body to mind, heart, soul, and spirit), like an acorn that holds the potential to become a grown oak tree.

The ground unconscious explains why people are unconsciously attracted to an opposite partner with whom they can grow in kind and degree to realize their full human potentials at all levels of their being and to eventually create their own offspring.[293]

The archaic unconscious

Is linked to the unique predispositions and instincts that individuals have inherited from their ancestral past.

This innate set of tendencies explains why most people feel more comfortable and resonant with a partner who shares their own heritage.[294]

The submerged unconscious

Is what Carl Jung called the shadow, or the subconscious.[295] It represents all experiences and memories that were once conscious and are now screened out of awareness, either through simple forgetting or a more forceful repression, negation, or dissociation.[296]

This subconscious explains why people feel attracted to a partner who had traumatic experiences similar to their own during their upbringing, and, more significantly, developed coping mechanisms that are different from their own.[297]

The embedded unconscious

Was called the "superego" by Freud, referring to culturally conditioned aspects of the self (I or ego) that can critically observe "it" parts of its existence, such as the pleasure-seeking body, behavior, thoughts, feelings, emotions, or even its essence—but never itself (until made conscious).[298]

This explains why people are attracted to an opposite and equal partner who sees beyond their limited identity, as it is their soul's deepest desire to be seen for who they truly are and awaken to their deepest essence.[299]

The emergent unconscious

Represents unique potentials that have not yet emerged, like the novel unfolding of a particular oak tree.[300]

This explains why people who struggle at a particular level of consciousness, spiritual, sexual, anima/animus complex, and other developmental lines, or who are less emotionally stable or available than others are attracted to a partner at the next higher level. See *Figure 30: Personality matrix*, on page 187.

Purpose and application of the module

1. Separate your observations and perceptions of your partner's reality/behavior from your primary emotional reactions.
2. Realize that your partner is not "creating" challenging primary emotions and vulnerable feelings in you, but rather "stimulates" or "triggers" already existing forms of your unconscious or "pushes buttons s/he has not installed."
3. Create a space between your primary emotional triggers and your unconscious defensive reactions so that you can respond in a sensible and vulnerable (emotionally available) way after you have calmed down.
4. Learn to "own" your primary emotional fight, flight, or freeze reactions without blaming/shaming your partner.

5. Get in touch with and express the underlying unconscious, vulnerable feelings that are protected by your primary emotional reactions.
6. Be clear about the shared values, imperatives, agreements, purposes, and boundaries between you and your partner that must be respected and maintained to create a safe container for emotional safety, vulnerability, and healing.
7. Prepare for the "Healing your Shadow/Unconscious" exercise in Module 19.

Kleenex/tissue box demonstration of emotional reactions

Use a box with tissues to demonstrate three unhealthy ways of reacting and one healthy way of responding to emotional triggers. You may have your assistant or a practitioner demonstrate with you:

1. Have the box thrown towards you, and then immediately throw it back to where it came from and defend yourself or blame the other to demonstrate a fight/dispute/blame reaction.
2. Let the box hit you and play the "poor-me victim" by saying, "Life is unfair"; "My partner is so mean to me"; "This always happens to me"; "I have no choice"; "S/he always hurts my feelings"; "I don't know what to do"; "I need to be rescued"; etc.
3. Dodge the box or let it bounce off yourself, like you are made of Teflon, avoiding confrontation because you are so spiritual, saying, spiritual people don't get angry"; "Nothing can touch me"; "I don't react because I am so present and surrender to everything (Omm)"; "What you resist persists"; etc. — which are all reactions that fall under the category of "spiritual bypassing" and being emotionally repressed or unavailable.
4. Catch the Box; pause; take responsibility for your behavior/action and emotional reaction; look inside; take out a tissue and look at it as a metaphor of your unconscious; and

see how you can grow and heal through the emotional trigger and vulnerable feelings.

Stuffed animal demonstration of emotional dis/identification

1. Hide a small stuffed animal or puppet under your shirt, in front of your chest/heart.
2. Pull it out at the collar to indicate emotions and feelings arising, and hold it in front of your face to indicate that you become identified with them.
3. Act out the emotion/feeling, play the victim, or spiritually bypass.
4. Look at the animal/puppet (emotion/feeling) and own it but disidentify from it without projecting it onto the other person or dissociating, denying, ignoring, repressing, or splitting it off.
5. Integrate the emotions and feelings: I have anger (or other emotional reactions) and feelings that were stimulated by you, but I am not my emotions and feelings. I own them and take responsibility by witnessing them.

Exercises: Emotional availability

The following are all paired exercises.

1. Print out the NVC worksheet on page 117 and the worksheet below.
2. Make the four agreements for confidentiality, responsibility, healthy boundaries, I-statements, and sharing, as outlined on page 556.
3. Read the questions in the worksheet below to practitioners, give examples, and answer questions.
4. Explain that if the words "like" (I feel "like" an idiot) or "that" (I feel "that" I can't trust you), etc., are placed before an emotion or feeling word, then usually no emotion or feeling is expressed. Other "killer" words that prevent intimacy are "always" and "never."

5. Explain the difference between interpretations and authentic emotions/feelings (see list in Nonviolent Compassionate Communication Worksheet on page 117.)

Exercise one: Differentiate observation, primary emotional reaction, and vulnerable feeling

1. Ask practitioners to pair up with their romantic partner, and individuals to pair up with someone who is already experienced with this kind of work.
2. Ask practitioners to choose who answers the questions below first. Questions 1–3 are especially important.
3. Allow at least 30 minutes for each practitioner.

Worksheet: Emotional availability

1. What was/is the situation that triggered a fight, flight, or freeze reaction in you?
2. State your primary emotional reaction: what did you do, what did you feel?
3. State the underlying unconscious vulnerable feeling(s) (see image and worksheet on page 117) that were protected by your primary emotional reaction? (You may think back to a similar childhood situation and how you felt then, or how a child may feel in such a situation.)
4. Were you able to separate the reality/behavior of your partner from your emotional reaction and vulnerable feelings, and own them, or did you project them onto him/her?
5. If so, in what way?
6. How did your partner react?
7. How was the situation resolved (including possibly ignoring/bypassing it)?
8. What is it about yourself that perceived the situation as hostile, unacceptable, abusive, threatening, uncomfortable, etc.?

9. What kind of support could you provide to yourself to better handle the emotional reaction and vulnerable feelings that were brought up in the uncomfortable situation?
10. What kind of support would you like to receive from your partner to better handle the emotional reaction and vulnerable feelings that were brought up in the uncomfortable situation?
11. Is there a characteristic or ability that you feel you need within yourself to stay present with, disidentify from, and integrate these feelings?
12. What is a "coherent narrative" that explains your emotional reaction and underlying vulnerable feelings? See endnote.[268]
13. How would you share this "coherent narrative" with your partner?
14. What are imperatives/agreements with your partner about shared values/visions, healthy boundaries, truthfulness, curiosity, openness, and vulnerability that must be met and not continually violated to create a safe container for the learning, healing, growing, and awakening practices to take place in a committed, undefended love relationship with a shared purpose?

Follow-up questions

1. How do you feel after doing this exercise and what insights did you gain?
2. How will this exercise impact your love relationships?

Additional information and resources

The 3-2-1 Shadow Process

Ken Wilber often mentions the 3-2-1 Process that uses shifts in perspectives as a way of identifying and integrating unconscious aspects of the self.

In this process, dissociation is believed to proceed from 1st-person to 2nd-person to 3rd-person:

1. Each part that we disown is at first an aspect of our "I" or 1st-person awareness. We are identified with it.
2. This part is then often unconsciously projected onto other people (2nd person). You are …. You make me ….
3. If the threat of this emotion or situation becomes unbearable, we banish it totally as a 3rd-person "It" aversion toward things that we can no longer face (but that still create irritation, reactivity, fear, phobia, rage, or aversion).

The reversal of dissociation towards disidentification and owning emotional reactions and vulnerable feelings thus goes from 3 to 2 to 1 as (3) face it, (2) talk to it, and (1) finally, BE it. Thus, the 3-2-1 shadow process.[301]

Books:

Undefended Love: The Way You Felt About Yourself When You First Fell in Love is the Way You Can Feel All the Time (2000) by Jett Psaris and Marlena S Lyons.
tinyurl.com/irpm473[302]

See all books by A. H. Almas/Diamond Approach
tinyurl.com/irpm477[303]

The Atman Project: A Transpersonal View of Human Development (1996) by Ken Wilber
tinyurl.com/irpm479[304]

Sex Purpose Love book reference

Page 108–113

Suggested movie: *Prince of Tides* (1991)

Watch this movie to see how the effects of childhood trauma and the repression of related memories and emotions negatively impact our ability to feel fully alive, to live on purpose, and to form healthy love relationships.

The film stars its director, Barbra Streisand, as New York psychiatrist Dr. Susan Lowenstein. She treats the emotionally scarred Sallie Wingo (Blythe Danner), a woman who tried to commit suicide. To solve the mysteries of her troubled client's past, Lowenstein asks Sallie's twin brother, Tom (Nick Nolte), an unemployed, aimless, and miserable football coach, to come to New York from South Carolina, where he lives in a strained relationship with his wife and daughters. As Lowenstein and Tom work together and fall in love, deep hidden secrets are revealed and healing takes place that transforms them to find new meaning in their life.

Practice Module 19
Healing your Shadow/Unconscious

*It's the old rule that drunks have to argue
and get into fights.
The lover is just as bad. he falls into a hole.
But down in that hole he finds something shining,
worth more than any amount of money or power.*

*Last night the moon came dropping its clothes in the street.
I took it as a sign to start singing,
falling up into the bowl of sky.
The bowl breaks. Everywhere is falling everywhere.
Nothing else to do.*

*Here's the new rule: break the wineglass,
and fall toward the glassblower's breath.*
~ Jalal Rumi ~

Module description

Learn and practice how to transform your relationship conflicts into opportunities for ongoing learning, healing, growing, awakening. Discover your true identity or essence through a simple, yet profound, six-step process. Take full responsibility for your primary emotional reactions to your partner's reality instead of becoming defensive. Get in touch with the underlying vulnerable feelings that are protected by your primary emotional reactions and make them conscious. Realize the false beliefs about yourself that are hidden below your vulnerable feelings. Face your deepest fears. State your false identity. Receive an affirmation and additional information about your true identity.

Heal your emotional wounds and psychological trauma by becoming fully present and by changing the ways you think about yourself and behave. Stop feeling responsible for your partner's emotional reactions to your reality, and instead meet him or her with love, compassion, and understanding in mutuality. Move towards ever-deepening intimacy, passion, and commitment by being less defensive. Feel, all of the time, the way you felt when you first fell in love. Enjoy an undefended love relationship.

Introduction

In Module 19, we combine the five-step process to uncover our false identity—from the book *Undefended Love,* by psychotherapists Jett Psaris and Marlena S. Lyons, whose work is grounded in A.H. Almas's Diamond Approach—with the "Transformation of Identity Matrix" that was created by "Feminine Power" originators, Katherine Woodward Thomas and Claire Zammit.

Many practitioners call this process a "miracle exercise" because it allows emotionally available and mindful couples to resolve their relationship conflicts without the help of a therapist; to deepen their love relationship; and to move towards feeling, all of the time, the way they felt when they first fell in love.

The first five steps of the exercise build on the insight that most of our defensive primary emotional fight, flight, and/or freeze reactions to our partner's reality protect vulnerable and more painful underlying feelings that were caused by childhood trauma, emotional wounding, and other forms of the unconscious that we covered in the previous Module 18. These vulnerable feelings operate in our unconscious because they are stored in the "timeless" amygdala and are not connected to the autobiographical memory function of the hippocampus, which was not online yet when we were young children or was disconnected through shock trauma. The resulting outward projections through blaming our partner or withdrawing to avoid reliving these painful feelings is rooted in false beliefs about ourselves and others that our Ego vigorously defends and that guide our ways of thinking and behaving. Underneath these defenses lie our deepest fears, which are the opposite or antithesis of love. These hidden and often unwarranted fears (fear=false evidence appearing real) are caused by three dynamics: (1) the fear of reliving the terror that we experienced as helpless and defenseless children, when we were neglected or mistreated by our caregivers on whom we totally depended for our safety and survival; (2) the shame of being somehow flawed (see fear-shame spiral on page 172); (3) the fear of losing our carefully constructed but ultimately false self-identity, which mystics and spiritual teachers refer to as Ego death, "to die before we die," as depicted in the hero's journeys and in many spiritual traditions.[305]

By recognizing and overcoming our deepest fear and shame, we can acknowledge and state our defended false identity that caused the defensiveness in the first place—such as, "I am .... "(e.g., invisible, too much, etc.); "I am not ...." (e.g., safe, lovable, etc.); or "I don't .... "(e.g., matter, belong, etc.).

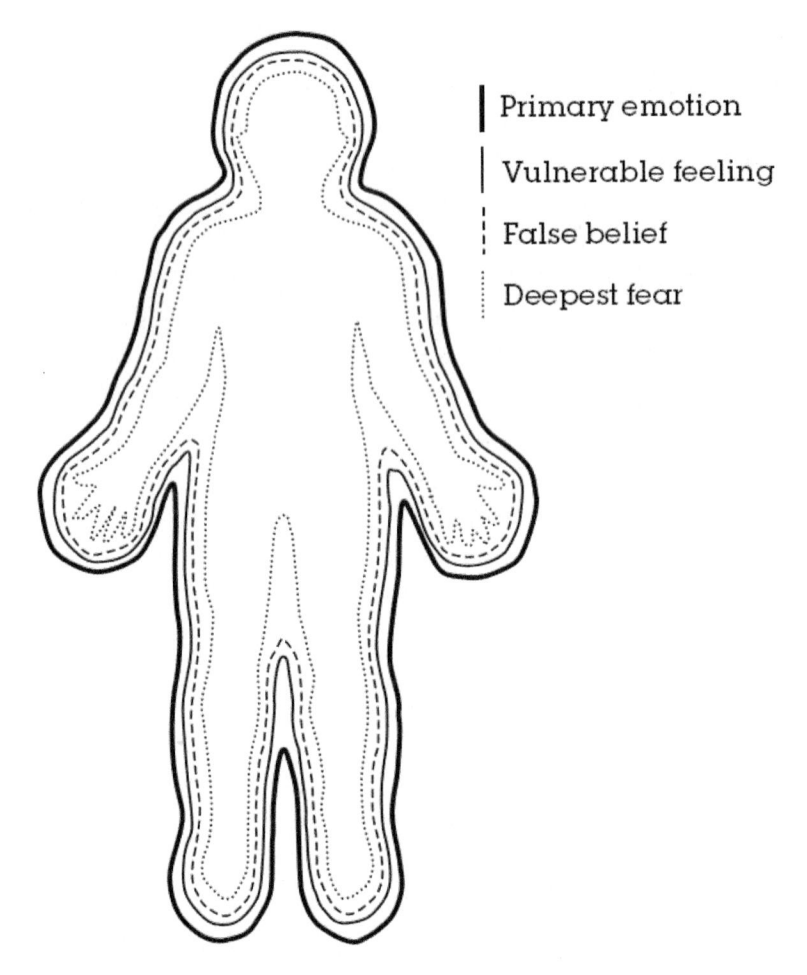

- Primary emotion
- Vulnerable feeling
- False belief
- Deepest fear

Figure 46: Layers of emotion, feeling, false belief, and fear

If the process unfolds correctly, the statements "miraculously" and "brilliantly" match one of the 21 false identities in the "Transformation of Identity Matrix" in the second worksheet below.

In the final step of the exercise, the practitioner who has worked through the process receives an affirmation with his or her true identity. Hearing the statement will either deeply move the practitioner (often to tears) or create a defensive response. Both responses are indicators that the affirmation reflects the true identity, or authentic nature, self, or essence of the practitioner. If it receives a neutral response, then most likely something went "wrong" in the process, and it is advised to repeat it, maybe with the help of the group facilitator or a trained practitioner.

After the exercise, the practitioners can find additional information in the "Transformation of Identity Matrix" PDF to gain deeper insights about how the false identity most likely shows up in their lives; the effects it has on others; the beliefs it creates about others; the beliefs about life in general; the ways of being that generate evidence to validate the false identity; the necessary skills and capacities to cultivate in order to evolve beyond the false identity; the gifts that developed based on the false identity; and deeper affirmations of the true identity.

Some practitioners may find the affirmations to be superficial, simple, or even laughable. They may think that to truly heal, they must relive the trauma of the past and understand what caused it in the first place. But, as we know from the latest therapeutic approaches such as Cognitive Behavioral Therapy (CBT), Mindful Behavioral Therapy (MBT), and especially the NeuroActive Relational Method (NARM), which is suggested as a supplement to this process, regression is not necessary and can even be harmful when it retraumatizes the clients and keeps them stuck in the past. Rather, these approaches suggest and have proven through evidence that we can only heal our relationship and attachment wounds in a relational context by facing and owning our primary emotions, vulnerable feelings, false beliefs, deepest fears, and false identities, and changing our thoughts, beliefs, and behaviors in the present, which ultimately changes the neuronal structure and activity in our bodies and brains for more aliveness and healthier relationships.

Thus, the results of this transformational psychospiritual "undefended love" process between couples are increasingly greater levels of inner peace and joy, and a deepening of intimacy, love, and connection.

Disclaimer

It is important to clarify that this process is obviously not suitable to address personality disorders (that we cover in Module 21), deeper trauma that was caused by physical or sexual childhood abuse, post-traumatic stress disorder (PTSD), or clinical depression and other serious mental illnesses such bipolar disorder or schizophrenia, all of which require diagnosis and treatment by a professional therapist or psychiatrist.

Agreements

In the *Undefended Love* book, it is suggested not to make agreements between couples to avoid defending, protecting, hiding, (spiritually) bypassing, or justifying (and thus outwardly projecting) any unconscious wounds and false identities. This is certainly a valid concern.

However, from an integral perspective, not having agreements is a performative contradiction, as it is an agreement in itself. Another implicit agreement is that both partners agree about the process in the context of a committed love relationship. It is therefore suggested to be clear about the shared purpose of the relationship and to have a vision, mission, and values statement as we will explore in Modules 22 to 25 to create the safe container for the undefended love practice.

Not having explicit agreements should not mean to have weak or unhealthy boundaries and to accept all kinds of abusive behavior from a partner, such as breaking agreements that were based on shared values, taking unjustified advantage, or being intentionally physically or emotionally abusive. This is especially important for relationships in which one partner is at the Green stage and the other at a Red or Purple/Magenta stage of development (see pre/post fallacy on page 185.) If the abuser does not see and change his or her behavior, the process in this module becomes a one-way street. It is therefore advised to end the relationship when the partner at the later stage has recognized and healed the wounds and underlying false identities that created the sexual, emotional, and spiritual attraction, and the porous boundaries in the first place, so that the relationship pattern does not repeat itself.

Purpose and application of the module

1. Deepen intimacy, passion, and commitment in your love relationships instead of blaming, arguing, fighting, making demands, or drifting more and more apart.
2. Realize that defensive emotional reactions to a partner's reality are not "caused" by him or her, but rather trigger or stimulate unconscious wounds and false identities.
3. Develop compassion for yourself and others, as nobody chooses their genetic predispositions and the childhood experiences that formed their unconscious mind and attachment wounds.
4. Engage in a mutual process that allows you to take responsibility for your own emotional reactions to your partner's reality and support him or her in doing them same.
5. Identify the vulnerable feelings, false beliefs, deepest fears, and false identities that underlie your primary emotional reactions.
6. Receive affirmations and detailed information to realize your true identity and to heal your unconscious wounds and defenses.
7. Support your awakening process by transforming needs into desires, desires into wants, wants into preferences, and preferences into no preference, by being present in the now and surrendering to what is.
8. Take full responsibility for your defensive emotional reactions to your partner's reality while maintaining your integrity by co-creating a relationship with a partner who shares your purpose, vision, mission, values, and lifestyle.
9. Move towards feeling, all the time, the way you felt when you first fell in love.
10. Avoid spending money for couples therapy by supporting each other in your healing process.

Integral Relationship Practice | 356

11. Seek professional help for deeper psychological and psychiatric issues that cannot be addressed by this process.

Exercise: Healing your shadow

The following is a paired exercise.
1. Print out the worksheets below.
2. Have yoga mats, blankets, and pillows available or ask the practitioners to bring them.
3. Make the four agreements for confidentiality, responsibility, healthy boundaries, and I-statements, as outlined on page 556.

Exercise one: Identify your false identity

1. Hand out the first worksheet below with the questions for the five phases of the process.
2. Demonstrate the exercise with your assistant or a participant. Then ask couples to pair up with their romantic partner, and individuals to pair up with someone who is already experienced in this kind of work.
3. Invite the practitioners who are more experienced to facilitate the process first. Once finished, they will switch roles with their partners.
4. The practitioners who first go through the process will lie down on a thick blanket, yoga mat, etc., with a pillow under their head and a thin blanket on top of them (ask practitioners to bring them if you can't provide them).
5. The practitioners who facilitate the process (facilitators) sit next to their partners, with the question sheet and a pen or pencil to take short notes on it.
6. The facilitators ask for permission to respectfully touch their partner's upper body during the exercise.
7. The practitioners going through the process will answer the first question. During your demonstration, you may do this on the practitioner's behalf by giving the example in the worksheet. During the actual process, instruct the practitioners not to read the examples.

8. Before step two, the practitioners going through the process close their eyes for the rest of the time and then answer all the remaining questions from the worksheet, as asked by the facilitators (remind them to listen for real feelings, not expressions such as "I felt like ..." or statements of interpretations versus feelings).
9. The facilitators take short notes in order to go back to earlier statements, if needed, and to show them to you or an assistant if the process went wrong at some point and prevented them from arriving at one of the 21 false identities.
10. Once the false identities are uncovered, the facilitators will raise their hand and you or your assistant will check to ensure that they did the process correctly before handing out the affirmation worksheets below, pointing to the false identities they uncovered.
11. The facilitators then read the corresponding affirmations to their partners and see how they "land." If there is a rejection or deep resonance, it is most likely correct. If there is no emotion, then maybe it is not the false identity, and they should review the process.
12. If the affirmation resonates, the practitioners will verbally repeat their affirmations two or three times after the facilitators, while anchoring them by gently squeezing the wrist or arm of their partners.
13. The facilitators may write the affirmations on the back of the worksheets and sign them as true.
14. When the practitioners are ready, they open their eyes and may share a hug with their partners.
15. They then switch and the previous facilitators are now guided by their partner through the process.
16. If both practitioners finish before the others, they can either repeat the process with different triggers, or answer the follow-up questions below or from Module 18.

Worksheets: Healing your shadow

Uncovering your false identity worksheet

1. State your complaint (something that triggered you) about your partner or ex-partner.
Example: You are always creating distance between us.
This can be a recurring event or one major event that triggers you. Don't go into too much of a story! (DO NOT read any of the examples to your partner!)

2. State your primary emotional reaction (usually fight, flight, or freeze).
Example: I feel angry, hurt, or confused (state a feeling, not an interpretation).
Anger, hurt, disgust, shame, fear/afraid. Protects deeper wound. Listen for "I felt like he/she is…."

3. State the vulnerable feeling below your reaction (that is protected by the primary reaction).
Example: I feel sad and alone (state a feeling, not an interpretation). This is the critical point to get in touch with the vulnerable feeling that the primary emotional reaction is protecting. (Feel into body, breath, touch. Ask, how may a child feel in such a situation?)

4. State the belief about yourself that underlies your vulnerable feeling

Example: Below the feeling of sadness, I realize that I believe that you don't care for me.

5. Recognize your deepest fear.

Example: When I realize that I believe you don't care for me, I see that my deepest fear is that I am not worth loving.

6. State your false identity.

Example: I am not loved, or I am unworthy of love, or I am not lovable (see affirmation 13, below).

Worksheet: Transformation of Identity Matrix

By Katherine Woodward Thomas, MA, MFT, and Claire Zammit, PhD.

Also see the related **NARM**[33] connection,[306] attunement,[307] trust,[308] autonomy,[309] and love-sexuality[310] adaptive survival styles in the respective endnotes below.

1. I'm Alone (I'm on my own)[306]
2. I'm Bad (I'm evil, I'm going to get in trouble, I'm selfish, it's my fault, I'm a disappointment)[308]
3. I Don't Belong (I'm lost)[309]
4. I'm a Burden (I don't need anyone, I'm responsible)[306]
5. I'm Crazy[307]

6. I'm Different (I am a freak, I'm weird)[306]
7. I'm Not Enough[307]
8. I'm a Failure (I'm a mess, I'm a screw-up)[309]
9. I Don't Have (I'm poor, I'm deprived, I'm impoverished)[307]
10. I'm Not Important (I'm not heard)[309]
11. I'm Inferior (I'm not as beautiful as ..., I'm not as smart as ...)[310]
12. I'm Invisible (I'm not seen, I don't exist)[307]
13. I'm Not Loved[310]
14. I Don't Matter[307]
15. I'm Powerless (I'm small and weak, I'm helpless, I'm not big enough)[308]
16. I'm Not Safe[308]
17. I'm Too Much[307]
18. I'm Unworthy (I don't deserve)[307]
19. I'm Not Wanted[310]
20. I'm Worthless (I'm not valuable, I'm disposable, I'm not special)[309]
21. I'm Wrong (I'm a mistake)[307]

1. I'm Alone (I'm on my own)

True Identity:

I was not born to be alone. I came here to love and be loved, and I have the power to create deep and meaningful connections with others.

2. I'm Bad (I'm evil, I'm going to get in trouble, I'm selfish, it's my fault, I'm a disappointment)

True Identity:

I deeply care about other people. I am here to contribute to the evolution and advancement of humankind, and I create openings for the flow of life to emerge in new and powerful ways for all.

3. I Don't Belong (I'm lost)

True Identity:

I am a part of all this, deeply related to all, and profoundly necessary to the well-being of the whole. Everyone, everywhere, belongs to me and I to them.

4. I'm a Burden (I don't need anyone, I'm responsible)

True Identity:

My feelings, needs, and desires are valid and essential to my own well-being as well as the well-being of others.

5. I'm Crazy

True Identity:

I can trust my knowing. I value my capacity for seeing things differently, recognizing how necessary my perspectives are to the well-being of all.

6. I'm Different (I am a freak, I'm weird)

True Identity:

I am profoundly gifted in unique and exceptional ways, and the world really needs what I have to offer.

7. I'm Not Enough

True Identity:

My very existence in and of itself provides extraordinary value and is a profound blessing to all.

8. I'm a Failure (I'm a mess, I'm a screw-up)

True Identity:

I am a powerful force of nature, here to have a great impact upon the world for the benefit and blessings of all beings.

9. Don't Have (I'm poor, I'm deprived, I'm impoverished)

True Identity:

I am deeply loved by all of Life, and it is right and good for me to have the best that life has to offer. Life grants me the power to generate profound levels of abundance and well-being everywhere I go.

10. I'm Not Important (I'm not heard)

True Identity:
My participation and presence matter and are important to the well-being and thriving of the entire community.

11. I'm Inferior (I'm not as beautiful as ... , I'm not as smart as ...)

True Identity:
All people come into the fullness of their power and their brilliance in my presence.

(For women) All women come into the fullness of their power, their radiance, their beauty, and their brilliance in my presence. All women everywhere are my sisters in shine.

12. I'm Invisible (I'm not seen, I don't exist)

True Identity:
I came here to be seen and have a profound impact on the world, and it is my responsibility to presence my visibility wherever I go.

13. I'm Not Loved

True Identity:
I am deeply loved by all of life. My very existence pleases the universe, and I now take my rightful place in the community as a beloved, embraced member of the tribe.

14. I Don't Matter

True Identity:
I am a loving, powerful presence on the planet, and I have significant and meaningful contributions to make. My life matters and is an important contribution to the well-being of the whole.

15. I'm Powerless (I'm small and weak, I'm helpless, I'm not big enough)

True Identity:
I am a powerful leader, here to serve the empowerment of all.

16. I'm Not Safe

True Identity:

I am deeply intuitive, and I can trust myself to intuitively know how to create safety and well-being for myself and others.

17. I'm Too Much

True Identity:

I am a profound light to the world and the vastness of my being blesses all.

18. I'm Unworthy (I don't deserve)

True Identity:

I am a humanitarian lover of the entire world. All of creation belongs to me, and I lovingly tend to the well-being of all beloved creatures on the earth, including myself.

19. I'm Not Wanted

True Identity:

Centered in the power and magic of who I am, I magnetize all manner of support and abundance into my life. My contribution blesses the world in profound and extraordinary ways. I am grateful for all that I am able to give and all that I'm able to receive.

20. I'm Worthless (I'm not valuable, I'm disposable, I'm not special)

True Identity:

I am a valued member of the tribe. I contribute extraordinary, valuable gifts and talents for the well-being of all. I own the full value of my unique gifts and talents, treasuring and esteeming them, and I deeply value the gifts and talents of others.

21. I'm Wrong (I'm a mistake)

True Identity:

There are no mistakes in nature. Who I am and what I have to contribute is profoundly necessary to the well-being of all.

A PDF with detailed descriptions of the false identities is available for download at the following:
tinyurl.com/irpm54[311]

Follow-up questions
1. How has your false identity impacted your love relationships?
2. What kind of support do you feel that you could provide to yourself to better handle the challenging feelings and false identity that were brought up in an uncomfortable situation?
3. What kind of support would you like to receive from your partner to better handle the challenging feelings and false identity that were brought up in an uncomfortable situation?
4. Is there a characteristic or ability that you feel you need within yourself to stay present with these challenging feelings and to heal your false identity?
5. What is a "coherent narrative" (see endnote[268]) that explains your emotional reaction, the underlying vulnerable feelings, your deepest fear, and your false identity?
6. How would you share this narrative with a partner?
7. What are imperatives/agreements with your partner about shared values/visions, healthy boundaries, truthfulness, curiosity, openness, and vulnerability that must be met and not continually violated to create a safe container for the learning, healing, growing, and awakening practices to take place in a committed, undefended love relationship with a shared purpose?

Additional information and resources

Undefended Love: The Way You Felt About Yourself When You First Fell in Love Is the Way You Can Feel All the Time (2000) by Jett Psaris and Marlena S Lyons. tinyurl.com/irpm480[312]

Healing Developmental Trauma: How Early Trauma Affects Self-Regulation, Self-Image, and the Capacity for Relationship (2012) by Laurence Heller, PhD, and Aline LaPierre, PsyD
tinyurl.com/irpm459[313]

The NARM healing cycle[314]
NARM Training tinyurl.com/irpm482[315]

Sex Purpose Love book reference
N/A

Suggested movie: *Good Will Hunting* (1997)

Watch this amazing movie, written by Ben Affleck and Matt Damon in their twenties, to see that knowledge without experience is blind, and to see how unresolved trauma limits our ability for empathy, intimacy, love relationships, and living on purpose.

The young immature genius Will Hunting (Matt Damon) lives in a small world in South Boston, where he can seemingly solve any problem with his mind but lacks any real-life experiences outside of his bubble.

After getting into trouble with the law again, Will is assigned to therapist Dr. Sean Maguire (Robin Williams), who tries to help him with his anger and emotional dissociation issues. Will further struggles with his unconscious daemons and avoidant attachment style after he falls in love Skylar (Minnie Driver), a Harvard student who plans on attending medical school at Stanford after she graduates. As Sean struggles with Will in their weekly sessions and finally breaks through to him, he is also transformed, and both break free and embark on a new life.

Practice Module 20
Forms, Levels, and States of Love

Sometimes life is too hard to be single, and sometimes life is too good not to be shared.
~ Elizabeth Gilbert ~

Module description

Learn and practice how to fall in love with someone good for you, and you for him or her, by understanding eight forms of love, six levels of dependence, and five states or phases of love. Realize that the eight forms of love are experienced through a combination of three essential ingredients: (1) various levels of "interior" intimacy (into-me-you-see) which are determined by the level of consciousness, and spiritual and emotional development of each partner; (2) various degrees of "exterior" passion, which are created through hormones when your primary sexual fantasies are met; (3) various degrees of dependence, ranging from unhealthy co-dependence to healthier forms of dependence, independence, and interbeing, to inter-becoming at higher levels of spiritual realizations and shared purpose.

See that when you draw lines to represent the degrees of intimacy, passion, and dependence that you and your partner experience, you can form three metaphorical triangles of love for each of you—one for the reality, one for the projected ideals, and one for your intentions in the relationship.

Successfully navigate the various states or phases of falling in love that are driven by "love" hormones. Understand that individuals can be in different phases and experience them in different durations and intensities as they get to know each other and become increasingly intimate, passionate, and committed. Co-create a lasting, healthy, and happy love relationship through understanding the form, dependence, and phase of love that you and your date or partner are in.

Introduction

In this module, the practitioners engage in three paired exercises to explore different forms, levels, and states of love. The forms of love are based on Robert Sternberg's triangular theory of love. The levels of love are based on the insight that lovers experience different degrees of unconscious emotional dependence on each other. The states of love are based on scientific findings about the unfolding hormone-driven chemistry between partners.

We can generally say that people love others who make them feel happy and alive through their appearance, status, and behavior. Some people feel additionally loved by those who extend themselves in support of their ongoing learning, healing, growing, and awakening.[316] And others feel an even deeper love towards those who also co-create more goodness, truth, beauty, and functioning in synergistic ways with them.

All three reasons for feeling loved have as their foundation various levels of intimacy, passion, and dependence that combine into eight forms of love, and typically advance through three brought phases or states of infatuation, romance, and commitment. Understanding the kind of love each partner is experiencing or yearning for, which of the eight basic forms of love are unfolding between a couple, the level of dependence and resulting commitment of each partner, and the phase or state of chemistry each lover is in provides us with the container for all the remaining modules, in which we explore multiple capacities for love on a biological, transformational, and transcendental level.

Three ingredients and eight forms of love

The three basic ingredients of love are *intimacy* (into-me-you-see), which is experienced to different degrees in the left-hand "I and We" quadrants; *passion*, which is experienced to different degrees in the right-hand "It and Its" quadrants, as shown in *Figure 5: The four dimensions of relating*, on page 33; and *dependence*, which is experienced through a mutually compatible unconscious fit between the lovers.

Intimacy is created through similar levels of consciousness, cognitive, moral, spiritual, and emotional development, as well as shared passions, values, and cultural backgrounds, such as language, heritage, religion, tribal identity, etc. Couples who experience mutual levels of intimacy may say, "We understand each other," "We click," "We resonate with each other," "We share the same values," "We see the world in the same way," or "We are best friends."

Passion is created when the primary fantasies (shown on page 166)—in males, for "sexy" females with good reproductive capabilities; in females, for successful attractive males with good productive capabilities—are met and couples are at similar levels of sexual development and share interests and lifestyle choices. Couples who experience mutual levels of passion may say, "We have a lot of chemistry," "We are physically attracted to each other," "We can't keep our hands off each other," "We have great sex," "We have fun together," "We like to do things together," or "We are a great team."

Dependence is created through mutual compatibilities in the various forms of the unconscious mind (see Module 18) and through the differences in coping mechanisms that each lover has developed in response to childhood trauma. Dependence ranges from co-dependence, dependence, independence, interdependence, and interbeing, to inter-becoming, and leads to various forms of commitment. Couples who experience mutual levels of dependence may say, "We complete/complement each other," "We can't live without each other," "We push each other's buttons," "We fight a lot," or "We are soulmates, twin flames, or worthy opponents." This unconscious dimension of love relationships is always experienced as mysterious, miraculous, or magical, as the "lovestruck" couple has no rational explanation for their magnetic push/pull.[317]

Integral Relationship Practice | 370

By drawing one line each for the level of intimacy, passion, and dependence, we can combine them into a metaphorical triangle as shown below.

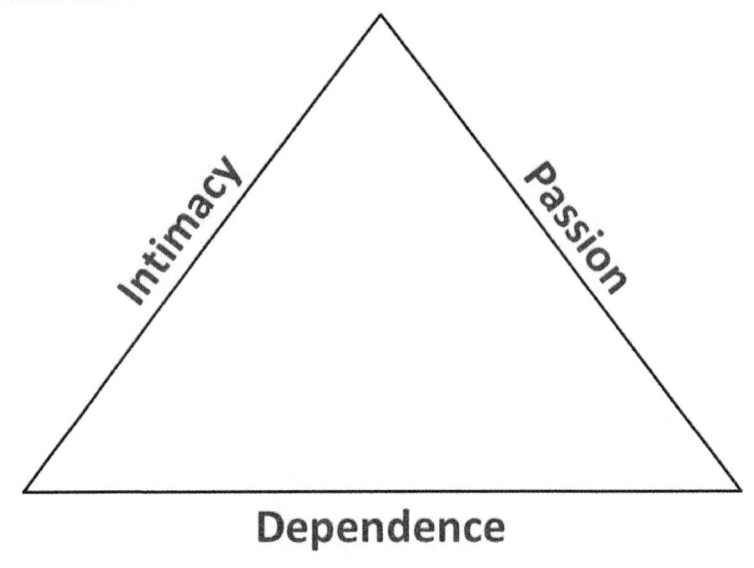

Figure 47: The triangle of love

If we draw one triangle for the experience of each partner to indicate the level of intimacy, passion, and dependence that they experience at any given time, the triangles will most likely be shaped differently. We can then superimpose the triangles to see how they line up for partner A and B.

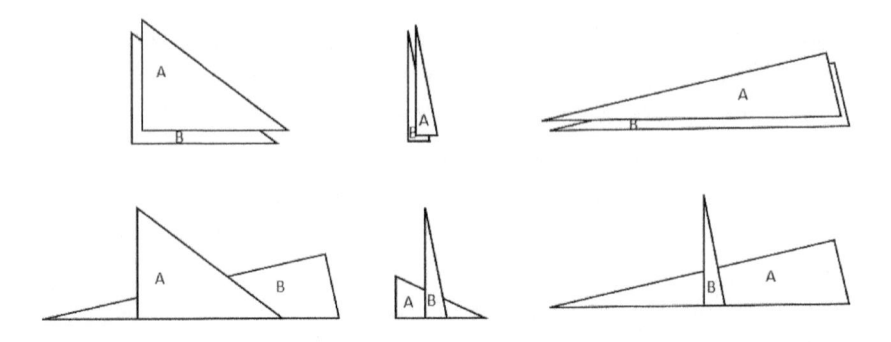

Figure 48: Compatible and incompatible triangles of love

The shape of the triangles is indicative of eight broad forms of love, as shown below, that each partner may experience.

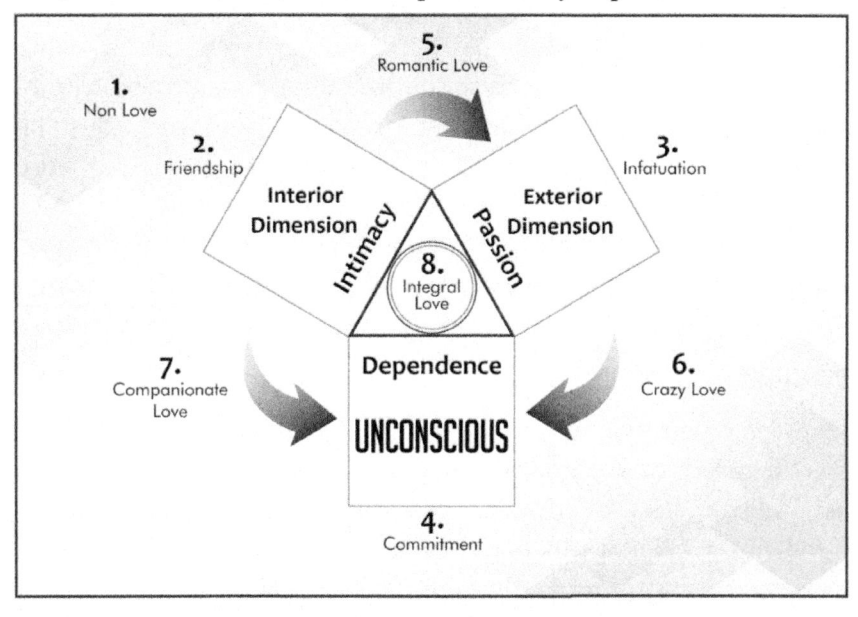

Figure 49: Eight forms of love

The Eight Forms of Love

Below are the descriptions of the eight forms of love that are indicated by the presence and levels of each side of the metaphorical triangles.

Some of the relationships are platonic in nature or may feel like love but are not—at least not in the healthy definition. Others denote actual love relationships by aligning two, and ultimately integrating, balancing, and harmonizing all three sides of the triangle in a healthy way.

The eight forms of love are loosely related to the different Greek words for love: Eros (romantic, passionate love), Philia (affectionate love), Agape (selfless, universal love), Storge (familiar love), Mania (obsessive love), Ludus (playful love), Pragma (enduring love), Philautia (self-love).[318]

1. Non-love

Is present if there is no mutual experience of intimacy, passion, or dependence between two individuals. However, sometimes people keep meeting at school, work, social groups, or in other environments for some time without feeling any attraction until noticing each other as potential mates, and one or more sides of the triangle may start to evolve and align between them. Hence "non-love" may grow into other forms of love over time if two people engage in fun or meaningful activities together on a regular basis, and if their first impression of each other is neutral or at least not negative.[319]

2. Friendship

Develops when two people share *intimacy* through an intellectual, interest-based, or spiritual resonance in kind and degree through their Lower Left quadrants. The quality and depth of their friendship are determined by the alignment of their respective interior lines (cognitive, communicative, worldviews, values, moral, spiritual, etc.), as well as shared interests and hobbies. Friendship is often the prerequisite for a woman to enter into a sexual relationship, while men tend to be more driven by their physical/sexual attraction in the right-hand quadrants that may (or may not) lead to friendship after sex. Vulnerability, truthfulness,[320] and honesty are vital factors for the development of mature friendships through intimacy, since integrity is the main ingredient for building trust.[321]

3. Infatuation[322]

Is experienced when a *passionate* physical attraction—triggered through the fulfillment of a man's or woman's primary phantasy in the right-hand quadrants—is the sole factor that draws an individual to a person of the opposite sex, and his or her body secretes the "falling-in-love" hormones that we discuss below.

For males, a seductive sexual female (a suitable sex object) is usually enough for them to experience sexual passion and to become infatuated. For most females, a combination of power, social status, wealth, wit, humor, and intelligence (since women want success objects), combined with physical attractiveness, kindness towards her, and dominant aggressive behavior towards others (protection), are usually the prerequisites to infatuation.

Unlike the left *intimacy* side of the triangle, which requires a mutual resonance between two people to develop into a friendship, infatuation can be a one-way street. It can be quite painful if the passionate sexual longings of one person are not met by an equal amount of fervor from the object of their desire. In any case, met or unmet infatuation may lead to sexual addiction, destructive behavior, emotional havoc, social isolation, depression, and financial ruin.

Increasing sexiness of individuals leads to deeper feelings of infatuation in the people who fall for them; for example, men losing their heads over much younger, curvaceous, or otherwise attractive women (e.g., poor Goethe at age 73, agonizing over Ulrike von Levetzow, age 18), or women losing their heads over powerful males (e.g., Monica Lewinsky and Bill Clinton). Like the propensity of certain people to become alcohol or drug addicts, while others don't, some people become infatuated more frequently, while others never experience this form of love.

4. Commitment

Arises between partners through various *levels of dependence* that result from a mutually compatible fit of their unconscious makeup. The energetic push/pull always appears to be mysterious to the lovers who are negatively afflicted or positively graced by it; nevertheless, it can be understood through insight.[323]

The two underlying dynamics for the appearance of dependence are often confused. One originates from pathological (unhealthy) split-offs, negations, repressions, or dissociations that create a sense of lack, neediness, and deficiency (see the submerged unconscious shadows and anima/animus complex in previous modules) that the lovers project onto each other. The second results from a sense of fullness, abundance, or wholeness, with the desire to share one's blessings, to complement, balance, harmonize, synergize, learn, grow, heal, awaken, and co-create in a partnership (see ground, embedded, and emergent unconscious).

Elizabeth Gilbert's grandfather observed "sometimes life is too hard to be single, and sometimes life is too good not to be shared," an insight which nicely illustrates the two motives that lead to commitment between two people. Since both dynamics tend to be unconscious and vary in kind and degree for different domains and phases of life (money, sexuality, time, work, family, spirituality, worldviews, feminine, masculine, etc.), neither partner can know for certain which parts of their hidden selves cause the unconscious attraction, and which of the six general facets of dependence (as outlined below, on page 382) may be the result.

5. Romantic love

Develops between partners who share *intimacy* and sexual *passion* but don't experience a deeper emotional dependence through a mutually compatible unconscious fit. This is the kind of love that most women and some men desire and is romanticized in countless romantic movies, novels, and love songs. Women who desire this kind of love dream of a supportive, wealthy, powerful, and generous partner with similar interests, values, and lifestyle choices as their own, who shares their passionate sexual attraction (chemistry). Men who desire romantic love desire a good-looking, typically younger, sexy, seductive woman who celebrates, appreciates, and admires him. Neither wants to be challenged by the other to heal, grow, and awaken to deeper realizations.[324] In other words, they want someone with "no baggage" who meets their primary fantasy and loves, cherishes, and accepts them for who they are, with all their emotional wounds, dysfunctions, and ignorance of their ego. This kind of love is called romantic, as it seeks to avoid all unpleasant aspects, work, and challenges that inevitably arise in any long-term partnership, instead of welcoming conflict as an opportunity for learning, healing, growing, and awakening.

Once the hormones that created the passion for one or both partners wear off—which usually takes between 3 and 24 months—romantic love relationships often either transform into friendships (for example, Elaine and Jerry in the sitcom *Seinfeld*), if there was a sufficient level of shared interests and intimacy to begin with, or the couple breaks up (now sometimes called "consciously uncouple") altogether when unconscious facets of the self creep up from the bottom of the triangle and neither partner wants to—or knows how to—deal with them in an effective way (typically through a healthier lifestyle, appropriate therapy, and/or a spiritual practice.)

6. Crazy love

Also called mania, develops when two people share *passion* through a strong sexual attraction and *dependence* through a pathological, mutually compatible, unconscious fit but have no intimacy that is rooted in shared values, lifestyle choices, interests, and worldviews. This kind of love is largely driven by elevated levels of testosterone, dopamine, and norepinephrine, and lowered levels of serotonin,[325] and can afflict people from all walks of life. These love relationships are characterized by an addictive emotional and sexual (co)dependence that is not mediated by much (or any) rational consideration. It is called "crazy love" because the afflicted lovers are initially "crazy about each other" and any uninvolved bystander finds the soon-to-follow drama that often involves emotional and physical abuse to be crazy.[326] Crazy love relationships can still be positive, as they may force addicted individuals who repeatedly engage in them, to eventually grow to higher levels of consciousness through their painful fights and devastating breakups. This may lead them to engage in healthier romantic and, eventually, Integral love relationships.

7. Companionate love

Develops if a couple shares *intimacy* and *commitment* but experiences no (more) sexual passion. This kind of love is often seen between conventional (Amber/Orange) and older couples. They may have gotten together because of religious or cultural conventions and pressures (such as arranged marriages), or to conceive and raise children in a traditional family environment (conformist stage), or they saw the benefits of marriage for their social status, careers, and material success (rational stage). Companionate love may arise out of an initial friendship but rarely out of romantic or crazy love. Couples who experience companionate love may advance towards an Integrally informed love relationship if they address the issues that prevent them from having a passionate sex life, by overcoming physical problems through exercise, partner yoga, healthy eating, or medication, and through the removal of emotional blocks with the support of self-help books,[327] a sex therapist, intimacy workshops, and tantric practices.[328]

8. Integral love

Develops when a couple experiences healthy *intimacy, passion,* AND *dependence,* and integrates them in a balanced and harmonized way. Partners who share this kind of love either feel incredibly blessed and lucky to have found each other—often without actually knowing why their relationship is so satisfying—or have reached later/higher stages of development (second-tier consciousness, anima/animus complex stage five, transcendental sexuality, and spirituality beyond the psychic level) that allow them to consciously co-create an integrally informed love relationship between opposites and equals.[329]

Three pairs of triangles

There are actually three pairs of differently shaped triangles for each partner:

1. One pair of triangles that represents the actual reality of the relationship for each of the partners.

2. A second pair of triangles for the ideals that each partner projects onto the other. These ideals might originate from experiences in previous love relationships (e.g., great sexual passion, a deep emotional bond, sharing of rewarding activities, intellectually stimulating conversations, or a divine spiritual resonance), or they may be ideals that are inspired through friends, romantic movies, romance novels, or porn. Nobody can be completely free from these projections, which increase in relation to how much the actual relationship deviates from positive memories of previous partnerships, or in relation to the individual's attachment to unrealistic romantic fairy tales and sexual fantasies. Both partners will then sooner or later try to align their mate with their own projected ideals. As the saying goes, "I love you — you're perfect — now change."

Men may expect their partner to stop nagging them and to be more supportive of their vision, to be less moody, to lose weight, have their breasts enlarged, or to be more accommodating in the bedroom. Women may expect him to become more emotionally available and to complain less about his job, to make more money, exercise more, be more supportive around the house, take care of the kids, spend more quality time with her, romance her more often, not lust after other women, and to be more considerate as her lover.

Hence the suggested Zen practices of "Beginner's Mind" to let go of these projections.[330]

3. The third pair of triangles indicate the intentions of each partner in the relationship. The difference between these intentions and the actual reality (first pair of triangles) represents the integrity of the relationship. For example, a woman may intend to stay with a man forever — only to end the partnership when he no longer makes her happy or doesn't produce in the way that she projected onto him (or as he promised to her). A man may intend to be faithful to his partner, to take care of her financially, and to be

emotionally available, only to hide his feelings and focus his attention, time, and money on his hobbies or on other women once the thrilling effect of the "romance hormones" are gone.

Polyamorous relationships

The dynamic between the triangles becomes especially interesting in polyamorous relationships, where more than two partners, each of them with their own three triangles, are lovingly involved with each other … just to make your head spin a little, if it isn't already.

Purpose and application of the module

1. Learn about the three main reasons why people feel loved, and the eight forms of love.
2. Realize that there are the reality, the projected ideals, and the intentions of love relationships.
3. Explore six levels of dependence that impact the depth of commitment in love relationships.
4. Successfully navigate the various phases or states of unfolding love relationships.
5. Practice forgiveness and conscious uncoupling work if you went through a painful breakup, to open to love again.

Exercises: Forms, levels, and states of love

The following are all paired exercises.
1. Print out the worksheets with the questions for the three exercises below.
2. Make the four agreements for confidentiality, responsibility, healthy boundaries, I-statements, and sharing, as outlined on page 556.

Exercise one: Eight forms of love

1. Share the answers to the following questions with your partner.
2. What does love and being "in love" mean to you? What is the difference for you?

3. Which of the eight forms of love did or do you experience?
4. How has the difference between the reality, projected ideals, and intentions impacted your love relationship?
5. Have you ever been in a polyamorous or other form of non-monogamous relationship? If yes, what forms of love did you experience with your different partners and how has it impacted your primary relationship?
6. What attracted you to your former partners (and your current partner) in the three dimensions of love (intimacy, passion, dependence), including your primary fantasy?

Levels of dependence

As mentioned above, there are six levels of dependence that lead to more or less committed relationships, as indicated by the base of the triangle.

Codependent relationships

Have a very long base of the triangle and develop between individuals with severe pathologies (usually from childhood trauma) and other forms of psychosis[331] and neurosis[332] that typically require treatment from a professional therapist or psychiatrist to be healed.[333] These lovers are often fused (along with the accompanying separation anxiety and jealousy attacks), engage in endless "seduce-and-withhold" games, and get entangled in the drama triangle (see page 132).

Dependent relationships

Are formed between couples with milder forms of shadow that create a sense of closeness or bond between them (long base of the triangle). Conflicts in these love relationships are often ignored, attributed to the differences between men (are from Mars) and women (are from Venus), accepted as the inevitable reality of any partnership, or—at best—dealt with and accepted through empathetic dialogue and compromise that may be supported by self-help books, workshops, or a marriage and family therapist.

Independent relationships

Are experienced by people who reach a high level of emotional and financial independence (very short base of the triangle) who often leave their partners unilaterally (or cause them to leave) to live alone and to claim their full authority (anima/animus complex stage four).

Some people at this level, especially women in the New Age and feminist movements, but also pathologically agentic men, see the pursuit of independence as the highest goal of any personal and spiritual development, as they strive to be autonomous, whole, complete, and self-fulfilled without a partner. Any desire to be in a healthy love relationship that may arise in them or others is seen as a weakness and regression towards "unevolved" dependent or codependent partnerships that they have escaped. This motivates individuals who are stuck at this level to move ever further towards pathological agentic ascending, or descending, instead of recognizing independence as a healthy and necessary (but ultimately transitory) prerequisite to enter the next stages of human relating, in which wholeness and partialness become increasingly balanced.

Interdependent relationships

These relationships have a short base of the triangle and are realized by couples who have the insight that nobody exists independently of others[334] and that a balanced and harmonized personality development at all levels of our being (body, mind, heart, and soul) always occurs by integrating the healthy aspects of the feminine-masculine polarities in their interior and exterior quadrants in self-other relationships.[335]

For them, sharing material resources by living together, and cherishing differing views that stem from a shared level of consciousness, take center stage. Unlike individuals in the independent stage, who pretend to be whole and complete and hence avoid partnerships that would challenge their ego (false separate sense of self), interdependent couples cherish their differences as the by-product of their "pretension to completeness"[336] and welcome opposing views to create synergy.

Interbeing relationships

Emerge between couples who have advanced into higher state-stages of spiritual development (causal, pure witness, nondual). They experience a devotional yearning for their "divine other" but attempt to transcend emotional or sexual neediness (moving from need to desire, to want, to preference, to no preference.) They attempt to be at peace and grounded in their essential "Being" in the "here and now" and are neither desperate for nor avoid a partnership.

In their love relationships with opposite and equal partners, each attempt to be present and surrender to what is, without any need to change the other, to accommodate, or to be accommodated (longer base of the triangle.)[337] Neither of them lusts for anybody else, nor do they fear being consumed or abandoned, which opens the possibility for mature monogamy[338] and undefended Love that is by definition devoid of any need, fear, or shame. These relationships may also have elements of spiritual bypassing.

Inter-becoming relationships

Are experienced between equal and opposite couples who have profound yearnings to realize their fullest human potentials in a deeply committed love relationship in which they value depth over span (very long base of the triangle).

They realize that we are not only human beings, but even more, human becomings, and see their love relationships as the best vehicle for ongoing learning, deep healing, personal growth, spiritual awakening, and, most importantly, being of service to others towards making the world a better place as a couple. They do this by owning their emotional reactions to each other's realities; advancing into new potentials and novelties through dialectical processes of differentiating and integrating (thesis, antithesis and synthesis); and sharing a purpose that creates more goodness, truth, beauty and functioning in service of others.

Exercise two: Six levels of dependence

1. Share the answers to the following questions with your partner.
2. What did or do you experience in your relationships on the scale of co-dependence, dependence, independence, interdependence, interbeing, and inter-becoming, as described above?
3. Have relationships ended for you when your own or your partner's level of dependence shifted?
4. What healing and growth potentials around the levels of dependence would you like to realize?

States of Falling in Love

All temporary experiences that come and go in a fluid way and are recognized as such by the self (e.g., I was angry, happy, sleeping, dreaming, awake, stoned, drunk, in love, etc.) are called states of consciousness, as we explored in Module 12, Spiritual Development. States must not to be confused with the vertical/hierarchical structure stages of consciousness development from which states are observed and interpreted, as shown in the Wilber-Combs Matrix on page 213.

Feelings such as sexual lust, infatuation, bliss of romance, conflict, emotional bonding, or pain/depression after a breakup or divorce are all temporary states (versus permanent stages) that are caused by elevated or lowered levels (imbalances) of specific chemicals in our body, called hormones and neurotransmitters.[339]

States or phases of love relationships as seen by several authors

Deepak Chopra lists four states in his book *A Path To Love*, on pages 62–131: attraction, infatuation, courtship, and intimacy.

John Gray lists five states in his book *Mars and Venus on a Date*, on pages 34–109: attraction, uncertainty, exclusivity, intimacy, and engagement.

Geoffrey Miller lists several states in *The Mating Mind*, on page 179:
infatuation, falling in love, ecstasy, jealousy or heartbrokenness, boredom, and forming attachment.

David Richo lists three phases in his book *How to be an Adult in Relationships*: romance, conflict, and commitment.

Another useful source lists six states: (1) two separate selves from a (2) symbiosis during exclusive bonding (romantic state), followed by (3) differentiation, disillusionment, regret, doubt, fear, and conflict when one or both partners move from "we" back to "me," and then (4) rapprochement after a back and forth between intimacy and independence, and finally (5) full commitment in the context of a larger "we."

Navigating states of love

Fortunately, all hormone-driven states of falling in and out of love are temporary states and not permanent stages; otherwise, we would never get anything done. The three major states/phases of attraction that are outlined below provide a very general overview of the intricate and mysterious role that chemicals play in the human experiences of lust, infatuation, romance, conflict, commitment, and breakups.

Phase 1 – Desire/Lust/Infatuation

Sexual urges and lust are driven by the sex hormone testosterone. It is present not only in males—even though levels in their bodies are usually ten times higher than in women's bodies, which leads men to think about and crave sex more often.[340]

Testosterone also plays a role in the sexual desires and emotional well-being of women; however, in females the dominant cuddle hormone is estrogen, which stimulates seductiveness, openness, and receptiveness, as well as longing for physical closeness, skin-to-skin contact, and sex.[341] Estrogen is also important for vaginal health: thick viscosity of lubrication, firm muscle tone, elasticity, thickness of vaginal walls, and healthy pH levels. As estrogen levels drop during and after menopause, often so does the frequency of intercourse, as a natural consequence of reduced lubrication, thinning vaginal walls, weakened vaginal musculature, and increased risk of bacterial infections.[342] Sometimes a role reversal in sexual appetites appears around midlife, when testosterone levels and the resulting libido naturally decrease in men, while the libido of women increases as the testosterone-masking effects of estrogen decline.[343]

At any rate, increased levels of testosterone create sexual desire and drive men and women to be out there looking for somebody, and healthy levels of estrogen make women seductive and receptive.[344]

Infatuation is experienced if we find a person who meets our sexual and romantic desires. Norepinephrine, which is similar to its better-known cousin adrenaline, increases physical energy, memory function for new stimuli (men really listen and remember what a woman says after they have fallen in love), perspiration, heart rate, and blood pressure, with the downside of lowered appetite, sleeplessness, and exhilaration. It also stimulates more "fight or flight" responses, which often lead new lovers to be overreactive or edgy, and easily to become jealous, possessive, or defensive.[345]

Phase 2 – Romance, uncertainty, and conflict

This is the truly lovestruck phase. After people become infatuated and enter the romance state, they can hardly think of anything else. They lose their appetite, need less sleep, spend hours at a time daydreaming about their new love, and engage in endless phone or video chat conversations, email exchanges, and text messaging, and try to spend as much time together as possible. In the infatuated romance state, a group of neurotransmitters called monoamines play an important role. These include the following:

Dopamine—also activated by cocaine, nicotine, heroin, and other addictive substances. It creates the drive to seek the rewarding stimulus and is therefore associated with any kind of major addiction, in our case to a member of the opposite sex.[346]

Serotonin—suspected to be one of love's most important chemicals. Lowered levels of serotonin allow for an increase of the love hormones testosterone, dopamine, and norepinephrine.[347] Similar to patients with obsessive-compulsive disorder (OCD), the serotonin-starved brains of lovers obsessively think about the object of their desire, which renders them temporarily insane, especially if their love is unrequited. Serotonin-enhancing antidepressants (aka selective serotonin reuptake inhibitors or SSRI's) such as Prozac, Celexa, Lexapro, Luvox, Paxil, or Zoloft can help in such situations, but are also known to lower a person's sex drive and romantic feelings towards others. So it is advisable to stay away from these medications, if possible.[348]

While lovers are crazy about each other, this phase also renders them temporarily insane, so that they ignore clear warning signs about incompatibilities and red flags.

The drug-induced romance phase typically lasts between 3 and 24 months, a time span which has evolutionary reasons. This was the period of time that made sense for our ancestors to try to get pregnant. If no offspring was produced, it was advantageous for them to move on to find a new partner. Even modern couples who don't want (more) children can't stay infatuated forever; otherwise, they wouldn't get any work done (which does not mean that they should no longer be romantic after the romance phase—quite the contrary).

Uncertainty and conflict often arise at the end of the romance phase, when the love hormones wear off and couples come to know each other better in day-to-day life and show more realistic versions of themselves. The key to navigating this phase successfully is to show curiosity and openness and to express feelings and unmet needs.

Exclusivity and engagement are entered into when couples make an agreement to no longer be open to other relationships and to date each other exclusively.

If lovers manage to resolve the inevitable conflicts that arise at the end of the romance phase in a constructive way and stay together,[349] they may reap the long-term benefits of being in a healthy love relationship, such as increased social status, financial stability, physical health, and sexual satisfaction, as well as personal and spiritual growth in the commitment phase that follows.

Phase 3 – Commitment

Two attachment hormones support couples in sustaining their relationship beyond the romance phase, especially if pregnancy occurs. These chemicals evolved through the descendants of committed parents who were more successful than those who separated in raising their young to maturity by staying together and supporting each other:

Oxytocin—is released during childbirth and causes the female breasts to produce milk. It helps cement the strong bond between mother and child. Oxytocin is also released in both sexes during orgasm and is thought to promote the bonding between adults who become sexually intimate. It also reduces stress, especially in women, and is believed to have many other health benefits for both sexes.[350]

Vasopressin—is the monogamy hormone that plays an important role in the long-term commitment between partners.[351] Levels increase before and during orgasm. The bonding effect of vasopressin was discovered when scientists injected different amounts into the bodies of prairie voles.[352]

Long-term partnerships can stay satisfying and exciting beyond the romance phase if the couples are compatible along crucial developmental lines; share common interests, values and passions; are dedicated to ongoing learning, healing, growing, and awakening in the context of their union; share a purpose that makes the world a better place; and engage in rewarding novel activities such as travel, hobbies, joint projects, realization of common dreams, participating in growth workshops, and a vibrant tantric sex life.[353]

Exercise three: States of falling in love

1. Share the answers to the following questions with your partner.
2. How did the states or phases of love from lust, desire, infatuation, romance, conflict, disillusion, rapprochement exclusivity, commitment, engagement, marriage, and possibly dissolution/divorce unfold for you and your partner(s)?
3. Why did your previous relationships end?
4. Who ended them?
5. How did your relationships end and what is your relationship with your former partners now?
6. What did you learn from the endings?
7. What kind of forgiveness or "conscious uncoupling" work did or do you need to do to open to love again?[354]
8. What do you want to do differently now and/or in your future relationships?

Follow-up questions

1. How do you feel after the three exercises?
2. What insights did you gain from the three exercises?
3. How will your experience of this module impact your love relationships?
4. What will you do differently?

Additional information and resources

Forgiveness Made Easy: The Revolutionary Guide to Moving Beyond Your Past and Truly Letting Go (2017) by Barbara J Hunt
tinyurl.com/irpm483[355]

Conscious Uncoupling: 5 Steps to Living Happily Even After (2016) by Katherine Woodward Thomas
tinyurl.com/irpm485[356]

Sex Purpose Love book reference

Page 83–86, 125–132

Suggested movies:

The Mirror Has Two Faces (1996)

Watch this touching and witty comedy, directed by Barbra Streisand, to see the various phases, states and forms of love that are experienced through various levels of emotional intimacy, sexual passion, and unconscious dependence.

Rose Morgan (Barbara Streisand) is a plain, plump English literature professor who feels that she can't compete with her gorgeous mother and sister. Gregory Larkin (Jeff Bridges) is a math professor who believes that sexual passion has ruined his life. The two Columbia University professors meet through a "personals" ad (this was before internet dating). After their intellectual friendship deepens, they decide to form a marriage that is solely based on intimacy and commitment (the left and bottom side of the triangle), while repressing any sexual passion (the right side of the triangle). This strategy only works until Rose develops more of her feminine side and, with the help of her mother, heals her childhood insecurities around her looks. Their marriage is nearly destroyed when Rose, to Gregory's shock, tries to consummate their relationship. While Gregory is in Europe on a lecture tour, Rose transforms herself into a sexy siren to integrate the passion side of the triangle to save her marriage.

When Harry Met Sally (1989)

Watch this beautiful, intelligent, touching, and revealing romantic comedy to see the multiple phases of love—from lust to infatuation, romance, conflict, commitment—and breakups, as the dynamics between emotional intimacy, sexual passion, and unconscious dependence unfold in the relationships of the couples who are portrayed.

At the center of the movie are the love lives of Harry Burns (Billy Crystal) and Sally Albright (Meg Ryan), who meet for a drive from Chicago to New York after they graduate from college. During their road trip, they argue about whether men and women can ever truly be strictly platonic friends. Ten years later, they meet again by chance and agree to form a friendship without having sex with each other, to avoid this complication between them. Their resolve is increasingly challenged, as their friendship deepens while they date other people and support each other with the challenges in their separate love lives.

Practice Module 21
Personality Disorders

*I don't know what living a balanced life feels like.
When I am sad I don't cry, I pour.
When I am happy I don't smile, I glow.
When I am angry I don't yell, I burn.
The good thing about feeling in extremes is when I love I give them wings but perhaps that isn't such a good thing, cause they always tend to leave and you should see me when my heart is broken
I don't grieve, I shatter.*
~ Rupi Kaur ~

Module description

Learn and practice how **not to** fall in love with someone who is bad for you, and you for him or her, unless you want to. Identify possible symptoms of personality disorders. Choose how to respond to people who display symptoms, especially in love relationships.

Distinguish between challenging "negative" emotional reactions that all couples experience in their love relationships from time to time and the erratic behaviors of people with more serious personality disorders and other pathologies. Understand that the former are caused when old wounds are triggered and can be usually healed through therapeutic work. Realize that the latter are marked by patterns of ongoing instability of moods, self-image, and behavior that usually cannot be addressed through therapy and result in impulsive actions and unstable relationships.

Accept that symptoms of personality disorders tend to worsen over time and are often defended by the afflicted individuals as being normal and appropriate, even though the expression of those symptoms have affected their day-to-day life, and especially their intimate love relationships, in negative and often devastating ways for many years. Learn how to identify the three most common personality disorders. Avoid the pattern of the "22 stages of decline" that relationships between highly conscious empaths who are in love with afflicted partners usually descend through. Prevent yourself from falling in love with people who have personality disorders (unless you want to, which can be quite exciting and transformational), and learn how to support them in managing their challenges by showing compassion while maintaining healthy boundaries.

Introduction

In Module 21 we turn to the challenges in love relationships between people with serious personality disorders (PDs) and empaths who fall in love with them (see "22 stages of decline" below).

This module is based on the observation that empaths at higher levels of consciousness development and inner complexity are often involved in social circles, groups, events, workshops, and trainings that focus on personal development, spirituality, authentic relating, NVC, relationship skills, female empowerment, sexuality (including tantra), psychological healing and trauma work, etc. These communities also frequently attract similarly complex people with personality disorders (sometimes including the creators and leaders themselves) who are attracted and captivated by the same topics. Alas, their capacity to learn, heal, change, grow, and awaken is severely impaired and limited because of their disorder, which is initially not apparent but shows up when they become romantically involved with others or become otherwise challenged. There is often an unawareness or denial in these circles about PDs, or a well-meant, and to an extent justified, reluctance or flat-out rejection by the leaders and participants to identify, name, diagnose, stigmatize, pathologize, or label people who are severely personally and relationally challenged in various ways; in addition, there is often a sincere (but erroneous) belief in these communities that everyone can change and heal to lead a happy, fulfilling life in a healthy relationship. As a result of this context, the empaths sometimes enter romantic relationships with afflicted participants, leaders, or teachers.

Initially, the three sides of the triangle of love (see *Figure 47: The triangle of love*, on page 370) in these relationships seem to be magically aligned, and the empaths fall deeply in love. They feel blessed that they finally found their true soulmate, twin flame, or sacred other. Someone who is open, beautiful, seductive, charming, sexy, smart, successful, complex, present, deep, emotionally available, vulnerable, exciting, compatible, committed, and evolved. He or she seems to be a dream come true.

Alas, once the empaths are hooked, the relationships increasingly become one-sided, with the empaths giving more and more time, energy, money, and support, and receiving less and less love, appreciation, and help in return, and eventually even being blamed for their partner's misery.

Of course, it also says a lot about the empaths' lack of knowledge, experience, boundaries, maturity, self-love, security, and purpose (which we try to remedy in this module and training) that makes them vulnerable to being attracted to and becoming sexually and emotionally addicted to charming and seductive partners with PDs. Thus, these relationships become the best opportunity for the empaths to learn, heal, grow, and awaken through the drama and emotional pain they will experience during the relationship and after it inevitably ends, when the empath burns out and the person with the PD blames him or her and moves on.[357] As the saying goes, it always takes two people to form a relationship, but only one to end it.

The DSM 5 and ICD 11

Individuals who have genetic predispositions[358] and became emotionally wounded or traumatized during their childhood may display symptoms of personality disorders that often increase over the course of their lives.

According to the American Psychiatric Association's Diagnostic and Statistical Manual on Mental Disorders (DSM 5), personality disorders represent "an enduring pattern of inner experience and behavior that deviates markedly from the expectations of the culture of the individual who exhibits it." Similarly, the WHO International Classification of Diseases (ICD 11) states that "to qualify for a diagnosis of personality disorder, problems in interpersonal relationships and impaired functioning must be present."[359]

These patterns and problems tend to be fixed and consistent across time and situations and are typically perceived to be appropriate by the afflicted individuals, even though these behaviors may affect their day-to-day life (and especially their love relationships) in negative and often devastating ways. The disorders are mostly incurable unless the afflicted persons are able and willing to make a prolonged and serious effort to heal. This is often not possible because of a lack of acknowledgment that there is a problem in the first place, or a lack of motivation, financial resources, or access to qualified therapists and psychiatrists.

Therefore, people with PDs often see no need or path to change—until they can no longer succeed through the behavior they grew accustomed to and become increasingly isolated, fall into depression, develop physical illnesses, or become suicidal. If they would or could change, their life as they know it would fall apart and they would have no frame of reference for how to navigate the world.

In some cases, therapists even refuse to treat certain conditions, such as borderline or narcissistic personality disorders, as they have repeatedly experienced that clients with these challenges are unwilling or unable to change, and often attack, blame, or discredit the therapists who tried to help for being wrong, abusive, or incompetent.

Three clusters

The DSM-5 lists ten personality disorders and allocates them to one of three groups or clusters.

- Cluster A (odd, bizarre, eccentric)—Paranoid PD, Schizoid PD, Schizotypal PD.
- Cluster B (dramatic, erratic)—Borderline PD, Histrionic PD, Narcissistic PD, Antisocial PD.
- Cluster C (anxious, fearful)—Avoidant PD, Dependent PD, Obsessive-compulsive PD.

While personality disorders differ from mental disorders like schizophrenia and bipolar disorders, they do, by definition, lead to significant impairments.

Cluster A and C symptoms

Below you find short descriptions of symptoms in people with disorders in Clusters A and C, who are much less or not seductive at all, easier to identify, and unlikely to show up in the forementioned circles. We will then turn to the first three disorders in cluster B, with descriptions of symptoms that highly seductive, charming, charismatic, and popular people may display, especially in intimate relationships.

Paranoid personality disorder (PPD)

This mental disorder is characterized by paranoia and a pervasive, long-standing suspiciousness and generalized mistrust of others. Individuals with this disorder may be hypersensitive and easily insulted, and they habitually relate to the world by vigilant scanning of the environment for clues or suggestions that may validate their fears or biases. Paranoid individuals are eager observers. They think they are in danger and look for signs and threats of that danger, potentially not appreciating other evidence.

They tend to be guarded and suspicious and have quite constricted emotional lives. Their reduced capacity for meaningful emotional involvement and the general pattern of isolated withdrawal often lend a quality of schizoid isolation to their life experience. People with PPD have a tendency to bear grudges, to be suspicious and self-referential, to interpret others' actions as hostile, and to have a tenacious sense of personal right.[360]

Schizoid Personality Disorder (SPD)

This is a personality disorder that is characterized by a lack of interest in social relationships, a tendency towards a solitary or sheltered lifestyle, secretiveness, emotional coldness, and apathy. Affected individuals may be unable to form intimate attachments to others and simultaneously demonstrate a rich, elaborate and exclusively internal fantasy world.[361]

Schizotypal Personality Disorder (STPD)

This is a mental disorder characterized by severe social anxiety, paranoia, and often unconventional beliefs. People with this disorder feel extreme discomfort with maintaining close relationships with people, mainly because they think that their peers harbor negative thoughts about them, so they avoid forming them. Peculiar speech mannerisms and odd modes of dress are also symptoms of this disorder. Those with STPD may react oddly in conversations, not respond, or talk to themselves.[362]

Antisocial Personality Disorder (ASPD)

This is also known as Dissocial Personality Disorder (DPD) and sociopathy. It is a personality disorder characterized by a pervasive pattern of disregard for, or violation of, the rights of others. An impoverished moral sense or conscience is often apparent, as well as a history of crime, legal problems, or impulsive and aggressive behavior.[363]

Avoidant Personality Disorder (APD)

Those affected display a pattern of social inhibition, feelings of inadequacy and inferiority, extreme sensitivity to negative evaluation, and avoidance of social interaction despite a strong desire to be close to others. Individuals with the disorder tend to describe themselves as uneasy, anxious, lonely, unwanted, and isolated from others. The behavior typically begins by early adulthood, and occurs across a variety of situations. People with avoidant personality disorder often consider themselves to be socially inept or personally unappealing, and avoid social interactions for fear of being ridiculed, humiliated, rejected, or disliked.[364]

Dependent Personality Disorder (DPD)

Formerly known as Asthenic personality disorder, it is characterized by a pervasive psychological dependence on other people. This personality disorder is a long-term condition in which people depend on others to meet their emotional and physical needs, with only a minority achieving normal levels of independence.

Obsessive–Compulsive Personality Disorder (OCPD)

This is a personality disorder that is characterized by a general pattern of concern with orderliness, perfectionism, excessive attention to details, mental and interpersonal control, and a need for control over one's environment, at the expense of flexibility, openness to new experiences, and efficiency.

Workaholism and miserliness are also often seen in those with this personality disorder. Rituals are performed to the point of excluding leisure activities and friendships. Persons affected with this disorder may find it hard to relax, always feeling that time is running out for their activities, and that more effort is needed to achieve their goals. They may plan their activities down to the minute—a manifestation of the compulsive tendency to keep control over their environment—and they dislike unpredictable situations they cannot control.

Cluster B symptoms that affect love relationships

The following three personality disorders have the greatest negative impact on love relationships, as the symptoms often only show up after the initial romance phase.

Borderline Personality Disorder (BPD)

This is a serious mental disorder which is marked by patterns of ongoing instability in moods, behavior, self-image, and functioning. The symptoms often result in impulsive actions and unstable relationships. A person with a BPD may experience intense episodes of anger, depression, and anxiety, lasting anywhere from only a few hours to a few days, followed by euphoria and exuberance.

Some people with BPDs also have high rates of co-occurring mental disorders, such as mood disorders, anxiety disorders, and eating disorders, along with substance abuse, self-harm, suicidal thinking and behaviors, and actual suicide attempts.

People with BPDs may experience extreme mood swings and can display uncertainty about who they are.

Other symptoms include the following:

• Seemingly ordinary events may trigger symptoms! For example, people with a BPD may feel angry and distressed over minor separations from people they feel close to, or when sudden changes of plans occur.

• Studies also show that people with this disorder may imagine they see anger in an emotionally neutral face and have stronger reactions to words with negative meanings than people who do not have the disorder.[365]

Relationships with people who have a BPD usually evolve through three stages, often in a cyclical pattern: (1) the vulnerable seducer, (2) the clinger, and (3) the hater. This evolution may take months, and sometimes even years, to cycle through. In the later periods, the personality often swings wildly back and forth from one phase to the next.[366]

There is an ongoing debate if BPDs can be treated. Some research shows that mindfulness practices and medication can support patients in better regulating emotions and improving their relationships. Another question is whether the diagnosis should be shared with patients. The jury is now leaning towards disclosing, even though there is often pushback from the patient.[367]

Histrionic[368] Personality Disorder (HPD)

According to a study by psychologist Krystle Disney and her collaborators at Washington University in St. Louis, the strongest predictors of divorce likelihood were, by far, histrionic personality disorder symptoms.[369]

People with this disorder show patterns of excessive attention-seeking emotions, inappropriately seductive and sexually provocative behavior, loud and inappropriate appearances, exaggerated behaviors, dramatic emotions with an impressionistic style that lacks (believable) detail, being easily influenced by others, having an excessive need for approval, and craving stimulation. Histrionic people are lively, dramatic, vivacious, enthusiastic, and flirtatious. Somewhat unsurprisingly, four times more women show symptoms of HPDs than men (see more below) and there is probably a higher than average rate among exhibitionistic actors and actresses, models, artists, and other attention-seeking public figures.

Associated behaviors in patients include egocentrism, self-indulgence, continuous longing for appreciation, and persistent manipulative behavior to have their own needs met. People with a HPD are usually high-functioning, both socially and professionally. They have good social skills and use them to manipulate others into making themselves the center of attention. A HPD also affects a person's social and/or romantic relationships, as well as their ability to cope with losses or failures. They may seek treatment for clinical depression when romantic or other close personal relationships end.

Individuals with a HPD often fail to see their own personal situation realistically, and instead dramatize and exaggerate their difficulties. They may frequently go through job changes and many consecutive sexual relationships, as they become easily bored and may prefer withdrawing from frustration instead of facing challenges and uncomfortable feelings. Because they tend to crave novelty and excitement, they may place themselves in risky situations. All these factors may lead to greater risk of developing clinical depression.

Some people with histrionic traits or other personality disorders change their seduction technique into a more maternal or paternal style as they age.

Narcissistic Personality Disorder (NPD)

People with narcissistic personality disorders (NPD) have significant problems with their self-worth, stemming from a powerful sense of entitlement. This leads them to believe that they deserve special treatment, have special powers, are uniquely talented, or that they are exceptionally brilliant or attractive. Their sense of entitlement can lead them to act in ways that fundamentally disregard and disrespect the worth of those around them. They are further characterized by their persistent grandiosity, excessive need for admiration, and disdain and lack of empathy for others. They often display arrogance, a sense of superiority, and power-seeking behaviors. They are sometimes found in New Age circles, believing that they are at the center of the universe, and create their own reality in magical ways (called New Age narcissism.)

People with a NPD are preoccupied with fantasies of unlimited success and power, so much so that they might end up becoming lost in their daydreams while they fantasize about their superior intelligence or stunning beauty. These people can get so caught up in their fantasies that they don't put any effort into their daily life and don't direct their energies toward accomplishing their goals.

Status is very important to people with a NPD. Associating with famous and special people provides them a sense of importance. Yet these individuals can quickly shift from overidealizing others to devaluing them.

People with a NPD often feel devastated when they realize that they have normal, average human limitations, that they are not as special as they think, or that others don't admire them as much as they would like. These realizations are often accompanied by feelings of intense anger or shame that they sometimes take out on other people. Their need to be powerful and admired, coupled with a lack of empathy for others, makes for conflicted relationships that are often superficial and devoid of real intimacy and caring.

A NPD is different from having a strong sense of self-confidence. People with NPDs typically value themselves over others to the extent that they disregard the feelings and wishes of others and expect to be treated as superior, regardless of their actual status or achievements. In addition, people with NPDs may exhibit fragile egos, an inability to tolerate criticism, and a tendency to belittle others in an attempt to validate their own superiority.

True NPD symptoms are pervasive, apparent in various situations, rigid, and remain consistent over time. However, the same is true of the self-judgments of afflicted people. They tend to vacillate between feeling like they have unlimited abilities, and then feeling deflated, worthless, and devastated when they encounter their normal, average human limitations.

Numbers of people with BPD, HPD, and NPD

According to the largest study ever conducted on personality disorders by the U.S. National Institutes of Health (NIH), 2.7% (some numbers suggest up to 5.9%) of the US population have BPD; 2–3% have HPD (according to Wikipedia);[370] and 6.2% have NPD.[371]

Of the people meeting the criteria for a BPD diagnosis, 53% were women and 47% were men.

Of the people meeting the criteria for a HPD diagnosis, 75% were women and 25% were men.

Of the people meeting the criteria for NPD, 62% were men and 38% were women.

As some people fit a mix of the diagnoses, we can assume that about 10% of the US population have BPD, NPD, and/or HPD.[372] Numbers in other countries may vary slightly but seem similar. Many more people may have certain traits of a PD, but not the full spectrum. Therefore, the number of people with some of these symptoms is likely higher than 10%.

Research on divorce rates shows that people with personality disorders have a greater likelihood of marital dissolution than people without them.[373] Because people with personality disorders are more likely to be single or serial dating, and roughly 40% of the US population live alone now,[374] about one in three singles may be afflicted and thus have difficulties forming or staying in a relationship.

Ultimately, the figures for PDs depend on where clinicians and statisticians draw the line between a "normal" personality and one that leads to the inability to form stable relationships. Characterizing personality disorders is difficult but diagnosing them reliably is even more challenging. For instance, how far from the norm must personality traits deviate before they can be counted as disordered? How significant is "significant impairment"? How is "impairment" to be defined? Which people have access to therapists and are seeking help (more men than women; and many may never be diagnosed)? Regardless of the answers to these questions, they are bound to include a large dose of subjectivity. Personal dislike, prejudice, or a clash of values can all play a part in arriving at a diagnosis of personality disorder, and it has been argued that the diagnosis sometimes amounts to little more than a convenient label for undesirables and social deviants.[375]

It is, therefore, important that a qualified and licensed mental health professional conducts a thorough assessment to determine whether or not a diagnosis of a PD or other mental disorder is warranted, and to help guide treatment options when appropriate.

On the other hand, just because someone denies having a PD (denials are extremely common) and refuses to be diagnosed and treated does not mean that he or she is healthy.

In the end, the best indicator for the psychological health and depth of embodiment of the spiritual realization of people is their ability to share their *biological, transformational, and transcendental purpose* in a healthy love relationship in such a way that the relationship provides more goodness, truth, beauty and functioning in the private and public spheres, as we will cover in Modules 22 and 23.

PDs in relationships

As mentioned above, the personality traits of people with PDs take on particularly maladaptive forms once the individuals enter intimate love relationships. Their behavior in normal day-to-day life is often similar to people who are mentally healthy. In fact, the often charming, winning, extroverted, charismatic, self-centered, clever, shameless, emotional, and needy ways make people with PDs frequently more popular and successful (at the expense of others) than healthy people.

However, their distorted sense of self, unstable emotions, and out-of-control behavior would challenge any long-term partner to be willing and able to put up with a great deal of turmoil and abuse, especially when life circumstances aggravate the already precarious hold on the feelings and behavior of their significant other with the PD. These relationships then have a pattern of going through 22 stages of decline (see below).

Healthy partners often feel betrayed when the initially seductive, considerate, and attentive person with whom they fell in love "disappears" as time goes by or turns against them in split loving/idealizing-hating/devaluating ways, which make the empaths feel confused, unloved, unseen, lonely, and less sure of themselves, causing their otherwise healthy sense of self, stable life, and independence to steadily decline.[376] To varying degrees, they find it difficult to express their rights, needs, and feelings, and find it almost impossible to set healthy boundaries, especially if their own boundaries weren't respected during their childhood.

Occasionally, people who have a partner with a PD experience recurrent flashes of the warmth and caring from the person with whom they first fell in love. They say that they long for the emotional connection they once had and insist they're committed to staying in the relationship—if only they felt more loved and appreciated.

In the end, the persons with the PD will exploit and abuse the empathetic "helpers" and eventually discard them, blaming them for being "unenlightened," "unevolved," "unloving," "selfish," "passive-aggressive," or "having taken advantage of them"—when, in fact, it was the other way around. And, to add insult to injury, the partner with the PD often publicly shames and denounces the empathetic helper.

Most people even side with the persons with PDs, especially if they are females, when they complain about their partners. They only experience their feminine, radiant, charming, and vulnerable side in public, and see them as the poor and abused victims when they hear about their troubled and miserable love lives, instead of recognizing their PDs as the main cause for the breakups. Famous examples include Princess Diana[377] or Marilyn Monroe.[378] Many people think that when women dump their male partners (70% of breakups are initiated by women), they must be losers, jerks, abusers, or worse. Otherwise, why would the women have left them in the first place? On the other hand, if men leave their partners, they also must be the jerks; otherwise, why would they have left their wives or girlfriends?

In defense of well-meaning and empathetic lovers with weak boundaries who continue to become enmeshed with unhealthy partners in codependent love relationships, PDs are often hard to spot, especially by lay people, but also by professionals (who are sometimes afflicted themselves—a reason why they chose to get into the helping profession in the first place), because, unlike other challenges to mental health, personality disorders do not represent a particular pattern of "illness" that can be "cured."

If you are in a relationship with such a person, it is vital to seek professional help and to work on your boundary issues to end an existing abusive relationship—even if it feels cruel and unloving—and to prevent such toxic relationships in the future. Living and sharing your purpose (as we will cover in Modules 22 and 23) and forming an Integral Love Relationship (as we will cover in Modules 24–26) is more important than trying to be the savior of one person and going down with him or her in the name of unconditional love and altruistic compassion.[379]

Purpose and application of the module

1. Understand why people with personality disorders (PDs) often show up in self-help groups and why these people are so seductive.
2. Recognize unhealthy patterns and behaviors in partners who may have PDs and ask them to get professionally diagnosed.
3. Meet others who show symptoms of personality disorders with love and compassion without getting entangled in unhealthy (sexual) love relationships.
4. Develop healthy boundaries that make you immune to falling in love with partners who have personality disorders.
5. Seek professional help if you are or were in a relationship with a partner with a PD to end your suffering.
6. Forgive yourself and your partner through the Forgiveness and/or Conscious Uncoupling processes. (See endnote 354.)
7. Support others who are or were in relationships with partners with PDs to see their own neediness, vulnerabilities, nativity, ignorance, idiot compassion, and lack of healthy boundaries, and to make better choices in the future.

Exercises: Personality disorders

The following are individual and paired exercises.
1. Print out the three worksheets for the individual exercises, and the questions for the paired exercises, found below.
2. Make the four agreements for confidentiality, responsibility, I-statements, and sharing, as outlined on page 556.
3. Hand out the worksheets.

Exercise one: BPD, HPD, and NPD symptoms

Read through the symptoms of BPD, HPD, and NPD in the worksheets below and rate those that apply to you and your (former) partner(s) on a scale from 0 (no symptoms) to 10 (severe

Integral Relationship Practice | 406

symptoms), and the level at which you find certain symptoms attractive in a partner at the same scale. Note that most (90%) of the symptoms must be present for a person to be diagnosed with the disorder by a health professional.

Worksheets: Personality disorders

Borderline personality disorder

	Symptoms:	Me	Partner	Attraction
1	Extreme mood swings (without obvious reasons)			
2	Display uncertainty about who they are (what they want)			
3	Rapid changes in interests and values			
4	Frantic efforts to avoid real or imagined abandonment			
5	A pattern of intense and unstable relationships with family, friends, and loved ones, often swinging from extreme closeness and love (idealization) to extreme dislike or anger (devaluation)			
6	Distorted and unstable self-image or sense of self			
7	Impulsive and often dangerous behaviors, such as spending sprees, unsafe sex, substance abuse, reckless driving, and binge eating			

8	Recurring suicidal behaviors or threats or self-harming behavior, such as cutting			
9	Intense and highly changeable moods, with each episode lasting from a few hours to a few days			
10	Chronic feelings of emptiness			
11	Inappropriate, intense anger or problems with controlling anger, sometimes hitting partner without a reason			
12	Having stress-related paranoid thoughts			
13	Having severe dissociative symptoms, such as feeling cut off from oneself, observing oneself from outside the body, or losing touch with reality			

Table 17: Borderline personality disorder

Histrionic personality disorder

	Symptoms:	Me	Partner	Attraction
1	Exhibitionist behavior			
2	Inappropriately seductive appearance or behavior of a sexual nature			
3	Impressionistic use of language style that lacks (believable) detail			
4	Constant seeking of reassurance or approval			
5	Excessive sensitivity to criticism or disapproval			
6	Pride of own personality and unwillingness to change, viewing any change as a threat			
7	Using somatic symptoms (of physical illness) to garner attention			
8	A need to be the center of attention			
9	Low tolerance for frustration or delayed gratification			
10	Rapidly shifting emotional states that may appear superficial or exaggerated to others			
11	Tendency to believe that relationships are more intimate than they actually are			
12	Making rash decisions			

13	Blaming personal failures or disappointments on others			
14	Being easily influenced by others, especially those who treat them approvingly			
15	Being overly dramatic and emotional			
16	Influenced easily by others or circumstances			
17	Emotional lability; shallowness			
18	Make-up: physical appearance is used to draw attention to self			
19	Exaggerated emotions; theatrical			

Table 18: Histrionic personality disorder

Narcissistic personality disorder

	Symptoms:	Me	Partner	Attraction
1	A grandiose sense of self-importance; exaggerates achievements and talents			
2	Dreams of unlimited power, success, brilliance, beauty, or ideal love			
3	Self-perception of being unique, superior, and associated with high-status people and institutions			
4	Sense of entitlement to special treatment and to obedience from others			

5	Unwilling or unable to empathize with others' feelings, wishes, or needs			
6	Needing constant admiration from others			
7	Exploitative of others to achieve personal gain			
8	Believes he or she is special and unique and can only be understood by, or should associate with, other special or high-status people (or institutions)			
9	Unreasonably expects special, favorable treatment or compliance with his or her wishes			
10	Exploits and takes advantage of others to achieve personal ends			
11	Intensely envious of others and believes that others are equally envious of them			
12	Has a pompous attitude of arrogance or acts that way			

Table 19: Narcissistic personality disorder

Exercise two

1. Share the answers to the following questions with your partner, even if you have not been in a relationship with a person with a PD.
2. How have aspects of PDs in yourself and/or your partners impacted your past and, if applicable, current relationship?

See 22 stages of decline (below) if you are an empath and are or were with a partner with a PD.
3. What attracted you to your former partners (and your current partner) in the three dimensions of love (intimacy, passion, dependence), including your primary fantasy? (See Module 20 above.)
4. What were/are the reality of the relationships, the projected ideals, and the intentions of the triangles of love? (See page 376 above.)
5. What forms of love did, or do, you experience, including primary fantasy and "commitment," from codependence to inter-becoming? (See page 379 above.)
6. How did the states or phases of love—lust/desire, infatuation, romance/conflict, exclusivity, commitment, engagement, marriage, and possibly dissolution/divorce—unfold for you and your partner(s) (see page 382 above.)
7. Why did your previous relationships end?
8. Who ended them?
9. How did your relationships end and what is your relationship with your former partners now?
10. What did you learn from the endings?
11. Was there any forgiveness or "conscious uncoupling" work that you did or still need to do to open up to love again? See endnote.[354]
12. What do you want to do differently now and/or in your future relationships?
13. What are imperatives/agreements with your partner about shared values/visions, healthy boundaries, and the fulfillment of needs that must be adhered to for creating a safe space/container for your ongoing learning, healing, growing, awakening, and sharing a purpose?

Additional information and resources

22 stages of relationship decline between empaths and partners with PDs.

1. The empath becomes attracted to a person with the PD. Their relationship starts. The empath loves deeply and unconditionally. He or she feels emotionally fulfilled even though the person with the PD plays no role to develop a stronger bond. The empath feels satisfied and thinks their love is reciprocated just by being around the person with the PD.
2. The empath believes the false notion that they have finally met the kind of love that many people never find. The person with the PD affirms this notion by creating an illusion that leads the empath to believe that what the partners have is special. The empath feels a deep bond from which it is almost impossible to break free.
3. Sometimes it appears that the person with the PD wants this relationship as much as the empath. Actually, what they want is someone who invests their time, energy and love and is in their complete control.
4. As time passes, the person with the PD will make the empath feel weak, unconfident, and bereft of the abilities to do even simple things. The person with the PD will never launch an open attack but instead use statements like "I don't want to hurt you but ..." to point out shortcomings. The person with the PD will try to take over anything that symbolizes control, such as handling bills or making decisions about purchases, and will look down on the empath for their interests and other things that form their identity. Gradually, the empath starts to believe that they are less capable and that they "need" someone like the person in their life. They falsely believe that no one else would want them.
5. For an empath, this relationship will be everything, as they are the ones who are in love. Out of love, they always want to soothe and cheer up the person with the PD, talk to them, help

them, and do whatever makes them feel good. The persons with the PD project themselves as the victim of their past, their relationships, and the circumstances. The empaths are givers; they try to make up for all the unfortunate things that have ever happened to the person with the PD.

6. The empath has a good and a clear heart and cannot imagine that the deep and unresolved wounds of the person with the PD are not the same as their own. Healing those wounds is different from healing their own.
7. The relationship is all about the person with the PD. The empath realizes this slowly, and a time comes when they feel afraid to talk or fight for their needs and desires. In their attempt to please, they don't want to voice their true needs. They would rather be likable than give any reason to be disliked. But, secretly they are not too happy.
8. The more devotion, love, care, affection, and effort the empath puts into the relationship, the person with the PD feels completely in control over the relationship. The empath literally dances to the tune of the person with the PD. As long as the empath continues to appease the person with the PD, it's impossible to detect any problem in the relationship. The problem occurs when the empath finally reaches the breaking point.
9. Finally, the empaths raise their voice because they can no longer keep up with the suppressing ways of the partner with the PD. Day after day their emotional needs remain unfulfilled. This happens because from the beginning of the relationship they have believed that their partner's emotional needs are all that matters. When they finally understand that their well-being also matters and speak out, they seem selfish. The person with the PD does not like it.
10. People with PDs are attention seekers. They derive satisfaction when people fuss around them. Their needs can never be met, they can never be satisfied. They may move on to other partners, open a new business, travel around the world, get

involved in new creative pursuits, and so on and so forth, but they will never be happy. The empath isn't aware of this fact.

11. When the empath finally bursts out with something like "My feelings also matter," the person with the PD is quick to call the empath "crazy," perhaps calling them overdramatic, needy, controlling, jealous, etc., and discount their concerns as being unfounded. This kind of dismissive behavior is the tactic used to gain control over the empath's mind.

12. The empath becomes confused. Why they have meted out such behavior is beyond their understanding. They start blaming themselves and wonder if they are at all worthy of being loved by anyone at all.

13. At this point, the empath is not able to understand that they are just being manipulated. Their partner has bent everything around them to create a twisted view of the circumstances, a view that lets them know "the truth"—that they are the one who is "right" and it's the empath who is tremendously "wrong" and wicked.

14. The empath will try to communicate with the person with the PD in all truthfulness. The person with the PD will, however, justify their behavior and pass the blame.

15. It is normal at this point for the empath to feel lost, confused, and hurt. But despite all the heartbreak, the empath will need to be calm and do some self-evaluation to figure out how they became so defenseless. This is how they will start transforming.

16. The empath needs to know that they are, by nature, healers. They have the inner strength to help others in the right ways, sometimes as a duty and sometimes when life brings them to such situations.

17. The empath must realize the bitter truth that not everyone deserves their love, care, and affection. Not everyone who seems distressed and unhappy is revealing their true self. There are some people who have sinister motives and have a very different outlook towards relationships and people than

their own. Not everyone they fall in love with can be trusted so quickly.
18. In this situation, the empath must realize that they too are in a very bad situation, not unlike situations of which the person with the PD always spoke of. But, in the empath's case, it will be different. They will make positive efforts and heal themselves. The person with the PD will not.
19. For the empaths, this will be a painful awakening. They will learn from the experience to move ahead.
20. The person with the PD will move on. In time, they will find another victim.
21. The person with the PD will continue as if nothing has happened and they are completely innocent. They won't remember, even for a moment, that someone loved them so deeply and intensely. They won't remember the powerful bond they once had with someone; they will just move on to find it somewhere else. A time will come when they will know they can neither connect with themselves nor with other people.
22. The empaths will be stronger, wiser, and more cautious about to whom they give their time, affection, and love.
From www.tinyurl.com/irpm90[380]

Books:

Stop Walking on Eggshells: Taking Your Life Back When Someone You Care About Has Borderline Personality Disorder (2020) by Paul T. Mason and Randi Kreger
tinyurl.com/irpm486[381]

The Borderline Personality Disorder Survival Guide: Everything You Need to Know About Living with BPD (2007) by Alex L. Chapman and Kim L. Gratz tinyurl.com/irpm488[382]

Stop Walking on Eggshells tinyurl.com/irpm491[383]

Sex Purpose Love book reference
Page 113–124

Suggested Movie: *Eternal Sunshine of the Spotless Mind* (2004)

Watch this movie to see the relationship between a needy, insecure empath with weak boundaries and a woman who has a borderline personality disorder descend through the 22 stages of decline.

After an impulsive decision to go to Montauk, introverted, and anxious Joel Barish (Jim Carrey) meets the free-spirited, impulsive, and unhinged Clementine Kruczynski (Kate Winslet) on the train home. She displays multiple symptoms of a borderline personality disorder and seduces him—a typical first step in such relationships—and he falls in love with her. As the movie jumps back and forth between different times of their relationship and Joel's childhood, we see more of the psychological issues that afflict them both.

At one point, Joel discovers that Clementine had broken up with him and had her memories of him erased from her brain by a firm called Lacuna. Heartbroken, Joel decides to undergo the same procedure, erasing her from his memory, as well, after he records a tape about his experience with her. Despite later hearing this tape, he becomes entangled with her again, seemingly having nothing learned from the breakup, a pattern which is emblematic of people with weak boundaries.

Practice Module 22
Biological and Transformational Purpose

You yourself are the eternal energy which appears as this universe. You didn't come into this world. You came out of it, like a wave from the ocean. You are not a stranger here.
~ Alan Watts ~

My vision for the future always centers around our children—it always centers around our children. So anytime anybody asks me what are the three most important issues facing the Congress, I always say the same thing: "Our children, our children, our children."
~ Nancy Pelosi ~

Module description

Learn and practice how to identify and share your biological purpose and transformational purpose in a healthy love relationship. Reveal your belief in creationism, evolutionary theory, intelligent design, or a co-creative life force that fundamentally shapes your views on your life's purpose, and the importance of love relationships and procreation.

Share your experiences and needs around your biological purpose or imperative of survival, procreation, group-forming, territorialism, competition and cooperation, and quality-of-life-seeking. Realize how the unique ways of living your biological purpose lead to what you desire in a partner and the formation of transactional, asymmetrical, need-based love relationships.

Gain insights about the dialectic of love between the first and second, third and fourth, and fifth and sixth chakras. Avoid getting into master-slave dynamics in your love relationships. See how advancing into living and sharing your transformational purpose of learning, healing, growing, and awakening with an equal and opposite partner leads to being-based transformational love relationships along the seven chakras and understand how these relationships typically unfold.

Introduction

Warning!

What we explore in the first part of this module frequently pushes women's emotional buttons, as it touches on what we may call "the collective female shadow" of their unconscious mate selection process that is based on the unacknowledged primary sexual fantasies with which most women would rather not be confronted. Some women may push back, as what we explore appears to them to be sexist, superficial, judgmental, unevolved, opportunistic, and stereotypical. They also may not want to face that their biologically driven mate selection process makes them co-responsible for creating and solving many of the wicked problems that humanity is facing, which they would rather deny and blame on men.

In contrast, men are usually fully aware and open to acknowledge (at least when women are not present) that they are attracted to and compete for mates with whom they can optimally share their biological purpose.

Ask the practitioners to look at their defensiveness and potential woundedness instead of projecting it onto you. Point out that you will cover advanced forms of transformational love in the second part of this module, and transcendental love in Module 23.

Meaning Making

How we make meaning of our lives and define, live, and share our purpose in love relationships is fundamentally shaped by our core beliefs and understanding of why and how the universe, our planet Earth, living things, and self-conscious human beings came into existence. There are three different general beliefs.

1. Creationism, which mostly resonates with people at a magical and mythic level of consciousness development is the belief that the universe and all living organisms were created by deities, human-like figures, or animals. Creationist myths can be found in nearly all known tribal and religious traditions and are regarded by their believers as being true to varying degrees.[384]
2. Evolutionary theory (ET), which resonates mostly with people at a rational level of consciousness, maintains that no God or other metaphysical force[385] or consciousness is necessary to explain how the universe—with our milky way, galaxy, solar system, and planet Earth—could emerge out of "nothing," as this "nothing" is actually filled with spaceless and timeless dark energy and matter that cannot be "observed."[386] ET further maintains that organisms on Earth descended from a common ancestral gene pool and produced increasingly complex and unique life-forms and, ultimately, human consciousness through mutations, sexual/natural selection, and migration.[387]
3. Intelligent design (ID)[388] resonates mostly with people at a post-rational level of consciousness development, but also with some believers at a pre-rational level. It is the response to the inherent problems of tribal and religious creation myths and belief systems on one end of the spectrum, and a criticism of naturalism, or scientific materialism, with the potential nihilism of positivist explanations of evolution, on the other. Critics such as Lawrence Kraus or Richard Dawkins see ID as simply a disguised form of creationism and vehemently argue against it.[389]

The Integral Relationship model proposes a fourth alternative, a co-creative and procreative impulse or life force, as the underlying cause and drive for the emergence of the universe, life, and human consciousness. This impulse or life force has no "intelligence," telos, or Omega Point. It rather is the force that drives the ongoing combining of entities which leads to novel forms through emergence, as argued for by evolutionary theorists. Aligning ourselves with this life force that we can all experience gives our lives meaning by making us fully responsible for our collective future through co-creation and procreation in healthy love relationships, instead of succumbing to cynical, nihilistic, individualistic hedonism, or relying on a God or higher intelligence for a better future.[390]

A 2014 Gallup poll found the following percentages for those living in the US in regard to each of the three core beliefs about the origin of the universe and development of human beings.[391]

1. Creationism (42%)
2. Intelligent design (31%)
3. Evolutionary theory (19%)

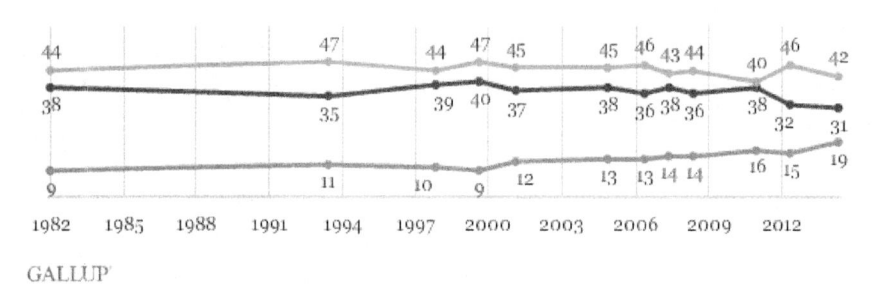

Figure 50: US statistics for origin of humans

A 2009 poll in Germany found the following numbers:
1. Creationism (16%)
2. Intelligent Design (4%)
3. Evolutionary Theory (69%)
4. Other Theories 3%
5. Don't know 7%

In the 2006 figure below, we see the percentages in the acceptance of evolutionary theory versus creationism in different countries.[392]

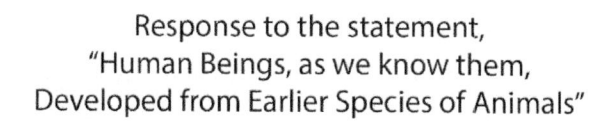

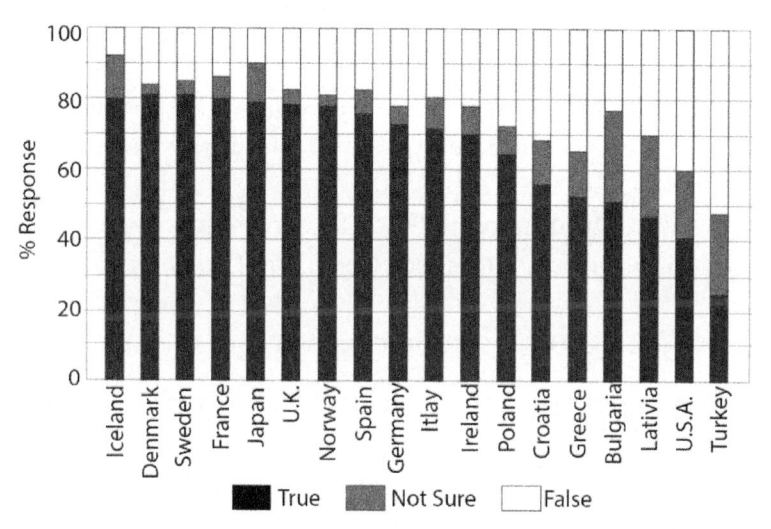

Response to the statement,
"Human Beings, as we know them,
Developed from Earlier Species of Animals"

Figure 51: Acceptance of evolutionary theory

Purpose and application of the module

1. See how your and your partner's beliefs about how the universe and humans came into existence lead to different views on your purpose and sharing it in a love relationship.
2. Learn about our biological purpose/imperative that we share with all living things.
3. Understand why fully living our biological purpose is best accomplished in asymmetrical transactional love relationships along the first six chakras.
4. See how this co-creation takes place in each of the four dimensions of our being/quadrants by balancing feminine and masculine polarities.

Integral Relationship Practice | 422

5. Avoid slipping into master-slave relationships.
6. Advance into living your transformational purpose that leads to transformational love.

Exercises: Biological and transformational purpose and love

The following are paired and group exercises.
1. Make the four agreements for confidentiality, responsibility, healthy boundaries, I-statements, and sharing, as outlined on page 556.
2. Give a short introduction to the beliefs in creationism, evolutionary theory, intelligent design, and co-creative life force.
3. Allow about 20–30 minutes or longer for each exercise.

Exercise one: Why are we here? What shall we do?

1. Share your beliefs about the origin of the universe and human beings with your partner.
2. Share how your beliefs have shaped the ways you make meaning of your life and your purpose.
3. Share how your beliefs impact your love relationship(s)?
4. Spend about 20–40 minutes time for this exercise.
5. Invite group sharing.

Exercise two: What is our biological purpose?

This is a group exercise.
1. Ask practitioners what they think their biological purpose is and write it on a whiteboard/flipchart.
2. Make sure they (or you) mention all six imperatives below.
3. Point out that all healthy humans are driven by a co-creative and procreative life force or impulse to live their biological purpose, even though the expressions vary widely, and that some avoid, repress, or are incapable of reproduction/procreation and group forming in healthy nuclear families.

Biological purpose

Our biological purpose or imperative[393] that we share with all living things is to perpetuate our existence through self-sustaining processes including:
1. Survival (food, shelter, safety)
2. Reproduction/Procreation (raising offspring)
3. Group forming (family/community)
4. Territorialism (home, neighborhood, city, county, state, country, continent)
5. Competition/Cooperation (altruism)
6. **Quality-of-life-seeking**

Figure 52: Biological purpose

Yes, it is this simple ....

Asymmetrical, transactional, need-based love relationships

Our biological purpose and the related desires are most effectively fulfilled when males compete for sexy females with the best reproductive capabilities, and females choose successful males with the best productive capabilities. (See *Figure 27: The primary sexual fantasy dynamic*, in Module 9, page 166.)

As one of many examples of this dynamic, Alison Armstrong writes in her book, *Making Sense of Men: A Woman's Guide to a Lifetime of Love, Care and Attention from All Men*:

> Four qualities in women (shiny hair, shapely body, sensuality, and sexual energy) will attract men who will want to have sex with them. Once women have charmed and enchanted the men who they are interested in [by meeting their primary fantasy] with their self-confidence, authenticity, passion, and receptivity, they will fall in love with them and make them happy by spending time, taking care, protecting, and contributing/providing.

	Sexual Attraction	Charmed and Enchanted
CAUSE	❹ Shiny Hair	❹ Self-Confidence
	❸ Shapely Body	❸ Authenticity
	❷ Sensuality	❷ Passion
	❶ Sexual Energy	❶ Receptivity
RESPONSE	▶ Want to have sex.	▶ Spend time with
	▶	▶ Take care of
	▶	▶ Protect
	▶	▶ Contribute to
	▶	▶ Make happy
	▶	▶ Fall in love with

Figure 53: Cause and response in male-female relationships

425 | Biological and Transformational Purpose

These differences in desires, attractors, and gender roles of males and females in the public and domestic spheres, based in our biological purpose, led to dialectical exchanges that evolved throughout human history in which males produce, protect, and create, and females reproduce, care, and direct/guide.

These desires and exchanges map onto the first six of the seven chakras:

Crown   -> Unity

Third Eye   -> Wisdom

Throat   -> Creativity

Heart   -> Care

Solar Plexus -> Power

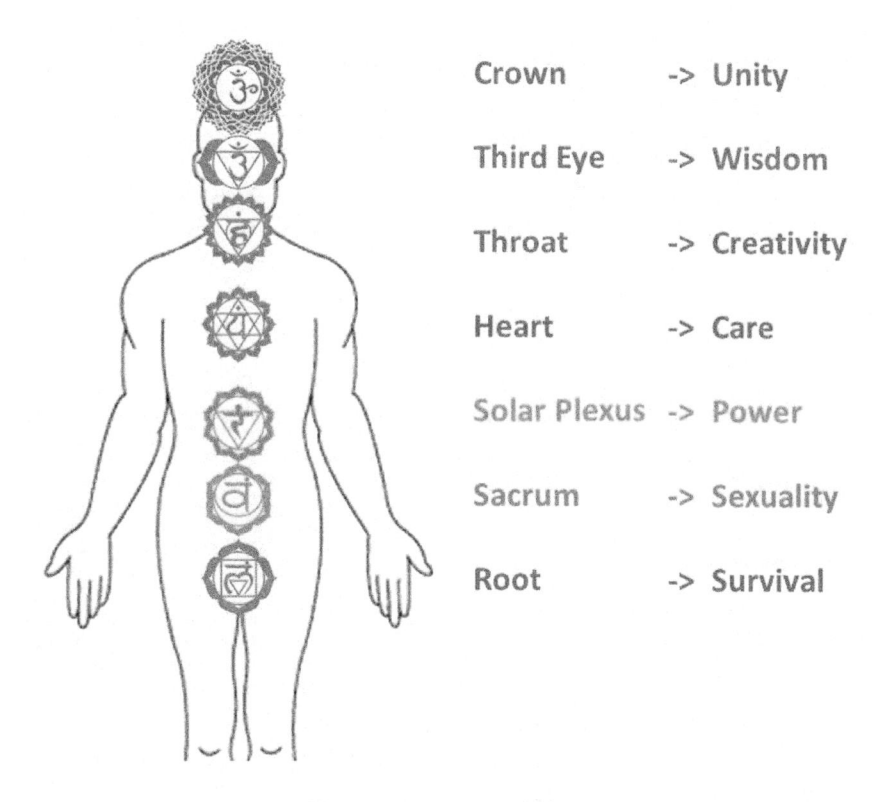

Sacrum   -> Sexuality

Root   -> Survival

Figure 54: Seven chakras

Root first chakra male providing in exchange for sacrum second chakra female sexuality that creates passion.

This pair of desires is related to and guided by instinctive processes in the reptilian parts of our brains, where the vital drives for survival and procreation are located.

Solar plexus third chakra male protection/safety/status in exchange for heart fourth chakra female care that creates dependence.

This pair of desires is related to and guided by the unconscious limbic parts of our brains,[394] where emotional memories of behaviors that made us feel safe, loved, and connected are stored, as are our traumatic experiences.[395]

Throat fifth chakra male self-expression and creativity in exchange for third eye sixth chakra female intuition, inspiration, and wisdom that creates intimacy.

The highest pair of desires is related to and guided by the neocortex of our brains, which allows for the development of self-consciousness, human language, autobiographical memory, abstract thought, and imagination.

Crown seventh chakra representing the differentiated unity of the couple.[396]

There is no mental concept, language, or dialectical exchange at this chakra, but rather present moment awareness, stillness, and surrender.

The seven chakras

In the Integral Relationship model, the chakras are defined as the felt "energy centers" or nerve bundles that are associated with major organs in our body, through which the co-creative and procreative impulse or life force yearns to co-create with a compatible opposite and equal mate. If this would not be the case, we would not be here as conscious human beings.

Chakra pioneer and psychotherapist Anodea Judith calls what we feel in each of the seven chakras "charge."[397] This charge can feel open, blocked, neutral, giving, receiving, empty, full, scarce, abundant, generous, withholding, passive, aggressive, feminine, masculine, etc. We will further explore this co-creative and procreative yearning and the charges along the seven chakras in Module 25.

Asymmetrical transactional love

The fulfillment of the divergent male and female desires in their partners along the even chakras leads to asymmetrical, transactional, need-based love relationships. Using the chakra system, we see that the female reward for the male contribution is always located at the next higher chakra, as shown in the image below. In other words, the male must first prove his ability to provide, protect, and create before receiving the rewards of sex, care, and wisdom.

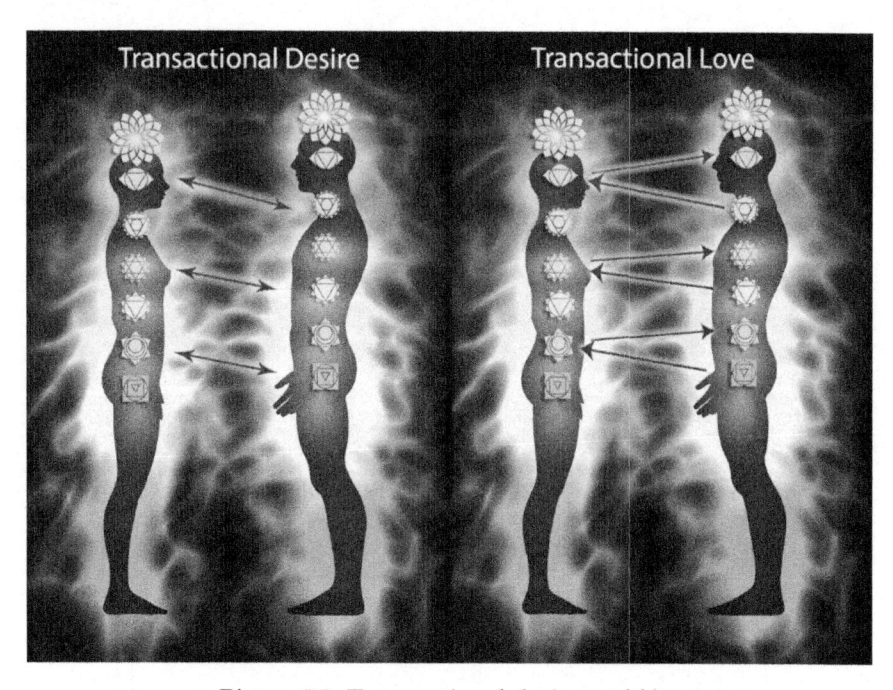

Figure 55: Transactional desire and love

These three pairs of exchange also correlate loosely with the Triangular Theory of Love (chakras 1–2=passion; 3–4=dependence; 5–6=intimacy), as shown in *Figure 47: The triangle of love*, on page 370.

Desires and consciousness development

If we put the divergent desires of males and females along the six chakra pairs, plus the seventh unity chakra, on a vertical Y axis, and the seven levels of consciousness development, from archaic to Integral, on a horizontal X axis (we will cover the transpersonal stage in the next Module), we arrive at a matrix with 49 intersections, as shown below.[398]

Chakras / Consciousness	Archaic	Magic	Egocentric	Mythic	Rational	Pluralistic	Integral
Crown male/female unity	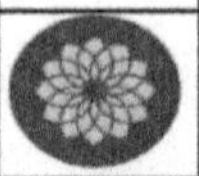 A-dual, fused, content	Bonded	Empowered	Devoted	Emancipated	Surrendered	Non-Dual integrated and differentiated
Third Eye male desire	 Improve chances of his offspring's survival	Further bonding and safety of the tribe	Increase his power and freedom	Create more stability and order by retaining and advancing rightful place in family and organization	Advance career and social status for good life of everyone	Deepen emotional intelligence and connect-ion to the feminine, animals and earth	Serve the greatest good for the largest number of people
Throat female desire	 Animalistic sounds and simple language to coordinate hunting and gathering	Chanting, story-telling, and magical ritual to entertain and protect	Gaining control over others through intimidation and anger	Make authoritative, patriarchal, absolute mythic statements	Reasonable, rational, logical, sensible, entertaining, confident, charismatic.	Truthful, sensitive, considerable, pluralistic, mystical, emotional	A-perspectival, multifaceted, inclusive, critical, complex
Heart male desire	 Appreciation	Participation	Submission and respect	Honoring	Support of his vision	Challenges (for his own good)	Complementing
Solarpl female desire	 Brutality towards others	Superstitious rituals Sacrifices Appease ghosts and Spirits	Aggressive Fighter Warrior Combat Possessive Controlling Macho Shameless	Arms and weapons Law and Order Heroic Soldier Art of War Laws	Modern Weapons Collateral Damage Peacemaking missions. Nation Building	Non-Violence Peaceful Warrior Protective Force	Moral considerations Spiral Wizardry
Sacrum male desire	 Fertility	Youthfulness	Uninhibitedness	Faithfulness	Physical fitness, Elegance	Tantric Lover	Transcendental, kundalini awakening
Root female desire	 Raw meat and other foods, Horde	Good cooked meat, Hunting, Tribe	Fast-food (Sugar, Fat Salt) Sub-stances, Gang	Carbs, Protein, Fruits, Vegetables Farming, Town, Family	Gourmet Food, Fine Wine, Dining Sub-urban Luxurious Living	Healthy Organic Foods No GMO Nature Communal Living	Sustainable foods and living Urban

Figure 56: Transactional love chakra-consciousness matrix

The exchange at each of the 49 intersections above takes place in each of the four dimensions of our being or quadrants, regardless of the couple being consciously aware of it or not.

This is illustrated in the image below, in which the seven levels of consciousness development (indicated by the seven long lines in each quadrant) are integrated with the seven chakras (indicated by the short lines for each level of consciousness) in each of the four dimensions of our being and relating (quadrants).

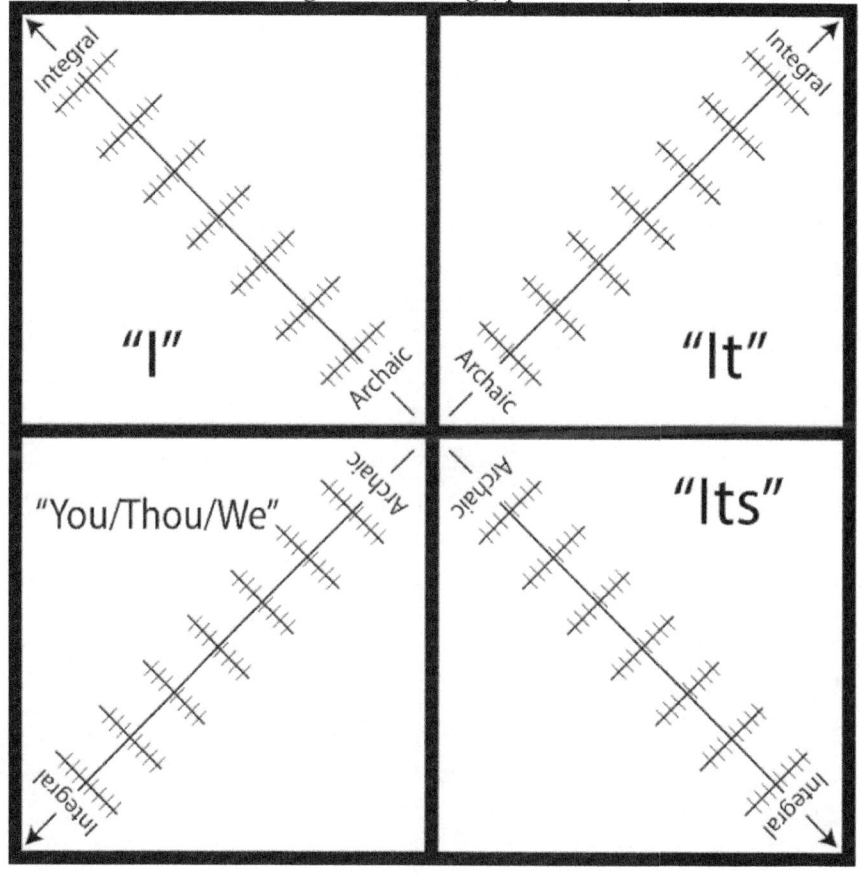

Figure 57: Four dimensions, chakras, and consciousness

We will further explore the co-creation in the four quadrants along the seven chakras in a guided meditation in Module 25.

Master-slave relationships

In an ideal romantic transactional love relationship, which most people are yearning for, both partners lovingly recognize and give each other what each of them desires and has been bargaining for in the respective chakra pair (females desiring providing, protection, and creativity; males desiring sex, care, and wisdom) in each of the four dimensions of their being and relating.

However, especially in modern and postmodern relationships, the dialectic can get quickly out of balance and break down completely when desires, expectations, and needs change and can no longer be fulfilled by one or both partners. This also happens when lovers withhold or lose what made them initially attractive to their partner, when the attractiveness of one partner increases or decreases, when needs and desires can be better met with someone outside the relationship, or when one partner evolves through better horizontal translation/integration or vertical transformation to higher levels of consciousness.

In most cases, the partner who still provides what their counterpart desires but no longer receives, in return, what they had bargained for, will become the slave and the other partner, the master—for example, when a woman is still sexual with her partner but he no longer provides for her, or when a man still protects but no longer receives her loving care.[399]

Social exchange theory

Especially in modern and postmodern biologically driven relationships, people often use levels of comparison to assess how rewarding their relationships are for them.

The Comparison Level (CL) is based on a person's expectation of the rewards they will reap from a relationship and how much they must invest to receive these rewards.

The Comparison Level for alternatives (CLalt) concerns a person's perception of whether an alternative potential relationship (or being single) would be more rewarding than staying in their current relationship.[400]

Exercise three: Dialectic of transactional love

1. Share the answers to the following questions with your partner.

2. What is or was the dialectical attraction/exchange/dynamic in your relationship(s) between you and your partner's first (survival) and second (sexuality), third (power) and fourth (heart), fifth (creativity) and sixth (wisdom), and seventh (unity) chakras?
3. At what level of consciousness is or was each dialectical exchange created? See the chakra-consciousness matrix above.
4. How is or was each of the dialectical exchanges expressed in the four dimensions of your being and relating (quadrants)?
5. Did the dialectic of love break down at some point in your current or past relationships?
6. If yes, why did it break down?
7. Are you or did you become the master or the slave in one or more chakra pairs in a current or past relationship?
8. What transactional forms of desire do you have and what kind of capacities to love would you like to develop in your current or future relationships?

Transformational purpose and transformational love

It is our transformational purpose to learn, heal, grow, and awaken. Biologically driven transactional love relationships have the potential to evolve into transformational love when equal and opposite partners awaken to their transformational purpose (TP), and support and challenge each other to evolve in the developmental lines that are shown in *Figure 30: Personality matrix*, on page 187, and covered throughout this manual.

This advancement allows them to move towards co-creation as opposite and equal partners at the level of each chakra in the four dimensions of their being and relating (quadrants) by balancing and harmonizing their healthy feminine and masculine polarities. Alas, relationships often end if only one partner awakens to their transformational purpose or if couples are not at the same level in major development lines.

Exercise four: Dialectic of transformational love

1. Share the answers to the following questions with your partner.
2. Have you and your current or former partner(s) awoken to living your transformational purpose and entered into a transformational love relationship?
3. If yes, at which chakras, lines (consciousness, spiritual, sexual, anima/animus), levels, and quadrants did you learn, heal, grow, and awaken?
4. If no, what are the reasons—e.g., just interested in romance, not at the same levels of development, too challenging or painful, etc.?
5. If yes, what have you learned together—for example, communication, relationship, or lovemaking skills?
6. In which developmental lines (consciousness, feminine-masculine, spiritual, sexual, anima/animus, etc.) have you grown together?
7. In what aspects of healing (fear-shame downward spiral, anima/animus complex, attachment styles, unconscious, false identities, personality disorders, etc.) have you supported each other?
8. What aspects of spiritual awakening and liberation realms (disidentification from, and integration of, the material, physical, mental, emotional, mystical/metaphysical) have you realized together?

Follow-up questions

1. How do you feel after exploring this module and engaging in the exercises?
2. What insights have you gained through the exercises?
3. What defenses came up for you?
4. With what purpose and capacity to love did you most resonate?
5. What kind of love relationship would you like to co-create?

Additional information and resources

A Universe from Nothing: Why There Is Something Rather than Nothing (2013) by Lawrence M. Krauss
tinyurl.com/irpm497[401]

The Mating Mind: How Sexual Choice Shaped the Evolution of Human Nature (2001) by Geoffrey Miller
tinyurl.com/irpm499[402]

Charge and the Energy Body: The Vital Key to Healing Your Life, Your Chakras, and Your Relationships (2018) by Anodea Judith
tinyurl.com/irpm501[403]

Sex Purpose Love book reference
Page 173–204 and 323–378

Suggested movie: *Quest for Fire* (1981)

Watch this movie to gain a deeper understanding of our evolutionary biological differences and purpose, and our capacity to love along the seven chakras.

The movie takes place in prehistoric times, as three tribesmen search for a new source of fire and, on the way, one of them also finds a mate. The new couple grows closer through intimate touches and glances, and a sense of deeper affection forms. As their relationship evolves, so too do her emotions and sexuality. At one point, she softly turns and lies on her back, and the invitation is clear but confusing for her partner. Face-to-face lovemaking is unheard of, and he is unsure of what to do. But she guides him and holds him, and soon he is upon her, looking in her eyes. We see, in one sensual and emotional moment, the shift from animal copulation to human lovemaking. It is a simple moment, but powerful in its presentation and what it means for human evolution, reminiscent of Geoffrey Miller's book, *The Mating Mind*, and Ferdinand Fellman's book, *The Couple*, in which the authors convincingly argue that human evolution in consciousness was caused through the intimate pair bond and face-to-face sexuality.

Practice Module 23
Transcendental Purpose and Love

As soon as you rise above mere survival, the question of meaning and purpose becomes of paramount importance in your life.
~ Eckhart Tolle, A New Earth ~

Find that place where your deepest gladness and the world's deep hunger meet.
~ Fredrick Buechner ~

Module description

Learn and practice how to awaken to, identify, live, and share your transcendental purpose that goes beyond your biological and transformational purpose. Reap the physical and psychological benefits from living your transformational purpose, such as increased lifespan, meaning, contentment, and love.

Remove psychological blocks that may prevent you from awakening to, identifying, living, and sharing your transcendental purpose. Align yourself with your natural talents for empathy, intelligence, creativity, or kinesthetic abilities. Understand how these talents became genetically encoded through the female sexual selection process of our ancestors and handed down to you through the process of meiosis. See how your physical and skill development formed the potentials for expressing your natural talents.

Use one or more of the five discovery methods that resonate most with you to identify or clarify your transcendental purpose. Recognize the depth of expression, level of calling, and stage of maturity of living and sharing your transcendental purpose. Focus your passion and skills where you can have the greatest impact to make the world a better place. Combine your strengths for creating more goodness, truth, beauty, and functioning with your soulmate who shares your transcendental purpose in an inter-becoming-based transcendental love relationship.

Introduction

We use the term transcendent(al)[404] purpose for different reasons. First, we use the term to indicate that it includes and goes beyond the terms and definitions that resonate with people at different stages of consciousness development, such as the following:

- Universe's Purpose (unity)
- Authentic Purpose (transpersonal)
- Evolutionary Purpose (integral)
- Soul's Purpose (pluralistic)
- Real/True Purpose (rational)
- Higher/God's Purpose (mythic)
- Unique Purpose (egocentric)
- Spirit's Purpose (magic)

We also call it transcendent(al)[405] because it transcends our biological and transformational purpose, as covered in Module 21, and is a priori[406] in the sense that the potentials to express it are present in us through genetically predispositioned talents[407] before our sense observations and language emerge.

And, finally, we call it transcendental as it aligns with the classical transcendentals[408] by always creating more goodness,[409] truth, beauty, and functioning,[410] as depicted by the four dimensions of our being and relating (quadrants) below, *and is in service of the biological purpose and the well-being of others.*

I = Beautiful / Aesthetics   It = Truth / Science

We = Good / Morals   Its = Functioning / Systems

Figure 58: The good, true, beautiful, and functional quadrants

These normative ethics[411] for the transcendental purpose are extremely important, as they have direct implications for our actions, ways of life, and institutions. Too often, horrible atrocities have been and are still committed in the name of following a higher power (God, spirit, or even evolutionary purpose), or simply following one's bliss, heart, calling, soul, or what makes one feel alive[412] in hedonistic ways.

When we awaken to and live our transcendental purpose, its impact on the world is dependent on several factors: the kind and degree of our natural talents; the ability to express them through our physical, brain, and skill development; our level of consciousness and spiritual development; our gender; and the opportunities, freedoms, and support that our social and cultural environment afford us.

Benefits of living and sharing our transcendental purpose

Researchers from Rush University Medical Center in Chicago described people with a purpose in life as "having the tendency to derive meaning from life's experiences and to possess a sense of intentionality and goal directedness that guides their behavior."[413]

Their research showed that the brains that functioned better at older age belonged to people who had indicated more purpose in life: "Living one's purpose actually affected cellular activity in the brain. Plaques and tangles still formed, but having a purpose seemed to increase the brain's protective reserve. Not only that, the stronger the purpose, the more it added to the reserve." The results held up even after the researchers controlled for differences in exercise levels, education, and other factors. Other studies linked a sense of purpose not only to slower rates of cognitive decline but also to lower rates of disability and death.[414]

These benefits are further enhanced when people find happiness and fulfillment through living their purpose in ways that serve the well-being of others by creating more goodness, truth, beauty, and functioning. The Dalai Lama and Arthur C. Brooks wrote about the importance of serving the well-being of others in *The New York Times*:[415]

> Americans who prioritize doing good for others are almost twice as likely to say that they are very happy about their lives. In Germany, people who seek to serve society are five times likelier to say they are very happy than those who do not view service as important. In one shocking experiment, researchers found that senior citizens who didn't feel useful to others were nearly three times as likely to die prematurely as those who did feel useful. This speaks to a broader human truth: We all need to be needed.

The Purpose Guides Institute[416] conducted extensive research on the topic and lists the following benefits for people who live their purpose:

1. Live up to seven years longer (NIH, 1998; Carlton, 2014)
2. Maintain healthier cell structures (UNC/UCLA, 2013)
3. Reduce their overall mortality rate by 23% (Mt. Sinai, 2015)
4. Experience better cardiovascular, neuroendocrine, and immune health (Institute on Aging, UW–Madison, 2006)
5. Double their likelihood of learning something new each day (Gallup/Healthways, 2013)
6. Have a 42% increase in the experience of contentment (Leider/Metlife, 2009)
7. Decrease the possible onset of Alzheimer's disease by 240% (Boyle/Rush, 2014)
8. Fight depression more effectively (*Journal of Clinical Psychology*, 1980)
9. Decrease rates of teen depression (PNAS, 2014)
10. Reduce death by coronary heart disease by 23% (Mt. Sinai, 2015)
11. Reduce death rate from stroke by 72% (Koizumi, 2008)
12. Quadruple the likelihood of being engaged at work (Gallup/Healthways, 2013)
13. Have a 47% increase in the experience of abundance (Leider/Metlife, 2009)
14. Report a 31% increase in the experience of feeling love (Leider/Metlife, 2009)
15. Experience an increase of meaning in times of dissonance (Stanford, 2014)
16. Are more tolerant towards other races (Harvard/Cornell/Carleton, 2014)
17. Have an increased appetite for education (Stanford, 2015)
18. Show an increase of philanthropy and volunteering by 50% (Gallup/Healthways, 2013)

Combining all these benefits with the fact that people in happy marriages enjoy greater physical and emotional health, financial stability, sexual satisfaction, and longevity,[417] makes identifying, living, and sharing one's transcendental purpose with an equal and opposite partner in a lifelong healthy love relationship (plus exercise and a healthy diet) a surefire way for a long and fulfilling life.

Genetic predisposition

The transcendental purpose became genetically predisposed as talents through females who selected male partners for their intelligence, creativity, kindness (towards them/aggressiveness towards others), and physical/practical skills. These four additional fitness indicators, on top of being tall, broad-shouldered, muscular, etc., vastly increased the ability of the males to provide, protect, entertain, and elevate their status compared with their duller competitors. We see this sexual selection even today in the attractiveness of males who are successful, tall, Ivy League-educated leaders; good-looking famous artists/actors, smart athletes, etc.

Sexual Selection for Intelligence, Creativity, Kindness/Empathy (towards partner), and Practical Skills

Figure 59: Sapiosexual woman

The genes of their offspring were then handed down to future generations through the process of meiosis.[418]

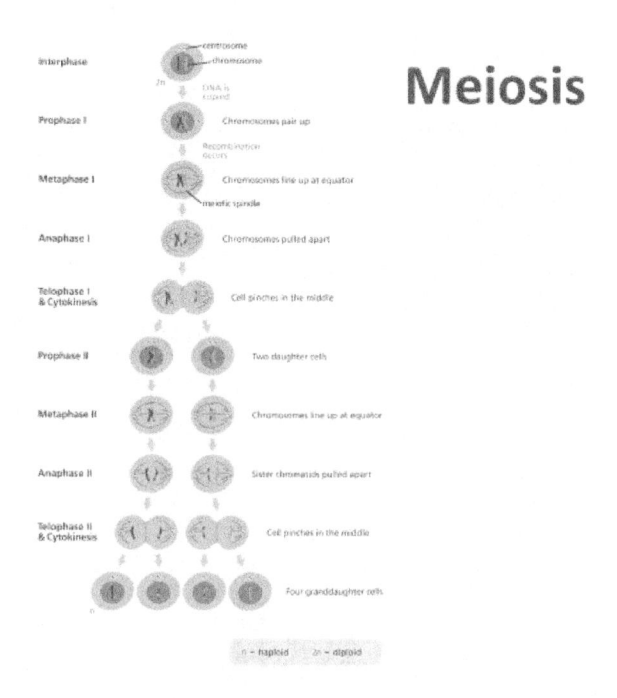

Figure 60: Meiosis

The genetically predisposed talents or potentials that are handed down this way vary vastly in people, in kind and degree, as shown in the metaphorical mountains below.

Empathy - Intelligence - Creativity - Practical

Figure 61: Genetically predisposed talents

To express our genetically predisposed talents in optimal ways, we needed a supportive family and social environment for healthy physical, brain, and skill development, as shown below by the metaphorical towers and the tree in the following image.

Figure 62: Skill development based on talents

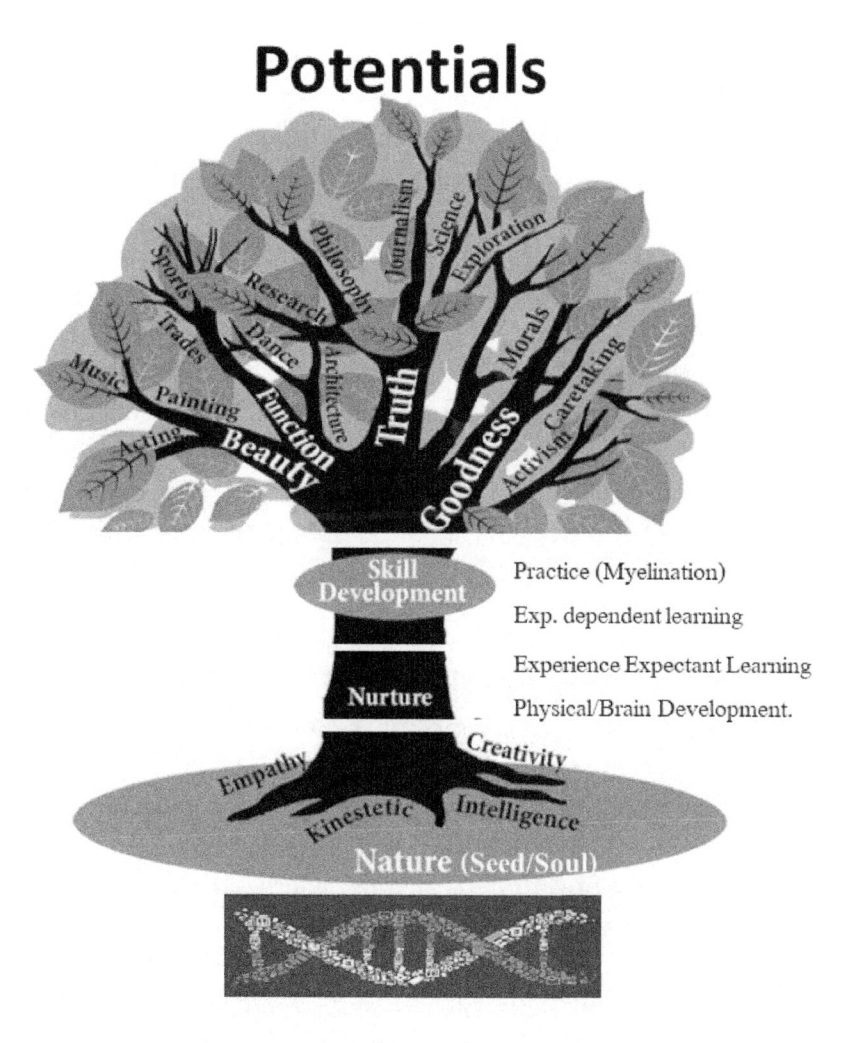

Figure 63: Development and expression of talents

Awakening to your transcendental purpose

Unlike the trajectory of our biological purpose, which unfolds naturally and involuntarily under normal conditions in physically and psychologically healthy humans from gestation to death (like any other "object-with-will" or living organism), we have to awaken to the fact that we have a transcendental purpose.

This awakening may happen spontaneously through a personal insight or aha moment, or may be triggered by an external event that, after brewing in our unconscious mind for a time, brings clarity about our role in creating a better world—beyond living our biological purpose. Some people awaken to their transcendental purpose gradually, when living their biological and even transcendental purpose no longer answers the deeper questions of their existence: What is the meaning of life? Why am I here? Where do I come from? What am I to do? What does it mean to be human? Why do I suffer? How can I be truly fulfilled and happy? What is my purpose? How can I contribute? Where will I go? How will I be remembered?

Once we are awakened to our transcendental purpose and live it, we can attract or find a compatible soulmate to share it with. This advancement transforms biological and transformational love into transcendental love.

Purpose and application of the module

1. Identify, live, and share your transcendental purpose.
2. Understand why your transcendental purpose ALWAYS creates more goodness, truth, beauty, or functioning that makes the world a better place.
3. Reap the many physical and mental health benefits of living and sharing your transcendental purpose.
4. See how the genetic predispositions that underlie the transcendental purpose were created by females who chose kind, smart, creative, and practical males for procreation.
5. Remove psychological blocks to identifying and living your purpose.
6. Use five discovery methods to identify your purpose.
7. Understand the depth of expression, levels of calling, and stage of maturity of your transcendental purpose.
8. Focus your transcendental purpose inside your circle of influence instead of your circle of concern.

9. Find out where your true nature and talents meet the world's deepest challenges and needs.
10. Create synergy with your soulmate who shares your transcendental purpose.

Exercises: Transcendental purpose and love

The following are individual, paired, and group exercises.
1. Print out the worksheets below.
2. Make the four agreements for confidentiality, responsibility, healthy boundaries, I-statements, and sharing, as outlined on page 556.

Removing psychological blocks

Purpose guides and coaches have discovered that most of their clients first need to remove psychological blocks—such as fears, shame, negative self-talk, false beliefs, and deeply rooted behavioral habits—as a first step to identifying and living their purpose.

An effective process to overcome this "immunity to change" was discovered by Harvard Graduate School of Education professors Robert Kegan and Lisa Laskow Lahey, who propose that when we fail at a goal we've set for ourselves, such as identifying and living our transcendental purpose, the failure isn't just the result of a lack of willpower; rather, it's likely that an "emotional immune system" is covertly at work, defending us from feelings of disappointment, fear, or shame.

Exercise one: Immunity to change

1. Share the answers to the following questions with your partner.
2. What are psychological blocks or other obstacles (e.g., financial, education, family, etc.) that prevent you from identifying, fully living, and sharing your purpose?
3. Use the Immunity to Change worksheet below to define your goals; what you are doing/not doing instead; your hidden

competing commitments; and your big (false) assumptions. Then, share your answers with your partner. See suggestions in endnote.[419]

Worksheet: Immunity To Change

Goal	Doing/Not Doing Instead	Hidden Competing Commitments	Big (false) Assumptions
Steps to take	Details	Details	Details
Take your emotions into account. Test the big assumptions that present the most significant obstacles in your life. Think of low-risk scenarios to take the first steps towards your goals.			

Voice dialogue

Voice dialogue was created in the early 1970s by Drs. Hal and Sidra Stone, a wonderful couple who shared their transcendental purpose. Their process was later adopted and popularized by Dennis Genpo Merzel Roshi as the Big Mind–Big Heart process.[420]

The Stones discovered the presence of numerous sub-personalities/voices (also called energy patterns or selves) within the human psyche: for example, the critic, the cynic, the protector, etc.[421]

Until we make them conscious, these unconscious voices often leak out and sabotage living and sharing our purpose with our soulmate in a healthy love relationship.

You can engage and disidentify (not dissociate, repress, split off, deny etc.) from these voices in a dialogue between them and your witnessing "higher" self that is not conditioned by your upbringing and learned behavioral patterns. This pure witnessing "higher" self or being is aligned with your soul's desire to feel fully alive and to share your purpose with your soulmate.

Exercise Two: Voice dialogue

Engage your partner or the practitioners in a group, using dialogues one and two below. The practitioner(s) will answer from the distinct voices that you select from the following worksheet.

Worksheet: Voice dialogue

There are four groups of distinct inner voices:

1. The Guardians

Are designed to protect the self—the small drop of conscious awareness that is taken over by the ego; the instinctual animalistic separate sense of self:

1. The Protector
2. The Controller
3. The Risk Manager
4. The Critic or Judge
5. The Skeptic Doubter or Cynic
6. The Victim
7. The Image Consultant

2. Resistance Voices

Are those whose only word is NO, which is usually not heard by the conscious self. However, it is felt almost continually as a string of moving and chronic tensions in the body, tiredness, sleepiness,

spacing out as in becoming absent, and a resistance to being attentive:
1. The Damaged Self
2. The Fixer
3. The Wounded, Vulnerable, or Innocent Child

3. The Voices of Freedom

Are voices designed to take the self beyond safety and comfort so that it can mature by living life with all its uncertainties and dangers:
1. The Desiring Mind
2. The Seeking Mind
3. The Mind that Seeks the Way
4. The Follower of the Way

4. Transcendent Voices

Represent qualities of being present in states of consciousness beyond the ego self. They are not in dialogue internally; instead, they become obvious when the ego noise is transcended. They can be intuited as inner knowingness, and sometimes they do manifest as a subtle whisper to the self. They are presented separately only for the purpose of clear learning and understanding.
1. The Way
2. Big Mind
3. Big Heart
4. Yin Compassion
5. Yang Compassion
6. The Master

Other voices to dialogue with

1. The Pusher
2. The Gatekeeper
3. The Pleaser
4. The Rule Maker
5. The Rational Mind
6. The Analyst

7. The Clown
8. The Rebel
9. The Caretaker
10. The Giver
11. The Perfectionist

Dialog one

You (as partner one) or group facilitator ask: I would like to talk to your inner [name voice, e.g., "skeptic"]. What is your name?
Voice (your partner or group says): I am the skeptic.
You: Nice to talk with you.
You: What is your role?
Voice: I protect you from ...
You: My partner would like to discover, live, and share his/her purpose with his/her soulmate .... What are your concerns/fears/objections?
Voice: My concerns are that ....
You: Why do you think that?
Voice: Because ....
You: I hear your concern. How do you know this is true?
Voice: ....
You: How can you absolutely know that this is true?
Voice: ....
You: What if it were not true?
Voice: ....
You: What would it take from you to be OK if I ...?
Voice: ....
You: How about if we ...?
Voice: ....

Dialog two

Have the following expanded dialogue in the same fashion as in Dialogue one above:
You (as partner one) or group facilitator:
I would like to talk to your inner [name voice, e.g., "gatekeeper"]. What is your name?

What is your role, your job?
How long have you been there?
When did we first meet?
What is your worst fear?
Is your job hard?
What makes it hard?
What would happen if you were not there?
Are you liked?
How are you perceived?
Do the other selves work along with you and support you?
When are you most active?
What do you say over and over?
Are there selves that oppose you?
What would you like to be done?
How do you feel right now?
Can you describe your appearance?

Five purpose discovery methods

There are five methods that have been developed by purpose guides and spiritual teachers to support you in discovering your natural talents and resulting transcendental purpose. We describe these five discovery methods as follows: (1) autobiographical or direct methods, (2) absent or indirect methods, (3) ego-transcending methods, (4) ego-affirming methods, and (5) Ikigai method.

Exercise three: Autobiographical methods

This can be a paired or group exercise.
Share with your partner or the group:
1. What activities and experiences made you feel happy, joyful, fulfilled, successful and in the flow of life over an extended period versus those that didn't?
2. When did you feel most passionate or fulfilled? What was going on in your life at this time?

3. When was your life most meaningful? What were you engaged in?
4. When did your life feel most aligned? When was there flow and ease?
5. When did you experience synchronicities and serendipity? What were you doing?
6. What would others say that your talents and purpose are?

The takeaway here is to follow your bliss and your heart and what makes you feel alive. This autobiographical method can be problematic when the ethical norms of creating goodness, truth, beauty and functioning in the service of the biological purpose and the well-being of others (as outlined above on page 437) become violated.

Books/Websites

StrengthsFinder 2.0 (2007) by Tom Rath
tinyurl.com/irpm502[422]

True Purpose: 12 Strategies for Discovering the Difference You Are Meant to Make (2009) by Tim Kelley
tinyurl.com/irpm505[423]

Clifton Strengths Test
tinyurl.com/irpm584[424]

Talent Dynamics Profile Test tinyurl.com/irpm585[425]

Exercise four: Absent method

Share with your partner after feeling back as far as possible to "your root":
1. What activities and people did you feel drawn to as a child?
2. What could you express and what couldn't you express?
3. What pains you the most about the world?
4. What absences do you want to absent?[426]

5. What do you want to create, improve, change, manifest, cure, end, or abolish, etc.?
6. What novelties do you want to advance into?
7. What is your vision, mission, and contribution for a better world?

The takeaway here is to follow your pain and your "blisters" (instead of your bliss, which can be misguiding) to where your true nature and talents meet the world's deepest challenges/needs.[427]

Books

The Soul's Code: In Search of Character and Calling. (1996) by James Hillman
tinyurl.com/irpm510[428]

What Were You Born to Do? Workbook (2013) by Curtis M. Adney
tinyurl.com/irpm512[429]

True Purpose: 12 Strategies for Discovering the Difference You Are Meant to Make (2009) by Tim Kelley
tinyurl.com/irpm514[430]

The Purpose Guides Institute Process.[431]

Exercise five: Ego-transcending method

Share with your partner:
1. Who are you if you are not your body, not your thoughts, not your feelings, not your experiences?
2. What is alive in you right now in this moment without pain of the past or fear of the future?
3. What would arise in you if you would act from that place of presence, surrender, and stillness?

The takeaway here is this:
"Do you have the patience to wait

Till your mud settles and the water is clear?
Can you remain unmoving
Till the right action arises by itself?"
Lao Tsu

Books

The Purpose Driven Life: What on Earth Am I Here For? (2002) by Rick Warren
tinyurl.com/irpm515[432]

Leading from the Emerging Future: From Ego-System to Eco-System Economies (2013) by Otto Scharmer and Katrin Kaufer.
tinyurl.com/irpm518[433]

Nature and the Human Soul: Cultivating Wholeness and Community in a Fragmented World (2008) by Bill Plotkin
tinyurl.com/irpm519[434]

A New Earth: Awakening to Your Life's Purpose (2005) by Eckhart Tolle
tinyurl.com/irpm520[435]

Evolutionary Enlightenment: A New Path to Spiritual Awakening (2011) by Andrew Cohen
tinyurl.com/irpm521[436]

Diamond Heart Series Books (1987) by A.H. Almaas
tinyurl.com/irpm523[437]

Man's Search for Meaning (2006) by Viktor E. Frankl
tinyurl.com/irpm525[438]

Exercise six: Ego-affirming methods

Share with your partner:
1. What are your limiting beliefs about yourself and about how God or the Universe wants to work through you?
2. What are you afraid to fully shine your light into the world?
3. Who are you *not* to be brilliant, gorgeous, talented, fabulous?

The takeaway here is to break free from your inner barriers, strengthen your Ego, stand up for yourself, magnetize the support you need to create your dreams, become rich and successful. This works mostly for truly brilliant and physically attractive women.

Books/Websites

The Law of Divine Compensation: On Work, Money, and Miracles (2014) by Marianne Williamson
tinyurl.com/irpm527[439]

Awakening to Your Life's Purpose (online courses) by Jean Houston tinyurl.com/irpm528[440]

Feminine Power (online courses) by Claire Zammit
tinyurl.com/irpm532[441]

Your Unique Self: The Radical Path to Personal Enlightenment (2012) Marc Gafni
tinyurl.com/irpm534[442]

The Japanese Ikigai (as conceived in the West)

Your purpose is where the four circles overlap.

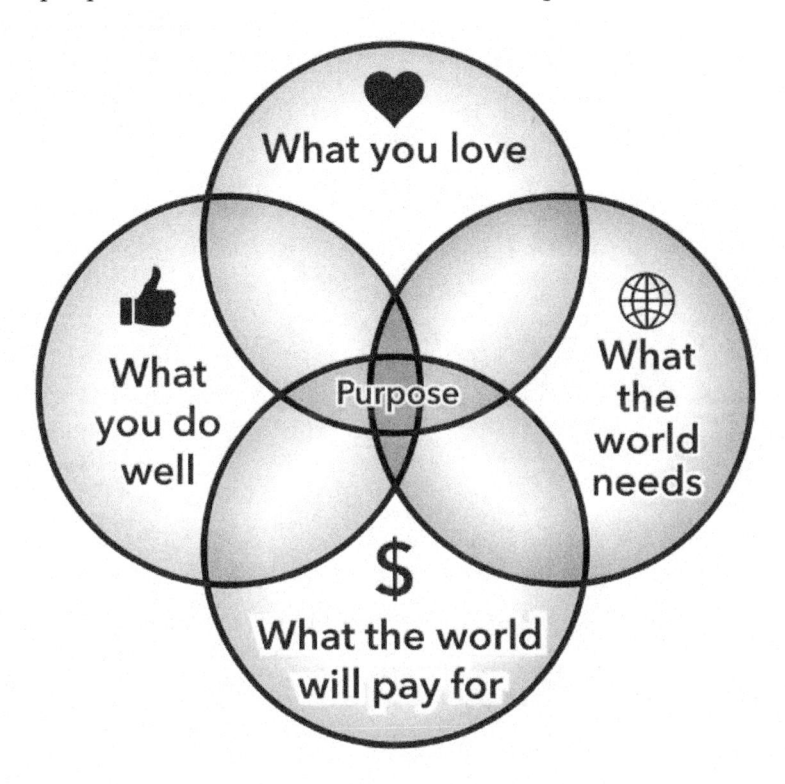

Figure 64: Ikigai

See real version at https://ikigaitribe.com/

The four circles map onto the four dimensions of our being and relating (quadrants), as shown below:

Integral Relationship Practice | 456

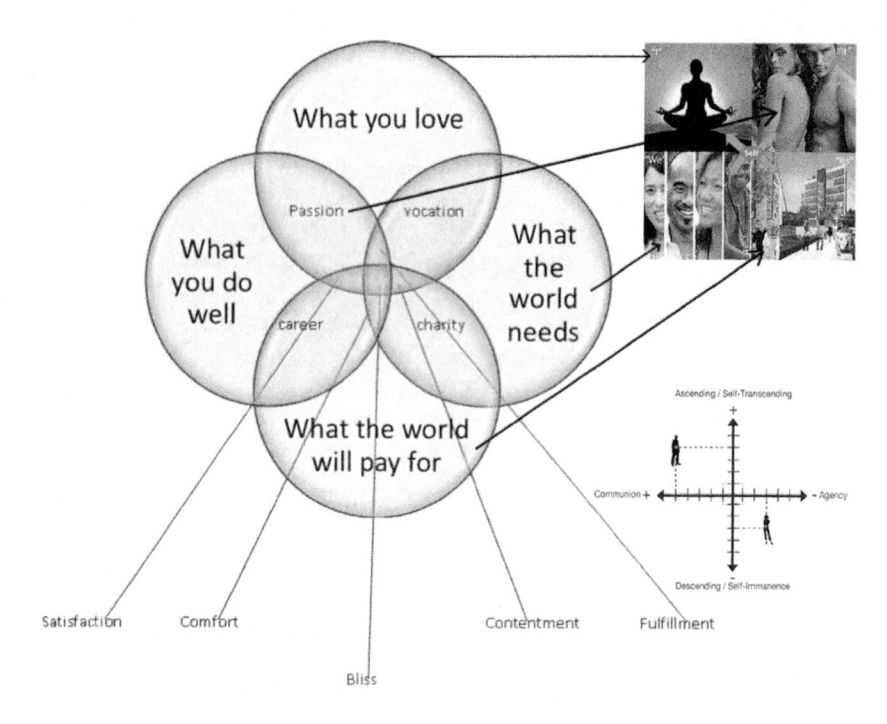

Figure 65: Ikigai and connection to the four dimensions

Exercise Seven: Ikigai

Share with your partner:
1. What do you love to do?
2. What you do well?
3. What does the world need from you to become a better place?
4. What does the world pay you for?
5. Where are the circles disjointed?
6. Do you do things that you are good at but don't love?
7. Do you do things that the world pays you for but does not really need?
8. How do you plan to move towards more alignment to live and share your transcendental purpose with your soulmate?

The takeaway here is to align and integrate the four dimensions of your being with living your purpose, including the difficult questions of making money, developing skills, acting in ethical ways, and doing what you love.

Exercise eight: Your transcendental purpose

Share with your partner:
1. Do you know what your transcendental purpose is?
2. If yes, how do you live/express/enact it, or how would you like to enact it?
3. If no, would you like to discover your purpose?
4. If no, why not?
5. What discovery method(s)—autobiographical, absent, ego-transforming, ego-affirming, and Ikigai—resonate most with you?

Depth of expression

There are five depth levels of expressing your transcendental purpose.[443]

Gross

When you enact your transcendental purpose at the gross level of depth, you create more goodness, truth, beauty, or functioning at the material, physical, or behavioral level (for example, as a grower and seller of healthy food, a physical therapist, a behavioral psychologist, or a music teacher).

Subtle

When you live out your transcendental purpose at the subtle level of depth, you create more goodness, truth, beauty, or functioning on the level of the mind (for example, as a language or math teacher).

Causal

When you enact your transcendental purpose at the causal level of depth, you create more goodness, truth, beauty, or functioning by challenging—and perhaps inspiring change in—the feelings, intuitions, values, and resulting meaning-making structures of people (for example, as a depth psychologist).

Pure Witness

When you enact your transcendental purpose at the pure witness level of depth, you create more goodness, truth, beauty, or functioning through being fully present and providing others with immediate or direct state experiences that they may then transform into permanently accessible stages through their own practices.

Nondual

When you enact your transcendental purpose at the nondual level of depth, you create more goodness, truth, beauty, or functioning by integrating all the previous levels (for example, as an Integral Relationship or Tantra Teacher).

With increasing depth, it becomes harder to find or attract paying clients, as you increasingly ask them to do the inner transformative work.

Exercise nine: Depth of expression

Share with your partner:
1. What is the depth level (gross, subtle, causal, pure witness, or nondual) of expression of your transcendental purpose?

Levels of callings

There are four levels of calling to express your transcendental purpose.

No calling

A shockingly large number of people do not feel any calling or purpose beyond living their biological purpose, and usually don't ask deeper questions about the meaning of their life and how to contribute to the well-being of others and a better world. Their mindset is that of consumers rather than contributors, and they are often part of the problems that humanity is needlessly creating rather than part of the solutions, especially if they do not procreate and raise children (or help to raise them).

Called to maintain/conserve

People who feel called to maintain something that already exists often follow in someone else's footsteps by living their life based on the expectations of parents, family, culture, and society, or they follow opportunities that are presented to them by others. This also includes spiritual lineages and religious traditions.

Called to innovate/improve

At this level, people are not content with the status quo, do not dwell on the past, and are willing to take controlled risks by taking the road less traveled to pursue their passion or follow their bliss. They believe that it is better to fail at living their own life than to succeed at living someone else's.

Called to invent/absent absences

At this level, people feel an irresistible and urgent calling to absent ills or other absences through advancements into novelty. Their passions are often fueled by pain, frustration, or deep concerns about maliciousness, injustices, falsehoods, ugliness, and dysfunction. They are consumed by conceiving radically and fundamentally new solutions to alleviate the suffering of others through compassionate action, deeper truths, better aesthetics, and more functional tools and systems that improve people's lives.

As with the depth of expression, it becomes harder to enact your transcendental purpose as the level of calling increases.

Exercise ten: Level of calling

Share with your partner:
1. What is the level of your calling (to maintain, improve, invent/absent absences) in enacting your purpose?

Stages of Maturity

The stages of maturity below were conceived by Bill Plotkin. He spent over 25 years developing eight Soulcentric/Ecocentric Stages of Human Development or Maturity.[444] His insights allow you to share your transcendental purpose with a partner who is in the same stage of maturity as you are, and to transition together with him or her through the stages.

The eight stages are not to be confused with the seven stages of consciousness development or altitude (from archaic to transpersonal) that we apply throughout this manual! Rather, Plotkin's stages have the potential to unfold at each level of vertical consciousness development from birth to death. Plotkin labels each by combining evocative human and earth archetypes to remind us that most stages can unfold at almost any age.

461 | Transcendental Purpose and Love

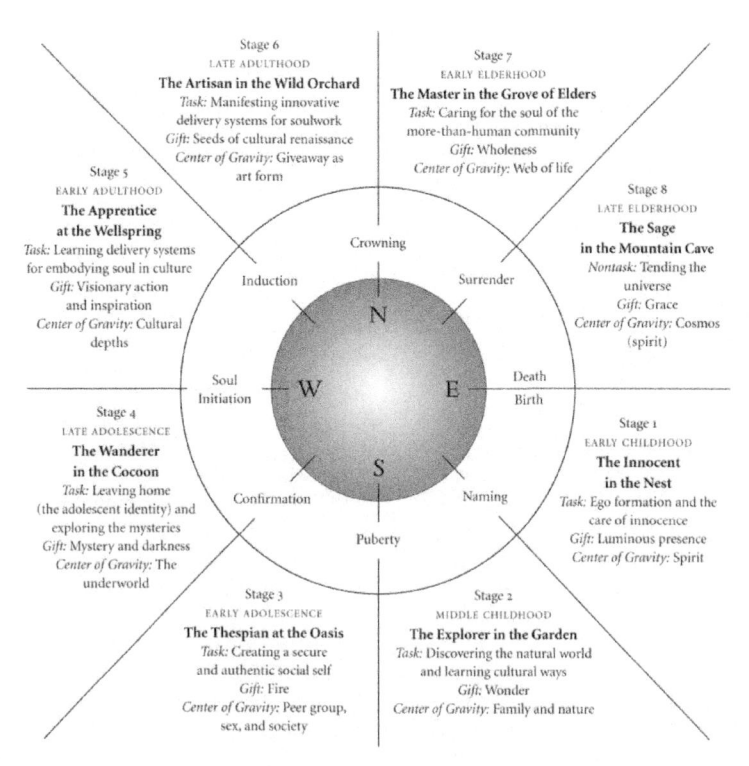

Stage 6
LATE ADULTHOOD
The Artisan in the Wild Orchard
Task: Manifesting innovative delivery systems for soulwork
Gift: Seeds of cultural renaissance
Center of Gravity: Giveaway as art form

Stage 7
EARLY ELDERHOOD
The Master in the Grove of Elders
Task: Caring for the soul of the more-than-human community
Gift: Wholeness
Center of Gravity: Web of life

Stage 5
EARLY ADULTHOOD
The Apprentice at the Wellspring
Task: Learning delivery systems for embodying soul in culture
Gift: Visionary action and inspiration
Center of Gravity: Cultural depths

Stage 8
LATE ELDERHOOD
The Sage in the Mountain Cave
Nontask: Tending the universe
Gift: Grace
Center of Gravity: Cosmos (spirit)

Stage 4
LATE ADOLESCENCE
The Wanderer in the Cocoon
Task: Leaving home (the adolescent identity) and exploring the mysteries
Gift: Mystery and darkness
Center of Gravity: The underworld

Stage 1
EARLY CHILDHOOD
The Innocent in the Nest
Task: Ego formation and the care of innocence
Gift: Luminous presence
Center of Gravity: Spirit

Stage 3
EARLY ADOLESCENCE
The Thespian at the Oasis
Task: Creating a secure and authentic social self
Gift: Fire
Center of Gravity: Peer group, sex, and society

Stage 2
MIDDLE CHILDHOOD
The Explorer in the Garden
Task: Discovering the natural world and learning cultural ways
Gift: Wonder
Center of Gravity: Family and nature

Crowning — Induction — Surrender — Soul Initiation — Death/Birth — Confirmation — Puberty — Naming

The Eight Soulcentric/Ecocentric Stages of Human Development
From Nature and the Human Soul © Bill Plotkin (New World Library, 2008)
soulcraft@animas.org

Figure 66: Bill Plotkin's Eight Stages of Maturity[vi]

Exercise eleven: Stages of maturity

Share with your partner:
1. Which of the eight stages of maturity above resonate most with you?

[vi] Stage 3: A Thespian is an actor or someone who acts in dramatic ways. Stage 6: An Artisan is a worker who practices a trade or handicraft.

Global challenges

The Millennium Project releases an annual report that assesses the 15 global challenges that are facing humanity and reports on which of the challenges are diminishing, staying the same, or increasing. The image below and the Millennium Project reports can provide an inspiration for you to identify, live, and share your transcendental purpose.

Figure 67: Millennium Project 15 global challenges

See report at tinyurl.com/irpm67[445]

Similar to The Millennium Project, the United Nations outlines 17 areas of concern that can provide you with inspiration for enacting and sharing your transcendental purpose. See *Figure 68* below.

Figure 68: United Nations global issues overview

See details at
tinyurl.com/irpm72[446] and tinyurl.com/irpm76[447]

Focus and circle of influence

Creating a mind-map, as shown below *in Figure 70*, can help you to move from your circle of concern or pain (shown in the outer circle), which is your driving force, to focusing on enacting/living your transcendental purpose inside your circle of influence and competence, which is in the inner circle. In other words, creating a mind-map can help you to think globally and to act locally (unless you are a world leader in your field).

This is where you will make the biggest difference, instead of going too broad and spending too much time worrying or elaborating about your circle of concern. As you make a difference with your soulmate and others, your circle of influence will eventually expand, and your circle of concern will diminish.

Integral Relationship Practice | 464

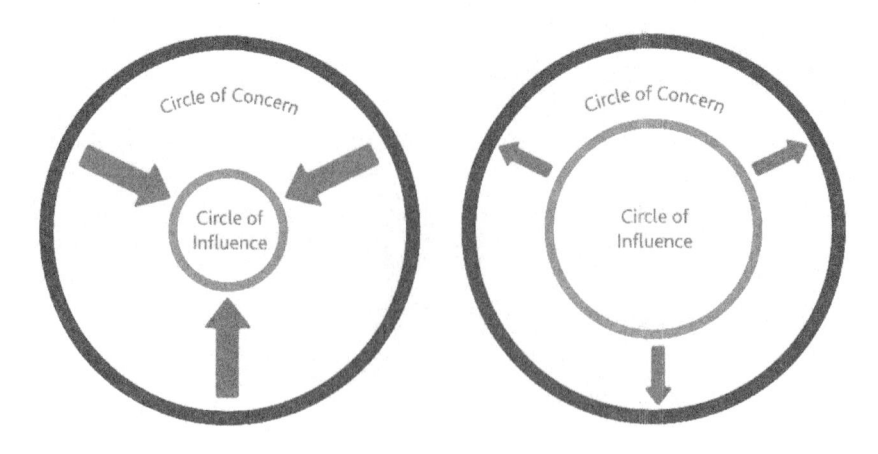

Figure 69: Circle of influence and concern

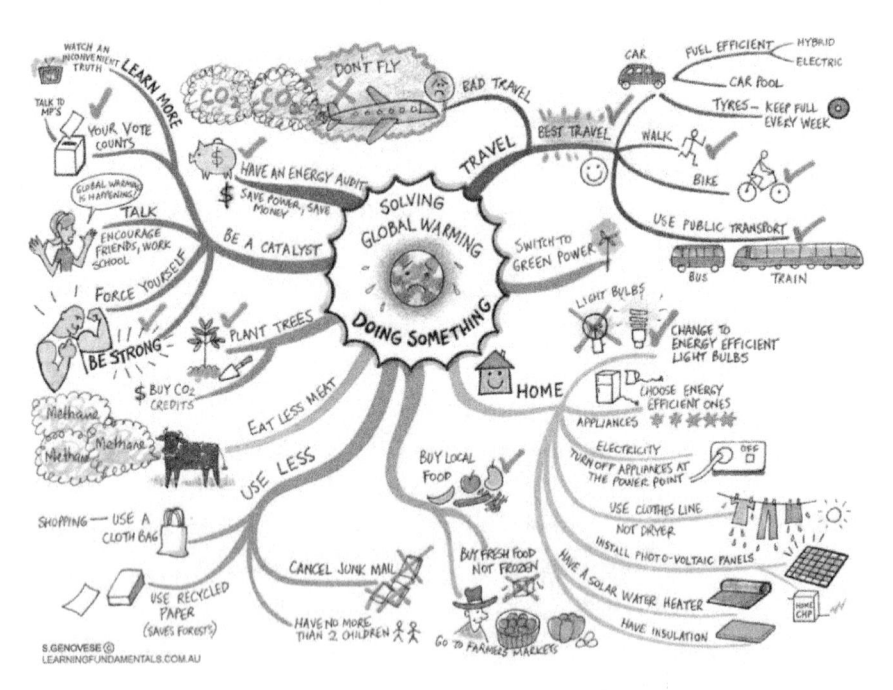

Figure 70: Example of enactment of purpose

See more mind-maps at tinyurl.com/irpm572[448]

Exercise twelve: Focus and circle of influence

Share with your partner:
1. Which challenges that humanity is facing concern and pain you the most?
2. What is your circle of influence in which you live/enact your transcendental purpose?

Sharing your transcendental purpose

Barbara Marx Hubbard calls sharing our purpose with others "supra-sexuality" or "vocational arousal."[449] She says that, "it could well be that nature is [has been for ages] inventing a passion as great as sex that I'm calling supra-sexuality. It's the passion to identify your own unique genius code [natural talents], to find partners in co-creation, to join not [only] our genes but our genius in the expression of our life purpose."

As we have seen above, under biological purpose in Module 22, and will further see in Module 26, in order for human evolution to progress, it continues to be vital that we also share our genes and not only our genius in healthy love relationships.[450]

The image below shows why soulmates with a shared transcendental purpose experience this "vocational arousal" because they complement each other's natural talents and skills, thus creating synergy and flow that is as exhilarating as great sex.[451]

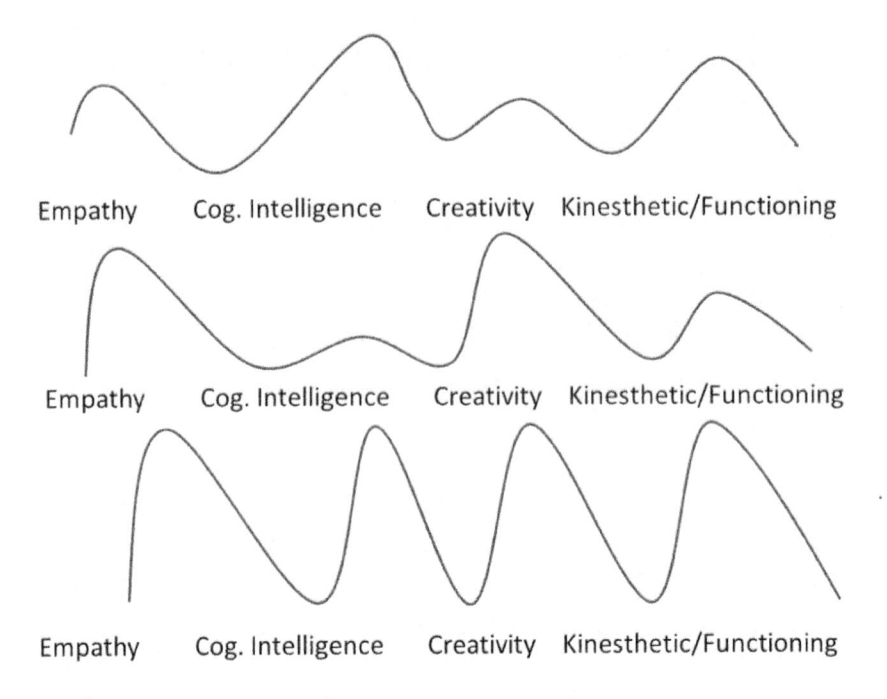

Empathy   Cog. Intelligence   Creativity   Kinesthetic/Functioning

Empathy   Cog. Intelligence   Creativity   Kinesthetic/Functioning

Empathy   Cog. Intelligence   Creativity   Kinesthetic/Functioning

Figure 71: Combining talents

Moving from transactional to transcendent(al) love

This synergistic "supra-sexuality" has the potential to shift need-based, asymmetrical transactional desires and love relationships (that we explored above in Module 22) to being and becoming-based symmetrical, transcendental desires and love relationships along the seven chakras, as shown below.

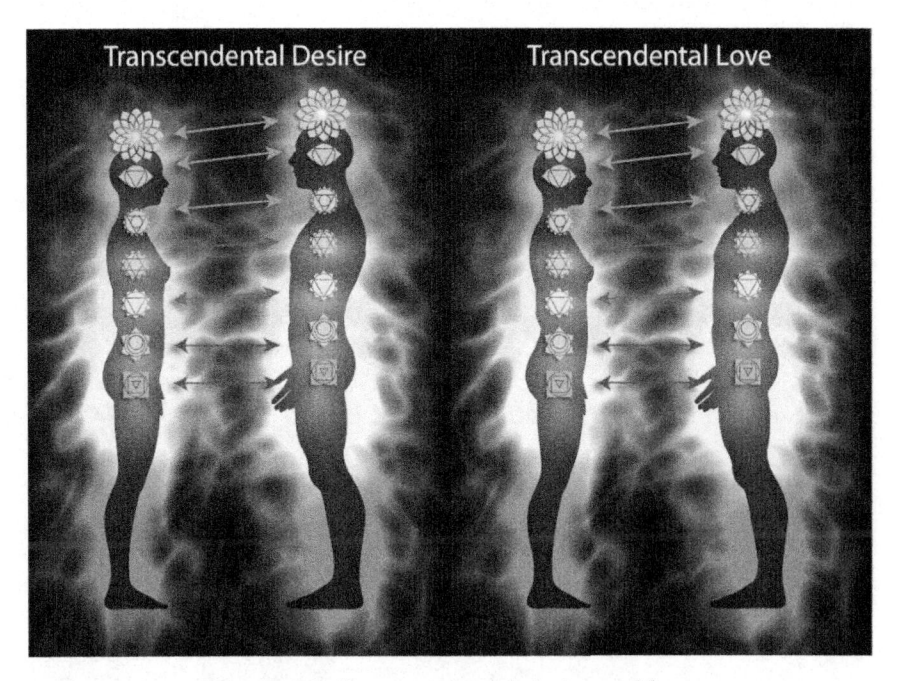

Figure 72: Transcendental desire and love

In these relationships, partners who are equal in their developmental lines and rights and responsibilities, and who complement each other in their talents, personality types, and feminine-masculine polarities love each other not only because they meet each other's biological desires and learn, heal, grow and awaken together, but, even more, because of that which is uniquely co-created between them at the level of their seven chakras in all four dimensions of their being and relating (quadrants) by balancing and harmonizing healthy feminine and masculine polarities, as shown below.

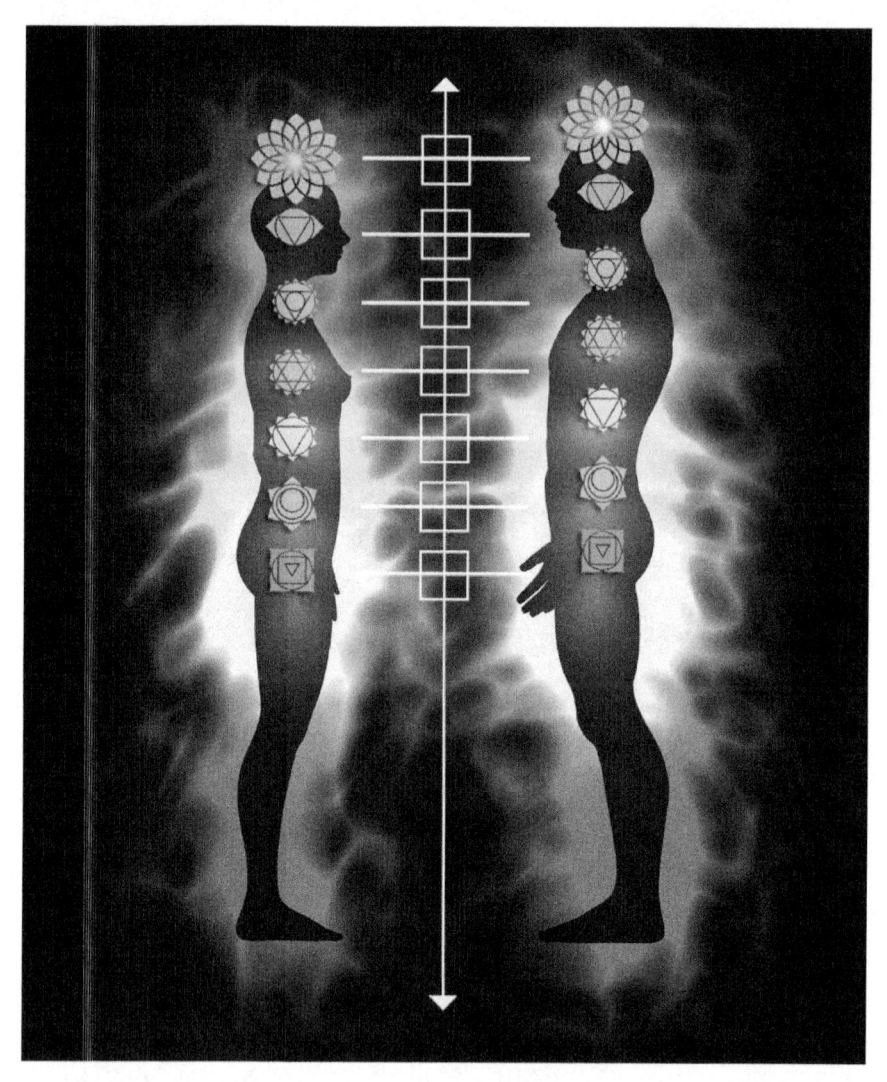

Figure 73: Co-created transcendental love between the seven chakras

Chakras/Consciousness	Transcendental Love
Crown male/female unity 	Co-created, non-dual inter-becoming and advancements into novelty through direct/immediate experience of the co-creative impulse and enacting *Transcendental Purpose*.
Third Eye male/female co-creation 	Co-created wisdom and vision how to best serve humanity and future generations as a couple by providing the greatest good for the largest number of people.
Throat male/female co-creation 	Co-created innovation through empathetic morals, compassionate ethical discourse, moving art, and humanistic systems.
Heart male/female co-creation 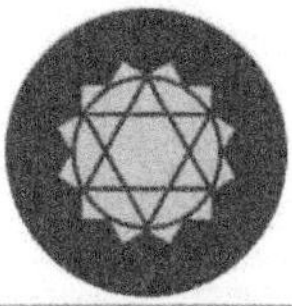	Co-created care and emotional intelligence and depth through self-validated intimacy and sharing of vulnerable feelings by each partner.
Solarpl. male/female co-creation 	Co-created "power with" versus "power over", social status, and safety through contributions from each partner.
Sacrum male/female co-creation 	Co-created sacred sexuality that nurtures the health of body, mind, heart, and soul of both partners.
Root male/female co-creation 	Co-created environmentally and socially responsible and sustainable lifestyle in which both partners assume equal rights and responsibilities for contribution, based on their abilities.

Figure 74: Transcendental love chakra matrix

Exercise thirteen: Sharing your transcendental purpose

Share with your partner:
1. Do you share your transcendental purpose with a (or your) partner?
2. If yes, what synergies do you create between your different talents, types, fem/masc. polarities etc.?
3. If no, would you like to share your TP with a/your partner or soulmate?
4. If no to #3, share why not.
5. If yes to #3, what would you like to co-create with your partner or soulmate?

Follow-up questions

1. How do you feel after exploring this module and the exercises?
2. What insights have you gained through the exercises?
3. How do these insights change your approach to co-creating a love relationship?

Additional information and resources

Immunity to Change: How to Overcome It and Unlock Potential in Yourself and Your Organization (2009) by Robert Kegan and Lisa Lahey
tinyurl.com/irpm536[452]

Sex Purpose Love book reference

Page 205–317 and 379–387

Suggested movie: *Cloud Atlas* (2012)

Watch this truly amazing, must-see epic science fiction movie, written and directed by the trans women Lana and Lilly Wachowski (who also created *The Matrix*) and Tom Tykwer, and based on the 2004 novel by David Mitchell. In the film, we see that living our transcendental purpose of creating more goodness, truth, beauty, and functionality in the context of healthy love relationships matters for creating a better world and future for humanity.

The movie moves in six different time periods, from 1849 to 2321. The main actors change gender and race throughout the movie, and some move from evil to neutral to good (and back). The main protagonists in each epoch are connected through their deeds, souls, or reincarnations, as indicated by their birthmarks. What makes the movie interesting and challenging to watch is that it jumps between the six time periods every few minutes to show the parallels of three main phases: enslavement, epic battles, and liberation. Watch the movie through the lens of stages of consciousness development and transformations between these stages from archaic to transpersonal. Notice the good, true, beautiful, and functional that is created by the "good" (heroic) characters through their words and deeds as they battle the "evil" villains. See how the positive actions of the soulmates ripple through the centuries. To quote Sonmi-451:

> Our lives are not our own. From womb to tomb, we are bound to others, past and present, and by each crime and every kindness, we birth our future. To be is to be perceived, and so to know thyself is only possible through the eyes of the other. The nature of our immortal lives is in the consequences of our words and deeds, that go on and are pushing themselves throughout all time."

In a more subtle way, you may also notice that Robert Frobisher's *Cloud Atlas* composition will be heard as an (1) initial piano performance, (2) a symphony, (3) a rendition by a jazz sextet, (4) nursing-home Muzak, (5) futuristic Korean street music, (6) a solemn hymn sung by a hoard of clones.

Integral Relationship Practice | 472

Figure 75: Cloud Atlas timeline and characters

Actor	Pacific Islands, 1849	Cambridge / Edinburgh, 1936	San Francisco, 1973	London, 2012	Neo Seoul, 2144	Big Island, 106 winters after The Fall (2321)
Jim Sturgess	**Adam Ewing**	Poor Hotel Guest	Megan's Dad	Highlander	Hae-Joo Chang	Adam (Zachry's Brother-in-Law)
Ben Whishaw	Cabin Boy	**Robert Frobisher**	Store Clerk	Georgette	—	Tribesman
Halle Berry	Native Woman	Jocasta Ayrs	**Luisa Rey**	Indian Party Guest	Ovid	Meronym
Jim Broadbent	Captain Molyneux	Vyvyan Ayrs	—	**Timothy Cavendish**	Korean Musician	Prescient 2
Doona Bae	Tilda Ewing	—	Megan's Mom, Mexican Woman	—	**Sonmi-451**, Sonmi-351, Sonmi Prostitute	—
Tom Hanks	Dr Henry Goose	Hotel Manager	Isaac Sachs	Dermot Hoggins	Cavendish Look-alike Actor	**Zachry**
Hugh Grant	Rev. Giles Horrox	Hotel Heavy	Lloyd Hooks	Denholme Cavendish	Seer Rhee	Kona Chief
Hugo Weaving	Haskell Moore	Tadeusz Kesselring	Bill Smoke	Nurse Noakes	Boardman Mephi	Old Georgie
Susan Sarandon	Madame Horrox	—	—	Older Ursula	Yosouf Suleiman	Abbess
Keith David	Kupaka	—	Joe Napier	—	An-kor Apis	Prescient
James D'Arcy	—	Young Rufus Sixsmith	Old Rufus Sixsmith	Nurse James	Archivist	—
Zhou Xun	—	—	Talbot (Hotel Manager)	—	Yoona-939	Rose
David Gyasi	Autua	—	Lester Rey	—	—	Duophysite
Robert Fyfe	Old Salty Dog	—	—	Mr. Meeks	—	Prescient

Table 20: Cloud Atlas cast and characters (main in bold)

Practice Module 24
Soulmates

Sometimes with the Heart
Seldom with the Soul
Scarce once with the Might
Few — love at all
~ Emily Dickinson ~

Module description

Learn and practice how to define, identify, and find or attract your soulmate. Connect with your soul's deepest desires and yearnings for a mate to co-create on the biological, transformational, and transcendental level of your being. Remove psychological blocks and other barriers to love.

Create your personal soulmate profile and dating strategy that allows you to chart your individual path that fits your personality to find, attract, or invite your soulmate. Realize that even if you don't meet your soulmate, taking the path towards him or her will immeasurably benefit you, others, and the world in whatever you do.

Introduction

Today, most people who are open to be in a love relationship want to be with a soulmate.[453] They envision everlasting love, romance, sexual attraction, and living happily ever after, once they fall in love, without having to do any ongoing work in their relationship. However, this vision is a magical fairytale fantasy that rarely, if ever, happens in real life.

From an Integral perspective, there are three kinds of soulmates. Biological soulmates are physically and sexually attracted to each other and share the same values and lifestyle choices to raise a family. Transformational soulmates additionally challenge and support each other to become the best versions of themselves through ongoing mirroring, learning, healing, growing, and awakening. Transcendental soulmates share the same passion and concerns about the world and complement each other in their talents to create synergy to improve the lives of others.[454]

The soul

In the Integral Relationship model, the soul is seen as the self that is not personal. Like an acorn that holds the potential to grow into a mature oak tree, the soul holds our unique physical, mental, psychological, and spiritual potentials to become fully human. The soul comes into existence at conception and encapsulates our unconditioned relational nature, before a conditioned, wounded, defensive, illusionary, and separate sense of self or Ego develops. This Ego (Latin for "I"), in the way we use it here, cannot love, as it always needs or wants something to be happy—and it always needs more!

In contrast, the soul is our unconditioned, authentic, natural, relational "we" self. The soul calls us to transcend our Ego (or, if you will, to develop an all-encompassing ego or self), to live a virtuous life, and to co-create and procreate with our soulmate to contribute to a peaceful and sustainable future for humanity by passing on our genes and genius, or memes,[36] to future generations. If that were not our soul's purpose—or more simply put, our true human nature—we would not fall in love, humans would not exist, and future generations would suffer and be doomed.

As a metaphor, we can see the soul as a unique stained-glass window or blueprint through which the co-creative and procreative life force (or God, spirit, eros, evolutionary impulse, elan vital, will to live, will to power,[455] etc.) shines as light or energy to inspire, drive, animate, and arouse us to live our biological, transformational, and transcendental purpose.

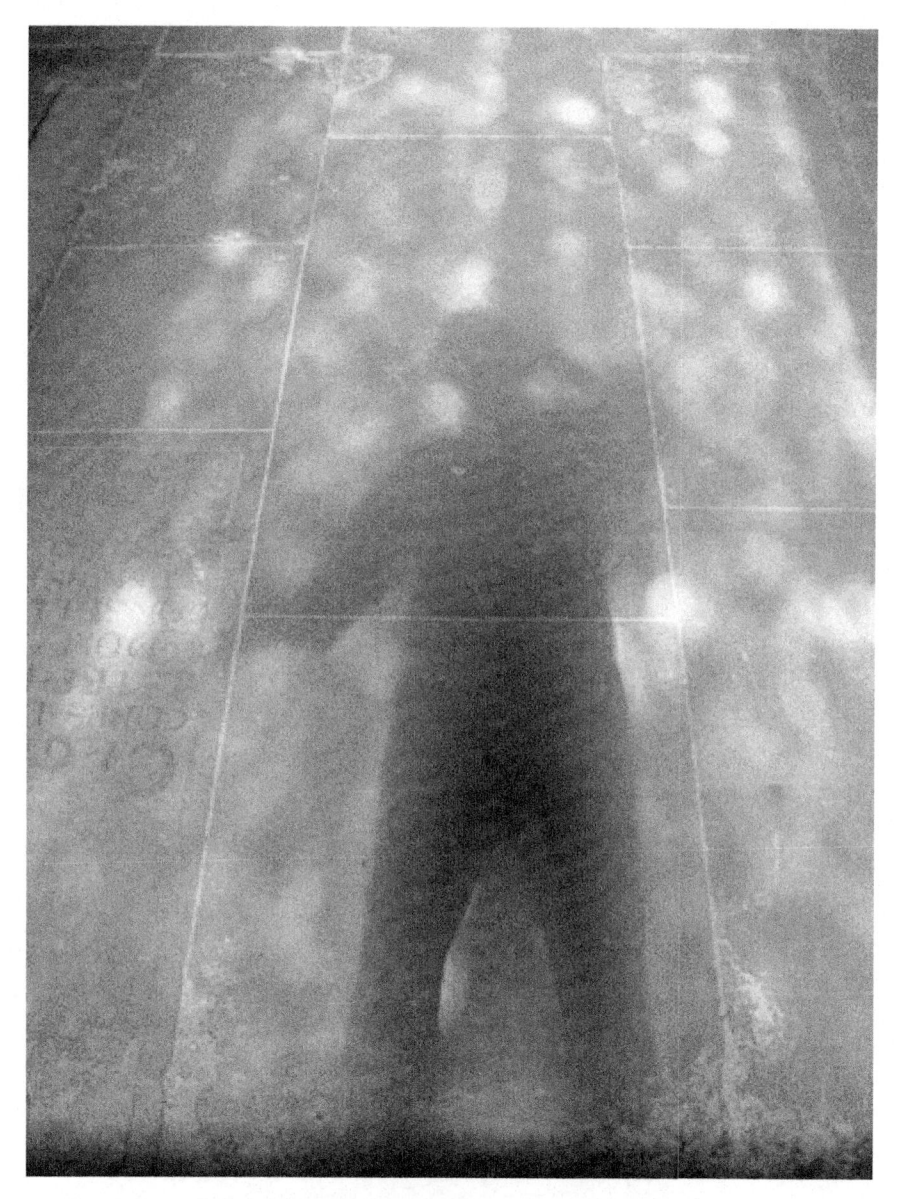

Figure 76: Metaphor of co-creative impulse

Unlike an acorn that has the potential to grow into an oak tree if placed in fertile ground, we humans are social animals who need others to survive and flourish after we are born, to know ourselves (we only know ourselves through the eyes of others), to realize our fullest human potentials, and to sustain humanity. Without others, we do not "exist."[456]

As the self develops (metaphorically shown below as the spiraling stained-glass windows), unconscious blind spots are created on the soul (glass)—via cover up, denial, repression, splitting off, and lack of integration of potentials (see the various forms of the unconscious on page 340)—through which the light cannot shine. We can only see the shadows through our defensiveness, diminished aliveness, unethical behaviors, lack of meaning and purpose, and avoidance of intimate relationships.

Soulmates have similar stained-glass windows, thus creating familiarity,[457] but with blind spots in different places, differences which initially create attraction through complementing and eventually create the opportunity for learning, healing, growing, and awakening when we are triggered and conflicts and defenses emerge after we project our blind spots onto our partner.

Figure 77: Metaphorical transformational soulmates development[458]

Three unfolding levels of soulmates

There are three levels of soulmate relationships that build on each other through transcending and including.

Biological soulmates

Are uniquely compatible in their DNA, values, needs, desires, and lifestyle choices to share their biological purpose or imperative to perpetuate their existence through the self-sustaining processes below:
1. Survival (food, shelter, safety)
2. Reproduction/Procreation (raising offspring)
3. Group forming (family/community)
4. Territorialism (home, neighborhood, city, county, state, country, continent)
5. Competition/Cooperation (altruism)
6. Quality-of-life-seeking

Transformational soulmates (or worthy opponents)

Are opposites and equals who are uniquely compatible to challenge each other to realize their fullest human potentials through ongoing learning, healing, growing, and awakening (or facing-up, cleaning-up, growing up, and waking up) through the following:

1. Ongoing learning and combining their knowledge to live their biological, transformational, and transcendental purpose in ever better ways. Common wisdom and research show that two heads are better than one.[459]
2. Ongoing healing that supports them in increasing their capacity for aliveness, empathy, cooperation, social interaction, and love.
3. Ongoing growing (in consciousness and the other developmental lines that are listed on page 105) to integrate new and advanced perspectives that increase the available

choices and wisdom to adequately respond to the challenges and opportunities that living their purpose presents.
4. Ongoing awakening that leads them to increasing levels of freedom, liberation, peace, and joy through present moment-to-moment awareness and surrender to what is, without attachment, desire, delusion, hatred/aversion.

Transcendental soulmates

Are uniquely compatible to co-create more goodness, truth, beauty, or functioning in service of the biological purpose and well-being of others by creating synergy between their different talents for empathy, cognitive intelligence, creativity/aesthetics, and practicality, as well as feminine-masculine polarities and types through the following:

1. Sharing the same joy, passion, concern, pain, desire, calling (to maintain, improve, or innovate), depth (gross, subtle, causal, pure witness, nondual), and maturity to make the world a better place.
2. Assuming equal rights and responsibilities in enacting their purpose by <u>BOTH</u> doing what they love to do and are good at, and what the world needs and pays them for.
3. Making feminine (care, compassion, feelings, relationships) and masculine (rights, justice, rationality, autonomy) validity claims to what is good, true, beautiful, and functional, and only proceed to (en)act(ment) when there is mutual understanding and agreement between them and all affected people, living and unborn.
4. Co-creating their love relationship as opposite and equal partners at the level of all seven chakras and loving not only each other but, even more, that which is uniquely co-created between them (see Module 25).

Purpose and application of the module
1. Learn about the soul and soulmates.
2. Differentiate between the Ego and the soul.
3. Gain an Integral understanding of biological, transformational, and transcendental soulmates.
4. Remove psychological blocks and other barriers to love that prevent you from finding/attracting and co-creating with your soulmate.
5. Create your soulmate profile by feeling into your head, heart, and gut.
6. Identify, find, attract, or invite your soulmate.
7. Live your transformational and transcendental purpose while you are single.
8. Deepen your soulmate connection with your partner.

Exercises: Soulmates
The following are individual, group, and paired exercises.
1. Print out the worksheets below.
2. Make the four agreements for confidentiality, responsibility, healthy boundaries, I-statements, and sharing, as outlined on page 556.

Exercise one: Ego versus soul
This can be an individual, paired or group exercise.
1. Ask practitioners to differentiate between the ego and the soul by feeling into their soul and filling out the right column in the list below.
2. Practitioners can do this individually and then share their answers with their partner or the group, or it can be a group exercise in which you write the answers on a whiteboard/flipchart.
3. See suggested answers in the endnote.[460]

The Ego–the conditioned, separate sense of self	The Soul–the unconditioned, relational self
Me	
Separation	
Blame	
Hostility	
Resentment	
Pride	
Complain	
Jealousy	
Projecting anger	
Power over	
Materialism	
Madness	
War	
Coldness	
Pain of past/fear of future oriented	
Intolerance	
Self-importance	
Stinginess	
Self-denial	
Social intolerance	
Complexity	
Doing	
Victim	

Table 21: Ego and Soul

Removing psychological blocks and barriers to love

Rumi wrote, "Your task is not to seek for love, but merely to seek and find all the barriers within yourself that you have built against it." So true!

Most relationship coaches have discovered that their clients first need to address psychological blocks such as fears, shame, negative self-talk, false beliefs, and deeply rooted behavioral patterns as a first step to finding, attracting, or inviting their soulmate.

Exercise two: Immunity to Change

This exercise is similar to the process on page 444.

Explore the psychological blocks and other obstacles (e.g., avoidant attachment style; still in love with someone else; too busy; not feeling attractive; being cynical, etc.) that prevent you from opening up to, defining, identifying, and attracting/finding/inviting your soulmate and co-creating with him or her.

Use the Immunity to Change worksheet below to define your goals, what you are doing/not doing instead, your hidden competing commitments, and your big (false) assumptions. See suggestions for filling out the form in endnote.[461]

Worksheet: Immunity To Change

Goal	Doing/Not Doing Instead	Hidden Competing Commitments	Big (false) Assumptions
Steps to take	Details	Details	Details

Take your emotions into account.
Test the big assumptions that present the most significant obstacles in your life.
Think of low-risk scenarios to take the first steps towards your goals.

Exercise three: Voice dialogue process

Do the Voice dialogue process on page 446 in the context of co-creating a soulmate relationship.

Defining your soulmate

You cannot find, attract, invite, or be invited by your soulmate if you don't know what your soul is yearning for. Because the soul is not speaking to us directly, we will first go broad by feeling into as many dimensions of co-creation on the material, physical, intellectual, emotional, and spiritual level as possible.

Exercise four: For singles–defining your soulmate

This can be a paired or group exercise.
Fill out the worksheet below by feeling into the following questions for each of the 16 soulmate desires and share the answers for each of them with your partner or the group.

1. What are your realistic desires and expectations for your soulmate that are aligned with what you bring to the relationship?[462]
2. How will you feel when your desires are met?
3. What are the obstacles, fears, blocks, etc., that prevent you from meeting your soul's desires in a mate and co-creating with him or her?

Exercise four: For couples–deepening your relationship

This can be an individual or paired exercise.
Fill out the form below by feeling into the following questions and sharing the answers with your partner:

1. What kind of (soulmate) relationship are you and your partner currently in—biological, transformational, and/or transcendental?
2. What would you like to co-create with your partner to deepen your soulmate relationship?
3. Are there any obstacles that you and your partner face as you co-create and deepen your soulmate relationship? If yes, what are they?
4. What do you want to improve to co-create (or deepen) your soulmate relationship with your partner?
5. What unrealized potentials do you see in yourself and your partner?

Worksheet: Defining your soulmate

Soulmate desire and what you contribute:	Positive feelings created:	Obstacles, fears, blocks, etc.:
1. Material/lifestyle/money (survival/safety):		
Desire:		
Contribute:		
2. Physical body (appearance, fitness, age, diet, hygiene, smell, sleep):		
Desire:		
Contribute:		
3. Sexuality (level, frequency):		
Desire:		
Contribute:		
4. Children/grandchildren:		
Desire:		
Contribute:		

5. Family/community:		
Desire:		
Contribute:		
6. Pets and animals:		
Desire:		
Contribute:		
7. Territory (where you live and are open to move to):		
Desire:		
Contribute:		
8. Profession/status:		
Desire:		
Contribute:		
9. Quality of Life (time, interests, passions, hobbies, dreams/vision for the future):[463]		
Desire:		

Contribute:		
10. Values/needs/ideals:[464]		
Desire:		
Contribute:		
11. Emotional intelligence/availability:		
Desire:		
Contribute:		
12. Learning together:		
Desire:		
Contribute:		
13. Healing/shadow work:		
Desire:		
Contribute:		

14. Growing (integration and transformation):		
Desire:		
Contribute:		
15. Spiritual awakening:		
Desire:		
Contribute:		
16. Shared transcendental purpose (co-creating good, true, beautiful, functional/practical):		
Desire:		
Contribute:		

Table 22: Soulmate worksheet

Use your answers to create a clear, captivating dating and relationship profile and vision map that focuses on the three most important things that your soul is yearning to co-create with your current soulmate or a future mate.

If you are single, this is important, regardless of whether or not you plan to use the profile for online dating, so that you become clear about who your soul is yearning for and wants you to find, attract, invite, or be invited by to co-create a soulmate relationship. You can then approach every potential qualifying soulmate with "beginner's mind" to stay open to potentials outside your profile/vision map.

Exercise five: Soulmate statement

This is an individual and group exercise.
Write down the statement or prayer with the three most important things that your soul is yearning for in a mate and share it with the group or your partner.
For example:

I am attracting/finding my soulmate who is at my level of development, shares my passion and purpose of _____, and wants to live, work and travel with me.

I am attracting/finding my soulmate who is on a Buddhist spiritual path, younger than me so that we can have children together and start a family, and who wants to live on a farm in _____, where we can grow our own food.

I am attracting/finding my soulmate who is a tall, successful entrepreneur and wants to start an international consulting firm for sustainable energy production with me that is based in _____.

Soulmate selection process

Most singles take a bottom-up approach to dating and relating. They prioritize physical/sexual attraction and biological transactional love first and then hope that, in time, transformational and transcendental love may arise. While that may sometimes happen, it is unlikely. More often, partners split up when one or both want to also share their transformational and transcendental purpose and realize that they are incompatible.

A better approach is a top-down process: to first identify and live your transcendental purpose, and then find/attract/invite a soulmate who also shares your transformational and biological purpose.

Finding, attracting, or inviting your soulmate

After deeply feeling into what your soul yearns for in a mate and creating your soulmate statement, you can ready yourself and open to finding, attracting, or inviting potential soulmates, or receiving their invitations.

Below are some suggestions for steps to take:
1. Get into shape (physically, financially, emotionally, spiritually, living your purpose.)
2. Do forgiveness and "conscious uncoupling" work—ideally on all past romantic relationships.[354]
3. Remove psychological blocks and barriers to love (see exercises above).
4. Learn whether you are a maximizer or a satisficer?[465] (The latter are happier!)
5. Consider mobility or prepare for mobility. Your soulmate may live in another city, state, country, continent. if you cannot move, make room in your home so that you can invite him or her.
6. For men: get over your fear of rejection (see books like *The Game* or *Stumbling Naked in the Dark*.)
7. For women: open to your soulmate (see, for example, *Calling In "The One"*).
8. Make compromises without compromising your values.
9. Make time and space in your life for dating and inviting your soulmate.
10. Be open and welcoming.
11. Smile at people.
12. Work with a dating coach.
13. Write your dating profile.
14. Take attractive pictures and post them with your dating profile.
15. Join groups and events where you can meet like-minded people.
16. Start your own relationship meetups/groups.

17. Tell your friends that you are open to find/attract your soulmate and share your statement.
18. Be active on social media.
19. Let go and live/improve your life.
20. Approach every potential mate with "beginner's mind."

Exercise six: Dating strategy for singles

This can be an individual, partner, or group exercise.
Share with your partner or group:
1. What is your clear soulmate statement?
2. Who are you inviting saying yes to?
3. What is your dating strategy?
4. Are you a satisficer or a maximiser and how does that impact your search/availability?
5. What obstacles have you faced in finding/attracting/inviting your soulmate?
6. What do you want to change, improve, or let go of to find/attract/invite your soulmate?

Identifying, qualifying, and choosing your soulmate

To identify and qualify your soulmate, you need to get your head, heart, and gut to say yes. In other words, align intimacy, passion, and commitment.

The best way to get to know and intimately connect with potential soulmates is to have conversations about the topics below, even before you go on a date:
1. What attracted you to me/my profile?
2. What do we feel most passionate and concerned about?
3. What is your desire/purpose for being in a relationship?
4. What is your life's purpose?
5. What inspires you to get up in the morning? What are your first thoughts?
6. What attracted you to your former partners?
7. Why did your relationships end?

8. Who ended the relationships?
9. What is your relationship with your former partners now?
10. What did you learn from the ending?
11. What do you want to do differently now?
12. What are your Love Languages?
13. What is your Enneagram Type, Attachment Style, and Anima/Animus complex?
14. Draw from the exercises and many dating and relating questions throughout this manual and in *Integral Relationships: A Manual for Men*.

Acceptance

If you are single or in a partnership with someone who is not (yet) your soulmate, the following insight from Robert Augustus Masters' book, *Transformation through Intimacy: The Journey Toward Mature Monogamy*, offers profound guidance:

> The passage from immature to mature [Integral] Relationships is not just a journey of ripening intimacy with a beloved other, but also a journey into and through zones of ourselves that may be quite difficult to navigate, let alone get intimate with and integrate with the rest of our being. But however much this passage might ask of us, it gives back even more, transforming us until we are established in the unshakable love, profound passion, and radically intimate mutuality that epitomize mature [Integral] Relationships. And even if we do not end up in such a relationship, our having taken the journey toward it will immeasurably benefit us [and others] in whatever we do.

Follow-up questions

1. How do you feel after exploring this module and the exercises?
2. What kind of soulmate are you ready for (biological, transformational, and/or transcendental)?
3. What insights have you gained through these exercises?

Additional information and resources

The Game: Penetrating the Secret Society of Pickup Artists (2005) by Neil Strauss
tinyurl.com/irpm541[466]

Stumbling Naked in the Dark: Overcoming Mistakes Men Make with Women (2003) by Bradley Fenton
tinyurl.com/irpm543[467]

Calling In "The One": 7 Weeks to Attract the Love of Your Life (2004) by Katherine Woodward Thomas
tinyurl.com/irpm544[468]

Sex Purpose Love book reference

Page 299–317 and 379–386

Suggested movie: *Grace and Grit* (2021)

Watch this movie that is based on Ken Wilber's book *Grace and Grit: Spirituality and Healing in the Life and Death of Treya Killam Wilber* (with many journal entries from Treya) to see what makes couples soulmates. One experience is that they usually recognize each other almost instantly, no matter if they are biological, transformational, or transcendental soulmates. A second quality is that they have removed all barriers to love and come from a sense of fullness instead of need or lack. A third quality is that they are devoted to facing all challenges in life and avoiding nothing to live together/procreate, to learn, heal, grow, and awaken together, and to make the world a better place.

The movie weaves together these experiences and qualities of soulmates through three narratives. The first voice is that of Treya herself, taken from her private journals that span from first meeting Ken in 1984 to her death in 1989 (she insisted that Ken use these journals in order to tell their extraordinary story). The second voice belongs to Ken, who was walking this difficult path alongside Treya, step by step, not yet aware of where their story would lead.

The third voice also belongs to Ken, but as the "omniscient narrator" who is lacing these narratives together and telling the story from the perspective of someone who has lived the full experience.
tinyurl.com/irpm85[469]

Practice Module 25
Co-Creation at the Level of the Seven Chakras

There's no such thing as being alone in the universe, and so there's no such thing as creating alone. Everything—every impulse, every creative gift of beauty, everything is a co-creation.
~ Gary Zukav ~

Module description

Learn and practice how to co-create a healthy sustainable Integral Love Relationship with your soulmate at the level of your seven chakras. Engage in a meditative breathing and movement exercise that allows you to feel into the co-creative life force of each of the seven chakras in your body. Notice the charge in each for your seven chakras.

Heal any unconscious wounds, trauma, or unrealized potentials that block, disconnect, or limit the co-creative life force from manifesting through each of your seven chakras. Feel into the yearning in each of your seven chakras to co-create with your soulmate in the four dimensions of your being by balancing and harmonizing healthy feminine and masculine polarities. Bring all the essential elements/dimensions of the Integral Relationship model into a functional whole.

Transform your relationships from need-based, asymmetric, transactional love to becoming-based, symmetric, transcendental love in which you not only love your partner but, even more, that which is uniquely co-created between the two of you at the level of each chakra by sharing your biological, transformational, and transcendental purpose.

Introduction

In this module, we bring our understanding of the essential elements/dimensions for co-creating an Integral Love Relationship (as we have explored in the previous 24 modules) into a functional whole.

These are (1) the four dimensions of being and relating; (2) eight levels of consciousness development and communication; (3) sex and gender difference; (4) avoiding the fear-shame downward spiral; (5) healthy feminine-masculine polarities; (6) developmental lines of spirituality; (7) sexuality; (8) anima/animus complex; (9) personality types; (10) attachment styles; (11) the unconscious and false identities; (12) forms and states of love; (13) personality disorders; and our (14) biological, (15) transformational, and (16) transcendental purpose and the resulting forms of love.

The integration of these elements/dimensions is best experienced through a guided meditation in which the practitioners learn about the seven chakras and feel into the unique yearnings that they have in each of them for co-creating in a love relationship with a compatible soulmate.

The seven chakras

As mentioned above, in the Integral Relationship model, the chakras are defined as the felt "energy centers" or nerve bundles that are associated with major organs in our body through which the co-creative and procreative impulse or life force yearns to co-create with a compatible opposite and equal soulmate.

Crown - Unity

Third Eye - Wisdom

Throat - Creativity

Heart - Love

Solar Plexus - Power

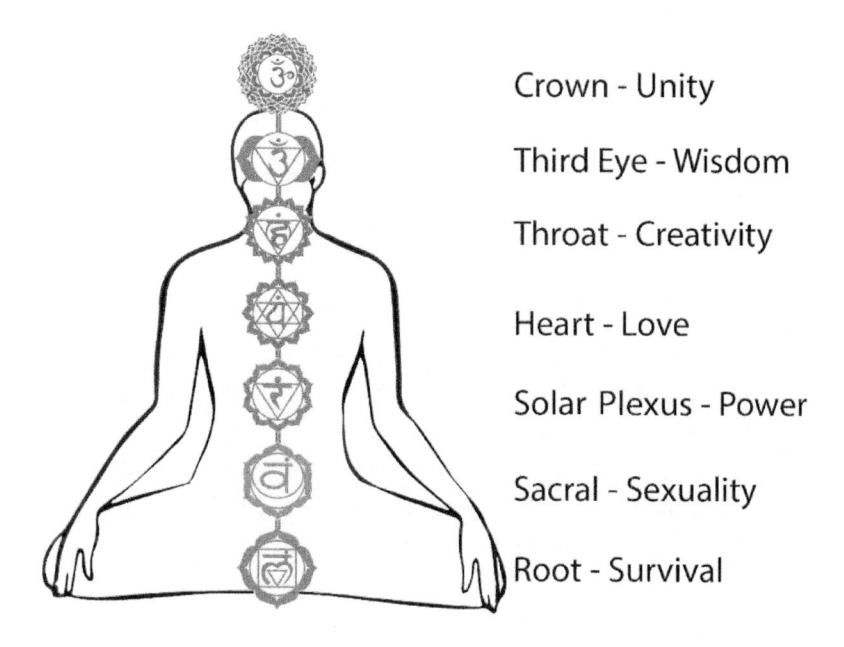

Sacral - Sexuality

Root - Survival

Figure 78: The seven chakras

The root chakra

Is felt at the base of the spine and connected to the legs. Through it, lovers experience the yearning to run towards each other, to feel safe with each other, to live in a comfortable home together, to share their resources, to be in a stable relationship, to be able to depend on each other, to feel grounded and strong, like a big tree with strong, well-nurtured roots in the ground.

Under relationship stress, primal fears around safety and survival arise. Partners may feel stuck, insecure, uprooted, downtrodden, lacking in purpose, or inclined to run away when the pain of staying is stronger than the fear of leaving.

The sacral chakra

Is felt below the navel. Through it, lovers experience the yearning to be physically and sexual intimate with each other, to create and procreate, to penetrate the world together, to increase their self-worth, to be adaptable, and to feel fully alive.

Under relationship stress—for example, during infidelity or withdrawal—strong emotional outbursts, jealousy, and even violence may arise. These responses may go along with feelings of paralyzing fear and shame, humiliation, lack of creating, loss of aliveness, and even suicidal thoughts.

The solar plexus chakra

Is felt between the navel and the bottom of the breastbone. Through it, lovers experience the proverbial butterflies in the stomach and the yearning to be powerful with each other, to be confident, focused, productive, and aligned, and to move in the same direction by getting things done and being in control of their lives.

Under relationship stress, couples feel that their stomach is in knots. They try to have power and control over each other instead of with each other, pull or push in opposite directions, be aggressive or passive aggressive towards each other. They may feel depressed and have a lack of self-esteem.

The heart chakra

Is felt in the center of the chest. Through it, lovers experience the yearning for love, compassion, trust, intimacy, vulnerability, and to integrate the lower and higher chakras and their inside and outside.

Under relationship stress, couples feel that their hearts are broken, often along with chest pain and a fast-beating, fluttering, or pounding heart. They close their hearts towards each other and feel distrust, resentment, anger, loss, frustration, anxiety, disconnection, disintegration, sadness, and despair.

The throat chakra

Is felt in the throat area and connected to the neck, mouth, and tongue. Through it, lovers experience the yearning to express themselves, share their truths, be heard, understood, and accepted, and to be creative with each other.

Under relationship stress, couples may endlessly argue with each other without reaching agreement, or feel anxious (to speak), speechless, shut down, deceived, resentful, and distrustful. They may lie to each other, give each other the silent treatment, or (often women) end arguments with words like "fine," "nothing," "go ahead," or "thanks a lot"—none of which actually mean what they say.[470]

The third eye chakra

Is felt between the eyebrows. Through it, lovers experience the yearning to share their vision, mission, goals, direction, values, knowing, and wisdom with their soulmate.

Under relationship stress, partners may feel alone or held back from pursuing their purpose, compromised in living their values, or unclear about their shared vision and mission. They may feel stuck, hopeless, and frustrated.

The crown chakra

Is felt at the top of the head, the highest of the seven main chakras.[471] Through it, soulmates experience the yearning to share their spiritual or higher self, their connection or unity with God, spirit, or the universe through presence and surrender. It is the chakra of liberation from suffering that is caused by desire, attachment, delusion, hatred, and aversion.

Under relationship stress, partners may blame each other for being attached to their Ego and outcomes; act from fear instead of love; be unenlightened; engage in spiritual materialism and bypassing; or not be present and surrendered in the here and now.

Purpose and application of the module

1. Learn about the seven chakras through which the co-creative life force yearns to co-create with an equal and opposite soulmate.
2. Feel into the charge or energy of each chakra through a guided meditation to heal unconscious wounds that block the co-creative life force from flowing freely through them.

3. Sense what your soul is yearning for in a mate at each of the seven chakras.
4. Note and share this yearning in each of the four dimensions of your being and relating at your level of development for each of the seven chakras.
5. Balance healthy feminine and masculine polarities along the seven chakras.

Exercises: Co-creation at the level of the seven chakras

The following are individual and paired exercises.
1. Print out the two worksheets below.
2. Make the four agreements for confidentiality, responsibility, healthy boundaries, I-statements, and sharing, as outlined on page 556.

Exercise one: Chakra charge meditation

See video of guided meditation at tinyurl.com/irpm98[472]
Guide the practitioners through the following mediation.
1. Assume the (meditation) position and look spiritual (joke).
2. Put your hand on your abdomen and take a few deep belly breaths, feeling your abdomen rise and fall (some practitioners need to learn how to breathe into their abdomen deeply and naturally.)
3. Close your eyes or lower your gaze.
4. Follow the sound of the bell, arising out of silence and fading back into silence. Ring the bell or chime.
5. Bring your attention into your physical body.
6. Wiggle your toes a little bit, feel the gravity of the earth that is keeping your body firmly grounded.
7. Relax every muscle in your body, starting from your feet, legs, and abdomen (deep breath); move your shoulders back a little to fully open your heart; continue with relaxing your chest, shoulders, arms, and hands.

8. Turn your head to the left, right, front, and back, and find that perfect balancing point for your head on top of your spine.
9. Relax every muscle in your face and release any tension you may hold in your jaw.
10. Feel into your first chakra, which is called the root chakra. It is located at the bottom of your spine, where you feel your connection with the earth.
11. Take a few deep breaths into your root chakra to activate it.
12. The root chakra is associated with survival, protecting, safety, providing food, home, money, material things, being grounded, and stability. It is connected to your legs and your fight, flight, freeze responses. The sound is Lam, and the color is red.
13. As you feel into your first root chakra, is it ... (mention the word-pairs below that resonate most with you for this chakra.)

Open or closed?	Connected or disconnected?
Giving or receiving?	Protected or inviting?
Empty or full?	Loud or quiet?
Abundant or scarce?	Flowing or static?
Active or passive?	Arrested or unrestrained?
Strong or weak?	Warm or cold?
Blocked or free?	Secure or anxious?
Blurry or clear?	Stable or volatile?
Engaged or avoidant?	Fearful or brave?
Directed or meandering?	Shameful or confident?
Guarded or vulnerable?	Balanced or unbalanced?
Generous or stingy?	Feminine or masculine?

14. Are there any fear, shame, shadow, wounds, trauma, trigger points, or unconscious parts that need healing and growth in your root chakra?
15. As you feel into your root chakra, what are you or your soul yearning for or desiring in your mate? What would you like to

Integral Relationship Practice | 504

co-create or manifest with your soulmate? What would you like to give and receive?
16. Hold this feeling or make a few short notes on your worksheet.
17. Pause here for about a minute.
18. If you like, move your lower body a little to move energy.
19. Feel into your second chakra, which is called the sacral chakra. It is located right below your belly button.
20. Take a few deep breaths into your sacral chakra to activate it.
21. Optional! For some practitioners it may be helpful to put their hand(s) on or right above the particular chakra that we feel into, or to cup it with their hands to better feel it. Other practitioners may feel that this would close, protect, or disturb the chakras. Use your intuition as to whether or not to offer this option.
22. The sacral chakra is associated with sexuality and creation, your sex organs, penetrating, being penetrated, and aliveness. The sound is Vam, and the color is orange.
23. As you feel into this second sacral chakra, is it ... (mention the word-pairs above that resonate most with you for this chakra.)
24. Are there any fear, shame, shadow, wounds, trauma, trigger points, or unconscious parts that need healing or growth in your sacrum chakra?
25. As you feel into this second sacral chakra, what are you or your soul yearning or desiring in your mate? What would you like to co-create or manifest with your soulmate? What would you like to give and receive?
26. Hold this feeling or make a few short notes on your worksheet.
27. Pause again for about a minute.
28. If you like, move your lower body a little to move energy.
29. Feel into your third chakra, which is called the solar plexus chakra. It is located between your naval and your breastbone.
30. Continue in the same fashion for the remaining five chakras by using the descriptions above or the worksheet below.

31. At the fifth chakra, invite the practitioners to make a long Om, Ham, or Ahh sound with you to feel the vibration and openness in their throat/voice box.
32. Invite the practitioners to share their experience after the meditation.

Worksheet: Chakra meditation

Chakra	Charge and yearning
7. Crown: Unity—Higher power, letting go, surrender, spirituality, liberation (from suffering). Om–Violet	
6. Third Eye: Vision—Values, understanding, imagination, wisdom, bigger picture, direction, freedom. Ksham–Purple	
5. Throat: Creativity—Communication, self-expression, honesty, truth, ideas, purpose. Ham–Blue	
4. Heart: Integration—Love, care, compassion, relationship, comfort, warmth, closeness, connection, sensitivity, openness, intimacy, vulnerability. Yam–Green	
3. Solar plexus: Power—Focus, action, getting things done, willpower, self-esteem, boundaries, being in control, direction, force. Ram–Yellow	
2. Sacral: Sexuality—Sex organs, penetrating, being penetrated, creation, aliveness, adaptability. Vam–Orange	
1. Root: Survival—Protection, safety. Providing food, home, money, material things, grounding, stability. Connection to legs, fight, flight, freeze. Sound: Lam; Color: Red	

Table 23: Chakra charge worksheet

Pointers to chakras and quadrants

The meditation is followed by a paired exercise in which the practitioners further differentiate their yearning to co-create with their soulmate by feeling into each of the four dimensions of their being (quadrants) at their level of development for each of the seven chakras. How this yearning manifests also depends on their desire to share their biological, transformational, or transcendental purpose. Each of the chakras and quadrants has potential shadow elements that are often projected onto a desired partner.

Below are examples and pointers for clarification and orientation about each of the chakra quadrants. You may use them to give examples to the practitioners based on their culture, personal experiences, and level of consciousness development.

1st root survival chakra

In the Upper Left "I" Interior quadrant, we locate feelings and thoughts around food, safety, physical well-being, physical health, money, and material goods. Many people have deep fears about poverty (or sometimes about having too much)—being concerned about not being able to "keep up with the Joneses," or about being robbed, or about lacking the intellectual capacities to provide sustenance and earne money.

The Upper Right "It" Exterior quadrant represents hormonal triggers of hunger and fear, as well as the ability of our body to perform work that provides sustenance.

In the Lower Left "We" Cultural quadrant, we locate values around food production: for example, do we honor sacred cows? Which animals and plants do we eat? Do we avoid GMOs? Do we eat industrially produced food, etc.? It also includes our eating habits and customary diets—such as fasting, vegetarianism, alcohol consumption, time of day we eat, etc.—and worldviews and ideologies about means of production and economic systems such as capitalism, socialism, or communism, as well as culturally conditioned types of work and professions that males and females typically perform around food production, and the role of the major breadwinner.

In the Lower Right "Its" Social quadrant, we find means of production such as construction of safe and comfortable dwellings (homes), farming, factories, and office buildings; infrastructure such as streets, airports, bridges, and waterways; as well as institutions such as hospitals, banking systems, stock markets, and government buildings.

Unconscious

Fear of poverty or shame around having too much; unhealthy attachment to material things and money; compulsive shopping and hoarding; greed and feelings of never having enough/always wanting more; concerns and guilt about consuming more resources than one deserves and so depriving others; extreme frugality, stinginess, or unhealthy Spartan living; eating disorders, especially around sugar, salt and fat; being too thin or too big; obsessing about food and material things; kleptomania.

2nd sacral sexuality chakra

In the Upper Left "I" Interior quadrant, we locate thoughts and feelings of shame, fear, and desire around sexuality, sexual orientation, body shame, and performance anxiety.

In the Upper Right "It" Exterior quadrant, we locate our biological sex; sex organs; sex hormones; physical aspects such as erections and lubrication; libido and frequency of sex; sexual positions and practices such as oral or anal sex; S&M; bodily fluids and odors; physical sexual turn-ons and turn-offs; cosmetic changes such as breast enlargements, shaving of pubic hair, intimate piercings, tattoos, etc.; and medications that treat erectile dysfunction or vaginal atrophy—the thinning, drying and inflammation of the vaginal walls due to the body having less estrogen—and other sexual stimulants.

In the Lower Left "We" Cultural quadrant, we locate norms and values around sexuality (such as who initiates the first contact);

rules and customs around premarital sex; display of sexuality in the media; acceptable levels of sexually explicit clothing and nudity; public displays of affection; sexual harassment; sex trafficking; and direct and indirect prostitution.

The Lower Right "Its" Social quadrant covers socially accepted environments for sexual conduct; sex toys and lingerie; locations of swinger clubs, sex bars, and brothels; sex trafficking rings; distribution of pornography through magazines, movies, or the internet; and romance novels and chick flicks (female porn).

Unconscious

Here we find repressed sexuality and avoidance, sex addictions, overly explicit sexual behavior; for example, in people with histrionic personality disorders (see Module 21); shame around sex organs or no shame at all (exhibitionism); the use of sexuality to manipulate; and psychologically caused erectile dysfunction, inability to orgasm, premature ejaculation, and other sexual trauma and dysfunction.

3rd solar plexus power chakra

In the Upper Left "I" Interior quadrant, we locate feelings of power and powerlessness, safety and lack of safety, significance, and insignificance. How much control do we feel we have over our own lives, and how much is controlled by our body, others, nature, and our social environment? In which areas of our lives are we free to choose and in control, and where are we constrained both emotionally and in our power? This chakra is also the center of anger issues.

In the Upper Right "It" quadrant, we locate the physical abilities to exert power, defend oneself physically, intimidate others or escape quickly, as well as empowerment of individuals, violent behavior, having control over one's own body (e.g., eating and exercise habits), and all "gut" feelings that are related to the abdominal area, such as having "butterflies," "knots," indigestion, or feeling punched in the stomach.

In the Lower Left "We" Cultural quadrant, we locate implicit and culturally created power structures—for example, men having power over women, superiors over underlings, parents and teachers over children, masters over slaves, certain social classes over others, police over citizens, military over nations, politicians/ruling parties over their constituencies, or the rich over the poor—and the media and entertainment industries, who have the power of controlling information over the masses.

In the Lower Right "Its" Social quadrant, we locate weapons to enforce power—such as knives, guns, bombs, tanks, planes, ships, fortresses, military complexes, etc.—and infrastructure such as gated communities, alarm systems, surveillance cameras, internet security systems, bodyguards, and armored cars.

Unconscious

Being extremely fearful (especially when there are no threats), overly aggressive (especially when not warranted), overconfident, reckless, passive-aggressive, rigid or having weak boundaries. Inflated ego, bragging about accomplishments, name-dropping, and pursuit of power and status at any cost. Feeling powerless, worthless, or as a victim of circumstance, having no freedom of choice. Being extremely modest and invisible.

4th heart integration chakra

In the Upper Left "I" Interior quadrant, we locate overall emotional availability and the capacity to love (being open-hearted); the capacity for self-validated intimacy and vulnerability; empathy and compassion; the ability to deal with heartbreaks; and feelings around goodness, truth and beauty.

In the Upper Right "It" quadrant, we locate physical tension in the chest area, skipping heartbeats, and heart racing that are caused by stress and challenging feelings and emotions (or other psychosomatic disorders); psychoactive and mood-altering legal and illegal drugs; and the capacity for kind and caring behavior.

In the Lower Left "We" Cultural quadrant, we locate acceptable expressions of feelings and love in the private and public sphere; the importance given to emotional expressions versus rational thought; justification of (un)ethical or (im)moral behavior; decision-making based on feelings versus rationality; following one's heart and finding truth in what feels right versus logic and reason.

In the Lower Right "Its" Social quadrant, we locate buildings, settings, spaces, places, centers, and environments, as well as groups and organizations that invite the expression of feelings and emotions, such as churches and other places of worship and celebration, cemeteries, retreat spaces, therapy centers, hospitals, sacred gardens, event centers and private homes, as well as authentic relating or 12-step groups or management models like "Theory U."

Unconscious

Being totally identified with and driven by irrational feelings or repressing feelings and being unable to use feelings and emotions as guides for considerate and sound decision-making; showing "idiot compassion"; emotional blackmail and manipulations in the name of following one's heart; inability to show empathy for self or others; and failing to integrate head and heart.

5th throat creativity chakra

In the Upper Left "I" Interior quadrant, we locate abilities to verbally express thoughts, feelings, intentions, and observations; eloquence, accuracy, creativity, logic, and intelligibility of speech; being self-assured and clear with an ability to reason and make rational arguments, the ability to make others laugh, entertain, and engage people with compelling storytelling, wit, and intelligence.

In the Upper Right "It" quadrant, we locate the voice box, vocal chords, and lungs that produce the sound, volume, and tone of the voice (women prefer men with deep resonant voices)[473]; physical skills to express creativity, such as singing, painting, sculpting, playing a musical instrument, or writing; and, very generally speaking, the functions of the left side of the brain.[474] Women feel attracted to men who display integrity by doing what they say they will.

In the Lower Left "We" Cultural quadrant, we locate languages and dialects, accepted forms of verbal expression (for example, in Europe, swearing and cursing in public and using obscene words in the media is widely accepted, while in the US, words like "fuck," "shit," "piss," "cunt," "cock," "motherfucker," etc., are frequently bleeped out),[475] grammatical rules, semiotics, hermeneutics, discourse ethics, dialectic, meaning-making, and mathematical formulas and rules, all of which vary from culture to culture and language to language.

In the Lower Right "Its" Social quadrant, we locate artifacts, written documents, libraries, the internet and social media, schools and universities, museums and exhibitions, concert halls and cultural centers, churches, temples and mosques, all of which signify and celebrate human (especially male) creativity.

Unconscious

Being a loudmouth; always needing to be the center of attention by speaking up and telling stories; always needing to be right; being overly quiet and insecure; having deep fears about public speaking or performing; not knowing what to say in private and social situations. Creativity that does not lead to beauty, goodness, truth or functioning; having no creative outlet; feeling uncertain about one's creative power and ability.

6th third eye vision chakra

In the Upper Left "I" Interior quadrant, we locate feelings and notions of wisdom, vision and intuition.

In the Upper Right "It" quadrant, we locate wise behavior.

In the Lower Left "We" Cultural quadrant, we locate wisdom and intuition about morals and ethics.

In the Lower Right "Its" Social quadrant, we locate institutions, organizations, and networks such as spiritual groups, think-tanks, wisdom circles, discussion groups, political organizations, research centers, and foundations, as well as systems and infrastructures like the internet and universities.

Unconscious

Being a "know-it-all" and obsessing over certainty, or being totally unsure or agnostic about everything, being unable to make value judgments and decisions that serve the well-being of self and others, elevating spiritual or ancient wisdom over modern pragmatic rational choices, or not seeing any wisdom in spirituality, religions, and moral philosophy, or being a cynic or nihilist.

7th crown unity chakra

In the Upper Left "I" Interior quadrant, the spiritual state experience of unconditional love or unity means a dropping away of any fear or shame between a couple, which opens the door for a deep sense of connection, intimacy, trust, and vulnerability that transcends the separate sense of self or ego.

In the Upper Right "It" quadrant, the experience of unity leads to "unconditional love" beyond age, body features, health conditions, race, skin color, and physical attractiveness. It is expressed through fully accepting our partner's behavior and reality, and acting in consistently supportive and caring ways towards him or her, unless there is physical abuse. Oneness on the physical level is mostly experienced during sex and orgasm.

In the Lower Left "We" Cultural quadrant, "unconditional love" is often romanticized in fairytales, poems, myths, books, plays, songs, and movies as "happily ever after." The lovers are willing to make personal sacrifices, such as entering into heroic fights, risking their lives, breaking cultural norms, or forsaking others to prove their undying devotion to their beloved. This usually entails the removal of all boundaries, including those which are culturally normed as healthy.

In the Lower Right "Its" Social quadrant, "unconditional love" is free from any societal conditions, norms, pressures, and anxieties, and is expressed through freely sharing material resources and social connections.

Unconscious

Confusing a-duality with nonduality. Being unaware of advanced spiritual state-stages. All forms of spiritual bypassing that are mentioned earlier. New Age narcissism, such as "everyone creates their own reality." Spiritual materialism or maintaining that nothing real exists. Being unaware of performative contradictions, such as being nonjudgmental or rejecting natural hierarchies and getting angry or defensive when challenged about them.

See *Sex Purpose Love*, page 329–378, for further details about chakras, quadrants, levels of consciousness development, fear-shame dynamic, and feminine-masculine polarities along the seven chakras.

For feminine-masculine polarities, see Module 11 and *Figure 34: Ascending, descending, agency, communion* on page 198.

515 | Co-Creation at the Level of the Seven Chakras

Figure 79: Seven chakra co-creation in the four dimensions of relating

Exercise two: Chakra co-creation

The following is a paired exercise.
1. Share with your partner what you want to co-create in the four dimensions of your being (quadrants) at the level of each chakra by balancing healthy feminine and masculine polarities.

Worksheet: Chakra co-creation in the four dimensions

Chakra	Co-Creation		
7. Shared spiritual practice—honors higher connection to consciousness, spirit	I (You–Partner–Co-Creation)	It (You–Partner–Co-Creation)	
	We (You–Partner–Co-Creation)	Its (You–Partner–Co-Creation)	
6. Shared values and vision—honors intuition, wisdom, seeing, understanding, imagination	I (You–Partner–Co-Creation)	It (You–Partner–Co-Creation)	
	We (You–Partner–Co-Creation)	Its (You–Partner–Co-Creation)	
5. Shared communication—honors communication, creativity (dialectic)	I (You–Partner–Co-Creation)	It (You–Partner–Co-Creation)	
	We (You–Partner–Co-Creation)	ITS (You–Partner–Co-Creation)	

4. Shared Love—honors heart, intimacy, empathy, care for self and others	I (You–Partner–Co-Creation)	IT (You–Partner–Co-Creation)
	We (You–Partner–Co-Creation)	Its (You–Partner–Co-Creation)
3. Shared power—honors life force, passion, "power with" versus "power over"	I (You–Partner–Co-Creation)	It (You–Partner–Co-Creation)
	We (You–Partner–Co-Creation)	Its (You–Partner–Co-Creation)
2. Shared sexuality	I (You–Partner–Co Creation)	It (You–Partner–Co-Creation)
	We (You–Partner–Co-Creation)	Its (You–Partner–Co-Creation)
1. Shared ground—honors earth. material, money, shelter, lifestyle	I (You–Partner–Co-Creation)	It (You–Partner–Co-Creation)
	We (You–Partner–Co-Creation)	Its (You–Partner–Co-Creation)

Table 24: Four dimensions chakra co-creation worksheet

See examples for filling out chakra one and two in the endnote.[476]

Integral Relationship

The insights from the above exercise connect the practitioners back to the image of an Integral Relationship in *Figure 2: Integral Relationship co-created along the seven chakras,* on page 6 of the Introduction to this manual. It shows a couple with a shared purpose who co-creates an Integral Relationship by balancing and harmonizing their healthy feminine and masculine polarities in the four dimensions of their being along their seven chakras in the safe container of intimacy, passion, and commitment.

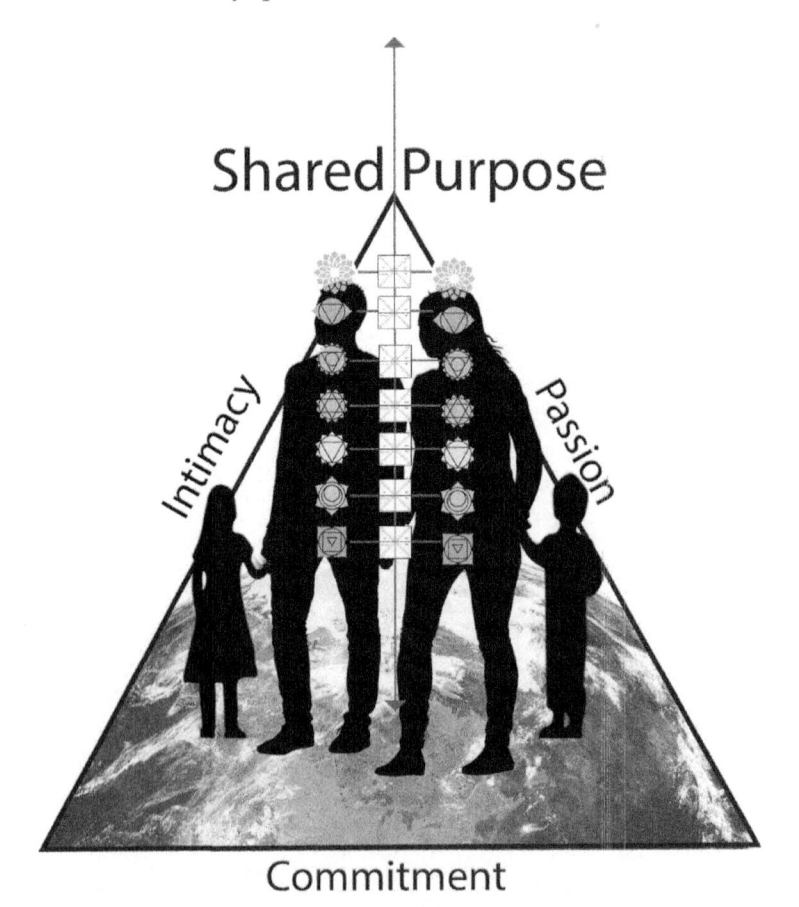

Figure 80: Integral couple making the world a better place

In summary we can define an Integral Love Relationship as co-created between (1) equal and opposite partners with the same rights and responsibilities in the domestic and public spheres who realize their fullest human potentials through ongoing (2) learning, (3) healing, (4) growing, and (5) awakening by (6) balancing and harmonizing their healthy feminine and masculine polarities in (7) the four dimensions of their being at (8) the level of their seven chakras and sharing their (9) biological, (10) transformational, and/or (11) transcendental purpose that creates more (12) goodness, (13) truth, (14) beauty, and (15) functioning to make the world a better place.

Follow-up questions

1. How do you feel after exploring this module and the exercises?
2. What insights have you gained through your experience?
3. Which of the essential elements/dimensions of an Integral Relationship to you plan to incorporate in your love relationship?
4. Where do you see learning, growing, healing, and awakening potentials in your life and relationships?
5. How do you and your partner (plan to) contribute to making the world a better place.

Additional information and resources

Charge and the Energy Body: The Vital Key to Healing Your Life, Your Chakras, and Your Relationships (2018) by Anodea Judith
tinyurl.com/irpm545[477]

Sex Purpose Love book reference

Page 391–462 and 475–509

Suggested movies:

Frida (2002)

Watch this exceptional movie to see soulmates who share their biological, transformational, and transcendental purpose along the seven chakras to co-create more goodness, truth, beauty, and functioning to make the world a better place.

The real-life biopic "Frida" is based on Hayden Herrera's 1983 biography of artist and political activist Frida Kahlo (1907–1954), which rescued her from obscurity and helped to transform her into a feminist icon.

We see how Frida (Salma Hayek) channeled the pain of a crippling injury from a bus accident at age 18 and her complex and tempestuous relationship with her mentor and husband Diego Rivera (Alfred Molina) into her work, as the young couple took the art world by storm. Through her provocative and romantic entanglements with women, her illicit and controversial affair with Leon Trotsky, and her provocative and uncompromising paintings, Frida lived a bold and uncompromising life, and, together with her husband Diego, became a true political (the good), artistic (the beautiful), and sexual (the truth) revolutionary.

Inside Bill's Brain: Decoding Bill Gates (2019)

Watch this three-part Netflix documentary as an option to see the importance of co-creation with others in trying to solve the significant problems that the world is facing.

No matter what you may think personally about Bill Gates, his connection to sex offender Jeffrey Epstein, and his divorce from his wife, Melinda French Gates, you may still find aspects of this series inspiring and informative.

See how Bill lived his calling early on to solve problems or absent absences, how he co-created with others, how he seemingly became more compassionate, how he met his wife Melinda, how they co-created their foundation, and how he became driven to make the world a better place by partnering with researchers and philanthropists. See his triumphs and, even more significantly, his failures, and how he deals with both. You may find it surprisingly fascinating.

Practice Module 26
Why Relationships Matter

Ideas move from mind to mind, but I don't know that these ideas are always selected with reference to what helps the listeners leave the most offspring in the next generation.
~ Holmes Rolston III ~

A better system will not automatically ensure a better life. In fact, the opposite is true: only by creating a better life can a better system be developed.
~ Václav Havel ~

Module description

Learn and realize why being in a healthy sustainable Integral Love Relationship not only matters for your own well-being and flourishing, but also for that of your soulmate, humanity, and future generations. Recognize that all functional systems are created by wholes who are parts of larger wholes, like whole humans who are parts of healthy couples, who are parts of functional families, who are parts of thriving communities, who are parts of successful societies/nations, who are parts of a peaceful and sustainable world and future of humanity. See why we can only practice our simultaneous wholeness and partialness at all levels of our being in a healthy love relationship.

Realize how the increasing number of singles around the world who are unable or unwilling to form healthy love relationships, and the resulting rapidly declining birthrates in modern and postmodern societies, are the underlying cause for the erosion of human bonds and social order, increasingly dysfunctional economic and political systems, environmental destruction, and civil and national wars. Become part of the solution instead of part of the problem by charting your personal path to relationship success, no matter if you are single or with a partner, and to teach it to others.

Introduction

Despite all the proven personal benefits of being in a healthy sustainable love relationship and the importance of nuclear families for thriving communities and flourishing societies, an increasing number of people in modern and postmodern societies feel that developing the necessary values and skills to share their life with their soulmate and to raise children are not worth the effort.[478]

For the first time since data was collected in 1976, there are now more unmarried than married people in the US. This trend of fewer marriages and more divorces is world-wide.[479] Some New-Agers, spiritual practitioners, and radical feminists even see the desire to be in a love relationship as a pathology, spiritually unevolved, or a modern form of enslavement. While being in a love relationship and becoming parents should be everyone's individual choice, it is important to bring awareness to the negative individual effects and the larger social and political consequences that will eventually negatively impact everyone, and to promote the development of healthy relationship skills in supporting couples and families.

In this final module, we will look at these negative consequences and why Integral Relationships matter for creating a peaceful and sustainable future for humanity.

What happened?

With the advent of modernity, and along with it the emergence of liberal democracy, feminism, freedom of speech, economic opportunity for all, globalism, and the influx of Eastern spirituality, most social theorists began to see societies as being composed of a collection of separate, self-interested, autonomous, and largely self-sufficient individuals. This became to be known as social atomism.[480]

It is referenced in almost every modern socioeconomic and political discourse, and sometimes in spiritual teachings, which primarily address the individual and society. This is like saying that atoms make up our bodies and ignoring holarchies of molecules, cells, cell tissues, and organs. Likewise, on a social level, social atomism frequently ignores the importance of couples, families, and communities for social cohesion.

This is understandable, as modernity largely rejects traditional conservative, religiously motivated family values, which are often associated with anti-liberalism, patriarchy, oppression and objectification of women, pro-life movements, marginalization of minorities such as members of LGBTQ+ communities, racism, and, in some countries, white supremacy. This rejection of traditional family values by modernity, without having a model other than singlehood to replace it, now leads to increasing social isolation and instability.

Starting in the 1960s, postmodernity tried to address this issue of social fragmentation and isolation by promoting communal living and the practice of polyamory, along with the advocacy for civil rights, social justice, nonviolence, environmental protection, world peace, and care for all living things on our planet.

Alas, these progressive communities and movements frequently turned out to be fragmented and unstable, and thus, unsustainable, because they were not rooted in shared values that arose out of stable couple and family relationships with children, and because members could join and leave at will, with little commitment to the community. Furthermore, the decline in birth rates that had begun in late modernity and accelerated in postmodernity and post-postmodernity to almost zero children per woman resulted in insufficient numbers of offspring to fuel the progressive and New-Age movements, whose members also stifled upward mobility by rejecting hierarchies and, at the same time, creating segregated education systems.[481] Consequently, for the first time in human history, cultural evolution became decoupled from biological evolution and, as a result—as we increasingly see today—liberal and socially progressive movements are struggling to advance.

On the other hand, we see that conservatives of the radical right who support autocratic leaders and often share traditional, religious, illiberal, nationalistic, and racist values increasingly out-procreate and out-vote left-leaning modern liberals and postmodern progressives of the radical left whose hopes for ongoing progress through cultural r/evolution become increasingly dwarfed.

The radicalization and widening chasm between the radical right and left holds the potential for new civil and international wars. This potential may be further fueled by the increasing number of frustrated males who can't meet the primary fantasies and other expectations of modern and postmodern women who could have a moderating and stabilizing effect on them, but whose expectations these men can no longer meet.[482]

Another negative effect of collapsing relationships and overall shrinking birth rates is the over-aging of societies, which produces more conservative voters and puts increasing strains on Social Security and healthcare systems that lay heavy financial burdens on younger, working generations and may soon become financially unsustainable.

The increasing number of singles has also a double negative effect on the environment. One effect is that they do not share resources like homes, appliances, utilities, vehicles, etc., in the way that couples and families do.[483] The other is that single males who want to be in a relationship need to compete financially with other males and females to be able to acquire the status symbols such as expensive cars and homes, and to pay for dates and travel, etc., in order to be attractive to the women they desire.

Finally, if we look at the global picture, we see that the populations of modern societies are beginning to shrink and, by 2100, may be half their current size, while countries in sub-Saharan Africa are projected to triple or quadruple in population by 2100, to three or even four billion.[484] This means that the shrinking and over-aging populations of modern and postmodern societies with declining economies must either economically support these young and exploding populations to provide them with local opportunities and to slow down their rates of reproduction through education and empowerment of women, or deal with unprecedented levels of migration and possible military aggression that holds the potential for further national and international conflicts.

To address these major interconnected challenges of anti-democratic movements, climate change/environmental destruction, over/under population, migrations, and civil wars/military conflicts that humanity is potentially facing, we need to dramatically increase co-creation and procreation between soulmates at modern and postmodern levels of development in Integral Relationships.

Purpose and application of the module

1. Learn why being in healthy Integral Love Relationships and having children matters beyond personal well-being.
2. Look at the benefits of sharing time, money, and sex in healthy love relationships.
3. Understand the importance of moving from social atomism to social holonism and from political liberalism to political relationalism.
4. Discuss the effects of population growth and over-aging societies on the future of humanity.
5. Map out your path to a healthy love relationship with your soulmate.

Time–money–sex

The three primary reasons why some people still want to be in a love relationship are, in the widest sense, time, money, and sex.

Time

We are social animals who crave and need human contact and physical exchange for our well-being. If deprived, our bodies feel stress and don't function optimally. Dopamine levels, which are vital for thinking and planning, drop and heightened levels of norepinephrine shut down immune functions and inhibit genes that lower inflammation.[485] It is important for couples to agree how to spend quality time together.

Money

Notwithstanding numerous age-old aphorisms insisting that money (alone) does not make us happy, recent research shows that people at higher income levels are more satisfied with life than people who are poor.[486] Hence, money (marrying up/sharing resources, etc.) is a natural sexual attractor and reason to be in a relationship. It is important for couples to share the same values and needs around money, as it is the number one reason for relationship conflicts, let alone the devastating fights over money during and after divorces.

Sex

We are sexual beings (otherwise we would not be here) and derive pleasure and many health benefits from having a healthy sex life.[487] Couples frequently report being happier with their sex lives than singles. It is therefore important to be in a relationship and for couples to share the same needs around their sexuality.

The three big reasons why people break up are … see above!

Exercises: Why relationships matter

The following are paired or group exercises.
1. Make the four agreements for confidentiality, responsibility, healthy boundaries, I-statements, and sharing, as outlined on page 556.

Exercise one: Time, money, sex

This is a paired exercise.
1. Share with your partner the roles that time, money, and sex play in your desire to be in a healthy love relationship?

2. How have these three primary reasons for relationships impacted who you were or are attracted to?
3. What conflicts have emerged in these three areas and how were they resolved?

Eight additonal reasons why relationships matter

Below are eight Ego-transcending reasons why being in a healthy love relationship matters not only for our own well-being and development, but also for that of others, society, and humanity.

1. They matter to our soulmate

There is overwhelming evidence that, in addition to exercise and a healthy diet, people who live their biological purpose in happy healthy long-term relationships enjoy greater physical health, emotional stability, sexual satisfaction, longevity (especially for men), financial stability, higher social status, and lowered stress hormones,[488] to name a few benefits.[489] Living and sharing our transcendental purpose provides many additional health benefits (see page 438) and makes modern and postmodern relationships sustainable.

Even if we may not be personally interested in all these benefits, it matters to our (potential) soulmate that we develop the openness and skills to be in a healthy love relationship.

2. They matter for future generations

Our existence is the result of billions of years of co-creation and procreation[490] by our ancestors that is driven by the co-creative life force, out of which our unique human capacities for ongoing learning, healing, growing, awakening, and creating more goodness, truth, beauty, and functioning emerged through the female sexual selection process. In our unconditioned nature or essence, we are the genetic and memetic[491] link between the past and the future through sharing our biological, transformational, and transcendental purpose with our soulmate.

We humans became the only known species that developed a separate sense of self or Ego and eventually the technology that allows us to mostly circumvent our natural or soul's purpose (oops). Thus, from a spiritual/soul perspective, it matters to future generations and to the future of humanity that we transcend our Ego to share our purpose with an equal and opposite partner.[492] Otherwise, we humans will be the next endangered species. As someone said, the question is not so much how to save humanity, but do we deserve to be saved?

3. They matter for the lifeworld and functioning systems

According to Jürgen Habermas, functioning societies consist of the *Lebenswelt* ("lifeworld" or "living environment") of couples, families, community, workplace, and voluntary organizations, out of which emerge impersonal and increasingly invisible social and political "systems" of power, money, and the media. The systems are intended to regulate the production and circulation of goods, services, and information, and, thus, to provide an integrating effect for communities who engage in rational ethical discourse to find consensus about their shared values and actions. Functioning societies depend on a fragile equilibrium between the lifeworld and the system.

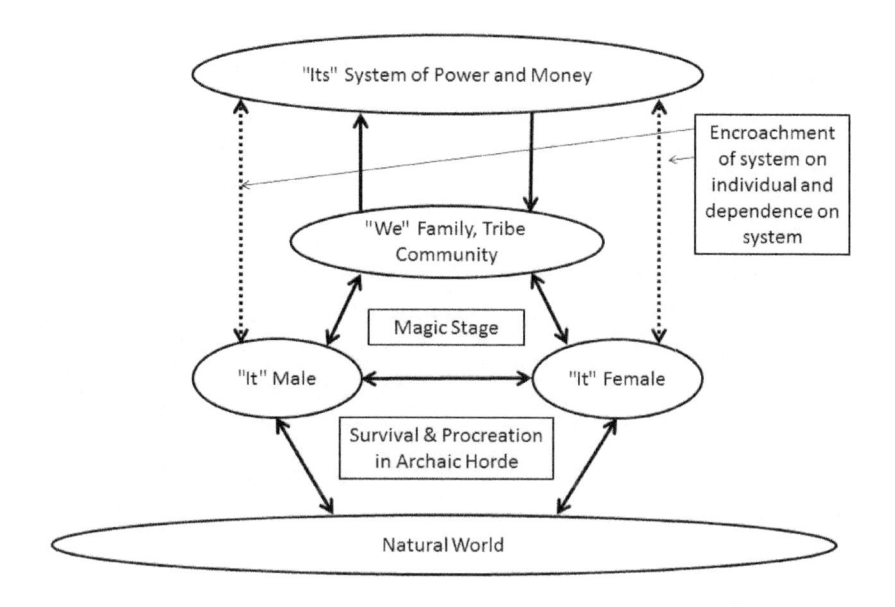

Figure 81: Natural world, lifeworld, and system

This equilibrium becomes out of balance when love relationships, families, and communities deteriorate because of liberal individualism; when individual freedoms become confronted with societal structures and order; and when the system—which is embedded in and depends on the lifeworld for its existence— encroaches upon, colonizes, displaces, and even destroys the lifeworld.

The resulting five "pathologies," according to Habermas, are as follows :

1. Decrease in shared meanings and mutual understandings.
2. Erosion of social bonds (disintegration of communities.)
3. Increase in people's feelings of helplessness and lack of belonging.
4. The consequent unwillingness of people to take responsibility for their actions and for social phenomena.

5. Destabilization and breakdown of social order and stability.

Similarly, in his 2021 book, *A World after Liberalism: Philosophers of the Radical Right*, Matthew Rose writes that right-leaning conservative anti-liberals recast liberalism's virtues of individualism into vices:

> In theory, liberalism protects individuals from unjust authority, allowing them to pursue fulfilling lives apart from government coercion. In reality, it severs deep bonds of belonging, leaving isolated individuals exposed to, and dependent on, the power of the state. In theory, liberalism proposes a neutral vision of human nature, cleansed of historical residues and free of ideological distortions. In reality, it promotes a bourgeois view of life, placing a higher value on acquisition than on virtue. In theory, liberalism makes politics more peaceful by focusing on the mundane rather than the metaphysical. In reality, it makes political life chaotic by splintering communities into rival factions and parties."

This view is echoed by Patrick Deneen in his 2018 book, *Why Liberalism Failed*, which elicited concurring responses from numerous reviewers and readers. As a review in *The Economist* observed, "Deneen does an impressive job of capturing the current mood of disillusionment and general worries about atomization and selfishness." Barak Obama endorsed Deneen's vision, writing, "Deneen offers cogent insights into the loss of meaning and community that many in the West feel, issues that liberal democracies ignore at their own peril." And David Brooks pointed out in the *New York Times*, "Deneen's book is valuable because it focuses on today's central issue. The important debates now are not about policy. They are about the basic values and structures of our social order."[493]

Because our socioeconomic and political systems depend on a functioning lifeworld that is created by couples, healthy nuclear families, and stable communities, the pathologies of liberalism, modernism, and postmodernism eventually give rise to instability and crises of the system itself. As Václav Havel wrote in *The Power of the Powerless*, "A better system will not automatically ensure a better life. In fact, the opposite is true: only by creating a better life can a better system be developed."

We already see the effects of social atomism and hyperindividualsim throughout the world in dysfunctional governments, impersonal shareholder-value-driven corporations, the growing military-industrial complex, increasingly unmanageable Social Security and healthcare systems, crumbling infrastructures, polarization in media outlets, the vulnerability of the internet and social media to misinformation and hackers. All of this led to the emergence of a new radical right whose views are summarized by Ezra Klein in an April 2022 *New York Times* opinion:

> Conservatives argue that our truest identities are rooted in the land in which we're born and the kin among whom we're raised. Our lives are given order and meaning because they are embedded in the larger structure and struggle of our people. Liberalism and, to some degree, Christianity have poisoned our cultural soil, setting us adrift in a world that prizes pleasure and derides tradition. We should celebrate the strength in cultural difference, reject the hollow universalist pieties of liberals and insist on the preservation of what sets people apart.[494]

Thus, healthy (Integral) relationships, functional families, and thriving communities matter if we want to move beyond the pathologies of intolerant, autocratic conservatism and hyperindividualistic liberalism, and avoid the breakdown of the system, or our total dependence on it, or the total control over us by moving towards holarchism (see below).

4. They matter for the environment and people's health

Population research in Western countries shows a rising number of singles living in one-person households who accelerate consumption, deplete resources, and degrade nature. Current studies show that solo-living consumes more land, energy, goods, and materials per person than living in shared housing.[495] The same is likely true for traveling, as couples share cars and rooms.

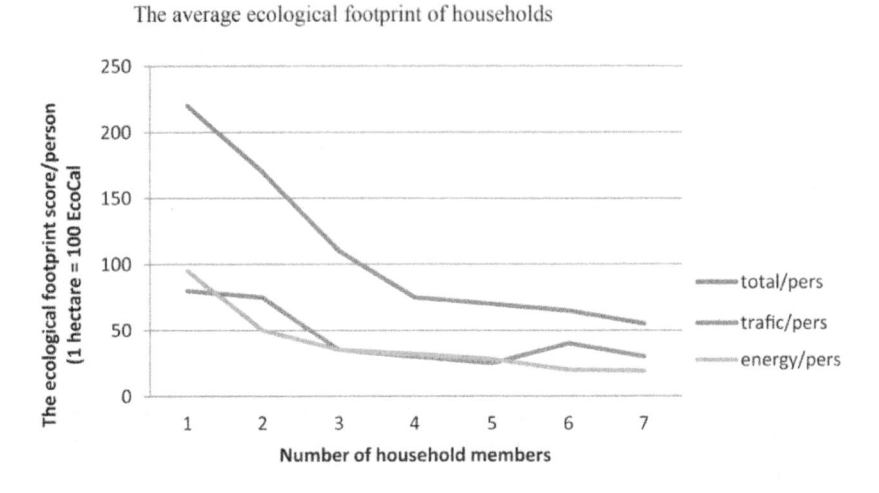

Figure 82: Ecological footprint of single versus family living

Couples are also less likely to smoke, drink, and eat junk food.[496] Thus, relationships matter for the environment and for our personal health.

5. They matter for sustainable populations and future generations

As we see in the images below, most countries now have, or are rapidly moving towards, fertility rates that are way below two children per woman; the exception for the next few decades is sub-Saharan Africa.

Total Fertility Rate 2022

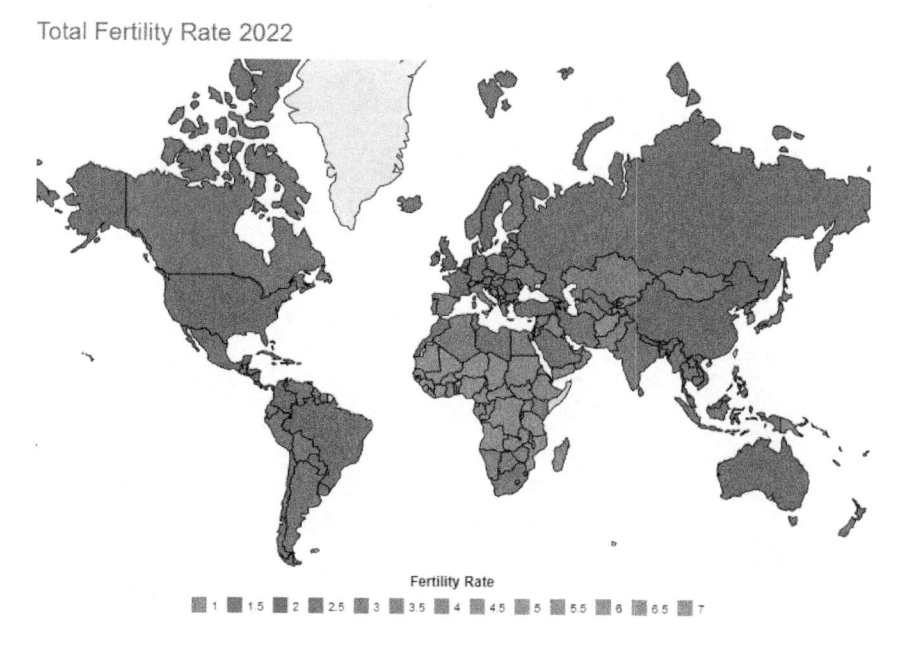

Figure 83: World fertility rate map

See the image above as an interactive map at tinyurl.com/irpm546[497]

See a country-by-country history and projection of fertility rates at tinyurl.com/irpm548[498]

Over-aging and shrinking societies, as shown below, lead to increasing instability and bankruptcy of social systems, economic decline, loneliness, and possible defenselessness against invading nations with younger populations and/or fascist autocratic or dictatorial leaders.

Integral Relationship Practice | 536

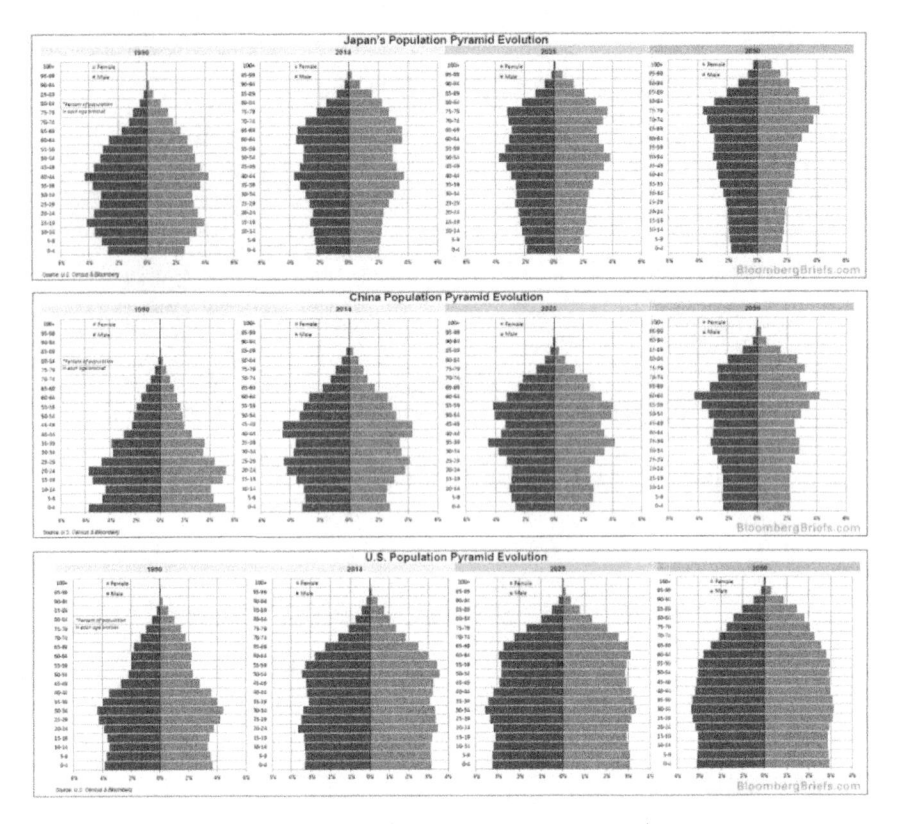

Figure 84: Japan, China, and US[499] populations age

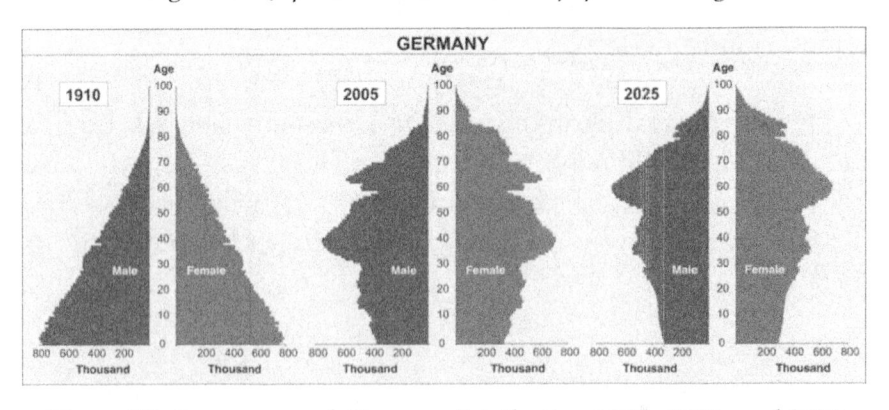

Figure 85: German population age distribution 1910, 2005, and 2025

In her 2022 book, *8 Billion and Counting: How Sex, Death, and Migration Shape Our World*, Jennifer D. Sciubba concludes that current population trends are unprecedented in human history and that nobody really knows what the effects will be. Countries with many working-age adults and few children and older people to take care of will potentially thrive economically during that demographic window but will eventually fall into recessions when these working people retire and there are not enough children to replace them. These societies then also become vulnerable to attacks by countries with younger and growing populations or to destabilization caused by an influx of immigrants with different value systems.

See a six-minute 2016 video about population growth at tinyurl.com/irpm549[500]
The creators of this video did not consider levels of consciousness development and estimated overly high birth rates for Europe.

Thus, co-creation and procreation matter so that there are enough younger people to sustain the economies and stability of societies, fuel Social Security systems, care for older people, and, if necessary, defend their countries.

6. They matter for cultural evolution

There is clear evidence that people at earlier levels of consciousness development procreate at much higher rates than people at later levels.[501] This now leads to a backward shift of the societal center of gravity towards earlier stages of consciousness development in many modern and postmodern societies, as they fail to support the children who are born into families at earlier levels to advance to later stages of consciousness. The decline of fertility rates at higher levels of consciousness development may also explain the reversal of the Flynn effect.[502]

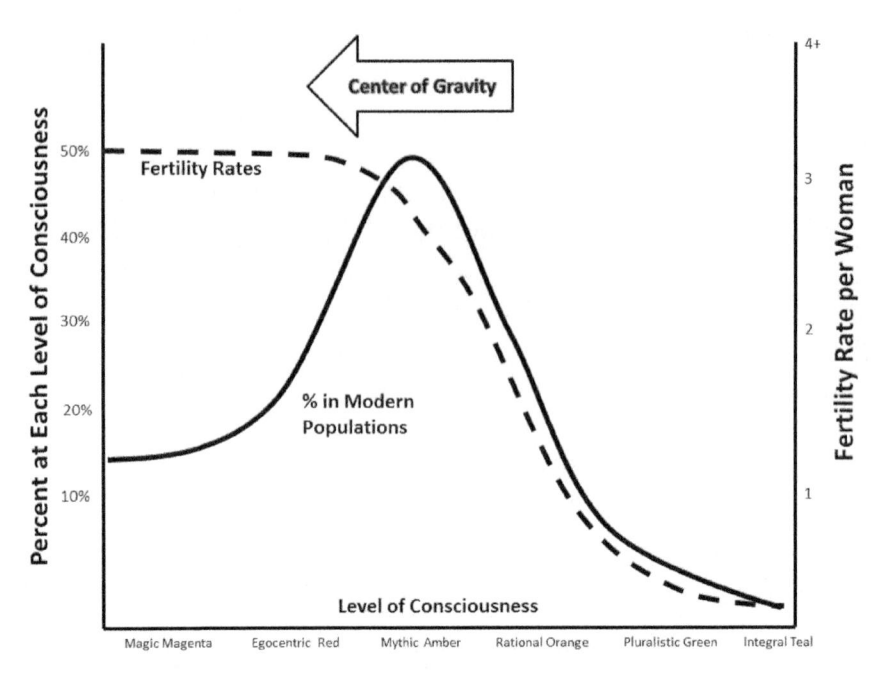

Figure 86: Fertility rates and overall decline in consciousness

Researchers in the US and Germany found that there is a strong negative correlation between societal secularism and both national-level fertility rates and individual-level fertility behavior. Rather than religious people at mythic levels and below becoming a smaller proportion of the world population, demographers project that because the religiously unaffiliated modern and postmodern members of societies have fewer children, they will make up a smaller proportion of the world population over time.[503]

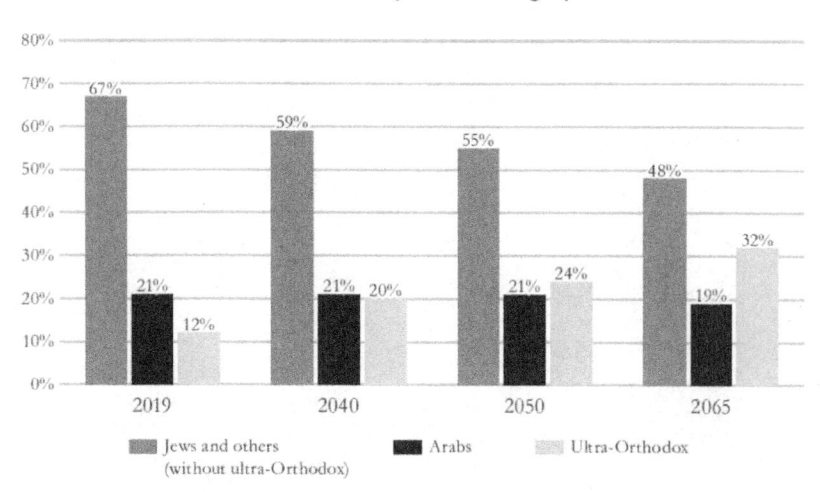

Israel's Projected Demographic Shift

Figure 87: Israel's projected demographic shift[504]

Thus, co-creation and procreation at later stages of consciousness development matter to shift the center of gravity beyond the limitations of the mythic, rational, and pluralistic stages towards a higher number of people at later stages of development.

7. They matter for communicative action

Traditionally, females had most rights and responsibilities in the domestic sphere, where they made feminine validity claims of care, compassion, relationships, and feelings to what is true, good, beautiful, and functional. Males had most rights and responsibilities in the public sphere and made masculine validity claims to rights, justice, autonomy, and rationality to guide and coordinate their actions in these four domains.

Integral Relationship Practice | 540

Figure 88: Female in domestic, and male in public sphere

As modern and postmodern females gain rights and responsibilities in the public sphere and males in the domestic sphere, it is essential that they both make feminine and masculine validity claims to coordinate their actions in both spheres.

Figure 89: Female and male in the domestic and public spheres

Thus, Integral Relationships matter to move towards gender equality in rights and responsibility through ethical discourse and communicative action in the domestic/private and public spheres.

8. They matter to counter social atomism

The misconception that humans are isolated, separate, self-interested, autonomous, and largely self-sufficient individual "social atoms," as suggested by modern liberalism, or products of cultural, social, or metaphysical (religious) "macro-systems," as suggested by premodern conservatism, instead of simultaneously whole and partial "holarchic" relational beings is the underlying cause for the many challenges in the private and public spheres that humanity is facing today and that are outlined above and in Module 23, on page 463.

To solve these wicked problems, we need to collectively advance to valuing and supporting couples and families over individuals in ways that transcend the traditional conservative, patriarchal family structures as promoted by the conservative radical right, the modern hyper-individualism as promoted by the liberal left, and the postmodern communalism as promoted by the progressive radical left—and move towards holarchism. This requires an understanding of holonic structures and the practice of Integral Relationships as outlined in this manual.

As mentioned above, holons are wholes that are parts for larger wholes who have their own unique properties. They are the foundation of all functional systems and societies. Balancing healthy feminine and masculine polarities are essential for individual holons (such as atoms, molecules, organs, and humans) and social holons (such as couples, families, communities, and societies) to maintain their simultaneous wholeness and partialness, as described in Module 11, page 183.

In the image below, we see that stacking social holons on top of individual holons is philosophically problematic because social holons are only relatively dependent on the lower, while individual holons are completely dependent on the lower for their existence. For example, we can have communities without families, but not organs without cells.

Integral Relationship Practice | 542

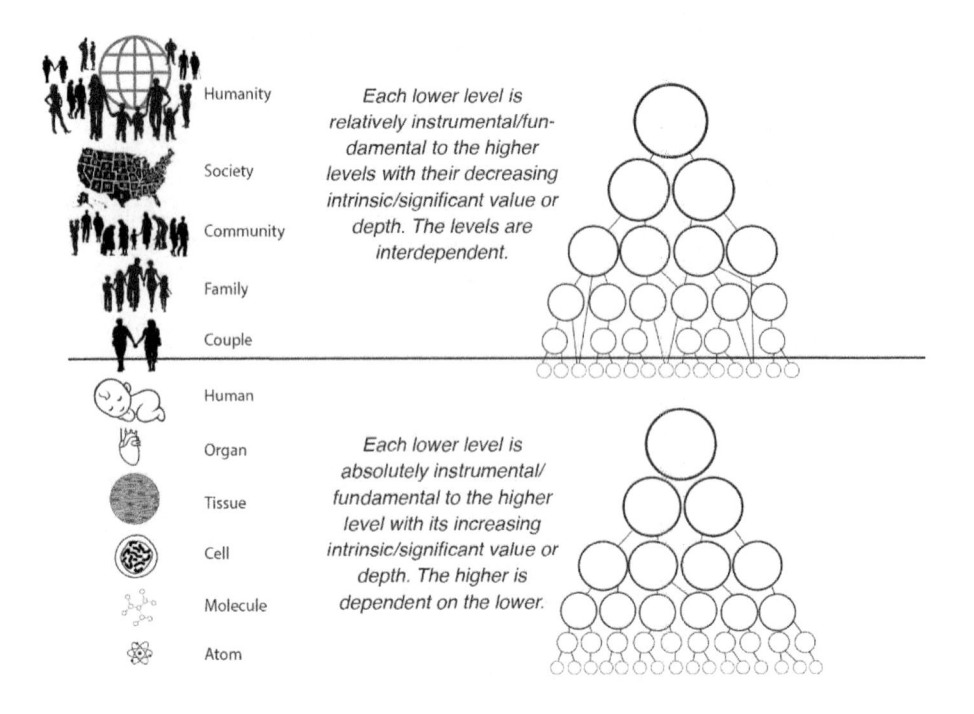

Figure 90: Individual and social holons

However, seen over time, functioning social holons also depend on the presence of the lower holons.[505] Denying this is the BIG fallacy.

The image below shows individual holons, from atoms to humans, and social holons, from couples to humanity, with their respective physical size, span (number), and depth, value, or love.

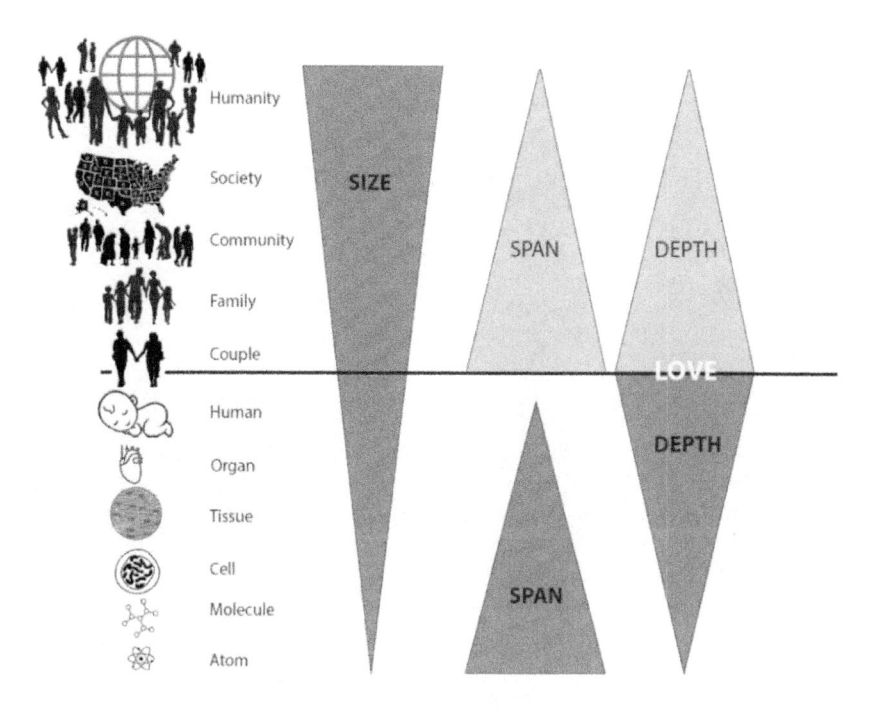

Figure 91: Size, depth, and span of individual and social holons

Until modernity emerged, humans gave the greatest value, depth, or love to co-creative and procreative couples, rather than to individuals, as shown above and below, as they were the foundation for nuclear families who were necessary for communities to flourish and survive. We still see this today in all religious traditions, with their creeds of "preach and breed."[503]

Integral Relationship Practice | 544

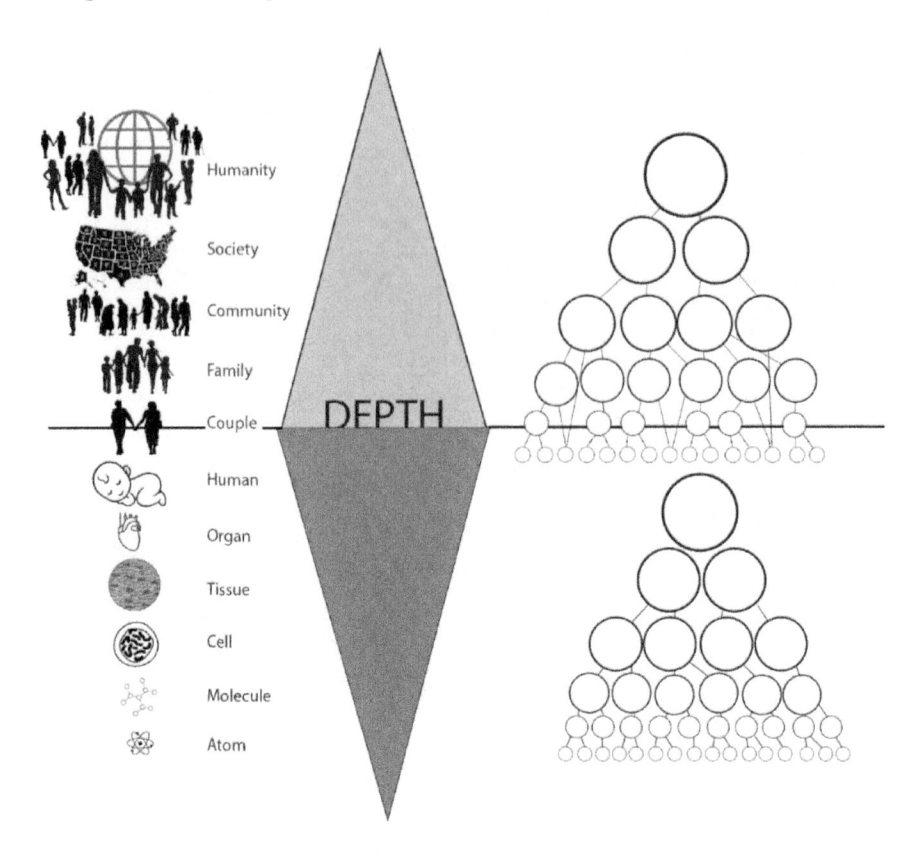

Figure 92: Holonic structure with highest depth given to couples

The image below shows collapsing holonic structures in modern and postmodern societies that focus on the individual instead of the couple, family, and community.

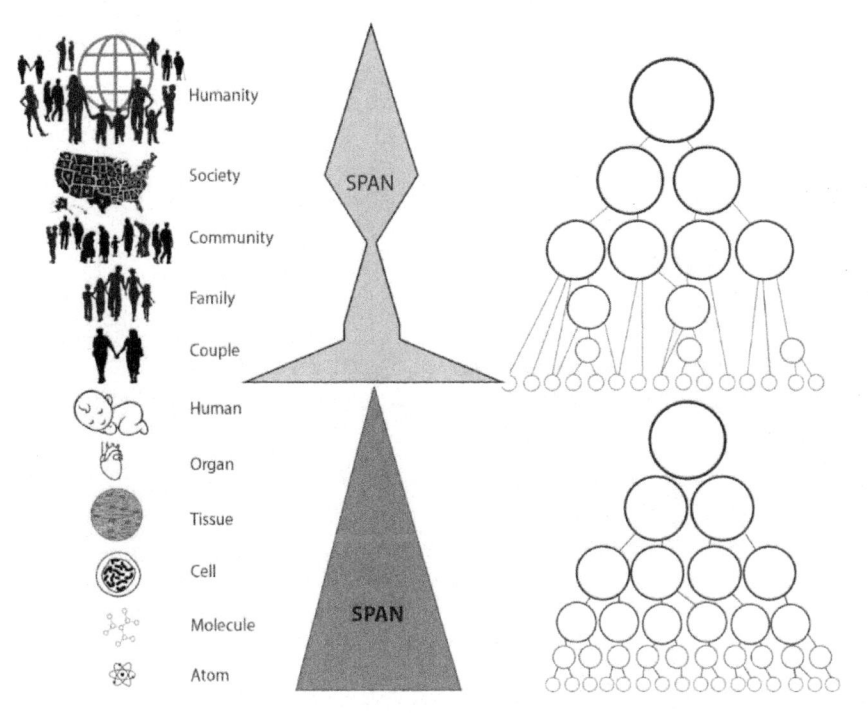

Figure 93: Collapsing social holons

Hence the importance of co-creation and procreation between couples in healthy Integral Relationships who form families and communities as the foundation for stable and sustainable societies and humanity, as shown in *Figure 91: Size, depth, and span of individual and social holons*, on page 543 above.

Exercise two: Why relationships matter

The following is a paired exercise.
Share with your partner which of the reasons why healthy love relationships matter resonate most with you and why?
1. Personal well-being, time, money, sex?
2. Serving your soulmate?
3. Passing on your genes and memes to future generations?
4. Stable sociopolitical and economic systems and protection from their encroachment?
5. Sharing resources and protecting the environment?

6. Preventing over-aging, collapsing, and defenseless societies?
7. Furthering cultural evolution instead of decline?
8. Practicing ethical discourse and communicative action in the domestic and public sphere?
9. Contributing to sustainable social holonic structures?

Exercise three: My path to an Integral Relationship

The following can be an individual or paired exercise.
Fill out the worksheet below and share your answers with your partner.

My Path to an Integral Soulmate Relationship

1. How would my soulmate, I, and the world benefit from being together? (Why do you want to be in a relationship?)

2. To me, a healthy soulmate relationship means:

3. What qualities do I want to develop to be attractive and ready for my soulmate?

4. What are possible inner and outer roadblocks, fears, and negative self-talk?

5. What is my Kosmic Address? (See personality matrix.)

6. What have I learned from my previous relationships and want to do different now?

7. What do I bring to a soulmate relationship? What do I look for in my soulmate?

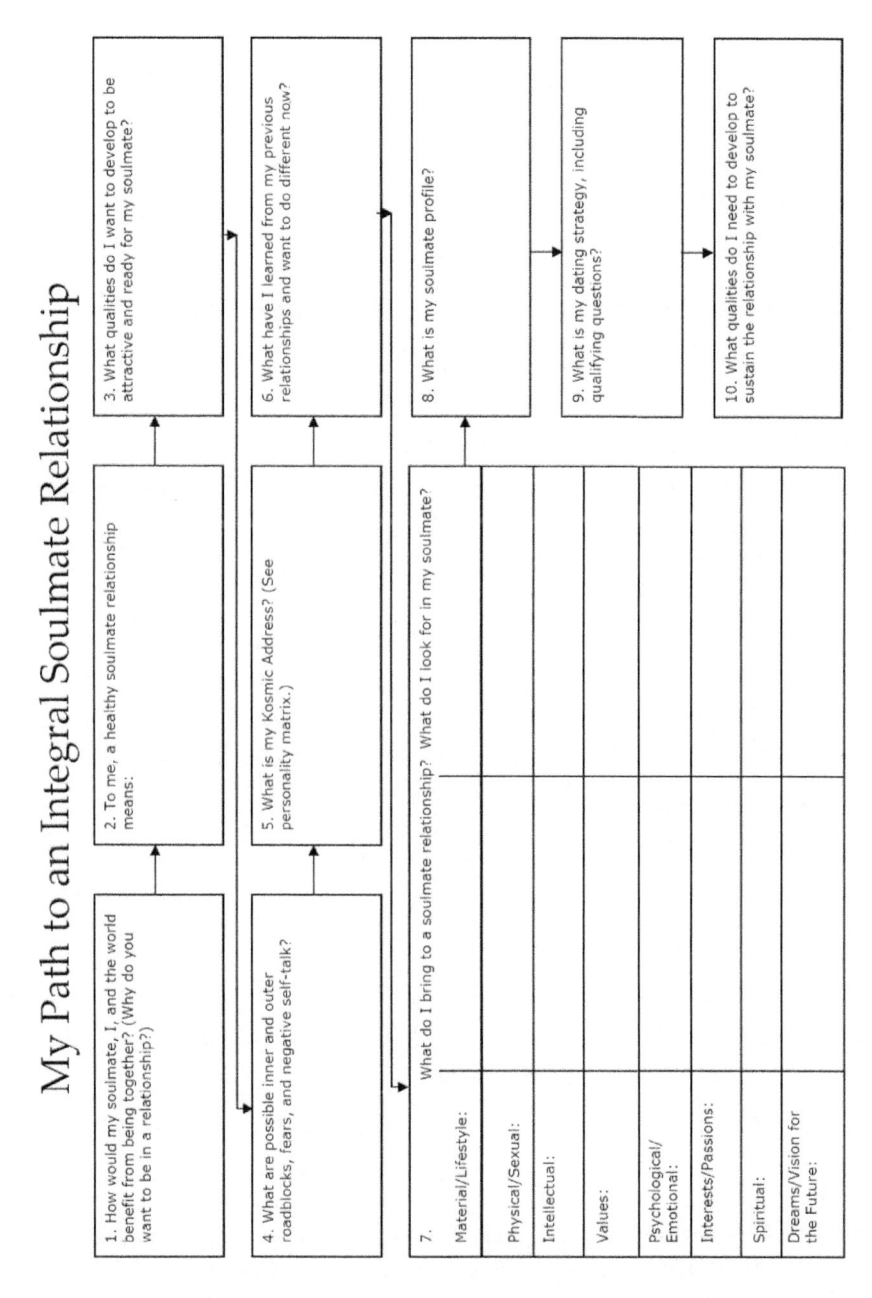

Material/Lifestyle:		
Physical/Sexual:		
Intellectual:		
Values:		
Psychological/Emotional:		
Interests/Passions:		
Spiritual:		
Dreams/Vision for the Future:		

8. What is my soulmate profile?

9. What is my dating strategy, including qualifying questions?

10. What qualities do I need to develop to sustain the relationship with my soulmate?

Table 25: My path to an Integral soulmate relationship

Download from tinyurl.com/irpm576[506]

Follow-up questions

1. How do you feel after exploring this module and doing the exercises?
2. What insights have you gained through these exercises?
3. What will be your next steps to find/attract your soulmate or advance your existing relationship?

Additional information and resources

All images and statistics from *Sex Purpose Love* are at tinyurl.com/irpm550[507]

The Couple: Intimate Relations in a New Key (2016) by Ferdinand Fellmann
tinyurl.com/irpm551[508]

Habermas: A Very Short Introduction (2005) by Gordon Finlayson
tinyurl.com/irpm552[509]

A World after Liberalism: Philosophers of the Radical Right (2021) by Matthew Rose
tinyurl.com/irpm554[510]

Why Liberalism Failed (2019) by Patrick J. Deneen
tinyurl.com/irpm558[511]

8 Billion and Counting: How Sex, Death, and Migration Shape Our World (2022) by Jennifer D. Sciubba
tinyurl.com/irpm563[512]

Dream Hoarders: How the American Upper Middle Class Is Leaving Everyone Else in the Dust, Why That Is a Problem, and What to Do about It (2017) by Richard Reeves tinyurl.com/irpm564[513]

Sex Purpose Love book reference

Page 403–508

Suggested movies:

Idiocracy (2006)

Watch this movie to see why co-creation and procreation in healthy Integral Love Relationships matter not only for our own well-being and development but even more for a peaceful and sustainable future for humanity.

The film tells the story of the two most average individuals in America, Joe Bauers (Luke Wilson), a US Army librarian, and prostitute Rita (Maya Rudolph). They are recruited to take part in a government hibernation experiment in the year 2005. Over the next five centuries, the most intelligent humans choose not to have children while the least intelligent reproduce indiscriminately, creating increasingly dumber generations. In 2505, Joe and Rita awaken in a dystopian Washington, D.C., now dumbed down by mass commercialism and mindless TV programming. Joe is eventually appointed Secretary of the Interior and later becomes the US president, after an IQ test identified him as the most intelligent person alive.

Unfortunately, we now see that this movie is not just a silly comedy but feels increasingly like a documentary, as it becomes a reality in front of our very eyes.

See the political, social, and ecological implications of the fact that people at postconventional levels of consciousness development procreate much less than people at earlier levels and how this may impact our future.[514]

Tomorrow Ever After (2016)

Watch this movie to see a reverse perspective from the dystopian world in the year 2505, as shown in *Idiocracy*. This touching micro-budget production holds up a mirror to our modern materialistic societies and fraught human relationships and suggests what we can do about it by furthering the Integral Relationship vision.

In the film, we see a historian from the year 2592 who time-traveled to 2015 New York. There, she has to navigate the societal woes that she had read about in history books as "The Great Despair," a horrible period filled with pain, exploitation, greed, pollution, and loneliness.

Throughout the story, she continues to act with the expectation that people will be good, caring, responsible, and helpful. In part, she is crushingly disappointed, and it keeps causing problems. In part, her expectation and her earnest, obvious intentions to do good cause some people around her to become more caring.[515]

Live Event Script
Hosting and facilitating Integral Relationship events

This section is for facilitators who want to host and lead live Integral Relationship groups, workshops, and trainings (events).

Goals of events

1. To create a safe, sacred environment and container for peak-state experiences through intimate and loving connections between the practitioners during the event.
2. To make participants welcome and comfortable.
3. To invite the participants to engage with each other before the event starts.
4. To provide value for participants through understanding and experiencing the Integral Relationship model by using the exercises and practices.
5. To ask for feedback from the participants, including testimonials and videos.
6. To build a database and generate referrals for future events and consultations.
7. To invite participants back to attend future events and consultations.

Marketing

1. Write your professional facilitator bio.
2. Use the module descriptions below with images from tinyurl.com/irpm405[516] or create your own images (for example, with Canva www.canva.com).
3. Add your photos and videos.
4. Mention date, time, duration, location (Google Maps), cost, sign-up information, and contact information for those who have questions.

Answer the following questions about your event in your offers:
1. What problem does joining the event solve for me?
2. What is it about?
3. Who is it for?
4. What do I gain/learn?
5. How will this improve my life?
6. How will it make me feel better?
7. Why should I join?
8. How is this different from similar events?
9. What is unique about this offer?
10. When and where is it (date, times, map, pictures of event location, etc.)?
11. How much does it cost?
12. Are there discounts (early bird, bring a person for free, group discount, work exchange, scholarships, etc.)?
13. When and how do I pay?
14. Who offers it and what is his/her/their credibility/competence?
15. What will we do? Theory, practice, etc.?
16. Do I get a certificate?
17. How many people will attend?
18. What kind of people will I meet there?
19. What is the gender balance?
20. What is the age distribution of the group?
21. Can I bring a friend or partner?
22. How do I join?
23. Where can I learn more?
24. Who answers my questions? How do I make contact?
25. What will happen after the event?

Where to promote your events:
1. Websites (your own and local event websites).
2. Facebook (run targeted ads and write personal messages with invitations to your FB friends).

3. Instagram (run targeted ads and write personal messages with invitations to your IG friends).
4. LinkedIn.
5. Twitter.
6. Meetup.com (can be quite effective, even for online events).
7. Eventbrite.
8. Email newsletter (build your database by asking people on social media to share their email address with you; send them a thank-you gift (e.g., the first chapters of the Integral Relationships books or your own books).
9. WhatsApp Group (collect phone numbers from participants on sign-up sheet).
10. Flyer.
11. YouTube videos about the event.
12. TicTok videos.
13. Magazine advertisements.

Event logistics and structure

1. Welcome table.
2. Business cards with holder.
3. Sign-up sheet on clipboard.[517]
4. Name tags with strings; paper for name tags; colored markers for name tags.
5. Bowl or basket for money, with a sign for the fee (e.g., $20) and some bills in the basket for change.
6. Pens and pencils (in a little bucket or glass).
7. Post-it Notes.
8. Chairs, Back Jacks, pillows, blankets.
9. Incense, candles, flowers, plants.
10. Whiteboard or flipchart, with markers.
11. Powered (Bluetooth) speakers for music.
12. Printouts of the worksheets for participants and facilitator (see link and barcode in page 565).
13. Printouts of Kosmic Address and Path to Healthy Relationship.

14. Affirmation sheet for love circle facilitator (see Preliminary Practice Module below).
15. Folder with the 14 dimensions and your website printed on the cover.
16. Bell/chime/singing bowl, clock, kitchen timer, raisins in a bowl.
17. Little puppet to demonstrate identification and disidentification (versus splitting off, repressing, denying, avoiding, bypassing, etc.).
18. Beanie Baby or talking stick to pass around when participants are sharing.
19. Socks for sock game (see Preliminary Practice Module below).
20. Props for exercises, as required (for example, hula hoops or colored hats).
21. Box with tissues.
22. Books for sale, with price sheets.
23. Water pitcher; beverages (tea, coffee); snacks (fruits, cookies, pretzels, nuts, etc.) paper towels; napkins; glasses; cups; plates.
24. If you use a PowerPoint presentation: computer, cable, projector, remote, screen, wireless clicker/laser pointer, power strip/extension cord, as needed.

Set up the event room

1. Prepare and print the handouts (worksheets for practitioners; facilitator sheets).
2. Set up the event room with chairs, Back Jacks, pillows, blankets, etc.
3. Prepare the registration desk.
4. Charge speaker and phone/MP-3 player, as needed.
5. Set up the facilitator area with a candle; books; bells/singing bowls; pillows; Bluetooth speaker; cable to connect MP-3 player; worksheets in multi-folder; Beanie Baby/puppet; raisins in a bowl; chestnut or acorn.
6. Prepare name tags.
7. Prepare dishes, beverages, and snacks.

8. Put tissue box in the event room.
9. Set up www.menti.com and write the code on the whiteboard.
10. Write the following questions on the whiteboard or flipchart:
    - What attracted you to this group/event?
    - What would you like to learn/attain?
    - What challenges do you face?
    - What questions do you have?
11. Send out WhatsApp and Meetup reminders.
12. Light incense and candles before practitioners arrive.
13. Play music when first participants arrive (for example, "Songs for the Inner Lover" or "Satsang," by Miten and Deva Premal).
14. Make sure the event phone is set on vibrate and is available before and during the event.

Welcome, registration, warm-up questions, and social time

1. Welcome participants.
2. Help with storing coats, shoes, bags, etc.
3. Point out bathroom and smoking area.
4. Collect the event fee as participants arrive (no payment after the event.)
5. Have participants enter name, email, and phone number on sign-up sheet.
6. Ask participants to write on their name tag, maybe with some ornaments or emojis (heart, smiley face, etc.).
7. Hand out Post-it Notes and the sheet with Personality Matrix and Path to a Healthy Relationship on the back.
8. Seat participants in the event room.
9. Facilitator should stay in the event room with the participants in order to facilitate the pre-event activities. It is important to engage the participants.
10. Ask participants to answer the four questions on the whiteboard by writing their answers on the Post-it Note and then handing them to you. You may answer the questions

during the event and enter them into a spreadsheet afterwards for analysis and answering the questions online.
11. Ask participants to pair up; distribute the sheet containing the four dimensions of being and related questions (see page 36); and ask the paired participants to give the answers to each other.

Event opening and agreements

1. Welcome the participants.
2. Ask participants to turn off their cell phones and put them away (no looking at messages/texting, etc.).
3. Inform participants about bathrooms, breaks, and other logistics.
4. Make the following four agreements to create a safe container for all participants to be open and vulnerable, and for you to be protected as a group facilitator:
- One: Participants may share about the exercises and their own experience, but not about what they learn about others.
- Two: Participants are responsible for their own level of participation, boundaries, and emotional reactions. Unless you are a licensed therapist or other helping professional, mention that you are not a clinician, that this is not a therapy group, and that you don't offer therapy. Encourage participants to give themselves the gift of a follow-up with a mental health or other professional if they experience any deep emotional or other form of disturbance.
- Three: When sharing, participants are asked to make "I-statements"—to speak about their own personal experience and feelings and to refrain from talking about others; sharing third-party "book" knowledge; making generalizations (such as, "all men/women/people, etc. are"); giving advice to others; and engaging in crosstalk or one-on-one discussions.
- Four: Participants are encouraged to signal to the group in a non-verbal way what they feel or want to express, by making the heart sign; placing their hands on their heart; bowing a

Namaste; or giving a thumbs-up, etc., in a kind and respectful way.
5. Ask for a show of hands that everybody agrees.
6. Strictly enforce these agreements by intervening when they are violated; otherwise, you may lose control of the group.
7. Instruct participants that if someone cries, it is important to leave them in their process until they ask for help (tissue, touch, hug, etc.). You, as the facilitator, may be the only one to intervene if participants are clearly in distress and need to be taken out of their process to avoid catharsis or re-traumatization.
8. Invite participants to briefly share their name, where they live, and what they do for a living (unless you facilitate a workshop or event that includes Module 1, in which they will be introduced to the group). They may pass around a talking stick or Beanie Baby as they speak.
9. Ask participants to share if they have any physical or other limitations that may prevent them from participating fully.
10. Explain (with follow-up practice) that when you say "Pass the Shush or Sushi," everyone will make a "shhhh" sound (especially important for Module 1.)
11. Bring practitioners up to date on the modules that you previously covered, especially Module 1: Four Dimensions of Being and Relating. Explain how the four dimensions enter into intimate contact and need to be balanced and harmonized for a healthy love relationship to flourish.
12. Also briefly explain the eight levels of consciousness development—from archaic, to magic, egocentric, mythic, rational, pluralistic, integral, and transpersonal.
13. Give a preview of the upcoming modules that you have not yet covered.
14. Introduce the exercise for the current event (provide as much theory as necessary and as little as possible.)
15. Give examples from your own life and/or demonstrate the exercise.

16. Ask if there are any questions before you start.
17. Remind participants about silencing their cell phones and ask that phones be put away.
18. Put your own phone on vibrate or mute.
19. Facilitate the module.
20. Take photos during the event.
21. Invite shares and questions at the end of the exercises.

End of Event

1. Describe future event(s) and invite participants to attend.
2. Facilitate the closing circle, inviting people to form a very tight circle by taking small steps forward.
3. Invite participants to look around and silently, through eye contact, acknowledge others with whom they connected and those who held space for the group.
4. Ask participants to share one word describing how they feel (besides hungry and tired) and/or what they are grateful for.
5. Invite people to put their left hand into the circle and halfway close their hands, so that a "vortex" is created (see picture below.)
6. Explain that this vortex is a symbol to show that we are always partial in our relationships (partner, family, community, society, country, humanity, galaxy, universe) while already whole (as our whole hands).
7. Invite participants to lift up their thumbs and see that they are all human thumbs (representing our sameness in our soul-needs and being-needs, e.g., for love and connection) while also looking slightly different (representing our individuality, dreams, desires, sexual preferences, particular individuals we are attracted to, etc.
8. Conclude by asking participants to lift up their hands at the count of three and, if they like, to share some hugs.

Figure 94: Closing circle with touching hands and thumbs up

After Event

1. Take group photos.
2. Offer books for sale.
3. Ask participants if they would be willing to give a short video testimonial (use a lavalier microphone, if possible, for better sound, e.g., Rhode smartLav+ tinyurl.com/irpm97)[518]
4. Ask participants to write a testimonial into a "Love Notes" book.
5. Ask participants to return their name tags and pens.
6. Ensure a neat closure of the event area (participants may return Back Jacks, pillows, chairs, blankets, dishes, etc.)
7. Collect leftover folders and handouts and restore or file them.
8. Enter sign-up sheet entries into database, e.g., Zoho.
9. Follow up with participants by phone, email, WhatsApp, or social media.
10. Enter filled-out Post-it Notes into an Excel sheet for analysis and future reference.

11. Answer Post-it Note questions in your social media, WhatsApp groups, and/or emails.

Afterword

Every reader finds himself. The writer's work is merely a kind of optical instrument that makes it possible for the reader to discern what, without this book, he would perhaps never have seen in himself.
~ Marcel Proust ~

As I finish this book, I am almost 65 years old and am looking back at a fulfilled life. I grew up in post–WWII Germany with my younger sister and brother in a traditional family. My parents were happily married for almost 50 years until my father passed away in 2006. I still talk to my 89-year-old mother every week and she never forgets to mention how grateful she is towards my dad for everything he did for her and our family.

In my youth, I spent a lot of time in the little rural village where my mother grew up. There, her parents and her younger brother and his wife ran the local inn, where many social events took place. My experiences of seeing multigenerational families working together on their farms and in their small businesses, and creating a flourishing local community with a church, kindergarten, school, soccer club, and choir had a deep impact on me, as did my parent's happy marriage. It showed me the importance of families and communities living and working together to lead happy, flourishing lives.

My big passion as a young man was making music. After I finished my schooling, I began playing keyboards in several bands, and later, in 1979, after returning from a six-month gig in Louisiana, I opened a music store in Germany. During that time, I married my first wife, and we had a daughter together. After our divorce in 1986, I met my second wife, and in 1995 we moved with our two daughters to Santa Rosa, CA, where our third daughter was born in 1997. My daughters are now all leaving their mark in the world — as schoolteacher, family physician, caretaker, and management consultant.

My second wife and I divorced after I met Eckhart Tolle in 2000 and wanted a deeper relationship than she was interested in and available for.

This was when my second "education" in relationships began, as my German role-models and two marriages did not prepare me at all for the demands of the postmodern, Northern Californian, New-Age women I was dating. To meet their expectations and sense of entitlement, I immersed myself in relationship books and engaged in all kinds of personal development groups, workshops, and practices that my lovers suggested to me.

Alas, despite their well-meaning and generous support, and despite my best efforts to accommodate the women I dated, there remained a deep cultural divide between my vision for a deeply committed marriage with a shared "higher purpose" to make the world a better place by leading a virtuous lifestyle, and their often more hedonistic, individualistic, and materialistic desires that did not resonate with me and that I could not fulfill, sometimes for financial and sometimes for ethical reasons. And I was not alone; many men that I talked with seemed challenged by the expectations of women who, in turn, often felt that there were no good men out there.

I developed a deep sense that my own inability and that of many others in my community to co-create healthy sustainable love relationships, and the unwillingness of younger people to have children, would soon have a negative impact on our own lives, our community, and, eventually, American society and the world at large.

This was when I was introduced to the work of Ken Wilber by my friend and fellow soulmate searcher, Liza, to whom this book is dedicated. Wilber's work allowed me to integrate my relationship experiences as a divorced father with the wisdom from the relationship teachings that I had studied—culminating in my first two books, *Integral Relationships: A Manual for Men*, and *Sex Purpose Love: Integral Couples Creating a Better World*. Out of these two books, which were generously endorsed by Ken Wilber and others, emerged the international integral relationship workshops and trainings on which the practices in this new book are based.

My hope is that the information and exercises contained in *Integral Relationship Practice* reach all singles and couples who are interested in co-creating healthy love relationships and those who want to support them as role models and teachers.

My ultimate dream is that the Integral Relationship vision will inspire the emergence of new forms of functional nuclear families and thriving communities—from the bottom up—which will create institutional, governmental, business, and nonprofit organizations that provide financial support, tax incentives, and educational and employment opportunities that would not be equally available to adults who decide to stay single and childless.

As harsh as this may sound to hyperindividualistic liberals of the radical left, I see this bottom-up approach as the only solution for progressing towards a sustainable and peaceful future for humans around the world at any level of consciousness development.

Thank you for helping to make this vision of a peaceful and sustainable future that is co-created by couples with children a reality by sharing this book and the information and practices that are contained in it with everyone you know.

Please contact me at martin@integralrelationship.com if I can be of any support to you as an Integral Relationship practitioner, helping professional, or group facilitator to make this vision a reality.

Appendix I
Links, updates, and resources

The links and references provided throughout the book, especially in the endnotes, were correct at time of printing.

For clickable links, images in the book, worksheets, updates, corrections, errata, additional resources, etc., visit www.integralrelationship.com/irp or scan the QR code below.

For a list with all URL's in this book, visit integralrelationship.com/irpurls or scan the QR code below.

Endnotes

[1] www.hai.org

[2] tinyurl.com/irpm567
www.nydailynews.com/opinion/ny-oped-mass-shootings-are-inseparable-from-our-boy-crisis-20220606-3v27opdsfffwvde5eni6usn32y-story.html

[3] Hannah Arendt writes in *The Origins of Totalitarianism*:

"What we call isolation in the political sphere, is called loneliness in the sphere of social intercourse. Isolation and loneliness are not the same .... While isolation concerns only the political realm of life, loneliness concerns life as a whole. Totalitarian government, like all tyrannies, certainly could not exist without destroying the public realm of life, that is, without destroying, by isolating men, their political capacities. But totalitarian domination as a form of government is not content with this isolation and destroys private life as well. It bases itself on loneliness, on the experience of not belonging to the world at all, which is the most radical and desperate experiences of man"

[4] MIT's Sherry Turkle reminds us in her book, *Alone Together: Why We Expect More from Technology and Less from Each Other*, that the root of the word "community" means literally "to give among each other" and argues that such a practice requires "physical proximity" and "shared responsibilities."

[5] McIntosh offers us a four-point thesis:

1. The only way to overcome cultural and political hyperpolarization is to grow out of it by becoming a more mature society. Polarization is pressing us to evolve or face further regression.

2. The growth we need can be achieved by increasing our collective cultural intelligence, which involves the practice of appreciating and affirming the values of the worldviews we oppose.

3. Affirming the values of America's three major worldviews—modernism, traditionalism, and progressivism—entails continuously distinguishing the positives from the negatives of each worldview.

4. As we come to see how these three major worldviews are interdependent parts of our overall cultural ecosystem, this restores our faith in progress and points to a new American Dream of cultivating cultural evolution on every front of its development.

www.stevemcintosh.com/books/developmental-politics/

[6] Ken Wilber (1949—) wrote that both books are fully grounded in Integral Theory of human growth and potentials and that they add new, interesting, and relevant material to it to provide a truly up-to-date overview of today's relationships and how to make them work from the very highest potentials possible.

[7] You can find all descriptions with an image at https://integralrelationship.com/ir-modules/

[8] Available for download at www.integralrelationship.com/irp. See Appendix I for details.

[9] A priori, Latin for "from the former," is traditionally contrasted with a posteriori. The term usually describes lines of reasoning or arguments that proceed from the general to the particular, or from causes to effects. Whereas a posteriori knowledge is knowledge based solely on experience or personal observation, a priori knowledge is knowledge that comes from the power of reasoning based on self-evident truths. From tinyurl.com/irpm590
www.merriam-webster.com/dictionary/a%20priori

[10] See the application of The NeuroAffective Relational Model (NARM) by Laurence Heller, PhD, and Aline LaPierre, PsyD, that we use in Modules 2, 3, and 19 to heal these wounds.

[11] A group of hormones are nicknamed the "feel-good," "love-and-cuddle hormones" because of the happy and sometimes euphoric feelings they produce.

www.health.harvard.edu/mind-and-mood/feel-good-hormones-how-they-affect-your-mind-mood-and-body

[12] See tinyurl.com/irpm593
www.sightonstress.com/the-power-of-eye-contact-a-free-and-easy-stress-reducer/

[13] www.youtube.com/watch?v=VTep0hla1L0

[14] www.youtube.com/watch?v=ZPtT3p8T6Cg

[15] www.youtube.com/watch?v=jMxlPS9aK7o

[16] www.youtube.com/watch?v=YsDF3e6XdRE or, www.allmusic.com/album/northern-seascape-mw0000046855

[17] https://drive.google.com/drive/folders/1krXcl712kEOu7hXfXbRn8eIHQ4ci7xAt

[18] www.amazon.com/Power-Now-Guide-Spiritual-Enlightenment/dp/1577314808/

[19] An Integral Life Practice includes exercises for the body, mind, spirit/soul, and shadow work, and also covers ethics, sexuality, work, emotions, and relationships.

See the book *Integral Life Practice: A 21st-Century Blueprint for Physical Health, Emotional Balance, Mental Clarity, and Spiritual Awakening* (2008) by Terry Patten, Ken Wilber, Adam Leonard, and Marco Morelli.

[20] Download from Google drive tinyurl.com/irpm587 https://drive.google.com/drive/folders/1krXcl712kEOu7hXfXbRn8eIHQ4ci7xAt

[21] Humanists stand for the building of a more humane, just, compassionate, and democratic society, using a pragmatic ethics based on human reason, experience, and reliable knowledge—an ethics that judges the consequences of human actions by the well-being of all life on Earth. https://americanhumanist.org/what-is-humanism/definition-of-humanism/

[22] Jürgen Habermas (1929—) is a German philosopher and sociologist in the tradition of critical theory and pragmatism. His work addresses communicative rationality and the public sphere. tinyurl.com/irpm589 https://en.wikipedia.org/wiki/J%C3%BCrgen_Habermas

[23] Wilber and, subsequently, I drew heavily from the work of Habermas, even though, unlike Wilber, I resonate with Habermas that there is no directionality and no progressive, strongly teleological realization of an ideal goal in the evolution of individual consciousness and societies. As we will see later, I relate evolution to a "non-intelligent" co-creative and procreative impulse, life force (NARM), "will to live" (Schopenhauer), or will to power to realize our full human potentials (Nietzsche), the sexual selection process, procreation, and the behaviors that females reward in males.

From https://iep.utm.edu/habermas/:

Moreover, while Habermas speaks of evolution, he uses the term differently than nineteenth-century philosophies of history (Hegel, Marx, Spencer) or later Darwinian accounts. His "social evolution" is neither a merely path-dependent accumulative directionality nor a progressive, strongly teleological realization of an ideal goal. Instead, he envisions a society's latent potentials as tending to unfold according to an immanent developmental logic, similar to the developmental logic that cognitive-developmental psychologists claim maturing people normally follow. Lastly, Habermas' theory of social evolution avoids worries about determinism by distinguishing between the logic and the mechanisms of development, such that evolution is neither inevitable, linear, irreversible, nor continuous.

For Habermas, the slow social learning in history is the sedimentation of iterated processes of individual learning that accumulates in social institutions. While there is no unified macro-subject that learns, social evolution is also not mere happenstance plus inertia. It is the indirect outcome of individual learning processes, and such processes unfold with a developmental logic or deep structure of learning: "the fundamental mechanism for social evolution in general is to be found in an automatic inability not to learn. Not learning but not-learning is the phenomenon that calls for explanation." Habermas posits a universal developmental logic that tends to guide individual learning and maturation in technical-instrumental and moral-practical knowledge.

He discerns this logic in the complementary research of Jean Piaget in cognitive development and Lawrence Kohlberg in the development of moral judgment. As social and individual learning are linked, such underlying logic has slowly created homologies—similarities in sequence and form—between: (1) individual ego-development and group identity, (2) individual ego-development and world-perspectives, and (3) the individual ego-development of moral judgment and the structures of law and morality. Habermas pays more attention to the last homology and later writings focus on Kohlberg, so it is instructive to focus there.

Kohlberg's research on how children typically develop moral judgment yielded a schema of three levels (preconventional, conventional, and postconventional) and six stages (punishment-obedience, instrumental-hedonism/relativism (what is in it for me), interpersonal accord and conformity "good-boy-nice-girl," authority legalistic law-and-order, social contract, universal ethical principles). Two stages correspond to each level. Habermas follows Kohlberg's three levels in claiming we can retrospectively discern preconventional, conventional, and postconventional phases through which societies have historically developed. Just as normal individuals who progress from child to adult advance through levels in which different types of reasons are taken to be acceptable for action and judgment, so too can we retrospectively look at the development of social integration mechanisms in societies as having been achieved in progressive phases in which legal and moral institutions were structured by underlying organizational principles.

Habermas slightly diverges from the six stages of Kohlberg's schema by proposing a schema of neolithic societies, archaic civilizations, developed civilizations, and early modern societies. Neolithic societies organized interaction via kinship and mythical worldviews. They also resolved conflicts via feuds, appealing to an authority to mediate disputes in a preconventional way to restore the status quo. Archaic civilizations organized interaction via hierarchies beyond kinship and tailored mythical worldviews backing such hierarchies. Conflicts started to be resolved via mediation, appealing to an authority relying on more abstract ideas of justice—punishment instead of retaliation, assessment of intentions, and so forth. Developed civilizations still organized interaction conventionally but adopted a rationalized worldview with postconventional moral elements. This allowed conflicts to be mediated by a type of law that, while rooted in a community's (conventional) moral framework, was separable from the authority administering it. Finally, with early modern societies, we find that certain domains of interaction are postconventionally structured. Moreover, a sharper divide between morality and legality emerges, such that conflicts can be legally regulated without presupposing shared morality or needing to rely on the cohering force of mythical worldviews backing hierarchies.

[24] The book, *Metatheory for the 21st Century*, edited by Roy Bhaskar, Sean Esbjörn-Hargens, Nicholas Hedlund, and Mervyn Hartwig, examines the points of connection and divergence between critical realism and integral theory, arguably two of the most comprehensive and sophisticated contemporary metatheories. It covers topics such as (1) "Beyond Nature and Humanity: Reflections on the Emergence and Purposes of Metatheories" by Zachary Stein; (2) "Healing the Half-World: The Emancipatory Potential of Meta-Level Social Science" by Mark G.

Edwards; (3) "Developing a Complex Integral Realism for Global Response: Three Meta-Frameworks for Knowledge Integration and Coordinated Action" by Sean Esbjörn-Hargens; (4) "Towards a Complex, Integral Realism" by Paul Marshal; (5) "Rethinking the Intellectual Resources for Addressing Complex 21st-Century Challenges: Towards a Critical Realist Integral Theory" by Nicholas Hedlund; (6) "After Integral Gets Real: On Meta-Critical Chiasma of CR and IT" by Michael Schwartz; (7) "Why I'm a Critical Realist" by Mervyn Hartwig; and (8) "Contributions of Embodied Philosophy to Ontological Questions in Critical Realism and Integral Theory" by Tom Murray.

tinyurl.com/irpm594

www.routledge.com/Metatheory-for-the-Twenty-First-Century-Critical-Realism-and-Integral-Theory/Bhaskar-Esbjorn-Hargens-Hedlund-Hartwig/p/book/9780415820479

[25] Hanzi Freinacht is a made-up character invented by two people—Emil Ejner Friis, a Danish philosopher and activist in the Danish Alternative Party, and Daniel Gortz, a PhD student in sociology at Lund University in Sweden.

tinyurl.com/irpm596

www.philosophyforlife.org/blog/on-metamodernism-and-the-listening-society

[26] www.stevemcintosh.com/

[27] tinyurl.com/irpm597 https://en.wikipedia.org/wiki/Clare_W._Graves

[28] A 1946 telegram that was signed by the Emergency Committee of Atomic Scientists, with Albert Einstein as chairman, read as follows:

"Our world faces a crisis as yet unperceived by those possessing power to make great decisions for good or evil. The unleashed power of the atom has changed everything save our modes of thinking and we thus drift toward unparalleled catastrophe. We scientists who released this immense power have an overwhelming responsibility in this world life-and-death struggle to harness the atom for the benefit of mankind and not for humanity's destruction. We need two hundred thousand dollars at once for a nation-wide campaign to let people know that a new type of thinking is essential if mankind is to survive and move toward higher levels. This appeal is sent to you only after long consideration of the immense crisis we face. ... We ask your help at this fateful moment as a sign that we scientists do not stand alone."

(Source: "Atomic Education Urged by Einstein," *New York Times,* May 25, 1946, p. 13.)

http://icarus-falling.blogspot.ca/2009/06/einstein-enigma.html for the

[29] *Spiral Dynamics: Mastering Values, Leadership and Change* (1996) by Prof. Don Edward Beck and Christopher C. Cowan

www.amazon.com/Spiral-Dynamics-Mastering-Values-Leadership/dp/1405133562/

[30] From https://en.wikipedia.org/wiki/Spiral_Dynamics

Ken Wilber briefly referenced Graves in his 1986 book (with Jack Engler and Daniel P. Brown), *Transformations of Consciousness*, and again in the 1995 *Sex, Ecology, Spirituality*, which also introduced his four quadrants model. However, it was not until the "Integral Psychology" section of the 1999 *Collected Works: Volume 4* that he integrated Gravesian theory, now in the form of Spiral Dynamics. Beck and Wilber began discussing their ideas with each other around this time.

AQAL "altitudes"

By 2006, Wilber was using SDi only for the values line, one of many lines in his All Quadrants, All Levels/Lines (AQAL) framework (adopted in this manual). In the book, *Integral Spirituality*, published that year, he introduced the concept of "altitudes" as an overall "content-free" system to correlate developmental stages across all of the theories on all of the lines integrated by AQAL.

The altitudes used a set of colors that were ordered according to the rainbow, which Wilber explained was necessary to align with color energies in the tantric tradition. This left only Red, Orange, Green, and Turquoise in place, changing all the other colors to greater or lesser degrees.

[31] Also see: tinyurl.com/irpm598 https://drtomhabib.com/intimate-couples-regression-and-lower-right-supporting-structures-thomas-a-habib
and The Trauma House by Dr. Katharina Klees tinyurl.com/irpm600
www.aufwindinstitut.com/workshop-traumahaus-konzept-2/

[32] See an animated Power Point Slide in Google Drive, courtesy of Robert Kaiser!

tinyurl.com/irpm604

https://docs.google.com/presentation/d/1dU6OpyBplbJPQXJhtP3dTH5Ns6mYql98/

[33] **NARM** stands for NeuroAffective Relational Model. It is outlined in the book *Healing Developmental Trauma: How Early Trauma Affects Self-Regulation, Self-Image, and the Capacity for Relationship* (2012) by Laurence Heller, PhD, and Aline LaPierre, PsyD.

The book is about restoring connection that fulfills our longing to feel fully alive in our relationships. An impaired capacity for connection to self and others, and the ensuing diminished aliveness, are the hidden dimensions that underlie most psychological and many physiological problems. Unfortunately, we are often unaware of the internal roadblocks that keep us from experiencing the connection and aliveness we yearn for. These roadblocks develop in reaction to developmental and shock trauma and the related nervous system dysregulation, disruptions in attachment, and distortions of identity. The goal of the NARM is to work with these dysregulations, disruptions, and distortions while never losing sight of supporting the development of a healthy capacity for connection and aliveness. It is a model for human growth, therapy, and healing that, while not ignoring a person's past, more strongly emphasizes a person's strengths, capacities, resources, and resiliency, and builds and expands upon our current capacity for connection to our body and emotions as well as to our capacity for interpersonal connection—capacities that are, as we will see, intimately related.

In the book and their trainings, the authors address conflicts around the capacity for connection and explore how deeper connection and aliveness can be supported in the process of healing developmental trauma. See tinyurl.com/irpm482 https://narmtraining.com/

Five Biologically Based Core Needs:

NARM recognizes five biologically based core needs that are essential to our physical and emotional well-being: the need for connection, attunement, trust, autonomy, and love-sexuality. When a biologically based core need is not met, predictable psychological and physiological symptoms result: self-regulation, sense of self, and self-esteem become compromised. To the degree that our biologically based core needs are met early in life, we develop core capacities that allow us to recognize and meet these needs as adults. Being attuned to these five basic needs and capacities means that we are connected to our deepest resources and vitality.

Although it may seem that humans suffer from an endless number of emotional problems and challenges, most of these can be traced to early developmental and shock trauma that compromise the development of one or more of the five core capacities. For example, when children do not get the connection they need, they grow up both seeking and fearing connection. When children do not get their needs met, they do not learn to recognize what they need, are unable to express their needs, and often feel undeserving of having their needs met.

To the degree that the internal capacity to attend to our own core needs develops, we experience self-regulation, internal organization, expansion, connection, and aliveness, all attributes of physiological and psychological well-being. Supporting the healthy development of the core capacities is central to the NARM approach. See endnotes 264 to 268 for details about the five adaptive survival styles.

[34] To bring into a harmonious or responsive relationship. Being "in tune."

Attunement is the reactiveness we have to another person. It is the process by which we form relationships. Dr. Dan Siegel says, "When we attune with others, we allow our own internal state to shift, to come to resonate with the inner world of another. This resonance is at the heart of the important sense of 'feeling felt' that emerges in close relationships. Children need attunement to feel secure and to develop well, and throughout our lives we need attunement to feel close and connected."

Attunement might look like an adult seeing a baby crying, recognizing that the baby is hungry, and then picking up the baby to feed her. In an adult relationship, attunement might be an adult who knows that "I'm fine" doesn't actually mean that and digs a little deeper to find out what's going on. tinyurl.com/irpm606
https://momentousinstitute.org/blog/what-is-attunement

[35] Richard Dawkins writes in his book, *The Selfish Gene*: "The evolution of the capacity to simulate [a version of the environment in the brain of animals] seems to have culminated in subjective consciousness. Why this should have happened is, to me, the most profound mystery facing modern biology. Perhaps consciousness arises when the brain's simulation of the world becomes so complete that it must include a model of itself."

Richard Frackowiak, with seven other neuroscientists, writes in *Human Brain Function*: "We have no idea how consciousness emerges from the physical activity of the brain, and we do not know whether consciousness can emerge from non-biological systems, such as computers."

Antonio Damasio elaborates in his 2010 book, *Self Comes to Mind*: "For the time being, the mental state/brain state equivalence should be regarded as a useful hypothesis rather than a certainty. It will take a continued accrual of evidence to lend it support, and, for what we need, an additional perspective, informed by evidence from evolutionary neurobiology aligned with varied neuroscience evidence."

German philosophical anthropologist Prof. Ferdinand Fellmann argues in his book, *The Couple,* that it is very likely that our ancestors became self-conscious human beings through erotic love relationships. He reasons that these relationships emerged when females began to enjoy sensuality and penetration with attractive males outside their procreative cycles and separated with them, as pairs, from the horde.

[36] A meme (rhymes with gene) is an idea, behavior, or style that spreads by means of imitation from person to person. It acts as a unit for carrying cultural ideas, symbols, or practices, that can be transmitted from one mind to another through writing, speech, gestures, rituals, or other imitable phenomena with a mimicked theme. Supporters of the concept regard memes as cultural analogues to genes in that they self-replicate, mutate, and respond to selective pressures.
https://en.wikipedia.org/wiki/Meme

[37] A genetic predisposition is a genetic characteristic which influences the possible phenotypic development of an individual organism within a species or population under the influence of environmental conditions.
https://en.wikipedia.org/wiki/Genetic_predisposition

[38] www.amazon.com/Everything-Love-Signs-Book-astrology/dp/1440528195

[39] www.amazon.com/All-Rules-Time-tested-Secrets-Capturing/dp/0446618799

[40] www.amazon.com/Game-Penetrating-Secret-Society-Artists/dp/0060554738

[41] www.amazon.co.uk/Pickup-Artist-New-Improved-Seduction/dp/0345518195

[42] www.nationalgeographic.org/article/development-agriculture/

[43] www.amazon.com/Art-Loving-Erich-Fromm/dp/0061129739

[44] www.amazon.com/Principles-Making-Marriage-Gottman-1999-12-01/dp/B01K92U968

[45] www.amazon.com/Men-Only-Straightforward-Guide-Inner/dp/B0035G04Q6

[46] www.amazon.com/Women-Only-about-Inner-Lives/dp/1590523172

[47] www.amazon.com/Mars-Venus-Collide-Relationships-Understanding/dp/0061242977

[48] www.amazon.com/Improve-Marriage-Without-Talking-About/dp/0767923189

[49] www.amazon.com/Making-Sense-Men-Lifetime-Attention/dp/1605309095

[50] www.amazon.com/Why-We-Love-Chemistry-Romantic/dp/B01L9DL6ZO

[51] www.amazon.com/Real-Love-Unconditional-Fulfilling-Relationships/dp/1592400477

[52] www.amazon.com/Getting-Love-You-Want-Couples/dp/0743495926

[53] www.amazon.com/New-Rules-Marriage-What-Need/dp/0345480864

[54] www.amazon.com/Passionate-Marriage-Intimacy-Committed-Relationships/dp/0393334279

[55] www.amazon.com/Hold-Me-Tight-Conversations-Lifetime-ebook/dp/B0011UGLQK

[56] www.amazon.com/He-Mr-Right-Everything-Before/dp/0307336735

[57] www.amazon.com/Intelligent-Womans-Guide-Online-Dating/dp/0615242472

[58] www.amazon.com/Stumbling-Naked-Dark-Overcoming-Mistakes/dp/0981484336

[59] www.amazon.com/Relationship-Roulette-Improve-Your-Lasting/dp/031338357X

[60] There isn't, as an eardrum and brain are necessary to "translate" the air waves into the qualia of sound.

[61] www.amazon.com/The-Way-of-Superior-Man-audiobook/dp/B07FXZBYJ9/

[62] www.amazon.com/Path-Love-Spiritual-Strategies-Healing/dp/060980135X

[63] www.amazon.com/Undefended-Love-Jett-Psaris/dp/1572242086

[64] www.amazon.com/How-Be-Adult-Relationships-Mindful/dp/1570628122

[65] www.amazon.com/Love-Awakening-Discovering-Intimate-Relationship/dp/0060927976

[66] www.amazon.com/Hearts-Wisdom-Practical-Growing-Through/dp/1573241555

[67] www.amazon.com/If-Buddha-Dated-Handbook-Spiritual/dp/0140195831

[68] www.amazon.com/Calling-One-Weeks-Attract-Love/dp/1400049296

[69] Sri Aurobindo, an Indian nationalist and freedom fighter, poet, philosopher, and yogi developed his vision and philosophy of human progress and a spiritual path, which he called "Integral Yoga." He wrote: "Man is a transitional being. He is not final. The step from man to superman is the next approaching achievement in the earth's evolution. It is inevitable because it is at once the intention of the inner spirit and the logic of Nature's process." Jean Gebser used the term to describe the emergence of a new structure of consciousness in the West, which he termed "Integral." Wilber adopted the term "Integral" for his theory that is based on Aurobindo and Gebser (among many others) in the late 1990s.

[70] In a dialog with Allan Combs, Ken Wilber gave four definitions for Integral: (1) the highest level of development possible; (2) the integration of all lower levels; (3) a horizontal integration of the four quadrants at any level; and (4) to be Integrally informed.

[71] For a long time, the Integral stage was seen by researchers as the highest level of human consciousness that integrated all lower levels. Later, higher stages were discovered (e.g., by Susanne Cook-Greuter); this now sometimes creates confusion, as "Integral" no longer stands for highest or most integrated.

[72] See, for example, Sean Hargens's failed MetaIntegral project, the demise of Integral Institute, and, to an extent, Integral Life, and the breakup of Andrew Cohen's former community.

[73] Ken Wilber writes in his 2016 book *Integral Meditation*:

"Martin Ucik, in his superb book written for men, *Integral Relationships*, uses the AQAL Framework to analyze relationships, especially when individuals are at different places in each of those fundamental areas. His extensive experience in the area led him to the conclusion (which most developmentalists would share) that individuals who are at different areas in 4 of the 5 major AQAL elements (namely quadrants, lines, states, and types) can still have fairly productive relationships. But for those who are different in that 5th element—namely, who are at different levels (different structure-stages of Growing Up)—his only advice is: 'Sorry.' He simply finds that levels are so different from each other—different truths, different needs, different values—that it is almost impossible for two partners at different levels to find enough mutual understanding and shared values to really stay together."

[74] www.themasculineman.com/compatibility-matrix/

[75] David Zeitler, at www.mindfulnesscoach.biz, added his insights to this, with which I only partly agree, but certainly consider:

The variance in development that we see here can also be explained by the fact that most women tend to spend more time in communion-oriented stages, while most men tend to spend more time in agency-oriented stages. This is why men "feel" like they are more "exclusion" oriented and why women "feel" more "inclusion" oriented. Also, the "repudiation/negation" subphase occurs at every level, so we all "exclude" the previous stage for a period when we grow to the next stage. If we want to see how women "exclude" in ways that men do not, we can look at how teenage girls constantly exclude other girls from the group (Carol Gilligan also noted this)—in this way, women are much more exclusionary than men, who created social hierarchies in order to be inclusive (their response to evolutionary pressures of men dying more in protection roles).

[76] See Jenny Wade *Changes of Mind*, page 268: "[For people in first-tier consciousness] differences in values threaten the ego to some extent, so they are unable to be tolerant or accepting of people at a different level of awareness." Spiral Dynamics maintains that humans operate 50% of the time from their central stage of development (center of gravity), 25% from the stage below, and 25% from the stage above.

[77] Ken Wilber does not tire of interpreting Carol Gilligan's work (see her book *In a Different Voice*) that women don't think hierarchically but

develop hierarchically. Alison Armstrong of PAX (www.understandmen.com) and her facilitators maintain that men go through four developmental stages—(1) page, (2) knight, (3) prince, and (4) king (which is more likely a vertical translation than a vertical transformation)—while she identifies no developmental stages in women and explicitly says that women don't develop. Also see her book, *The Amazing Development of Men: Everyman's Journey from Knight to Prince to King*.

[78] www.amazon.com/Integral-Psychology-Consciousness-Spirit-Therapy/dp/1570625549

[79] This article provides a good overview of their work.

tinyurl.com/irpm608

www.perspegrity.com/papers/STAGES%20background_Murray.pdf

[80] tinyurl.com/irpm611

https://integral-review.org/issues/vol_16_no_1_ofallon_murray_stages_speciality_inventories.pdf

Old/new general inventory sentence stem questions:

1. Raising a family…
2. When I am criticized…
3. Change is…
4. A man's job…/These days, work…
5. Being with other people…
6. The thing I like about myself is…
7. My mother and I…/My co-workers and I…
8. What gets me into trouble is…
9. Education…
10. When people are helpless…
11. Women are lucky because…/What I like to do best is…
12. A good boss…
13. A girl has a right to…/We could make the world a better place if…
14. The past…
15. When they talked about sex…/Privacy…
16. I feel sorry…

17. When they avoided me…

18. Rules are…

19. Crime and delinquency could be halted if…

20. Men are lucky because…/Business and society…

21. I just can't stand people who…

22. At times I worry about...

23. I am…

24. If I had more money…

25. My main problem is…

26. When I get mad…

27. People who step out of line… (at work…)

28. A husband has a right to…/A partner has the right to…

29. If my mother…

30. If I were in charge…

31. My father…

32. If I can't get what I want…

33. When I am nervous…

34. For a woman career is…/Technology…

35. My conscience bothers me if…

36. Sometimes I wished that…

[81] https://antoinette555.files.wordpress.com/2019/08/the_stages_matrix_roadmap.pdf

[82] http://integralleadershipreview.com/15583-integral-theory-making-and-the-need-for-empirical-rigor-observations-from-the-field-of-adult-development/

[83] www.amazon.com/Truth-Dating-Finding-Love-Getting/dp/193207306X/

[84] www.amazon.com/Integral-Relationships-Manual-Martin-Ucik/dp/B08W5QW2D6/

[85] www.amazon.com/Sex-Purpose-Love-Integral-Relationships/dp/B08W7DPT6L

[86] Carl Rogers (1902-1987) maintained that for people to "grow," they need an environment that provides them with genuineness (openness

and self-disclosure), acceptance (being seen with unconditional positive regard), and empathy (being listened to and understood).

See www.simplypsychology.org/carl-rogers.html and

https://en.wikipedia.org/wiki/Carl_Rogers

[87] https://en.wikipedia.org/wiki/Marshall_Rosenberg

[88] See studies and books by Deborah Tannen that discuss how men interrupt women more often than the other way around:

tinyurl.com/irpm613

www.amazon.com/Deborah-Tannen/e/B000AQ3YWU%3Fref=dbs_a_mng_rwt_scns_share

[89] Also see tinyurl.com/irpm587 https://drive.google.com/drive/folders/1krXcl712kEOu7hXfXbRn8eIHQ4ci7xAt for print versions in German, English, and Turkish.

[90] We typically speak of bad feelings and negative emotions when they are challenging and difficult to stay present with. We then have a tendency to push them away or repress them, or to project them onto others (you make me feel that way.) This disconnects us from our own and the feelings of others. If we don't see feelings and emotions as bad or "negative" and own and embrace them instead, we can appreciate them as as an opportunity to look at our wounded self, unmet needs, or violation of our values and agreements that caused them in the first place, and thus welcome them as "positive," or even better, not label them at all.

[91] See tinyurl.com/irpm614

http://mindfulneeds.com/whatismfn/difference-between-needs-and-strategies/

[92] The term emotion is derived from the Latin term, *emovere*, which means to stir, to agitate, to move outward. Hence, an emotion is referred to as a stirred-up state of the organism. Emotion is often defined as a complex state of feeling that results in physical and psychological changes that influence thought and behavior.

[93] https://worldhappiness.report

[94] https://en.wikipedia.org/wiki/Manfred_Max-Neef%27s_Fundamental_human_needs

[95] www.amazon.com/Nonviolent-Communication-Language-Life-Changing-Relationships/dp/189200528X/

[96]

Synopsis of the difference between ethical and moral discourse		
	Ethics	Morality
Basic concept	Good/bad	Right/wrong just/unjust
Basic unit	Values	Norms
Basic question	What is good for me or us?	What is just? What ought I to do and why? What is right?
Validity	Relative and conditional	Absolute and unconditional
Type of theory	Prudential, teleological	Deontological* (duty, obligation, or rule)
Aims	Advice, judgment preference ranking	Established, valid norms, discovering duties

Table 26: Difference between ethics and morals

* Deontology is the study of that which is an "obligation or duty," and consequent moral judgment on the actor on whether he or she has complied. See: https://en.wikipedia.org/wiki/Deontological_ethics

[97] www.yourdictionary.com/tacit

[98] https://youtu.be/igh9iO5BxBo

[99] https://youtu.be/1P0Z1yq-2FQ

[100] https://en.wikipedia.org/wiki/Karpman_drama_triangle

[101] *Man's Search for Meaning* (2006 Edition) by Viktor E. Frankl www.amazon.com/Mans-Search-Meaning-Viktor-Frankl/dp/0807014273/ (older copy page 86)

[102] https://powerofted.com/drama-triangle

[103] https://commonoutlook.com/learning/book-reviews/getting-to-yes-review

www.beyondintractability.org/bksum/fisher-getting

[104] You can find colored baseball caps that we use for the exercises in Module 7 and 8 in the US at:

tinyurl.com/irpm616

www.orientaltrading.com/bright-baseball-caps-a2-15_32.fltr

In Germany:

tinyurl.com/irpm617

www.textilwaren24.eu/caps-muetzen

In the UK:

tinyurl.com/irpm619

www.ethicstar.com/cheap-caps.html

[105] www.amazon.com/Getting-Yes-Negotiating-Agreement-Without/dp/0143118757

[106] www.amazon.com/Nonviolent-Communication-Language-Life-Changing-Relationships/dp/189200528X/

[107] https://en.wikipedia.org/wiki/Double_bind

[108] tinyurl.com/irpm621

https://en.wikipedia.org/wiki/Bohm_Dialogue

tinyurl.com/irpm622

http://dialoguestudies.org/wp-content/uploads/2015/02/Bohmian_Dialogue_a_Critical_Retrospective_of_Bohm_s_Approach_to_Dialogue_as_a_Practice_of_Collective_Communication.pdf

[109] https://en.wikipedia.org/wiki/Discourse_ethics

[110] George Lakoff, has argued about the importance of making the "symbolic-semantic-neural" unconscious, conscious:
"Language gets its power because it is defined relative to frames, prototypes, metaphors, narratives, images, and emotions. Part of its power comes from its unconscious aspects: we are not consciously aware of all that it evokes in us, but it is there, hidden, always at work. If we hear the same language over and over, we will think more and more in terms of the frames and metaphors activated by that language. Cultural narratives and frames are instantiated physically in our brains. We are

not born with them, but we start growing them soon, and as we acquire the deep narratives, our synapses change and become fixed. A large number of deep narratives can be activated together. We cannot understand other people without such cultural narratives. But more important, we cannot understand ourselves—who we are, who we have been, and where we want to go."

The Turkish poet Murathan Mungan said about identity: "Identity is a concept of our age that should be used very carefully. All types of identities--ethnic, national, religious, sexual or whatever else, can become your prison after a while. The identity that you stand up for can enslave you and close you to the rest of the world."

Ken Wilber further explains the relationship between "free will" and developmental levels and structures, in his following claim about individual choices:

"Worse, he can introspect all he wants, and yet he still won't realize this. He is simply a mouthpiece for a structure that is speaking through him. He thinks he is original; he thinks he controls the contents of his thoughts; he thinks he can introspect and understand himself; he thinks he has free will and yet he is just a mouthpiece. He is not speaking; he is being spoken. The same is true for dozens of other aspects of subjectivity and awareness: they are the products of impersonal structures and intersubjective networks and worse, structures and networks that cannot themselves be seen by subjectivity or awareness (not directly anyway)."

[111] tinyurl.com/irpm624

www.nytimes.com/2021/01/31/opinion/change-someones-mind.html?smid=url-share

or

tinyurl.com/irpm626

https://docs.google.com/document/d/1DcphKaH2eKlu99Mg8mm_NzvHlDlOHzlD/

[112] www.amazon.com/Habermas-Short-Introduction-Gordon-Finlayson/dp/0192840959

[113] www.amazon.com/Pragmatism-Introduction-Michael-Bacon/dp/0745646654

[114] www.amazon.com/Metatheory-Twenty-First-Century-Ontological-Explorations/dp/0415820472

[115] www.amazon.com/Complex-Integral-Realist-Perspective-Towards/dp/0815362188

[116] https://centreforcriticalrealism.com/

[117] A lesbian is a female homosexual

Gay is a term that primarily refers to a homosexual person—is often used to describe homosexual males, but lesbians may also be referred to as gay.

Bisexuality is romantic and sexual attraction toward both sexes.

Transgender is an umbrella term for people whose gender identity differs from what is typically associated with the sex they were assigned at birth.

Two-Spirit is a modern umbrella term used within some indigenous communities to describe people who are seen as having both male and female spirits within them.

Queer is an umbrella term for sexual and gender minorities that are not heterosexual or cisgender. Cisgender means a person whose gender identity corresponds to their sex assigned at birth, or the antonym of transgender. Cis is the Latin-derived prefix for 'on this side of', which is the opposite of trans-, meaning 'across from' or 'on the other side of

Questioning are people who are unsure, still exploring, and concerned about applying a social label of their gender, sexual identity, sexual orientation, or all three.

Intersex is a variation in sex characteristics that does not allow individuals to be distinctly identified as male or female.

Asexuality (or nonsexuality) is the lack of sexual attraction to anyone.

Ally is a person who considers themselves a friend to the LGBTQ+ community.

Pansexuality, or omnisexuality, is sexual attraction, romantic love, or emotional attraction toward people of any sex or gender identity.

Agender genderless, gender free, non-gendered, or ungendered are people who identify as having no gender or gender identity.

Gender Queer is an umbrella term for gender identities that are not exclusively masculine or feminine.

Bigender is a gender identity where the person moves between feminine and masculine gender identities, behaviors, "female" and "male" personas, possibly depending on context.

Gender variance, gender nonconformity, gender diversity, gender atypicality refers to behaviors or gender expressions by people who do not match masculine or feminine gender norms.

Pangender people are those who feel they identify as all genders.

https://ok2bme.ca/resources/kids-teens/what-does-lgbtq-mean/

[118] tinyurl.com/irpm587

https://drive.google.com/drive/folders/1krXcl712kEOu7hXfXbRn8eIHQ4ci7xAt

[119] The stark contrasts between romance novels and pornography underscore how different female and male erotic fantasies are. These differences reflect human evolutionary history and the disparate selection pressures women and men experienced, say the authors of this thought-provoking book.

[120] Rudder was a co-founder of OkCupid. From 2009–2011, OkCupid published statistical observations and analysis of members' preferences and connections. The blog posts were written by Rudder and gained widespread media attention. After the sale to IAC, Rudder assumed day-to-day control of OkCupid as president and general manager until he left in 2015.

[121] The NBC sitcom *Seinfeld* offers great examples of the objectification of females as sex objects and the shaming of males for being flawed, especially the bald, short, stocky, dimwitted, unsuccessful, and opportunistic character of George Costanza (Jason Alexander). *Entertainment Weekly*'s TV critic, Ken Tucker, has described the main four characters as "having a group dynamic rooted in jealousy, rage, insecurity, despair, hopelessness, and a touching lack of faith in one's fellow human beings." https://en.wikipedia.org/wiki/Seinfeld

[122] tinyurl.com/irpm627

https://dqydj.com/income-by-sex/

[123] Ibid. 10% of males make more than US $151,425.00; 5% make more than US $206,691.00+; and 1% make more than US $428,500.00.

[124] See Lori Gottlieb, *Marry Him: The Case for Settling for Mr. Good Enough*. In a 2010 interview with CNN, Gottlieb said the following:

"There's a survey in the book where men and women are asked, 'If you got 80 percent of everything you wanted—of your ideal traits in a mate or partner—would you be happy?" The majority of women said, "No, that's settling," and the majority of men said, "Eighty percent? I'd be thrilled; that's a catch." So, the question is: is getting less than everything we want truly settling? And more important, semantics aside: is getting anything less than everything we want going to make us less happy? The answer is no, and it probably will make you more happy." http://edition.cnn.com/2010/LIVING/02/24/lori.gottlieb.marry.him/index.html which shows that many women stay single because they don't find men that they deem good enough.

Also see endnote 482 for Pew Research statistics about singles and dating.

[125] www.amazon.com/Evolution-Human-Sexuality-Donald-Symons/dp/0195029070/

[126] www.amazon.com/Myth-Male-Power-Warren-Farrell-ebook/dp/B076HVLZGH/

[127] www.amazon.com/Warrior-Lovers-Fiction-Evolution-Sexuality/dp/0300093543/

[128] www.amazon.com/Evolution-Desire-Strategies-Human-Mating/dp/046500802X/

[129] www.amazon.com/Mating-Mind-Sexual-Choice-Evolution/dp/038549517X

[130] www.amazon.com/Seduction-Redefined-Creative-Collaboration-Masculine/dp/0981831877

[131] www.amazon.com/Dataclysm-Identity-What-Online-Offline-Selves/dp/0385347391

[132] www.youtube.com/watch?v=vwKLTVCJn6Q

[133] www.youtube.com/watch?v=rCGTYld8Yjk

[134] https://oru.academia.edu/LenaGunnarsson

[135] For a detailed article, see: tinyurl.com/irpm629 www.mercurynews.com/2016/11/08/bay-area-filmmakers-new-film-the-red-pill-is-a-bitter-one-for-feminists-to-swallow/

[136] In the Netflix series, *Inside Bill's Brain: Decoding Bill Gates*, Gates' then-wife, Melinda French Gates, says in an interview that she did not feel safe when Bill was not home.

tinyurl.com/irpm631

www.netflix.com/watch/80184678?trackId=255824129

[137] See scene in the movie *As Good as It Gets* in which Jack Nicholson's character says, "You make me want to be a better man."

tinyurl.com/irpm632

https://youtu.be/LrtpRNsdfYs

[138] tinyurl.com/irpm587

https://drive.google.com/drive/folders/1krXcl712kEOu7hXfXbRn8eIHQ4ci7xAt

[139] https://youtu.be/-4EDhdAHrOg

[140] www.amazon.com/Improve-Marriage-Without-Talking-About/dp/0767923189

[141] www.amazon.com/Passionate-Marriage-Intimacy-Committed-Relationships/dp/0393334279

[142] www.amazon.com/Making-Sense-Men-Lifetime-Attention/dp/1605309095

[143] www.ted.com/talks/brene_brown_listening_to_shame

[144] See tinyurl.com/irpm633

www.encyclopedia.com/social-sciences/encyclopedias-almanacs-transcripts-and-maps/femininitymasculinity for a history and research about the feminine and masculine polarities.

[145] tinyurl.com/irpm635

https://drive.google.com/drive/folders/1krXcl712kEOu7hXfXbRn8eIHQ4ci7xAt

[146] Inspired by Jim Cruzen. See conversation with him and his partner at tinyurl.com/irpm639

https://youtu.be/PF9ENbdc-R0
tinyurl.com/irpm640

www.facebook.com/Conscious-Dance-Academy-1699644220068415/

[147] See for example tinyurl.com/irpm641

www.amazon.com/hula-hoops/s?k=hula+hoops

[148] www.youtube.com/watch?v=XVnmllLhfDw

[149] https://youtu.be/q3rmnjtrSGw

[150] www.ted.com/talks/trevor_copp_and_jeff_fox_ballroom_dance_that_breaks_gender_roles

[151] If we experience the four polarities (a=agency, c=communion, t=self-transcendence, s=self-immanence) in the four dimensions of our being and relating (quadrants), we arrive at 16 possibilities:

Upper Left:
ULA=independence, introverted, introspection, keeps thoughts and feelings hidden from others, uncompromising.

ULC=emotional closeness, share ideas, open communication, teamwork, compromising, care, and responsibility.

ULT=striving for wisdom, presence, and emptiness.

ULI=striving for compassion, fullness, and surrender.

An easy way to relate to the four polarities in the UL is to think about communication. ULA, you don't want to talk; ULC, you want to talk; ULT, you want to be heard and understood; ULI, you want to hear and understand.

Lower Left:
LLA=individualism, survival of the fittest, there is only one right way to see the world.

LLC=cultural diversity, all living things have a right to be, there are many ways to see the world.

LLT=the most qualified with the widest perspective should lead and make decisions.

LLI=the most caring with the deepest connection should lead and make decisions.

An easy way to relate to the four polarities in the LL is to think about your neighborhood. LLA, you don't care about your neighbors and prefer them to look and think like you; LLC, you know and connect with your neighbors and appreciate cultural diversity; LLT, you want to grow and lead your community; LLI, you want to fit into your community.

Upper Right:
URA=you don't like to be physically close, touched, or intimate.

URC=you love physical closeness, touch, and intimacy.

URT=you see your body as servant that needs to be controlled and disciplined around its desires for food, comfort, relaxation, and sex.

URI=you see your body as a temple and guide that is full of wisdom that points to its own needs that you surrender to.

An easy way to relate to the four polarities in the UR is to think of sex. URA, you don't want to have sex; URC, you want to have sex; URT, you want to be on top and empty yourself; URI, you want to be at the bottom and be filled up.

Lower Right:

LRA=prefer to be single, live and work alone, avoid family events and social gatherings, people should be responsible for themselves and their fate.

LRC=enjoy social gatherings, team worker, social systems should support the poor and underprivileged, we are all in this together.

LRT=aspires to climb the social and corporate ladder. Cares about social status, influence, and wants to be a leader.

LRI=cares about the well-being of all people in family, community, and society.

An easy way to relate to the four polarities in the LR is to think of your workplace. LRA, you prefer to work alone and take full responsibility for producing results; LRC, you would rather work in a team and share goals and responsibilities with others; LRT, you enjoy a hierarchical structure with a clear chain of command and responsibilities; LRI, you enjoy flat or no hierarchies and would rather be part of a team than the leader.

Since every quadrant can be looked at from the inside and the outside (see Ken Wilber, *Integral Spirituality*, page 33–49), you may even be able to take this further, but this would be beyond the scope of this manual, so we leave it at the sixteen possible energies.

[152] www.amazon.com/Intimate-Communion-Awakening-Sexual-Essence/dp/155874374X/

[153] www.amazon.com/Sex-Seasoned-Woman-Pursuing-Passionate/dp/0812972740

[154] www.amazon.com/New-Passages-Mapping-Your-Across/dp/0345404459

[155] Spiritual materialism is a term coined by Chögyam Trungpa in his book *Cutting Through Spiritual Materialism*. He uses the term to describe mistakes spiritual seekers commit which turn the pursuit of spirituality

into an ego-building and confusion-creating endeavor, based on the idea that ego development (growing up or being mature) is counter to spiritual progress.

Conventionally, it is used to describe capitalist and spiritual narcissism, commercial efforts such as "new age" bookstores and wealthy lecturers on spirituality; it might also mean the attempt to build up a list of credentials or accumulate teachings to present oneself as a more realized or holy person. Author Jorge Ferrer equates the terms "spiritual materialism" and "spiritual narcissism," though others draw a distinction that spiritual narcissism is believing that one deserves love and respect or is better than another because one has accumulated spiritual training instead of the belief that accumulating training will bring an end to suffering. https://en.wikipedia.org/wiki/Spiritual_materialism

[156] https://en.wikipedia.org/wiki/Metaphysics

[157] From the book *Healing Developmental Trauma*, page 26-27:

"The limitation of what we take to be our personal identity is addressed in many esoteric traditions and has been popularized by well-known authors such as Eckhart Tolle and Ken Wilber. Psychodynamic orientations work to solidify the sense of identity and strengthen the ego, whereas esoteric orientations hold that Ego is an illusion that separates us from Being and keeps us from experiencing the spaciousness, fluidity, and fullness of our essential nature. Both perspectives are important. Esoteric approaches address the limitations of what they call Ego but generally do not incorporate the clinical awareness of the importance of attachment and developmental trauma in the creation of our sense of self. In addition, esoteric approaches do not address the primary role of nervous system dysregulation in the formation of the fixed identifications that come to be confused with identity.

NARM integrates both psychological and esoteric traditions and adds a biologically based approach that at times helps to solidify a person's sense of identity and at other times supports the exploration of the fluid nature of identity. The NARM approach holds that the most immediate access to spiritual dimensions is through a regulated physiology. Whereas for hundreds of years, the body, particularly in Western traditions, was seen as an impediment to spirituality, it is a NARM premise that a coherent biological/psychological self is a springboard to the higher Self. It is only when individuals have a solid sense of who they are that they can open to the fluid nature of Self.

The meditation technique of Vipassana is one important tool in the mindfulness process that can lead to the awareness and direct experience of the fluid nature of the Self. Because it is a powerful tool, however, it can potentially opens meditators to painful or overwhelming affective states that they are not equipped to process. We have worked with many individuals who during meditation retreats became anxious and overwhelmed by their emotions. Any system of self-exploration that does not take into consideration trauma and attachment issues and the resulting disrupted functioning of the nervous system creates the danger of dysregulating and re-traumatizing its practitioners.

One of Eckhart Tolle's core principles is that nothing that happened in the past can keep us from being fully in the present moment. Although theoretically true, this orientation can be hurtful to those who have experienced trauma and suffer from significant nervous system disorganization. Traumatized individuals, which includes most of us to differing degrees, need both top-down and bottom-up approaches that address nervous system imbalances as well as issues of identity. Many people recognize the 'power of now,' as Tolle calls it, but because of their nervous system dysregulation they are unable to remain in the present moment. Falling short of this ideal becomes another reason for individuals with trauma to feel bad about themselves."

[158] Depersonalization can consist of a detachment within the self, regarding one's mind or body, or being a detached observer of oneself. Subjects feel they have changed, and that the world has become vague, dreamlike, less real, lacking in significance or being outside reality while looking in. It can be described as feeling like one is on "autopilot" and that the person's sense of individuality or selfhood has been hindered or suppressed.

Chronic depersonalization refers to depersonalization/derealization disorder, which is classified by the DSM-5 as a dissociative disorder, based on the findings that depersonalization and derealization are prevalent in other dissociative disorders including dissociative identity disorder. https://en.wikipedia.org/wiki/Depersonalization

[159] The mirror test—sometimes called the mark test, mirror self-recognition (MSR) test, red spot technique, or rouge test, attempts to

determine whether an animal possesses the ability of visual self-recognition. It is the traditional method for attempting to measure physiological and cognitive self-awareness. However, agreement has been reached that animals can be self-aware in ways not measured by the mirror test, such as distinguishing between their own and others' songs and scents. https://en.wikipedia.org/wiki/Mirror_test.

[160] https://youtu.be/ZPtT3p8T6Cg

[161] https://en.wikipedia.org/wiki/Spiritual_bypass
www.robertaugustusmasters.com/spiritual-bypassing/

[162] www.apa.org/topics/mindfulness/meditation

[163] www.mindful.org/10-things-we-know-about-the-science-of-meditation/ and www.mindful.org/five-ways-mindfulness-meditation-is-good-for-your-health/

[164] 24-item self-report questionnaire designed to measure your BIS/BAS motivational systems
http://expfactory.org/experiments/bis_bas_survey/preview

[165] See video with Dr. Siegel at tinyurl.com/irpm642
https://youtu.be/BGYUbc73JwY

[166] Extended descriptions at tinyurl.com/irpm643
www.move2focus.net/integration/

[167] In Buddhism, the Four Noble Truths are:

1. Dukkha (suffering, incapable of satisfying, painful) is an innate characteristic of existence in the realm of samsara.

2. Samudaya (origin, arising) of this dukkha, which arises or "comes together" with taṇha ("craving, desire or attachment").

3. Nirodha (cessation, ending) of this dukkha can be attained by the renouncement or letting go of this taṇha.

4. Magga (path, Noble Eightfold Path) is the path leading to renouncement of tanha and cessation of dukkha.

[168] www.amazon.com/Power-Now-Guide-Spiritual-Enlightenment/dp/1577314808/

[169] www.amazon.com/Integral-Spirituality-Startling-Religion-Postmodern/dp/1590305272/

[170] www.amazon.com/Integral-Meditation-Mindfulness-Grow-Wake/dp/1611802989/

[171] www.amazon.com/Cutting-Through-Spiritual-Materialism-Chogyam/dp/1570629579

[172] www.amazon.com/SQ21-Twenty-One-Skills-Spiritual-Intelligence/dp/159079298X/

[173] www.amazon.com/Spiritual-Bypassing-Spirituality-Disconnects-Matters/dp/1556439059

[174] www.amazon.com/Love-Awakening-Discovering-Intimate-Relationship/dp/0060927976/

[175] www.amazon.com/Journey-Heart-Path-Conscious-Love/dp/0060927429/

[176] www.amazon.com/Toward-Psychology-Awakening-Psychotherapy-Transformation/dp/1570628238/

[177] www.amazon.com/Perfect-Love-Imperfect-Relationships-Healing/dp/1590303865/

[178] www.amazon.com/Evolutionary-Enlightenment-Path-Spiritual-Awakening/dp/1590792092

[179] www.amazon.com/Neurobiology-We-Relationships-Interact-Learning/dp/159179949X

[180] www.ncbi.nlm.nih.gov/pmc/articles/PMC4769029/

[181] See tinyurl.com/irpm644

www.webmd.com/sex-relationships/features/10-surprising-health-benefits-of-sex. Researchers found that sex (1) relieves stress, (2) boosts the immune system, (3) burns calories (85 or more in 30 minutes), (4) improves cardiovascular health, (5) boosts self-esteem, (6) improves intimacy, (7) reduces pain (through release of oxytocin), (8) reduces risk of prostate cancer, (9) strengthens pelvic floor muscles, and (10) helps you to sleep better. Also see Patricia Love and Steven Stosny in *How to Improve your Marriage Without Talking About It* page 148–150.

[182] "Kundalini" literally means coiling, like a spring or snake, at the base of the spine. It conveys the sense of an untapped energy potential or great reservoir of creativity that can be moved up the spine, often during sexual activity. When kundalini energy moves through the body, consciousness necessarily changes with it. From a psychological perspective, it can be thought of as a rich source of psychic or libidinous energy in our unconscious.

Integral Relationship Practice | 596

---

[183] The PC or pubococcygeus muscle is found in males and females. It stretches from the pubic bone to the tailbone, forming the floor of the pelvic cavity. It is the same muscle that you use to stop the flow of urine. It can be strengthened by squeezing and holding it for a few seconds 30–50 times in a row three times a day.

[184] tinyurl.com/irpm647 https://pubmed.ncbi.nlm.nih.gov/21910541/ and tinyurl.com/irpm648 https://pubmed.ncbi.nlm.nih.gov/23107993/

[185] www.youtube.com/watch?v=YsDF3e6XdRE

[186] www.allmusic.com/album/northern-seascape-mw0000046855

[187] See blog about monogamy and non-monogamy at tinyurl.com/irpm653

https://integralrelationship.com/survey-and-question-what-motivates-monogamy-and-non-monogamy-at-integral-and-higher-stages/

[188] tinyurl.com/irpm657

www.psychologytoday.com/us/blog/the-polyamorists-next-door/201805/polyagony-when-polyamory-goes-really-wrong

[189] University of British Columbia professor Joseph Henrich used his areas of expertise—psychology, anthropology, and economics—to demonstrate the social harm associated with men taking multiple wives. Implicit in his argument is an endorsement of monogamy, which, he wrote in a 64-page affidavit, "seems to redirect male motivations in ways that generate lower crime rates, greater GDP per capita, and better outcomes for children."

In the Western tradition, the earliest we can trace laws about monogamy is to Athens, when the first notions of democracy began to be instituted. The argument is that it's meant to create equality among citizens so that, essentially, there'll be wives available to all Athenian men, rather than having all the rich men take many wives. We can think of it as a first kind of effort to level the playing field. By saying that both the king and the peasant can only have one wife each, it's the first step toward saying that all men were created equal; however, men were still allowed to have slave concubines just as long as they were non-Athenian women.

The core of the argument is that polygyny—when men marry multiple wives— takes up all the women and creates an underclass of men that have no access to partners, and those guys cause trouble. They commit crimes and engage in substance abuse.

A Stanford economist argues that when men can't invest in getting another wife, they then invest more in their own production. Rather than basically saving up in order to get a second wife or a third wife, they invest more in the children of the one wife they have, and in other types of economic production.

There is also less equality for women and more strife in the home. When women are in short supply, it increases male competition, and so men use violence against women to control the household. Also, if you have one male with lots of wives, there are all sorts of stepmothers and unrelated adults in the same household as children, and that increases the likelihood of violence. The biggest risk factor for spouses killing each other is a large age difference, and in polygamous households you inevitably end up with a large age difference between at least some of the spouses. tinyurl.com/irpm658
www.salon.com/2011/07/23/monogamy_4/

[190] www.amazon.com/Mars-Venus-Bedroom-Lasting-Romance/dp/0060927933/

[191] www.amazon.com/Passionate-Marriage-Intimacy-Committed-Relationships/dp/0393334279

[192] www.amazon.com/Transcendent-Sex-When-Lovemaking-Opens/dp/0743482174

[193] www.amazon.com/Intimate-Communion-Awakening-Sexual-Essence/dp/155874374X

[194] www.amazon.com/Finding-God-Through-Sex-Awakening/dp/1591792738

[195] www.amazon.com/Dear-Lover-Womans-Guide-Deepest/dp/1591792606/

[196] See Leslie Temple Thurston, *The Marriage of Spirit*, page 52: "This androgynous soul form includes both the masculine and feminine frequencies, both negative and positive, and both conscious and unconscious. The second schism is the splitting away of the soul. It institutes the division between conscious-unconscious, negative-positive, and masculine-feminine. The individual is split into the masculine frequencies if in a male body or the feminine frequencies if in a female body."

[197] Carl Gustav Jung (1875 - 1961) was a Swiss psychiatrist, influential thinker, and founder of analytical psychology.

[198] The Anima and Animus are, in Carl Jung's school of analytical psychology, the totality of the unconscious feminine psychological qualities that a male possesses (anima) and the masculine ones possessed by the female (animus). Jung was not clear if the anima/animus archetype was totally unconscious, calling it "a little bit conscious and unconscious." Jung gave as an example a man who falls head over heels in love, then later in life regrets his blind choice as he finds that he has married his own anima–the unconscious idea of the feminine in his mind, rather than the woman herself. The anima is usually an aggregate of a man's mother but may also incorporate aspects of sisters, aunts, and teachers. The anima and animus are one of the most significant autonomous complexes of all. They manifest by appearing as figures in dreams, as well as by influences in the interactions between the sexes. Jung said that confronting one's shadow self is an "apprentice-piece," while confronting one's anima and animus is the "masterpiece." See www.en.wikipedia.org/wiki/Anima_and_animus

[199] In psychology, a *complex* refers to unconscious associations or strong unconscious impulses that underlie an individual's behavior. Complexes explain why some people get angry or sad about a situation while others don't, or why one person is emotionally attracted to or repulsed by a certain person's aura and behavior while others are not.

[200] See Ayala Malach Pines' *Falling in Love,* page 98—100 for a theory about how males have to suppress their emotional, but not their physical (or sexual) attachment to their mother in order to identify with their father. This attachment is then transferred to women in later life. Females have to become sexually detached from their mother but not emotionally in order to identify with father. This attachment is then transferred to men in later life. Also see John Welwood, *Love and Awakening,* pages 182—184, and on page 199.

[201] Though soulmates and twin flames are both related to deep soul connections between two people, the relationships themselves are different. The connection between soulmates is powerful and often comes easily. Soulmates overlap and deeply understand or resonate with each other in their purpose, while challenging each other to heal their childhood wounds and trauma because of their similar experiences and different coping mechanisms. Soulmates often end up together because they are very compatible. Twin flames, on the other hand, complement and teach, inspire, and challenge each other to grow to realize their

fullest human potentials. This may lead them to become soulmates if they share the same purpose, or to find or attract their soulmate.
tinyurl.com/irpm659

https://hellorelish.com/articles/soulmate-vs-twin-flame.html

[202] See Harville Hendrix, *Getting the Love You Want,* page 35—36: "It was as if you had merged with the other person and became more whole," as well as page 48—60.

[203] www.amazon.com/Female-Authority-Empowering-Psychotherapy-Approach/dp/0898624606

[204] www.amazon.com/Different-Voice-Psychological-Theory-Development/dp/0674970969/

[205] www.amazon.com/The-Way-of-Superior-Man-audiobook/dp/B07FXZBYJ9/

[206] www.amazon.com/dp/1699443386

[207] www.amazon.com/King-Warrior-Magician-Lover-Rediscovering/dp/0062505971/

[208] www.amazon.com/Fire-Belly-Being-Sam-Keen/dp/0553351370

[209] www.amazon.com/Iron-John-Book-about-Men/dp/0306824264

[210] A 1996 behavioral genetics study of twins (related to the Big Five personality traits) suggested that heritability and environmental factors both influence all five factors to the same degree. Among four twin studies examined in 2003, the mean percentage for heritability was calculated for each personality and it was concluded that heritability influenced the five factors broadly. The self-report measures were as follows: openness to experience was estimated to have a 57% genetic influence; extraversion 54%; conscientiousness 49%; neuroticism 48%; and agreeableness 42%.
https://en.wikipedia.org/wiki/Big_Five_personality_traits

[211] Neuro-Linguistic Programming, or NLP, is a method that originated in the 1970s to improve therapeutic and personal successes by replicating effective patterns of behavior and communication. The model soon became popular in sales, education, and change management to create better rapport with customers, students, and employees and can also be applied to improve success with a woman. NLP identifies three basic learning and communication modalities in people: auditory, visual, and kinesthetic.

Auditory types connect through verbal exchange and might say "I hear what you say," or "let me tell you something." They learn and communicate through words.

Visual types like to see/show things and might say "I see what you mean" or "let me show you how I see things." They learn and communicate through images.

Kinesthetic types like to feel and touch and might say "this really touches me" or "don't you feel what is going on." They learn and communicate through shared feeling and hands-on experiences.

[212] According to the Myers-Briggs type indicator, all people can be classified using a scale of four opposing criteria:

Extroversion–Introversion

Sensing–Intuitive

Thinking–Feeling

Judging–Perceiving

The 16 possible combinations of the four either/or criteria determine a type. For example:

ISTJ - Introvert Sensing Thinking Judging

www.myersbriggs.org/

You can identify your own and your partner's types with their associated strengths and weaknesses by taking an online Myers-Briggs typology test: for example, at www.humanmetrics.com/personality, or search for the many other options.

[213] Human Design is a New-Age-inspired practice. It combines astrology, the I Ching, Kabbalah, and Vedic philosophy, centering around the division of personalities into five energy types alleged to indicate how someone is supposed to exchange energy with the world: manifestors, generators, manifesting generators, projectors, and reflectors. https://en.wikipedia.org/wiki/Human_Design

[214] The DISC theory describes personality through four central traits:

Dominance: active use of force to overcome resistance in the environment.

Inducement: use of charm in order to deal with obstacles.

Submission: warm and voluntary acceptance of the need to fulfill a request.

Compliance: fearful adjustment to a superior force.

https://en.wikipedia.org/wiki/DISC_assessment

[215] The Big Five personality traits is a suggested taxonomy, or grouping, for personality traits, developed from the 1980s onward, in psychological trait theory. These five overarching domains have been found to contain and subsume most known personality traits and are assumed to represent the basic structure behind all personality traits.

https://en.wikipedia.org/wiki/Big_Five_personality_traits

[216] The HEXACO model of personality structure is a six-dimensional model of human personality that was created by Ashton and Lee and explained in their book, *The H Factor of Personality*. The six factors, or dimensions, include Honesty-Humility (H), Emotionality (E), Extraversion (X), Agreeableness (A), Conscientiousness (C), and Openness to Experience (O) … HEXACO. Each factor is composed of traits with characteristics indicating high and low levels of the factor. The HEXACO model shares several common elements with other trait models (like The Big Five) and is also unique due to the addition of the Honesty-Humility dimension.

tinyurl.com/irpm660

https://en.wikipedia.org/wiki/HEXACO_model_of_personality_structure

[217] Factor analysis is a statistical method used to describe variability among observed, correlated variables in terms of a potentially lower number of unobserved variables called factors. For example, it is possible that variations in six observed variables mainly reflect the variations in two unobserved variables. https://en.wikipedia.org/wiki/Factor_analysis

[218] www.audible.com/pd/Why-You-Are-Who-You-Are-Audiobook/B07946LTV5

[219] www.amazon.com/Factor-Personality-Self-Entitled-Materialistic-Exploitive_And/dp/1554588340

[220] www.amazon.com/Love-Languages-Secret-that-Lasts/dp/080241270X/

[221] www.5lovelanguages.com/quizzes/

[222] The origins of the Enneagram

Some authors believe that variations of the Enneagram symbol can be traced to the sacred geometry of Pythagorean mathematicians and mystical mathematics.

Plotinus, in the Enneads, speaks of nine divine qualities that manifest in human nature.

It may have entered esoteric Judaism through the philosopher Philo, later becoming embedded in the branches of the Tree of Life in the Kabbalah (Nine-Foldedness).

Variations of the Enneagram symbol appear in the Sufi tradition, with specific reference to the Naqshbandi Order ("Brotherhood of the Bees"). Also see tinyurl.com/irpm662 https://sufipathoflove.com/enneagram-in-sufism/

Possible relationship with Christianity through medieval references to the Evagrius' catalogue of various forms of temptation (Logismoi) which, much later, in medieval times, was translated into the seven deadly sins.

Franciscan mystic Ramon Llull taught a philosophy and theology of nine principles in an attempt to integrate different faith traditions.

Jesuit mathematician Athanasius Kircher has an Enneagram-like drawing that forms part of a 17th-century text.

tinyurl.com/irpm664

www.integrative9.com/enneagram/history/

[223] See A.H. Almaas Facets of Unity: The Enneagram of Holy Ideas.

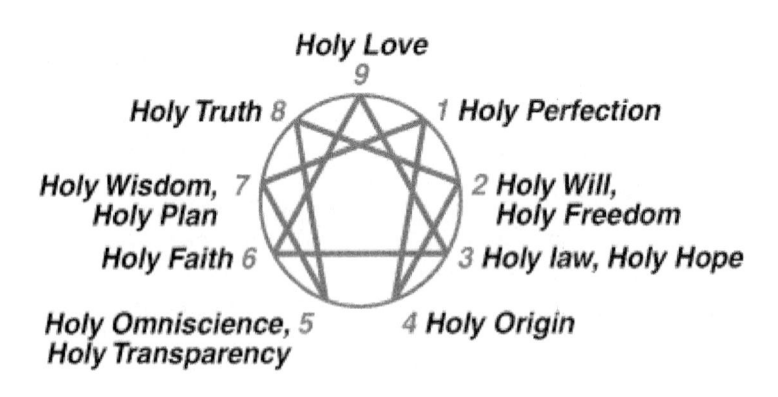

Holy Love 9
Holy Truth 8
1 Holy Perfection
Holy Wisdom, 7
Holy Plan
2 Holy Will,
Holy Freedom
Holy Faith 6
3 Holy law, Holy Hope
Holy Omniscience, 5
Holy Transparency
4 Holy Origin

Figure 95: Enneagram holy ideas

Source:

tinyurl.com/irpm665

www.enneagraminstitute.com/the-traditional-enneagram

Also see tinyurl.com/irpm666

www.diamondapproach.org/glossary/refinery_phrases/enneagram-holy-ideas

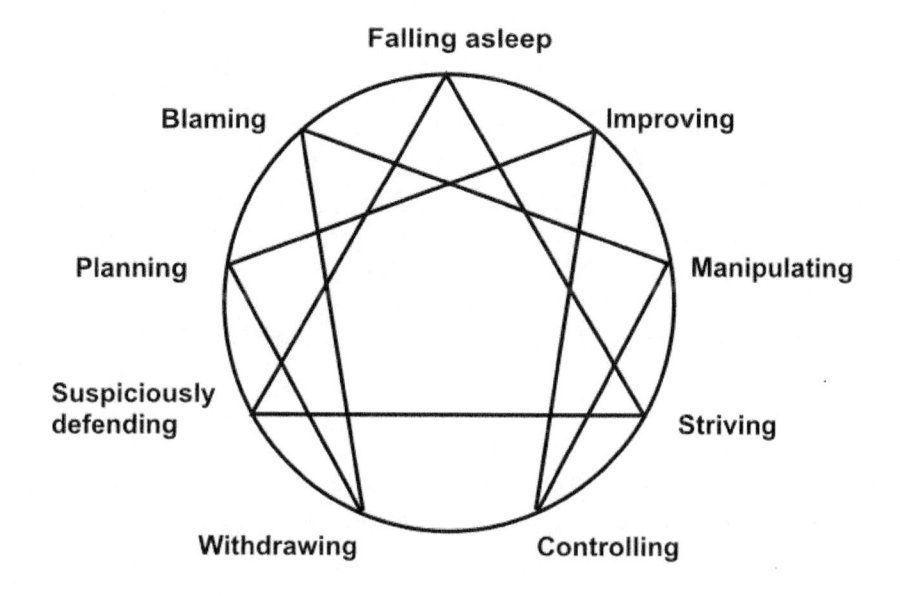

Figure 96: Enneagram specific reactions

Source:

tinyurl.com/irpm668

www.diamondapproach.org/glossary/refinery_phrases/enneagram-specific-reactions

Integral Relationship Practice | 604

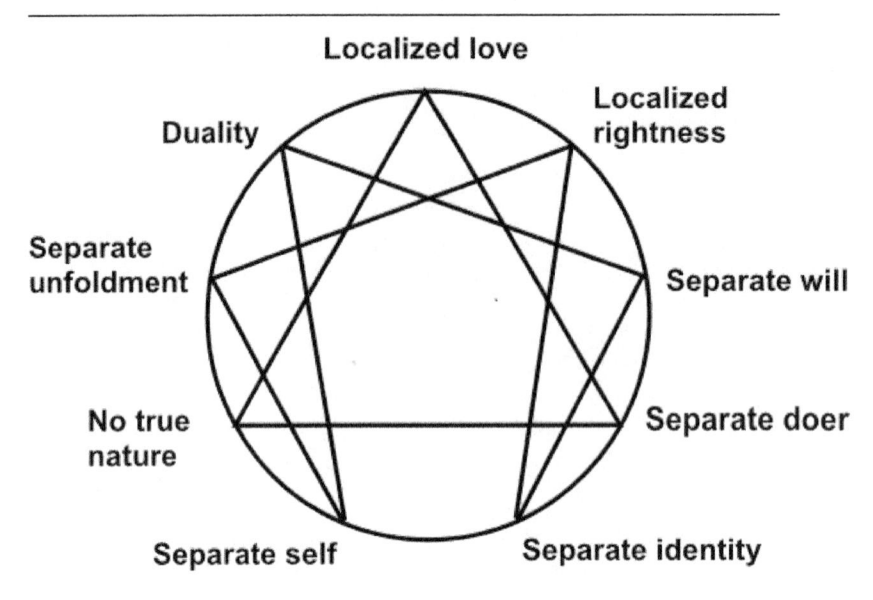

```
                    Localized love
                              Localized
          Duality             rightness

Separate
unfoldment                    Separate will


 No true
  nature                      Separate doer


      Separate self    Separate identity
```

Figure 97: Enneagram specific delusions

Source:

tinyurl.com/irpm671

www.diamondapproach.org/glossary/refinery_phrases/enneagram-specific-delusions

[224] www.enneagraminstitute.com/the-enneagram-type-combinations

[225] www.enneagraminstitute.com/ivq

[226] Two tests that seem to be especially useful are at tinyurl.com/irpm674 www.enneagraminstitute.com and tinyurl.com/irpm264 www.9types.com

[227] Don Richard Riso and Russ Hudson integrate the horizontal types (e.g., Enneagram), vertical growth (levels/stages) and "states" in their book *The Wisdom of the Enneagram* (see page 75–87). This book also has a simple test in the front that you can take with your partner.

A simple, playful, and fun book for couples and the whole family is *The Enneagram Made Easy* by Renee Baron and Elizabeth Wagele. www.amazon.com/Enneagram-Made-Easy-Discover-People/dp/0062510266

[228] Even though it is strongly suggested not to type other people unless they request your help to type themselves, some Enneagram groups, e.g., www.facebook.com/groups/enneagramopenings/, allow typing of

celebrities when specific reasons are given. Below is a shortened lists of celebrities from www.thechangeworks.com/images/Famous.pdf

Type 1 (Reformers/Perfectionists): Harry Belafonte, Noam Chomsky, Hillary Clinton, Anne Frank, Harrison Ford, Jodie Foster, Al Gore, Martin Luther, Immanuel Kant, Nelson Mandela, Pope John Paul II, Colin Powell, Yitzak Rabin, Ayn Rand, Condoleezza Rice, Eleanor Roosevelt, Donald Rumsfeld, George Bernard Shaw, Martha Stewart, Meryl Streep, Margaret Thatcher, Harry Truman, Carl Sagan.

[229] **Type 2 (Helpers):** Alan Alda, Brigitte Bardot, Lynne Cheney, Diana–Princess of Wales, Mia Farrow, Jesus Christ, Yoko Ono, Dolly Parton, Nancy Reagan, Mother Teresa, Desmond Tutu.

[230] **Type 3 (Achievers):** Muhammad Ali, Lance Armstrong, Halle Berry, Tony Blair, David Bowie, Bill Clinton, David Copperfield, Tom Cruise, Michael Dell, F. Scott Fitzgerald, Mick Jagger, Michael Jordan, Lady GaGa, Carl Lewis, Andrew Lloyd Webber, Paul McCartney, Madonna, Demi Moore, Benjamin Netanyahu, Jacqueline Kennedy Onassis, Elvis Presley, Arnold Schwarzenegger, O.J. Simpson, Will Smith, Sylvester Stallone, Sting, Andy Warhol, Vanessa Williams, Oprah Winfrey, Tiger Woods.

[231] **Type 4 (Individualists):** Ingmar Bergman, Maria Callas, Prince Charles, Eric Clapton, James Dean, Fyodor Dostoyevsky, Bob Dylan, William Faulkner, Hermann Hesse, Michael Jackson, Janis Joplin, Marilyn Manson, Michelangelo, Claude Monet, Jim Morrison, Edith Piaf, Prince, Vincent Van Gogh, Orson Welles, Oscar Wilde, Kate Winslet, Virginia Woolf.

[232] **Type 5 (Investigators/Thinkers):** Ken Wilber, Agatha Christie, Marie Curie, Charles Darwin, Robert DeNiro, René Descartes, Emily Dickinson, Joe DiMaggio, Amelia Earhart, Albert Einstein, T. S. Eliot, Bill Gates, Stephen Hawking, Alfred Hitchcock, Franz Kafka, Stanley Kubrick, George Lucas, John Nash, Isaac Newton, Edward Norton, John D. Rockefeller, Jean-Paul Sartre, Nikola Tesla, Jules Verne.

[233] **Type 6 (Loyalists):** Woody Allen, George H. W. Bush, Ellen DeGeneres, Jane Fonda, Hugh Grant, Che Guevara, Tom Hanks, Dustin Hoffman, Robert Kennedy, David Letterman, Michael Moore, Paul Newman, Richard Nixon, Sydney Pollack, Robert Redford, Julia Roberts, Chris Rock, Meg Ryan, Bruce Springsteen, Jon Stewart.

[234] **Type 7 (Enthusiasts/Explorers):** Mel Brooks, Michael Caine, Pierre Cardin, George Clooney, Francis Ford Coppola, Billy Crystal, Salvador Dali, Leonardo DaVinci, Leonardo DiCaprio, Thomas Edison, Goethe, Whoopie Goldberg, Steve Jobs, Elton John, Jack Nicholson, Franklin Roosevelt, Martin Scorsese, Steven Spielberg, Barbra Streisand, Elizabeth Taylor, Tina Turner, Robin Williams.

[235] **Type 8 (Challengers):** Humphrey Bogart, Napoleon Bonaparte, Marlon Brando, Julius Caesar, Sandra Bullock, Al Capone, Johnny Cash, Fidel Castro, Winston Churchill, Russell Crowe, Morgan Freeman, Indira Gandhi, George Gurdjieff, Ernest Hemingway, Charlton Heston, Jimmy Hoffa, Saddam Hussein, Billy Idol, Lyndon Johnson, Sean Penn, Pablo Picasso, Frank Sinatra, Socrates, Donald Trump, John Wayne.

[236] **Type 9 (Mediators/Peacemakers):** Jennifer Aniston, Ingrid Bergman, Kevin Costner, Matt Damon, Dalai Lama, Dwight Eisenhower, Queen Elizabeth II, Gerald Ford, Carl Jung, Stan Laurel, Abraham Lincoln, Andie MacDowell, Jerry Seinfeld.

[237] tinyurl.com/irpm252

www.enneagraminstitute.com/the-enneagram-type-combinations

[238] Also see tinyurl.com/irpm403

https://drdaviddaniels.com/relationships-intimacy/enneagram-types-in-relationship/

Dr. Khaled ElSherbini added these descriptions for various type combinations:

1 2 6 dutiful types

4 6 8 intense types

1 3 5 objective types

2 7 9 positive types

3 7 8 assertive types

4 5 9 withdrawn types

For more visit tinyurl.com/irpm400

https://enneagramegypt.com/

[239] See www.lynnroulo.com/enneagram-love-types-go-well-together/

[240] The descriptions were adopted from material on tinyurl.com/irpm255

www.enneagraminstitute.com/how-the-enneagram-system-works/

[241] See for example:

tinyurl.com/irpm416

www.enneagraminstitute.com/ivq

tinyurl.com/irpm680

similarminds.com/variant.html

tinyurl.com/irpm683

http://personalitycafe.com/enneagram-personality-theory-forum/149408-instinctual-variant-test-final-version.html

[242] https://enneagramegypt.com/

[243] https://drdaviddaniels.com/

[244] www.enneagram.com/

[245] https://theenneagraminbusiness.com/

[246] https://tests.enneagraminstitute.com/

[247] https://app.trueself.io/profile/questions

[248] www.enneagraminstitute.com/the-enneagram-type-combinations

[249] https://drdaviddaniels.com/relationships-intimacy/enneagram-types-in-relationship/

[250] www.lynnroulo.com/about/enneagram/enneagram-type-combinations/

[251] www.enneagraminstitute.com/ivq

[252] http://similarminds.com/variant.html

[253] https://youtu.be/7TO8uqMi0Mg

[254] www.youtube.com/channel/UC1a8stigiVibE7glqqnClgg

[255] https://youtu.be/L_wKhSdhO78

[256] https://play.google.com/store/search?q=enneagram&c=apps&hl=en

[257] www.amazon.com/s?k=Enneagram&ref=nb_sb_noss_2

[258] www.amazon.com/Wisdom-Enneagram-Psychological-Spiritual-Personality/dp/0553378201/

[259] www.amazon.com/Facets-Unity-Enneagram-Almaas-2000-09-05/dp/B01N8YAS36

[260] www.amazon.com/gp/product/0997183179/

[261] www.amazon.com/gp/product/1731357966

[262] www.amazon.com/Enneagram-Love-Work-Understanding-Relationships/dp/0062507214/

[263] tinyurl.com/irpm675

https://theenneagraminbusiness.com/fascinating-or-fun/the-enneagram-according-to-pooh/

The Enneagram in the Movies (and a little TV):

tinyurl.com/irpm677

https://foldedandunfolding.wordpress.com/2016/01/11/the-enneagram-in-the-movies-and-a-little-tv/

Other Enneagram Movies:

tinyurl.com/irpm679

https://enneagrammaine.com/the-movie-list/

[264] Three forms of attachment styles were discovered by John Bowlby in the second part of the last century when he observed the behavior of babies after a stressful separation from their caregivers (usually parents). A fourth type "disorganized/disoriented" was added, based on research by developmental psychologist Mary Ainsworth.

[265] https://en.wikipedia.org/wiki/Strange_situation

[266] See Ayala Malach Pines, *Falling in Love*, page 109–120: "'Attachment theory' describes how children learn to feel close (attached) to their primary caregiver (usually the mother) while also feeling safe to explore their individuality. If the primary caregiver is consistent, stable, trustworthy, and responsive, the toddler develops a sense of security in love and as an adult will be comfortable and satisfied in love relationships. If not, an adult will display a pattern of anxiety and ambivalence or may even avoid intimate love relationships altogether."

[267] https://youtu.be/apzXGEbZht0

[268] From *HuffPost*:

It is truly amazing how much fog, depression, confusion, and anxiety begins to lift when the story one narrates starts to be one's own. It needn't be a pretty story or even a wholly accurate story—just one's own.

Storytelling is an important part of self-development. The (coherent) narration that has gone awry can be addressed and realigned in psychotherapy.

There is compelling research evidence that the coherence of a primary caregiver's autobiographical, relational story is a key component in parenting (and love relationships). (See the works of Robert Karen and Daniel Siegel.)

What researchers found was that a strong predictor of stable, secure attachment was the primary ability of adults to recount a coherent story of their own lives. That story doesn't need to be historically accurate. It does not need to be positive. It is not necessary to have had a happy childhood. All that is necessary is being able to tell both yourself and an interviewer a story that hangs together, that makes sense.

This is how coherence is described by attachment theory researcher Mary Main (paraphrased by Arieta Slade):

[A] coherent interview is both believable and true to the listener; in a coherent interview, the events and affects intrinsic to early relationships are conveyed without distortion, contradiction, or derailment of discourse. The subject collaborates with the interviewer, clarifying his or her meaning, and working to make sure he or she is understood. Such a subject is thinking as the interview proceeds and is aware of thinking.

tinyurl.com/irpm462

www.huffpost.com/entry/personal-narrative-healing_b_862285

Prompt: Write a coherent narrative, a story that makes sense of one of the traumas from your list. Describe what happened in the traumatic incident and how you felt. Then write about how you think this event impacts you in your life today.

Tips for Writing a Coherent Narrative: From

tinyurl.com/irpm463

https://ecourse.psychalive.org/wp-content/uploads/2016/05/Coherent-Narrative.pdf

Write as an adult. Maintain an adult perspective as you write your story. Write about events from your childhood in the past tense. Recognize that even though old emotions may be stirred up, these painful memories are not happening to you now. Do not write from a victimized point of view.

Write rationally. In order to develop coherence, your narrative must make logical sense. Writing rationally activates your linear, logical, language-based, left brain. If your narrative is logical, you will have more of a feeling of resolve after writing.

Write autobiographically. It's important to include specific, autobiographical memories when writing your coherent narrative. These are your stories, and you should be in them. Autobiographical memories are stored in the right side of your brain, and it is crucial to include them in order to develop coherence and integrate your brain.

Write intuitively. It's okay to write about things you think happened. A lot of our early or traumatic memories are hazy; they are implicit, not explicit, memories. If something feels right or true to you on an intuitive level, you should include it in your narrative. You don't need to be 100% sure it happened that way.

Write with feeling. It's important to include details of how you felt, as you write about your memories. Recalling emotions and bodily sensations can be an important part of resolving old traumas.

Write about how the past influences your present. Make connections. Notice how patterns or feelings from the past may be playing out in your life today. Are there elements of your early relationships that may be affecting how you feel with your partner? Is there a way you felt as a child that you may be projecting onto your own kid? When you make connections between how you felt in the past and how you feel in the present, you can begin to see the world more clearly. When you feel triggered in your daily life, you can return to your coherent narratives. Understanding where your feelings originated, you can then choose not to react impulsively to the old emotions.

Write with balance. Based on the adaptations your brain made to your early attachments, you are probably more comfortable writing from either a right- or left-brain perspective. You may feel overwhelmed or flooded with emotions and images when you write, or you may feel very rational but lack a sense of how you felt in the stories you are telling. It's important to find a balance—to acknowledge the emotions, while maintaining a rational perspective. This is how you integrate your brain and get the full benefits of writing a coherent narrative.

Write with self-compassion. Maintain a compassionate attitude toward yourself as you write. If you feel stirred up from writing about a painful or traumatic experience, be kind to yourself in the process. Recognize that suffering is part of the human experience, and you are not alone in your suffering. Seek out a friend or a therapist to talk to. A lot of people suffer from guilty feelings as they expose details from their family life.

Don't go with the guilt. You have a right to tell your story and make sense of your own life.

[269] Download Adult Attachment Interview from tinyurl.com/irpm684

https://drive.google.com/file/d/1TdnEUItRTffmKh6sqSby4bYb_V0iqz7v

[270] To learn more about how to write a "coherent narrative" and develop an "earned secure attachment," see the online course "Making Sense of Your Life: Understanding Your Past to Liberate Your Present and Empower Your Future" with Dr. Lisa Firestone and Dr. Daniel Siegel at tinyurl.com/irpm686

www.psychalive.org/what-is-your-attachment-style/.

[271] www.attachmentproject.com/

[272] www.greatist.com/health/attachment-style-quizzes#7

[273] www.dianepooleheller.com/attachment-test/

[274] www.web-research-design.net/cgi-bin/crq/crq.pl

[275] https://youtu.be/WjOowWxOXCg

[276] www.amazon.com/Attached-Science-Adult-Attachment-YouFind/dp/1585429139/

[277] www.amazon.com/Polysecure-Attachment-Trauma-Consensual-Nonmonogamy/dp/1944934987

[278] www.amazon.com/Developing-Mind-Second-Relationships-Interact/dp/1462520677/

[279] www.amazon.com/Attachment-Disturbances-Adults-Treatment-Comprehensive/dp/0393711528

[280] www.amazon.com/Attachment-Psychotherapy-David-J-Wallin/dp/1541457919

[281] www.amazon.com/Healing-Developmental-Trauma-Self-Regulation-Relationship/dp/1583944893

[282] www.cdc.gov/violenceprevention/aces/about.html

[283] https://en.wikipedia.org/wiki/Adverse_Childhood_Experiences_Study

[284] www.huffpost.com/entry/personal-narrative-healing_b_862285

[285] https://ecourse.psychalive.org/wp-content/uploads/2016/05/Coherent-Narrative.pdf

[286] www.amazon.com/Mom-Want-Hear-Your-Story/dp/1081439793/

Integral Relationship Practice | 612

---

[287] www.amazon.com/Dad-Want-Hear-Your-Story/dp/1070527718/

[288] www.storyworth.com/questions

[289] Adopted from the introduction to the book, *Healing Developmental Trauma: How Early Trauma Affects Self-Regulation, Self-Image, and the Capacity for Relationship* (2012) Laurence Heller, PhD, and Aline LaPierre, PsyD

tinyurl.com/irpm459

www.amazon.com/Healing-Developmental-Trauma-Self-Regulation-Relationship/dp/1583944893

[290] Almost all couples and many therapists/teachers confuse challenging emotional reactions to other people's reality as a failure of setting healthy boundaries and defending ourselves. Instead, emotional reactions such as anger or fear are **always** caused either by our own pain or violations of our values and being-needs. It is an attempt by our unconscious to protect ourselves from re-experiencing the emotional hurt that was inflicted on us in our past, most likely during childhood. Instead of projecting the emotional fight, flight, flight, or fawn reactions on the other person (usually through blame, "shoulding," or violence), we can learn to own our emotions and feelings and make "I" statements. This **does not mean** that we must like, agree, condone, or accept their behavior at all, especially if it violates our values or human decency, because that would make us into a passive doormat. It simply means that we separate the behavior of the other person from our emotional reaction to their reality and own it. We can also learn to show empathy and/or compassion and take the others person's perspective and view. Then, without projecting, we may state our needs and desires and either accept, change, or leave the situation.

[291] MRI scans have revealed that the main activity in the brain of a person who is in love is not occurring in the cortex, the seat of conscious awareness and logical thinking, but in the reptile and limbic brain system (the Caudate Nucleus and the Ventral Tegmental Area), which are the seat of powerful emotions and long-term memories. They may direct us to choose a person who can help us master unresolved childhood issues.

Roy Bhaskar writes in *Reflections on MetaReality: Transcendence, Emancipation and Everyday Life*, page 2652–66: "Nonduality is a property of consciousness; reciprocity is a property of animate being, vitality, and life; co-presence is a principal of property of all being (including matter). Reciprocity in fact works via the principles of co-presence. Since what happens in the case of reciprocation is that some aspect or part of the reciprocating being with a similar, attuned to or (one might say) on the same wavelength, frequency, or level of vibration as that to which it reciprocates, resonates to the impulse which activates it. As the reciprocating being is itself a concrete universal, then the modes of resonance will depend on which feature of that particular concrete universal is involved. It is the psychic being which typically mediates and links the levels of conscious transcendental identification and enfolded co-presence."

Additional evidence that lovers resonate with each other in mysterious ways is provided by experiments that see correlations in brain and heart activity between physically isolated pairs.

Even though not directly focused on lovers, Rupert Sheldrake's research into Morphic Resonance (the hypothesis that living organisms draw upon and contribute to a collective memory of their species) may also hold answers why humans sometimes feel magically "in-tune" with, or powerfully drawn to, a specific lover, which cannot be explained by their reproductive, cultural, social, and psychological compatibility.

Also see Ayala Malach Pines, *Falling in Love,* page 178, and Helen Fisher, *Why We Love,* page 69–72.

[292] See Ken Wilber, *The Atman Project,* Chapter 11, under "Types of Unconscious." tinyurl.com/irpm479.

[293] The unrealized stages of these future growth potentials are not actively suppressed or involuntarily repressed; they just have not developed yet. Examples are certain aspects of a child's sexual impulses and preferences that have not emerged yet due to their young age. Even though each human, just like a tree, will develop its own unique qualities, the deep structures are embedded in the as-yet unrealized potential of their kind. In case of the child, we know it will become an adult, in the case of the acorn, it is already determined that it will not become a dandelion or a birch tree.

[294] These are embedded in their reptilian brain stem and DNA, and existed a priori, before language is learned, conceptual knowledge is developed, and personal events are remembered. This facet of the

unconscious causes people to experience and respond to the world in a manner similar to the ways that their forefathers did.

[295] The term subconscious is used in many different contexts and has no single or precise definition. This greatly limits its significance as a meaning-bearing concept, and, in consequence, the word tends to be avoided in academic and scientific settings. As the saying goes, you can't be a little pregnant, just as you can't be a little conscious. See www.en.wikipedia.org/wiki/Subconscious

[296] See Deepak Chopra, *The Path of Love*, page 177; Marlena Lyons and Jett Psaris, *Undefended Love* (a book that focuses on the submerged unconscious in relationships and how to uncover our true essence, especially page 57-59); John Welwood, *Love and Awakening*, page 31–48 and page 196 (in opening to our anger, we also find other feelings underneath it—sorrow, fear, or hurt—that are calling for attention and concern), and Harville Hendrix *Getting The Love You Want*, page 36–39.

[297] These are the elements of our existence that are considered to be incompatible with the ego (which is a mask and is often referred to as our false sense of self or false identity). If we are faced with these elements, we react defensively or aggressively, out of fear of re-experiencing the hurt that made us repress the memory of the event in the first place. As psychologists know, "anger masks fear, and fear masks hurt."

[298] The following poem describes our desire to be seen beyond our mask or false self:

The Mask I Wear:

Don't be fooled by me.

Don't be fooled by the face I wear

For I wear a mask.

 I wear a thousand masks—masks that I'm afraid to take off, and none of them are me.

Pretending is an art that's second nature with me

But don't be fooled, for God's sake, don't be fooled.

I give you the impression that I'm secure

That all is sunny and unruffled with me, within as well as without

that confidence is my name and coolness my game,

that the water's calm and I'm in command,

and that I need no one.

But don't believe me. Please!

My surface may be smooth but my surface is my mask,

My ever-varying and ever-concealing mask.

Beneath lies no smugness, no complacence.

Beneath dwells the real me in confusion, in fear, in aloneness.

But I hide this.

I don't want anybody to know it.

I panic at the thought of my weaknesses and fear exposing them.

That's why I frantically create my masks to hide behind.

But I don't tell you this. I don't dare. I'm afraid to.

I'm afraid you'll think less of me, that you'll laugh and your laugh would kill me.

I'm afraid that deep-down I'm nothing, that I'm just no good and you will see this and reject me.

I idly chatter to you in suave tones of surface talk.

I tell you everything that's nothing and nothing of what's everything, of what's crying within me.

So when I'm going through my routine do not be fooled by what I'm saying

Please listen carefully and try to hear what I'm not saying

Hear what I'd like to say but what I cannot say.

It will not be easy for you, long felt inadequacies make my defenses strong.

The nearer you approach me the blinder I may strike back.

Despite what books say of men, I am irrational;

I fight against the very thing that I cry out for.

You wonder who I am, you shouldn't. For I am every man and every woman who wears a mask.

  - Author unknown. Variations can be found in several publications and on the Internet.

[299] It is the inner voice (judge, protector, skeptic, controller, seeker, etc.), that consciously represses, but is unconscious of its own existence. Others—especially a soul mate—may recognize this embedded unconscious "self" and mirror it back, until the subject of the previous level of awareness becomes the object of the subject of the next level.

[300] The difference is that the ground and archaic unconscious are based in the past (in our examples above, the evolution of oak trees throughout history, and the resulting givens for its growth as an oak tree—both unconsciously embedded in the acorn. The emergent unconscious is in the future; for example, people who reject ideas of higher levels of consciousness development, such as Amber rejecting Orange, don't do this by actively repressing views from a higher altitude. They have simply not evolved to higher levels of consciousness yet, and hence are unconscious of them.

[301] https://integrallife.com/the-3-2-1-shadow-process/

[302] www.amazon.com/Undefended-Love-about-Yourself-First/dp/1572242086/

[303] www.amazon.com/A-H-Almaas/e/B000APJFS8/

[304] www.amazon.com/Atman-Project-Transpersonal-Human-Development/dp/0835607305

[305] Ego death is a "complete loss of subjective self-identity." The term is used in various intertwined contexts, with related meanings. In Jungian psychology, the synonymous term psychic death is used, which refers to a fundamental transformation of the psyche. In death and rebirth mythology, ego death is a phase of self-surrender and transition, as described by Joseph Campbell in his research on the mythology of the Hero's Journey. It is a recurrent theme in world mythology and is also used as a metaphor in some strands of contemporary western thinking.

Zen practice is said to lead to ego-death. Ego-death is also called "great death," in contrast to the physical "small death." According to Jin Y. Park, the ego death that Buddhism encourages makes an end to the "usually-unconsciousness-and-automated quest" to understand the sense-of-self as a thing, instead of as a process. Meditation is learning how to die by learning to "forget" the sense of self. Enlightenment occurs when the usually automatized reflexivity of consciousness ceases, which is experienced as a letting-go and falling into the void and being wiped out of existence; when consciousness stops trying to catch its own tail, I become nothing, and discover that I am everything.

https://en.wikipedia.org/wiki/Ego_death

[306] NARM connection survival style

The identity and physiology of adults with early trauma are impacted by the distress and dysregulation they experienced in early life. Early shock and attachment trauma create a distorted template for lifelong psychological, physiological, and relational functioning. Because of their early trauma, both the thinking and the spiritualizing subtypes disconnect from bodily experience and personal relationships. Although initially protective, sustained disconnection from the body and other people creates increasing dysregulation that leads to psychological and physiological symptoms.

The thinking subtype

As a result of early trauma, thinking subtypes have retreated to the life of the mind and choose theoretical and technical professions that do not require significant human interaction. These individuals tend to be more comfortable behind a computer, in their laboratory, or in their garage workshops where they can putter undisturbed. They can be brilliant thinkers but tend to use their intelligence to maintain significant emotional distance.

The spiritualizing subtype

These subtypes are prone to spiritualizing their experience. As a result of either early shock or relational trauma, they did not feel welcomed into the world and grew up believing that the world is a cold, loveless place. Because other humans are often experienced as threats, many individuals with this subtype search for spiritual connection, are more comfortable in nature and with animals, and feel more connected to God than to other human beings. To make sense of the pain of their lives, they often become spiritual seekers trying to convince themselves that someone loves them; if people do not, then God must.

These individuals are often extremely sensitive in both positive and negative ways. Having never embodied, they have access to energetic levels of information to which less traumatized people are not as sensitive; they can be quite psychic and energetically attuned to people, animals, and the environment and can feel confluent and invaded by other people's emotions. They are also unable to filter environmental stimuli—they are sensitive to light, sound, pollution, electromagnetic waves, touch, etc.; therefore, they often struggle with environmental sensitivities.

False identity

Regardless of age, connection types, at some level, often feel like frightened children in an adult world. Because of their inadequate sense of self, they often try to anchor themselves in their roles as scientist, judge, doctor, father, mother, etc. When functioning in a role, they feel comfortable, and they know what the rules are; being outside a specific role can feel frightening.

Isolation

Many connection types feel alone and isolated without realizing how they avoid human contact and isolate themselves; some are aware of their fear of people but believe that it is other people who are the source of the threat they feel. Ambivalence is characteristic of individuals with this survival style, particularly in personal relationships. They simultaneously have an intense need for, and an extreme fear of, contact. They tend to withdraw or break contact in emotionally disturbing or stressful situations.

Growth strategies for the connection survival style

This survival style's deepest longing for connection is also its deepest fear. The therapeutic key is to explore this profound internal conflict as it expresses in the moment-by-moment process of therapy and how it plays out in these clients' symptoms and lives. There is a functional unity between the difficulty of feeling body and emotions and the impaired capacity to make interpersonal connection. Clients with a Connection Survival Style know that at a deep level their survival strategy is not really serving them, but it is frightening to live without it. tinyurl.com/irpm686.

[307] NARM attunement survival style

Because of the lack of environmental attunement, individuals with this survival style do not learn to attune to their own needs, emotions, and body and become so adapted to scarcity that later in life, they are unable to recognize and express their own needs or allow fulfillment. For people with this survival style, there is a conflict between, on one hand, the expression of the need for physical or emotional nourishment, and the expectation of disappointment on the other.

Depending on the timing and severity of the attachment and nurturing difficulties, two different subtypes develop. Both subtypes live with a feeling of emptiness and deprivation, but they have different strategies for coping with that experience.

The inhibited subtype

When attachment and nurturing losses are early and/or more severe, the tendency is to foreclose the awareness of one's needs. The shame-based identification of these individuals is that needs are bad and wrong and that they are not entitled to have their needs fulfilled. These individuals often develop a counter-identification that is based on being proud of how little they need and how much they can do without. The extreme example of this strategy is anorexia.

The unsatisfied subtype

When the attachment and nurturing disruption is later or less severe, the unsatisfied type develops a tendency to be left with a chronic sense of feeling unfulfilled. In contrast to the inhibited type who will not express needs, the unsatisfied type can be very demanding of people in their lives while living with the continual feeling that there is never enough.

A good example to illustrate the difference between the inhibited and unsatisfied types is the state of their cupboards: the cupboards of the inhibited subtype tend to be nearly empty, and these individuals become anxious if their cupboards are too full while the cupboards of the unsatisfied subtype are overflowing, and they become anxious when supplies start to diminish.

False identity

Individuals with this survival style identify so strongly with the early experience of deprivation that they come to see the world through the prism of scarcity. Their resignation to deprivation and the depression of their needs, which is an adaptation to scarcity, impacts both their psychology and their physiology. Remembering that depression and resignation were originally life-saving, the identity of individuals with this adaptive survival style develops around making sense of, and coping with, their underlying resignation and depression. An identity develops around longing for fulfillment while at the same time, not being able to allow fulfillment.

Giving to get

Becoming caretakers is the coping mechanism both subtypes have in common. Caretaking is a pride-based strategy that allows them to see themselves as being without needs: "I don't have needs; everyone needs me." By developing relationships and work situations in which other people depend on them, they do not have to confront the shame they feel about needing or the rejection they fear will happen if they express their needs.

Growth strategies for the attunement survival style

NARM has developed a new orientation to help individuals with this survival style move toward resolution. The challenge for Attunement individuals is to learn how to attune to their own needs, to express them appropriately, and to tolerate more charge, fulfillment, expansion, and aliveness. The overall arc of therapy shifts from reliving experiences of abandonment and scarcity to learning how to tolerate fulfillment and expansion. We explore with these clients how there has been an adaptation to scarcity, to lack of attunement, and to abandonment that has affected both their sense of self and their physiology. tinyurl.com/irpm686.

[308] NARM trust survival style

There are two basic strategies that individuals with the Trust Survival Style use in their struggle to exercise their power: they become seductive and manipulative, or they become overpowering.

The seductive subtype

Individuals with the Trust seductive subtype use an "as if" strategy. They act as if they care, as if they are present to others, as if they love. They are experts at reading what people need. The "as if" quality is reflected in their chameleon-like ability to be all things to all people. Many people are taken in and believe the "as if" presentation of individuals with this survival subtype, but at some point, realize they are being used and betrayed by them.

Seductive subtypes know what people want to hear and say it convincingly. They have an uncanny knack for knowing people's vulnerabilities and can make them feel as if they are the center of the universe. They can skillfully:

- Manipulate or maneuver others to do their bidding.

- Seduce and charm: "I know what you need. I'll take care of you."
- Exert a charismatic attraction.
- Manipulate by presenting the image that will best meet their goals.

The overpowering subtype

The overpowering subtype develops as a result of the extreme helplessness these individuals have experienced in situations of abuse and horror. As children, their smallness, vulnerability, and dependency were used against them, and their vulnerability became intolerable. At some point, as they grow older, they make the decision to "turn the tables." They react to their parents' abuse by saying, "Never again! From now on, I'm the one in control." They take control and become the abusers.

Overpowering subtypes live with an underlying feeling of impotence and powerlessness. In reaction, they attempt to gain power over others by:

- Developing physical strength.
- Building empires, becoming rich and powerful.
- Developing their martial arts skills or owning guns.
- Being "one up."
- Gaining power over others then using it for their own purposes.
- Inspiring confidence in others and using it to control them.
- Being power hungry and competitive—always trying to be at the top.
- Having lived with intolerable fear as children, they present an image designed to evoke fear in others.

False identity

Individuals with the Trust Survival Style are very concerned with their image. They tell themselves that as long as they maintain a good front, as long as no one knows what is really going on inside, they are safe. The more negatively seductive subtypes feel about themselves, the harder they work at maintaining a good image. The more fearful overpowering subtypes feel about themselves, the harder they work at inciting fear in others. Sadly, both subtypes become experts at presenting a false image because they have lost touch with their core, with their sense of self.

Relationship and sex

Individuals with this survival style will not allow themselves to be emotionally close to anyone because closeness stirs up feelings of dependency and triggers the fear of being controlled, as they were in early life. They will stay in a relationship as long as they feel that they are in control and can successfully dominate their partner. To this end they often choose Attunement types as partners: Attunement types are caretakers who are happy to serve while Trust types are more than happy to be served.

Both men and women with this survival style use their sexuality as a weapon and sex as an arena for conquest. Women view men in terms of status, power, and money; they use sexual conquest to seduce high-status males in order to gain personal power. Men rank women according to their physical beauty and enhance their power with the sexual conquest of the most beautiful women.

People with this survival style strive to dominate the partner they are with. They find it difficult to sustain a relationship with a truly warm and loving partner; when they are with a loving partner, they can become sadistic, impotent, or break off the relationship. If two individuals with the Trust Survival Style come together, their lives become a power struggle full of ploys, subtle or direct, to dominate the other. Trust types are also attracted to needy partners, whose dependency they encourage. Their strategy is different from that of the Attunement type, who rescues needy partners in order to take care of them. Unlike Attunement types, whose identity revolves around being caregivers, Trust types want power over the needy partner.

Growth strategies for the trust survival style

For individuals with the Trust Survival Style, coming to therapy is an admission that they need help. The more strongly an individual uses the strategies of this survival style, the more unlikely it is that they will seek therapy—which, for them, evokes their core fear of vulnerability and betrayal.

When Trust types do come to therapy, they will probe for the therapist's weaknesses and work to stay in a one-up position. Individuals with this survival style are difficult to work with because they tend to stop therapy the moment that they feel threatened. Because they feel threatened by the therapeutic situation, they will often try to assert their dominance by finding an issue (for example, money, time, or payment policies) to do battle over and get special treatment. When working with individuals with this survival style, therapists must be careful not to get hooked into their seemingly endless attempts at one-upmanship. Individuals with the Trust Survival Style need therapists who are clear and direct, who have strong boundaries, and who will not get pulled into their power games. At the same time, it is essential that the therapist express understanding and empathy for the real suffering that these clients experience. tinyurl.com/irpm686.

[309] NARM autonomy survival style

In adults who have developed this adaptive survival style, self-assertion and overt expressions of independence and autonomy are experienced as dangerous and to be avoided. The major fears that fuel this survival adaptation are the fears of being criticized, rejected, and abandoned.

Paralyzed by Internal Conflict

What was once a struggle with their parents is now internalized so that individuals with the Autonomy Survival Style spend their lives playing out the conflict between the internalized demanding parent and the withholding child. As a result, they feel paralyzed and bound by the internal contradictions inherent in the interplay of these two roles. Extreme ambivalence and a resulting immobilization are characteristics of this survival style.

Fear of intimacy

Given their childhood experience, it is easy to understand how love and intimacy are associated with fears of invasion, of being controlled, smothered, crushed, or overwhelmed. These individuals long for closeness but associate it with losing their independence and autonomy.

Individuals with the Autonomy Survival Style are placaters and are afraid to expose their true feelings. Instead, they play the role of the "good boy" or the "nice girl" because they feel that since playing this role won their parents' "love," it will win other people's love as well. A key statement for this adaptive survival style is, "If I show you how I really feel, you won't love me—you'll leave me." Because they are afraid to stand up for themselves, they blame others for taking advantage of "their good nature." Unfortunately, playing the role of the "good boy" or "nice girl" puts them in a no-win situation. Playing a role brings constant disappointment, resentment, and anger because, given that they are not authentic, they cannot feel loved for who they really are even when people respond favorably to the persona they have created. They develop a distrust of the world, a cynical belief that no one can really accept them as they are.

Relationship and sex

In personal relationships, these individuals allow frustrations to build without addressing them until they reach a point where they can no longer tolerate the accumulated resentments. They usually have escape strategies that allow them to leave relationships without confrontation: They withdraw without explanation, or they make their partner miserable so that the partner rejects them. This rejection by the other allows them to achieve "freedom" without the guilt of saying no, while at the same time reaping the secondary benefit of being the "innocent" injured party.

Rumination

The tendency to brood and ruminate is typical of this survival style. These individuals ruminate after personal encounters, berating themselves about whether they did or said the right thing, chastising themselves for any "mistakes" they feel they made in the interaction, wondering if they said the right thing or hurt the person's feelings.

Ambivalence toward authority

A key aspect of the Autonomy Survival Style identity is a deep-seated ambivalence toward authority. Overtly, Autonomy types are deferential to authority, but covertly they harbor resentments and rebellious impulses. When dealing with authority, they feel that the only options they have are to submit to it or rebel against it. This "submit or rebel" dilemma leaves them in a no-win situation that has profound implications for the therapeutic relationship.

Growth strategies for the autonomy survival style

In the therapeutic process with individuals with the Autonomy Survival Style, it is important to keep in mind how paralyzed they feel as a result of their own internal contradictions. Not realizing how much pressure they put on themselves or how they constantly judge themselves, they experience their internal struggle as resulting from external circumstances. Growth takes place when they become aware that the pressures they experience are primarily the result of their own internal demands. tinyurl.com/irpm686

[310] NARM love-sexuality survival style

When individuals experience misattunement to their love and sexuality needs, one of two subtypes develop—the romantic subtype or the sexual subtype—each favoring one aspect of the love-sexuality split.

The romantic subtype

These individuals romanticize love and marriage. They are openhearted but often disconnected from their sexuality and may even be terrified of it; they have difficulty integrating a vital sexuality into their love relationships. In the early stages of a relationship, they can feel more sexual, but as the relationship deepens, their sexual feelings diminish. Less integrated romantic subtypes, having disconnected from their sexual impulses, can become the moral crusaders, the self-appointed guardians of public morality who attempt to enforce their moral code on others. In the repressed romantic subtype who professes a strong and often judgmental position about the sexuality of others, the sexual impulses have been driven underground and are sometimes expressed in covert and secret acting out.

The sexual subtype

Individuals with the sexual subtype have a tendency toward seductive behavior as a way to make themselves desirable. They seek out and use attractive partners to bolster their own self-esteem and measure sexual satisfaction by the frequency, rather than by the depth, of their experience.

Their seductiveness is not used for control, as with the Trust type, but as a way to prevent real intimacy. Because of their fear and avoidance of intimacy, they often have the feeling that they are incapable of loving. Sexual subtypes consider themselves sexually sophisticated, and sexual potency and performance are important to them. Frequently, however, their sexuality is mechanical and disconnected, centered more on conquest and performance than on heart connection.

For this subtype, the love-sexuality split results in both alienation from deep sexual pleasure and obsession with genitally focused sexuality. Individuals in this sexual subtype may be obsessed with sex and pornography; they may be highly promiscuous, constantly seeking the sexual satisfaction that their rigid, defended bodies will not allow them to fully experience.

In relationship, they experience an initial period of intense sexuality, but as the possibility of a heart connection develops, they often lose sexual interest or break off the relationship. They can be sexual with relative strangers but not with the person they love. This split is reflected in their inability to maintain a strong sexual connection beyond the early courting period. As a relationship progresses and the partner becomes less of a stranger and more like family, sexual subtype individuals cannot maintain a sexual charge. They cope by changing relationships relatively frequently to maintain their sexual interest or by staying in one relationship and feeling sexually frustrated. Sometimes, they will stay in one relationship to fulfill their need for love but have affairs to fulfill their sexual needs.

False identity

The identity of Love-Sexuality types is based on looks and performance; their highest priority is to look good and perform well. Individuals with this survival style spend their lives compensating for their early heartbreak and rejection by trying to perfect themselves. Having experienced rejection, their mantra becomes, "I will be so perfect, so attractive, that everyone will be drawn to me, and I will never have to face rejection again." They are often driven and demanding and hold high standards of perfection for themselves and others. Their pride-based identifications involve the relentless pursuit of perfection, whereas their shame-based identifications, often unconscious, reflect a sense of hurt, rejection, and feeling flawed.

Relationship and sex

Love-Sexuality types, focusing more on surface image than on the core of the relationship, choose partners who reflect well on them. They like to bathe in the narcissistic glow of their partner's good looks and accomplishments.

Individuals with the Love-Sexuality Survival Style have a tremendous fear of vulnerability. They may be aware of strong feelings of affection for their partner but will show marked restraint in revealing them. When feeling wounded, their rigid pride reveals itself; they wait for their partner to initiate reconciliation. Having invested energy in creating an image of perfection, they fear that nobody could possibly love them if their flaws were revealed. They also fear that they are not capable of loving anyone, and they constantly question whether love is even possible.

Growth strategies for the love-sexuality survival style

Individuals with the Love-Sexuality Survival Style come to therapy with concerns about their love relationships. They realize how difficult it was for them to feel both sexual and loving toward the same person. At first, they can often only relate to their lack of sexual feelings or love as boredom. They come to see that their inability to maintain a sexual and loving relationship with the same partner has to do with a lifelong love-sexuality split that had remained unresolved. tinyurl.com/irpm686.

[311] https://katiedejong.com/wp-content/uploads/2018/05/Identifying-Core-Negative-Beliefs-Transformation-of-Identity-Matrix.pdf

[312] www.amazon.com/Undefended-Love-about-Yourself-First/dp/1572242086/

[313] www.amazon.com/Healing-Developmental-Trauma-Self-Regulation-Relationship/dp/1583944893

[314] The NARM Healing Cycle

Most therapeutic and personal growth traditions tend to focus on either top-down or bottom-up aspects of the circular flow of information, working either from the body to the brain or from the brain to the body.

NARM views the mindful bottom-up experience of the body as the foundation of the healing process. The body is our connection to reality, the platform from which NARM works. By paying attention to the body, we are more easily able to recognize the truths and fictions of our personal narrative. As shock states held in the nervous system are discharged, we come into more contact with our body. A positive cycle is established in which the more self-regulated we become, the more we are in touch with our body, and the more in touch with our body we are, the greater our capacity for self-regulation.

While NARM is grounded in bottom-up somatic mindfulness, it uses the mindful awareness of survival styles to bring a process of top-down inquiry to our sense of self which includes our fixed beliefs (identifications and counter-identifications), our self-hatred, self-rejection, and judgments. NARM also uses inquiry to help dissolve the fixed, narrow ideas about others and the world that limit our life. Since many of our identifications develop in the first five years of life, distortions in identity keep us seeing ourselves and the world from a child's perspective.

As the NARM process unfolds, a healing cycle is set in motion in which nervous system regulation increases and distorted identifications and beliefs diminish and eventually resolve. In a positive healing cycle, the increasing nervous system regulation helps dissolve painful identifications, and as painful identifications and judgments dissolve, increasing capacity for self-regulation becomes possible.

THE NARM HEALING CYCLE

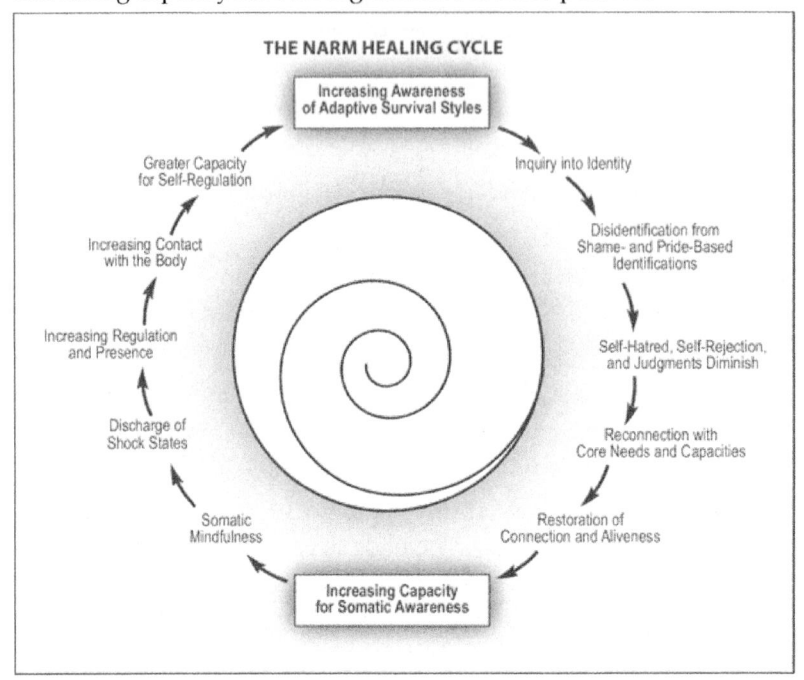

- Increasing Awareness of Adaptive Survival Styles
- Inquiry into Identity
- Disidentification from Shame- and Pride-Based Identifications
- Self-Hatred, Self-Rejection, and Judgments Diminish
- Reconnection with Core Needs and Capacities
- Restoration of Connection and Aliveness
- Increasing Capacity for Somatic Awareness
- Somatic Mindfulness
- Discharge of Shock States
- Increasing Regulation and Presence
- Increasing Contact with the Body
- Greater Capacity for Self-Regulation

Figure 98: The NARM healing cycle

[315] https://narmtraining.com/

[316] Scott Peck defined love in his book *The Road Less Traveled* as "The will to extend one's self for the purpose of nurturing one's own or another's spiritual growth." John Welwood in *Love and Awakening* page 49 – 59 calls soul mates "worthy opponents." The book, *Undefended Love,* by Marlena Lyons and Jett Psaris (based on A.H. Almaas's (Hameed Ali) Diamond Heart Work,) is an excellent tool for using relationships to awaken to your soul's essence (also see Modules 18 and 19).

[317] Romancing the Unconscious

Dr. Ayala Malach Pines, couples therapist, professor, and head of the Department of Business Administration at the School of Management at the Ben-Gurion University in Israel, and author of ten books, aptly summarizes the attraction of the unconscious and the potentials for healing and growth in her excellent book, *Falling In Love,* on pages 194–195 [quoted by permission]:

Unconscious forces more than logical considerations dictate with whom we fall in love.

An intimate relationship provides one of the best opportunities for mastering unresolved childhood issues.

The unconscious choice is of a person with whom we can reenact childhood experiences; thus, the person combines the most significant traits of both parents.

Negative traits of both parents have more of an impact on romantic choices—especially in obsessive loves—than do positive traits, because the injury or deprivation caused by them needs healing.

The more traumatic the childhood injury, and the greater the similarity between the lovers and the injuring parent, the more intense the experience of falling in love is.

In falling in love, there is a return to the primal symbiosis with the mother, a perfect union with no ego boundaries. This is why we only fall in love with one person at a time. The return to the lost paradise creates the expectation that the lover will fill all our infantile needs.

Because falling in love is dictated by an internal romantic image, lovers feel as if they have known each other forever. And because it involves a re-enactment of specific and powerful childhood experiences, lovers feel that the beloved is "the one and only" and that the loss of the beloved will be unbearable.

When a couple falls in love, their unconscious choice is mutual and complementary, enabling both partners to express their own core issues. Together, they create their core issue as a couple, the issue around which most of their later conflicts center.

Understanding the connection between unresolved childhood issues and later problems reduces the feelings of guilt and blame and helps both partners take responsibility for their parts in the relationship problem.

Couples who listen to each other's feelings, express empathy, and give each other the things they ask for, can keep the romantic spark alive indefinitely.

Expressing empathy and granting the partner's wishes is the best way to grow. As partners grow, their relationship grows. And growth is the antithesis to [relationship] burnout.

Although no two relationships are ever the same, psychologists have noticed common patterns of the unconscious fit in couples:

Parent and child—often have shared issues with dependency and trust.

Master and slave—have problems with authority and control.

Distancer and pursuer (also known as "seduce and withhold/withdraw")—are in desperate need—and at the same time deeply afraid—of intimacy and have found their perfect match. One is pursuing—but never quickly enough to get really close; the other is running—but never fast enough to really get away. As one moves closer, the other withdraws, only to reverse the roles for the next episode.

Idol and worshipper—insist on putting the other on a pedestal. This often indicates issues with competition and inadequacy.

Babes in the wood—look alike, share the same interests, and—more importantly—dislike the same things.

Cat and dog—look on the surface as they should have never even met. They argue incessantly over anything and avoid intimacy by living in a war zone.

You may recognize elements of these opposite pairs in your own love relationship or that of others.

[318] See *The New Psychology of Love,* edited by Robert J. Sternberg and Karin Weis page 149–170; *Styles of Romantic Love* by Clyde and Susan S. Hendrick; and *Why We Love* by Helen Fisher, page 94, where they list the styles as follows:

Eros — a passionate physical and emotional love based on aesthetic enjoyment, the stereotype of romantic love.

Ludus — a love that is played as a game or sport, a conquest.

Storge — an affectionate love that slowly develops from friendship, based on similarity.

Pragma — love that is driven by the head, not the heart; undemonstrative.

Mania — highly volatile love; obsession; fueled by low self-esteem.

Agape — selfless altruistic love; spiritual; motherly love.

Also see "A Duplex Theory of Love," by Robert J. Sternberg page 184–199, who lists them as the following:

Non-love, friendship, infatuation, empty love, romantic love, companionate love, fatuous love (silly, stupid, ridiculous, meaningless, or foolish love), consummate love (complete, perfect, and highest form of love).

[319] See Ayala Malach Pines, *Falling in Love*, page 3–11: "Repeated exposure is yet another requirement for a romantic spark to turn into the steady flame of a love relationship. If the first impression is negative, it is best to cut contact." Also see Helen Fisher, *Why Him Why Her?* (page 144–146) and the service Over 40 Dating, where singles meet over several consecutive weekends for social activities to get to know each other in a "natural" setting.

[320] Truthfulness refers to the subjective truth about the interior of a person, while "truth" refers to the objective "factual" truth in the exterior. The answer to the question of whether you had intercourse with a woman during a business trip would be an objective, factual truth. If you are in love with her or not would be subjective truthfulness. People can only be truthful to their level of consciousness (and, by definition, not about their unconscious). Children and adults are deeply conditioned to lie, because telling the truth has often negative consequences. This is often a big challenge in relationships, where telling the truth or being truthful would hurt the other partner and may get him or her to leave.

[321] See Susan Campbell, Truth in Dating: *Finding Love by Getting Real, and Saying What's Real: 7 Keys to Authentic Communication and Relationship Success*.

[322] Lovers who regress to a state devoid of any useful discrimination, or of being completely carried away by unreasoned passion or "love" that leads to addictive love.

[323] Many mystics, poets, philosophers, theologians, and even scientists have pointed to this mystery; as the mathematician Blaise Pascal (1623-1662) mused, "the heart has reasons that reason cannot know."

[324] When women who seek this form of love speak of healing, learning, growth, and awakening in a partnership, they often mean that *men* need to do so to adapt the female perspective and so no longer challenges them emotionally. These women say: "I am done growing, very evolved, and happy. I love myself way too much to have a partner to make my life miserable again." They may be right in some cases if they date men who are less conscious or balanced/integrated in their development, but all too often it is just an avoidance to take responsibility for their own uneven development and sometimes lack of physical self-care. And to assume that women in general are more evolved than men because they are often the majority in self-help and spiritual groups ignores the different developmental lines, levels of consciousness development, and the fact that most of their teachers are males who get into trouble if they date their students.

[325] See Helen Fisher, *Why We Love,* page 52–56.

[326] Women initiate domestic violence about as often as men do when either of them feels powerless to resolve their conflicts through nonviolent means (such as talking things through). The myth that males are more abusive than women stems from the fact that women report physical abuse more often to the authorities than their partners, while males feel shame to do so in the first place, and are often laughed at and ridiculed if they do report physical abuse to the police. See, for example, Warren Farrell, *Does Feminism Discriminate Against Men* page 33–39, and *Women Can't Hear What Men Don't Say,* page 123–162, and the movie, *The Red Pill.*

[327] David Schnarch's *Passionate Marriage* is a classic.

[328] The movie *The Mirror has Two Faces* is a touching and funny example of a couple that tries to avoid crazy love and moves from companionate to integral love. Any kind of couples Tantra workshops or the excellent HAI workshops about love intimacy and sexuality (www.hai.org) are recommended.

[329] See *The New Psychology of Love,* edited by Robert J. Sternberg and Karin Weis, page 185, under intimacy about the qualities of integrally informed relationships, which they describe as:

Desire to promote the welfare of the loved one.

Experienced happiness with the loved one.

High regard for the loved one.

Being able to count on the loved one in times of need.

Mutual understanding with the loved one.

Sharing of one's self and one's possessions with the loved one.

Receipt of emotional support from the loved one.

Giving of emotional support to the loved one.

Intimate communication with the loved one.

Valuing of the loved one.

[330] See Shunryu Suzuki, *Zen Mind, Beginner's Mind*, which suggests to approach life, and hence our relationships, without the thought of gaining anything special. Or, as Eckhart Tolle mentioned: "The ego cannot love, it always wants something."

[331] The three primary causes for psychosis are *functional* (mental illnesses such as schizophrenia and bipolar disorder), *organic* (stemming from medical, non-psychological conditions, such as brain tumors or sleep deprivation), and *psychoactive drugs* (e.g., barbituates, amphetamines, and hallucinogens).

[332] Such as obsessive-compulsive disorders, chronic anxiety, or phobias.

[333] Below is an alphabetical list of psychotherapies. The list contains some approaches that may not call themselves psychotherapy but have a similar aim to improve mental health and well-being through talk and other means of communication. Choosing the best therapy and practitioner is essential to the success of the treatment. See Ken Wilber, *Integral Psychology*, page 98–100 for more information.

Adlerian therapy	Analytical psychology
Art therapy	Autogenic psychotherapy
Behavior therapy	Biodynamic psychotherapy
Bioenergetic analysis	Biosynthesis
Brief therapy	Classical Adlerian psychotherapy
Co-Counseling	Cognitive analytic psychotherapy
Cognitive behavioral psychotherapy	Concentrative movement therapy
Contemplative psychotherapy	Core process psychotherapy
Daseins analytic psychotherapy	Depth Psychology

Dialectical behavior therapy	Emotional Freedom Techniques (EFT)
Encounter groups	Eye Movement Desensitization and Reprocessing (EMDR)
Existential analysis	Family systems therapy
Feminist therapy	Focusing
Freudian psychotherapy	Gestalt therapy
Gestalt theoretical psychotherapy	Group therapy
Holotropic breathwork	Humanistic psychology
Hypnotherapy	Integrative psychotherapy
Internal Family Systems Model	Jungian psychotherapy
Logo therapy	Multimodal therapy
Narrative therapy	Neuro-linguistic programming (NLP)
Object relations theory	Personal construct psychology (PCP)
Positive psychotherapy	Postural Integration
Primal integration	Process oriented psychology
Primal therapy	Provocative therapy
Psychedelic psychotherapy	Psychoanalysis
Psychodrama	Psychodynamic psychotherapy
Psycho-organic analysis	Psychosynthesis
Pulsing (bodywork)	Rational emotive behavior psychotherapy
Re-evaluation counseling	Reality therapy
Reichian psychotherapy	Rogersian (or Rogerian) psychotherapy
Rolfing	Sophia analysis
Self-relationship (or sponsorship)	Systemic therapy
SHEN therapy	T Groups
Transactional analysis (TA)	Transpersonal psychology

Table 27: Different forms of therapy

[334] See Polly Young Eisendrath and Florence Wiedemann, *Female Authority*, page 222–223: "Thus we claim that personality is always a tandem development of self-other conceptions and never a discovery of an independent self. The fallacy of individualism, a misleading notion that we are separate units contained in private bodies like machines in little houses, leads to endless confusion about human relationship and a general repression of dependence and vulnerability. We have encountered many people–especially women–who literally believe that living alone is a condition of psychological independence. In other words, they have confused personal agency (choice, etc.) with the social condition of living alone. The idea of "living alone" is, itself, a distortion based on misconceptions about privacy because people never live alone. As organisms, we have a variety of both biological and psychological needs that prevent us from being able to survive in isolation."

[335] See Christian de Quincey, *Radical Knowingm* page 176–180: "I as subject am never reflected in things (objects) only in other "I's" such as you." Famous feminist activist Gloria Steinem, who had quoted Irina Dunn as saying, "A woman needs a man like a fish needs a bicycle," married David Bale in 2000 at age 66.

[336] See Robert Kegan in *In Over Our Head*, page 313: "Couples in 4th order consciousness begin with the premise of their own completeness and see conflict as an inevitable by-product of interaction of two psychologically whole selves, while couples in 5th [Integral] order of consciousness begin with their "own tendency" to pretend to completeness (while actually being incomplete) and see conflict as the inevitable, but convertible by-product of the pretension to completeness."

[337] Adyashanti, a married Zen teacher in an interview with Bert Parlee stated: "The proof of the depth and embodiment of your realization is seen in your love relationship. That's where the proof is in the pudding. If it all collapses in your relationship, you have some work to do. And people do have a lot of difficulties in their relationships."

[338] See Robert Augustus Masters book *Transformation through Intimacy: The Journey Towards Mature Monogamy*.

[339] For a comprehensive explanation of how hormones influence our romantic experiences, see Helen Fisher, *Why We Love*; Theresa L. Crenshaw, *The Alchemy of Love and Lust*; and John Gray, *Why Mars And Venus Collide* page 53–75. In the movie, *What the bleep do we know*, during

the wedding scene you can see an entertaining animated segment that illustrates the function of hormones in our addiction to love.

[340] See Louann Brizendine, *The Female Brain,* page 91.

[341] See Theresa L. Crenshaw, *The Alchemy of Love and Lust,* page 164–174 and 190.

[342] See Theresa L. Crenshaw, *The Alchemy of Love and Lust,* page 213–217: "If you are with a woman in or past menopause, it is important to be sensitive to her changed emotional and physical needs, and to apply skill, care, and (if necessary) plenty of good lubricant to make sex pleasurable, safe, and rewarding for both of you."

[343] See Nancy W. Collins and Mason Grigsby, *Love at Second Sight,* page 208–209. Their research showed that in first-time marriages, men were looking for sexual attractiveness (40%) while women focused on good providers (30%). Single men over 50 look for common interests (34%) in a mate and only 13% look for sex, while sex tops the list of female requirements at 36%. The recent "cougar" movement is another indicator for this role reversal in which older women seek younger men for sex.

Testosterone patches and vaginal estrogen creams may help to restore the sex drive in males and receptivity and vaginal health in women.

[344] See Helen Fisher, *Why We Love,* page 80–83.

[345] See Helen Fisher, *Why We Love,* page 53–54.

[346] See Helen Fisher, *Why We Love,* page 52–53. Also, researchers at Florida State University examined the nature of love by studying the brains and behavior of male prairie voles, picked for their habit of lifelong monogamy and aggression towards other females once they have found a mate. The scientists found that males became devoted to females only after they had mated. The bond coincided with a huge release of the feel-good chemical dopamine inside their brains. Brandon Aragona, who led the study, demonstrated that dopamine was the voles' love drug by injecting the chemical into the brains of males who had not yet had sex with female companions. Immediately, they lost interest in other females and spent all their time with their chosen one. Further experiments showed that dopamine restructured a part of the vole's brain called the nucleus accumbens, a region that many animals have, including humans. The change was so drastic that when paired-up males were introduced to new females, although their brains still produced

dopamine on sight, the chemical was channeled into a different neural circuit that made them go cold towards the new female.

[347] See Theresa L. Crenshaw, *The Alchemy of Love and Lust*, page 131–132, and Helen Fisher, *Why We Love*, page 54–55.

[348] See Helen Fisher, *Why We Love*, page 188–190.

[349] See David Richo, *How to be in Adult in Relationship*, page 126–152, and the many other relationship books (see Appendix I in *Integral Relationships: A Manual for Men*) that deal with conflict resolution.

[350] See John Gray, *Why Mars and Venus Collide*, page 221: "Women today long for romance, because romance is the most powerful oxytocin producer. It is a powerful antidote to the stress of working in a testosterone-oriented work world." Also see tinyurl.com/irpm688 womentowomen.com/sexualityandfertility/healthbenefitsofsex.aspx

[351] Individual differences in social behavior are regulated by genetics, epigenetics, and patterns of short-term change in peptides and steroids. While many factors contribute to the expression of social behaviors across species, at present the best studied are variations in steroids and more recently in oxytocin and vasopressin pathways. Comparative analyses, especially in closely related yet behavioral distinct species, have been useful in identifying mechanisms through which evolutionary and proximate pressures could shape the features of social monogamy. Each of the social behaviors reviewed here, as well as several others related to social monogamy, such as the social regulation of reproduction, are adaptive and exist along a continuum. Where an individual or a species falls on that behavioral continuum is controlled at least in part by peptide and steroid systems and the interactions among these. Further adding to these variations, experiences across the life cycle serve to change and refine these systems. The same hormones necessary for the expression of the features of social monogamy, also are implicated in the development of a nervous system capable of being epigenetically tuned to high levels of sociality. tinyurl.com/irpm691 www.frontiersin.org/articles/10.3389/fevo.2018.00202/full

[352] See Theresa L. Crenshaw, *The Alchemy of Love and Lust*, page 102–105 and Helen Fisher, *Why We Love*, page 89–91.

Males rely on a second bonding hormone in addition to oxytocin, a chemical called vasopressin. It has been demonstrated that dopamine, oxytocin, and vasopressin play an important role in human society, for instance, in love, social attachment, and reward. There are great similarities between voles and humans. Vasopressin is associated with male voles' territoriality and aggression towards others after they bonded and had sex with a female.

tinyurl.com/irpm693

www.nationalzoo.si.edu/Publications/ZooGoer/2004/3/monogamy.cfm

[353] See John Gray, *Why Mars and Venus Collide*, with many tips on how to reduce stress that kills romance; Helen Fisher, *Why We Love*, page 181–208, with tips how to make romance last; *Passionate Marriage* by David Schnarch on how to remove emotional blocks that prevent a satisfying sex life; *The Exceptional 7 Percent* by Gregory K. Popcak about the nine secrets of the worlds happiest couples; and *What Makes Love Last: How to Build Trust and Avoid Betrayal* by John Gottman and Nan Silver.

[354] See *Forgiveness Made Easy* by Barbara J. Hunt tinyurl.com/irpm695

www.forgivenessmadeeasy.co.uk,

Below is a very short basic outline of her process.

Step One: Eye to Eye

Close your eyes and allow yourself to imagine you are sitting beside a fire and invite the person you wish to forgive to join you at the fireside.

Allow yourself to experience any feelings that arise.

Step Two: Heart to Heart

Maintaining eye contact with the person, allow yourself to say everything that needs to be said to that person.

Confess the full extent of your resentment — every last drop.

Allow yourself to experience any feelings that arise.

Step Three: Shoe to Shoe

In your imagination, switch positions with that person. If you can, put on their shoes and stand or sit as they would, then speak back as them.

Allow yourself to experience any feelings that arise.

Switch shoes again, back to yourself and reply again until you feel the conversation is complete at that level.

Step Four: The Balcony

Let the conversation continue between you, but from a very high, wise, compassionate, authentic, "integral" or higher perspective.

Gain insights into why the other person acted the way they did. They may show remorse or ask for your forgiveness. You want to go "high" enough that it feels as if you have transcended your egos.

You can even ask the other person to say out loud what you wish they'd said to you—that you needed to hear—in real life, now.

Allow yourself to experience any feelings that arise.

Step Five: The Haggling

In your imagination, tell the other person all of your payoffs and the costs of holding onto your resentment and what you've got out of resenting them.

Allow yourself to experience any feelings that arise.

Step Six: The Forgiveness

When you're ready, say some significant words that express your forgiveness.

Allow yourself to experience any feelings that arise.

Step Seven: Completion

Set a new intention for your relationship with this person, especially if you are still in relationship with them; for example, tell them, "From now on how I choose to treat you is….."

Allow yourself to experience any feelings that arise.

Conclusion

When you're ready, imagine the person you've been speaking to dissolving back into white light, allowing the fire to go out.

Check in with your body and your heart to see how you're feeling.

Take a deep breath and when you're ready, you can open your eyes.

Power Point at tinyurl.com/irpm696

https://drive.google.com/file/d/1tb1S0tHb9tg2ZB2YHKJ9HX6EQotrX_Vf/view?usp=sharing

Conscious Uncoupling

From tinyurl.com/irpm697

www.consciousuncoupling.com/wp-content/uploads/2017/04/CUguide.pdf

Step One: Find Emotional Freedom:

Something has been broken, and it's more than just your heart. It may be your feeling of not being safe in the world, your inability to make sense of your life, or even having lost your very faith in life and love.

Step Two: Reclaim Your Power and Your Life

You may find yourself going over your breakup story again and again, laboriously trying to piece together a narrative that weaves the fragmented, jagged, and ill-fitting bits of memory and information into one cohesive whole.

Step Three: Breaking the Pattern, Healing Your Heart

You may be feeling disheartened by what appears to be a repeat of old painful childhood hurts, as though you're somehow cursed when it comes to finding happiness in love. Understanding ourselves as the source of our experience means that we have the power to start creating new and different experiences moving forward.

Step Four: Becoming a Love Alchemist.

It is a true accomplishment to be at this point of your conscious uncoupling journey, where you're finally ready to clear the air of old hurts and resentments and move forward in life with a clean slate, which is particularly helpful if you are raising children together.

Step Five: Creating Your Happy Even After Life

Make wise, healthy, and life-affirming decisions as you take on the essential task of reinventing your life and setting up vital new structures that will allow you and all involved to thrive in the aftermath of your breakup.

[355] www.amazon.com/Forgiveness-Made-Easy-Revolutionary-Letting/dp/199981956X/

[356] www.amazon.com/Conscious-Uncoupling-Steps-Living-Happily/dp/0553447017

[357] Eckhart Tolle, (in relationship with Kim Eng) writes in *The Power Of Now*, page 127 (page 153 in the paperback edition), "Three failed relationships in as many years are more likely to force you into awakening than three years on a desert island shut away in your room"—and on page 132 (page 159 paperback edition): "Humanity is under great pressure to evolve because it is our only chance of survival as a race. This will affect every aspect of your life and close relationships in particular. Never before have relationships been as problematic and conflict ridden as they are now. As you may have noticed, they are not here to make you happy or fulfilled. If you continue to pursue the goal of salvation through a relationship, you will be disillusioned again and again. But if you accept that the relationship is here to make you conscious instead of happy, then the relationship will offer you salvation, and you will be aligning yourself with the higher consciousness that wants to be born into this world. For those who hold on to the old patterns, there will be increasing pain, violence, confusion, and madness."

[358] Genetic epidemiologic studies indicate that all ten personality disorders (PDs) classified on the DSM-IV axis II are modestly to moderately heritable. Multiple lines of evidence suggest that dysfunction in the serotonin (5-HT) system is associated with impulsivity, aggression, affective lability, and suicide.

tinyurl.com/irpm698

www.ncbi.nlm.nih.gov/pmc/articles/PMC3181941/

[359] The ICD-11 shows considerable alignment with the DSM-5 Alternative Model for Personality Disorders.

tinyurl.com/irpm699

www.frontiersin.org/articles/10.3389/fpsyt.2021.655548/full

The 2016 ICD-10 describes personality disorders as deeply ingrained and enduring behavioral patterns, manifesting as inflexible responses to a broad range of personal and social situations. They represent extreme or significant deviations from the way in which the average individual in a given culture perceives, thinks, feels and, particularly, relates to others. Such behavior patterns tend to be stable and to encompass multiple domains of behavior and psychological functioning. They are frequently, but not always, associated with various degrees of subjective distress

and problems of social performance.
https://icd.who.int/browse10/2016/en#F60.2

[360] https://en.wikipedia.org/wiki/Paranoid_personality_disorder

[361] https://en.wikipedia.org/wiki/Schizoid_personality_disorder

[362] https://en.wikipedia.org/wiki/Schizotypal_personality_disorder

[363] https://en.wikipedia.org/wiki/Antisocial_personality_disorder

[364] https://en.wikipedia.org/wiki/Avoidant_personality_disorder

[365] www.nimh.nih.gov/health/topics/borderline-personality-disorder/index.shtml

[366] To learn more about relationships with people who have a BPD visit the following websites:

tinyurl.com/irpm701

https://bpdfamily.com/content/how-borderline-relationship-evolves

For women: tinyurl.com/irpm703

http://gettinbetter.com/casanova.html

For men: tinyurl.com/irpm705 http://gettinbetter.com/anycost.html

For Families: tinyurl.com/irpm707

https://bpdfamily.com/

[367] tinyurl.com/irpm709

www.medscape.com/viewarticle/947850?src=WNL_trdalrt_210323_MSCPEDIT&uac=397912HK&impID=3266487&faf=1#vp_2

[368] Borrowed from Late Latin histriōnicus ("pertaining to acting; scurrilous, shameful; wretched"), ("pertaining to acting and the theatre"), from histriō ("actor, player")
https://en.wiktionary.org/wiki/histrionic

[369] tinyurl.com/irpm710

www.psychologytoday.com/blog/fulfillment-any-age/201306/two-warning-signs-your-relationship-may-not-last

[370] tinyurl.com/irpm712

https://en.wikipedia.org/wiki/Histrionic_personality_disorder

[371] tinyurl.com/irpm713

www.ncbi.nlm.nih.gov/pubmed/18557663

[372] tinyurl.com/irpm716

www.ncbi.nlm.nih.gov/pmc/articles/PMC3864176/

[373] Using data from a large, nationally representative community sample, Whisman, Tolejko, and Chatav (2007) found that each of the seven PD's assessed (Paranoid, Schizoid, Antisocial, Histrionic, Avoidant, Dependent, and Obsessive-Compulsive) was associated with a significantly increased occurrence of marital disruption.

tinyurl.com/irpm718

www.ncbi.nlm.nih.gov/pmc/articles/PMC3569846/

[374] tinyurl.com/irpm720

www.statista.com/statistics/242284/percentage-of-single-person-households-in-the-us-by-state/

tinyurl.com/irpm721

www.pewresearch.org/social-trends/2021/10/05/rising-share-of-u-s-adults-are-living-without-a-spouse-or-partner/

[375] tinyurl.com/irpm723

www.psychologytoday.com/blog/hide-and-seek/201205/the-10-personality-disorders

[376] tinyurl.com/irpm725

https://stopwalkingoneggshells.com/

"She was a curious mixture of incredible maturity and immaturity, like a split personality," said one of her friends. "It was so extraordinary how she handled ordinary people, but at the same time she did silly and childlike things. She was very impulsive."

Indeed, Diana's unstable temperament bore all the markings of one of the most elusive psychological disorders: the borderline personality. This condition is characterized by an unstable self-image; sharp mood swings; fear of rejection and abandonment; an inability to sustain relationships; persistent feelings of loneliness, boredom, and emptiness; depression; and impulsive behavior such as binge eating and self-mutilation. Taken together, these characteristics explain otherwise inexplicable behavior. Throughout her adult life, Diana experienced these symptoms severely and chronically. While she received periodic treatment for some of her problems—her eating disorder and her depression—neither Diana nor anyone close to her came to grips with the full extent of her illness.

Yet she tended to define herself in terms of the approval of others. "I think essentially that she was an ill person," said Dr. Michael Adler of the National AIDS Trust. "She was very, very insecure. She didn't believe in herself. There was not a sort of real center to her personality. Her identity was created for her, and she increasingly got herself into personal problems, which highlighted her inadequacies."

tinyurl.com/irpm729

www.nytimes.com/books/first/s/smith-diana.html

[378] While for many, Marilyn Monroe is one of the most enduring sex symbols of our time, behind her perfect curves and sultry personality lay a complex and troubled woman. And more than that—it is likely that the iconic actress suffered from borderline personality disorder, says science journalist Claudia Kalb. She explains: "What is clear is that Monroe suffered from severe mental distress. Her symptoms included a feeling of emptiness, a split or confused identity, extreme emotional volatility, unstable relationships, and an impulsivity that drove her to drug addiction and suicide—all textbook characteristics of a condition called borderline personality disorder."

tinyurl.com/irpm730

www.dailymail.co.uk/news/article-3448841

[379] Integral therapist Dr. Mark Forman shared in a personal conversation that supporting each other as equals in the healing and growing process in a love relationship is fine. It becomes unhealthy when one person is constantly in the support role (as a lay or professional therapist, mentor, teacher, coach, etc.), and the other is the receiver. This becomes especially problematic if the "giver" requires some feedback or support, and is rejected and shamed by their partner as needy, unevolved, immature etc.

[380] https://themindsjournal.com/stages-relationship-empath-narcissist/

[381] www.amazon.com/Stop-Walking-Eggshells-Borderline-Personality/dp/1684036895

[382] www.amazon.com/Borderline-Personality-Disorder-Survival-Guide/dp/1572245077

[383] https://stopwalkingoneggshells.com/

[384] A 2014 Gallup survey reports, "More than four in 10 Americans continue to believe that God created humans in their present form 10,000

years ago, a view that has changed little over the past three decades. Half of Americans believe humans evolved, with the majority of these saying God guided the evolutionary process. However, the percentage who says God was not involved is rising."

The debate is sometimes portrayed as being between science and religion, but as the United States National Academy of Sciences states: "Today, many religious denominations accept that biological evolution has produced the diversity of living things over billions of years of Earth's history. Many have issued statements observing that evolution and the tenets of their faiths are compatible. Scientists and theologians have written eloquently about their awe and wonder at the history of the universe and of life on this planet, explaining that they see no conflict between their faith in God and the evidence for evolution. Religious denominations that do not accept the occurrence of evolution tend to be those that believe in strictly literal interpretations of religious texts." tinyurl.com/irpm731

http://en.wikipedia.org/wiki/Creation%E2%80%93evolution_controversy

[385] The term metaphysics was used by the followers of Aristotle, arguably the father of Western science, to describe his substantial work that went beyond his inquiries regarding the physical world, which he called "the knowledge of immaterial being." Today it is typically interpreted as "things beyond science" such as values, ethics, morals, aesthetics, potentials, absences, and the explanation of supernatural phenomenon.

[386] See for example the 2012 book by Lawrence M. Krauss, *A Universe from Nothing: How There is Something Rather Than Nothing*. The main theme of the book is how a universe could and plausibly did arise from a deeper nothing—involving the absence of space itself—and may one day return to nothing via processes that can be comprehensible and do not require any external control or direction.

[387] See https://en.wikipedia.org/wiki/Evolution

[388] Intelligent design (ID) is the view that it is possible to infer from empirical evidence that "certain features of the universe and of living things are best explained by an intelligent cause, not an undirected process such as natural selection."
tinyurl.com/irpm732

www.newworldencyclopedia.org/entry/Intelligent_design

[389] See for example a debate between Richard Dawkins and Dephak Chopra at tinyurl.com/irpm734 https://youtu.be/BiwLrxPb1fE?t=697 (starting at 00:11:37.)

[390] Ultimately—and this is the main point here—it does not matter for the validity of the co-creative and procreative ILR model if you believe that a mythic God, the purely physical "four fundamental forces," or an intelligent evolutionary impulse, spirit, eros, or other unknowable intelligent force or creator brought the universe and ultimately humans into existence, as long as you are open to the idea that the meaning of life is to follow our genetically predisposed biological, transformational, and transcendental purpose that is driven by the co-creative impulse to procreate and to co-create more good, truth, beauty and functioning with a compatible life partner, instead of repressing co-creation and procreation in the name of nihilism, rationalism, hyper-individualism, or New-Age narcissism, and pursuing a childless, single, hedonistic lifestyle.

[391] May 8–11, 2014 Gallup Poll about evolution, creationism, intelligent design tinyurl.com/irpm738

www.gallup.com/poll/21814/evolution-creationism-intelligent-design.aspx

[392] Source tinyurl.com/irpm743

https://en.wikipedia.org/wiki/Level_of_support_for_evolution

[393] Biological imperatives:

Reproduction:

In order for species to persist, they must by definition reproduce to ensure the continuation of their species. Without reproduction the species ceases to exist. The capacity for reproduction and the drive to do so whenever physiological and environmental conditions allow it are universal among living organisms and are expressed in a multitude of ways by the spectrum of living organisms.

Territorialism:

Territorialism is a fairly fundamental feature of all living organisms, by simple virtue of the fact that we live in a physical universe. Bacteria evidently acquire territory as they spread out in a petri dish. Observing living organisms in nature suggests that the step before procreation is to establish a territory within which they may hunt, breed, and ensure the growth of their offspring.

Group Forming:

It is observable that most organisms form groups in order to enhance their chances of survival. Groups can be of simply two or of huge numbers. Group-forming is complex and involves territorialism; notions of identity; culture. Group-forming is what leads us as humans to form families, clans, tribes, and nations.

This group-forming in humans is the result of biology: due to the size of our brains, children are dependent on their parents for much longer than most animals; the result of this is that the biological couplings necessary for reproduction linger so that the parents can ensure the survival of the offspring.

This necessary parental investment and larger brain-size, coupled with our ability to communicate, precipitates the evolution of social constructions such as the family. After several generations, many more families exist with varied connections to each other; a common ancestry, evidenced by their phenotype, unites these clans.

Out of family clans, tribes form multiple generations later. As a result, non-biological group-forming can take place where tribes can split due to geography and demand for resources.

Competition:

Competition is one of the environmental factors that constitute natural selection. Individual organisms compete for food and mates; groups of living organisms compete for control of territory and resources; species though, do not so much compete, as passively adapt to their environment.

Quality-of-Life-Seeking:

A living organism's need to improve their quality-of-life seems to serve the purpose of improving their chances of survival. Quality-of-life-seeking also includes reducing the levels of stress experienced by an individual organism. Stress can cause both physiological and mental illness. Stress can be due to crime; threat and acts against the person; threat and acts against property. Health, in general, comes under this category: individual organisms that seek to maintain and improve their health are improving their chances of survival.

tinyurl.com/irpm744

http://psychology.wikia.com/wiki/Biological_imperative

[394] The limbic system is not a separate system but a collection of structures that includes the olfactory bulbs (smell is very important in the sexual selection process), hippocampus, hypothalamus, amygdala, etc. The limbic system supports a variety of functions including emotion, behavior, motivation, long-term memory, and olfaction. Emotional life is largely housed in the limbic system, and it has a great deal to do with the formation of memories.

[395] "What we really seek is familiarity—which may well complicate any plans we might have had for happiness. We are looking to recreate, within our adult relationships, the feelings we knew so well in childhood. The love most of us will have tasted early on was often confused with other, more destructive dynamics: feelings of wanting to help an adult who was out of control, of being deprived of a parent's warmth or scared of his anger, of not feeling secure enough to communicate our wishes. How logical, then, that we should as grown-ups find ourselves rejecting certain candidates for marriage not because they are wrong but because they are too right—too balanced, mature, understanding, and reliable—given that in our hearts, such rightness feels foreign. We marry the wrong people because we don't associate being loved with feeling happy."

tinyurl.com/irpm745

www.nytimes.com/2016/05/29/opinion/sunday/why-you-will-marry-the-wrong-person.html

[396] The concept of Differentiated Unity emerged in classic Greek philosophy with Plato, who saw the different virtues of the Philosopher as part of one soul (or God, if you will.) In modern sociology, the term is often used to describe individual humans as parts of the unity of a couple or the unity of societies. In Integral theory, it means that every individual whole is part of a larger whole or unity.

[397] See my conversation with Anodea Judith at tinyurl.com/irpm746

https://youtu.be/bECj_5POLX0 and her website https://anodeajudith.com/

[398] This matrix is inspired by the Wilber-Combs Lattice that we covered in Part 1. It follows the same idea: that the seven chakras have been present, felt and identified since Archaic times, just as spiritual state-

stages from gross to nondual have been available and experienced by certain people throughout human evolution and were then interpreted from their particular stage of consciousness development.

[399] The first problem, as we know from our own love life and the stories of others, is that those needs that make us feel loved when fulfilled by our partner, and all those needs and desires of our partner that we help to fulfill, are manifold and change over time. We grow older. We may have children. And over time, it can happen that individuals develop to the next higher stage of consciousness, or they progress in other developmental lines, for example, sexually, spiritually, morally, or physically. Or we go through major changes by undergoing some psychological healing, for example, around our Anima or Animus complex or other shadows and wounds.

Needs may also change through better vertical translation and integration at different levels of consciousness development. Think, for example, of all the ways we mature and the various needs that change in their urgency as we progress or regress through Maslow's famous "hierarchy of needs": (1) physiological, (2) safety, (3) love/belonging, (4) esteem, (5) self-actualization, and (6) self-transcendence needs. Or consider all the ways we change as we shift between the six basic human needs, as defined by Tony Robbins: (1) certainty and comfort, (2) uncertainty and variety, (3) significance, (4) love and connection, (5) growth, and (6) contribution.

As a result, as Hegel pointed out, these needs and desires-based relationships are not stable. A man who would give all his material resources and income to a woman to have her meet his desire for sex in exchange may no longer be attractive to her. Similarly, once she would have augmented her status through him by becoming a princess or queen, his status would become less of an attractor. The same would hold true if he augmented her quality of life through his creativity that meets all her desires. He may still be creative, but she may no longer desire it and thus no longer provide her support and wisdom to him.

On the other hand, a woman who would liberally meet her partner's desire for sex, care, and wisdom/intuition, may lose her attractiveness and be no longer provided for, protected, and inspired in the ways she desires, as the male could get what he wants without having to satisfy her desires in return. In other words, he would own her and thus, again in the somewhat obscure Hegelian sense, destroyed what he initially desired and needed to define himself.

To overcome this problem in transactional love relationships, a dialectic emerges in which females—because of their deep-seated fears of abandonment and desire to have their quality of life improved—constantly challenge males through negation, or what Hegel called sublation, in the material, power, and creativity domains to improve and provide more. Men experience this as "yes, but" and nagging, and demands to constantly improve and do better to continue to be desirable.

This forces males—because of their shame of not being good enough to get sex, care/approval, and intuition/wisdom—to come up with ever better solutions to provide females with increasing amounts of material resources, safety, status, and creativity.

On the other hand, females often feel under enormous pressure to constantly increase their sexual attractiveness and skills, their ability to care, and their capacity to provide ongoing wisdom and intuition to remain attractive and get what they desire from males. An analytical look at magazines and commercials that cater to each sex provide ample and vivid examples of the pressures that are put on each sex to become and stay desirable as mates.

So, on further investigation of need and desire-based love relationships, we see that they are fragile and can get quickly out of balance for several reasons: the first is when needs change and can no longer be fulfilled by the partners. The second is when lovers withhold or lose what made them initially attractive to their partner. The third is when the attractiveness of one partner increases, for example, if a man begins to earn way more money, or increases his status, or becomes a star, or when a woman increases her sexual attractiveness, her capacity to care, or her ability to provide wisdom and intuition. The fourth reason is when needs and desires begin to be met in different ways, for example, a man having a more attractive sex partner outside the relationship, or a woman embarking on her own successful career, or turning her care towards children and/or animals.

The one whose desires are no longer met could now either leave the relationship or suck it up. As long as leaving is not an option because of personal circumstances (such as children, or financial, emotional, or sexual dependence), societal pressures (traditional marriage, public shame, discrimination, etc.), or fears of abandonment and the resulting emotional pain caused by hormonal withdrawal symptoms (being heartbroken), the one who still provides but no longer receives will become the slave and the other the master.

A woman may be forced to be sexually available without being adequately provided for, be expected to show recognition, appreciation, and care without feeling safe and protected, or offer her intuition and wisdom while no longer being creatively inspired and entertained by her partner.

A man who still provides, protects, and inspires may no longer be rewarded with sex, care, and intuition.

This traps both lovers. The master in transactional "love" relationships gains authority and rights without responsibility but becomes dependent on the slave to get his needs and desires met, while the slave has to fulfill the needs and desires of the master without having authority or rights and no longer gets his or her needs and desires met. Following Hegel's argument, we can see that unless authority or rights and responsibilities are commensurate and reciprocal, no actual normative status for a healthy sustainable love relationship exists.

Thus, the creation of transactional love relationships requires twice the work. First, we need to get an image of our partner's needs and desires without their self-image by judging him or her as needy, selfish, or sexist. Only in this way can we expect to have our needs and desires met by the other onto whom we project them. Secondly, we need to integrate the expectations of the other into our self-image to avoid becoming a mere object of his/her needs, desires, and expectations.

While transactional love relationships are a great opportunity for learning, healing, and growing, and to learn to give and receive love (unconditionally), they often become exhausting for couples who are not able or willing to do this kind of work, and simply want the ongoing perfect romance. They either descend into frustrating power struggles, endless fights, or passive-aggressive behaviors, which can lead to physical and mental abuse, or they can try to get their unfulfilled needs and desires met outside the relationship. Both typically lead to devastating and painful separations and divorces. Consequently, an increasing number of modern and postmodern people get divorced and become serial daters who chase one romantic relationship after the next, through calling in "The Next One," and then consciously (or hatefully) uncouple when their partner is no longer desirable, as we see prominently in the broken marriages of Hollywood star couples, less visibly in many family court rooms around the world, and in the scores of people who have given up on love relationships altogether.

We can therefore say that need-based and desire-driven transactional love relationships have two phases at the level of each chakra pair. The first phase is the involuntary emergence of loving feelings in various degrees of sexual passion, emotional dependence, and verbal intimacy, which in combination lead to one of the eight forms of being in love as indicated by the "triangles of love" in Module 20. The second phase is the actual capacity to love, which is the ability and willingness of each partner to fulfill the other's needs and desires in kind and degree after the love-struck phase has passed, and to receive his/her gifts with openness, gratitude, and appreciation, instead of rejecting them or taking them for granted. Both capacities, to give and to receive, are part and parcel of transcending fear—which is the opposite of love. As Rumi wrote, "Our task is not to seek for love, but merely to seek and find all the barriers within ourselves that we have built against it."

[400] For more see tinyurl.com/irpm63 www.tutor2u.net/psychology/reference/relationships-social-exchange-theory

[401] www.amazon.com/Universe-Nothing-There-Something-Rather-dp-1451624468/dp/1451624468

[402] www.amazon.com/Mating-Mind-Sexual-Choice-Evolution/dp/038549517X

[403] www.amazon.com/Charge-Energy-Body-Healing-Relationships/dp/1401954480

[404] For the philosophers among you: as adjectives, the difference between transcendental and transcendent is that transcendental is concerned with the a priori or intuitive basis of knowledge, independent of experience, while transcendent is surpassing usual limits.

[405] In classical philosophy, transcendental or transcendence means climbing or going beyond. It was initially used with reference to God as completely outside of and beyond the world, contrasted with immanence, with God manifested inside the world.

In the second meaning, which originated in medieval philosophy, transcendental is a quality of being which cannot be predicated on any actually existing thing insofar as it exists. Primary examples of the transcendentals are unity, truth, and goodness, which, taken together, lead to beauty and functioning.

In modern philosophy, Kant called "all knowledge transcendental if it is occupied, not with objects, but with the way that we can possibly know objects even before we experience them." He also equated transcendental with that which is "… in respect of the subject's faculty of cognition." Something is transcendental if it plays a role in the way in which the mind "constitutes" objects and makes it possible for us to experience them as objects in the first place. Ordinary knowledge is knowledge of objects; transcendental knowledge is knowledge of how it is possible for us to experience those objects as objects. Kant argues for a deep interconnection between the ability to have self-consciousness and the ability to experience a world of objects. Through a process of synthesis, the mind generates both the structure of objects and its own unity.

In phenomenology, the "transcendent" is that which transcends our own consciousness—that which is objective rather than only a phenomenon of consciousness.

Jean-Paul Sartre also speaks of transcendence in his works. In *Being and Nothingness*, Sartre utilizes transcendence to describe the relation of the self to the object-oriented world, as well as our concrete relations with others.

In everyday language, "transcendence" means "going beyond," and "self-transcendence" means going beyond a prior form or state of oneself. Mystical experience is thought of as a particularly advanced state of self-transcendence, in which the sense of a separate self is abandoned.

Adopted from

tinyurl.com/irpm747

https://en.wikipedia.org/wiki/Transcendence_(philosophy)

[406] A priori knowledge is independent of all particular experiences, as opposed to a posteriori knowledge, which derives from experience. The Latin phrases a priori ("from what is before") and a posteriori ("from what is after") were used in philosophy originally to distinguish between arguments from causes and arguments from effects. tinyurl.com/irpm749

https://en.wikipedia.org/wiki/A_priori_and_a_posteriori

[407] See *The Complexity of Greatness: Beyond Talent or Practice,* page 3

Genes serve to drive people to seek the kinds of experiences that build high levels of skill and knowledge that in turn fuel creative achievements. Genes are intimately involved in manifestation of excellent performance. It is through genetic expression that performance at any level takes place, and there is good evidence for both structural and functional changes as the skills involved in excellent performance develop. These changes take place through extended adaptations of genetic expression to continual exposure to the stress of training. Stating this is far from contending, however, that the genetic expression patterns that emerge with training are inevitable or determined by the genes. If anything, the genetic expression patterns themselves are determined by the environmental exposure or training, but this picture is muddied as well by the Genes are intimately involved in manifestation of excellent performance. It is through genetic expression that performance at any level takes place, and there is good evidence for both structural and functional changes as the skills involved in excellent performance develop. These changes take place through extended adaptations of genetic expression to continual exposure to the stress of training. Stating this is far from contending, however, that the genetic expression patterns that emerge with training are inevitable or determined by the genes. If anything, the genetic expression patterns themselves are determined by the environmental exposure or training, but this picture is muddied as well by the possibility that it is the genes that drive the exposure to the training. At bottom, this is to say that gene– environment interaction and correlation are at the root of individual differences in performance.

[408] The transcendentals (Latin: transcendentalia, from transcendere "to exceed") are the properties of being, nowadays commonly considered to be truth, beauty, and goodness. The concept arose from medieval scholasticism. Viewed ontologically, the transcendentals are understood to be what is common to all beings. From a cognitive point of view, they are the "first" concepts, since they cannot be logically traced back to something preceding them.
https://en.wikipedia.org/wiki/Transcendentals

[409] "The good is the opposite of evil. Evil is the conscious desire to produce suffering where suffering is not necessary. To self-consciously exploit the vulnerability of other people and to elevate their suffering

beyond what they or anyone else is unable to tolerate. The truth exists in service of an ideal. The pursuit of impulse pleasure and putting your language in service of it is one root to totalitarianism and slavery, because you are the puppet of an ideology, or another thinker or your own impulsive desires." (Jordan P. Peterson)

[410] For Plato and Aristotle, the cosmic values of truth (that which defines reality), goodness (that which fulfills its purpose), and beauty (that which is lovely) were objective in nature and knowable by the noble seeker. Since human beings had the internal capacities of logos (reason), ethos (morality), and pathos (emotion), these internal capacities corresponded to the cosmic values and brought forth human fulfillment.

[411] Normative ethics is the study of ethical behavior and is the branch of philosophical ethics that investigates the questions that arise regarding how one ought to act, in a moral sense.

tinyurl.com/irpm750

https://en.wikipedia.org/wiki/Normative_ethics

[412] As Walter White in the final episode of the hit television series, "Breaking Bad," admits to his wife, "I did it for me. I liked it. I was good at it. And I was really—I was alive." https://youtu.be/FaqxAEx46Zk

[413] tinyurl.com/irpm752

www.sciencedaily.com/releases/2010/03/100301165619.htm

[414] tinyurl.com/irpm753

www.huffingtonpost.com/ashton-applewhite/purpose-in-life-brain_b_8555918.html
tinyurl.com/irpm755

www.alzheimers.net/1-25-16-how-purpose-impacts-your-brain/

[415] tinyurl.com/irpm756

www.nytimes.com/2016/11/04/opinion/dalai-lama-behind-our-anxiety-the-fear-of-being-unneeded.html?smid=fb-share&_r=0

[416] www.purposeguides.org/

[417] A burgeoning literature suggests that marriage may have a wide range of benefits, including improvements in individuals' economic well-being, mental and physical health, and the well-being of their children.
tinyurl.com/irpm757

Integral Relationship Practice | 656

---

https://aspe.hhs.gov/report/effects-marriage-health-synthesis-recent-research-evidence-research-brief

A major survey of 127,545 American adults found that married men are healthier than men who were never married or whose marriages ended in divorce or widowhood. Men who have marital partners also live longer than men without spouses; men who marry after age 25 get more protection than those who tie the knot at a younger age, and the longer a man stays married, the greater his survival advantage over his unmarried peers.

tinyurl.com/irpm758

www.health.harvard.edu/newsletter_article/marriage-and-mens-health

[418] Meiosis is a specialized type of cell division that reduces the chromosome number in human cells by half. Human cells contain 23 X-shaped chromosome pairs (not to be confused with the 23rd X or Y chromosome part in males that defines sex) that are made up of 46 chromatids (the two lines that make up the X). Half of the 46 chromatids are of maternal origin and half of paternal origin. Meiosis produces haploid gametes (ova/eggs or sperm) that contain one set of 23 single chromosomes (half of the 46 chromatids that make up the 23 Xs so to speak). When two gametes (an egg and a sperm) fuse, the resulting zygote is once again diploid (23 + 23 chromatids to make up 23 X-shaped chromosome pairs), with the mother and father each contributing 23 chromatids each. This same pattern, even though with different numbers of chromosomes, occurs in all organisms that utilize meiosis.

[418] **There are four groups of distinct inner voices.**

The Guardians are designed to protect the self—the small drop of conscious awareness that gets taken over by the ego, the instinctual animalistic separate sense of self:

[419] Example for transcendental purpose immunity to change

Goal	Doing/Not Doing Instead	Hidden Competing Commitments	Big (false) Assumptions
Live my transcendental purpose.	Hedonistic Pursuits.	I'm committed to being loyal, having fun and staying safe.	Seeking pleasure, avoiding risks, and being loyal

		I'm afraid to be alone and broke.	is the path to happiness.
Work with a Purpose Guide. Get a new degree. Save money for starting my own business. Find a life partner who shares my purpose.	Going out to have fun with friends. Staying in a dysfunctional relationship. Working in an unfulfilling but safe job.	My friends depend on me and I need to balance work with play and leisure time. I made a commitment to my partner. I promised my colleagues I would not quit, and I committed to pay back my student loans.	If I neglect my old friends they will no longer like and support me, and I will not have fun. If I would lose my partner, I could not bear the pain and won't find someone else. If I quit at work, nobody else can do my job and I will go broke.

Table 28: Transcendental Purpose immunity to change examples

[420] There are many videos on YouTube for example tinyurl.com/irpm761

https://youtu.be/3gZ37piq57w. Also see videos with Dennis Genpo Merzel Rôshi for example tinyurl.com/irpm764

https://youtu.be/n22a1Hf4rjk

You may also purchase a audio and video series with Drs. Hal and Sidra Stone at tinyurl.com/irpm765

www.voicedialogue.com/voice-dialogue-videos-audios/

[421] Also see John Kessler - Integral Polarity Practice https://theippinstitute.com/

[422] www.amazon.com/StrengthsFinder-2-0-Tom-Rath/dp/159562015X

[423] www.amazon.com/True-Purpose-Strategies-Discovering-Difference/dp/0615267939

[424] www.gallup.com/cliftonstrengths/en/252137/home.aspx/

[425] www.tdprofiletest.com/home/

[426] See "Absence" in Roy Bhaskar's critical realism glossary:

Absence is closely related to change and hence to cause. For a change in something is the absence of something that was present, or the presence of something that was absent; and to cause something is to make a change, either of the first sort, which is what Bhaskar calls "absenting" something, or of the second sort, which Bhaskar calls "absenting absence." Either way, to cause something is to make something — either a presence or an absence — absent.
tinyurl.com/irpm767

www.criticalrealism.com/glossary.php

[427] Theologian Frederick Buechner defines vocation as the place where "your deep gladness and the world's deep hunger meet." Your deep gladness is the call of one's true, enduring, and authentic self, the pursuits that engender, not necessarily always happiness, but profound joy.

[428] www.amazon.com/Souls-Code-Search-Character-Calling/dp/B001Q3M5YO

[429] www.amazon.com/What-Were-You-Born-Workbook/dp/1883692091

[430] www.amazon.com/True-Purpose-Strategies-Discovering-Difference/dp/0615267939

[431] **Purpose Guiding Process**

Jonathan Gustin, a psychotherapist, meditation teacher, and Integral mentor who founded The Purpose Guides Institute (www.purposeguides.org/) developed the following 12-step process that supports his clients to identify their natural talents (or what he calls their *Soul's Purpose*.) He describes the process as follows:

1. Care of the Soul

In this first step, explore ways to prepare for crossing the threshold between the life you live now and the life that is calling you. Cultivate a "Miracle Morning" ritual that prepares you for living a life that harmonizes with your Soul. Clear space in your life, so that something utterly new, mysterious, and generative may appear. Recognize your own soul right now and begin to let it animate your being. Practice "soul-embodiment" right now and how this differs from ongoing preparation for purpose awakening. Construct a "purpose altar" in your home to become an "axis mundi" (the world center, or the connection between Heaven and Earth) for your purpose journey. Identify the most frequent traps and detours that occur on the road to a purpose-driven life.

2. Prepare for the Journey

Create a road map for the eight facets of your Soul's Purpose: Vision, Values, Powers, Essence, Giveaway, Task, Message and Delivery System. Integrate the three worlds of consciousness, which correspond to the triple purpose of life: To "Wake Up, Grow Up, and Show Up." Don't be disturbed by life's vicissitudes. Transform everyday disappointments into spiritual turnarounds.

3. Default Purpose

Realize that the purpose that moves your life forward, when you are not living from soul, is your default purpose: a combination of bequeathed values from your upbringing and the defense mechanisms you learned during childhood. A default purpose leads you away from your authentic purpose, whereas the Soul's purpose draws you forward into living your destiny. As long as your strongest driving desire comes from a default purpose, your ability to fulfill your destiny is thwarted. Distinguish between the two types of Purpose which propel you: Default vs. True, Defensive vs. Evolutionary, Inherited vs. Revealed, Socially Conditioned vs. Soul Conditioned, Unconscious vs. Intentional, Scarcity Based vs. Love Based, etc. Identify your specific default purpose that veils your True Purpose. Practice moment-to-moment attention in order to recognize the interactions, self-talk and behaviors that are rooted in your default purpose. Practice Purpose-Inquiry effectively: "What would Soul do?"

4. Discern your Purpose

When seeking your purpose, there are two approaches: direct vs. indirect, or inductive vs. deductive. The indirect path to purpose engages your mind's intelligence to detect or infer what your true purpose is. Discover "soulprint hints" from your history. See how your emotions, especially your passions, devotions and fervors, provide clues to your destiny. Find the hidden evidence pointing towards your deepest purpose in your fantasies, aspirations, daydreams and the ways you wish to be remembered. Look for soul clues in your readings, movies, hobbies, and even the heroes you've been choosing.

5. Encountering Resistance

Identify the parts of yourself that have resistance to living your deepest purpose, including the Critic, Skeptic, Controller, Rebel, Achiever, Protector, and Image Consultant. When one of these parts exhibits resistance during your attempts to embrace your soul's purpose, you may experience tension, anxiety, paralysis, fear, or find yourself in a state of constant distraction. Realize that resistance to your Soul's deepest purpose is natural. Distinguish between the real and imagined risks of living your true purpose from the perspective of the voices of resistance. Uncover the authentic concerns of these parts of yourself. Work with your voices of resistance so that you can live your life's destiny.

6. Evolutionary Spirituality

Evolutionary Spirituality is the journey of co-creating the future through embodying your Soul's unique purpose. Realize if you have been creating from the past, present, or future, and what the wisdom of the future, specifically 10 years from now, has to share with you. See how the purpose of evolution and the purpose of soul are identical: to midwife more goodness, truth, beauty, [and functioning]. Realize how Soul is the place where the future is arising out of the present and how life is an evolving process and as such, our soul-work is part of that never ending development. Relinquish attachment to the ego's agenda in both—the spirituality of being and the spirituality of becoming.

7. Soul-Quest Preparation

Go on a daylong solitary ceremony in nature, where you will fast and pray for a Vision of your purpose. Leave the comfort and security of your home to go into wild nature to explore your soul's purpose, because humans have always gone to nature to find their calling: the Buddha awakened under a tree; Jesus went to the desert; Mohammad was fasting and praying in a cave when the Koran came to him; and Moses went to the top of a mountain to bring a vision for his people. Use this ancient, nature-based ceremony that has been practiced throughout the ages and allow wild nature to mirror your wild soul to you, revealing undiscovered layers of depth in your being through immersion in nature, fasting from food and company, and transformational practices. Become an open vessel capable of being filled with your Soul's sacred calling.

8. Receiving Soul

Aristotle coined the term "entelechy" to describe the full actualization of a life form. He said that the entelechy of an acorn is an oak tree. It is the entelechy of the acorn that guides its development. This theory is sometimes called the "acorn theory of soul". It proposes that you already possess the full potential and potency of your Soul, and that the task is to fully actualize your Soul. See that the dictum, "You can be anything you want to be" is dead wrong because your calling is inborn, and that your mission is to obey the imperatives of your Soul and not your ego. Use the Entelechy Process for listening to the "oak tree of yourself and use Meditation to awaken hidden dimensions of your Soul.

9. High-Definition Purpose (The Giveaway)

Embody your soul's gifts, so you can freely share them with the world by contributing to the development of another person. Performing your Giveaway is both a deeply fulfilling, and at the same time impassioned response to the world's needs. The theologian Frederick Buechner put this eloquently: "... our calling is where our deepest gladness and the world's hunger meet."

10. Acting Purposefully

Walk your path. Identify what undermines living your purpose, such as the time you kill, the knowledge you neglect to learn, the connections you fail to build, the health you sacrifice along the path, the people around you who don't support and love your efforts. Instead, make purposeful choices, practice for rooting out what is not purposeful for your evolution, live purposefully immediately and learn from the wisdom of authentic failures.

11. Soul-Quest Incorporation

After your soul-quest, re-enter your former life after returning from your soul-quest and bring your unique gifts to your people. Keep the flame of your Vision alive in the midst of an often-indifferent world. Protect your Vision from fading into a memory. Deepen and embody your purpose in your relationships, work, and ordinary life.

12. Embodiment

Mark Twain noted, "The two most important days in your life are the day you are born and the day you find out why." Embrace the challenge before you to live your life in accordance with the deepest truths you have been graced to know at the core of your being. As the poet David Whyte wrote, "Hold to your own truth at the center of the image you were born with." Switch your focus from discovering your purpose to living your purpose with wild abandon as a demonstration of love and service to Life. Discern whether you have received sufficient information about your life purpose. Absorb what has been revealed to you during your soul-encounters. Construct a purpose statement that accurately distills the essence of your purpose.

[432] www.amazon.com/Purpose-Driven-Life-What-Earth/dp/031033750X

[433] www.amazon.com/Leading-Emerging-Future-Ego-System-Eco-System/dp/1605099260

[434] www.amazon.com/Nature-Human-Soul-Cultivating-Fragmented/dp/1577315510

[435] www.amazon.com/New-Earth-Awakening-Purpose-Selection/dp/0452289963

[436] www.amazon.com/Evolutionary-Enlightenment-Path-Spiritual-Awakening/dp/1590792092

[437] www.amazon.com/Elements-Real-Diamond-Heart-Book/dp/0936713011

[438] www.amazon.com/Mans-Search-Meaning-Viktor-Frankl/dp/0807014273/

[439] www.amazon.com/Law-Divine-Compensation-Money-Miracles/dp/0062205420

[440] https://evolvingwisdom.com/programs/life-purpose-personal-power/

[441] https://femininepower.com/

[442] www.amazon.com/Your-Unique-Self-Personal-Enlightenment-ebook/dp/B00A7KCM04

[443] Also see Joanna Macy tinyurl.com/irpm769 www.joannamacy.net/main who has similar ideas around depth of expression.

[444] Plotkin drew from his own experiences and twenty other categories of sources that inspired him. See *Nature and the Human Soul: Cultivating Wholeness and Community in a Fragmented World*, page 56–58 for details.

[445] www.millennium-project.org/projects/challenges/

[446] www.un.org/en/sections/issues-depth/global-issues-overview/

[447] www.un.org/development/desa/disabilities/envision2030.html

[448] https://learningfundamentals.com.au/resources/

[449] See a video about *Suprasexuality: Uniting Genius in Co-creating the Future* with Barbara Marx Hubbart and Patricia Albert at tinyurl.com/irpm770

https://youtu.be/NnhYrlPkJwM.

[450] As much as I agree with Barbara Marx Hubbard about vocational arousal, I disagree with her and all "intelligent design" idealists, including Plato, Hegel, Teilhard de Chardin, Wilber, Cohen, McIntosh, etc., that there is a given or automatic movement Evolution/Eros/Telos towards more consciousness or goodness, truth, beauty, and functioning that is independent from our sexual selection process and sustainable procreation by people at higher levels of consciousness, and at least 10% of the population at any level of consciousness development living their transcendental purpose.

[451] Synergy is created through interaction or cooperation that gives rise to a whole that is greater than the simple sum of its parts. The derives from the Greek word synergos, meaning "working together." In the natural world, synergistic phenomena are ubiquitous, ranging from physics (for example, the different combinations of quarks that produce protons and neutrons) to chemistry (a popular example is water, a compound of hydrogen and oxygen), to the cooperative interactions among the genes in genomes, the division of labor in bacterial colonies, the synergies of scale in multi-cellular organisms, as well as the many different kinds of synergies produced by socially-organized groups, from honeybee colonies to wolf packs and human interactions. In the context of organizational behavior, following the view that a cohesive couple or group is more than the sum of its parts, synergy is the ability of a couple or group to outperform even its best individual member.

From https://en.wikipedia.org/wiki/Synergy

[452] www.amazon.com/Immunity-Change-Potential-Organization-Leadership/dp/1422117367

[453] 73% of Americans believe in soul mates. tinyurl.com/irpm774 www.scienceofpeople.com/soulmate/

[454] The following article was authored by Scott Andrews, Founder of www.AspireNow.com

It aptly describes how to recognize a soulmate:

"You can almost always spot soulmates, because they make each other more powerful as a team than they were apart! This is the **first** way to spot your soul mate.

If you are in a relationship, and you're having to rationalize how much this other person helps you (or hinders you) then they are **not** your soulmate. Take the word soul, add the definition with the definition for mate, and you've got a strong definition of a soulmate: "the core spiritual nature, immortal, inseparable even from death, mated to be together."

Considering this definition, let us also consider the **second** way to spot your soul mate:

They are both aware of their spiritual nature. In most cases, these two will have their eyes first upon this higher calling or power (God/Spirit), second upon each other, third upon their purpose <u>together</u>. Their family, career, and other things will always follow in some priority after these three.

The **third** was to spot a soulmate is to recognize how the journeys of the two interrelate. All soulmates are on a spiritual life journey. These journeys, when the souls coincide for maximum impact, almost always run parallel or coincide in such a way that it creates a relationship that is more about the union, or the team, than the individual. They put the team/partnership journey above their individual journey and desires. The reason for this is that the individual's dream is complementary to the union in a soul mate relationship. At the same time, the relationship works in a way that each person's individual journey is fully supported. With soulmates, there is trust and respect. With trust and respect comes the ability to realize aspirations - both as a couple and as individuals.

The **fourth** way to spot your soulmate is to recognize how each partner brings real love into the other's life. If a person does not bring real love to you, but instead causes significant conflict, grief, angst, lack, and failure, then it is highly unlikely that this person is your soul mate. A soulmate helps to awaken your soul and makes it easier for you to learn the lessons you are meant to learn. A key difference is that the soulmate is not the lesson, they help you learn your lessons and support that growing process.

The **fifth** way to spot a soulmate is that they possess harmonious and complementary natures. Sometimes, when people are coming from ego, rather than spirit, the relationship becomes about what they have (possessions) rather than who they are (experiences). Soulmates are about experiences far more than possessions, because they realize that they cannot take their possessions with them. Your soul does not own your possessions, but it owns your experiences."

Reprinted with permission from the author.

[455] The "will to power" is a central concept in the philosophy of nineteenth-century German philosopher, Friedrich Nietzsche, as a psychological, biological, or metaphysical principle that is neither good nor bad. It is a basic drive found in everyone that can be channeled toward different ends. Philosophers, scientists, and journalists direct their will to power into a will to truth. Artists channel it into a will to create beauty. Saints direct it towards creating goodness. Craftsmen and politicians aim to create functioning tools and systems. Nietzsche clearly doesn't advocate the pursuit of power. Instead, he praises those expressions of it he views as creative, beautiful, and life-affirming, and he criticizes expressions of the will to power that he sees as ugly or born of weakness. One particular form of the will to power that Nietzsche devotes much attention to is what he calls "self-overcoming." Here the will to power is harnessed and directed toward self-mastery and self-transformation, guided by the principle that "your real self lies not deep within you but high above you." Adopted from tinyurl.com/irpm775 www.thoughtco.com/nietzsches-concept-of-the-will-to-power-2670658

[456] Existence is the ability of an entity to interact with physical or mental reality. In philosophy, it refers to the ontological property of being.

[457] See below from *Grace and Grit: Spirituality and Healing in the Life and Death of Treya Killam Wilber,* page 9–11 in which Ken Wilber and Treya share about their first encounter on Aug. 3, 1983.

Ken wrote:

Love at first touch. We hadn't said five words to each other. And I could tell by the way she was looking at my shaved head that it definitely was not going to be love at first sight. I, like almost everybody, found Treya quite beautiful, but I really didn't even know her. But when I put my arm around her, I felt all separation and distance dissolve; there was some sort of merging, it seemed. **It was as if Treya and I had been together**

for a lifetime. This seemed very real and very obvious, but I didn't know quite what to make of it. Treya and I still hadn't even talked to each other, so neither of us knew the same thing was happening to the other. I remember thinking, oh great, it's four in the morning and I'm having some sort of weird mystical experience right in the kitchen of one of my best friends, merely by touching a woman I've never met before. This is not going to be easy to explain ....

I couldn't sleep that night, as images of Treya poured over me. She was indeed beautiful. But what exactly was it? There was an energy that seemed literally to radiate from her in all directions; a very quiet and soothing energy, but enormously strong and powerful; an energy that was very intelligent and suffused with exceptional beauty, but mostly an energy that was *alive*. This woman said *LIFE* more than anybody I had ever known. The way she moved, the way she held her head, the ready smile that graced the most open and transparent face I had ever seen — God she was alive!

Treya wrote:

To be touched like that, like he touched me, first through his words and what it showed of him, the soft depth of his brown eyes, and then an easy melting body to body, something clearly happened there, I closed my eyes to try to sense it, beyond words but palpable, real, even if mostly inexpressible.

I feel my heart open, I trust him more than I trust the universe. Fascinating lying in bed this morning. Feeling little wavelets of vibration, very clear and distinct. Sensation in my arms and legs, but mostly localized in the lower half of my trunk. What is happening when this goes on? Are things loosening up, held tensions from the past dissolving?

I focused on my heart, felt an opening very, very, clearly, from thinking of that sensation I had with Ken last night. An amazingly powerful surge from my heart, that then goes down into the center of my body, and then up toward the top of my head. So pleasurable and blissful it's almost painful, like an ache, a longing, a reaching out, a wanting, a desire, an openness, a vulnerability. Like how I would feel perhaps all the time if I weren't protected, if I dropped my defenses ... and yet it feels wonderful, I love the feeling, it feels very alive and very real, full of energy and warmth. Jolts my inner core alive.

tinyurl.com/irpm776

www.amazon.com/Grace-Grit-Spirituality-Healing-Killam/dp/1570627428

[458] Image: Thanksgiving Square Chapel - Dallas, TX tinyurl.com/irpm778

https://thanksgiving.org/thanksgivingsquare/

[459] Two heads are better than one if the competency and confidence of the individuals involved matches.

tinyurl.com/irpm779

www.scientificamerican.com/article/are-two-heads-better-than/

[460] Ego-Soul Worksheet suggested answers

The Ego—the conditioned, separate sense of self	The Soul—the unconditioned, relational self
Me	We/Us
Separation	Unity
Blame	Understanding
Hostility	Friendliness
Resentment	Forgiveness
Pride	Humility
Complain	Gratefulness
Jealousy	Co-happiness (Mudita)* or compersion**
Projecting anger	Owning anger
Power over	Power with
Materialism	Spiritualism
Madness	Sanity/Wisdom
War	Peace
Coldness	Sympathy/Warmness
Pain of past/fear of future oriented	Now orientation
Intolerance	Tolerance
Self-importance	We-importance
Stinginess	Generosity/Altruism
Self-denial	Self-acceptance

Social intolerance	Social acceptance
Complexity	Simplicity
Doing	Being
Victim	Creator

Table 29: Ego versus soul

*Mudita means joy; especially sympathetic or vicarious joy. Also: the pleasure that comes from delighting in other people's well-being.

https://en.wikipedia.org/wiki/Mudita

** An empathetic state of happiness and joy experienced when another individual experiences happiness and joy. Vicarious joy associated with seeing one's partner have a joyful romantic or sexual relation with another.

https://en.wiktionary.org/wiki/compersion

[461] Immunity to Change:

Goal	Doing/Not Doing Instead	Hidden Competing Commitments	Big (false?) Assumptions
Find or attract my soulmate	Hedonistic Pursuits	My life is good as it is.	Nobody will love me.
Get into shape (physically, financially, emotionally, spiritually). Be open and welcoming. Smile at people. Work with a dating coach. Write my dating profile. Take pictures and post my dating profile.	Hanging out with friends. Work more. Watch TV. Play with my pet. Go on vacations. Play computer games.	I should not need a partner to be happy. When I do not search or look, he/she will come. I need to work harder and become more successful so (s)he will be attracted to me. I need to be there for my	There are no good partners out there. I am not ready for a relationship. I will have to change my life. I will never fall in love again. I will be left and heartbroken. I cannot deal with rejection (mostly for men).

Join groups and events where I can meet likeminded people. Start my own meetups/groups. Tell my friends. Be active on social media. Create a vision map. Do the "Calling in 'The One' Process."		friends, family. I waste my time with dating. I will look like a loser/failure if I admit that I am single and looking.	I am afraid of being harassed and/or rejecting.* Nobody shares my passion. Nobody wants what I want. All good men/women are taken. People are only interested in their primary fantasy.
* This is often a reason for attractive women who get a lot of attention and offers from men to close themselves down. One solution is to say, "Thank you for having the courage to approach me. You have good taste and seem to be a nice / good / friendly person. I am looking for an equal partner who (name your three most important criteria—e.g., who wants to have children with me, is on an integral level of consciousness development, and shares my passion and purpose to do good by healing people through holistic bodywork). What are you looking for in a partner? What are you passionate and concerned about?" A conversation can follow to get to know each other better and to support each other in finding a compatible partner.			

Table 30: Soulmate immunity to change examples

[462] See *Marry Him: The Case for Settling for Mr. Good Enough* (2011) by Lori Gottlieb for having realistic expectations.

tinyurl.com/irpm781

www.amazon.com/Marry-Him-Case-Settling-Enough/dp/045123216X

[463] List of passion and interests:

Passion/Interest	Must Have	Can't Tolerate	Would Like	Can Tolerate	Want to Develop	Needs Discussion

Integral Relationship Practice | 670

activism						
animals						
antiques						
appearance						
art						
bathroom/hygiene						
camping						
children						
concerts						
cooking/food						
dancing						
dining out						
environmental concerns						
entertainment						
family						
fishing/hunting						
friends						
future						
gaming						
gardening/plants/landscaping						
golfing						
groups						
hiking						
hobbies						
holidays						
home-improvement/decorate						
household						
massage						
material lifestyle						
money/investing						
movies/videos/DVD						
museums						

music (playing and listening)						
nightclubs						
painting						
past						
performing arts						
personal growth						
pets						
philosophy						
physical health						
politics						
reading						
religion						
romance						
sensuality						
sexuality						
shopping						
spirituality						
sports (watching and active)						
travel and sightseeing						
tv, videos, streaming						
vacations						
vehicles/transportation						
video games						
volunteering						
wedding						
wine tasting						
work						
writing						

Table 31: List of passions and interests

[464] List of values and ideals:

Capacity/Value/ Ideal	*Must Have*	*Can't Tolerate*	*Would Like*	*Can Tolerate*	*Want to Develop*	*Need to Discuss*

Integral Relationship Practice | 672

attentiveness						
availability						
beauty						
charity						
commitment						
compassion						
creativity						
effortlessness						
even temper						
faithfulness						
generosity						
gentleness						
good humor						
consistency						
hope						
hospitality						
integrity						
joy						
justice						
kindness						
love						
mercy						
monogamy						
patience						
perfection						
playfulness						
richness						
self-control						

self-sufficiency						
service						
simplicity						
trust						
truth						
understanding						
uniqueness						
wholeness						

Table 32: List of capacities, values, and ideals

[465] **Satisficers** are individuals who are pleased to settle for a good enough option, not necessarily the very best outcome in all respects. A satisficer is less likely to experience regret, even if a better option presents itself after a decision has already been made. Compared to satisficers, **maximizers** are more likely to experience lower levels of happiness, regret, and self-esteem. They also tend to be perfectionists.

tinyurl.com/irpm782

www.psychologytoday.com/us/blog/science-choice/201506/satisficing-vs-maximizing

tinyurl.com/irpm783

www.psychologistworld.com/cognitive/maximizer-satisficer-decision-making-quiz

tinyurl.com/irpm785

https://freakonomics.com/podcast/nsq-maximizer-satisficer/

[466] www.amazon.com/Game-Penetrating-Secret-Society-Artists/dp/0061240168

[467] www.amazon.com/Stumbling-Naked-Dark-Overcoming-Mistakes/dp/0981484336/

[468] www.amazon.com/Calling-One-Weeks-Attract-Love/dp/1400049296

[469] https://integrallife.com/grace-and-grit-film-release-everything-you-need-to-know/

[470] tinyurl.com/irpm786

www.ocf.berkeley.edu/~jonc/classic/woman_dict.html

Integral Relationship Practice | 674

---

[471] Some systems have additional chakras that are located outside the human body. The "earth" chakra is located below the root chakra and reaches into the earth, while several chakras above the crown chakra stretch up into the entire universe and beyond the sphere of understanding or experience (and are thus impossible to talk about).

[472] tinyurl.com/irpm787

www.youtube.com/watch?v=ZPtT3p8T6Cg

[473] In many primates, including humans, the vocalizations of males and females differ dramatically, with male vocalizations and vocal anatomy often seeming to exaggerate apparent body size. These traits may be favored by sexual selection because low-frequency male vocalizations intimidate rivals and/or attract females.

tinyurl.com/irpm789

http://rspb.royalsocietypublishing.org/content/283/1829/20152830

A female's comment under a Barry White song on YouTube: "Just listening to that voice could get me pregnant."

[474] See tinyurl.com/irpm790

https://en.wikipedia.org/wiki/Lateralization_of_brain_function.

[475] The FCC has never maintained a specific list of words prohibited from the airwaves during the time period from 6 am to 10 pm, but it has alleged that its own internal guidelines are sufficient to determine what it considers obscene. https://en.wikipedia.org/wiki/Seven_dirty_words.

[476] Examples for chakra one and two:

2. Shared Sexuality	I (You—Partner—Co-Creation)	IT (You—Partner—Co-Creation)
	We practice sexuality to heal our unconscious, deepen our intimacy (in-to-me-you-see), and awaken spiritually by facing everything and avoiding nothing.	We have a healthy diet, don't use substances, are height-weight proportional. We keep our body and skin clean. We make ample time for lovemaking.

	We (You—Partner—Co-Creation)	Its (You—Partner—Co-Creation)
	We respect each other's boundaries and are monogamous (polyamorous, etc.). We are tolerant towards people with different sexual orientations and practices. We keep our sex life private.	Our love-room (bedroom) is aesthetically pleasing with warm colors, soft sheets, candles, incents, music, massage oil.
1. Shared Ground - Honors Earth. Material, money, shelter, lifestyle.	I (You—Partner—Co-Creation) We want to feel physically safe and comfortable while having an ecologically and socially responsible lifestyle.	Its (You—Partner—Co-Creation) We are vegetarians and exercise regularly and do frequent medical checkups so that we consume less resources and can perform our work in optimal ways.
	We (You—Partner—Co-Creation) We support liberal values of equal rights, responsibilities, and opportunities for all humans (our community etc.) to have safe shelter, food security, sanitation, and access to education. We are politically active and donate time and money for such causes.	Its (You—Partner—Co-Creation) We live ecologically responsibly in an urban area with public transportation and earn money through responsible work that creates benefits (what exactly) for others.

Table 33: Examples co-creation at the 1st and 2nd chakra

[477] www.amazon.com/Charge-Energy-Body-Healing-Relationships/dp/1401954480

[478] Singles Nation: Why Americans Are Turning Away from Marriage.

For the first time since the Bureau of Labor Statistics began tracking the number of single people in 1976, they outnumber married people. About 50.2 percent or 124.6 million American adults are single (unmarried). In 1950, that number was around 22 percent.

tinyurl.com/irpm792

www.census.gov/newsroom/stories/unmarried-single-americans-week.html

[479] tinyurl.com/irpm794

https://ourworldindata.org/marriages-and-divorces

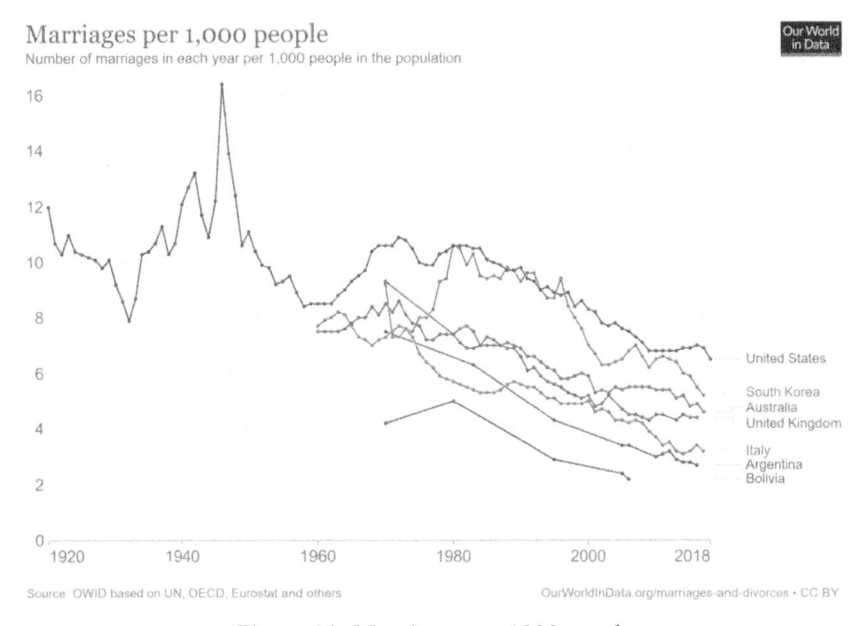

Figure 99: Marriages per 1000 people

[480] According to the philosopher Charles Taylor, the term "atomism" is used loosely to characterize the doctrines of social contract theory which arose in the seventeenth century and also successor doctrines which may not have made use of the concept of social contract, but which inherited a vision of society as in some sense constituted by individuals for the fulfilment of ends which were primarily individual. Certain forms of utilitarianism are successor doctrines in this sense. The term is also applied to contemporary doctrines which harken back to social contract theory, or which try to defend in some sense the priority of the

individual and his rights over society, or which present a purely instrumental view of society.

https://en.wikipedia.org/wiki/Atomism_(social)

[481] See the book *Dream Hoarders: How the American Upper Middle Class Is Leaving Everyone Else in the Dust, Why That Is a Problem, and What to Do About It* (revised edition 2018) by Richard V. Reeves

The separation of the upper middle class from everyone else is both economic and social, and the practice of "opportunity hoarding" — gaining exclusive access to scarce resources — is especially prevalent among parents who want to perpetuate privilege to the benefit of their children.

tinyurl.com/irpm795

www.amazon.com/Dream-Hoarders-American-Leaving-Everyone/dp/0815734484

[482] See an extensive 2020 Pew Research Center report that states that nearly half of U.S. adults say dating has gotten harder for most people in the last 10 years. Half of single American adults are not on the dating market at all. Of those who say they are currently looking for a relationship or dates, 61% are men compared with 38% women. The gender differences are heavily concentrated among older singles. While men and women younger than 40 are roughly equally likely to not be looking for a relationship or dates (33% and 39%, respectively), a majority of older women (71%) say they aren't looking to date right now, compared with 42% of men 40 and older.

Most older single women are not looking to date

% of single adults in each group saying they are ___ for a committed relationship and/or casual dates

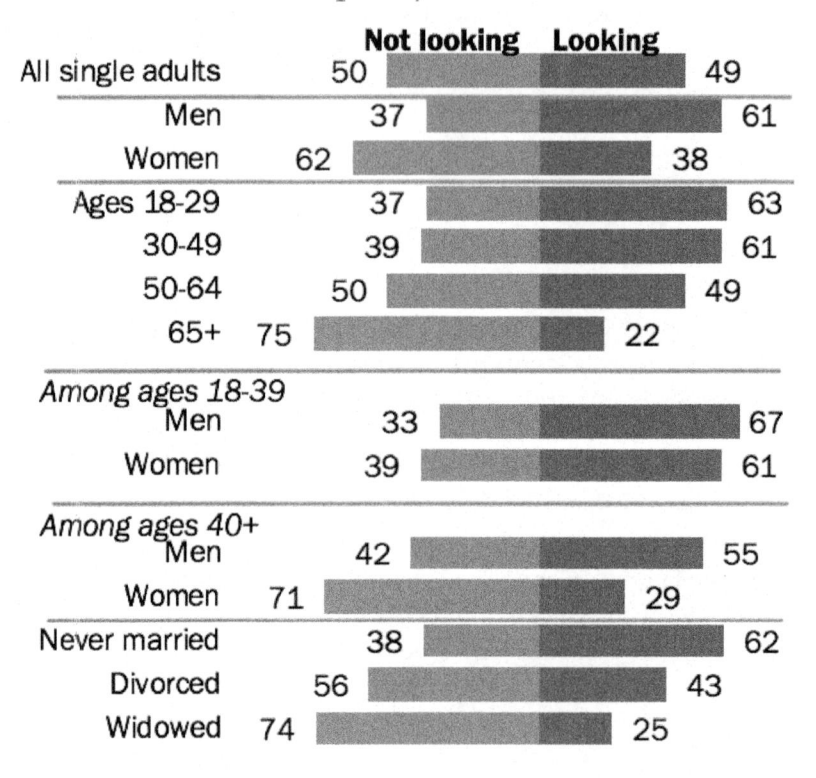

	Not looking	Looking
All single adults	50	49
Men	37	61
Women	62	38
Ages 18-29	37	63
30-49	39	61
50-64	50	49
65+	75	22
Among ages 18-39 Men	33	67
Women	39	61
Among ages 40+ Men	42	55
Women	71	29
Never married	38	62
Divorced	56	43
Widowed	74	25

Note: "Single adults" are those who are not married, living with a partner or in a committed romantic relationship. "Divorced" does not include respondents who are separated. Share of respondents who didn't offer an answer not shown.
Source: Survey of U.S. adults conducted Oct. 16-28, 2019.
"Nearly Half of U.S. Adults Say Dating Has Gotten Harder for Most People in the Last 10 Years"

PEW RESEARCH CENTER

Figure 100: US statistic men and women looking for a partner

Women who have found it difficult to date are much more likely than men to say a major reason for their difficulty is that it's hard to find someone who meets their expectations (56% vs. 35%) and that it's hard to find someone looking for the same kind of relationship as them (65% vs. 45%).

Women say it's hard to find someone who is looking for the same kind of relationship and meets their standards

% saying each of the following is a major reason it has been difficult to find people to date, among daters who have found it very or somewhat difficult in the past year

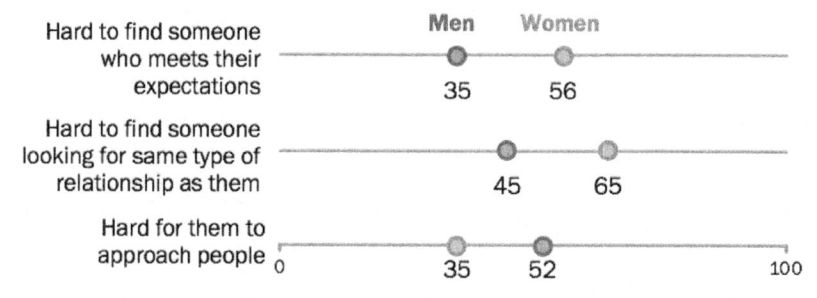

	Men	Women
Hard to find someone who meets their expectations	35	56
Hard to find someone looking for same type of relationship as them	45	65
Hard for them to approach people	35	52

Note: "Daters" are those who are not married, living with a partner or in a committed romantic relationship and have indicated that right now they are looking for: a committed romantic relationship only, casual dates only or either a committed romantic relationship or casual dates. Only reasons with a statistically significant difference between men and women are shown.
Source: Survey of U.S. adults conducted Oct. 16-28, 2019.
"Nearly Half of U.S. Adults Say Dating Has Gotten Harder for Most People in the Last 10 Years"

PEW RESEARCH CENTER

Figure 101: US statistic men and women looking for a partner

tinyurl.com/irpm796

www.pewresearch.org/social-trends/2020/08/20/personal-experiences-and-attitudes-of-daters/

[483] Think about your household's monthly expenses. There are the big-ticket items—your rent or mortgage, your health care, maybe a student loan. Then there's the smaller stuff: the utility bills; the internet and

phone bills; Netflix, Hulu, and all your other streaming subscriptions. If you drive a car, there's gas and insurance. If you take the subway, there's a public transit pass. You pay for food, and household items like toilet paper and garbage bags and lightbulbs. You buy furniture and sheets and dishes.

Now imagine paying for all those things completely on your own. If you live by yourself—or as a single parent or caregiver—you don't have to imagine. This is your life.

tinyurl.com/irpm798

www.vox.com/the-goods/22788620/single-living-alone-cost

[484] See tinyurl.com/irpm799

www.populationpyramid.net/sub-saharan-africa/2100/ and tinyurl.com/irpm800

www.thelancet.com/pdfs/journals/lancet/PIIS0140-6736(20)31522-1.pdf

[485] In recent years, a vast scientific literature has emerged linking loneliness to depression, anxiety, alcoholism, and drug abuse. There is even a growing body of epidemiological work showing that loneliness makes you more likely to fall ill: it seems to prompt the chronic release of hormones that suppress healthy immune function. Biochemical changes from loneliness can accelerate the spread of cancer, hasten heart disease and Alzheimer's, or simply drain the most vital among us of the will to go on. The ability to measure and detect it could help identify those at risk and pave the way for new kinds of interventions.

tinyurl.com/irpm801

www.technologyreview.com/2020/09/04/1008008/neuroscience-loneliness-pandemic-covid-neurons-brain/

Lonely people also had significantly higher levels of norepinephrine coursing through their blood and shutting down immune functions like viral defense, while ramping up the production of white blood cells called monocytes.

tinyurl.com/irpm802

www.npr.org/sections/health-shots/2015/11/29/457255876/loneliness-may-warp-our-genes-and-our-immune-systems

[486] Studies found that people at higher income levels are more satisfied with life. Interestingly, even at annual income levels above $120,000, this

positive correlation still applied. There is no saturation point, a higher income equals more happiness at all levels. These studies even showed that where incomes are increased by the same percentage, the impact is stronger at higher income levels than at lower income levels.

tinyurl.com/irpm803

www.forbes.com/sites/rainerzitelmann/2020/07/06/does-money-make-people-happy/?sh=7b28d5b7574d

[487] Researchers found that sex: (1) relieves stress, (2) boosts the immune system, (3) burns calories (85 or more in 30 minutes), (4) improves cardiovascular health, (5) boosts self-esteem, (6) improves intimacy, (7) reduces pain (through release of oxytocin), (8) reduces risk of prostate cancer, (9) strengthens pelvic floor muscles, and (10) helps you to sleep better. tinyurl.com/irpm804

www.webmd.com/sex-relationships/guide/sex-and-health#1 and tinyurl.com/irpm806

www.womenshealthnetwork.com/sexual-health/

Also see Patricia Love and Steven Stosny in *How to Improve your Marriage Without Talking About It*, page 148–150.

[488] Until women began to enter the workforce, they were more often able to turn to nurturing and relaxing "tending and befriending" strategies with their partners, family, and friends when they felt stressed. These comforting activities triggered the release of the "cuddle hormone" oxytocin. Oxytocin naturally counters the harmful stress hormones cortisol and epinephrine, which increase blood pressure and blood sugar levels and weaken the immune system.

"In the modern environment one is exposed to various stressful conditions. Stress can lead to changes in the serum level of many hormones including glucocorticoids, catecholamines, growth hormone and prolactin. Some of these changes are necessary for the fight or flight response to protect oneself. Some of these stressful responses can lead to endocrine disorders like Graves' disease, gonadal dysfunction, psychosexual dwarfism and obesity. Stress can also alter the clinical status of many preexisting endocrine disorders such as precipitation of adrenal crisis and thyroid storm."

tinyurl.com/irpm808 www.ncbi.nlm.nih.gov/pmc/articles/PMC3079864/

Males, on the other hand, typically resorted to masculine fight-or-flight strategies to lower the stress hormones that arose for them in the public sphere and at home. Alas, fight-or-flight produces the stress-reducing hormones in much smaller amounts, and males got the short end of the stick, unless they received frequent care and sex from a loving and supportive partner at home. tinyurl.com/irpm809

www.webmd.com/women/features/stress-women-men-cope#2

[489] A burgeoning literature suggests that marriage may have a wide range of benefits, including improvements in individuals' economic well-being, mental and physical health, and the well-being of their children. tinyurl.com/irpm810

https://aspe.hhs.gov/report/effects-marriage-health-synthesis-recent-research-evidence-research-brief

A major survey of 127,545 American adults found that married men are healthier than men who were never married or whose marriages ended in divorce or widowhood. Men who have marital partners also live longer than men without spouses; men who marry after age 25 get more protection than those who tie the knot at a younger age, and the longer a man stays married, the greater his survival advantage over his unmarried peers. tinyurl.com/irpm811

www.health.harvard.edu/newsletter_article/marriage-and-mens-health

[490] The origin of sexual reproduction can be traced to early prokaryotes, around two billion years ago (Gya), when bacteria began exchanging genes via conjugation, transformation, and transduction. tinyurl.com/irpm812

https://en.wikipedia.org/wiki/Evolution_of_sexual_reproduction

[491] Memetics is the study of information and culture based on an analogy with Darwinian evolution. Proponents describe memetics as an approach to evolutionary models of cultural information transfer. Memetics describes how an idea can propagate successfully, but doesn't necessarily imply a concept is factual.

[492] I asked Eckhart Tolle once why he wrote in *The Power of Now*: "Nothing matters, but everything is honored." He went to great length to explain that we honor the creator (God) behind the creation without Ego desire or attachment to what is created. In my interpretation, he suggests that we transcend our ego to allow the co-creative and procreative impulse or life-force to manifest through our relational soul's purpose to sustain the human race and create more goodness, truth, beauty, and functioning.

Adyashanti said after a couples retreat that he facilitated with his wife: "The depth and embodiment of your spiritual realization will be seen in your love relationships. That is where the proof is in the pudding. If it all collapses in your relationships, you have some work to do. And people have a lot of problems in their relationships."

[493] Also see Ezra Klein, May 2022 interview with Patrick Deneen

tinyurl.com/irpm814

www.nytimes.com/2022/05/13/podcasts/transcript-ezra-klein-interviews-patrick-deneen.html

[494] tinyurl.com/irpm815

www.nytimes.com/2022/04/03/opinion/putin-ukraine-liberalism.html?smid=url-share

[495] tinyurl.com/irpm817

www.researchgate.net/publication/297048728_The_Environmental_Impact_of_Singles'_Consumer_Behaviour_Is_the_Lifestyle_of_Singles_Inevitably_Environmentally_More_Damaging

[496] Research consistently shows that marriage and long-term relationships are good for your physical, mental, and financial health.

tinyurl.com/irpm819

www.theguardian.com/lifeandstyle/2016/apr/17/couples-healthier-wealthier-marriage-good-health-single-survey-research

tinyurl.com/irpm820

www.ncbi.nlm.nih.gov/pmc/articles/PMC5830314/

[497] https://worldpopulationreview.com/country-rankings/total-fertility-rate

[498] www.macrotrends.net/countries/USA/united-states/fertility-rate

[499] tinyurl.com/irpm821

www.cdc.gov/nchs/data/nvsr/nvsr70/nvsr70-17.pdf

[500] https://youtu.be/QsBT5EQt348

[501] See tinyurl.com/irpm822

https://integralrelationship.com/ccpc with many graphics that is frequently updated.

[502] In his telling 2017 book, *Dream Hoarders: How the American Upper Middle Class Is Leaving Everyone Else in the Dust, Why That Is a Problem,*

and What to Do about It, Richard Reeves describes the separation of upper middle-class children from ordinary American kids. He looks at three forms of opportunity hoarding, in particular: exclusionary zoning, unfairness in college admissions, and the allocation of unpaid internships.

tinyurl.com/irpm564

www.amazon.com/Dream-Hoarders-American-Leaving-Everyone/dp/081572912X

Also see the 2019 BBC article, "Has Humanity Reached 'Peak Intelligence'?" about the reversal of the Flynn effect which maintained that IQ test scores increase over time: "Whatever the cause of the Flynn effect, there is evidence that we may have already reached the end of this era—with the rise in IQs stalling and even reversing. If you look at Finland, Norway, and Denmark, for instance, the turning point appears to have occurred in the mid-90s, after which average IQs dropped by around 0.2 points a year. That would amount to a seven-point difference between generations.

tinyurl.com/irpm824

www.bbc.com/future/article/20190709-has-humanity-reached-peak-intelligence

[503] A 2021 study proposes and explores a new fertility determinant: societal secularism. Using country-level data from multiple sources and multilevel data from 58 countries in the World Values Survey, the author documents a strong negative relationship between societal secularism and both country-level fertility rates and individual-level fertility behavior. Secularism, even in small amounts, is associated with population stagnation or even decline absent substantial immigration, whereas highly religious countries have higher fertility rates that promote population growth. This country-level pattern is driven by more than aggregate lower fertility of secular individuals. In fact, societal secularism is a better predictor of highly religious individuals' fertility behavior than that of secular individuals, and this pattern is largely a function of cultural values related to gender, reproduction, and autonomy in secular societies. Beyond their importance for the religious composition of the world population, the patterns presented in the study are relevant to key fertility theories and could help account for below-replacement fertility.

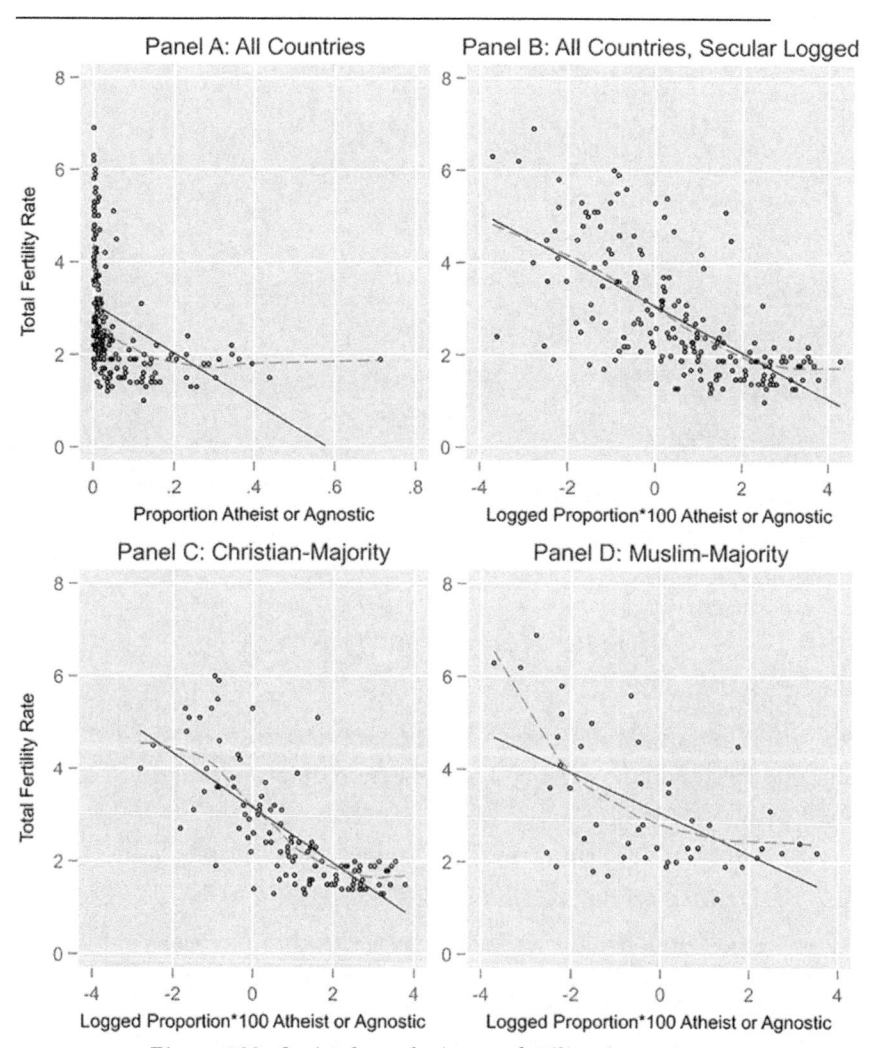

Figure 102: Societal secularism as fertility determinant

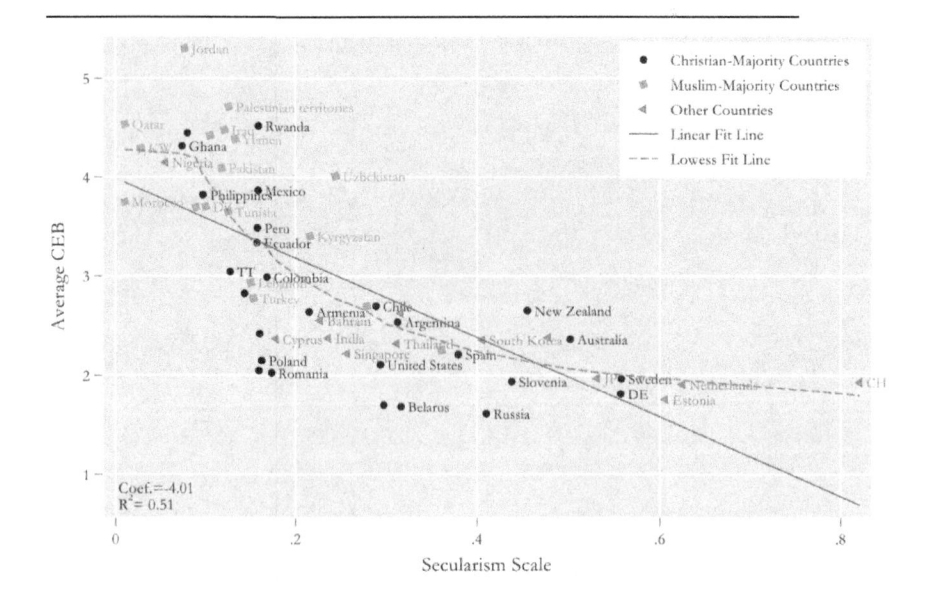

Figure 103: Secularism in various countries

tinyurl.com/irpm825

https://journals.sagepub.com/doi/full/10.1177/23780231211031320

See country by country history and projection of fertility rates at tinyurl.com/irpm826

www.macrotrends.net/countries/USA/united-states/fertility-rate

Also see Dr. Michael Blume tinyurl.com/irpm827

www.blume-religionswissenschaft.de/english/pdf/Biological_Success_of_Religion_Blume.pdf and his German book *Religion und Demografie: Warum es ohne Glauben an Kindern mangelt* (2014) by Dr. Michael Blume tinyurl.com/irpm828

www.amazon.com/Religion-Demografie-Glauben-Kindern-mangelt/dp/1499110251

[504] From the 2022 book *8 Billion and Counting* by Jennifer D. Sciubba

tinyurl.com/irpm563

[505] Ken Wilber does not get tired to maintain that stacking social holons on top of individual holons, as shown below in this module, is problematic or a fallacy, because the social holarchy of couples, families, communities, societies, and humanity are not co-created (or emerge) in

the same way as individual holons do, such as cells that form tissues, that form organs, that form humans.

His reasoning is threefold:

1. Social holons have no single governing force, will, purpose, or "consciousness."

2. Social holons can exist even if we remove the smaller holons that they are created from. For example, a community can exist without families (at least for some time).

3. Individual holons can more or less autonomously form, join, or leave social holons, while this freedom of movement is not available to holons that are parts of individual holons.

See more in *Sex Purpose Love*, page 435–445

[506] https://drive.google.com/drive/folders/1krXcl712kEOu7hXfXbRn8eIHQ4ci7xAt

[507] https://integralrelationship.com/splstatistics/

[508] www.amazon.com/Couple-Intimate-Relations-Development-Humanities/dp/3643907702/ about the primacy of the couple.

[509] www.amazon.com/Habermas-Short-Introduction-Gordon-Finlayson/dp/0192840959

[510] www.amazon.com/World-after-Liberalism-Philosophers-Radical/dp/0300243111

[511] www.amazon.com/Why-Liberalism-Failed-Politics-Culture/dp/0300240023/

[512] www.amazon.com/Billion-Counting-Death-Migration-Shape/dp/1324002700

[513] www.amazon.com/Dream-Hoarders-American-Leaving-Everyone/dp/081572912X

[514] See a 4-minute clip from the movie about reproduction at tinyurl.com/irpm833

www.youtube.com/watch?v=sP2tUW0HDHA and a 16-minute critique that is not differentiating between cognitive IQ, which is now declining in many countries, and consciousness development at

tinyurl.com/irpm836

www.youtube.com/watch?v=522T2axRBcU

[515] tinyurl.com/irpm837

www.tomorroweveraftermovie.com/

[516] https://integralrelationship.com/ir-modules/

[517] Available for download at www.integralrelationship.com/irp. See Appendix I for details.

[518] tinyurl.com/irpm839

www.rode.com/microphones/smartlav-plus

Index

A

accusation, 25
  betray, 25
Adyashanti, 207
Almaas, A.H., 602, 628
Amber, 376
American Psychiatric Association's Diagnostic and Statistical Manual on Mental Disorders (DSM), 394
Anchor, 18
Andrews, Scott, 664
Anima/Animus, 161, 175, 255, 258, 376, 493
  Anima Development in Men. *See Anima Animus*
  Animus Development in Women. *See Anima Animus*
  five stages in anima/animus complex, 262, 268
Anodea Judith. *See* chakras
Arendt, Hanna, 109
Armstrong, Alison, 580
attachment styles, 319, 326, 333
  anxious-avoidant, 332
  anxiously attached, 331
  avoidant, 331
  securely attached, 330
  test, 322
Aurobindo, Sri, 578

B

Bateson, Gregory
  Double Bind Theory, 146
Bateson, Gregory, 146
benefits of living, 438
Bergson, Henri, 51
biological Purpose, 417, 424, 436, 479
Bohmian dialog, 148
BPD, 401
brain, 56, 219
  behavioral approach system (BAS), 221
  behavioral inhibition system (BIS), 221
  Hippocampus, 56
  Hypothalamus, 56
  Limbic, 56
  Reptilian, 56
breathing in, 17
Brown, Brené, 172
Bühler, Karl, 129
  organon model, 129

C

Canva, 551
Chakras, 13, 53, 98, 156, 235, 425, 426, 429, 467, 480, 497
Chant, 20
climate change, xxix, 527
cognitive, 52, 130
Cohen, Andrew, 231
collective environment, 30
  social, 31
color-coding, 54
  Amber, 75, 137, *See* Mythic

Beige, 49, 62, 95, *See* Archaic
Green, 73, 92, 99, 110, 137, 175, 187, 354, see Pluralistic
Infrared, 54, 62, 100, *See* Archaic
Magenta. *See* Magic
Orange, 87, 99, 175, 186, *See* Rational
Purple, 63
Teal, 73, *See* Integral
Turquoise, 54, 73, 95, 97, *See* transpersonal
Yellow, 73
communication, 125
  integral and transpersonal, 145
  need-based, 139
communication styles, 137
communications
  communicative action, 149
  Three domains, 149
compassion, 81, 91
  idiot compassion, 86
compatibility matrix, 98
compatible pathologies, 339
competency, 96
complexity, 68
complexity difference in man/women, 102
connect with each other, 13
  eye gazing, 13
  handholding, 13
  hugging. *See* hugs
consciousness, xxxiv
  levels of consciousness, 91
  second-tier, 146
  self-conscious, 67
  stages of consciousness, 49
consciousness development
    and unconscious, 616
    sexes grow through stages differently, 100
consciousness growth in male-female, 101
contraception
    abortions, 160
contradictions, 87
Cook-Greuter, Susanne, 103
Coronavirus pandemic, xxix
creativity chakra. *See* Throat chakra

D

Darwin, Charles, 102
David Deida
    Feminine Masculine Polarities, 184
David Emerald. *See* The Empowerment Dynamic
Deneen, Patrick J., xxxii
depolarized society, xxxiv
dialectic, 430
Dickinson, Emily, 475
dilemma, 147
disasters, xxix
    droughts, xxix
    floods, xxix, 537
    megastorms, xxix
    wildfires, xxix
disidentification, 11
divorcing well, 266
Dopamine, 384
downward spiral, 171, 173
    fear-shame, 171
    Ten phases of fear-shame, 173
dragged down, 97
Dreaded drama triangle, 132

E

persecutors, 133
rescuers, 133
victims, 132, 140

Eckhart Tolle, 233
Ego, 10, 98, 104, 202, 290, 342, 380, 476
   Ego affirming, 62
   ego development, 11
   ego impairments
      selfish hedonism, 10
   Ego impairments, 10
Ego Affirming Method, 453
Ego Transcending Method, 450
ego versus Soul Exercise, 481
egocentric, 307
Egocentric, 436
ego-transcending, 529
Einstein, Albert, 29, 71, 159
elements of integral relationships, 498
ElSherbini, Dr. Khaled. *See Anima Animus*
embracing each other. *See* Hugs
emotional availability, 337
emotional complexity, 102
emotional reactions, 115
   anger, 118
   disgust, 118
   fear, 118
   joy, 118
   sadness, 118
   shame, 118
   surprise, 118
empathy guess, 121
Enneagram, 175, 276, 287, 289, 309, 493
   achiever/seeker, 296
   challenger/boss, 297
   enneagram test, 292
   enthusiast/adventurer, 296
   helper/caretaker, 296
   investigator/thinker, 296
   Levels of development, 297
   loyalist/defender/hero, 296
   peacemaker/preservationist, 297
   reformer/perfectionist, 295
   romantic/aesthete, 296
enneagraminstitute.com, 604
environment
   control or dominate. *See* Integral
   surrender. *See* transpersonal
era, 82
   metamodern, 92
   postmodern, 82
essential dimensions, 2
existentialism, 82
expressing transcendental purpose, 457

F

Farrell, Warren, xxx
fatigue, 119
fear of isolation, 267
feelings
   interpretations, 119
   satisfied, 118
   unsatisfied, 118
Feminine Masculine Polarities, 541
Feminine-masculine polarities, 198
five forms of pluralism, 87

five spiritual stages, 216
flourishing garden, 2
flourishing societies, xxxv, 524
fluidity, 101
forms of love
  commitment, 373
  companionate love, 376
  crazy love, 375
  friendship, 372
  infatuation, 372
  integral love, 376
  non-love, 372
  romantic love, 374
four dimensions, 29, 46, 215, 421, 429, 455, 590
four dimensions of Sexuality, 236
Four Polarities
  Agency, 201
  Ascending, 200
  Communion, 202
  Descending, 201
four quadrant questions, 36
four quadrants, 29, 31, 429, 573, 578
  quadrant absolutism, 33, 137
Freud, 342

G

Gandhi, Mahatma, 109, 110
Gebser, Jean, 52, 53, 578
Gebser, Jean, 103
gender roles, 75, 159, 163
  matriarchy, 85
  matrifocal, 75
  patriarchal, 75
general beliefs, 418
genetic predisposition, 440

Gilbert, Elizabeth, 367
Gilligan, Carol, 579
Graves, Clare, 103
Graves, Clare W., 52, 53
guided meditation, 16

H

Habermas, Jürgen, 45, 52, 53, 81, 569
Harding, Mary Esther, 183
harmonize, 91
Havel, Václav, xxxiii, 523, 533
Hegel, Friedrich, 102
Hegelian dialectic, 147
Hendrix, Harville, 599
Hezinger, Mark, 275
holarchism, 533, 541
holistic, 85
holons, 202
Holy grail, 126
HPD, 401, 509, *See* Personality Disorders
hugs
  The A-Frame, 14
  The Burper, 15
  The Butt Grab, 15
  The Grind, 15
human evolution, 649
Human evolution, xxvi, 231, 433, 465
Human potentials, 5
Hyperindividualism, xxxiv
hyperindividualistic, 533

I

idealism, 81
immunity to change, 445
individual awareness, xxx

ingredients of love, 368
  dependence, 369
  intimacy, 369
  passion, 369
inner peace, xxx, 353
Integral Relationship, 518
integration chakra. *See* Heart chakras
intimacy, 590, 595
intrigued, 47

J

Journey, 20
Jung, Carl, 256, 337, 341, 597, 598
  Anima/Animus, 598

K

Karpman, Stephen B., 132
Kegan, Robert, 50, 104, 470, 635, *See* immunity to change
Kohlberg, Lawrence, 103
Krishnamurti, Jiddu, xxix
Kundalini, 240, 595

L

Lahey, Lisa Laskow. *See* immunity to change
layers of emotion, 352
layers of veils, 14
levels of dependence, 379
levels of soulmates, 479
  biological, 479
  transcendental, 480
  transformational, 479
LGBTQ, 525
list of needs, 117

Loevinger, Jane, 103
looking, 20
  inside out, 20
  outside in, 20
love circle, 20
  love circle affirmations, 21
love languages, 275, 286
  acts of service, 278
  gifts, 278
  physical touch, 279
  quality time, 278
  words of affirmation, 278
love relationships, 475
  sustainable relationships, xxxii, 1
Love, Patricia, 595
love-and-cuddle hormones, 13
  Oxytocin, 13, 220
Love-and-cuddle hormones, 568
  Oxytocin, 681
lovestruck, 369, 384
lust and desire, 383
Lyons, Marlena, 628

M

Maslow, Abraham, 103
  hierarchy of needs, 121
materialistic, 76
Max-Neef, Manfred, 122
McIntosh, Steve, xxxiv
McLaughlin, Mignon, 171
measurement of attractiveness, 167
Meiosis, 441
memories, 220
  explicit, 221
  implicit, 220
men as hero, 264

metacognition, 210, 218
metamodernism, 52
Mind
  Subcortical system, 220
mindfulness meditation, 9, 13, 207, 217, 228
money, 528
Movie, 47, 69, 79, 89, 107, 123, 142, 158, 169, 182, 205, 232, 252, 273, 287, 317, 335, 348, 365, 388, 416, 433, 470, 494, 520, 549
  American Beauty, 107
  As Good As It Gets, 335
  Bliss, 252
  Cloud Atlas, 470
  Eternal Sunshine of the Spotless Mind, 416
  Frida, 520
  Gandhi, 123
  Good Will Hunting, 365
  Grace and Grit, 494
  Groundhog Day, 79
  Her, 47
  I Heart Huckabees, 232
  Idiocracy, 549
  Inside Bill's Brain Decoding Bill Gates, 520
  Into the Wild, 69
  Little Miss Sunshine, 182
  Love Actually, 287
  Marriage Story, 273
  Prince of Tides, 348
  Quest for Fire, 433
  Same Time, Next year, 89
  The Imitation Game, 158
  The Invention of Lying, 142
  The Mirror Has Two Faces, 388
  The Red Pill, 169
  The Tree of Life, 205
  Tomorrow Ever After, 549
  When Harry Met Sally, 388
  Winnie the Pooh, 317
Mr. Right, 78
myths, 71

N

Namaste, 14
narcissism, 64, 81, 203, 514
NARM, 63
nondual awareness, 9, 209
  casual/deep sleep, 210
  gross/waking, 209
  nondual. *See* Nonduality
  pure witness, 211
  subtle/dreaming, 210
Nonduality, 212
non-monogamy, 249
nonviolent communication, 81, 109, 113, 127, 141, 177
nonviolent protest, 124
  non-cooperation campaign, 124
Norepinephrine, 384

O

opposite sex, 161
Orange, 376
Oxytocin, 386, 595

P

paradoxes, 87
Passionate Marriage, 244
Patriarchal, xxxiv
Peck, Scott, 628

Pelosi, Nancy, 417
personality dirsorders in relationships, 403
personality disorders, 93, 97, 216, 256, 298, 302, 321, 391, 399
   Antisocial(ASPD), 396
   Avoidant(APD), 396
   Borderline(BPD), 398
   Dependent(DPD), 397
   Histrionic(HPD), 399
   Narcissistic(NPD), 400
   Obsessive-Compulsive(OCPD), 397
   Paranoid(PPD), 395
   Schizoid(SPD), 396
   Schizotypal(STPD), 396
Personality Matrix, 186, 216, 243, 271
personality types, 281
phases of love, 367
physical body, 17
   Abdomen, 16
   Arms, 17
   Chest, 17
   Tongue, 17
physical pleasures, 238
physiological challenges, 10, 338
Piaget, Jean, 102
Pierre Teilhard de Chardin, 51
Pines, Ayala Malach, 598, 608
Plotkin, Bill. *See* stages of maturity
polarities
   integrating with quadrants, 590
Polarities, xxxi
   Feminine, xxxi
   Masculine, xxxi
Polarization, xxxii

polyagony, 250
post-Integral stages, 93
postmodernity, xxxi
power chakra. *See* Solar plexus chakra
primary fantasy, 372
Primary Fantasy, 166
Proust, Marcel, 561
Psaris, Jett, 88, 628
psychological challenges, 338
purpose discovery methods, 450

Q

quadrants, 203

R

radical conservatism, xxxii
realism, 149
reasons for communicating, 128
relational context, 202
   self-adaptation, 203
   self-immanence, 203
   self-preservation, 203
   self-transcendence, 202
relationships, 30
   conflicts, 58, 72, 107, 136, 138
   cougar, 100
   intimate, 33
   limitations of statistics about, 7
   master-slave, 429
   polyamorous, 378, *See* polyagony
   romantic, 29
   sustainable love relationship, 183
relationships skills, 21
relationships terminology, 7

relativism, 85
religions, 229
river-flow method, 184
Robert Augustus Masters. See Spiritual Bypassing
Rogers, Carl. See nonviolent communication
Rolston, Holmes, 523
Rosenberg, Marshall, 110
Roy, Bhaskar, 52
Rumi, Jalal, 319, 349

S

Sagan, Carl, 49
self-governance, xxxiii
selfhood and reality, 230
Serotonin, 385
Seven chakras, 498
    Crown chakra, 501
    Heart chakra, 500
    Root chakra, 499
    Sacral chakra, 499
    Solar plexus chakra, 500
    Third eye chakra, 501
    Throat chakra, 500
sex, 528
sexual development, 235
    five stages of sexual development, 238
sexual fantasy, 143
sexual preferences, 239
sexuality chakra. See Sacral chakra
shadow/unconscious, 341, See unconscious
    Healing, 349
Shadow/Unconscious, 216
Shaw, George Bernard, 125

Siegel, Dan. See attachment styles
Siegel, Daniel, 221
    nine domains of integration, 223
single women, 266
social atomism, 524, 541
    social holons, xxxi, 541
Social atomism
    social holons, 686, 687
Social realm, 43
Sock game, 26
Sonmi, 471
soul, 476
soul-mate
    how to find, 664
soulmates, 475
Soulmates
    Soulmate selection, 490
Spiral Dynamics, 58
Spiral Dynamics (SD), 579
spiritual
    definition, 208
spiritual bypassing, 208, 216, 244, 379
stages of conciousness
    Amber, 186
stages of consciousness, 139
    Archaic, 49, 69, 139
    consciousness ladder, 55
    Egocentric, 49, 65, 79, 127, 140
    Integral, 91, 92
    Magic, 49, 140
    Mythic, 71, 72, 127, 140
    Pluralistic, 81, 110, 127, 141
    Rational, 71, 72, 127, 141
    Transpersonal, 91, 107
stages of maturity, 461
stages of sexual development
    fucking, 238

having sex, 239
making love, 240
repressed sexuality, 238
tantric transcendent sexuality, 240
state of pure being
   free yourself, 9
states of love, 383
Steinem, Gloria, 183
stop criticizing, 174
Stosny, Steven, 595, 681
stress hormone, 13
   cortisol, 13, 160, 220
Stress hormone
   cortisol, 681
survival chakra. *See* Root chakra
synergy, 198
   feminine communion, 199
   feminine descending, 199
   masculine agency, 199
   masculine ascending, 199

T

tantric, 241
Tantric, 94, 97
ten phases of fear-shame
   anger, 180
   Cave-shaming, 179
   complaining, 178
   emasculating, 180
   emotionally unfaithful, 180
   fixing, 179
   nagging, 179
   sexually unfaithful, 180
   stops romancing, 178
   withdrawing, 179
The Big Five, 277

The Empowerment Dynamic (TED), 134
The Imitation Game, 132
The Japanese Ikigai, 455
therapeutic approaches, 353
   Cognitive Behavioral Therapy, 353
   Mindful Behavioral Therapy, 353
   NeuroActive Relational Method, 353
Thurston, Leslie Temple, 597
time, 527
Tolle, Eckhart, 9, 435
Tolle, Eckhart, 13
transactional love, 427
transcendental love, 497
transcendental purpose, 435
   stages of maturity, 460
transcendental Purpose, 436, 443, 457, 465
   levels of calling, 458
transformational purpose, 431
transpersonal level of consciousness, 93
trapped in time, 79
   time loop, 79
trauma. *See* unconscious wounds
Turquoise, 93

U

uncharted, 19
unconscious
   archaic unconscious, 341
   embedded unconscious, 342
   emergent unconscious, 342
   ground unconscious, 341

submerged, 341
Unconscious, 337
unconscious wound. *See* psychological challenges
undefended love, 353
unity chakra. *See* Crown chakra
use of language, 130
   implicit, 130

V

Vasopressin, 386
vision chakra. *See* Third eye chakra
vulnerable, 119

W

Wade, Jenny, 579
waning levels, 173
Warren Farrell, 632
webmd.com, 595
Welwood, John, 598, 628

Spiritual Bypassing, 217
wikipedia.org, 598
Wilber, Ken, 46, 51, 54, 91, 341, 494, 578, 579, 591, 613
   Wilber-Combs matrix, 213, 242
Wilson, Jim, 20, 246
   Northern Seascape, 20
Wittgenstein, Ludwig, 145
women as sex object, 269
women as wife, 269
world happiness report, 121

Y

yearnings, 10, 381
Yellow. *See* Integral

Z

zones of being and relating, 43
Zukav, Gary, 497

Printed in Great Britain
by Amazon